REPRINTS IN SOCIAL AND ECONOMIC HISTORY

Selected by Professor S. B. Saul, B. Com., Ph.D.

DEPARTMENT OF ECONOMIC HISTORY
UNIVERSITY OF EDINBURGH

Commentaries on the productive forces
of Russia

Tegoborski, Ludwik.

JOHNSON REPRINT CORPORATION
New York • London
1972

The work reprinted here is complete in two volumes;
a third volume was planned by the author but was never published.

Library of Congress Catalog Card Number: 79-38881

First reprinting 1972, Johnson Reprint Corporation

Johnson Reprint Corporation   Johnson Reprint Company Ltd.
111 Fifth Avenue   24/28 Oval Road
New York, N.Y. 10003   London, NW1 7DD, England

Printed in the U.S.A.

COMMENTARIES

ON

THE PRODUCTIVE FORCES

OF

RUSSIA.

BY

M. L. DE TEGOBORSKI,

PRIVY COUNCILLOR AND MEMBER OF THE COUNCIL OF THE
RUSSIAN EMPIRE.

IN TWO VOLUMES.

VOL. I.

LONDON:

LONGMAN, BROWN, GREEN, AND LONGMANS.

1855.

Lonoon:
A. and G. A. Spottiswoode,
New-street-Square.

TRANSLATOR'S PREFACE.

WHETHER war or commerce may now be destined to give the tone to our relations with Russia for many a day to come, it surely concerns us to be able to form something like a rational estimate of the material resources of that immense empire — the primary elements of her power for good or for evil. And yet, down to the present date, there exist in our language but few sources of correct information upon that important subject. The consequently prevailing ignorance, often felt and regretted, is not unfrequently accompanied, even in generally well-informed quarters, by a sort of vague surmise that it results from a system of sedulous concealment on the part of the mysterious power whose strength and weakness are, we believe, much more frequently declaimed upon than placed in the scales of an even balance. " It has seldom happened," says an able writer in one of our principal reviews, " to any nation to engage in hostilities with a foreign power whose real strength and resources are so imperfectly known. No other empire than that of Russia *ever succeeded in keeping so vast a portion of the globe a secret and a mystery to the rest of mankind.*" There does not, however, seem to be just cause for imputing to Russia any such intention; nor is it easy to perceive the sufficient ground which should induce her to entertain it. Whatever may be the mysteries of her diplomacy — with which we meddle not, — we find that those publicists who have restricted their inquiries to an analysis of the effective components of her material welfare, do not complain that — with the exception of her finances, as to which she has certainly not been unnecessarily communicative * — there is any

* Yet in this department, too, she has of late given signs of a greater disposition to publicity. See, *inter alia*, a remarkable letter in the *Revue des Deux Mondes* for

A 2

department of her statistics in which secrecy is either maintained or desired. On the contrary, it would appear that,
ever since the commencement of the present century, but
especially during the last twenty years, the Russian government has not only made great exertions to obtain correct
information for itself with regard to the condition and resources of the Empire, but has been at no small pains to
diffuse this information amongst its subjects, and to excite
amongst the latter a taste for its acquisition. For this purpose reports by the various ministries regarding the matters
which concern their several departments are published at
frequent intervals ; chairs of statistics have been established
in the different universities ; in 1843 the " Materials for
a Statistical Account of the Russian Empire " emanated
from the Ministry of the Interior ; the official " Tables of
Commerce," which have annually appeared for the last fifty
years contain more information than is to be found in the
analogous documents of most other states ; and, altogether,
scarcely a month or a week passes without some valuable contribution to our knowledge of the country issuing
from the press through one or other of the various official
journals.* With all this, however, it must be acknowledged
that our positive information upon many important points is
still but meagre and defective ; and we fear it is likely to
remain so for a long while to come. The immense area,
the thinness and unequal distribution of the population, and
the low degree of culture hitherto attained by the bulk of the
latter as compared with those peoples which are the heirs of
an earlier civilisation, throw such constant impediments in
the way of procuring accurate returns, that a statistical
account of the Russian Empire such as Mr. M'Culloch has
given us of our own, belongs to the number of those tasks
which the present generation will gladly bequeath as a legacy

last November, in which the author of the following work corrects some misstate-
ments contained in a very clever but partizan article, which had shortly before
appeared in the same journal, from the pen of the late M. Léon Faucher. Although the information here conveyed does not come in the shape of official
authority, it cannot for a moment be supposed that the writer would have seen
fit to publish anything which the Russian government was desirous of con-
cealing.

  * See Baron von Reden's two valuable works, *Das Kaiser-Reich Russland*, and
Russlands Kraft-Elemente und Einfluss-Mittel.

to the next. All that the most painful and conscientious
statist can really accomplish is to lay before his readers such
approximations to the truth as the imperfect materials within
his reach enable him to form and justify; and if a writer
professing to give an impartial account of the productive
powers of the country, shall industriously collect, carefully
discriminate, and scientifically combine these materials, we
apprehend that he will perform in full all he can be presumed
to have undertaken.

There have been various works upon Russia published on
the continent within the last few years, which, if translated
into English, might assist in enabling such of us as are
willing to read and learn, to substitute a discriminating
judgment for the vague and vacillating notions which too
generally prevail regarding the resources of that ill-understood
and anomalous Empire. From amongst these, the Editor of
the present volume, glad if he shall thus have rendered an
acceptable service to the public, has selected Tengoborski's
"Études sur les Forces Productives de la Russie;" because,
relying not so much upon his own slight and superficial
knowledge as on the opinion of more competent judges, he
believes that, for the purpose just mentioned, the work in
question possesses a higher value than any other which has
hitherto appeared — at least in the more accessible languages
of Europe — from the pen of either foreigner or native.
Occupying a high official position in the Department of the
Finances, the able author (already favourably known to the
public by a valuable work on the finances of Austria), im-
pelled apparently by *le désir de tout connaître en étant
obligé de le décrire,* had set himself the task of a laborious
inquiry into the productive powers of the empire, and has
here communicated the result of his "Studies" in a comprehensive series of tables and commentaries, to which it
will be hard to refuse the merit of talent, fairness, and moderation. There is throughout the book a remarkable absence of leanings and prejudices; the figures appear to have
been drawn from the most reliable sources, and to have been
carefully and conscientiously sifted; whilst the opinions expressed bear the internal stamp of honesty and candour. It
is easy to perceive that the writer entertains unbounded con-

fidence in the future destinies of his country, regarding it
as a field for the measureless development of elements of
strength and greatness which are still in their infancy ; but
he does not seek to convey the idea that its present condition,
as compared with that of the longer civilised portions of
Europe, is in many respects otherwise than backward ; and
when he observes an evil, instead of labouring to disguise it
—as many of us conceive that a good patriotic Russian
would be apt to do,—he seeks to estimate its intensity, and
calmly discusses the means of its removal. The impartiality of his statements has indeed found general recogni-
tion ; and we see French and German publicists resorting
to the book as a store-house of facts, even where they exhibit
no undue inclination to assent to the inferences of the author.
To claim for it an immunity from error would of course be
absurd. Traversing a field so extensive and varied, occasional mistakes must have been reckoned on, even had
the writer's materials been *in pari casu* with those of statists
whose survey is confined within narrower limits. But,
apart from such inaccuracies as might, perhaps, be detected
in the " *Statistique générale de la Belgique* " itself, the work
is exposed to this farther source of error, that the scantiness of
positive has constrained the author, in the course of his comprehensive survey, to the occasional assumption of merely *probable* data. And although it must be allowed that in such cases
the boldness he displays in his calculations does not exceed
the caution and sagacity with which he bases his units, and
that he appears thoroughly desirous that his probable error
shall at least not be on the side of exaggeration, it must be
borne in mind that such " guesses at truth "—as to the
uniform successfulness of which the author does not conceal
his own scepticism—are entitled at best to no more than a
qualified and provisional assent, awaiting future modification
from the more abundant store of facts which each successive
year will no doubt help to accumulate ; for, in this department of science, quite as much as in any other, it is only by
successive limitations of error that we can hope for gradual
progress in the path which leads towards truth. Meantime,
the occasional occurrence of such problematical ciphers—for
which there is nothing else (except quiet ignorance) to sub-

stitute at present — will be found neither to affect the value of the copious particulars with which the volume teems, nor to detract from the character of the work as exhibiting an entire synoptical view of all that is now best ascertained regarding the important subjects which it describes and discusses ; and no one who is in the least degree aware of the labour and difficulties attending every inquest of the sort — no one who has ever attempted to collect for his own information the statistics of a single county, parish, or village, will withhold his admiration from what has here been accomplished for the length and breadth of an area so vast, that the very figures of arithmetic almost cease to convey to the mind any definite notion of its extent.

For the reader's convenience, the Translator has frequently added, within brackets, the English equivalents of the Russian money, weights, and measures mentioned throughout the volume. As this, however, has not been done invariably, and as errors of calculation may also have occasionally crept in, tables of these equivalents are here subjoined. The geographical measure has not been converted in the text ; so it will be necessary to bear in mind that the *mile* spoken of is always the geographical mile of 4 minutes of the equator, or 15 to a degree. The rouble mentioned is constantly the silver rouble, unless paper currency* be specified.

* In order to facilitate the circulation of money in the Russian empire, the Empress Catherine II. instituted (1768) a bank with a capital of one million roubles based upon gold and silver, against which, bank-notes (termed assignats) of the value of from 25 to 100 roubles were issued to a like amount. As these were declared a legal tender in all public and private payments, as they were instantly convertible into coin at their nominal value, and as they supplied a felt want in the ordinary transactions of business, they soon gained the confidence of the public, and—from the superior convenience of paper to metal for many purposes—occasionally stood at a small premium. It was thus found possible to augment the issues to the extent of 100 millions of roubles, without any material diminution of their current value. Unfortunately, the too great facilities thus presented for *making money* tempted the Russian Government (which, like some others nearer home, occasionally found its exchequer emptier than it could have wished) to extend these paper issues beyond its ability to redeem them with coin upon demand. No sooner was this perceived by the public, than the notes fell to a discount ; and the fall was both great and rapid. In 1787 they had stood nearly at par; but the following year they were at 92; in 1793 they had fallen to 74 ; and in 1796 they were down at 68 ; from this quotation they rallied in 1802 to $71\frac{4}{10}$, and in

The second volume, concluding the work, is in a state of forwardness, and no undue delay in bringing it out is likely to occur.

MONEY.

1 Silver rouble (=100 kopecks) =   3s. 2d. sterling.

WEIGHT.

1 Pound (= 96 zolotniks)   =   0·90 lbs. avoird.
1 Pood (= 40 lbs.)- - - = 36·08 ,,   ,,
1 Berkowetz (= 10 poods) = 360·8 ,,   ,,

DRY MEASURE.

1 Tchetwerik (= 8 garnietz) = 0·72 imp. bushels.
1 Tchetwert (= 8 tchetweriks) = 0·72 imp. quarters.

LIQUID MEASURE.

1 Vedro (= 10 crouchkas) =   2·7 imp. or 3¼ wine gallons.
1 Oxhoft (=18 vedros) -   = 48·6   ,,   58½ ,,   ,,

LONG MEASURE.

1 Arschine (= 16 verschoks) =   28 inches.
1 Sagène   (=   3 arschines) =   7 feet.
1 Verst   (= 500 sagènes)   = 1,166 yards.

SUPERFICIAL MEASURE.

1 Dessiatine (= 2,400 square sagènes) = 2·69 imp. acres.

1803 they rose to 80; but this was the culminating point of the short reaction from their first rapid depreciation. From that date they again sunk rapidly—to 60 in 1806; to 50 in 1809; to 33$\frac{3}{10}$ in 1811; and in 1815, upon Bonaparte's return from Elba, they stood for a short time as low as 20½. After the restoration of peace, measures were taken by government to bring the finances and currency into a normal condition, and assignats to the nominal amount of about 200 millions of roubles were bought up at the price of the day and burned; but it was not until 1839 that the latter object was fully accomplished by the return to a metallic (silver) currency, of which the silver rouble formed the unit—the legal relation of the existing paper currency to silver being at the same time fixed at the rate of 350 kopecks of the former to 100 kopecks of the latter, which was somewhat above the current price of the day and the average value of paper for the ten years preceding. Since then the old assignat has vanished from circulation ; but in some provinces it is still the custom to keep accounts in paper roubles, which are then understood to be =$\frac{2}{7}$ of the silver currency.

CONTENTS

OF

THE FIRST VOLUME.

CHAP. III.

CLASSIFICATION OF THE SOIL IN REGARD TO CULTURE.

CHAP. IV

POPULATION.

CHAP. V.

PRODUCTS OF THE SOIL, AND THEIR GROSS VALUE.

PRODUCTS OF THE ANIMAL KINGDOM.

PART II.

INTELLECTUAL PRODUCTIVE FORCES.

CHAPTER I.

AGRICULTURE.

General Considerations on the Importance of Agriculture for Russia. — Com-
plaints as to its backward Condition. — Causes. — Three-shift Rotation.—
Atmospheric Influences.— Disproportion between Value of Land and
Value of Labour. — Influence of Serfage and the Corvée. — Erroneous No-
tions. — Corvée still indispensable. — Its Conversion into a Money Rent a
Question of Circumstances.— Distribution of Lands by Hearth (Tiàglo).—
Distribution of Rural Population in large Villages. — Classification of
Landowners.— Boundaries of Estates not well ascertained. — Large Extent
of Land in Litigation.— Prices of Grain, and their great Fluctuations.—
Estimate of Quantity raised in Russia. — Comparisons. — Duties of the
State in regard to Agriculture. — Crown Lands. — Catile. — Relative Ex-
tent of Meadow Land. — Measures for improving Stock-farming. —
Causes of its backward State. — Want of Markets for Meat. — Importance
of a Trade in Salt Provisions and Dairy Produce. — Breeds. — Numbers.
— Horses.— Circumstances favourable to their Rearing. — Causes of De-
terioration of Breeds. — Government Remedies and their Results.—
Numbers — Sheep. — Progress of Sheep-farming. — Influence of Aus-
tralian Wool. — English Market. — Precarious Condition of Russian Wool
Trade. — Consumption of Wool. — Exportation. — Swine. — Meadow
Culture. — Draining and Irrigation. — Flax and Hemp. — Influence of
English Linen Manufacture. — Flax Culture in Ireland. — Defects in Rus-
sian Culture, Preparation, and Assortment. — Prices. — English Importa-

COMMENTARIES

ON THE

PRODUCTIVE FORCES OF RUSSIA.

OF PRODUCTIVE FORCES CONSIDERED AS THE BASIS OF PUBLIC WEALTH.

THE wealth and material well-being of nations, upon which their power and financial prosperity depend, are primarily determined by the productive forces which each country possesses within itself.

Without entering upon any analysis of the nature and causes of the wealth of nations, or of the modes of its formation and distribution, — an inquiry which belongs to the domain of political economy proper, — we will at once refer the whole productive forces which constitute the elements of a country's wealth to one or other of two categories, namely, the physical or natural, and the moral and intellectual.

To the former belong the extent and fertility of its soil, the nature and quality of its productions, its geographical and topographical position, and the influence of climate; to which we may add the physical forces of the population, and the different races of animals by which the country is inhabited.

In the latter we include the degree of intelligence at which a given people has arrived, its national character, manners and customs, its inclination or aptitude for this or that sort of productive labour. These moral qualities, in their turn, are themselves greatly dependent on various outward circumstances, — on the physical conditions of the country — on the influences of food and climate — of origin and historical traditions — of social and political organisation. Thus it is matter of trite observation that warm climates have a tendency to enervate their populations — a tendency often fostered by the fertility of the soil and the facility of procuring a subsistence ; whilst more industry and a greater capacity for labour is found amongst the children of the north, where Nature is less prodigal of her bounties. The effect of institutions—social, economic, administrative — is very great; moral and intellectual influences may paralyse the development of physical forces; they may also to a certain extent make up for the want of them; but, upon the whole, the results which we are warranted to anticipate must always be more or less subject to physical conditions. History, no doubt, supplies us with several examples of countries which, although very moderately endowed with natural productive forces, have nevertheless become great and prosperous, as, in modern times, Holland and the Republic of Venice ; but even in such exceptional cases we will always be sure to find that, along with the political causes to which such results may in no small degree be ascribed, there has likewise been some material or local cause in concurrent operation. If the mercantile and enterprising spirit of the Dutch has spread fertility over sterile tracts ravished by man's skill from the waves,—if it has evoked rich and populous cities from the depths of the ocean, and carried their country to that high pitch of prosperity which we have seen it attain,—it must not be forgotten that those peaceful conquests have been materially promoted by the geographical position of the land, which rendered it the natural mart of a large intermediate commerce. Though the genius of man may triumph over many natural obstacles, his power is not unlimited ; and in an absolute absence of the natural elements of wealth, the most creative genius will devise in vain. We could not convert Iceland or Lapland into rich and prosperous territories, though we were to people them with the most intelligent, the most industrious, and the most laborious of mankind.

Countries may become wealthy by agriculture, by commerce, by manufactures, or by the simultaneous concourse of all the three ; but the degree of relative importance attaching to one or other of these sources of prosperity must always depend, more or less, on the physical conditions of the given country. A just appreciation of these is one of the most important problems devolving on the statesman. In relation to great states, at any rate, we may affirm it as a general rule, that their wealth and prosperity depend primarily on the mass of the natural productive forces of which they can dispose ; and this is the goal from which we shall accordingly start, in proceeding to study the financial resources of Russia.

PART I.

PHYSICAL AND MATERIAL PRODUCTIVE FORCES.

CHAPTER I.

Extent and Geographical Position. — Classification of Territory in regard to Geographical Position.—Extent and Geographical Position of each Province and
Government. — Arrangement of these according to their Extent. — Observations on their comparative Extent.

ACCORDING to the recent work (published in 1848) of M.
Arsénieff, one of our most distinguished geographers and
statists (*Statistitscheskie Otsherki Rossii*), the Empire of Russia
occupies a superficial extent of 367,200 geographical square
miles, extending from the 35th to the 208th (or, including the
islands and possessions in America, to the 225th) degree of
longitude (counting eastward from Ferro), and from the 38th
to the 78th degree of north latitude. Its greatest length from
west to east, or from Kalisch to the port of Petropavlovsk at
the extremity of Kamtchatka, is 14,410 versts, or 2072 geographical miles. Its greatest breadth from north to south,
namely, from Kola in Lapland to the frontier of Persia, is
4860 versts, or 699 geographical miles.

European Russia, without Nova Zembla, and including the
kingdom of Poland, extends from the 41st to the 70th degree
of northern latitude, and from the 35th to the 85th degree of
east longitude, and occupies a superficies of 99,275 geographical
square miles * ; an extent which considerably exceeds half of the
entire surface of Europe. The extent of European frontier is
estimated by M. Reden, in his Comparative Statistics, at 2528
geographical miles, of which 1382, or more than half, are maritime, and 1146 dry frontier.† M. Reden reckons the posses-

---

* We have obtained this figure by calculating the extent of thirty-seven
governments, of which a geographico-statistical account was given in a memoir
by the astronomer Struve, read before the Geographical Society on 1—13 August,
1845, and adding the extent of the other provinces of European Russia, according
to the Comparative Statistics of M. Reden, some figures of which we have corrected in conformity with more recent information.

† Vergleichende Cultur-Statistik der Gross-Staaten Europa's, von Freiherrn
von Reden, pp. 14, 15.

sions of the five great powers, Russia, Great Britain, France, Austria, and Prussia, in the four quarters of the globe, to cover a surface of 500,000 square miles, of which he assigns to Russia 359,524 [*]; so that the possessions of the latter would exceed, in the proportion of 18 to 7, those of the other four put together.

Sernoff, who, in 1833, estimated the whole superficies of the Russian empire at no more than 330,755 geographical square miles, has classed its geographical position in the following manner: —

Degrees of North Latitude.			Extent in Geographical Square Miles.
From	78 to 75	- - - - - -	3,132·55
„	75 „ 70	- - - - - -	21,050·22
„	70 „ 65	- - - - - -	61,878·77
„	65 „ 60	- - - - - -	79,228·62
„	60 „ 55	- - - - - -	75,953·72
„	55 „ 50	- - - - - -	62,134·29
„	50 „ 45	- - - - - -	22,565·56
„	45 „ 40	- - - - - -	4,135·85
„	40 „ 38	- - - - - -	675·28
		Total as above - -	330,755·86

We perceive, from this classification, that the greater portion of the empire, namely, 279,195 square miles, or 84 per cent. of its whole surface, is situated between the 50th and 70th degrees of north latitude.

The academician Struve has distributed the empire, in regard to climate, as follows: —

In the frigid zone	-	-	64,226 geographical square miles.
In the temperate zone	-	-	266,529 „ „
Total as above	-	-	330,755 „ „

of which European Russia occupies

In the frigid zone - - - 11,026 geographical miles, including Nova Zembla.
In the temperate zone - - 90,710 geographical miles, including the Caucasian provinces.

Total - 101,736 [†]

Siberia, with the isles of the Eastern Ocean, contains, according to the same estimates,

In the frigid zone	-	-	53,200 geographical square miles.
In the temperate zone	-	-	175,819 „ „
Total	-	229,019 „ „

---

[*] This figure is 7676 square miles less than that of M. Arsénieff.
[†] This figure is 2,461 square miles higher than what we have given on p. 3. See explanatory note.

In this last figure are comprehended neither the steppes inhabited by the Kirghiz Caïssaks, nor the possessions of the Russo-American Company.

It results, from these calculations, that little more than a tenth of the surface of European Russia belongs to the frigid zone, and nearly nine-tenths to the temperate zone, according to the meaning attached by geographers to that classification; whilst nearly a fourth of Siberia is situated within the former, and more than three-fourths within the latter.

We here present, on the authority of M. Struve, the table, already referred to, of the extent and geographical position of thirty-seven governments of European Russia, arranged according to their elevation in north latitude.

GOVERNMENTS.	Extent in Geographical Sq. Miles.*	North Latitude.		Longitude.	
		From	To	W.	E.
		° ′	° ′	° ′	° ′
Government of Olonetz - -	2,732	64 35	60 8	47 28	59 20
St. Petersburg -	941	60 54	57 59	45 10	51 46
Nowgorod - -	2,213	61 21	57 5	47 55	57 43
Esthonia - -	370	59 42	58 19	39 39	45 54
Jaroslaw - -	660	59 4	56 44	55 1	58 51
Livonia - -	884	59 4	56 34	39 28	45 13
Twer - - -	1,223	58 53	55 54	49 33	56 4
Pskow - -	816	58 12	55 56	44 58	49 59
Courland - -	496	57 46	55 41	38 38	45 2
Wladimir - -	862	57 14	55 6	55 16	60 54
Witebsk .. -	810	57 27	54 46	43 24	49 32
Moscow - -	589	56 42	54 49	52 54	56 55
Kowno - -	758	56 27	54 48	38 47	45 2
Smolensk - -	1,019	56 36	53 13	48 30	53 25
Wilna - -	768	55 50	53 23	41 34	46 4
Riazan - -	766	55 45	53 0	56 15	59 18
Kalouga - -	573	55 23	53 18	51 7	54 59
Toula - - -	555	55 53	52 47	53 39	56 50
Penza - - -	690	54 54	52 38	60 19	64 25
Mohilew - -	885	55 12	51 57	46 32	50 24
Tambow .. -	1,202	55 11	51 20	56 9	61 22
Minsk - -	1,622	55 6	51 14	42 52	48 17
Orel - - -	859	54 0	51 47	50 31	56 44
Grodno - -	692	54 3	51 31	40 7	43 32
Tschernigow -	1,000	53 18	50 15	48 4	52 17
Koursk - -	818	52 24	50 13	51 0	55 57
Woronèje - -	1,209	52 53	49 33	55 7	60 45
Wolhynia - -	1,297	52 2	49 27	41 18	47 7
Carried forward - -	27,309				

* In order to diminish the number of figures we have omitted fractions, suppressing those *under* half a mile, and giving a complete mile instead of a fraction of *more* than half a mile.

GOVERNMENTS.	Extent in Geographical Square Miles.	North Latitude.		Longitude.	
		From	To	W.	E.
		° ′	° ′	° ′	° ′
Brought forward - - -	27,309				
Government of Kiew - -	914	51 29	48 28	46 4	50 50
Kharkow - -	985	51 17	48 36	51 34	57 56
Poltawa - -	897	51 8	48 44	48 26	53 49
Country of the Don Cossacks -	2,943	51 18	46 7	55 16	62 29
Government of Podolia - -	774	49 50	47 22	43 50	48 35
Ekathérinoslaw -	1,206	49 12	46 51	50 58	57 36
Kherson - -	1,332	49 6	46 8	46 44	51 59
Bessarabia - -	858	48 37	44 51	43 41	48 10
Tauride (comprehending the Sea of Azow) - -	1,208	47 43	44 8	49 8	54 49
Total extent of the thirty-seven Governments - - -	38,426				

In copying this table, M. Reden, in his Comparative Statistics, adds the extent of fifteen provinces or governments of European Russia, of which the area has not yet been determined with mathematical precision. These we here subjoin with their latitude according to Piadischeff's Atlas, rectifying their extent in conformity with more recent information:—

GOVERNMENTS.	Extent. Sq. Miles.	North Latitude.	
		From	To
		° ′	° ′
Government of Archangel with Nova Zembla - - - - - -	15,519	78 0	61 20
Grand Duchy of Finland * - -	6,873	70 10	59 45
Government of Wologda - -	6,967	64 30	58 20
Perm - - -	6,073	61 50	55 30
Wiatka - - -	2,500	60 0	55 30
Kostroma - - -	1,496	59 12	56 40
Nijni Nowgorod -	876	57 10	54 30
Kazan - - -	1,128	56 45	54 10
Orenburg - - -	6,773	56 20	47 0
Simbirsk - - -	1,315	55 45	52 35
Kingdom of Poland - - -	2,294	55 5	50 10
Government of Saratow - - -	3,525	53 15	48 0
Astrakhan - - -	2,860	49 40	44 40
Stavropol, with the country of the Black Sea Cossacks - - - - -	2,650	46 50	41 40
Total superficial extent of these provinces	60,849		

* According to the Statistics of Rein, published at Helsingfors in 1843.

The other figures, with the exception of the superficial extent of Poland, are borrowed from the Statistics of M. Arsénieff.

In the order of their extent, the provinces of European Russia included in the two preceding tables would be arranged as follows:—

	Sq. M.		Sq. M
Government of Archangel, including Nova Zembla	- 15,519	Brought forward -	79,179
Wologda - - -	6,967	Government of Tschernigow -	1,000
Grand Duchy of Finland -	6,873	Kharkow -	985
Government of Orenburg -	6,773	St. Petersburg	941
Perm -	6,073	Kiew -	914
Saratow -	3,525	Poltawa -	897
Country of the Don Cossacks -	2,943	Mohilew -	885
Government of Astrakhan -	2,860	Livonia -	884
Olonetz -	2,732	Nijni-Nowgorod	876
Stavropol -	2,650	Wladimir -	862
Wiatka -	2,500	Orel -	859
Kingdom of Poland - -	2,294	Bessarabia -	858
Government of Nowgorod -	2,213	Koursk -	818
Minsk -	1,622	Pskow - -	816
Kostroma -	1,496	Witebsk -	810
Kherson -	1,332	Podolia -	774
Simbirsk -	1,315	Wilna -	768
Wolhynia -	1,297	Riazan -	766
Twer - -	1,223	Kowno -	758
Woronèje -	1,209	Grodno -	692
Tauride (including Sea of Azow)	1,208	Penza -	690
		Jaroslaw -	660
		Moscow -	589
Ekathérinoslaw	1,206	Kalouga -	573
Tambow -	1,202	Toula -	585
Kazan -	1,128	Courland -	496
Smolensk -	1,019	Esthonia -	370
		Total extent -	99,275
Carried forward -	79,179		

The extent of the Russian possessions in Asia is distributed in M. Reden's Comparative Statistics in the following manner.

1. Transcaucasian Provinces —   Geogr. Sq. M.

Georgia -	-	-	-	-	-	- 1,475
Armenia	-	-	-	-	-	- 1,350

2. Siberia —

Government of Omsk and Tobolsk	-	-	-	24,900
Tomsk -	-	-	-	60,400
Jenisseisk, Irkoutsk, and Okhotsk, together with Kamtschatka			-	- 123,300
Steppes of the Kirghiz, tributary to Russia		-	-	30,000
The Islands -	-	-	-	- 1,110
Total	-	-	-	- 242,535

The extent of the colonies in America is estimated at 17,500 geographical square miles.

On inspecting the table of the superficial extent of all the governments of Russia in Europe, we perceive that there are enormous disproportions betwixt them in this respect; for, even setting aside the two extreme members of the series, namely the government of Archangel and that of Esthonia, the former of which is forty-four times the size of the latter, there are still governments which stand to each other as to superficial extent in the proportion of 10 or even 14 to 1. Thus, for example, the government of Wologda is almost fourteen times as large as that of Courland. The territorial extent of a single government, that of Archangel, exceeds by nearly a third the superficies of the whole Austrian Empire, Hungary included; and several of them are from four to ten times as large as the most considerable States of the Germanic Confederation, Prussia alone excepted.

This immense extent of empire is attended with many inconveniences in regard to administration and finance. It opposes great obstacles to internal communication, to the exchange of the productions of the soil and of industry, and consequently to the progress of national wealth. It also presents great varieties of result from administrative and financial legislation; for a measure or regulation which is of easy execution in one of the Baltic provinces, having an extent of three or four hundred square miles, may often be attended with very different practical results in the governments of Wologda or Archangel,—the former with a surface of nearly seven thousand, the latter, of more than fifteen thousand square miles, and with an exceedingly thin and scattered population.

For a considerable portion of the empire, nature has obviated the difficulties resulting from these great distances by a very extensive network of river communication, the utility of which we shall afterwards have occasion to refer to. During four or five months of the year, likewise, land transport by means of sledges is facilitated by the abundance of snow.

This brief sketch of the extent and the geographical position of Russia is sufficient to make us perceive the great importance of those undertakings which have for their object to multiply our means of communication, and to complete by canals, roads, and railroads, the facilities afforded by our lakes and watercourses. The great importance of those matters has not escaped the attention of Government, as we may perceive from the immense works now being executed at a vast expense under the direction of a ministry created specially for that branch of administration. The utility of these works will depend in great measure on the systematic order which will be followed in their execution: they are intended to embrace the *ensemble* of the great strategetical, commercial, financial, and industrial interests of the empire, and the urgency of the constructions undertaken or to be undertaken will be measured by the importance of the interests which call for them, and the practical advantages which may be anticipated as their result.

CHAP. II.

CLIMATE, NATURAL FERTILITY, AND CONFIGURATION OF THE SOIL.

Configuration of Soil. — Mountain Chains. — Climate. — Direction of Isothermal, Isotheral, and Isochimenal Lines. — Hydrographic System. — Natural Fertility of Soil. — Classification of Empire into Zones and Regions. — Region of the Steppes. — Region where Black Mould (*tschernozième*,) predominates. — Future importance of the Steppes. — Classification of Governments according to their Fertility.

EUROPEAN RUSSIA is essentially a country of plains. The principal mountain chains are found on the east and south. The Ural mountains, which extend from the country of the Kirghiz to the icy ocean, form a natural frontier between Russia in Europe and her Asiatic possessions. The whole mountainous portion of the governments of Orenburg and Perm belongs to that chain. The mountains of the Caucasus extend from the Caspian to the Black Sea, and, like the Ural mountains on the north, separate Europe from Asia on the south; to this system belong the mountains of the government of Stavropol and the Crimea. Some spurs of the Carpathians extend into the north of Bessarabia, and lose themselves by degrees in slight eminences in the governments of Kiew and Podolia. Another branch of the Carpathian system stretches away into the kingdom of Poland, where it is lost near the territory of the city of Cracow. The heights of Finland and of the governments of Olonetz and Archangel belong to the Scandinavian system. The principal chain of mountains traversing Finland is termed the Maanselkä. The only mountains occupying the central portion of the empire are the Waldaï, which scarcely deserve the name, and might be considered rather as an elevated *plateau :* their culminating point does not rise to more than 175 toises above the level of the ocean. The whole remainder of the country is a flat intersected by a few hills. The sources of the Volga, near Lake Seliger in the government of Twer, do not rise in height to more than 895 feet. The city of Moscow, situated between the Upper Volga and the basin of the Oka, that is, on the southern slope of the Waldaï heights, stands at an elevation of not more than 384 feet. The city of Kazan, situated towards the middle of the course of the Volga, stands only 65 feet above the level of the sea.

Central Russia alone forms a plain (for most part of great fertility) of about 18,000 square miles in extent, that is, almost one and a half times as large as the whole Austrian Empire, and almost twice as large as France. According to the most recent calculations, the extent of the plains of European Russia would stand to that of countries more or less mountainous in the proportion of 14 to 1.*

This configuration of the soil, and other physical and geographical causes, exercise a sensible influence upon our climate.

It is well known that the vicinity of large bodies of water tempers the heats of summer and the extreme rigour of winter. But the greater portion of Russia is remote from these great reservoirs of a moderate and less variable temperature. For Western Europe every west wind is a sea wind, softened by contact with the waters of an ocean of which the temperature never descends below + 7° of Reaumur, whilst it is a continental wind for Asia and the East of Europe. The Asiatic continent presents an immense surface, separated from the ocean, on the west, by the entire extent of Europe, and not interrupted, like the European continent, by the numerous gulfs which mitigate the temperature of that part of the globe. The plains of Asia are exposed on the north to the winds which arrive from the polar regions, and are covered on the south by chains of mountains which intercept the hot winds of the tropics. All these circumstances contribute to the asperity of the climate of this part of the world, the vicinity of which must necessarily exercise a very sensible influence on the temperature and atmospheric variations of a large portion of European Russia. The atmosphere is chilled by the icy wind arriving from the arctic regions, which sweeps unopposed over all the Russian plains; whilst the east winds, entering from the plain of central Asia by the interval which separates the Ural mountains from the Caspian Sea, frequently occasion droughts which extend over a vast extent of territory. From the concurring operation of these causes it results that, at similar latitudes, our climate is much more severe than that of the western countries of Europe, and that it becomes so considerably colder in proportion as we approach the east.

By instructions from the Ministry of Domains, there has been prepared a statistico-agricultural atlas of European Russia, which contains, along with much other interesting information, a climatological chart founded on a long series of meteorological observations, on which is indicated the direction of the isothermal lines, as well for the mean temperature of the year, as for

* See Reden's Vergleichende Cultur-Statistik, p. 70.

the temperatures of summer and of winter. From this chart we perceive that all the isothermal lines follow, with slight deviations, a direction constantly more and more inclined towards the south in proportion as we advance towards the east,—in other words, that, to find the same elevation of temperature as we approach the east, we must at the same time approach nearer to the equator. This inclination is especially marked in those lines, termed "isochimenal," which indicate the mean temperature of winter. Thus, for example, at the bay called Tscheskaya-Gouba, in the government of Archangel, in 67° of latitude, and in the Ural mountains at the source of the little river Ouy, in the government of Orenburg, in 55° of latitude, the mean winter temperature is alike — 12°, although there is between the two localities a difference of 12° of latitude ; that is, the one is 180 geographical miles nearer the equator than the other. At the mouth of the Dwina, in latitude 65°, and at Orenburg, between 51° and 52°, which is more than 220 geographical miles nearer the equator, the mean temperature of winter is — 10° ; at St. Petersburg, in latitude 60°, and at Woronèje, in latitude 52°, it is — 6° ; at Souwalki, government of Augustow, in the kingdom of Poland, latitude 54°, and in the environs of Kherson, latitude 47°, it is — 2°.

The isothermal lines, which indicate the mean temperature of the year, have a less marked inclination than the preceding. The greatest deviation towards the south from the line parallel to the equator is 9°, or 135 geographical miles. Thus, for example, at about 15 miles to the north of Archangel, in the latitude of 65°, and at 15 miles to the east of Nijnitiagoulsk, in the government of Perm, in latitude 57°, the mean temperature of the year is 0° ; at the mouth of the Onéga, in the government of Archangel, between 63° and 64°, and at the upper part of the river Ural in the government of Orenburg, in latitude 54°, the mean annual temperature is + 1 ; in the environs of Revel, in 59°, and at 25 miles to the south of Saratow, in 50°, it is + 4° ; to the south-west of Warsaw, between 51° and 52°, and at 10 miles to the north-west of Stavropol, between 45° and 46°, it is + 7° ; at 15 miles to the south-west of Odessa, between 45° and 46°, and in the environs of Derbent, between 41° and 42°, it is + 9.

The lines termed isotheral, which indicate the mean temperature of summer, are those which least deviate from parallelism to the equator, that is, their inclination towards the south in proportion as we approach the east, is much less considerable. The greatest difference of latitude betwixt districts possessing the same mean summer temperature does not exceed 4°. Sometimes the difference does not exceed one degree.   Thus, at St. Petersburg, in latitude 60°, and in the environs of Perm, on the north, between 58° and 59°, the mean temperature of summer is +13°;' at Pskow, in 58°, and to the south of Oufa in the government of Orenburg in 54°, it is + 14°; in the environs of Wilna, in latitude 55°, and at 7 miles to the north of Saratow in 52°, it is + 15°; a little to the south of Lublin, towards the Austrian frontier, between 50° and 51°, and at Taganrog in 47°, it is +17°.

As the mean temperature of the year decreases at equal latitudes in proportion as we approach the east, so the difference between summer and winter temperature becomes much more considerable as we proceed in that direction.   This may be perceived by inspecting the following table, which we borrow from an article on the Climate of Russia, lately published by M. Wesselowski.

NAMES OF PLACES.	North Latitude.	East Longitude.	Elevation, in Feet.	Mean Temperature.*	Difference between Summer and Winter Temperature.
	° ′	° ′		°	°
Saint Petersburg -	59 56	47 57	0	+ 2·9	18·8
Moscow - - -	55 45	55 13	384	+ 3·6	21·2
Kazan - - -	55 47	66 47	64	+ 2·0	24·9
Ekatherinburg - -	56 50	78 14	820	+ 0·7	24·9
Bogoslowsk - -	59 45	77 39	600	− 0·7	26·8
Barnaoul - - -	53 19	101 36	400	− 0·3	28·3
Tomsk - - -	56 29	102 49	300	− 0·3	25·6
Irkoutsk - - -	52 17	121 55	1,300	− 0·5	27·0
Nertschinsk - ·	51 55	134 12	2,100	− 3·2	34·6
Jakoutsk - - . -	62 1	147 23	–	− 8·8	42·2

In consequence of this oriental and continental situation of Russia, which deprives it of the softening influences exerted on the climate of western Europe by the vicinity of the Atlantic Ocean, and the gulfs which proceed from it, the winters with us are much more severe than there, when compared with the mean temperature of the whole year.   In none of the countries of Western Europe, where the mean temperature of the year attains the height of + 7·2° or + 7·6°, does the mean temperature of winter sink (except it may be rarely) below zero: in Russia, again, it is only in places which have a mean annual temperature of + 8·5° or + 9°, that the mean temperature of winter rises above the freezing point.   In support of this observation, M. Wesselowski cites the following examples:—

* Reaumur's scale.

	Mean Temperature of the Year.	of Winter.
Odessa - - - -	+ 7·2°	− 1·8°
Nikolaïew - - -	+ 7·5	− 2·7
Kherson - - -	+ 7·9	− 1·9
Astrakhan - - -	+ 8·0	− 2·2
Kizliav - - - -	+ 8·6	− 1·5
Simferopol - - -	+ 8·5	+ 0·9
Sevastopol - - -	+ 9·4	+ 1·8
Tiflis - - - -	+ 9·9	+ 2·1

Those who are desirous of thoroughly studying the subject of Russian climate will find a great deal of detailed information in the meteorological observations of Messieurs de Humboldt and Kupfer, and in the interesting brochure of M. Wesselowski, from which we have borrowed the foregoing figures.

In regard to her hydrographic system, Russia, although less favoured by nature than many other countries, possesses nevertheless a considerable number of important rivers. The Volga, the Ural, the Emba, and the Terek, which fall unto the Caspian Sea; the Petschora, which discharges itself into the Arctic Ocean; the Onega and the Dwina, into the White Sea; the Neva, the Tornea, the Düna, the Niémen, and the Vistula which empty themselves into the Baltic; the Dniester, the Dnieper, and the Kouban, into the Black Sea; and the Don, into the Sea of Azow, form, along with their tributaries, the basis of a very extensive system of fluvial communication, which is so much the more valuable inasmuch as the mouths of all our principal rivers, with the exception of the Vistula and the Niémen, are situated within our own territory. The Vistula and the Dniester are the only rivers which have their source without the limits of the empire. Most of the principal rivers, flowing through a flat country, have a slow and regular course which opposes no invincible obstacles to their navigation; but, on the other hand, there are frequent shallows and a scarcity of water, resulting from the absence of those numerous little affluents which are continually feeding the larger rivers in countries of greater inclination. This deficit of water frequently impedes the operations of commerce both internal and external. Amongst the rivers which we have enumerated there are also some which are not yet navigable, or which are so only during the augmentation of the waters,—a period which is usually of shorter duration in flat countries than in mountainous, where the melting of the snow proceeds with less rapidity. In regard to foreign commerce, our fluvial system presents one grave disadvantage, namely, that, with the exception of the Dwina, the navigation of which is open for only a small portion of the year, all the principal rivers which wash our territories empty themselves into seas which are either entirely closed, as the Caspian, or which, like the Black Sea and the Baltic, have their egress through straits which are under the dominion of other states. The only way of modifying this disadvantage is by means of treaties, and of those international relations which tend more and more to secure to every country freedom of maritime navigation. To the physical impediments of our maritime commerce we must add that during great part of the year all our northern ports are closed by ice.

European Russia contains, in its northern portion, a great number of lakes, of which the more considerable are,—Ladoga, the largest in Europe, with a superficial extent of 324 square miles; Onega, in the government of Olonetz, with a surface of 229 square miles; Saïma, Payna, Etsäri, Pyhäjärsi, Saïjani, 26 miles long by 3½ in breadth; and Kolkis, in Finland; Enare-Fräsk, in Lapland, dependent on the Grand Duchy of Finland*; Lake Peipus, situated between the governments of Esthonia, Livonia, Pskow, and St. Petersburg; Ilmen, in the government of Nowgorod. To these we may add the White Lake (Belo Osero), in the government of Nowgorod, and Kubensk, in that of Wologda, which, although much smaller than most of the preceding, are of great importance for fluvial communication. In the 37 governments of which we have given, at page 5., the territorial extent, the lakes occupy 824 square miles, or more than 2 per cent. of the surface. These lakes complete the natural system of river communication, the utility of which is, however, limited by the great length of our winters.

There are also in the southern parts of the empire a great number of saliferous lakes, from whence salt is extracted in large quantities: the most important of these is Elton, in the government of Saratow.

Southern Russia also contains several lagunes in the north of the Crimea, and along the coasts of the governments of Kherson and Bessarabia, in the environs of Perekop and Otschakow, and along the mouths of the Danube.

In such a vast empire as Russia there must necessarily be much variety in the quality of the land; but in general,

* Finland is, besides these, covered with an infinity of small lakes, formed in the cavities of its rocky soil. According to Rühs (see his Statistics of Finland, published at Stockholm in 1827), nearly a third of the surface of that province is occupied by lakes and marshes.

throughout European Russia, the soil is abundantly fertile. "There is," says a Report from the Department of Rural Economy to the Ministry of Domains, "but a very small portion of our soil not susceptible of cultivation. We have but very little stony ground: it is only in the north that such occurs. Moving sands occur partially along the banks of rivers, and, to a greater extent, in the south-eastern portion of the steppes, that is to say, on the confines of the empire; but in that part of the steppes, what we more frequently meet with is land with a saline base. Still, those lands which are unsuitable for culture occupy but a small space compared with the whole immense extent of the empire; and we must observe, that a considerable portion of our territory is covered with an eminently fertile soil, which we term *tschernozième* (black earth or humus), the like of which is not found in any part of Western Europe. The region covered with this soil extends northward, on the west side, to latitude 51°, and on the east side to 57°; southward, it extends, on the west to 47°, and on the east to 54° of north latitude; embracing (according to an approximative estimate) a superficies of 87,000,000 of dessiatines (= 234,000,000 of acres). This immense surface forms a precious treasure for agriculture. On the other hand, the rivers which wash our territory flow, for most part, over a bed which is but slightly depressed beneath their banks, and often inundate extensive valleys of excellent meadow land."

This natural fertility of our soil is partly counteracted by the atmospheric influences of our climate, especially by frequent droughts. The direction of our isothermal lines determines the limits of the different cultures. Thus, for example (as we learn farther from the Report just quoted), whilst in Norway, wheat is cultivated up to the 70th degree of north latitude, with us the limit of that culture descends in Finland to 63°; in the government of Archangel, to below 62°; in the government of Olonetz to below 61°; in that of Wologda, to below 59°; and in that of Wiatka, to 57°.

The Agricultural Gazette contained (supplement to No. 1. 1834) an interesting article, which classifies the empire, in regard to physical culture, in eight zones, as follows:—

1. The *icy zone*, which embraces Nova Zembla, the northern extremity of Siberia, and a part of the circle of Kola in the government of Archangel. The countries embraced in this zone, rendered uninhabitable by the rigour of the climate and the absence of vegetation, are visited only by hunters and fishers, who come principally from the government of Archangel.

2. The *marshy zone.*—In this zone the land is alternately

stony, marshy, and covered with moss and heath. The soil is exceedingly ungrateful, and the rigour of the climate enhances the difficulties of culture. It is the home of the rein-deer, which have replaced most of the other domestic animals. Fish and rein-deer flesh form the principal food of the inhabitants, and the chase of marine and furred animals their principal means of subsistence. They also hunt the swan and wild-goose, which arrive there in numbers during the moulting season, and breed in the mossy marshes. These two birds of passage, and two or three others, are the only birds known in this region.

3. *Zone of forests and of cattle-rearing.*—This commences where the former terminates. The chase, especially of the squirrel, continues to be the principal resource of the inhabitants. It is only in the southern part of this zone, which is rich in forage, that the rearing of cattle begins to acquire importance, and that we find some traces of agriculture. The northern part is inhabited only by nomades.

4. *Zone where agriculture properly so called commences*, termed also *Barley zone*, for this, from the shortness of the summer, is the only grain which can be successfully cultivated. Still, the potatoe begins to acclimatise, and likewise a few garden vegetables. As, however, the amount of agricultural products is but limited, a large portion of the population subsists by the rearing of cattle, the chase, fishing, and wood-floating. This zone extends southwards to the city of Jarensk in the government of Wologda, that is, to the 63rd degree of north latitude.

5. *Zone of rye and flax.*—The culture of these grains succeeds better than any other. This zone, which embraces the principal portion of the empire, extends southward to the centre of the government of Tschernigow, in latitude 51°. The climate is in general sufficiently favourable to agriculture;—more rigorous towards the east in the direction of Siberia, and becoming milder by degrees in proportion as we advance towards the west. In the Baltic provinces the cold is tempered by the vicinity of the sea, and the climate is in general less harsh than in the other parts of that zone which are situated under the same latitude. In this region the forests are visibly diminishing, with the exception of those districts where, from want of the means of transporting timber, it would be unprofitable to fell them. This part of Russia is particularly favoured in regard to river communication. The soil is in general abundantly fertile; but agriculture is far behind in its modes of cultivation, with the exception of the Baltic provinces, where it is considerably more advanced than in the rest. Rye and flax being the principal products of this zone, the culture of wheat is a matter of second-

ary consideration.   The fruits of the garden succeed only in the west,—principally in the governments of Grodno and Wilna. The apple is almost the only garden fruit cultivated with success in the central parts of this zone.

6. *Zone of wheat and of garden fruits,*—thus designated because the climate is more favourable for these productions, and because they are cultivated in greater abundance here than in the preceding region.   This zone, which extends southwards to Ekathérinoslaw, or to the 48th degree of north latitude, is considered with reason the granary of the empire.   The provinces which it embraces supply the provisions of St. Petersburg and of a great part of the army, besides furnishing cereals in considerable quantities for exportation.   Besides wheat and other cereals, millet, buck-wheat, and hemp are cultivated in this zone with much more success than in the preceding one.   The culture of tobacco begins to acquire importance, and is much more extensive than in other parts of the empire.   The rearing of cattle and the distillation of spirits are the chief branches of rural economy.   The rearing of bees forms also an object of some importance.   The difference of climate, in proportion as we approach or recede from the east, is much more sensible here than in the preceding zones.   In the western governments, as Kiew and Podolia, the climate is exceedingly healthy and favourable to vegetation, whilst the eastern portions are subject to the harsh temperature of the plains of Asia.   Accordingly, many products which are cultivated with success in these western governments do not thrive under similar latitudes in the countries lying farther east.   A considerable portion of this region is occupied by the *steppes*.   These may be classed into the grass-bearing, the pasturage, the heathy, and the sandy and stony.*   The deficiency of wood, which is very perceptible in a great part of the country comprised in this zone, has been attributed to different causes,—as the hardness and quality of the soil, which render it unfavourable to sylviculture, the dryness of the climate in the southern districts, the saline substances which are hurtful to vegetation.   Some writers, amongst whom

---

* M. Hermann estimates the extent of the steppes of the whole empire at nearly a third of its total superficies.   This calculation seems exaggerated.   M. Arsénieff reckons the extent of the steppes of European Russia at 17,728 square miles, which would make about $\frac{2}{11}$ of the total surface; but he has omitted several governments of which considerable portions belong to this region.   M. Brinken, who has taken a deal of trouble to determine precisely the limits of the steppes in European Russia, gives, in his work upon the rewooding of these countries, a geographical and geognostical map, according to which their extent would exceed 21,000 square miles, — which we take to be the nearest approach to correctness that has been made.

is M. Hermann, attribute this want of timber to the destruction of forests by the nomadic populations; but this opinion finds contradictors, in the number of whom is M. Baer, author of the Preface to M. Koeppen's Report on the forests and waters of the Volga.* In part of these countries the re-timbering has become almost impossible, but in many of them we think it might succeed by dint of perseverance, especially if government, which has already bestowed great attention on the subject, continues its fostering care, by applying sufficient pecuniary means to the promotion of such enterprises, where the eventual profits appear too remote to invite the speculations of private parties. It is a question of much importance for the future of these countries, and one to which we shall have occasion to return in the sequel. The deficiency of water is likewise a great obstacle to the advancement of culture and population. In no country would artesian wells be of such great utility as here. It is long since this object began to attract the notice of government; but great obstacles have been met with in the nature of the soil, and the geognostical conformation of the rocks: of the numerous attempts which have been made since 1832, very few have hitherto been successful: still, they have not been abandoned. The difficulties which the steppes present to the cultivation of the soil are partly compensated by the advantages which they offer for the rearing of sheep and cattle, and by their numerous salt lakes and salt marshes, which supply a large part of Russia with salt.

7. *Zone of maize and of the vine.* — This zone embraces Bessarabia, New Russia, the country of the Don Cossacks, the government of Astrakhan, the provinces of the Caucasus, and the Crimea; of which, however, the southern portion belongs rather to the eighth zone. Independently of all the productions of the preceding zones, the vine is cultivated with success in several parts of this region, and the culture of maize is widely diffused. The steppes still extend over a large portion of its surface. They are partly utilised as pasture, for the rearing of cattle, which here, also, constitutes an important branch of rural economy; but they contain a large extent of soil which is totally unproductive. The upper part of Bessarabia is a mountainous country, partially wooded, and with a very fertile soil; the lower part is composed almost entirely of steppes; the slopes along the rivers are favourable to the culture of the vine. The government of Kherson forms a plateau intersected by deep and narrow valleys. The soil is very hard, and is exposed to frequent droughts, which occasion deficient harvests. This

* Beiträge zur Kenntniss des russischen Reiches, vol. 4

province is also frequently ravaged by locusts. The government of Ekathérinoslaw suffers less from these plagues; still a portion of it, on the eastern side, is frequently a prey to droughts. The northern part of the government of the Tauride is a country of steppes, occupied principally in the rearing of cattle. This country is particularly rich in salt marshes. The southern part of the Crimea has a real garden climate. The vine, the olive, the caper-shrub, and many other plants which require a mild temperature, are cultivated with success. This part of the Crimea lies, therefore, in the following zone. The southern portion of the government of Woronèje is composed almost exclusively of steppes which are suitable for culture. The south-western portion of the country of the Don Cossacks is more suited for agriculture than the rest of that country. In the lands in the vicinity of the Don and its affluents, the vine is cultivated at intervals; this province likewise furnishes anthracite, iron, and a little lead. The soil of the government of Astrakhan is in great part very sandy; it presents but meagre pasturage; but it is tolerably adapted to the culture of the vine. The northern side of the government of Stavropol contains sandy tracts of country and salt marshes. Its nomadic inhabitants find their chief occupation in the rearing of cattle. The southern part, bordering on the Terek and the Kuban, contains at intervals land suitable for agriculture, and producing good wheat. In this respect its western side is far superior to its eastern. The vine is cultivated in the environs of Kizliar. The country of the Black Sea Cossacks is very similar in character to the other countries of the government of Stavropol, with the exception of a rather considerable tract of flat land in the neighbourhood of the sea. The cultivation of gardens and the rearing of sheep are carried on to a considerable extent in this zone; but this part of Russia is essentially deficient in forests. More care ought to be devoted to the working of coal, of which extensive strata have been discovered.

8. *Zone of the olive, the silkworm, and the sugar-cane.* — This zone embraces the transcaucasian provinces, a mountainous country with great variety of climate according to situation. The valleys abound in plants peculiar to warm climates; the heights are covered with pastures, and are adapted to the culture of cereals. The vine, the mulberry, and many other fruits, are cultivated in the temperate valleys. In those where the climate is warmer, and especially in the provinces conquered from Persia, cotton and rice are cultivated with success, though in many cases irrigation is requisite. The olive grows only in the western districts. The sugar-cane is cultivated in the

c 2

lower districts near the Kour, which have a very warm climate and an eminently fertile soil; but it is not probable that the cultivation will ever become very extensive. The trans-Caucasian provinces produce also cochineal, assafœtida, madder, and safflower, the culture of which may, with time, become of great importance. Silk is one of their principal products.

M. Arsénieff divides European Russia, as regards its agriculture, into eight regions, which we shall here briefly indicate.

1. *Northern Region.*

This region extends from the gulfs of Bothnia and Finland to the northern part of the Ural mountains. It embraces Finland and the governments of Archangel, Wologda, and Olonetz,— a total extent of 31,620 square miles, or nearly a third of all European Russia. In this region, the cultivated land and meadows do not occupy above 2 per cent. of the surface ; nor do they suffice for the subsistence of its very thin population. The soil is generally ungrateful, and, from the rigour of the climate, cultivation is difficult. The forests, which in the three northern governments occupy nearly three-fifths of the surface, constitute the principal riches of these regions. In Finland they occupy somewhat more than a fifth of the surface.

2. *Region of the Alaoune Heights.* (*Alaounskoe prostranstvo.*)

This is the name given by Russian geographers to the elevated plateau which separates the basins of the Dniéper and the Wolga, whose waters flow in a southerly and south-easterly direction from that of the Dwina, the course of which is towards the west. This region comprehends the governments of St. Petersburg, Nowgorod, Twer, Smolensk, and Pskow, and occupies an extent of 6,233 square miles. It possesses a much larger proportion than the preceding of arable lands. These occupy nearly a fifth of its surface ; but, from the fault of both soil and climate, their fertility is not great. It is comparatively deficient in meadow and in good pasture land. The meadows have not one-sixth part of the extent of the arable land. More than half the surface is occupied by forests.

3. *Region of the Baltic.*

In this region, which covers an extent of 1724 square miles, are comprised the governments of Livonia, Courland, and Esthonia. The cultivable land does not occupy more than about $7\frac{1}{2}$ per cent. of its surface. It is not in general very fertile, and would not suffice for the subsistence of the inhabitants, if the natural powers of the soil were not enhanced by a more rational mode of culture than prevails in the other parts of Russia. The extent of the meadows is more in proportion to that of the cultivated land than in the preceding regions. Nearly half the surface is occupied by forests.

4. *Lower Region.* (*Nizmennoe prostranstvo.*)

The slight elevation of this region is characterised by the number of rivers, large and small, which descend to it from the Alaoune heights and the regions of the Carpathians, as also by very extensive marshes. It embraces the governments of Witebsk, Mohilew, Minsk, Grodno, Wilna, and Kowno, and occupies an extent of 5,533 square miles. In respect to the quality of its soil, it is one of the poorest. The arable land occupies more than a third of its surface; the meadows are not numerous; their extent may be to the cultivable land nearly in the proportion of 1 to 3. Forests take up about a third of the surface, and lands unsuitable for culture, including marshes, occupy nearly a seventh.

5. *Region of the Carpathians.*

This region, of about 5,862 square miles in extent, occupies the lowest heights descending from the Carpathian mountains, which extend, constantly lowering, from the frontiers of Gallicia to the affluents of the Upper Dniéper; that is, to the rivers Dessna, Soula, Psla, and Worsla, and, in a south-easterly direction, to the waters which pertain to the basin of the Don. It embraces the Ukraine and Little Russia, namely, the governments of Kiew, Wolhynia, Podolia, Tschernigow, Poltawa, and Kharkow.

This is one of the most fertile, and by nature the most favoured parts of Russia. In the portion situated beyond the Dniéper, the cultivated land occupies, in the governments of Kiew and Podolia, more than half, and in that of Wolhynia, about a third of the surface. The meadows occupy, in the government of Kiew, less than a tenth; in that of Wolhynia, about 12 per cent.; and in that of Podolia, nearly a fifth of the surface. The forests occupy, in the government of Kiew, more than a fifth; in that of Wolhynia, nearly two-fifths; and in that of Podolia, 12 per cent. of the superficies. In the portion on this side the Dniéper, the arable lands occupy, in the government of Tschernigow, more than three-fifths; in that of Poltawa, more than two-fifths; and in that of Kharkow, nearly two-fifths of the surface. The meadows occupy, in the government of Tschernigow, $12\frac{1}{2}$ per cent., and in those of Poltawa and of Kharkow more than a fourth of the surface. The forests occupy, in the government of Tschernigow, nearly a fifth; in

that of Poltawa, 12 per cent. ; and in that of Kharkow, 11 per
cent. of the surface.   Throughout this region, the soil proper
for culture is composed in great part of black humus (tschernozième) of exceeding fertility.

6. *Region of the Steppes.*

The steppes extend from the mouth of the Danube, along the
shores of the Black Sea and the Sea of Azow, and across the
lower parts of the Don, the Volga, and the Ural, on to the plains
of Central Asia.   This region occupies an extent of 17,728 square
miles.*   It embraces the governments of Bessarabia, Kherson,
Ekathérinoslaw, Tauride, Stavropol, Astrakhan, and the country
of the Don Cossacks.   It is distinguished from every other part
of Russia by the peculiar character of its soil.   The greater
part of this vast country is without wood and without water.
Pasture and prairie occupy the larger portion of its extent.

7. *Central Region.*

This region extends from the central part of the Volga to the
upper portions of the Khoper, the Don, the Oka, and the
Dessna.   It occupies a superficies of 11,126 square miles, and
embraces thirteen governments, namely, Jaroslaw, Kostroma,
Wladimir, Nijni-Nowgorod, Penza, Tambow, Woronèje, Koursk,
Orel, Kalouga, Moscow, Toula, and Riazan.   It is one vast
plain, of which the soil is partly mediocre, partly of a fair amount
of fertility, but in general suitable for the culture of cereals.

8. *Region of the Ural.*

This region occupies the whole eastern part of European
Russia, and extends from the government of Astrakhan to that
of Archangel.   It embraces the governments of Simbirsk, Kazan, Wiatka, Perm, and Orenburg,—a total extent of 16,597
square miles.   The soil is in general fertile.   The arable land
occupies about 14 per cent., the meadows nearly 10 per cent.,
and the forests nearly half of the surface.

In the following chapter the reader will find tables of classification of the soil of each government.   Here we shall confine
ourselves to the addition of a few words upon the region of the
Steppes.

This region, which occupies about a fifth of the whole possessions of the Russian empire in Europe, or more than twice the
extent of France, is, both from its immense extent and from its
geographical position, called to take an important part in the

* See note, p. 17.

gradual development of the productive forces of Russia, and deserves on that account our particular consideration.

The opinions which we have heard expressed with regard to the agricultural capabilities of these countries are various and conflicting. Some consider the larger portion of the steppes as unfertilisable deserts; others, dazzled by the prosperity of some isolated colonies, believe nothing wanting but hands and judicious culture to convert them into rich and fertile plains. We have always thought it probable that the truth must lie somewhere betwixt these two extreme opinions, and we have been confirmed in our surmise by the perusal of a paper of M. Koeppen, inserted in the "Beiträge zur Kenntniss des russischen Reiches,"—a statistical journal which has for some years been published at St. Petersburg, under the editorship of Messieurs Baer and Helmersen. Those who take an interest in the matter will find there a number of instructive facts bearing upon the quality of the soil, the character of the vegetation, the most appropriate culture, and the atmospheric influences of these regions; and we place the more confidence in the writer's opinions, because they are based upon a long series of observations and agronomic experiments made upon the spot. The reader will also find very interesting information on this part of Russia in the work of M. Haxthausen*, who has drawn it from the best sources, and completed it from observations collected during his travels in the South of Russia.

Amongst other peculiarities of the steppes, a very prominent and the most distinctive one is the absence of timber. In the north of Russia, the soil covers itself of its own accord with trees and heaths, and immense forests are the product; in the provinces of the south, herbaceous vegetation invades the soil with a force of increase which is rarely to be met with in the other countries of Europe. Herbs, which elsewhere are scarcely twelve inches high, attain in the steppes a height of five or six feet or more. In some places the stratum of soil proper for vegetation is not deep enough to admit of trees taking root; in others, it is the vigorous growth of the grasses which prevents the development of forest vegetation unaided by the care of man. Opinions differ greatly as to the possibility of wooding it anew. Upon comparing all the information which we possess upon this point, it may, we conceive, be laid down as certain, that in part of the steppes sylviculture is impossible, or at least too difficult and costly to warrant the attempt†, whilst in other portions partial

* Studien über die innere Zustände, das Volksleben und insbesondere die ländlichen Einrichtungen Russlands.

† After long experiments made on the domains of the Duke of Anhalt-Koethen at Askanianova, in the government of Tauride, M. Teetzmann, the

plantations and sowings would be a very practical undertaking, holding out a fair promise of large ultimate benefit. The most suitable localities for such improvements would be the banks of rivers, and the numerous ravines formed by the infiltration of rain water.

The traces of ancient forests still to be found in many districts show that the present nakedness of the steppes in regard to forest vegetation does not proceed solely from natural causes, as climate and soil, but must be attributed, in part at least, to the destruction of forests which once existed. Professor Haxthausen observed, during his travels in the government of Saratow, that the rivers Irguiss, Jarouslan and Aktouba were still bordered with fine forests of oak, birch, poplar, and aspen, but that no pines (nadelholz) were to be met with. According to the best information he was able to obtain, the forests along the banks of the Irguiss were impenetrable thickets about sixty years ago; since then they have been greatly wasted. The same author observes, speaking of this government, " If the necessary ways of communication were established, if the small rivers were rendered navigable, which would be a matter of little difficulty, if what remains of the forests were preserved and new ones were planted, if peat-bogs, which ought not to be rare, were searched for and worked, this country could not fail, from the extraordinary fertility of its soil and its favourable geographical position, to become in a short time one of the richest provinces of the empire."

The partial attempts at sylviculture, which have been perfectly successful in some German settlements situated in districts the most thoroughly stripped of their timber, and which have been successful also with some private proprietors, show that the rewooding of a portion of the steppes is by no means impossible, and that the great thing required would be to undertake the culture on a large scale, and to pursue it with system and perseverance, making a careful selection of the proper districts, and adapting the species of trees to be sown or planted as well to the depth as to the quality of the soil. Parties have often allowed themselves to be too easily discouraged by a want of success arising from some local accident. M. Lowschine, formerly governor of Odessa, succeeded, says M. Haxthausen, in forming a thriving plantation upon a bed of barren sand.

The same publicist observes that in travelling through the

registrar of the property, made a calculation, from which it would appear that rewooding would cost 1428 silver roubles per dessiatine (£84 sterling per imperial acre). But this estate is situated in one of the most unfavourable localities for sylviculture.

governments of Simbirsk and Saratow, he often met with brush-wood composed chiefly of dwarf oak; and he thinks that these might often be turned to good account in the formation of quickset hedges, as in Vendée and the north of Westphalia, the introduction of which would be of great service to cultivation.

The upper stratum of the soil presents every variety of composition, from shifting sands and saline impregnations up to the most fertile composts. As this stratum generally rests upon a basis not very accessible to infiltrations, it is upon its thickness that the degree of its fertility depends. Where it is not deep enough to retain the moisture, it easily becomes saturated with rain water and is as easily dried up by evaporation. This is of course an immense impediment to culture in countries where droughts are so frequent and of such long duration, that it is nothing uncommon for twenty months to pass without a single copious shower of rain. It is not so bad as this in *all* the steppes; but such is at least their predominant character in several governments of the south and east. This infrequency of rain, joined to the want of reservoirs, forms notoriously one of the chief drawbacks of the country; but the vegetation of that part of the steppes which is used merely for pasture possesses a peculiar character by which the deleterious influence of drought is diminished. Nature here exhibits her wonderful variety of resource. Spring vegetation generally lasts in these countries for about three months; if this period pass without a sufficiency of rain, the herbage does not attain its natural height; it is dried up whilst its sap is still in full vigour, and in this state it affords a substantial food for cattle for the space of nine months. These pastures are particularly suitable for sheep. When, on the other hand, the spring rains happen to be in excess, the vegetation becomes too rank: the herbage attains four times its natural height; and a plant called *stipa capillata* sends forth strong prickles, which penetrate into the flesh of the sheep, causing them acute pain, and often proving fatal; the pasture at the same time becomes less wholesome and nourishing; so that, by a strange anomaly, in this country, where the general complaint is of drought, those proprietors who have heavy stocks of sheep prefer a dry season to a superabundance of moisture. The vegetation of the pasturage steppes presents another peculiarity, namely, that it is not equally spread over the surface of the soil, but is found scattered as it were in little islands. A continuous sward is to be met with only in very low valleys.

M. Teetzmann, registrar of estates to the Duke of Anhalt-Koethen, whose memoir is appended to Mr. Koeppen's work already mentioned, divides the steppes into two categories,—the *perpetual* (ewige Steppen), and the *accidental* (zufällige Steppen). The former, in which the permeable stratum of the soil is exceedingly thin, will, in his opinion, never be susceptible of much culture, and timbering is there out of the question; for the culture even of fruit trees is very difficult and requires incessant attention.   In the latter category he ranks that portion of the steppes where the permeable stratum of the soil is thicker, more appropriate for agriculture, and at the same time more favourable to forest vegetation, of which we still find traces in those valleys which do not rise more than twelve or eighteen feet above the level of the sea.

As for the culture of esculent plants according to a rational system of husbandry, it seems to result, from the experiments which have been made, that this is totally impracticable; but though the systems of three-shift or alternate rotations, pursued in other countries, cannot be applied here, satisfactory results may be obtained in good situations by proceeding in a manner appropriate to the local circumstances.   Grain is sown in the same field for several years successively; the land is then left fallow and allowed to sward itself; the first year there is a plentiful crop of weeds; during the second and third these gradually disappear, and the pasture becomes more nourishing.   When it is found that the soil has sufficiently recruited, it is again converted into corn land; and this agronomic cycle is renewed every ten, twelve, or fifteen years, according to situation and natural fertility.

M. Teetzmann gives a statistical table of the harvests on the estates of the Duke of Anhalt-Koethen during the ten years from 1832 to 1841, from which it appears that rye and wheat gave at an average 6 returns, barley 7, and millet 23.   Some years there was a return from rye of 16, from wheat and barley of 15, and from millet of no less than 64; but, on the other hand, in the course of the same decennial period, there was one year where the harvest was a complete failure, and there were others where it barely returned the seed.   To appreciate the above facts at their real value, we must observe that the estates in question are situated within what M. Teetzmann terms the *perpetual steppes*.

M. Haxthausen divides the steppes geognostically into five classes or formations: —

1. The calcareous tertiary formation predominates in Bessarabia, in Podolia, and in a small part of the government of Kherson.

2. Chalk forms the basis of the soil in the north, and embraces the steppes in the governments of Kharkow, Woronèje, Tam-

bow, part of the country of the Don Cossacks, and of the government of Saratow.

3. The granitic basis, which is derived from the Carpathians, extends along the Black Sea and the sea of Azow on to the Caucasus.

4. The mud steppes extend on the south-east along the Kouban and the Terek.

5. The steppes with a saline basis extend on the east to the river Taïk.

The steppes of the three first formations stand at a much higher elevation above the level of the sea than the two latter, which, according to Pallas, evidently formed the bottom of the waters that once united the Caspian and Black Seas. They are every where covered with a stratum of humus of greater or less thickness. The mud steppes are exceedingly fertile except where they are marshy. The steppes whose basis is granitic are covered for the most part with a thick but short herbage, whilst those having a cretaceous or calcareous basis produce herbs that attain a height of six or seven feet; meadow flowers and weeds are found in the utmost profusion; the river banks are covered with reeds, which, in the mud steppes, attain a height almost inconceivable. We find there also quantities of burdocks (a species of cynarocephalous plant, Fr. *Glouteron*, Germ. *Klette*), which attain a height of thirty or forty feet, and are used for firewood.

The future importance of the country of the steppes is chiefly concentrated in the districts situated above the Black Sea and the sea of Azow between the Carpathians and the Don.

The steppes with a saline basis, which stretch towards the east, besides being difficult of culture, are situated out of the path which the gradual development of the productive forces of the empire will naturally follow; and M. Haxthausen rightly considers that, both from their physical constitution, and their geographical situation, they will attain to no great importance for at least a long while to come.

The countries of the steppes contain a large portion of the *tschernozième*, that exceedingly fertile soil of which we have already spoken (p. 15.). The region in which this soil predominates, extends from the Ural mountains in the environs of Oufa, the capital of the government of Orenburg, westward to the environs of Krzemieniec in Podolia, taking a sweep to the south and passing by the governments of Kazan, Riazan, Orel, Kiew, and Wolhynia. The space occupied by soil of this quality embraces, according to information collected by the Ministry of Domains, the greater part of the government of Orenburg, a

considerable part of that of Kazan, the governments of Simbirsk
and of Penza, part of the government of Saratow; on the right
bank of the Volga, the government of Tambow, the country of
the Don Cossacks, great part of the government of Ekathérin-
noslaw, the governments of Poltawa, of Kharkow, and of Wor-
nonèje, part of the governments of Toulan and of Riazan, great
part of the government of Orel, part of the governments of
Tschernikow and of Kiew, the northern parts of the governments
of Kherson and of Bessarabia, Podolia, and a part of Wolhynia;
altogether about 18 per cent. of the whole surface of European
Russia.* We cannot consider the whole extent of soil ranked
in this category as being of exceeding fertility; for it is frequently intersected by marshes, and it also embraces a large
proportion of that region of the steppes where agriculture suffers
from frequent droughts; but the whole of the southern portion
of Russia, which is still very thinly peopled in proportion to the
extent and fertility of its soil, has a great future before it, when
we consider the immense reserve of productive forces which it
possesses within itself, and which are capable of being developed
with the progress of culture and the various successive improvements of which the country is susceptible. The following
quotation is from M. Haxthausen's work already mentioned.
Speaking of the future prospects of the provinces bordering on
the Black Sea and the Sea of Azow, which he terms Pontine
Countries (*pontische Landstriche*), he proceeds:—" The future
historical importance of the Pontine Countries for the civilised
European world consists, in my opinion, in the following circumstances. A time will come when the greater part of civilised
Europe will have an excess of population, which it will be unable to feed without having recourse to the importation of cereals.
It will then find reserved for it two granaries of abundance,—
the United States of America, and the region of black earth in
the centre and south of Russia. Here we find a country which
(taking into account that portion of the steppes not hitherto
brought under cultivation) comprehends 20,000 to 25,000 square
miles of the most fertile soil in the world, still very thinly
peopled, and with very little chance of being peopled up to its
resources at any time within the next century. There will arise
in that country immense magazines of corn for Europe, when
means of communication have been properly organised for enabling grain to be transported without difficulty or loss of time

* According to the approximative calculation already noticed (p. 15.), the
tschernozième occupies an extent of 87,000,000 dessiatines = 17,259 square miles,
which comes to 18 per cent. of the total surface (95,710 square miles, without
Nova Zembla). M. Haxthausen's estimate, 20,000 square miles, appears excessive.

or great expense, and at all seasons of the year, to the ports of
the Black Sea and the Sea of Azow.

" But these countries are of immense and immediate importance to Russia herself. What they already are, may enable us
in some measure to predict what they will become. A glance
at the map of Russia will make us understand this. The north
of the empire, or the region of forests, conveys its products partly
to the North Sea by way of Archangel, but in much larger
quantities, by means of its northern and north-eastern affluents,
to the majestic current of the Volga. By this route they reach
either the northern countries situated along the banks of this
river, or St. Petersburg and the Baltic by canal, or lastly, descending the Volga, they reach the southern countries situated
along its banks. The industrial countries of the centre of Russia
all carry their products to the Volga; it is by this great artery
of the empire that, descending the stream, they find their outlets as far as the Caspian Sea and beyond it; ascending the
river, they reach the Baltic by means of canals. The fertile
countries of the Volga and its southern affluents, convey the
produce of their soil upon this great highway of communication, provision the industrious but less fertile districts, and
send the surplus to Astrakhan and St. Petersburg. But besides
this system of communication, there is an immense country with
an eminently fertile soil, which stretches in a line from below
Penza to Kiew, and the rivers of which flow neither towards the
north nor towards the east, nor towards the Volga nor towards
the Baltic, but towards the south,—to the Black Sea. This
sea, then, is the sole natural outlet for the whole of that country, which embraces an extent of from 8 to 10,000 square miles.
So long as Russia was not in possession of the steppes and of
the shores of the Black Sea, it was impossible for these fine
countries to prosper; they must, if we may use the expression,
stifle in their own fatness. Accordingly, it is only since Russia
has come into incontested possession of her southern coasts, that
the culture and population of the countries in question have
begun to make evident progress. But it is not alone on the
provinces of the interior of Russia that these ports of its southern coast exercise an incalculable influence. They have likewise
become ports of exportation for the Polish provinces, and even
for Eastern Gallicia. None of these countries had formerly outlets for their produce except by the tedious road which leads to
the Baltic. It is not yet sixty years since all their corn went to
Danzig, Memel, and Koenigsberg; now it goes to Odessa.*

* Great part of the grain of the kingdom of Poland and of the neighbouring
provinces of the empire continues down to the present date to be exported from

Russia has already made great efforts to promote her commerce on the southern coasts of her empire, and to people and cultivate the contiguous steppes. The first part of her task has been surprisingly successful, within the short space of sixty years at the utmost; as regards the second part, the results hitherto attained have been less important."

In considering the various provinces of the empire separately in regard to the natural fertility of their arable land, they may be classed in the following manner.

Soil in general of great fertility.

Government of Podolia.	Government of Tambow.
„ Poltawa.	„ Woronéje.
„ Kharkow.	„ Koursk.
„ Bessarabia.	„ Simbirsk.
„ Saratow.	„ Kazan.
„ Penza.	

A large portion of the soil very fertile.

Government of Kiew.	Country of the Don Cossacks.
„ Wolhynia.	Government of Toula.
„ Tschernigow.	„ Riazan.
„ Ekathérinoslaw.	„ Orel.
„ Tauride.	„ Wiatka.
„ Kherson.	„ Orenburg.
„ Stavropol.	

Soil in part pretty fertile.

Government of Mohilew.	Government of Perm.
„ Minsk.	„ Nijni Nowgorod.
„ Grodno.	Kingdom of Poland.
„ Kowno.	

Soil mediocre.

Government of Smolensk.	Government of Jaroslaw.
„ Witebsk.	„ Kostroma.
„ Esthonia.	„ Wladimir.
„ Livonia	„ Kalouga.
„ Courland.	„ Moscow.
„ Wilna.	

Soil very meagre, or ungrateful, either from its own qualities or from the climate.

Government of Archangel.	Government of Twer.
„ Wologda.	„ Pskow.
„ Olonetz.	„ Astrakhan.
„ St. Petersburg.	Grand Duchy of Finland.
„ Nowgorod.	

the Baltic, which is the most natural outlet for all the countries bordering on the Vistula and the Niémen and their tributaries. The exportation of grain from Gallicia by way of Odessa is inconsiderable, and can take place only when prices at that port are high. (*Author's Note.*)

In the trans-Caucasian provinces the soil is in general very fertile, and suitable for the culture of all the cereals; and vegetation is very vigorous.

Southern Siberia contains very fertile districts, particularly in the neighbourhood of rivers. In this respect the government of Jenisseisk takes the first rank; next comes that of Tobolsk; the others likewise contain vast tracts suitable for agriculture. It is only the provinces of Okhotsk, Jakoutsk, and Kamtschatka of which the soil is mostly unproductive or very difficult of culture, with the exception of those districts which lie in the neighbourhood of the river Kamtschatka. What is chiefly wanting in Siberia is hands for the culture of the soil.

As a natural consequence of the immense extent of the empire and of the zones which it embraces, the productive soil is very unequally distributed; some governments contain very little arable land, whilst in others it exists in disproportion to the means of labouring it. This we will have occasion to observe more in detail in the following chapter.

CHAP. III.

CLASSIFICATION OF THE SOIL IN REGARD TO CULTURE.

Extent of Cultivable Land — Meadows — Forests — Unproductive Land.— Comparisons with France, Austria, and Prussia.—Tables of the Extent of Cultivated Land, Meadows, and Forests in the various Governments.—Observations, Comparisons, and Inferences.

THOSE writers, foreign as well as native, who have occupied themselves with this branch of statistics, differ greatly from each other in their estimates with regard to the classification of the soil of European Russia. Schubert, in his work entitled *Staaten-Kunde*, published in 1835, did not reckon the cultivated soil of this part of the empire at more than 61½ millions of dessiatines, whilst Hermann, in 1809, had reckoned it at 63,147,000. Seblowski, in 1832, calculated the extent of the cultivated fields at 75 millions of dessiatines, and, adding the amount of ground occupied by gardens and in the culture of flax and hemp, he carried the total cultivated land to about 85 or 90 millions of dessiatines. Upon comparing this last calculation with the number of our agricultural population, with the extent of cultivable land enjoyed by the peasants in the various parts of Russia, and with the most recent official data as to the results of surveys and the quantities of grain sown which we have been able to procure, we think we may with perfect safety admit, as the *minimum* extent of cultivated soil, 90 millions of dessiatines = 17,854 geographical square miles, or about 18 per cent. of the total surface. This estimate appears to be justified by the following calculation:—

According to the statistical work of M. Arsénieff, published in 1848, which is founded on official documents, the cultivable lands occupy, in forty-five governments, an extent of 72,386,755 dessiatines (see the recent work of M. Koeppen, *Der Bauernstand in Russland*, p. 105.). This estimate does not include any of the following provinces,—Bessarabia, the Tauride, the governments of Ékathérinoslaw and of Stavropol, the country of the Ural Cossacks, the kingdom of Poland, and the grandduchy of Finland.

In the kingdom of Poland, the arable land occupied in 1846, 5,444,000 dessiatines; in Bessarabia, more than a million *; in the governments of Stavropol, Ekathérinoslaw, and Tauride, (according to an approximative calculation founded on the quanty of grain sown, the extent of productive soil belonging to the state domains, the agricultural population, and other statistical data,) nearly 3 millions; in the country of the Uralian Cossacks, about 130,000; in Finland, nearly 1½ per cent. of the surface, or 520,000 dessiatines.

The assumption of these figures gives a result of 82,480,755 dessiatines; but, taking into consideration that, for the greater number of governments the official figure of the extent of cultivable land is based upon old surveys made in the last century, and that since that period a pretty considerable extent of soil then uncultivated has been gained to culture by the draining of marshes and clearing of forests, especially in those governments where the cultivable land was scarce, and population has considerably augmented, we may safely add 10 per cent. at least to the above result, which would bring the total extent of land in

---

* M. Arsénieff approximatively reckons the cultivated land in Bessarabia at 500,000 dessiatines only; but this calculation is evidently very far below the truth. The proof of this is furnished by the author himself. We read in his statistical description of this province that in 1845 there were sown there 458,868 tchetwerts of cereals. There is generally reckoned in Russia, for seed, one tchetwert per dessiatine, and M. Arsénieff himself adopts this proportion. It is notorious that with us, in almost every government, a certain portion of the cultivable soil is always lying fallow : in some districts this portion generally amounts to a third, in others it is as much as a half : in order, then, to sow 458,868 tchetwerts, there must be at least 688,000 dessiatines of arable land. Adding the fields cultivated with potatoes, of which there were harvested that year 127,289 tchetwerts, together with the melonries, orchards, and vegetable gardens, and taking into consideration the progress of population and culture, we do not see how we can admit less than a million of dessiatines.

cultivation to 90,729,000 dessiatines. We have therefore adopted approximatively the number of 90 millions of dessiatines as *minimum*.

In Austria the cultivated soil occupies, according to the official statistics of 1846, 39,710,435 joch*, = 4,152 geographical square miles, or 34·3 per cent. of the whole surface (12,104 square miles).

It occupies in Prussia, according to Förster and Weber's statistics, 48,319,892 morgen †, = 2,249 square miles, which gives a proportion to the entire surface (5,077 geographical square miles) of 44·3 per cent.

In France, according to the agricultural statistics of 1840, all sorts of culture, fallows included, occupied an extent of 26,078,022 hectares ‡, which gives, upon a total surface of 52,768,610 hectares, a proportion of 49·4 per cent.

Here, then, is the proportion which subsists between the cultivated land and the entire surface in the four principal states of continental Europe.

France	-	49·4 per 100	Austria	-	34·3 per 100
Prussia	-	44·3 „ 100	Russia	-	18 „ 100

Thus, the relative extent of our productive soil to the total surface is to that of Austria as 9 to 17 ; to that of Prussia, nearly as 2 to 5 ; and it is more than one-third of the proportion of France.

In the forty-five governments of which the statistics are given in the work of M. Arsenieff already cited, the meadows occupy 44,835,944 dessiatines; in Bessarabia, according to an approximative calculation, they occupy 1,200,000 dessiatines; in the governments of Ekathérinoslaw, Tauride, and Stavropol, according to a calculation equally approximative, they occupy 7,000,000 ; in the kingdom of Poland, according to the official

* Arable land - - - - - - 36,951,164 joch.
  Vineyards - - - - - - 1,759,271
  Gardens (reckoned approximatively) - - 1,000,000

                               Total   - - 39,710,435

† Arable land - - - - - - 47,295,716 morgen.
  Vineyards and gardens - - - - 1,024,176

                               Total   - - 48,319,892

‡ Culture of cereals - - - - - 13,900,262 hectares.
  Vines - - - - - - - 1,972,340
  Various - - - - - - - 3,442,139
  Fallows - - - - - - 6,763,281

                               Total   - - 26,078,022

data of 1846, they occupy 1,046,000; in the country of the
Uralian Cossacks, about 200,000; in Finland, 1,070,000.*
The assumption of these figures gives a total of 55,352,000
dessiatines; but, as the greater part of these data is founded
upon old surveys, and as, since that period, in a number of
governments, pasture lands and part of the forest lands have been
converted into meadows, we may perhaps admit approximatively for the total extent of meadow land, 60 millions of
dessiatines, which would be 12 per cent. of the entire surface.

In Austria the meadows occupy 10,595,152 joch†, or 9·1
per cent. of the entire surface; in Prussia, 14,326,429 morgen,
or 13·1 per cent; and in France, 5,774,745 hectares, or nearly
11 per cent. In this respect, therefore, the classification of
our soil, compared with that of other countries, does not offer
any very striking difference. The relative extent of the
meadows to the entire surface is, in Russia, a thirteenth less
than in Prussia, an eleventh greater than in France, and a
third greater than in Austria. We possess, moreover, in
our steppes, immense tracts of pasturage, which are suitable for
the rearing of cattle.

In the forty-five governments above mentioned, 179,110,415
dessiatines are occupied by forests. The governments of
Kherson, Ekathérinoslaw, Stavropol and Tauride, the country
of the Don Cossacks, the greater part of the government of
Saratow, and the southern part of Bessarabia, being situated
within the steppes, are essentially bare of forests. In Bessarabia, the state forests have an extent of 21,930 dessiatines,
and according to an article in the Russian *Dictionnaire Ency-
clopédique*, the total extent of the forests in that province would
amount to 255,000 dessiatines. In the governments of Ekathérinoslaw, Stavropol, and Tauride, the state forests occupy an extent
of 186,482 dessiatines. Adopting, in regard to each of these
governments, the same proportion for the lands belonging to individuals or communities, and combining this calculation with
other statistical data, we will obtain for the whole extent of
forests in these three governments about 400,000 dessiatines.
The country of the Uralian Cossacks is almost totally naked of
timber. In the kingdom of Poland the forests occupied, according to the official statistics of 1846, an extent of 3,206,000 des-

* The meadows occupy in Finland, according to official information, 3·09 per
cent. of the surface ; which gives, for 6,873 square miles, = 34,645,418 dessiatines,
1,070,000 dessiatines.

† The meadows and gardens together occupied in Austria, according to the
official statistics of 1846, an extent of 11,595,152 joch. We have deducted for
the gardens, calculating approximatively, a million of joch, which ¦we have added
to the cultivable land.

siatines; in the Grand Duchy of Finland they occupy, according to the most recent statistical data, 21·54 per cent. of the surface, that is, 7,462,000 dessiatines.

These figures taken together give a total of 190,433,000 dessiatines, or 38½ per cent. of the whole surface. But considering that in those governments where the quantity of cultivable land is smallest a considerable part of the forests has been cut down and cultivated or converted into meadow land since the period when the old surveys were made, we can scarcely consider that the amount of soil under forest exceeds 180 millions of dessiatines, or 36 per cent. of the entire surface.

In Austria, according to the official statistics of 1846, the forests occupy an extent of 35,421,817 joch (including 114,462 joch of olives and chestnuts), or 30·6 per cent. of the surface; in Prussia, 23,800,000 morgen, or 21·8 per cent.; in France, 8,804,550 hectares, or 16·6 per cent.*

We perceive, from these comparisons, that, taken in its entire extent, Russia is the most thickly wooded country of all the large European states.

If we deduct from the total surface of 99,275 square miles, = 500,425,000 dessiatines,—

1. For cultivable land - - - -	90,000,000	
2. For meadows - - - - -	60,000,000	
3. Forests - - - - - -	180,000,000	
4. For pasture land (approximatively estimated at 10 per cent. of the surface) - - - - -	50,000,000	380,000,000

There will remain of uncultivated and unproductive soil, including roads, canals, lakes, and rivers, together with land occupied by buildings   -   -   -   -   - } 120,525,000

Or 24 per cent. of the total surface.

---

* In the "Kritische Blätter für Forst und Jagdwissenschaft" (vol. 5, part 2, for 1831) M. Pfeil, a superior officer in the Prussian administration of woods and forests, estimates the forests of France at not more than 9 per cent. of its surface; but the incorrectness of this estimate appears from the most recent and complete official data, which we find in the agricultural statistics published in 1840 and 1841. These exhibit the extent of woods and forests in each of the several departments, and their total extent is made to amount to 8,804,550 hectares viz ;—

Forests belonging to the crown - -	52,972 hectares.
„ to the state - -	1,048,907
„ to communes and individuals	7,333,966
Forest land - - - -	368,705
Total, ut supra -	8,804,550

Which gives, on the entire surface (52,768,610 hectares), 16⅔ per cent. In the same article M. Pfeil estimates the extent of the forests in Prussia at 24 per cent. of the surface; whilst according to the statistics of Förster and Weber they do not occupy above 23,800,000 morgen of a surface which extends to 109,104,730 morgen; giving the proportion of 21·8 per cent., which we have adopted.

In Austria the unproductive soil occupies an extent of 17,667,702 joch, or 15·3 per cent.; in Prussia, 5,685,695 morgen, or 5·2 per cent.; in France, 2,930,216 hectares, or 5·5 per cent.

These estimates of the unproductive soil of those countries are founded on the following calculations:—

AUSTRIA.

(According to the official statistics of 1846.)

	JOCH.
Cultivable land - - - - -	36,951,164
Vineyards - - - - -	1,759,271
Meadows and gardens - - - -	11,595,152
Olive and chestnut plantations - - -	114,462
Pasture lands - - - - -	12,377,233
Forests - - - - - -	35,307,355
Total productive soil - - -	98,104,637
Total surface, 12,104 geog. sq. m. = -	115,772,339
Remains for unproductive soil = 15·3 per cent. of surface - - - - - -	17,667,702

PRUSSIA.

(According to Förster and Weber's statistics.)

	MORGEN.
Arable land - - - - -	47,295,716
Vineyards, orchards, and gardens - -	1,024,176
Meadow land - - - - -	14,326,429
Pasture land - - - - -	16,972,714
Forests - - - - - -	23,800,000
Total productive soil - - -	103,419,035
Total surface, 5,077 geog. sq. m. = -	109,104,730
Remains for unproductive soil = 5·2 per cent. of surface - - - - - -	5,685,695

FRANCE.

(According to the agricultural statistics of 1840.)

	HECTARES.
Miscellaneous cultures, fallows included - -	26,078,022
Meadow land - - - - -	5,774,745
Pasture land - - - - -	9,181,076
Woods and forests - - - -	8,804,551
Total productive soil - - -	49,838,394
Total surface - - - -	52,768,610
Remains for unproductive soil = 5·5 per cent. of surface - - - - - -	2,930,216

As our estimate, more or less approximative, of the extent of pasture land, rests upon exceedingly vague notions, the comparison will be more exact if we place the latter in the class of unproductive land. This classification, which is at the same time more rational for the appreciation of the agricultural condition of a country, will give out the following comparative results.

M. Schnitzler, in his *Statistique générale de la France* (tome iv. p. 35.), slumps together the pasture and unproductive land, which occupies in France, according to this classification, 12,111,316 hectares, or about 23 per cent. of the entire surface. In Austria the pasture and unproductive land, taken together, occupy an extent of 30,044,935 joch, or 26 per cent. of the entire surface. In Prussia they occupy 22,658,409 morgen, or 20·8 per cent. of the surface.

In Russia, when we deduct from the entire surface (500,425,000 dessiatines) the cultivable land, the meadows and the forests, which occupy together 330,000,000 dessiatines, there remain, for unproductive land, pasture included, 170,425,000, or nearly 34 per cent.

According to the foregoing calculations, the total surface of the four principal states of the European continent would be arranged as follows: —

NATURE OF THE LAND.	Proportion per cent.			
	Russia.	Austria.	Prussia.	France.
Cultivable land - - - - -	18	34·3	44·3	49 4
Meadow land - - - - -	12	9·1	13·1	11
Forests - - - - - -	36	30·6	21·8	16·6
Pasture land, marshes, *landes*, heaths, lakes, rivers, roads, and land occupied by buildings - - - -	34	26	20·8	23

From these comparisons we may perceive that, as regards the proportional extent of our productive soil, we are still greatly behind other countries. It is especially the heaths, the stony land, and the marshes of the north, together with the sands and uncultivated steppes of the southern and eastern regions, that remove from culture such a large portion of the soil. But on this point we may observe, *first*, that, with the exception of the marshy districts of the government of Archangel, which occupy an extent of about 48 millions of dessiatines, and which seem to have but little chance of ever attaining any value, a large portion of the marshes and sandy land may, in the course of time, be gained to culture by means of draining and irrigation*; and, *secondly*, that, setting aside partial clearings rendered necessary by local circumstances, there are still many districts where lands suitable for culture lie idle for want of hands to labour them, — especially the steppes of the south of

---

* Hitherto it has been chiefly by the clearing of forests, even at the expense of their waste, that the culture of the soil has been sought to be extended.

Russia, which contain in this respect considerable resources for the future.

On comparing the absolute extent of cultivated land in the four principal states of continental Europe, we obtain the following result:—

Dessiatines.

European Russia - - - - - -	90,000,000
France 26,078,000 hectares (1 dessiatine = 1·092 hect.) -	23,881,000
Austria, 39,710,000 joch (1 joch = 0·527 dessiat.) - -	20,928,000
Prussia, 48,320,800 morgen (1 morgen = 0·233 dessiat.) -	11,480,000

Thus the absolute extent of cultivated land in European Russia is to that of France nearly in the proportion of 15 to 4; to that of Austria as 9 to 2; and to that of Prussia nearly as 8 to 1. It exceeds by about 47 per cent. the extent of the whole Austrian empire; by more than 85 per cent. the whole of France; and it is about thrice the entire extent of Prussia. This relative superiority in regard to extent of our cultivated soil must go on augmenting with time, seeing that we have still a vast extent of territory waiting to be brought under the dominion of the plough, whilst the other countries have a much smaller reserve of land capable of becoming arable.

The other portions of the soil present, in regard to the absolute cipher of their extent, the following comparative results:—

NATURE OF THE LAND.	Russia.	Austria.	Prussia.	France.
	Dessiatines.	Dessiatines.	Dessiatines.·	Dessiatines.
Meadow land - -	60,000,000	5,583,645	3,338,060	5,288,228
Forests - - -	180,000,000	18,667,298	5,545,400	8,062,775
Pastures, *landes*, heaths, marshes, &c.	170,425,000	15,833,680	5,278,943	11,090,927

It results from these figures that the extent of our meadows is to that of those of Austria as 100 to 9·3; to that of those of Prussia as 100 to 5·5; and to that of those of France as 100 to 8·8.

Our forests exceed in extent more than thrice the total superficies of the Austrian empire, nearly four times that of France, and more than seven times that of Prussia.

The agricultural classification of the soil in the different provinces and governments exhibits results worthy of remark.

We present the table of that classification for forty-five governments according to the statistics of M. Arsénieff, as being the only document of the sort that we possess founded on official information; and to this we subjoin four supplementary tables of our own.

General Table of the Agricultural Classification of the Soil, in Forty-five Governments, according to M. Arsénieff's Statistics.

GOVERNMENTS.	Total Superfices.	Land under Cultivation.	Meadows.	Forests.
	Dessiatines.	*Dessiatines.*	*Dessiatines.*	*Dessiatines.*
1. Archangel - -	78,215,760	78,867	156,312	29,532,712
2. Astrakhan - -	14,414,400	21,787	384,574	120,365
3. Courland - -	2,494,800	489,710	313,877	975,264
4. Esthonia - -	1,895,040	236,660	258,344	477,792
5. Grodno - -	3,487,680	1,232,598	315,207	798,996
6. *Jaroslaw* - -	3,321,360	1,047,697	205,771	1,646,283
7. *Kalouga* - -	2,887,920	1,227,566	151,942	1,240,910
8. *Kazan* - -	5,685,120	1,886,108	472,401	2,990,403
9. Kharkow - -	4,964,400	1,912,159	1,299,996	544,615
10. Kherson - -	6,713,280	1,400,000	2,000,000	90,000
11. Kiew - -	4,601,520	2,343,994	443,478	989,055
12. *Kostroma* - -	7,539,840	1,513,313	303,605	5,320,604
13. *Koursk* * - -	4,123,370	2,080,006	535,997	529,306
14. Kowno - -	3,820,320	2,052,320	500,000	803,995
15. Livonia - -	4,299,120	414,057	553,258	1,928,428
16. Minsk - -	8,174,880	2,820,000	1,546,000	3,304,470
17. *Mohilew* - -	4,455,360	1,580,987	154,548	1,851,402
18. *Moscow* - -	2,968,560	1,144,062	253,431	1,330,187
19. *Nijni- Nowgorod* -	4,415,040	1,621,615	246,302	2,390,294
20. *Nowgorod* - -	11,153,520	1,132,002	225,092	7,425,030
21. Olonetz - -	14,026,320	331,112	95,970	9,942,789
22. *Orel* - - -	4,324,320	2,179,678	331,414	1,286,936
23. *Orenburg* - -	28,128,240	2,135,538	3,928,128	10,984,545
24. Country of the Don Cossacks - -	14,832,720	2,309,469	9,540,033	421,291
25. *Penza* - - -	3,477,600	1,458,380	422,050	1,416,005
26. Perm - - -	30,607,920	2,573,057	1,992,940	19,927,680
27. Podolia - -	3,895,920	2,064,937½	772,662	473,540
28. Poltawa* - -	4,516,550	1,998,833	1,214,480	578,430
29. *Pskow* - -	4,077,360	1,292,092	195,145	2,226,723
30. *Riazan* - -	3,860,640	1,693,977	288,068	1,412,106
31. *St. Petersburg* -	4,883,760	543,172	175,500	2,741,956
32. Saratow - -	17,766,000	2,526,986	6,512,584	1,203,080
33. *Simbirsk* - -	6,627,600	2,427,181	1,512,640	2,156,660
34. *Smolensk* * - -	5,136,670	1,848,243	220,063	2,537,088
35. *Tambow* - -	6,058,030	2,153,211	1,604,315	1,773,421
36. *Toula* - -	2,792,160	1,912,036	208,655	472,259
37. Tschernigow -	5,034,960	3,190,591	629,635	965,645
38. *Twer* - - -	6,163,920	1,604,794	268,666	3,410,811
39. *Wiatka* - -	12,600,000	2,606,938	432,708	9,491,346
40. Wilna - -	3,865,680	1,169,191	334,692	1,767,435
41. *Witebsk* - -	4,082,400	1,547,347	108,038	1,624,302
42. *Wladimir* - -	4,344,840	1,630,576	253,144	2,104,079
43. *Wolhynia* - -	6,531,840	2,108,257	776,265	2,438,865
44. *Wologda* - -	35,113,680	739,337	378,689	32,912,961
45. *Woronèje* - -	6,093,360	2,106,314	2,319,325	521,350
TOTAL - -	418,473,780	72,386,755 or 17·3 %	44,835,944 or 10·7 %	179,081,414 or 42·8 %

* In these three governments we have rectified the figures of the first column.

In the governments printed in italics the data, in regard to the extent of cultivated land, meadows and forests, rest upon the old general survey of last century. The first operations of this survey began in the government of Moscow in 1766, and in that of Kharkow in 1769; they were continued subsequently in the other governments, and the greater part were finished before 1800. There are only two governments, namely, Wiatka and Perm, in which the survey was entirely effected in the present century; in the former of these two governments it was commenced in 1804 and finished in 1835, and in the latter it occupied from 1822 to 1843. In the governments of Saratow, Simbirsk, Kazan, and Orenburg it was commenced last century, and was not finished in Kazan till 1803; in Simbirsk till 1821; and in Saratow and Orenburg till 1835. There are twenty governments which have not as yet been surveyed; namely, Archangel, Esthonia, Livonia, Courland, Minsk, Grodno, Wilna, Kowno, Kiew, Wolhynia, Podolia, Tschernigow, Poltawa, Bessarabia, Kherson, Ekathérinoslaw, Tauride, Stavropol, Astrakhan, and the country of the Don Cossacks. The agricultural classification of the greater part of these governments, which we find in M. Arsénieff's statistics, is founded on official information collected by the local authorities.

It is evident that during the time which elapsed whilst the surveys were going on, and which has elapsed since their termination, cultivation must have necessarily undergone numerous changes. In many districts it has been extended by the clearing of forests and steppes; in others a part of the meadows has been converted into arable land, whilst forests and pasture land have been converted into meadow. It would be impossible to determine the precise results of these changes; but we have endeavoured to estimate them approximatively, by taking into view the periods at which the surveys were respectively finished, the progress of population, the number of the peasants belonging to the Crown, to the appanages, and to private parties, the extent of the Crown domains, the quantity of seed required for these lands, the number of head of cattle, the local circumstances which have favoured the clearing of forests and of steppes, and the causes which have called these into action. We present the results of these calculations in the following amended Tables, to which we have added the provinces not comprehended in M. Arsénieff's agricultural statistics.

In regard to those governments for which this author has founded his classification of the soil upon other data, we have modified his figures but partially, and on the faith of more recent information. We have at the same time to observe that, in several governments of which the survey dates from a pretty recent epoch, as, for example, in those of Saratow, Wiatka, and Orenburg, where it was not fully terminated till 1835, but in which there still remained a great deal of land to be cleared, and where, from that cause, the population has considerably augmented, the culture of the soil has undergone important changes, and a considerable addition has been made to the lands in cultivation; whilst, on the other hand, in other districts where the survey was finished at the end of last or at the commencement of the present century, but where the population was much denser at an early period, the state of culture has remained pretty stationary.

In the course of our last journey through the interior of Russia, we observed, with some degree of surprise, that in several governments, even of the more populous, as, for example, in those of Moscow, Wladimir, Kalouga, and Nijni-Novgorod, in which a great part of the forests has been destroyed since the survey was finished, this destruction has not been turned to account for the extension of agriculture: we find large tracts of old forest land, where the trees have been cut down, covered with brushwood and serving at the very best for pasture.

From our own observations, and from new information which we have been enabled to procure since the first edition of this volume was published, we have introduced some changes into the following recapitulatory tables: —

Supplementary Table, No. I. Land in Cultivation.

GOVERNMENTS.	Total Extent of Surface.	Quantity of Land in Cultivation.	Number of Dessiatines of Cultivated Land to 100,000 Dessiatines of Surface.
	Dessiatines.	*Dessiatines.*	
1. Toula - - - -	2,792,160	2,000,000	71,629
2. Tschernigow - - -	5,034,960	3,191,000	63,377
3. *Podolia* * - - - -	3,895,920	2,440,000	62,630
4. *Koursk* - - - -	4,123,370	2,503,000	60,703
5. Orel - - - -	4,324,320	2,400,000	55,500
6. Kowno - - - -	3,820,320	2,060,000	53,922
7. *Kiew* - - - -	4,601,520	2,353,000	51,135
8. *Woronèje* - - -	6,093,360	3,007,000	49,349
9. Kingdom of Poland - -	11,563,627	5,445,000	47,087
Carried forward -	46,249,557	25,399,000	

* In the governments printed in italics the cipher of the extent of land in cultivation has been rectified from statistical information collected from the local authorities.

Governments.	Total Extent of Surface.	Quantity of Land in Cultivation.	Number of Dessiatines of Cultivable Land to 100,000 Dessiatines of Surface.
	Dessiatines.	*Dessiatines.*	
Brought forward -	46,249,557	25,399,000	
10. Riazan - - - -	3,860,640	1,800,000	46,624
11. Penza - - - -	3,477,600	1,600,000	46,009
12. Kalouga - - - -	2,887,920	1,300,000	45,015
13. Poltawa - - - -	4,516,560	2,000,000	44,281
14. Moscow - - - -	2,968,560	1,300,000	43,792
16. Kharkow - - -	4,964,400	2,100,000	42,301
16. Grodno * - - -	3,487,680	1,470,000	42,148
17. Wladimir - - -	4,344,840	1,800,000	41,428
18. Tambow - - - -	6,058,030	2,500,000	41,268
19. Nijni-Novgorod - -	4,415,040	1,800,000	40,770
29. Witebsk - - - -	4,082,400	1,600,000	39,193
21. Smolensk - - -	5,136,575	2,000,000	38,936
22. Mohilew - - - -	4,455,360	1,700,000	38,156
23. Simbirsk - - - -	6,627,600	2,500,000	37,721
24. Kazan - - - -	5,685,120	2,100,000	36,939
25. Taroslaw - - -	3,321,360	1,200,000	36,130
26. Minsk - - - -	8,174,880	2,820,000	34,496
27. Wolhynia - - -	6,531,840	2,110,000	32,303
28. Pskow - - - -	4,077,360	1,300,000	31,883
29. Wilna - - - -	3,865,680	1,170,000	30,266
30. Bessarabia - - -	4,319,280	1,300,000	30,098
31. Twer - - - -	6,163,920	1,670,000	27,093
32. *Wiatka* - - - -	12,600,000	2,973,000	23,595
33. Kostroma - - -	7,539,840	1,600,000	21,221
34. Kherson - - - -	6,713,280	1,400,000	20,854
35. *Courland* - - -	2,494,800	496,000	19,881
36. Ekathérinoslaw † - -	6,078,240	1,200,000	19,743
37. Country of the Don Cossacks - - - -	14,832,720	2,310,000	15,574
38. Saratow - - - -	17,766,000	2,530,000	14,241
39. Tauride ‡ - - -	5,861,520	750,000	12,795
40. Esthonia - - - -	1,895,040	240,000	12,665
41. *Orenburg, with the country of the Uralian Cossacks* - - - -	34,135,920	4,115,000	12,055
42. Novgorod - - -	11,153,520	1,300,000	11,656
43. St. Petersburg - - -	4,883,760	550,000	11,262
Carried forward - -	275,626,842	84,003,000	

* To the government of Grodno M. Arsénieff assigns 1,232,598 dessiatines of arable land, whilst in the statistics of the War Ministry we find the extent stated at 1,713,363 dessiatines.   On combining the figure of the population, the quantity of grain sown, the extent of land possessed by the crown peasants, and by those of individual proprietors, we have considered that we might adopt the mean of the two numbers.

† In this government there are required about 750,000 tchetwerts of seed corn, which implies at least 750,000 dessiatines under culture. Adding fallows, potato land, melon land, vineyards, and gardens, we think we may estimate the land in culture at 1,200,000 dessiatines, as minimum.

‡ In 1845 there were sown with cereals in this government 430,864 dessiatines. Adding for fallows, vineyards, gardens, and potato land, we may carry the whole

GOVERNMENTS.	Total Extent of Surface.	Quantity of Land in Cultivation.	Number of Dessiatines of Cultivated Land to 100,000' Dessiatines of Surface.
	Dessiatines.	*Dessiatines.*	
Brought forward -	275,626,842	84,003,000	
44. Livonia - - - -	4,299,120	415,000	9,653
45. Perm - - - -	30,607,920	2,589,000	8,459
46. Stavropol* - - -	13,356,000	750,000	5,615
47. Olonetz - - - -	14,026,320	370,000	2,638
48. Wologda - - -	35,113,680	800,000	2,278
49. Grand Duchy of Finland -	34,645,418	520,000	1,501
50. Astrakhan - - -	14,414,400	150,000	1,041
51. Archangel - - -	78,215,760	80,000	102
Total - - -	500,305,460	89,677,000	17,924

From the above table it appears that, in regard to the relative extent of land in cultivation, there exist extraordinary disproportions betwixt different parts of the empire. Thus, for example, in the governments of Toula, Tschernigow, Podolia, and Koursk, the cultivated land exceeds three-fifths of the whole territorial extent; whilst in that of Astrakhan it amounts only to a hundredth, and in that of Archangel to a thousandth, part of the surface; proportions so small, as not to be met with in any other country of the European continent. The difference between the governments of Archangel and of Toula is as 1 to 70·2; but the former of these governments, with its heaths and marshes covering nearly three-fifths of its surface, and that of Astrakhan, with its immense steppes, which occupy more than nine-tenths of its whole extent, are, both the one and the other, in such exceptional circumstances, that for purposes of comparison they must be set aside. Striking off these two governments, the greatest difference, namely, that between Finland and the government of Toula, is nearly as 1 to 48. If we remove from the scale the government of Finland likewise, which, from its rocky surface, so thickly studded with lakes, is also in an exceptional condition, the greatest difference, being that between the governments of Wologda and Toula, is reduced in the proportion of 1 to 31. Still such divergent proportions in the distribution of the soil are not found in any

extent of land in cultivation to 750,000 dessiatines at least ; especially as during the last eight years cultivation must have rather increased than fallen off.

* In this government the *arable* lands occupy, according to the statistics of the Ministry of War, only 659,797 dessiatines; but, on consultnig other data, and allowing for vineyards, gardens, and orchards, we are of opinion that we may slump the whole extent of cultivated land in this government at about 750,000 dessiatines.

other country. In the empire of Austria, which, from the
extent and variety of its possessions, presents such great inequalities in this respect, the difference between the provinces
containing the largest and those containing the smallest proportion of cultivated land stands only in the proportion of 6 to
1.   Thus, for example, in Moravia and Silesia, the provinces
containing the largest proportion of land in cultivation, such land
represents but 48 per cent. of the entire surface ; whilst we
possess eight governments, namely, Toula, Tschernigow, Podolia,
Koursk, Orel, Kowno, Kiew, and Woronèje, embracing an
extent of 6,887 geographical square miles, equal to nearly three-
fourths of the area of France, where the cultivable lands exceed
this proportion.   The first named of these governments has an
excess of one-half in relative extent of cultivated land over those
provinces of Austria which are in this respect the most richly
provided.   On the other hand, those countries of the Austrian
empire which are in this respect the poorest, namely, the countries of the littoral, where the arable lands do not exceed 8 per
cent. of the area, are more favoured than the last six governments of the preceding table, and they exceed the relative extent of cultivated ground in the government of Archangel in
the proportion of 80 to 1.

The average proportion of two-fifths of the surface for arable
land may be considered as sufficient to ensure the subsistence of
the inhabitants, even in countries where the population is compact, if the soil be not exceedingly ungrateful.   We have nineteen governments which exceed this proportion and thirty-two
which come short of it.   In the seven governments standing
first in the table the arable land exceeds half the surface ; in
twelve governments it varies from 40 to 50 per cent. ; in eleven
it is from 30 to 40 per cent. ; in four it is between 20 and
30 per cent. ; in nine it is between 10 and 20 ; and in eight
governments it is below 10 per cent.

It may not, however, be superfluous to observe, that we have
comprehended in this table only those lands which are actually
under culture; and that there are various governments, especially in the region of the steppes, where a large portion of the
lands still unreclaimed are very capable of being brought under
culture; so that several of the most fertile provinces, as the governments of Saratow, Kherson, Ekathérinoslaw, Tauride, Stavropol, and the country of the Don Cossacks, where the *arable*
soil undoubtedly occupies more than a half of the territorial
extent, appear to disadvantage in the agricultural classification
because their arable land *now laboured* does not amount to one-
fourth of their area.

When we take into view the territorial extent of each province, we find twenty-six governments, which, in the present
condition of our population, may be considered as amply provided
with arable lands, since these exceed the average proportion of a
third, occupy an extent of nearly 125 millions of dessiatines, or a
fourth of the entire surface, and embrace about two-thirds of the
cultivated land of European Russia; so that the other twenty-five
governments, the cultivated land of which is below this average,
occupy three-fourths of the surface, and represent only a third of
the whole cultivated land of this part of the empire.

We may consider the nineteen governments in which the
cultivated land exceeds the proportion of 40 per cent. as being
very amply provided.   To this category belong the governments
of Toula, Tschernigow, Podolia, Koursk, Orel, Kowno, Kiew,
Woronèje, the kingdom of Poland, Riazan, Penza, Kalouga,
Poltawa, Moscow, Kharkow, Grodno, Wladimir, Tambow, and
Nijni-Novgorod, which, taken together, occupy about 17 per
cent. of the total area, and more than half of all the soil in cultivation.   The eight governments in which the cultivated land
does not amount to 10 per cent. of the surface, namely, Livonia,
Perm, Stavropol, Olonetz, Wologda, Astrakhan, Archangel, and
Finland, occupy an extent of about 224 millions of dessiatines,
or more than 45 per cent. of the total surface.   Of this number,
the two governments of Astrakhan and Archangel, in which the
arable land amounts only to a hundredth and a thousandth part
respectively of the surface, occupy by themselves alone an extent of 92,630,000 dessiatines, or 18½ per cent. of the total area.

These great inequalities in the distribution of the cultivated
land, joined to the immense distances, which render communication so difficult, must of necessity impede the natural development of the numerous sources of wealth which Russia, favoured
in so many other respects, possesses within herself.

In regard to geographical position, we observe that all those
districts which possess little cultivated land are found in the
north and at the south-eastern extremity of European Russia,
and that the twenty governments where arable land is most
abundant occupy for most part the centre and the western portion of the empire.

Supplementary Table, No. II.   Meadow Land.

GOVERNMENTS.	Total Extent of Surface.	Extent of Meadows.	Number of Dessiatines of Meadow to 100,000 Dessiatines of Surface.
	Dessiatines.	Dessiatines.	
1. Country of the Don Cossacks - - - -	14,832,720	9,540,000	64,317
2. Woronèje - - -	6,093,360	2,400,000	39,387
3. Saratow - - -	17,766,000	6,513,000	36,660
4. Stavropol * - - -	13,356,000	4,000,000	29,949
5. Kherson - - -	6,713,280	2,000,000	29,792
6. Bessarabia - - -	4,319,280	1,200,000	27,782
7. Tauride * - - -	5,861,520	1,600,000	27,297
8. Tambow - - -	6,058,030	1,650,000	27,237
9. Kharkow - - -	4,964,400	1,350,000	27,194
10. Poltawa - - - -	4,516,560	1,215,000	26,901
11. Simbirsk - - -	6,627,600	1,600,000	24,141
12. Ekatherinoslaw * - -	6,078,240	1,400,000	23,033
13. Twer † - - -	6,163,920	1,290,000	20,928
14. Podolia - - -	3,895,920	773,000	19,841
15. Kowno ‡ - - -	3,820,320	750,000	19,632
16. Pskow § - - -	4,077,360	800,000	19,621
17. Minsk - - -	8,174,880	1,546,000	18,912
18. Grodno - - -	3,487,680	520,000	14,910
19. Koursk - - -	4,123,370	613,000	14,866
20. Taroslaw - - -	3,321,360	492,000	14,813
21. Esthonia - - -	1,895,040	260,000	13,720
22. Orenburg, with the country of the Uralian Cossacks -	34,135,920	4,452,000	13,042
23. Kingdom of Poland - -	11,563,627	1,500,000	12,972
Carried forward - -	181,846,387	47,464,000	

* In the governments of Stavropol, Tauride, and Ekathérinoslaw, which are steppe countries, it is very difficult to calculate with any degree of precision the extent of meadow land properly so called ; the steppes are used sometimes for culture, sometimes for the growth of hay, sometimes for pasture ; and the proportion employed for one or other purpose depends on the system of rural economy pursued, namely, whether this be the culture of cereals or the rearing of domestic animals—a point which differs greatly from one locality to another.   There is nothing like a steady rational system of husbandry to be found, except in some German colonies.   Of the extent of meadow assigned above from approximative calculation to these three governments, it is probable that a large portion is common pasturage.

† By the old survey, the meadows occupy 268,666 dessiatines; our own figure is founded on statistical data published under the superintendence of the local authorities, and nearly coincides with that of the Ministry of War, which is 1,277,088 dessiatines.

‡ M. Arsénieff allows for meadow only 500,000 dessiatines, equal nearly to a fourth of the arable lands ; more recent data collected by the local authorities, give the extent of meadow compared with cultivated land as 1 to 2.   Private information, which we have been able to procure, authorises us to strike the medium at 750,000 dessiatines, as given above.

§ The extent of meadow land in this government has been calculated approximatively from recent information derived from the local authorities.

Governments.	Total Extent of Surface.	Extent of Meadows.	Number of Dessiatines of Meadow to 100,000 Dessiatines of Surface.
	Dessiatines.	Dessiatines.	
Brought forward -	181,846,387	47,464,000	
24. Penza - - - -	3,477,600	450,000	12,940
25. Livonia - - - -	4,299,120	555,000	12,910
26. Courland - - -	2,494,800	314,000	12,586
27. Tschernigow - - -	5,034,960	630,000	12,513
28. Wolhynia - - -	6,531,840	777,000	11,896
29. Kiew - - - -	4,601,520	445,000	9,671
30. Orel - - - -	4,324,320	400,000	9,250
31. Kazan - - - -	5,685,120	500,000	8,795
32. Moscow - - -	2,968,560	260,000	8,758
33. Wilna - - - -	3,865,680	335,000	8,666
34. Toula - - - -	2,792,160	220,000	7,879
35. Riazan - - -	3,860,640	300,000	7,771
36. Mohilew - - -	4,455,360	300,000	6,733
37. Kalouga - - - -	2,887,920	193,000	6,683
38. Perm - - - -	30,607,920	1,993,000	6,511
39. Wladimir - - -	4,344,840	280,000	6,444
40. Nijni-Nowgorod - -	4,415,040	280,000	6,342
41. Astrakhan * - - -	14,414,400	800,000	5,550
42. Smolensk - - -	5,136,575	280,000	5,451
43. Kostroma - - -	7,539,840	340,000	4,509
44. Nowgorod - - -	11,153,520	470,000	4,214
45. St. Petersburg - - -	4,883,760	200,000	4,095
46. Wiatka - - -	12,600,000	500,000	3,968
47. Grand Duchy of Finland -	34,645,418	1,071,000	3,091
48. Witebsk - - - -	4,082,400	120,000	2,940
49. Wologda - - -	35,113,680	450,000	1,282
50. Olonetz - - -	14,026,320	110,000	784
51. Archangel - - -	78,215,760	157,000	201
Total - - -	500,305,460	60,194,000	12,031

* In a statistical table published in the Russian *Biblioteka dla Tchtenia* for October, 1852, in which the writer has rectified some of our figures by calculations founded on the progress of population and the rearing of domestic animals, the extent of meadow land in the government of Astrakhan is given at 1,794,000 dessiatines; but it is evident from the notes, that in this extent the writer comprehends the pasturage.

We have already observed on the difficulty of determining even approximately the extent of meadow in the country of the steppes, where it is frequently confounded with pasture. This difficulty is excessive in the government of Astrakhan, in consequence of the carelessness of its nomade inhabitants, who rather allow their sheep and cattle to remain at pasture summer and winter, than give themselves any trouble about hay. We consider that we may estimate the extent of meadow land, properly so called, that is, land from which a hay harvest is gathered, at somewhat more than 800,000 dessiatines; which is more than double the extent (384,574 dess.) given by M. Arsénieff from the old survey. This augmentation seems justified by the changes in the movement of population and by the progress of cultivation.

We see figuring at the head of this table a province (the country of the Don Cossacks) 2943 geographical square miles in extent, of which nearly two-thirds are occupied by meadow land. Again, in the two governments of Olonetz and Archangel, the meadows do not occupy a hundredth part of the entire surface. Next to the country of the Don Cossacks, the largest proportion of meadow land is found in the governments of Woronèje, Saratow, Stavropol, Kherson, Bessarabia, Tauride, Tambow, Kharkow, and Poltawa. In the two first of these governments they occupy more than a third, in the following seven more than a fourth of the surface.

Assuming as *minimum*, the proportion of 10 per cent. of meadow land to be requisite in a good distribution of the soil, we find that, according to the above table, there are twenty-eight governments, occupying an extent of about 204 millions of dessiatines, or more than two-fifths of the total extent of European Russia, in which the meadows exceed this proportion, and twenty-three in which they fall short of it. Of the latter, there are fourteen, occupying together more than 94 millions of dessiatines, or nearly a fifth of the surface, in which the extent of meadow land varies from 5 to 10 per cent., and nine in which it is below 5 per cent. These nine, which may be considered as very poor in herbage, occupy an extent of 202 millions of dessiatines, or more than two-fifths of the total surface of this part of the empire.

The governments which, in proportion to their territorial extent, are most scantily provided with meadow land, are those of Witebsk, Wologda, Olonetz, and Archangel*, where that part of the soil does not occupy so much as even 3 per cent. of the total surface. These four governments occupy together 131 millions of dessiatines, or upwards of 26 per cent. of the territorial extent of European Russia.

But the comparison betwixt the different governments will be more complete when we exhibit the extent of meadow side by side with that of arable land.

---

* In the government of Archangel, there are fine meadows along the banks of the rivers ; their extent exceeds that of the arable lands, in the proportion of 2 to 1. The rearing of cattle constitutes the principal branch of rural economy, and it is only relatively to the immense extent of its entire surface that this government can be called poor in herbage.

Supplementary Table, No. III. *Proportion of Meadow to Arable Land.*

Governments.	Arable.	Meadow.	Number of Dessiatines of Meadow to 100 Dessiatines of Arable Land.
	Dessiatines.	*Dessiatines.*	
1. Witebsk - - - -	1,600,000	120,000	7·5
2. Toula - - - -	2,000,000	220,000	11·
3. Smolensk - - - -	2,000,000	280,000	14·
4. Kalouga - - - -	1,300,000	193,000	14·8
5. Wladimir - - - -	1,800,000	280,000	15·6
6. Nijni-Nowgorod - -	1,800,000	280,000	15·6
7. Riazau - - - -	1,800,000	300,000	16·7
8. Orel - - - - -	2,400,000	400,000	16·7
9. Wiatka - - -	2,973,000	500,000	16·8
10. Mohilew - - - -	1,700,000	300,000	17·6
11. Kiew - - - -	2,353,000	445,000	18·9
12. Tschernigow - - -	3,191,000	630,000	19·7
13. Moscow - - - -	1,300,000	260,000	20·
14. Kostroma - - - -	1,600,000	340,000	21·3
15. Kazan - - - -	2,100,000	500,000	23·8
16. Koursk - - - -	2,503,000	613,000	24·5
17. Kingdom of Poland - -	5,445,000	1,500,000	27·5
18. Penza - - - -	1,600,000	450,000	28·1
19. Wilna - - - -	1,170,000	335,000	28·6
20. Olonetz - - - -	370,000	110,000	29·7
21. Podolia - - - -	2,440,000	773,000	31·7
22. Grodno - - - -	1,470,000	520,000	35·4
23. Nowgorod - - -	1,300,000	470,000	36·2
24. Kowno - - - -	2,060,000	750,000	36·4
25. St. Petersburg - - -	550,000	200,000	36·4
26. Wolhynia - - - -	2,110,000	777,000	36·8
27. Jaroslaw - - - -	1,200,000	492,000	41·
28. Minsk - - - -	2,820,000	1,546,000	54·8
29. Wologda - - - -	800,000	450,000	56·3
30. Pskow - - - -	1,400,000	800,000	57·1
31. Poltawa - - - -	2,000,000	1,215,000	60·8
32. Courland - - - -	496,000	314,000	63·3
33. Simbirsk - - - -	2,500,000	1,600,000	64·
34. Kharkow - - - -	2,100,000	1,350,000	64·3
35. Tambow - - - -	2,500,000	1,650,000	66·
36. Perm - - - -	2,589,000	1,993,000	77·
37. Twer - - - -	1,670,000	1,290,000	77·2
38. Woronèje - - - -	3,007,000	2,400,000	79·8
39. Bessarabia - - - -	1,300,000	1,200,000	92·3
40. Orenburg - - - -	4,115,000	4,452,000	108·2
41. Esthonia - - - -	240,000	260,000	108·3
42. Ekathérinoslaw - - -	1,200,000	1,400,000	116·7
43. Livonia - - - -	415,000	555,000	133·7
44. Kherson - - - -	1,400,000	2,000,000	142·9
45. Archangel - - - -	80,000	157,000	196·3
46. Grand Duchy of Finland -	520,000	1,071,000	206·
47. Tauride - - - -	750,000	1,600,000	213·3
48. Saratow - - - -	2,530,000	6,513,000	257·4
49. Country of the Don Cossacks	2,310,000	9,540,000	413·
50. Stavropol - - - -	750,000	4,000,000	533·3
51. Astrakhan - - - -	150,000	800,000	533·3
Total -	89,777,000	60,194,000	67

The foregoing table gives an average for all European Russia of 67 dessiatines of meadow to 100 dessiatines of cultivable land. In Austria, the proportion is as 267 to 1000; in Prussia, as 296 to 1000; and in France, as 221 to 1000.

It is difficult to fix the proportion of the relative extent of meadows required under a good system of husbandry, because that depends much upon local circumstances—upon the fertility of the arable land, upon the quantity of manure that it requires, the mode of culture, the quality of the meadows themselves, the plentifulness of the harvests, the quality of the pasture land.

We may admit as a general rule that, in those countries where a rational system of husbandry is most widely diffused, and green crops take the place of fallows, the proportion of 1 to 3 is sufficient for supporting the proper quantity of cattle. Thus, for example, in Lombardy, one of those countries in which agriculture is most advanced and most flourishing, the extent of meadow is to that of arable land nearly in the proportion of 4 to 14. We must add, however, that in that country, the natural fertility of the soil is admirably seconded by a system of irrigation, the most perfect hitherto known.

In Russia, where the three-field system, which exhausts the soil, is that which is still most generally followed—where in most districts the hay harvests are much less frequent and less abundant in consequence of the rigor of the climate, the length of the winters, and the frequent droughts, we may take it as a general rule that the requisite proportion is that of 1 to 2; that is, the meadows ought to be at least one-half as extensive as the arable lands. Those countries where the meadow land does not exceed in extent one-third of the cultivable land, may be considered as but unfavourably situated for the rearing of cattle to produce manure for the soil. Those, on the contrary, where the meadows occupy an extent equivalent to two-thirds of the arable land may be classed amongst the provinces which are richly provided with herbage. It must be understood, however, that these general calculations cannot be applied indiscriminately to every part of Russia. Thus, for example, in the countries belonging to the black humus (*tschernozième*) district, the soil is so fertile of itself that it requires no manure; so that cattle, with the exception of what are necessary for field labour, are raised there only for the sake of their milk, and for sale, and form a branch of rural economy quite independent of the culture of the soil.

In the report of the Department of Husbandry to the Ministry of Domains which we have already had occasion to refer to, it is stated that the three-field system cannot be carried on without exhausting the soil, except in localities where for every dessiatine of arable land there is at least another dessiatine of meadow yielding 150 poods of good hay. According to this maxim, it would be only the twelve last provinces given in the preceding table which would be favourably situated in this respect; but we cannot adopt the rule, for we find it at variance with facts. We perceive, on referring to the official statistics of Austria, that in that country, where the three-field system is still most generally adopted, there exists on an average little more than a quarter of a dessiatine of meadow to each dessiatine of cultivable land, or, deducting gardens and vineyards, nearly three-tenths of the former to one of the latter. Laying out of account all the provinces of that empire where the system of alternate culture is more or less in operation, and taking only those three—namely, Hungary, Gallicia, and Bohemia—where the three-field system is predominant, and where instances of a rational system of husbandry are still the exception, and not the rule, we obtain the following results:—

Cultivable land	-	-	-	24,545,503 joch.
Meadow land (gardens included)		-	-	7,207,604 „

This gives 294 joch of meadow to 1000 joch of arable land, or a little less than $\frac{3}{10}$ joch of the former to 1 joch of the latter, being the same proportion as for the whole empire. In Bohemia and in Hungary there does not exist nearly a quarter of a joch of meadow to a joch of arable land. It is evident that, in those provinces where the three-field system prevails, which have on an average only three-tenths, and in some cases less than a quarter, of the extent of meadow land considered necessary to support the system, the soil ought long ago to have been entirely exhausted, and agriculture to have been completely ruined; but this is by no means the case. Complaints are general as to the want of outlets for produce; but the want of meadow land has never been considered as a preponderating cause of the precarious condition of agriculture in these provinces. In France, where the three-field system is still predominant—for the fallows there occupy 26 per cent. of the land in culture, and nearly 33 per cent. of that portion of the cultivable land employed in the growth of cereals—there is not reckoned much more than the fifth part of a hectare of meadow to a hectare of arable land; and, if we subtract from the cultivated area vineyards and miscellaneous culture, we shall find only 28 hectares of meadow to 100 hectares of corn land. Yet it cannot be alleged that agriculture in France is in a state of rapid decay, notwithstanding the enormous assessments of every description to which it is subject.

In Prussia, where the three-field system likewise predomi-nates in several provinces, there are not three-tenths of a morgen of meadow to each morgen of arable land.

In Russia, the great quantities of cattle which are raised even in those provinces where the extent of meadow land is very much below that of arable, may serve, we think, to prove that parity in the extent of these two descriptions of soil is not a condition absolutely necessary to the three-field system of culture.

For all these reasons we have considered ourselves entitled to adopt with us the proportion of 1 to 2, as the normal proportion betwixt the extent of meadow and that of arable land.

Agreeably to this rule, founded on general considerations and liable to be modified by local circumstances, there would, according to the preceding table, be twenty-four governments favourably situated in regard to the relative extent of their meadow lands. Of this number, there are twelve in which the extent of the meadows exceeds that of the arable land. On the other hand, the table exhibits twelve governments in which the extent of meadow does not equal a fifth of that of the lands in culture. Amongst these is one—namely Witebsk—where the meadows do not amount to one-tenth of the cultivable area. *Per contra,* we find at the other extremity of the table three provinces—the country of the Don Cossacks, and the governments of Stavropol and Astrakhan—where the extent of meadow land is more than quadruple that of the lands in cultivation. Such extraordinary varieties of proportion are without parallel in the agricultural condition of other countries. Thus, for example, if we take the empire of Austria, we find that in Bohemia, which is the province least favoured in regard to meadows, the extent of the latter is to that of the cultivable fields nearly in the proportion of 10 to 43*, whilst in the province which is richest in herbage—the Tyrol—the proportion of meadow to cultivable land is as 23 to 13, or less than double.

We shall perceive, on examining the following table, the same disproportions in regard to our forests:—

---

* In Dalmatia, the meadows do not amount to a tenth of the extent of the arable land ; but this province, from the configuration and quality of its volcanic soil, stands in an exceptional position.

Supplementary Table, No. IV. Forests.

GOVERNMENTS.	Total Extent of Surface.	Extent of Forests.	Number of Dessiatines of Forest to 100,000 Dessiatines of Surface.
	Dessiatines.	Dessiatines.	
1. Wologda - - -	35,113,680	32,000,000	91,133
2. Wiatka - - - -	12,600,000	9,000,000	71,429
3. Olonetz - - - -	14,026,320	9,700,000	69,156
4. Kostroma - - -	7,539,840	5,000,000	66,314
5. Perm - - - -	30,607,920	19,927,000	65,104
6. Nowgorod - - -	11,153,520	7,000,000	62,760
7. St. Petersburg - - -	4,883,760	2,400,000	49,142
8. Kazan* - - -	5,685,120	2,627,000	46,208
9. Nijni-Nowgorod - -	4,415,040	2,000,000	45,300
10. Livonia - - - -	4,299,120	1,928,000	44,846
11. Smolensk - - -	5,136,575	2,200,000	42,830
12. Wilna - - - -	3,865,680	1,600,000	41,390
13. Minsk - - - -	8,174,880	3,300,000	40,368
14. Wladimir - - -	4,344,840	1,700,000	39,127
15. Courland - - -	2,494,800	975,000	39,081
16. Archangel - - -	78,215,760	29,500,000	37,716
17. Twer - - - -	6,163,920	2,300,000	37,314
18. Moscow - - - -	2,968,560	1,100,000	37,055
19. Wolhynia - - -	6,531,840	2,400,000	36,743
20. Mohilew - - -	4,455,360	1,600,000	35,912
21. Witebsk - - -	4,082,400	1,460,000	35,763
22. Pskow† - - -	4,077,360	1,400,000	34,336
23. Penza - - - -	3,477,600	1,100,000	31,631
24. Simbirsk - - -	6,627,600	2,000,000	30,177
25. Orenburg - - -	34,135,920	10,000,000	29,295
26. Kingdom of Poland - -	11,563,627	3,206,000	27,725
27. Riazan - - - -	3,860,640	1,000,000	25,902
28. Orel - - - -	4,324,320	1,100,000	25,438
29. Esthonia - - -	1,895,040	460,000	24,274
30. Jaroslaw - - -	3,321,360	805,000	24,237
31. Tambow - - - -	6,058,030	1,450,000	23,935
32. Grodno - - - -	3,487,680	760,000	21,791
33. Grand Duchy of Finland -	34,645,418	7,460,000	21,532
34. Kiew - - - -	4,601,520	950,000	20,645
35. Toula - - - -	2,792,160	440,000	15,758
36. Kalouga - - -	2,887,920	454,000	15,721
37. Kowno - - - -	3,820,320	600,000	15,705
Carried forward - -	388,335,450	172,902,000	

* In those governments, of which the names are printed in italics, the figure exhibiting the extent of forests has been corrected in conformity with the most recent information, collected by the local authorities.

† M. Arsénieff, following the old survey, gives the extent of the forests in this government at 2,226,723 dessiatines; but a great part of these forests has since then been destroyed by conflagrations and clearances. Founding our calculations on the most recent information derived from the local authorities, we do not think their present effective extent can be slumped at more than 1,400,000 dessiatines, the number given above.

This observation applies equally to several other governments, especially those of Moscow, Wladimir, and the countries bordering on the Volga.

Governments.	Total Extent of Surface.	Extent of Forests.	Number of Dessiatines of Forest to 100,000 Dessiatines of Surface.
	Dessiatines.	*Dessiatines.*	
Brought forward - -	388,335,450	172,902,000	
38. *Tchernigow* - - -	5,034,960	789,000	15,670
39. *Podolia* - - - -	3,895,920	470,000	12,064
40. *Koursk* - - - -	4,123,370	479,000	11,617
41. Kharkow - - -	4,964,400	500,000	10,072
42. Woronèje - - -	6,093,360	500,000	8,206
43. Saratow - - - -	7,766,000	1,200,000	6,754
44. Bessarabia - - -	4,319,280	255,000	5,904
45. *Poltawa* - - - -	4,516,560	252,000	5,579
46. *Tauride* - - - -	5,861,520	244,000	4,163
47. Country of the Don Cossacks - - - -	14,832,720	420,000	2,832
48. *Kherson* - - - -	6,713,280	120,000	1,788
49. *Ekathérinoslaw* - -	6,078,240	102,000	1,678
50. Stavropol - - -	13,356,000	113,000	846
51. Astrakhan - - -	14,414,400	120,000	833
Total - -	500,305,460	178,466,000	35,671

On casting a glance at the preceding table, we perceive from the extent occupied by forests in many of the governments, that there is no country in Europe so richly wooded as part of Russia; but the distribution presents great inequalities; for whilst some governments possess such an immense extent of forests as far to exceed their means of utilising them, there are others in which the want of timber is very sensibly felt. Thus, for example, in the government of Wologda, which covers an area of 6967 geographical square miles, exceeding almost by two-fifths that of the whole Prussian monarchy, the forests occupy more than nine-tenths of the total surface. There is not in all Europe a country which can be compared for the immensity of its forests to this single government; those of all Hungary and Transylvania put together do not occupy an area of more than 7,500,000 dessiatines, which is not equal to one-fourth of the extent of the forests of Wologda. It is equal to somewhat more than a quarter of the extent of those of Archangel, and somewhat more than a third of those of Perm; and is greatly exceeded by those of Wiatka, Olonetz, and Orenburg, each apart. The forests of Wologda exceed in extent, in the proportion of 6 to 1, and those of Archangel, in the proportion of 5 to 1, those of all Prussia. On the other hand, in the governments of Stavropol and Astrakhan, the extent of forests does not amount to one-hundredth part of the surface; and in the country of the Don Cossacks and the governments of Ekathérinoslaw and Kherson, it is only 3 per cent. of the area.

When forests are properly managed, it is considered sufficient for the wants of the country if they cover a fifth part of the surface. In Russia there are thirty-four governments in which they exceed this proportion, and only seventeen in which they fall short of it. Amongst the former, there are three in which they cover more than two-thirds of the area; three in which they cover more than half; seven, in which their extent varies between 40 and 50 per cent.; and eleven in which they occupy between 30 and 40 per cent. of the entire surface. We must however observe, that estimates founded on the experience of other countries as to the relative extent of forest land requisite for the wants of the population, are not strictly applicable to Russia. M. Boulmerincq, one of our best-informed foresters, is of opinion, that,—taking into consideration, *first*, the severity of our climate and the length of our winters; *secondly*, the want of economy which is observed amongst us in the employment of wood as fuel, and the considerable quantity which is used in the drying of grain*; *thirdly*, the influence of climate upon forest vegetation, which proceeds in Russia much more slowly on account of our easterly position (M. Boulmerincq estimates the difference between the progress of forest reproduction in Russia and in Germany to be in the proportion of 2 to 3);—we may add 50 per cent. to the estimates made for other countries. Adopting this opinion, M. Koeppen classes in the category of very badly timbered countries all those governments where the forest land does not occupy at least 22·5 per cent. of the surface. He considers as moderately provided with timber those in which the forest land occupies from 22·5 to 37·5 per cent. of the surface; and, as richly wooded, those in which the relative extent of forest land exceeds the proportion of 37·5 per cent. According to this classification we would have in Russia only sixteen governments richly provided with timber; fifteen, which would be regarded as moderately, and twenty which must be considered as very badly timbered. In the last-named category, we find, amongst others, the governments of Kowno, Grodno, Kiew, and the Grand Duchy of Finland, where the forests, nevertheless, occupy more than a fifth of the area, and where the want of

---

* It is but too true that wood is not economised in Russia, and that a great deal is wasted; but, in regard to firewood, the want of economy is largely compensated by the excellent construction of our stoves, which do not allow so much caloric to escape as the slightly built stoves made use of in other countries; as, for example, in the south of Germany. We may take it for certain that, in proportion to the number and size of the houses, there is not more firewood burned at St. Petersburg than at Vienna, in spite of the great difference of climate. On the other hand, almost all our country houses, and the greater part of our town houses being built of wood, we use a great deal more wood in building than is consumed in other countries.

timber has not been felt hitherto. But estimates of this sort cannot be correct, even approximatively, without we take into consideration the number of the inhabitants. We are of opinion that, in the present state of our relative population, we may still consider as very well wooded all those countries where the forests cover more than 25 per cent. of the surface, and that the same proportion might also suffice for our wants in future, notwithstanding the progress of population, if our forests were better economised. In this category are found, according to the preceding table, twenty-eight governments. Of course, even in those countries where this proportion is maintained, a deficiency of wood might be felt in certain localities where the forests were wasted by irregular cuttings. In this position we find, amongst others, the governments of Moscow and Wladimir, and a part of the countries in the neighbourhood of the Wolga. But, these partial devastations apart, we think that, as a general rule, we can consider as void of resources in their forests only those governments where the former do not occupy more than 15 per cent. of the surface. In this latter class are comprised the last thirteen governments of our table. The governments which are most abundantly wooded occupy the whole north, and a large portion of the west and centre of the empire; those which are least favoured in this respect are situated in the south and east.

The following table exhibits the absolute and relative extent of the uncultivated land in each government, that is, the remainder of its area after deducting the space occupied by cultivated land, meadows, and forests.

Supplementary Table, No. V.   *Land not in Culture.*

GOVERNMENTS.	Total Extent of Surface.	Pastures, *Landes*, Heaths, Marshes, Roads, Lakes, Rivers, and Ground occupied by Buildings.	Proportion per Cent. to total Area.
	Dessiatines.	*Dessiatines.*	
1. Wiatka - - -	12,600,000	127,000	1·
2. Woronèje - - -	6,093,360	186,360	3·1
3. Toula - - -	2,792,160	132,160	4·7
4. Wologda - - -	35,113,680	1,863,680	5·3
5. Podolia - - -	3,895,920	212,920	5·5
6. Minsk - - -	8,174,880	508,880	6·2
7. Nijni-Nowgorod - -	4,415,040	335,040	7·6
8. Tambow - - · -	6,058,030	458,030	7·6
9. Kostroma - - -	7,539,840	599,840	8·
10. Simbirsk - - -	6,627,600	527,600	8·
Carried forward -	93,310,510	4,951,510	

Governments.	Total Extent of Surface.	Pastures, *Landes*, Heaths, Marshes, Roads, Lakes, Rivers, and Ground occupied by Buildings.	Proportion per Cent. to total Area.
	Dessiatines.	*Dessiatines.*	
.Brought forward - -	93,310,510	4,951,510	
11. Kazan - - -	5,685,120	458,120	8·1
12. Tschernigow - -	5,034,960	424,960	8·4
13. Penza - - -	3,477,600	327,600	9·4
14. Orel - - - -	4,324,320	424,320	9·8
15. Moscow - - -	2,968,560	308,560	10·4
16. Kowno - - -	3,820,320	410,320	10·7
17. Pskow - - -	4,077,360	477,360	11·7
18. Kingdom of Poland -	11,563,627	1,412,627	12·2
19. Smolensk - - -	5,136,575	656,575	12·8
20. Koursk - - -	4,123,370	528,370	12·8
21. Wladimir - - -	4,344,840	564,840	13
22. Twer - - - -	6,163,920	903,920	14·7
23. Country of the Don Cossacks - - -	14,832,720	2,562,720	17·3
24. Kiew - - - -	4,601,520	853,520	18·5
25. Wolhynia - - -	6,531,840	1,244,840	19·1
26. Mohilew - - -	4,455,360	855,360	19·2
27. Riazan - - -	3,860,640	760,640	19·7
28. Wilna - - -	3,865,680	760,680	19·7
29. Perm - - - -	30,607,920	6,098,920	19·9
30. Kharkow - - -	4,964,400	1,014,400	20·4
31. Grodno - - -	3,487,680	737,680	21·2
32. Nowgorod - - -	11,153,520	2,383,520	21·4
33. Witebsk - - -	4,082,400	902,400	22·1
34. Poltawa - - -	4,516,560	1,049,560	23·2
35. Jaroslaw - - -	3,321,360	824,360	24·8
36. Olonetz - - -	14,026,320	3,846,320	27·4
37. Courland - - -	2,494,800	709,800	28·5
38. Kalouga - - -	2,887,920	940,920	32·6
39. Livonia - - -	4,299,120	1,401,120	32·6
40. St. Petersburg - -	4,883,760	1,733,760	35·5
41. Bessarabia - - -	4,319,280	1,564,280	36·2
42. Saratow - - -	17,766,000	7,523,000	42·3
43. Orenburg - - -	34,135,920	15,568,920	45·6
44. Kherson - - -	6,713,280	3,193,280	47·6
45. Esthonia - - -	1,895,040	935,040	49·3
46. Ekathérinoslaw - -	6,078,240	3,376,240	55·5
47. Tauride - - -	5,861,520	3,267,520	55·7
48. Archangel - - -	78,215,760	48,478,760	62
49. Stavropol - - -	13,356,000	8,493,000	63·6
50. Grand Duchy of Finland	34,645,418	25,594,418	73·9
51. Astrakhan - - -	14,414,400	13,344,400	92·6
TOTAL - -	500,305,460	171,968,460	34·4

The governments at the two extremities of the above scale present very extraordinary results. In the government of Wiatka, where the forests occupy nearly three-fourths of the entire area, the totally unproductive land does not exceed a hundredth part of the superficies; in the government of Astrakhan, again, it occupies more than nine-tenths; so that there remains for cultivated land, meadows, and forests, little more than 7 per cent. of the whole area. But it must be observed that, in the government of Wiatka, the forests, remote from means of communication, are in part unproductive, whilst in the government of Astrakhan a great part of the uncultivated land is utilised as pasture. Thus, as regards the productive forces of these two governments, neither is the situation of the one so advantageous, nor that of the other so void of resources as would appear from the statistical classsification of their soil. Moreover, it must be observed, that the government of Astrakhan abounds in land suitable for cultivation, and standing in want of nothing but hands to till it; it reckons only one hundred inhabitants to the geographical square mile.

Countries where the unproductive soil does not occupy more than 10 per cent. are in general considered as being in a satisfactory normal condition. From the above table it appears that in European Russia fourteen governments, occupying together an extent of about $113\frac{1}{2}$ millions of dessiatines, or $22\frac{1}{3}$ per cent. of its entire surface, are included in this category. In fifteen governments, embracing an extent of 111 millions of dessiatines, or 22 per cent. of all European Russia, the uncultivated land occupies between 10 and 20 per cent. of the surface. In eight governments, embracing an extent of 48 millions of dessiatines, it occupies from 20 to 30 per cent. of the surface. In four governments, namely, Kalouga, Livonia, St. Petersburg, and Bessarabia, this portion of the soil may be reckoned at about a third. In other four, namely, Saratow, Kherson, Esthonia, and Orenburg, occupying a territory of $60\frac{1}{2}$ millions of dessiatines, or more than 12 per cent. of all European Russia, the proportion of unproductive soil varies between 40 and 50 per cent. of the surface. It occupies more than a half in the five governments of Stavropol, Tauride, Ekathérinoslaw, Archangel, and Astrakhan, and also in the Grand Duchy of Finland, which provinces, taken together, cover an extent of $152\frac{1}{2}$ millions of dessiatines, or more than three-tenths of European Russia. In the government of Archangel, it is brushwood and marshes; in Bessarabia, Ekathérinoslaw, Stavropol, Tauride, Saratow, Kherson, Orenburg, and Astrakhan, it is the steppes by which the larger portion of the surface is occupied. A considerable portion of these steppes, not hitherto converted into cultivable land, may become so in the course of time—part of the soil being very fertile. Meantime, this portion is used as pasture, and offers great resources for the grazing of cattle. In Finland, it is rocks and lakes which withdraw so large a portion of the area from culture.

It is to be regretted that our agricultural statistics are not
sufficiently complete to furnish us with the extent of the pasture
lands in the different governments. The want of this prevents
us from forming any numerical estimate, however loose, of the
extent of area *entirely unproductive*,—that is, which cannot be
turned to any account whatever. In the general classification
of the soil of European Russia, (page 35.), we have adopted
from approximative calculations the proportion of a tenth for
land used as pasture. This tenth of the total surface figures at
about a third in the third column of the immediately preceding
table, which gives the extent of uncultivated soil in each government; but it is evident that the proportion between the land
which serves for pasture, and that which remains totally unproductive, is not alike in all the governments, but varies to infinity.
Thus, for example, we may admit without hesitation that in
several governments, especially in the eastern and southern provinces, and in all the countries of the steppes in general, more
than half the uncultivated land, and frequently more than two-
thirds of it, is used for pasture; whilst in some of the northern
governments the greater portion of the lands ranked in that
category is entirely sterile.

The following recapitulatory table presents a synoptical view
of the comparative results of the preceding tables:—

*Recapitulatory Table of the Cultivation of the Soil expressed in
per-centages of the total Surface.*

GOVERNMENTS.	Land in Cultivation.	Meadows.	Forests.	Pastures, Marshes, *Landes*, Heaths, Roads, Canals, Lakes, Rivers, and ground occupied by Buildings.
1. Toula - - - -	71·6	7·9	15·8	4·7
2. Tschernigow - - -	63·4	12·5	15·7	8·4
3. Podolia - - -	62·6	19·8	12·1	5·5
4. Koursk - - -	60·7	14·9	11·6	12·8
5. Orel - - - -	55·5	25·4	9·3	9·8
6. Kowno - - -	54	15·7	19·6	10·7
7. Kiew - - - -	51·1	9·7	20·7	18·5
8. Woronèje - -	49·3	39·4	8·2	3·1
9. Kingdom of Poland -	47·1	13	27·7	12·2
10 Riazan - - -	46·6	7·8	25·9	19·7
11. Penza - - -	46	13	31 6	9·4
12. Kalouga - - -	45	6·7	15·7	32 6
13. Poltawa - - -	44·3	26·9	5·6	23·2
14. Moscow - - -	43·8	8.8	37	10·4
15. Kharkow - - -	42·3	27·2	10·1	20·4
16. Grodno - - -	42·1	14 9	21.8	21·2
17. Wladimir -· - -	41·4	6·5	39.1	13

GOVERNMENTS.	Land in Cultivation.	Meadows.	Forests.	Pastures, Marshes, *Landes*, Heaths, Roads, Canals, Lakes, Rivers, and Ground occupied by Buildings.
18· Tambow - - -	41·3	27·2	23·9	7·6
19· Nijni-Nowgorod - -	40·8	6·3	45·3	7·6
20. Witebsk - - -	39·2	2·9	35·8	22·1
21. Smolensk - - -	38·9	5·5	42·8	12·8
22. Mohilew - - -	38·1	6·8	35·9	19·2
23. Simbirsk - - -	37·7	24·1	30·2	8
24. Kazan - - - -	37	8·8	46·2	8
25. Jaroslaw - - -	36·1	14·8	24·3	24·8
26. Minsk - - - ·	34 5	18·9	40·4	6·2
27. Wolhynia - - -	31·9	19·6	34·	14·2
28. Pskow - - - -	32·3	11·9	36·7	19·1
29. Wilna - - - -	30·2	8·7	41·4	19·7
30. Bessarabia - - -	30·1	27·8	5·9	36·2
31. Twer - - - -	27·1	20·9	37·3	14·7
32. Wiatka - - -	23·6	4	71·4	1
33. Kostroma - - -	21·2	4·5	66·3	8
34. Kherson - - -	20·9	29·8	1·7	47·6
35. Courland - - -	19·8	12·6	39·1	28·5
36. Ekathérinoslaw - -	19·7	23·1	1·7	55·5
37. Country of the Don Cossacks - - -	15·6	64·3	2·8	17·3
38. Saratow - - -	14·2	36·7	6·8	42·3
39. Tauride - - -	12·8	27·3	4·2	55·7
40. Esthonia - - -	12·7	13·7	24·3	49·3
41. Orenburg - - -	12·1	13	29·3	45·6
42. Nowgorod - - -	11·7	4·2	62·7	21·4
43. St. Petersburg - -	11·2	4	49	35·8
44. Livonia - - -	9·7	12·9	44·8	32·6
45. Perm - - - -	8·5	6·5	65·1	19·9
46 Stavropol - - -	5·6	30	0·8	63·6
47. Olonetz · - - -	3·6	0·8	69·2	27·4
48. Wologda - - -	2·3	1·3	91·1	5·3
49. Grand Duchy of Finland	1·5	3·1	21·5	73·9
50. Astrakhan - - -	1	5·6	0·8	92·6
51. Archangel - - -	0·1	0·2	37·7	62
In all together -	18	12	35·8	34·2

We perceive from this table that there are twenty-one governments, namely, Toula, Tschernigow, Podolia, Koursk, Orel, Kowno, Kiew, Woronéje, Riazan, Penza, Kalouga, Poltawa, Moscow, Kharkow, Grodno, Wladimir, Tambow, Witebsk, Mohilew, Simbirsk, Jaroslaw, and the Kingdom of Poland, embracing together an extent of about 103 millions of dessiatines, or more than a fifth of the entire area of European Russia, in which the cultivated land predominates. In the country of the Don Cossacks, occupying an extent of nearly 15 millions of dessiatines, the meadow land exceeds in extent all the other parts of the soil. In the seventeen governments of Nijni-Nowgorod, Smolensk, Kazan, Minsk, Pskow, Wolhynia, Wilna, Twer, Wiatka, Kostroma, Courland, Nowgorod, St. Petersburg, Livonia, Perm, Olonetz, and Wologda, embracing a territory of 166 millions of dessiatines, or a third of European Russia, it is the forests that occupy the greater portion of the surface. In the ten governments of Bessarabia, Kherson, Ekathérinoslaw, Saratow, Tauride, Esthonia, Orenburg, Stavropol, Astrakhan, and Archangel, and likewise in the Grand Duchy of Finland, occupying amongst them an extent of nearly 217 millions of dessiatines, or upwards of two-fifths of European Russia, the larger portion of the area is occupied by uncultivated land.

This excessive variety in the distribution of the soil, which is not found in the same degree in any other country, must necessarily exercise a great influence not only on the system of culture and on the progress of rural economy, but also on the well-being of the populations, and in general on the whole economical and social condition of the different provinces of the Empire. The relations of these different portions of the soil to the number of the inhabitants will form the subject of the following chapter.

CHAP. IV.

POPULATION.

Progress of Population. — Excess of Births over Deaths. — Absolute Population. — Proportion betwixt the Sexes. — Comparisons with other Countries. — Relative Population. — Comparisons. — Inferences. — Urban Population. — Comparisons. — Origin and Foundation of Towns in Russia, and different Classes of their Inhabitants. — Their Revenues. — Urban Population of the Asiatic Provinces. — Statistical Tables. — Observations.

In an empire like Russia, in which there is still so much land in a state of nature, — so many productive forces in reserve, — where the national activity is not stinted for aliment, but hands are wanting for the work, — the movement followed by population must necessarily be in a strongly marked ascending direction. The best information which we possess upon this subject is that which has been so carefully collected by M. Koeppen, Member of the Academy of Sciences of St. Petersburg. The ordinary annual increase of the population, as shown by the researches of this learned academician, exceeds the proportion of 1 per cent. M. Reden, in his comparative statistics of the principal

states of Europe, gives a table of the births and deaths in
Russia amongst the population belonging to the Greek Church
for the period from 1801 to 1833 inclusive, and for the years
1841—1843 : from this table it results that the total cipher of
the births, during the 33 years from 1801 to 1833, amounted
to 49,456,800, and that of the deaths to 32,767,600, which
gives for the population of that communion an increase of
16,689,200 individuals, or at the rate of 505,700 per annum.
The cipher of the births exceeded that of the deaths by 51 per
cent.   During the years 1841 to 1843, the cipher of the births
amounted at an average to 2,209,900, and that of the deaths to
1,731,700, which gave for the births an excess of only 478,200
individuals, or $27\frac{2}{3}$ per cent.   This temporary decrease in the
progress of population during these three years was occasioned
by epidemic diseases which prevailed in some parts of Russia in
1841 and 1842.   During these two years the annual excess of
births over deaths was at an average only 351,500 individuals,
or 19·4 per cent.; but the three following years, 1843, 1844,
and 1845, presented a very visible improvement :

The cipher of births amounted during that triennium to -	7,972,848
And that of deaths to - - - - -	5,403,932
Excess of births - - - - -	2,568,916
	or $47\frac{1}{2}$ per cent.

The triennium from 1846 to 1848 presents the following
results : —

Total number of births - - - - -	8,172,999
„ deaths - - - - -	7,337,555
Excess of births - - - - -	835,444
	or $11\frac{4}{10}$ per cent.

The decrease of the ascending movement of population during
this latter triennium was owing to the ravages of the cholera
in the year 1848, when the number of deaths exceeded that of
the births by 295,943, or 10·4 per cent.

Taking the entire decennium from 1841 to 1850, we obtain
the following results : —

Births - - - - - - -	26,502,000
Deaths - - - - - - -	21,047,000
Excess of births - - - - -	5,455,000
	or 26 per cent.

The annual movement presents the following results : —

	Population.	Excess of Births over Deaths.	Increase per cent. of Pop.
At the end of 1840	50,231,000	395,000 or 19·2 per cent.	0·8
1841	50,626,000	314,000 15·1	0·6
1842	50,940,000	842,000 47·3	1·7

	Population.	Excess of Births over Deaths.	Increase per cent. of Pop.
1843	51,782,000	972,000 or 55·6 per cent.	1·9
1844	52,754,000	755,000 40·3	1·4
1845	53,509,000	583,000 28·7	1·1
1846	54,092,000	538,000 24·8	1
		Excess of Deaths over Births.	Decrease per cent.
1847	54,630,000	296,000 or 10·4	0·5
		Excess of Births over Deaths.	Increase per cent.
1848	54,334,000	566,000	1
1849	54,900,000	785,000	1·4
1850	55,685,000		

We have obtained these figures by taking for the basis of our calculation the population of 1846, according to the data furnished M. Koeppen, in a Memoir read before the Academy of Sciences at St. Petersburg, and combining it with the figures given by the registers of births and deaths during the years 1841—1850, published in the St. Petersburg Almanac.

According to the above table, the total increment of the population during ten years would be 5,454,000, or 10·8 per cent., which is somewhat more than 1 per cent. per annum, notwithstanding the great mortality caused by the cholera, which prevailed throughout the empire during several years of this period. Thus the calculations of M. Koeppen, who estimates the ordinary increase of the population at upwards of 1 per cent. per annum are completely justified. On consulting, however, the statistical information collected at the Ministry of the Interior on the occasion of the last census, we obtain for the total population of European Russia in 1851 no more than 55,033,000 inhabitants, that is, 652,000 less than that resulting from the preceding table : this may proceed either from some incorrectness in the antecedent data upon which M. Koeppen had based the number of inhabitants in 1846, adopted by us as our basis, or from irregularities in the keeping of some of the registers; and as statistical returns become more exact and complete with the progress of time, we prefer adopting the figure resulting from the later inquiries, namely, 55,033,000 inhabitants in 1851.

It is very difficult to ascertain with precision the progress of population in each different government, owing to the frequent variations in the cipher of the floating population, which moves about from one province to another, either to colonise or in search of work. We perceive from the statistical observations of M. Koeppen *, founded on the census of 1816 and of 1834,

* Quelques mots au sujet des données statistiques sur la population de la Russie: St. Petersbourg, 1850.

and referring only to seven governments, namely, Moscow, Wladimir, Kostroma, Nowgorod, Nijni-Nowgorod, Twer, and Jaroslaw, that in the space of these eighteen years the population augmented, in the government of Moscow 23 per cent., or nearly $1\frac{1}{3}$ per cent. per annum, and in that of Nowgorod, 30 per cent., or $1\frac{2}{3}$ per cent. per annum, whilst in the governments of Jaroslaw, Wladimir, and Nijni-Nowgorod, the increase was only from 9 to 10 per cent., or about $\frac{1}{2}$ per cent. per annum, which shows that the rate of augmentation is very unequal. Going back to a more remote epoch, M. Arsénieff gives the population of 31 governments in 1790, compared with that of 1846. From these comparisons it results that, taking the governments in certain groupes, we obtain for the progress of population the following results:—

The number of inhabitants has augmented during the said period of fifty-six years,

In the three northern governments of Archangel, Wologda, and Olonetz, in the proportion of somewhat more than 40 per cent., equivalent to an annual increase of $\frac{7}{10}$ per cent.;

In the five governments of the Alaoune region, namely, St. Petersburg, Nowgorod, Twer, Smolensk, and Pskow, at the rate of about 30 per cent., or $\frac{1}{2}$ per cent. per annum;

In the three Baltic governments of Esthonia, Livonia, and Courland, at the rate of 50 per cent, or $\frac{9}{10}$ per cent. per annum;

In the governments of Witebsk and Mohilew, belonging to the lower region (nizmennoe prostranstvo), at the rate of 25 per cent., or $\frac{2}{5}$ per cent. per annum;

In the thirteen governments of the central region, Jaroslaw, Kostroma, Wladimir, Nijni-Nowgorod, Penza, Tambow, Woronèje, Koursk, Orel, Kalouga, Moscow, Toula, and Riazan, at the rate of 55 per cent., or nearly 1 per cent. per annum;

In the five governments of the Uralian region, Simbirsk, Kazan, Wiatka, Perm, and Orenburg, at the rate of 115 per cent., or 2 per cent. per annum.

Of these last five, it is in the government of Orenburg that the most marked progress has taken place. The population of that government rose during these fifty-six years from 355,000 to 1,706,000 inhabitants, that is, it almost quintupled itself,— a circumstance which must be attributed chiefly to immigration from governments where there is a deficiency of arable lands. Next to Orenburg, the greatest progress is found in the government of Perm, where the population has nearly doubled.

Thus, the progress of population has been most rapid in the central and Uralian regions, and slowest in the Alaoune, and in two governments of the lower region. The latter are the least fertile, and the least copiously endowed with productive forces. In some countries of the region of the steppes, the progress of population has been equally rapid. M. Haxthausen cites three districts of the government of Saratow, namely, Nicolaïewsk, Nowoi-Oussen, and Zarew, in which the increase of population between the seventh and eighth census, that is, between 1816 and 1834, amounted to 48 per cent., or nearly 3 per cent. per annum, —an increase which likewise is partially owing to immigration from other governments where arable land is less abundant.

In the kingdom of Poland, the population augmented during the decennial period from 1829 to 1839 by 500,000 individuals, or 13 per cent., which gives an annual increase of $1\frac{3}{10}$ per cent.; and during the eleven following years, 1840—1851, it augmented by 423,000, or 9·6 per cent., giving an annual augmentation of $\frac{4}{5}$ per cent. This decrease of progress is explained by the ravages of the cholera. In Finland the ordinary increase is at the rate of about 1 per cent. per annum.

Combining all these data, and especially taking into consideration the excess of births over deaths since 1840, we think we may adopt the rate of 1 per cent. for the ordinary annual increase of population throughout European Russia.

In Austria, according to recent official statistics, the population amounted in 1841 to 35,550,684 inhabitants, and at the end of 1851 to 38,388,000, which presents for the ten years an augmentation of 2,837,316 inhabitants, or 0·8 per cent. per annum : but the actual progress of the population was much greater, for the figure taken from the official statistics of 1841 was exaggerated, especially as regards the population of Hungary and Transylvania.* We may approximately estimate the increase of population in the Austrian Empire at 1 per cent. per annum, the proportion admitted by all the native statists, which would give on the population of 1851 (38,380,000 inhabitants) an increase of 384,000 individuals. In Prussia, according to the statistical tables of Hoffmann and Dieterici, founded upon official data, the annual increase of the population from 1816 to 1849 was at the average rate of 1·46 per cent. In France, during the space of twenty years, from 1821 to 1841, it augmented 12·37 per cent. †, or at the rate of 0·62 per cent. per annum. In England, according to the comparative statistics of M. Reden, the mean annual increase during the decennium

* See a work published at Vienna in 1852, under the title of " Handbuch der Statistik des oesterreichischen Kaiserstaats, by M. J. Hain, Secretary to the Direction of Administrative Statistics," vol. i. p. 504.

† According to the census of 1821, the population of France amounted to 30,462,000; in 1841, it had risen to 34,230,000, showing an augmentation of 3,768,000, or 12·37 per cent.

from 1831 to 1840 was at the rate of 1·11 per cent.; since then it has remained stationary from the effect of emigration. The excess of births over deaths in Austria, without including Hungary and Transylvania *, during the years 1841 to 1846 was at an average 230,000, or 32 per cent. per annum; in Prussia, during the triennium from 1841 to 1843, it was 175,000, or 40 per cent. per annum: in France, during the same triennial period, the annual average was 164,000, or 20 per cent. †; in Russia, without including Finland and the kingdom of Poland, the mean of the decennium from 1841 to 1850 gives 563,000, or 27 per cent.

If to the cipher of the population of European Russia in 1851 (55,033,000 inhabitants), we add 1 per cent., we may estimate the actual population (at the end of 1852) at about 55½ millions.

In 1849, the population of Finland amounted, according to the official statistics of that province, to - - - -	1,524,000
Increase of population in 3 years, at 1 per cent. - - -	45,000
Population at the end of 1852 - - - - -	1,569,000
Population of the kingdom of Poland in 1851, according to official returns - - - - - - -	4,852,000
Increase at 1 per cent. - - - - - -	48,000
Population at the end of 1852 - - - - -	4,900,000

Adding these two figures to the preceding, we obtain for the total population of European Russia, 61,969,000 inhabitants.

The population of the Russian possessions in Asia amounted in 1838 (according to a statistical memoir of M. Koeppen presented to the Academy of Sciences at St. Petersburg, on 30th October, 1840), to 4,638,000 souls.

Adding for 14 years an annual increment at the rate of ½ per cent., we obtain the cipher of 4,962,000 inhabitants.‡

This cipher, added to the total population of European Russia, gives 66,931,000 inhabitants for the whole empire; or, if we add the American possessions, with a population of about 60,000, together with the army and navy, we may carry the total cipher of the population of the empire to 68,000,000. This is nearly twice the population of France, and more than

---

* The registers of births and deaths for these two provinces have not hitherto been published.

† According to M. Schnitzler's statistics, founded on official tables.

‡ According to the census of 1851, the population subject to personal impost had, during the 18 preceding years, augmented in the four governments of Enisseisk, Tomsk, Tobolsk, and Irkoutsk only to the extent of 6 per cent., which gives an annual rate of increase of not more than ⅓ per cent.; but the rate of increase being much higher in the trans-caucasian provinces, we may admit for the whole Russian possessions in Asia an average annual increase of ½ per cent.

that of Austria and the whole states of the German Zollverein put together.

M. Reden, in his comparative statistics of the five great powers of Europe, makes their total population in 1846 amount to 180 millions; in this total Russia figures, including her possessions in Asia, at 64 millions, or more than a third.

Admitting for 1853 the cipher of 68 millions, according to the preceding calculation, and for the ordinary increase of population the rate of 1 per cent. per annum, it would require only sixty-six years to double the actual population, which would then amount to 136 millions. By the same calculation, the population of the whole empire would in thirty-nine years reach the cipher of 100 millions. But this increase must always depend more or less on the progress of cultivation, and on the successive development of the productive forces of the country.

It is a fact, evidenced by the statistics of every country, that the number of males born exceeds that of females, but that the rate of infantine mortality is greater amongst males than amongst females. We shall borrow our examples from the statistics of Prussia, which furnish very special data upon this point. During the period of three years, from 1841 to 1843, the male births in Prussia exceeded the female in the proportion of nearly 5·8 per cent. ; but the excess of deaths amongst male children below one year old was 21 per cent., and amongst children between one and three years old it was nearly 4 per cent. For children between three and five years of age, the female deaths present an excess of 2 per cent. Between the ages of five and twenty, the ciphers are found pretty nearly in equilibrio, — presenting, however, a slight excess of deaths amongst the females. Between twenty and twenty-five the mortality again becomes much greater on the male side ; between twenty-five and forty the chances turn in their favour ; between forty and fifty-five there are more deaths amongst males than amongst females ; but after the age of fifty-five, the cipher of female deaths almost always exceeds that of male, and the difference becomes almost constantly greater and greater in proportion as we advance in the scale of years. Thus, for example, in the number of individuals dying betwixt the ages of seventy and seventy-five the cipher of females exceeded that of males in the proportion of 8 per cent., which proves that a much greater number of females than of males attain an advanced age. During this triennium the excess of deaths amongst the masculine over those amongst the feminine population amounted to 5·9 per cent.

In Austria, during the period from 1830 to 1840, the difference of births in favour of male children, amounted, according to the official statistics, at an average, to 6·7 per cent. ; in France (from 1840 to 1843), to 5·8 per cent., and in England (from 1839 to 1842), to 5 per cent. The excess of mortality for the same sex was, in Austria, during a period of twenty-one years (1830 to 1851), 3 per cent. ; in France (from 1840 to 1843), 1⅖ per cent.; and in England (1838 to 1842) 3 per cent. In Russia, according to the statistical tables published in the St. Petersburg Almanac, under the superintendence of the Academy of Sciences, the cipher of masculine births during the decennial period from 1841 to 1850 exceeded that of female in the proportion of 5·3 per cent.*, and the cipher of deaths amongst the male population presented an excess of only 2·8 per cent.

As the St. Petersburg Almanac for 1852 and 1853 gives a statement of the deaths amongst the population belonging to the Greek Church during the years 1849 and 1850, classified according to the ages of the deceased, which was not done formerly, we avail ourselves of this document for the preparation of the following comparative table of the mortality in Russia and in Prussia according to the age and sex of the deceased.

Mortality of Male Population.

					To 100 Deaths.	
					In Russia.	In Prussia.
Under	5 years of age	-	-		52·4	50·2
From	5 to 10	-	-	-	5·7	4·4
	10	20 †	-	-	6·1	4·1
	20	25	-	-	3	3·1
	25	30	-	-	3·1	2·5
	30	35	-	-	2·8	2·3
	35	40	-	-	3·1	2·4
	40	45	-	-	2·9	3
	45	50	-	-	3·3	3
	50	55	-	-	3	3·2
	55	60	-	-	3·2	3·5
	60	65	-	-	2·8	4·4
	65	70	-	-	2·8	4·1
	70	75	-	-	2·1	3·8
	75	80	-	-	1·6	3·2
	80	85	-	-	1	1·7
	85	90	-	-	0·6	0·8
Above 90		-	-	-	0·5	0·3

* Some localities occasionally present very extraordinary results in this respect. Thus, for example, there were born at Odessa, in 1841, 1,772 males and 1,461 females, giving an excess of 21·3 per cent. in favour of the male sex.

† In the Russian statistics the deaths between 10 and 20 years are divided into two classes, namely, from 10 to 15, and from 15 to 20; in the Prussian, the division runs from 10 to 14 and from 14 to 20. We are thus obliged, for the sake of exactness of comparison, to lump, in both cases, the two classes into one.

Mortality of Female Population.

				To 100 Deaths.	
				In Russia.	In Prussia.
Under 5 years of age	-	-		52·3	46
From 5 to 10	-	-	-	5·7	4·6
10 20	-	-	-	5·5	4·5
20 25	-	-	-	3	2·7
25 30	-	-	-	3·2	2·8
30 35	-	-	-	2·9	2·9
35 40	-	-	-	3·2	2·9
40 45	-	-	-	3	3·1
45 50	-	-	-	3·3	2·8
50 55	-	-	-	3	3·3
55 60	-	-	-	3·5	3·7
60 65	-	-	-	3·1	4·9
65 70	-	-	-	2·9	4·6
70 75	-	-	-	2·2	4·6
75 80	-	-	-	1·5	3·4
80 85	-	-	-	0·8	1·9
85 90	-	-	-	0·5	0·9
Above 90	-	-	-	0·4	0·4

We perceive from this table that the relative mortality is greater in Russia during the periods of infancy and adolescence, and that this difference is also greater for the female sex. Thus, for example, as regards infants under five years of age, the difference does not exceed 2·2 per cent for males, whilst it attains the proportion of 6·3 per cent. for females. Taking together the two first classes, embracing the ages from five to twenty, we find for the male sex a difference of 3·3 per cent., and for the female sex a difference of 2·1 per cent. We find that in Russia the proportion of deaths amongst females up to the age of five years exceeds by 1·7 per cent. that of female deaths in Prussia up to the age of ten years. As natural consequence of a higher rate of mortality in childhood and early life, deaths in Russia become less numerous compared to the total cipher in a population of more advanced age. Up to the age of forty, the difference continues on the side of Russia: after that limit, it is, for almost every class, on the side of Prussia.

It were very desirable that infant mortality up to the age of five years should be subdivided in the Tables published by the Academy of Sciences, as is done in Prussia, into four classes, namely, still-born, under a year, from one to three, and from three to five: this would be of much importance for hygienic police, and for medical statistics. On the other hand, the Prussian statistics, from which we have drawn our information, stop at the age of 90, and all the individuals dying after that age are comprehended in one class, whilst the lists published in the

St. Petersburg Almanac carry on their classification to the age of 150, and present numerous examples of extraordinary longevity. Thus, in 1850, there were reckoned 105 females and 106 males, who died at an age between 100 and 105 ; 35 females and 57 males who died between 105 and 110; 16 females and 21 males who died between 110 and 115; 14 females and 12 males between 115 and 120 ; 2 females and 2 males between 120 and 125 ; 1 female (in the government of Kherson) and 1 male (in the government of Ekatherinoslaw), who died above the age of 125 ; and 1 female (in the government of Woronèje) and 1 male (in the government of Tambow) who died past the age of 140.*

The following Table presents the result of the movement of the population of the Greek Church in the eparchies of European Russia during the years 1849 and 1850 :

Names of Eparchies.	Average Excess of Births over Deaths.	Proportion per Cent.
1. Orenburg - -	34,976	81·5
2. Country of the Don Cossacks - -	13,881	77·9
3. Minsk - - -	13,661	71
4. Riazan - - -	26,386	70·9
5. Astrakhan - -	2,329	60·2
6. Kalouga - -	16,632	58·3
7. Koursk - -	29,242	56·2
8. Lithuania - -	11,392	56
9. Kostroma - -	15,525	49·5
10. Toula - - -	18,945	48·8
11. Orel - - -	25,220	48·7
12. Perm - - -	31,452	48
13. Mohilew - -	10,081	44·8
14. Tschernigow - -	19,361	42·8
15. Smolensk - -	16,541	41·4
16. Penza - - -	14,561	40·3
17. Tambow - -	23,803	38·8
18. Saratow - -	25,308	37·9
19. Wiatka - - -	25,941	37 7
20. Wladimir - -	14,526	35·7
21. Twer - - -	17,912	35·1
22. Kiew - - -	17,980	32·7
23. Woronèje - -	19,533	28·6
24. Kazan - - -	10,092	27·2
25. Nijni-Nowgorod -	12,803	26·9
26. Jaroslaw - -	8,874	26·5
27. Nowgorod - -	8,254	26·2
Carried forward -		

* It must, however, be observed that, in consequence of the incomplete condition of the registers of births during last century, it is impossible with us to prove the age of centenarians in a manner so positive as that of younger individuals.

Names of Eparchies.	Average Excess of Births over Deaths.	Proportion per Cent.
Brought forward -		
28. Archangel - -	2,095	25·8
29. Simbirsk - -	11,988	25
30. Wolhynia - -	10,875	24·5
31. Wologda - -	7,772	24·5
32. Podolia - -	11,325	23·5
33. Moscow - -	12,660	23
34. Pskow - - -	6,255	22·1
35. Poltawa - -	13,430	20
36. Polotsk - - -	2,609	17
37. Olonetz - - -	1,365	13
38. Kischenew - -	1,978	6·5
39. St. Petersburg - -	216	0·7
Total average excess of births - -	567,779	
	Average Excess of Deaths over Births.	
40. Kherson - -	425	0·8
41. Kharkow - -	593	0·9
42. Ekathérinoslaw -	32,133	79·4
Total average excess of deaths - -	33,151	
Total average excess of births ut supra - -	567,779	
Nett average excess of births - - -	534,628	

From this table we perceive the striking contrasts which the movement of the population presented during the years 1849 and 1850. Thus, for example, in the governments of Orenburg, Minsk, Riazan, Astrakhan, and the country of the Don Cossacks, there was an excess of births over deaths of from 60 to 81 per cent., whilst in the government of St. Petersburg this excess did not attain the rate of even 1 per cent., and in the government of Ekatherinoslaw, the number of deaths exceeded that of births in the proportion of 80 per cent. This unfavourable result of the movement of population in the last-named government, as well as in those of Kherson and Kharkow, proceeds from the famine and epidemic diseases which prevailed in these governments in 1849. During the following year (1850) the number of births presented an excess over the deaths,

In the government of Kharkow of 26,102, or of 50 per cent.
In that of Ekathérinoslaw   „   18,008,   „   62 per cent.
And in that of Kherson   „   22,059,   „   63 per cent.

As regards the existing population, the number of the female
sex exceeded the males, in Austria (in 1841), by 4·5 per cent. ;
in Prussia (in 1843), by 0·4 per cent. ; in France (in 1841), by
2·1 per cent. ; and in England (in 1841), by 4·9 per cent. In
Russia the statistical information collected by the ministry of
the interior for the year 1850, presents in all the governments
of European Russian taken as a whole, an excess of the female
sex of 2·1 per cent. ; but the numerical proportion of the sexes
varies greatly from one province to another. In the following
thirty-six, namely, the governments of Archangel, Courland,
Esthonia, Jaroslaw, Kharkow, Kazan, Kowno, Kostroma,
Livonia, Minsk, Mohilew, Nijni-Nowgorod, Nowgorod, Olonetz,
Orenburg, Orel, Penza, Perm, Poltawa, Pskow, Saratow,
Simbirsk, Smolensk, Tambow, Twer, Toula, Tschernigow,
Wilna, Witebsk, Wladimir, Wologda, Wolhynia, Woronèje,
Wiatka, and the country of the Don Cossacks, the female sex
predominates : in all the other provinces the numerical majority
is on the side of the male population.

The excess of female population is most considerable in the
governments of

	Per Cent.			Per Cent.
Nowgorod, where it is	- - 14·7	Archangel, where it is	-	- 8·1
Wladimir „	- - 14·5	Olonetz „	-	- 8·2
Nijni-Nowgorod „	- - 11·7	Orel „	-	- 6·9
Kostroma „	- - 11·3	Tschernigow „	-	- 7·1
Wiatka „	- - 11	Kazan „	-	- 5·8
Wologda „	- - 10·1	Kowno „	-	- 5·5
Courland „	- - 9·8	Esthonia „	-	- 5·5
Livonia „	- - 9·3			

The governments which present the greatest excess of male
population are,

	Per Cent.			Per Cent.
St. Petersburg, where it is	- 39·2	Astrakhan, where it is	-	- 9·3
Tauride „	- - 12·6	Moscow „	-	- 7·4
Bessarabia „	- - 10·4	Kherson „	-	- 6·4

In the governments of Siberia and in the Trans-Caucasian
provinces, the female population exceeded the male (according
to old data collected by the academician Koeppen) after the
eighth census, in the proportion of 2·5 per cent.; and in the
kingdom of Poland, according to the official statistics of 1851,
the female population presents an excess of 5·8 per cent.

Similar inequalities in the numerical relations betwixt the
two sexes do not exist, to our knowledge, in any other country.
They proceed with us from the frequent changes of locality
amongst the male population who travel from one province to
another, either in search of work, or in the pursuit of some
branch of commerce or industry, whilst the female population
is more sedentary. In other countries, such changes of locality
occur more equally in the case of both sexes.

The following comparative summary exhibits the result of the preceding observations: —

Excess of Births over Deaths.

In France - - - - - 164,000 individuals, or 20 per cent.
„ Prussia - - - - - 175,000 „ 40 „
„ Austria (exclusive of Hungary and
    Transylvania) - - - - 230,000 „ 32 „
„ Russia (exclusive of Finland and
    the kingdom of Poland) - - 563,000 „ 27 „

Annual Increase of Population.

In France - - - 0·6 per cent. | In England - - - 1 per cent
„ Russia - - - 1 „ | „ Prussia - - - 1·5 „
„ Austria - - - 1 „ |

Excess of Male over Female Births.

In England - - - 5 per cent. | In Prussia (nearly) - 6 per cent.
„ Russia - - - 5·3 „ | „ Austria - - - 6·7 „
„ France - - - 5·8 „ |

Excess of Deaths amongst Male over those amongst Female Population.

In France - - - 1·8 per cent. | In Austria - - - 3 per cent.
„ Russia - - - 2·8 „ | „ Prussia (nearly) - 6 „
„ England - - - 3 „ |

Excess of Female Population.

In Prussia - - - 0·4 per cent. | In Austria - - - 4·5 per cent.
„ France - - - 2·1 „ | „ England - - - 4·9 „
„ Russia - - - 2·1 „ |

The population of European Russia (61,969,000 inhabitants), distributed over a surface of 95,710 geographical square miles*, gives 647 inhabitants to the square mile, without reckoning the army.

In Austria, the population at the end of 1851 being reckoned at 38,388,000 inhabitants, we may reckon it for 1852, adding 1 per cent., at 38,770,000, which gives, for an area of 12,104 geographical square miles, 3,203 inhabitants to the square mile.

* In the table of the area of European Russia, given at p. 7., the government of Archangel, including Nova Zembla, is stated at 15,519 square miles ; but as the latter, approximately calculated to embrace an extent of about 3,500 square miles, presents little interest in a statistical point of view, we throw it out of our comparative calculations, and admit, according to M. Arsénieff, only 12,000 square miles for the area of this government. In the same table, the government of Tauride figures, in conformity with M. Struve's statistics, at an extent of 1,208 square miles; but in this extent is included the Sea of Azow, with a superficies of 46 square miles, regarded by M. Struve as a lake enclavé in the government. The latter area we also throw out, in order to render our tables of the relative population more exact. By this means, the area of European Russia, without Nova Zembla, is reduced to 95,710 geographical square miles; and it is to this cipher that all our future comparisons and calculations will apply.

In Prussia, the population at the end of 1849 amounted to - - 16,331,000
Increase to the end of 1852, 3 years, at 1 per cent. per annum - 490,000

Total for 1852 - - - - - - 16,821,000

This amount of population distributed over an area of 5,077 square miles gives 3,313 inhabitants to the square mile.

In France, the population in 1846 amounted, according to M.
Reden, to - - - - - - - 35,050,000
Add for 6 years, at $\frac{2}{3}$ per cent. per annum (less cholera year) - 1,260,000

Population for 1852 - - - - - 36,310,000

This, for an area of 9,584 geographical square miles, gives 3,789 inhabitants to the square mile.

In Great Britain, the population in 1846 amounted, according to M. Reden, to 27,905,000 : as since that period the excess of births over deaths has been balanced by emigration, we leave that figure without augmentation, which gives, on an area of 5,767 geographical square miles, a population of 4,839 inhabitants to the square mile.

Comparative Table.

	Absolute Population in 1852.	Number of Inhabitants per geog. sq. mile.
Great Britain - - -	27,905,000	4,839
France - - -	36,310,000	3,789
Prussia - - -	16,821,000	3,313
Austria - - -	38,770,000	3,203
European Russia - -	61,969,000	647

Thus the absolute population of this part of the empire exceeds, by nearly 60 per cent., that of Austria, and by more than 70 per cent. that of France ; it surpasses that of England in the proportion of 122 to 100, and that of Prussia, in the proportion of nearly 4 to 1. On the other hand, we are still very far behind other countries in the density of our population, since we have not attained one-fifth of the relative population of Austria, which, next to our own, is the lowest in the scale. It must not, however, be left out of view that there are in Russia, in the governments of the north, and in the Steppes of the south and east, immense tracts of country totally uninhabited ; in the governments of Archangel, Olonetz, and Wologda, which have an area of 21,750 square miles (without Nova Zembla), the marshes (*tundern*) and the sterile soil incapable of culture occupy an extent of about 7,000, and the forests an extent of about 13,000 square miles. We may admit that at least four-fifths of these immense forests remain to this day intact ; the sound of the axe has never been heard in them, nor has the foot of the shepherd penetrated their recesses : in a statistical point of view, then, all this portion of the forest land is in effect without the territory of the empire. One half of Finland, where the uncultivated soil, the lakes, and the marshes occupy nearly three-fourths of the surface, might also be ranked in the same category; in the countries of the steppes we may reckon at least 10,000 square miles of uncultivated and uninhabited surface; and thus there would be nearly 30,000 square miles to subtract from the total area of European Russia, which would reduce the remaining more or less inhabited portion to about 65,700 square miles for a population of nearly 62 millions of inhabitants, which would give 944 inhabitants to the square mile. Still, this is but a very weak relative population, when compared with that of other European countries. But the comparison will be more conclusive, in a statistical point of view, if we throw entirely out of view the forests, pastures, and unproductive soil, and take as our basis the cultivated land and meadows of which the extent, expressed in geographical square miles, is as follows: —

		Absolute Population.	Arable Land, Vineyards, Gardens, and Meadows.	Population to the Square Mile of productive Land.
Austria	-	38,770,000	5,259 *	7,372
France	-	36,310,000	5,785 †	6,277
Prussia	-	16,821,000	2,905‡	5,790
Russia	-	61,969,000	29,757	2,082

From this comparison it appears that the density of our population in relation to the productive soil, is to that of Prussia as 10 to 28; to that of France, as to 10 to 30; and to that of Austria, as 10 to 35.

The productive soil, under which we comprehend the arable land, meadows, vineyards, and gardens, when reduced to dessiatines §, and distributed amongst the population, gives the following results: —

			Population.	Productive Soil. Dessiatines.	Number of Dessiatines to each Inhabitant.
Austria	-	-	38,770,000	26,510,000	0·68
France	-	-	36,310,000	29,162,000	0·80
Prussia -	-	-	16,821,000	14,644,000	0·87
Russia -	-	-	61,969,000	150,000,000	2·42

* According to the official statistics of 1846 — Cultivable land, 36,837,717 joch; rice-fields, 113,447; vineyards, 1,759,271; meadows and gardens, 11,595,152; total, 50,305,587 joch = 5,259 geographical square miles (1 geographical square mile = 9,564·8 joch.)

† According to the agricultural statistics of 1840, cultivated land, fallows included, 26,078,022 hectares; natural meadows, 4,198,197; artificial meadows, 1,576,547; total, 31,852,766 hectares = 5,785 geographical square miles (1 geographical square mile = 5,506 hectares).

‡ According to Förster and Professor Weber's statistics: cultivable lands 47,295,716 morgen; vineyards, gardens, and orchards, 1,024,176; meadows, 14,326,429; total, 62,646,321 morgen = 2,905 geographical square miles (1 geographical square mile = 21,565 95 morgen).

§ 5,040·8 dessiatines = 1 geographical square mile.

Thus, there is in Russia for each inhabitant nearly thrice as much productive soil as in Prussia or France, and three and a half times as much as in Austria.

These comparisons show upon what a broad basis the future progress of the population of European Russia rests, even laying out of account the soil which may be gained to cultivation by the draining of marshes, the fertilisation of uncultivated *landes* and steppes, and the clearing of forests in districts too largely timbered. Thus, whilst other countries, as England and part of Germany, are already beginning to suffer from an excess of population, which brings an increase of proletarianism in its train, the progress of population will, for a long period to come, be with us a source of power and wealth, if only it be supported by the successive development of our productive forces. Still, we must not dissemble that there are special circumstances which will prevent the relative density of our population to our productive soil from ever attaining, except in some specially favoured districts, the same figure which it reaches in the most populous countries of Europe. The fertility of our cultivable lands, seconded even by all the improvements of which their culture is susceptible, will always be counteracted by influences inherent in our soil and geographical position which render defective harvests, both of grain and of provender, so frequent and so general. The population of small states may be augmented without inconvenience beyond the scope of the natural productive forces of their territory; it may find the means of subsistence in manufacturing industry and in foreign commerce; but in an empire so vast as that of Russia, and with such a geographical position, the progress of population must essentially depend on the abundance of the products of the soil. Whatever may be the progress of our industry, we can scarcely anticipate that we will ever have occasion to exert it on account of others in the way of working up exotic raw materials into goods for foreign exportation. China, and other Asiatic states, offer us some facilities in this respect; but commerce with these states is too limited in its resources to serve as the basis of subsistence for any large amount of population.

The population of the Russian possessions in Asia (4,962,000 inhabitants) distributed over an area of 241,425 square miles, without reckoning the islands, gives but 21 inhabitants to the square mile; and if we set apart the trans-caucasian provinces, with an area of 2,825 square miles, and a population of 2,200,000, which gives 779 inhabitants to the square mile, the remaining population is at the rate of no more than 12 inhabitants to the square mile. Siberia is another new world that has to be overcome by the conquests of culture and civilisation. Its population remains as yet grouped in those districts which lie along the banks of navigable rivers and the highways of communication; the rest is but a desert; but it is a desert of which a considerable portion contains within itself large sources of wealth waiting only for the hand of man to develope them. It is well known that all Southern Siberia enjoys a temperate and wholesome climate, a soil of exceeding fertility, and a very vigorous vegetation. The great impediments to population and culture in our Asiatic possessions are, first, the immense distances which separate from each other, and from European Russia, those districts which are most favourably situated in regard to their natural productive forces; and secondly, the want of external outlets. All the principal rivers of Siberia flow from south to north, and fall into the Frozen Ocean; they are, consequently, useless for external traffic. The Amur, the only river which could place Siberia in communication with the Eastern Ocean, flows mostly beyond our frontiers. The commerce carried on with China by land does not possess the elements of development to such an extent as to exercise much influence on the future prosperity of so vast a country.

M. Haxthausen perceives great prospects for the development of the productive forces of Russia in the working and clearing of the immense forests of the north, and in the culture of the steppes of the south. In his work, which we have already repeatedly quoted, he sketches the basis of a vast plan of colonisation which might, in his opinion, be carried out by means chiefly of the numerous class of soldiers who have served out their time in the army. The following is an extract from his proposals for colonising the forest countries of the northern governments:—

" The first thing required would be to form cuttings in the vast forests in order to open roads in straight lines of 50 to 60 versts in length, and 100 feet in breadth, separated from each other by a distance of 50 or 60 versts, and starting from the rivers in the inhabited districts of the country. Alongside of these roads, and at intervals of 15 versts, there would have to be burned a portion of the forest extending to from 3 to 6 square versts *, and a village formed of from 60 to 80 houses; there would thus be four villages along each of these new roads. The trees cut down for the opening of the roads might be partly employed in the construction of wooden trams to be laid down along one side of the road, such as are found in Austria † and

---

* A Russian verst is equivalent to 1,166 English yards, or 5 furlongs 12 poles; a square verst is = 280 English acres.

† In Austria these wooden tram-roads exist only provisionally and for very short distances, solely with a view to the working of the forests.—*Author's note.*

in North America.   The four villages would thus possess easy means of communication with each other, with the rivers, and with the inhabited parts of the country.

" As soon as the first routes were opened, and the new villages well settled, which might probably occupy a period of five years, there would be another operation to undertake, namely, to trace in the same manner cross roads between each of the villages already established on the main roads and the corresponding villages of the parallel roads, and to burn anew, at distances of 15 versts, a space of two versts square, for the establishment of a new village.   There would thus be opened up around the forests a stripe of wood 60 versts deep, in the form of parallelograms 60 versts long by 15 broad, each therefore embracing an extent of about 80 square miles.

" We would leave to the future the ulterior extension of this colonisation, which would gradually advance into the interior of the forests, in proportion to the progress of population, to the increasing demands for timber on account of the crown, and to the more easy outlet afforded by the new means of communication for the produce of the forests."

M. Haxthausen dwells upon the immense advantages of a colonisation of this sort; he indicates the order and means of execution, and he calculates the cost.   In another passage, he dwells upon the future importance, rural and woodland, of the northern governments, (Archangel, Olonetz, and Wologda), and then proceeds as follows: — " It is evident that government ought to feel a great interest in the increase of the population of these northern districts, and in extending culture more equally into their interior.   To possess a territory of 12,000 square miles of land capable of culture and yet almost totally uncleared, is of itself an immense loss to the state.   To this must be added, that the crown itself is proprietor of the greater part of these forests, to an extent, namely, of more than 10,000 square miles, of which more than nine-tenths is merely nominal property. Here there have existed for centuries trees which grow, fade, and die, and are replaced by a new generation destined to die in their turn, untouched by man's hand, and useless to his wants. Of what immense advantage would it not be for Russia, were this boundless territory to be peopled with the 6 or 8 millions of laborious and industrious inhabitants who might unquestionably find there the means of subsistence!   Experience teaches us that in the temperate countries of the north the populations are exceedingly robust: and the North Russian is already distinguished from the other races of the empire by his stronger constitution.

" The timber with which these countries are covered possesses a value not turned to account hitherto, but greater in
amount than all the gold-washings of Siberia. Assuming that
there exist on an average no more than 300 trees per dessiatine,
representing on the spot a value of only 100 roubles, (in Germany a dessiatine of such fine larch as I have seen in the government of Wologda would be worth from 2,000 to 3,000 silver
roubles), that would give to the whole crown forests in this
district a value of 5,555 millions of silver roubles,—a capital of
which it would certainly be worth while to draw the interest.
The actual population of these northern countries remains concentrated, along the banks of the rivers, within a very narrow
circle; and for centuries it has made no advances into the interior. As early as the times of the republic of Nowgorod we
find a Russian population wherever it exists at present; nothing,
at least, beyond the banks of a few small rivers seem to have
been peopled more recently. The population has no doubt
augmented; it is, indeed, exceedingly compact in those parts
which have been brought into a state of effective culture; but it
has not conquered a greater extent of territory. The inhabitants of the narrow limits which lie along the rivers, never
penetrate into the forests further than from 10 to 15 versts, for
the purpose of cutting the wood necessary for the construction
of small vessels. These are floated down the rivers in spring
when the waters are high, and the greater part are conveyed to
Archangel. Pitch and tar are also manufactured. It is evident
that in this way nothing beyond a mere stripe of the forests is
turned to account. The axe never reaches their interior, and
only a few isolated huntsmen have occasionally penetrated their
gloomy recesses.

" Whence, then, does it proceed that the present population,
yearly on the increase as it is, does not advance further into the
interior of the forests? The answer is simple : in the present
state of things, such a step holds out but little prospect of
reward to private enterprise. An individual attempts nothing
from which he does not expect real and immediate advantage.
This axiom is of application in every country, but in none so
thoroughly as in Russia."

We are of opinion that the author of this project is mistaken
with regard as well to the facility of its immediate execution, as
to the importance of its prospective advantages in a material and
financial point of view; still we by no means consider the idea
as void of practical utility; and, as a question of the future, it
is quite worthy of consideration.

M. Haxthausen communicated his project, at the time, to a

Russian statesman, and gives us (vol. ii. p. 128.) an extract from
the answer which he received in consequence.

Independently of the financial reasons which, in the opinion
of this statesman, prevent government at present from thinking
of the colonisation of these impenetrable forests, some doubts
might be raised as to the immediate opportuneness of the measure,
in respect the crown still possesses in its vast domains millions
of dessiatines of unoccupied land (*poustoporojnnvie*) requiring
hands for its culture; still, it would be very desirable to undertake by degrees the working of these forests, which represent at
this moment a dead capital of very large amount; and nothing
could better pave the way for this, than a gradual colonisation
appropriate to local circumstances; in regard to the possibility
of the plan of colonisation proposed by M. Haxthausen, " a plan
so vast would infallibly miscarry in face of the extreme rigour of
the climate, the difficulty of procuring supplies of food, the mor-
bific exhalations of the tarns and marshes,—destructive causes
which would infallibly carry off two-thirds of the pioneers. But
further, the colonisation itself would require to be compulsory.
Now, M. Haxthausen has had too good an opportunity of appreciating the spirit of the Russian government,—its paternal
spirit, whatever its detractors may say of it—not to be aware of
its necessary repugnance to any measure of this kind; never—
I appeal to the testimony of facts—has this so much decried
government dreamed of establishing new colonies by compulsion.
Moreover, the soil, under that degree of latitude, is very far
from being so fertile as M. Haxthausen supposes. Agriculture
is there in a precarious condition, and any returns to be anticipated from that source would be far from compensating, with
the rapidity which he assumes, the immense cost of the colonising."

Undoubtedly, in these huge forests, there must be marshy and
insalubrious districts, as well as districts in which the fertility
of the soil is very slender; but we think M. Haxthausen is correct
in his observation, that on an area of 10,000 square miles there
must also be districts which are at once healthy and fertile. In
northern climates, moreover, marshy districts do not exert such
a pernicious influence on health as they do in warm latitudes,
where their emanations are more intense and deleterious. The
severity of the northern climate not being a cause of insalubrity
in itself, the main thing required would be to make a good
selection of districts at once healthy and fertile. M. Haxthausen is of opinion that both these conditions are satisfied in a
large part of the territory extending into the interior of the
forests from either bank of the Soukhona; but he recognises

the necessity of preceding the execution of his plan by a general exploration of the district, to be executed by well trained forest officials. The difficulty of procuring supplies does not seem insurmountable, since the colonisation would necessarily commence in the neighbourhood of districts already inhabited, and would not be extended until communications betwixt the colony and these districts were fully established; whilst the culture of the soil conceded to the colonists would also furnish subsistence to some extent. As to the proposal for employing compulsion, M. Haxthausen does not regard that expedient as a *sine quâ non;* he is of opinion that, on an appeal from the government, a sufficient number of volunteers would present themselves from amongst the discharged soldiers; and he cites the success of the military colonies already existing, some of them dating from the reign of the Empress Anne, that is to say, from the first half of the eighteenth century. But all these colonies were established in regions much more accessible to culture, and enjoying a climate much more temperate, than that of those northern latitudes. So long as there remain vast regions to be peopled in the southern and eastern provinces, it will always be easier to attract voluntary settlers in these directions, than to induce populations to emigrate into the forests of the north. The plan sketched by M. Haxthausen could not, in our opinion, be carried into execution, without granting to the colonists great encouragements and considerable subsidies; and it would entail upon the state expenses greatly exceeding the author's estimate. We do not deny that the success of such an enterprise might largely compensate the expense, and that a colonisation which should diffuse culture over those regions, and enable us to work the virgin forests which represent a property now utterly unproductive, would be an invaluable conquest for the development of national wealth; but it is only for a distant future that its fruits could ripen, and in Russia there is still so much to be done for posterity, that it is impossible to take in hand with everything at once. Government, however omnipotent in its means of action, must for the moment confine its activity and financial resources to those improvements of which the want is more sensibly felt, and from which it may expect more prompt and immediate results.

In regard to colonisation, there are two facts demonstrated by experience which never ought to be lost sight of. Small colonies always remain in a precarious state of isolation, and their influence on the weal of the surrounding districts is very limited. On the other hand, colonies undertaken on a large scale, from which alone important results can be expected, never do succeed, except the colonists carry along with them some common bond, — a certain homogeneity of manners, which establishes amongst them a community of interests, and thus favours the establishment of a strong communal organisation. Many beautifully arranged enterprises have failed just for want of such a community of interest and such a corporation spirit. We might cite, for example, the pauper colonies attempted in the Low Countries, which have proved a failure, notwithstanding that the undertaking was projected by men who had made the subject their special study, and was placed under the charge of parties who devoted themselves with ardour to their task. Now, as a substitute for this corporation spirit, there is nothing to be found in Russia but military organisation. This M. Haxthausen appears to have perfectly comprehended; for his whole plan is based upon the enrolment of soldiers whose period of service has expired; and he justifies it by the example of military colonies already existing. But the organisation of these colonies was guided by a double aim, — a military and an agricultural. The union of these two objects at once helped to compensate the cost of their establishment, and to facilitate their administration; an administration, be it observed, entirely military, and little applicable, in our opinion, to the colonisation of forest lands in the north of the empire.

For the rest, we agree with M. Haxthausen, that, entirely to abandon the care of the cultivation of these countries to the hand of time and the stimulus of those private interests which may be developed with the progress of population, would be to renounce for ever the hope of an important result. A strong impulse and large encouragement on the part of Government would here be so much the more indispensable, because more than nine-tenths of the territory belong to the State.

We subjoin a table of the population of European Russia for 1851, by provinces and governments, including Finland and the kingdom of Poland, founded on information collected by the Ministry of the Interior at the time of the last census. We must, however, observe, that the limits of the governments of Orenburg, Saratow, Simbirsk, and Astrakhan having been changed in consequence of the creation of a new government, namely, that of Samara, and the extent of their present superficies not being yet determined with precision, we have been obliged to take, for all these governments, the statistical data of the year 1850 according to the old limits : —

Provinces and Governments, arranged in the order of their absolute population.	Population in 1851.	Extent in geographical sq. miles.	Number of inhabitants per geographical square mile.
1. Kingdom of Poland - -	4,852,000	2,294	2,111
2. Orenburg * - - -	2,130,000	6,773	314
3. Wiatka - - - -	1,929,000	2,500	772
4. Perm - - - - -	1,879,000	6,073	309
5. Saratow - - - -	1,861,000	3,525	528
6. Koursk - - - -	1,728,000	818	2,112
7. Kiew - - - - -	1,701,000	914	1,861
8. Tambow - - - -	1,685,000	1,202	1,402
9. Woronèje - - - -	1,669,000	1,209	1,380
10. Poltawa - - - -	1,665,000	897	1,856
11. Podolia - - - -	1,596,000	774	2,062
12. Grand Duchy of Finland -	1,554,000	6,873	226
13. Moscow - - - -	1,526,000	589	2,591
14. Wolhynia - - - -	1,495,000	1,295	1,154
15. Twer - - - - -	1,411,000	1,223	1,154
16. Orel - - - - -	1,408,000	859	1,639
17. Tschernigow - - -	1,392,000	1,000	1,392
18. Kazan - - - -	1,390,000	1,128	1,232
19. Riazan - - - -	1,372,000	766	1,791
20. Simbirsk - - - -	1,203,000	1,315	915
21. Kharkow - - - -	1,184,000	985	1,202
22. Nijni-Nowgorod - - -	1,175,000	877	1,340
23. Wladimir - - - -	1,171,000	862	1,358
24. St. Petersburg - - -	1,145,000	970	1,180
25. Toula - - - -	1,115,000	555	2,009
26. Smolensk - - - -	1,084,000	1,019	1,064
27. Penza - - - -	1,066,000	690	1,545
28. Kostroma - - - -	1,047,000	1,496	700
29. Stavropol† - - - -	1,004,000	2,650	379
30. Ekathérinoslaw - - -	994,000	1,206	824
31. Minsk - - - -	980,000	1,622	604
32. Kalouga - - - -	976,000	573	1,703
33. Jaroslaw - - - -	961,000	660	1,456
34. Kowno - - - -	935,000	758	1,234
35. Kherson - - - -	919,000	1,332	690
36. Bessarabia - - - -	902,000	858	1,051
37. Nowgorod ‡ - - -	890,000	2,213	402
38. Grodno - - - -	870,000	693	1,255
39. Wologda - - - -	866,000	6,967	124
40. Livonia - - - -	836,000	853	980
41. Mohilew - - - -	835,000	885	944
42. Wilna - - - -	819,000	768	1,066
43. Country of the Don Cossacks §	798,000	2,943	271
44. Witebsk - - - -	733,000	810	905
45. Pskow - - - -	673,000	809	832
46. Tauride - - - -	665,000	1,163	572
Carried forward - -	60,089,000	77,244	

* With the Cossacks of the Ural and Orenburg and their families.

† With the mountaineers and Cossacks of the line, according to returns collected by the Ministry of War.

‡ With the colonised military and their families.

§ According to statistics of the Ministry of War.

Provinces and Governments, arranged in the order of their absolute population.	Population in 1851.	Extent in geographical sq. miles.	Number of inhabitants per geographical square mile.
Brought forward -	60,089,000	77,244	
47. Courland - - - -	530,000	496	1,069
48. Esthonia - - - -	302,000	376	803
49. Olonetz - - - -	278,500	2,784	100
50. Archangel - - - -	252,000	12,000	21
51. Astrakhan, without the nomade populations - -	207,000	2,860	72
Total -	61,658,500*	95,760	644

We perceive from this table, that, next to the kingdom of Poland, the governments possessing the largest absolute population are those of Orenburg, Wiatka, Perm, Saratow, Koursk, Kiew, Tambow, Woronèje, Poltawa, Podolia, and Moscow. These eleven governments, each of which contains a population of more than $1\frac{1}{2}$ millions, embrace, along with Finland and the kingdom of Poland, more than 25 millions of inhabitants, or five-twelfths of the whole population of European Russia.

In regard to density of population the provinces and governments rank in the following order:

Provinces and Governments.	Inhab. per Sq. Mile.	Provinces and Governments.	Inhab. per Sq. Mile.
1. Moscow - -	2,591	6. Kiew - - -	1,861
2. Koursk - -	2,112	7. Poltawa - -	1,856
3. Kingdom of Poland -	2,111	8. Riazan - - -	1,791
4. Podolia - -	2,062	9. Kalouga - -	1,703
5. Toula - - -	2,009	10. Orel - - -	1,639

* For the sake of completeness we here subjoin the population in 1850 of the four governments of Orenburg, Saratow, Simbirsk, and Astrakhan, as given above according to their former limits, together with their population and that of the government of Samara in 1851, according to the new limits.

	In 1850.	In 1851.
Orenburg - - - - -	2,130,000	1,520,800
Saratow - - - - -	1,860,800	1,497,300
Simbirsk - - - - -	1,202,600	1,061,900
Astrakhan (without the nomade populations)	207,800	266,000
Samara - - - - -		1,341,000
	5,401,200	5,687,000
		5,401,200
Increase for 1851 -		285,800

This figure added to the foregoing table (61,658,500 inhabitants) gives a total population in 1851 of 61,944,300 inhabitants.

Provinces and Governments.	Inhab. per Sq. Mile.	Provinces and Governments.	Inhab. per Sq. Mile.
11. Penza - - -	1,545	32. Witebsk - -	908
12. Jaroslaw - -	1,456	33. Pskow - - -	832
13. Tambow - -	1,402	34. Ekathérinoslaw -	824
14. Tschernigow - -	1,392	35. Esthonia - -	803
15. Woronèje - -	1,381	36. Wiatka - -	772
16. Wladimir - -	1,358	37. Kostroma - -	700
17. Nijni-Nowgorod -	1,340	38. Kherson - -	690
18. Grodno - -	1,255	39. Minsk - - -	604
19. Kowno - - -	1,234	40. Tauride - -	572
20. Kazan - - -	1,223	41. Saratow - -	528
21. Kharkow - -	.1,202	42. Nowgorod - -	402
22. St. Petersburg - -	1,180	43. Stavropol - -	379
23. Twer - - -	1,154	44. Orenburg - -	314
24. Wolhynia - -	1,154	45. Perm - - -	309
25. Courland - -	1,069	46. Country of Don Cossacks	271
26. Wilna - - -	1,066	47. Finland - -	226
27. Smolensk - -	1,064	48. Wologda - -	124
28. Bessarabia - -	1,049	49. Olonetz - -	100
29. Livonia - -	980	50. Astrakhan - -	72
30. Mohilew - -	944	51. Archangel - -	21
31. Simbirsk - -	915		

In his General Political Manual of the States of Europe M. Schubert asserts that those countries which reckon less than 1,000 inhabitants to the geographical square mile belong to the class of badly peopled countries, and that those only can be ranged in the category of well-peopled countries which reckon more than 2,400 inhabitants to the square mile. According to this definition, Russia would contain only a single government, namely, that of Moscow (which has a relative population of 2,500), that could be ranked amongst the well-peopled countries; twenty-seven provinces or governments would belong to the class of averagely, and twenty-three to the class of very poorly, peopled.

M. Koeppen adopts for Russia the following classification: *provinces exceedingly well peopled*, those which reckon more than 1,400 inhabitants to the square mile; *of medium population*, having from 700 to 1,400 inhabitants to the square mile; and *weakly peopled*, all those having less than 700 inhabitants to the square mile. Applying this classification to the foregoing table, there would be thirteen provinces and governments in the first, twenty-four in the second, and fourteen in the third class.

In no country of the world is the population so unequally distributed as it is in Russia. It varies in the different governments, as we perceive, from 21 to 2,591 inhabitants to the square mile, or in the proportion of 1 to 123; or, if we lop off from the scale the three least peopled governments, namely,

Astrakhan, Olonetz, and Archangel, there still remains, between the two extremities, a difference in the proportion of 1 to 21.

In Austria, according to the official statistics of 1846, the relative population varied from one province to another, from 1,746 to 7,120 inhabitants to the square mile, or in the proportion of 1 to 4; in Prussia, from 1,926 to 5,500, or in the proportion of 1 to 3; in France, the *minimum* population, calculated by departments, is 1,278, and the *maximum* (setting aside the department of the Seine, which reckons, including the population of Paris, 128,111 inhabitants to the square mile) 9,936, which gives nearly the proportion of 1 to 8.

The inconveniences resulting from this disproportion betwixt the population of the different parts of the empire cannot fail to be felt in every branch of the public service. If it be easy for the administration of a government like Moscow, Toula, Courland, or Esthonia, to intervene promptly with its authority whenever the interests of the State or of social order require, the task is of by no means the same facility in such a government as Archangel, Wologda, Perm, or Orenburg, where days, or, during the season of bad roads, weeks may elapse, before a particular fact reach the knowledge of the authorities. In regard to police, this inconvenience is partly balanced by other circumstances. In provinces of large extent and small population, manners being simpler and interests less complicated, offences are less frequent, and there are less frequent calls for the intervention of the authorities than in countries where the population is more dense. But the case is widely different as regards the administration of finance. In that department, the difficulties arising from long distances are felt at every step; the collection and control of the taxes, direct and indirect, are rendered more difficult and costly, and the taxes themselves are less productive. As regards the development of their resources, too, analogous inconveniences are found from the difficulty of communication and interchange.

The following table exhibits the distribution of cultivated soil and population by provinces and governments: —

Table of Cultivated Land and Population by Provinces and Governments.

PROVINCES AND GOVERNMENTS. (Arranged in the order of their relative extent of cultivated land.)	Cultivated land expressed in dessiatines.	Population in 1851.	Number of dessiatines of cultivated land to each inhabitant.
1. Country of the Don Cossacks -	2,310,000	798,000	2·89
2. Minsk - - - -	2,820,000	980,000	2·88
3. Tschernigow - - - -	3,191,000	1,392,000	2·29
4. Kowno - - - - -	2,060,900	935,000	2·20
5. Witebsk - - - -	1,600,000	733,000	2·18
6. Simbirsk - - - -	2,500,000	1,203,000	2·08
7. Mohilew - - - -	1,700,000	835,000	2·04
8. Orenburg - - - -	4,115,000	2,130,000	1·93
9. Pskow - - - -	1,300,000	673,000	1·93
10. Smolensk - - - -	2,000,000	1,084,000	1·85
11. Woronèje - - - -	3,007,000	1,669,000	1·80
12. Toula - - - - -	2,000,000	1,115.000	1·79
13. Kharkow - - - -	2,100,000	1,184,000	1·77
14. Orel - - - - -	2,400,000	1,408,000	1·70
15. Grodno - - - -	1,470,000	870,000	1·69
16. Wiatka - - - -	2,973,000	1,929,000	1·54
17. Wladimir - - - -	1,800,000	1,171,000	1·54
18. Nijni-Nowgorod - - -	1,800,000	1,175,000	1·53
19. Podolia - - - -	2,440,000	1,596,000	1·53
20. Kostroma - - - -	1,600,000	1,047,000	1·53
21. Kherson - - - -	1,400,000	919,000	1·52
22. Kazan - - - -	2,100,000	1,390,000	1·51
23. Penza - - - -	1,600,000	1,066,000	1·50
24. Tambow - - - -	2,500,000	1,685,000	1·48
25. Nowgorod - - - -	1,300,000	890,000	1·46
26. Koursk - - - -	2,503,000	1,728,000	1·45
27. Bessarabia - - - -	1,300,000	902,000	1·44
28. Wilna - - - -	1,170,000	819,000	1·43
29. Wolhynia - - - -	2,110,000	1,495,000	1·41
30. Perm - - - -	2,589,000	1,879,000	1·38
31. Kiew - - - - -	2,353,000	1,701,000	1·38
32. Saratow - - - -	2,530,000	1,861,000	1·36
33. Kalouga - - - -	1,300,000	976,000	1·33
34. Olonetz - - - -	370,000	278,500	1·33
35. Riazan - - - -	1,800,000	1,372,000	1·31
36. Jaroslaw - - - -	1,200,000	961,000	1·25
37. Ekathérinoslaw - - -	1,200,000	994,000	1·21
38. Poltawa - - - -	2,000,000	1,665,000	1·20
39. Twer - - - - -	1,670,000	1,411,000	1·18
40. Tauride - - - -	750,000	665,000	1·13
41. Kingdom of Poland - -	5,445,000	4,852,000	1·12
42. Courland - - - -	˙496,000	530,000	0·94
43. Wologda - - - -	800,000	866,000	0·92
44. Moscow - - - -	1,300,000	1,526,000	0·86
45. Esthonia - - - -	240,000	302,000	0·79
46. Stavropol - - - -	750,000	1,004,000	0·75
47. Astrakhan - - - -	150,000	207,000	0·72
48. Livonia - - - -	˙415,000	836,000	0·50
49. St. Petersburg - - -	550,000	1,145 000	0·48
50. Grand Duchy of Finland -	520,000	1,554,000	0·33
51. Archangel - - - -	80,000	252,000	0·32
Total -	89,677,000	61,658,500	1·45

We perceive, from the preceding table, that the majority of the governments present no very striking inequalities in the relation of the extent of cultivated land to the cipher of the population. In twenty-four governments it exceeds the proportion of one dessiatine without attaining that of two dessiatines to each inhabitant. There are but seven governments in which it exceeds the proportion of two dessiatines to an inhabitant; and of these seven there are two, the government of Minsk and the country of the Don Cossacks, in which it nearly reaches three dessiatines. In the ten last governments in the table, it falls beneath the proportion of one dessiatine to each inhabitant; and of these ten there are two, namely, the government of Archangel and the Grand Duchy of Finland, in which there is less than one-third of a dessiatine to each inhabitant. Of the same ten, there are six, namely, the governments of Moscow, St. Petersburg, Wologda, Archangel, Astrakhan, and the Grand Duchy of Finland, which do not produce grain enough for their own consumption. The Baltic provinces provide for their own wants in consequence of the good culture of the arable lands; and Livonia even exports a part of its grain in years when there is a good harvest. On the other hand, amongst the thirty-four governments which have more than one dessiatine of cultivated land to each inhabitant, there are nine, namely, Jaroslaw, Kalouga, Kostroma, Nowgorod, Olonetz, Pskow, Twer, Wilna, and Wladimir, in which, either from the mediocrity of the soil, or from the negligent system of agriculture, the harvest does not ordinarily suffice for the home consumption. To the same category belong, also, the governments of Minsk, Mohilew, and Witebsk, which yet have more than two dessiatines of cultivated land for each inhabitant; whilst there are seven having less than a dessiatine and a half, namely, Kiew, Koursk, Tambow, Poltawa, Riazan, Saratow, and Wolhynia, which, in consequence of the fertility of their soil, furnish grain in considerable quantities both to the other provinces and for foreign exportation.

If, in reference to agricultural statistics, an acquaintance with the numerical relation of the population to the extent of cultivated land be a point of the utmost importance, it is no less important for a general appreciation of the progress of commerce, of industrial activity, and of national wealth, to establish, were it but approximately, the proportions betwixt the rural and urban populations.

The statistics of our towns are still very inexact and incomplete, partly from the carelessness of the local authorities, whose duty it is to furnish the returns, but partly, likewise, from difficulties inherent in this branch of official statistics.

These difficulties proceed in a great measure from the mobility of the floating population, which changes frequently, according to the season, to an extent seldom found in any other country. To cite but one example. In the town of Rybinsk, which in winter does not reckon more than six or seven thousand inhabitants at the utmost, the population, during the navigation season, is frequently more than decupled by the affluence of hands, who are attracted by the active commerce which is then carried on.*

In the large towns, the frequent changes of domicile, and the comings and goings of individuals who arrive upon business, or for service, or in quest of work, are apt to occasion mistakes, and make the same individuals figure twice or thrice in the population lists. It would require a great deal of exactness and continuous attention on the part of the authorities to avoid errors of this sort; whilst our municipal functionaries are still, in the greater number of towns, but little versed in business of the sort; and it will be a work of time to develope their intelligence, and to accustom them to greater order and exactness.† In the present condition of that part of our statistics, it

* M. Haxthausen asserts that the population of Rybinsk amounts in summer to no less than 130,000; but this number we regard as somewhat exaggerated.

† Statistics in general, as an administrative science, is but of modern date. In no country did its improvement commence until men's eyes become opened to its importance as a compass without which the financier, the administrator, and the statesman, can but grope their way, instead of boldly steering. It is only within a very recent period that, in the majority of states, statistical bureaux have been organised upon a large basis, and furnished with the necessary means for collecting *data* as exact as possible on every branch of social cconomy. If we compare the *Statistique Agricole de la France*, published 1840-41, in 4 vols. 4to., or the annual publications of the *Administration des Douanes*, which have appeared annually since 1840, with earlier works of the same description, or if we compare the statistical works of Messieurs Hoffman and Dieterici in Prussia, or of M. Czoernig in Austria, with the statistical publications which appeared twenty or thirty years ago, we will at once perceive the immense improvements which have been introduced into this branch of the service, and the importance which is now attached to a multiplicity of details formerly utterly disregarded.

To form a just idea of the importance attached in France for some time past to statistical works, and of the care which is bestowed on their preparation and verification, it is only necessary to peruse the report presented to the king on 30th May, 1840, by M. Gouin, the Minister of Commerce and Agriculture, on the occasion of the publication of the *Statistique Agricole*. We find, amongst other information, that more than 100,000 individuals contributed to the collection of the materials from which the work was prepared.

If, in this branch of science, we have remained in the rear of other countries, we have at least not been stationary. In every new publication we perceive marked improvements, better typography, better arranged system, and much complementary matter on details which were entirely wanting in preceding works: indeed, when we take into view the prodigious difficulties which are presented to works of this nature by distance alone, in consequence of the immense extent of our territories, we cannot but allow that our recent progress has been very considerable.

is only with the qualification " errors excepted " that we can adopt its data as the basis of our calculations and comparisons.

According to the Statistics of the Towns, published in 1842 by the Ministry of the Interior, there were, in 1840, in European Russia, including the kingdom of Poland and the Grand Duchy of Finland, 733 towns, of which

3	contained upwards of 100,000 inhabitants:						
	St. Petersburg	-	-	-	-	470,202	
	Moscow	-	-	-	-	349,068	
	Warsaw	-	-	-	-	140,471	
							959,741
5	upwards of 50,000 inhabitants:						
	Odessa	-	-	-	-	60,055	
	Riga	-	-	-	-	59,960	
	Cronstadt	-	-	-	-	54,717	
	Wilna	-	-	-	-	54,499	
	Toula	-	-	-	-	51,735	
							280,966
17	from 25,000 to 50,000 inhabitants:						
	Kiew	-	-	-	-	47,424	
	Astrakhan	-	-	-	-	45,938	
	Woronèje	-	-	-	-	43,800	
	Kischenew	-	-	-	-	42,636	
	Saratow	-	-	-	-	42,237	
	Kazan	-	-	-	-	41,304	
	Sévastopol	-	-	-	-	41,155	
	Berditschew	-	-	-	-	35,592	
	Kalouga	-	-	-	-	35,290	
	Jaroslaw	-	-	-	-	34,913	
	Orel	-	-	-	-	32,600	
	Nijni-Nowgorod		-	-	-	31,921	
	Koursk	-	-	-	-	30,469	
	Kharkow	-	-	-	-	29,395	
	Nikolaïew	-	-	-	-	28,664	
	Eletz	-	-	-	-	25,880	
	Akermann	-		-	-	25,339	
							614,557
73	of from 10,000 to 25,000 inhabitants			-	1,044,924	
153	„ 5,000 to 10,000 „			-	1,061,862	
286	„ 2,000 to 5,000 „			-	955,512	
132	„ 1,000 to 2,000 „			-	195,545	
56	„ under 1,000 „			-	37,333	
8	of which number of inhabitants unknown					
						3,295,176
733 *	with a population of		-	-	5,150,440	

Adding to this cipher 5 per cent. for the increase of the population from 1840 to 1852 †, we may carry the present total urban population to 5,400,000 inhabitants, which gives an average of 7,367 inhabitants to a town.

* Besides these, there are reckoned in forty-seven governments of European Russia, 1252 small towns or villages called *Miestetschka* and *Possady*.

† In the large towns, the urban population—being recruited not only by the excess of births over deaths, but likewise by immigration from the country—

On distributing the 733 towns over 95,710 square miles of territory (without Nova-Zembla), we find one town to $130\frac{1}{2}$ square miles. In Austria, there are reckoned 776 towns: the territorial extent of that empire being 12,104 square miles, this gives an average of one town to $15\frac{2}{3}$ square miles.* In Prussia, 979 towns to an extent of 5080 square miles give one town to $5\frac{1}{5}$ square miles. In France, M. Schnitzler reckons 901 towns, without the *bourgs*, on an extent of 9,616 square miles, which gives one town to $10\frac{2}{3}$ square miles.

Thus the relative cipher of our towns to territorial extent is to that of France as 1 to 12; to that of Prussia, as 1 to 24; and to that of Austria, as 1 to 8. On the other hand, the cipher of average urban population is higher with us. In Austria the proportion is no more than 6,190 inhabitants *per* town; in Prussia, it is 4,730; in France, 7,256; in Russia, 7,367.

The total population of the towns, properly so called, not being separately denoted in the statistics of either Austria or France, but being slumped with that of the burghs, which, for reasons already mentioned, we have thrown out of the account, we have determined the cipher in the following manner, and apprehend that it cannot differ, at any rate very widely, from the reality.

In Austria there were reckoned in 1843, according to the official statistics, 449 towns of more than 2000 inhabitants, containing at that period a population of 3,915,800. There remained, therefore, out of 776 towns, 327 which reckoned less than 2,000 inhabitants. Assuming for the latter an average population of 1,500, which gives 490,500 inhabitants for the whole, and adding the latter cipher to the preceding, we obtain for the population of the whole towns of the Austrian monarchy

---

increases sometimes at a more rapid rate than 1 per cent. per annum; but on the other hand, there are a number of small towns in which it remains stationary, or even, from local circumstances, follows a decreasing movement. On comparing the urban populations of a large number of governments, we are convinced that we cannot admit, upon the whole, a larger rate of increase than $\frac{1}{2}$ per cent., which, for the period from 1840 to 1852, less the two cholera years, gives 5 per cent.

* It must be observed that there are in Austria 2,467 burghs termed *Markt-flecken*, which are not included amongst the towns, but which reckon for most part considerably above 1000 inhabitants. The largest of these burghs are found in Hungary, where some of them reckon upwards of 30,000 inhabitants. The official statistics of 1843 contain all the burghs counting more than 2,000 inhabitants: of these there are 449 containing a population of 2,147,600. Of this number there are 37 in Hungary and 4 in Italy, each with a population of more than 10,000. In six of these, the population exceeds 20,000, and in three it is above 30,000. We have taken none of the burghs into our comparison, because in Russia there are likewise small burghs, the majority containing 1000 inhabitants and upwards, but of which the official statistics do not give the population. Adding the burghs to the towns there would be in Austria one town or burgh to each $3\frac{3}{4}$ square miles.

in 1843, the number of 4,406,300 inhabitants.   Adding to this, 9 per cent., or 396,600 inhabitants for the increase of population during 9 years, the total number of inhabitants of the 776 towns would amount in 1852 to 4,802,900 souls, which affords to each town an average population of 6,190.*

In France M. Schnitzler estimated the population in 1846 of 901 towns together with 476 burghs, each reckoning more than 3,000 inhabitants, at eight millions.   Adding 6 per cent. for the increase of the population during 6 years, we obtain a present total of 8,480,000 inhabitants, from which we must deduct 1,900,000 for 476 burghs, reckoning at an average 4,000 inhabitants *per* burgh.   This leaves for 901 towns a population of 6,580,000 inhabitants, which gives an average of 7,303 inhabitants per town.

In Prussia there were reckoned in 1843, according to the official census (see Dieterici's Statistical Tables, published in 1843), 4,246,173 inhabitants of towns.   Adding 9 per cent. for the increase of population during 9 years, we obtain for the total urban population of 1852 the number of 4,628,000 inhabitants, which, distributed over 979 towns, gives an average population for each town of 4,727 inhabitants.

The following are the comparative results of the foregoing statistics : —

Number of Towns.

					Sq. Miles.
Prussia	-	- 979		on an area of	5,080
France	-	- 901	(with the burghs 1,377)	„	9,616
Austria	-	- 776	(„ 3,242)	„	12,104
Russia	-	- 733	(with the small burghs 1,985) „		95,710

This gives

			Sq. M.	Sq. M.
In Prussia 1 town to		5½	
„ France 1	„	10⅔	(with the burghs, 1 town or burgh to 7)
„ Austria 1	„	15½	(„ 1 „ 3¾)
„ Russia 1	„	130½	(with the small burghs 1 town or small burgh to 48 sq. m.)

Absolute Cipher of urban Population in 1852.

			Inhabitants.	Inhabitants.
France	-	-	6,580,000	(with the burghs 8,480,000)
Russia	-	-	5,400,000	
Austria	-	-	4,803,900	(with the burghs 9,400,000)
Prussia	-	-	4,628,000	

Average Population of a Town.

			Inhabitants.	Inhabitants.
Russia	-	-	7,367	
France	-	-	7,303	(with the burghs 6,158 per town or burgh)
Austria	-	-	6,190	(„ 2,900 „)
Prussia	-	-	4,641	

* The proportion of 1 per cent., which we have adopted for the annual increase of the urban population in Germany and France, is founded on statistical data of the preceding periods.

Proportion of urban Population to total Number of Inhabitants.

In Prussia, out of 100,000 inhabitants there belong to the towns 27,587
„ France	„	„	„	17,728
„	„	„	(with burghs)	22,991
„ Austria	„	„	„	12,310
„	„	„	(with burghs)	24,282
„ Russia	„	„	„	8,710

In other words there are

In Prussia, for 100 inhabitants of towns,	262 inhabitants of country.
„ France	„	„	464	„	„
„ Austria	„	„	712	„	„
„ Russia	„	„	1,148	„	„

The comparison would be more exact if we knew the population of the burghs in Russia; but those small burghs, termed with us *Miestetschka* and *Possady*, are, for the most part, in a state so little advanced in regard either to material condition or to commercial and industrial movement, that we can scarcely assimilate them to the towns, and their population belongs much more to the agricultural class than to that of the bourgeoisie.

In regard to Austria and Prussia, the numerical superiority of the urban population in the latter country is merely apparent; for in it there were raised to the rank of towns, by virtue of the organic laws of 1808 and 1831, a large number of small burghs which do not possess all the elements necessary for a well-constituted municipal organisation; whilst in Austria there are, as we have already had occasion to observe, a number of wealthy and populous burghs of from 10,000 to 20,000 inhabitants, and which might therefore be properly reckoned in with the urban population, which have not been included amongst the towns.

Taking the above numbers as they result from the official statistics, we perceive that the relative cipher of our urban population rises only to a third of that of Prussia, that it amounts to three-fourths of that of Austria, and that it exceeds the half of that of France: adding the burghs to the urban population of Austria, there would be an urban population in that country exceeding ours in the proportion of 8 to 3. All this proves that municipal life is still very little developed in our country: agricultural interests will there prevail over all others to the end of the chapter: this is inherent in the constituent elements of our welfare, in our geographical situation, and in other causes to which we shall afterwards have occasion to advert.

On comparing the importance of the towns in regard to population, we obtain the following results:—

Towns of more than 100,000 Inhabitants.

Inhabitants.

In Russia, three: St. Petersburg, Moscow, and Warsaw, reckoning
together (1850) a population of - - - - 1,055,000 *
In Austria, five: Vienna, Milan, Venice, Pesth with Buda, and
Prague, with a population of - - - - 952,000
In Prussia, two: Berlin and Breslau, with a population of - 455,600

Towns of between 50,000 and 100,000 Inhabitants.

In Russia, five: Odessa, Riga, Wilna, Cronstadt, and Toula, with 281,000
In Austria, five: Léopol, Trieste, Debretzin, Padua, and Verona,
with - - - - - - - 299,000
In Prussia, four: Cologne, Koenigsberg, Dantzig, and Magdeburg,
with - - - - - - - 305,000

Towns of between 25,000 and 50,000 Inhabitants.

In Russia, 17, with a population of - - - - 614,000
In Austria, 14 „ - - - - 483,000
In Prussia, 10 „ - - - - 372,000

Towns of between 10,000 and 25,000 Inhabitants.

In Russia, 73, with a population of - - - - 1,086,000
In Austria, 53 „ - - - - 840,000
In Prussia, 42 „ - - - - 653,000

Towns of between 5,000 and 10,000 Inhabitants.

In Russia, 153, with a population of - - - - 1,104,000
In Austria, 95 „ - - - - 690,000
In Prussia, 106 „ - - - - 792,000

Towns of between 2,000 and 5,000 Inhabitants.

In Russia, 286, with a population of - - - - 993,000
In Austria, 277 „ - - - - 924,000
In Prussia, 425 „ - - - - 1,395,000

Towns of less than 2,000 Inhabitants.

In Russia, 188, with a population of - - - - 242,000
In Austria, 324 „ - - - - 521,000
In Prussia, 290 „ - - - - 568,000

Thus Austria possesses two more towns with a population
exceeding 100,000 inhabitants than Russia possesses; but the
joint population of our three largest towns exceeds by 103,000,
or more than 10 per cent., that of the five largest towns of the
Austrian monarchy.

The population of the two Prussian towns of more than
100,000 inhabitants attains only two-fifths or thereby of that
of our three largest towns.

* For the three capitals, where population makes very rapid progress, we have
added 10 per cent. to the cipher of the population of 1840; but for the whole
other towns we have adopted, for the reason given in note †, p. 90., a
supplement of only 4 per cent. for the increase during the decennial period 1840
to 1850. For the urban population of other countries we add 1 per cent. per
annum to the latest official returns to which we have access.

We have the same number of towns as Austria has containing a population of between 50,000 and 100,000, with a nearly similar amount of population. Prussia has one fewer of towns belonging to this class, but their average population is higher by 35 per cent. On the other hand, the difference is greatly in our favour in regard to towns of the third and fourth rank; and it is particularly remarkable for towns of between 10,000 and 25,000 inhabitants. Our towns of that class exceed in number by two-fifths those of Austria, and by three-fourths those of Prussia; their population exceeds by 246,000, or nearly 30 per cent. that of the Austrian, and by 433,000, or 66 per cent. that of the Prussian.

Our towns of medium population, those of from 5,000 to 10,000 inhabitants, exceed in number by about two-thirds those of Austria, and by one-half those of Prussia; for the total cipher of the population, they exceed by 414,000 inhabitants, or by 60 per cent. those of Austria, and by 312,000, or 39 per cent. those of Prussia. For towns of from 2,000 to 5,000 inhabitants we are, with a slight difference in our favour, nearly on the level of Austria; but we are greatly inferior to Prussia in regard as well to the number of towns as to the total cipher of their population. In regard to the small towns of less than 2,000 inhabitants, the difference of both Austria and Prussia is still greater. These little nuclei of industry and retail commerce are still much less numerous with us than in either of the two other countries.

From the annexed table of the urban population in 1851, by provinces and governments, we perceive that the two governments of St. Petersburg and Moscow, and the kingdom of Poland, contain 1,465,500 inhabitants of towns, or more than a fourth of the urban population of all European Russia: this is explained by the circumstance that the three capitals are situated within these districts.

On examining the column which indicates the proportion between the number of towns and the extent of territory, we find sixteen governments in which there is not a town to 100 square miles of surface: of this number there are two, namely, the government of Archangel and the country of the Don Cossacks, where there is not a town to 1000 square miles of surface. In the government of Astrakhan, there is but one town to 715 square miles; in that of Wologda one to 536; in that of Olonetz one to 398; in that of Stavropol, one to 373; and in that of Perm, one to 370. The governments in which the relative number of towns is greatest, that is, where we reckon one town to less than 50 square miles, are seven in

Table of the Urban Population of European Russia.

Provinces and Governments arranged according to the Number of the Urban Population.	Number of Towns.	Urban Population in 1851.	Total Population in 1851.	Proportion per Cent. of Inhabitants of Towns to whole Population.	Area in Square Miles.	One Town to Square Miles.
1. St. Petersburg -	13	592,000	1,145,000	51·7	970	75
2. Kingdom of Poland - -	85	480,000	4,852,000	9·9	2,294	27
3. Moscow - -	15	393,500	1,526,000	25·8	589	39
4. Kherson - -	12	217,700	919,000	23·7	1,332	111
5. *Saratow* * - -	14	182,000	1,861,000	9·8	3,525	252
6. Kiew - -	12	166,800	1,701,000	9·8	914	76⅔
7. Bessarabia - -	12	146,600	902,000	16·3	858	71½
8. Kharkow - -	16	135,400	1,184,000	11·4	985	61½
9. Orel - - -	13	129,600	1,408,000	9·2	859	71½
10. Koursk - -	18	115,800	1,728,000	6·7	818	45½
11. Tauride - -	15	114,200	665,000	17·2	1,163	77½
12. Tambow - -	12	111,100	1,685,000	6·6	1,202	100
13. Poltawa - -	17	107,000	1,665,000	6·4	897	53
14. *Simbirsk* - -	13	105,800	1,203,000	8·8	1,315	101
15. Wolhynia - -	12	105,200	1,495,000	7·	1,295	108
16. Tschernigow -	19	100,300	1,392,000	7·2	1,000	53
17. Livonia - -	12	95,800	836,000	11·4	853	71
18. Kalouga - -	14	93,800	976,000	9·6	573	41
19. Toula - -	12	91,200	1,115,000	8·2	555	46
20. Ekathérinoslaw -	13	87,400	994,000	8·8	1,206	93
21. Twer - -	13	86,400	1,411,000	6·1	1,223	94
22. Podolia - -	14	85,400	1,596,000	5·4	774	55
23. Woronèje - -	14	83,450	1,669,000	5·	1,209	93
24. Grodno - -	25	83,300	870,000	9·6	693	27¾
25. Grand Duchy of Finland - -	31	81,500	1,554,000	5·2	6,873	207
26. Jaroslaw - -	11	79,200	961,000	8·2	660	60
27. Kazan - -	13	78,900	1,390,000	5·7	1,128	87
28. Riazan - -	12	77,300	1,372,000	5·6	766	64
29. Penza - -	13	76,000	1,066,000	7·1	690	53
30. Wilna - -	9	75,500	819,000	9·2	768	85⅓
31. Nijni-Nowgorod -	13	74,300	1,175,000	6·3	877	67½
32. Witebsk -	12	74,100	733,000	10·1	810	67½
33. Wladimir - -	15	70,400	1,171,000	6·	862	57½
34. Minsk - -	11	69,600	980,000	7·1	1,622	147½
35. Courland - -	11	64,200	530,000	12·1	496	45
36. Perm - -	16	62,100	1,879,000	3·3	6,073	370
37. *Orenburg* - -	17	58,300	2,130,000	2·7	6,773	398
38. Smolensk - -	12	54,500	1,084,000	5·	1,019	85
39. Mohilew - -	12	51,900	835,000	6·2	885	74
Carried forward	623	4,977,550	52,477,000		57,404	

* For governments printed in Italics, see Note * p. 84, and corresponding portion of text.

Provinces and Governments arranged according to the Number of the Urban Population.	Number of Towns.	Urban Population in 1851.	Total Population in 1851.	Proportion per Cent. of Inhabitants of Towns to whole Population.	Area in Square Miles.	One Town to Square Miles.
Brought forward	623	4,977,550	52,477,000		57,404	
40. *Astrakhan* - -	4	51,700*	207,000	25·	2,860	715
41. Kowno - -	10	47,700	935,000	5·1	758	76
42. Wiatka - -	13	43,900	1,929,000	2·3	2,500	192
43. Stavropol - -	7	43,200	1,004,000	4·3	2,650	373
44. Pskow - -	11	42,200	673,000	6·3	809	73½
45. Kostroma - -	20	41,200	1,047,000	3·9	1,496	75
46. Wologda - -	13†	40,700	866,000	4·7	6,967	536
47. Nowgorod -	11	32,500	890,000	3·7	2,213	201
48. Esthonia - -	5	28,400	302,000	9·4	376	75
49. Archangel - -	8	27,200	252,000	10·8	12,000	1,500
50. Country of the Don Cossacks -	1	20,000	798,000	2·5	2,943	2,943
51. Olonetz - -	7	16,900	278,500	6·1	2,784	¦398
Total - -	733	5,413,150	61,658,500	8·7	95,760	130½

number, namely, the kingdom of Poland, the governments of Moscow, Grodno, Koursk, Toula, Kalouga, and Courland.

In regard to the numerical proportion of the urban population to the total number of inhabitants, the governments arrange themselves in the following order : —

To 1,000 *Inhabitants of the entire Population.*

		Inhab. of Towns.				Inhab. of Towns.
1. St. Petersburg	-	- 517	9. Livonia	-	•	- 114
2. Moscow	-	- 258	10. Archangel	-	-	- 108
3. Kherson ‡	-	- 237	11. Witebsk	-	-	- 101
4. Tauride	-	- 172	12. Kingdom of Poland	··		- 99
5. Bessarabia	-	- 163	13. Saratow	-	-	- 98
6. Astrakhan §	-	- 140	14. Kiew	-	-	- 98
7. Courland	-	- 121	15. Kalouga	-	-	- 96
8. Kharkow	-	- 114	16. Grodno	··	-	- 96

* Without the nomade populations. We must also observe that the urban population is stated too high in the official statistics of 1850. According to last census, the total population of this government within its new limits amounted to 266,000 inhabitants, of which 37,300 were inhabitants of towns, which does not give a proportion of 14 per cent.

† For this government we do not possess complete data for 1851, and have therefore been obliged to take the urban population from the statistics of the towns published in 1842, adding for increase since that period.

‡ This government owes its high relative cipher to the increase of Odessa.

§ See note (*) *suprà.*

	Inhab. of Towns.			Inhab. of Towns.
17. Esthonia	94	35. Olonetz		61
18. Orel	92	36. Wladimir		60
19. Wilna	92	37. Kazan		57
20. Simbirsk	88	38. Riazan		56
21. Ekathérinoslaw	88	39. Podolia		54
22. Toula	82	40. Grand Duchy of Finland		53
23. Taroslaw	82	41. Kowno		51
24. Tschernigow	72	42. Woronèje		50
25. Penza	71	43. Smolensk		50
26. Minsk	71	44. Wologda		47
27. Wolhynia	70	45. Stavropol		43
28. Koursk	67	46. Kostroma		39
29. Tambow	66	47. Nowgorod		37
30. Poltawa	64	48. Perm		33
31. Nijni-Nowgorod	63	49. Orenburg		27
32. Pskow	63	50. Country of the Don Cossacks		25
33. Mohilew	62	51. Wiatka		23
34. Twer	61			

According to this table, there are only eleven governments in which the number of the inhabitants of the towns exceeds a tenth of the entire population; of this number, the government of St. Petersburg presents, in consequence of the capital being included in it, the very large proportion of 517 inhabitants of towns to 1,000 of the entire population. In thirty-two governments, the proportion of urban population runs between 5 and 10 per cent., and in eight it is below 5 per cent.; in the country of the Don Cossacks, and in the governments of Orenburg and Wiatka, it does not reach even 3 per cent.

On comparing the male and female populations of the towns, we find that the former commonly exceeds the latter, sometimes —especially in towns of the first and second class—by a very considerable proportion, as, for example, by 30 to 50 per cent. At St. Petersburg, there were reckoned in 1851, 396,000 male individuals out of a population of 592,000, which gives the proportion of 67 males to 33 females; at Moscow, out of 393,500 inhabitants, 241,300, or more than 61 per cent., belonged to the male sex. M. Haxthausen cites, as one of the most striking of these contrasts, the town of Rybinsk, of which the total population amounts in summer, according to him, to 130,000 inhabitants, whilst the number of females does not exceed 2,500. These proportions betwixt the numbers of the two sexes present an anomaly nowhere else met with. In Germany, and other countries, it is precisely in towns of the first and second class that the female population almost invariably exceeds the male. The cause of this difference is, that in other countries many females from the country go to the towns in quest of work or service, whilst in Russia it is chiefly the male population that moves

about, whilst the country female population remains at home.*
According to returns collected at the Ministry of the Interior
for the year 1850, there were in European Russia twenty governments, namely, Courland, Jaroslaw, Kharkow, Kowno,
Kostroma, Livonia, Mohilew, Nowgorod, Orel, Orenburg,
Penza, Pskow, Simbirsk, Smolensk, Tambow, Tschernigow,
Twer, Wiatka, Wilna, and Wladimir, in which the female population of the towns exceeded the male population. In several
of these governments, and especially in those which border on
the governments of Moscow and St. Petersburg, the higher
number of the female population is explained by the emigration
of the men to the two capitals.

Taking the entire population of the Russian towns according
to the official statistics of 1850, exclusive of Finland and the
kingdom of Poland, the number of the male population then exceeded the female by 354,300 individuals, or 17 per cent.†

In the kingdom of Poland, on the other hand, the female exceeds by nearly 4 per cent. the male population of the towns,
and in the Grand Duchy of Finland the urban population presents an excess of females of about 17 per cent.

The classification of our towns according to the extent of
their population, and the numerical comparisons which we have
exhibited betwixt them and those of France, Austria, and Prussia, do not show to our disadvantage, if we take the absolute
cipher of their number, and of their population, that is, if we
leave out of view the extent of our total territory, and the number of our entire population. But with us the wealth and prosperity of the towns are not always in proportion to the number
of their inhabitants. This is often seen in their exterior. The
larger number of our towns, even of those whose population is
most considerable, are badly built; the greater part of the
houses are of wood; frequently it is only the churches and
public buildings that are constructed of stone or brick; the streets
are ill paved, or more frequently not paved at all. With the
exception of a few towns especially favoured by their situation,

* It does not clearly appear from the official statistical tables whether or not in
some towns the garrison be included in the urban population; but admitting that
to be the case, still, the civil male population would exceed the female by a very
large proportion. Thus, for example, at St. Petersburg, deducting 20,000 men
for the guards quartered in its environs, there would remain for the year 1851 a
male population of 366,000 souls, the female population for the same year being
only 196,000 souls, which gives for the male population an excess of 170,000 souls,
or 87 per cent.

† In this calculation are not included the country of the Don Cossacks, nor the
government of Stavropol, with regard to which our information for the year in
question is defective.

and which are so many centres to which the great interests of our home and foreign commerce converge, we seldom find the bustle and animation produced by commerce and industry.

In general, the origin and foundation of our towns, their constituent elements, and their condition, give them a peculiar character very different from that of other towns of the European Continent. In Germany, France, Italy, and the other countries of Europe, the greater number of the larger towns date from the middle ages, or a still earlier period; they were founded spontaneously, as it were, by a concourse of circumstances peculiar to the times and places which called them into being. They were corporations, associations formed in the midst of feudal institutions, sometimes with the view of affording better means of resistance to the oppression of the great feudatories, and sometimes with a view to commercial and industrial interests. Frequently there was the union of a political with a material object, as in the case of the Hanse towns of Germany. This community of interests developed from the outset a municipal spirit, which has been the cause of their strength and their prosperity. A similar spontaneity of origin has been wanting to the greater part of our towns. With the exception of a few ancient cities, to which the political or commercial interests of a more remote epoch converged, as Moscow, Kazan, Wladimir, Souzdal, Jaroslaw, Rostow, Nowgorod, Wologda, Nijni-Nowgorod, Kiew, Riga, Archangel, and some provincial capitals, the major part of the Russian towns are of modern foundation. They have arisen at the fiat of government, and frequently much less for the sake of existing interests than with a view to the future. The Empress Catharine II. erected into towns a great number of villages of which the situation, favourable to commerce, contained the germ of their prosperity, and several of these foundations, due to the foresight of government, have been completely successful. A considerable number of these paltry villages have become rich and populous cities. Amongst the creations of the enlightened reign of this empress, M. Haxthausen very properly cites the city of Kharkow. It was a miserable hamlet, founded at the beginning of the seventeenth century by a Cossack of the same name, which had become by degrees a tolerably populous village. In 1780, the Empress erected it into the rank of a town and provincial capital; it is now one of the finest cities of Southern Russia, and reckons more than 30,000 inhabitants. Odessa is another still more striking example of the well-inspired creations of this Empress. Founded in 1794, on the locality of an ancient Greek colony, it rose in less than half a century to the rank of one of the richest and largest cities of the empire, and contains at this moment a population of more than 60,000. On the other hand, there are also to be found amongst these numerous foundations, improvised towns which still remain in a precarious state of existence, and can be considered only as the stakes and pickets driven in over an immense space of ground to trace the march of coming culture and prosperity. M. Haxthausen, one of the best observers amongst those foreign travellers who have lately penetrated into the interior of Russia, has justly observed that on arriving at one of our modern towns, it is easy to distinguish the three æras of their foundation.

" When, travelling in the interior of the empire," says he, " we approach a Russian town, we do not, as in the countries of Romanic or Germanic origin, pass through a suburb of gardens, but enter, first, a Russian village, being the remains of the old village which was destined to be converted into a town: here still dwell the old peasants, and employ themselves principally in gardening, to supply the town with vegetables, carrying on their culture, not in enclosed grounds, but in the open fields. Passing through the village, we enter the town of Catharine II., built like one of the outer quarters of Moscow: it is composed of long, broad, unpaved streets, running between two rows of log houses one story high, with their gable ends turned to the street: here is concentrated the industrial life of the Russian population: here dwell the carters, the cartwrights, the corn-dealers: here are the inns, the alehouses, the shops, &c. Issuing from this second *quartier*, we enter the modern European town, with its straight and sometimes paved streets, and its spacious squares: we see on all hands buildings like palaces; but this part of the town has generally a deserted appearance: the streets present little bustle or animation, with the exception of the droschkies stationed in the squares and at the corners of the streets, with which no provincial capital, or even large district village, is ever unprovided. The most ancient edifices of this quarter are the public buildings: the greater number of the private houses date subsequently to 1815." *

In other European countries we have also seen villages and small burghs raised to the rank of towns by the will of the sovereign power; but in the majority of such cases the elements of these municipal corporations were already in existence, *de*

---

* M. Haxthausen states, that it is chiefly since the war of 1813 that the Russian nobility has got into the way of spending a portion of the year in the provincial towns; and he considers this period as a new æra for the development of town life in Russia.

facto, and the intervention of authority consisted solely in superadding a legal form.   Thus, for example, in Austria, in a number of ancient villages the population had largely increased, and, in the train of their commercial and industrial progress, government established in these villages periodical markets, erecting them into burghs termed *Marktflecken*, that is, *places destined for markets:* but these, before they acquired their municipal privileges, had become in fact considerable towns, with populations of ten or twenty thousand inhabitants or more. With us, on the contrary, the form has often preceded the fact; this has arisen from the influence which the sovereign power is called on to exert over the destinies of the empire,—an influence founded not merely on the form of the government, but like-wise on historical tradition, on custom, and on the requirements and interests of social order.   Since the time of Peter the Great, it is the government which in Russia marches at the head of civilisation; and government is sometimes obliged to slacken its pace in order not to get too far ahead of the wants, the ideas, and the manners of the people.   Of this truth, mis-apprehended by those who judge our country according to pre-conceived ideas, we have perfect evidence, not only in the history and present condition of our towns, but also in all our institutions: and this will appear to every one who takes the trouble to subject them to unprejudiced study and observation.

Many of these towns, some provincial capitals not excepted, owe the limited degree of prosperity they have attained solely to their being the seats of authority, and to the public establish-ments, which give them somewhat of the appearance of a city. M. Haxthausen correctly observes that there is essentially wanting to our towns of recent foundation, and even to some of the older, the nucleus of that burgess class which is composed of artisans, heads of industrial establishments, and persons carrying on some business, — the class designated in Germany the *Handwerkerstand*, and which forms in other countries a large proportion of the town population.   Industry on a small scale, — the industry of trades, has its seat with us rather in the country than in the towns: it is exercised in community in the villages; and these carry to the fairs the products of their labour: hence fairs are in Russia of more consequence than they are elsewhere.   In other countries it is for most part the artisans of the towns that supply the country with their articles; with us, on the contrary, it is often the shoemakers, the joiners, the smiths of the villages, that provide for the wants of the towns.   This scarcity of artisans, so general in small towns, is felt even in large cities.   We do not here speak of those workmen accumulated by the thousand in large manufactories, whose number has increased with us within the last twenty years to an extent perhaps exceeding the requirements of our industry, but we speak of those who learn a business which they carry on upon their own account, giving employment to a certain number of apprentices and journeymen, who become masters in their turn. We find, for example, at Petersburg furniture-warehouses in elegance not a whit behind those of Paris : we find them of every sort and for every class of the population : but when we have a trifling order that we want executed, or an article of any sort that we want mended, we find the utmost difficulty in procuring a workman, and are obliged to pay him two prices for his work. We may convince ourselves in another manner of this scarcity of artificers, by collating the trade-statistics of other countries, and taking for point of comparison some of the commonest trades. Thus, for example, in Prussia, the shoemakers, glovers, joiners, cartwrights, glaziers, smiths, locksmiths, and braziers, amounted in 1843 to 322,760 masters and journeymen out of a population of 15,471,765, which gives 21 workmen to 1000 inhabitants ; and, taking the statistics of the towns, this proportion amounts in the large towns to 40 per 1000 of the total urban population, which is the triple, quadruple, and even more, of what we find in the towns of Russia. Let us take, for example, Jaroslaw, one of the oldest, most populous, and most industrial cities of the empire, occupying by the number of its inhabitants the eighteenth place on the list of towns. The different trades above specified number in this town only 370 artisans, masters and men, out of a population of nearly 35,000, which gives the proportion of only 10 artisans to 1,000 inhabitants. In towns of more recent foundation, and in the small towns in general, we would frequently not find for the same trades 5 workmen to 1,000 inhabitants ; for example, throughout the whole government of Kharkow, there were reckoned in 1838 only 5,859 artisans of every sort, including apprentices and male children, for a population of 1,148,000 inhabitants, which gave only five individuals of that class (male children included) to every 1000 inhabitants, whilst in Prussia there were reckoned in 1843, for all trades, 710,200 masters and journeymen in a population of 15,471,765, which gives an average of 46 artisans for every 1,000 inhabitants.*

---

* Not having before us complete statistics of the working population of all Russia, we have been obliged to take for comparison some isolated data, which, however, may serve as average examples.

The middle classes, or those which live in the enjoyment of a certain amount of ease, being less numerous in Russia than in other countries, in proportion to the entire population, it is evident that the demand must be smaller for workmen belonging to certain trades; but that is not the sole cause of the smaller number of artisans in our towns; a concurring one is the circumstance already adverted to, that the most common trades are carried on much more in community in the country than under a master in the towns.

As much as the *idea of association* is innate in the mind of the Russian peasant, and reproduces itself in every phase of his existence*, so much is the *corporation spirit*, the municipal spirit, which has formed the nucleus of a strongly organised *bourgeoisie* in the old cities of Germany and Western Europe repugnant to his manners and to his character. This is one of the most remarkable peculiarities of the Russian people, and forms, in our opinion, one of the principal causes of the small progress of our towns, and of their municipal life.

If the system of village industry ingrained in the manners of our people is not favourable to the prosperity of our towns, it has, on the other hand, this advantage, that it will preserve us for a long time to come from proletarianism, that scourge of modern society, which possibly contains the germ of its dissolution. This is a question to which we shall have occasion to return in a future chapter, when we come to speak of our industry in a more general point of view. We allude to it here only in reference to the present condition of our towns.

M. Haxthausen observed, during his travels in the south of Russia, that in that part of the empire the absence of bustle and municipal life which characterise the greater part of our towns is most remarkable in those urban *communes* where the Russian population predominates; and that those towns in which the majority of the inhabitants belong to other nations are favourably distinguished in regard to substance, social condition, and industrial and commercial activity. To give more weight to his observations, the author refers to an article on the same subject published in the *Journal du Ministère de l'Intérieur* (livraison du mois de Janvier, 1843).

---

* It may be observed amongst the workmen, even of the humblest trades. No sooner are they united for any work, however small may be their number, than they commence by forming an *Artel* (a sort of workmen's association peculiar to Russia), and choosing a preses, who makes their bargains for them, disposes of their work, receives their payments, and whose directions they obey with a truly exemplary discipline.

In order to form a proper idea of the social and material condition of the towns of European Russia, we must likewise take into consideration the elements of which the urban population, taken as a whole is composed.

According to the census of 1851, the male population of the towns of European Russia, exclusive of Finland and the kingdom of Poland, amounted to 2,601,700 souls; of which 163,264 belonged to the class of merchants, and 1,494,107 to the class of burgesses (*mieschstchanie*); making together 1,657,371 souls, or 63⅔ per cent. of the whole male population. The remainder of the male population of the towns was composed of clergy, nobility, and peasants. In almost all the large towns, the number of the latter is very considerable. They go to settle there either as workmen or as domestics, or to carry on some petty commerce. Thus, for example, in the town of Jaroslaw, previously to 1840, there were reckoned 7,550 peasants (wives and children included) out of a population of about 32,000 inhabitants; of which they consequently formed nearly a quarter. In many towns, also, a large proportion of the burgess class still belongs by habits and occupation to the condition of cultivators; and this is what gives to our towns that rustic appearance which strikes the foreign traveller.

Of the total 497,578 houses, which in 1840 were contained in the 733 towns of European Russia, including Finland and the kingdom of Poland (which gives at an average 679 houses to a town), there were then reckoned, according to the official statistics, not more than 59,370, or somewhat less than 12 per cent., built of stone or brick, the remaining 438,208 being built of wood. The number of stone, therefore, was to that of wooden houses nearly in the proportion of 2 to 15. This explains the frequent occurrence of fires, which often consume entire towns, notwithstanding the existence of a well-organised body of firemen; and proves the necessity of encouraging, in every possible way, the erection of stone and brick houses. Amongst other things, it would be exceedingly desirable that, without prejudice to all the government supervision necessary to ensure solidity in the construction of public buildings, we should eliminate from our regulations with respect to the manufacture of bricks every thing that can impede that branch of industry, or enhance the cost of an article of which the price has risen within the last few years more than 50 or 60 per cent.

The following table, prepared from the official statistics of 1840, gives the numerical return of the town houses in each government, distinguishing those built of stone or brick from those built of wood: —

Governments arranged in the Order of their relative Number of Stone or Brick Houses.	Number of Houses in the Towns.		Total.	Number of Stone or Brick Houses to 1000 of the whole.
	Stone or Brick.	Wooden.		
1. Tauride - - - -	8,101	4,627	12,728	636
2. Kherson - - -	10,872	7,415	18,287	595
3. Esthonia - - -	730	1,629	2,359	309
4. St. Petersburg - -	3,753	9,194	12,947	290
5. Moscow - - - -	4,475	14,500	18,975	236
6. Kingdom of Poland -	6,750	22,380	29,130	232
7. Livonia - - - -	1,521	5,438	6,959	219
8. Wilna and Kowno ·	1,667	7,788	9,455	176
9. Ekathérinoslaw - -	2,454	11,491	13,945	176
10. Country of the Don Cossacks	453	2,363	2,816	161
11. Jaroslaw - - -	1,261	7,636	8,897	142
12. Twer - - - -	2,027	12,514	14,541	139
13. Courland - - -	292	2,425	2,717	108
14. Nowgorod - - -	750	7,025	7,775	96
15. Wiatka - - - -	412	4,301	4,713	87
16. Bessarabia - - -	1,195	14,460	15,655	76
17. Wladimir - - -	553	7,519	8,072	69
18. Woronèje - - -	540	7,710	8,250	65
19. Kazan - - - -	618	9,073	9,691	64
20. Astrakhan - - -	301	4,745	5,046	60
21. Pskow - - - -	372	5,783	6,155	60
22. Kostroma - - -	419	6,723	7,142	59
23. Kalouga - - -	622	10,131	10,753	58
24. Wolhynia - - -	567	9,327	9,894	57
25. Riazan - - - -	361	5,951	6,312	57
26. Toula - - - -	762	13,325	14,087	54
27. Minsk - - - -	371	6,641	7,012	53
28. Koursk - - - -	706	13,011	13,717	51
29. Podolia - - - -	445	8,268	8,713	51
30. Tambow - - - -	515	9,656	10,171	51
31. Orel - - - -	769	14,507	15,276	50
32. Grodno - - - -	212	4,096	4,308	49
33. Smolensk - - -	529	10,178	10,707	49
34. Saratow - - - -	614	12,782	13,396	46
35. Nijni-Nowgorod - -	351	7,501	7,852	45
36. Orenburg - - -	442	10,458	10,900	41
37. Grand Duchy of Finland -	323	8,105	8,428	38
38. Perm - - - -	349	11,460	11,809	30
39. Wologda - - -	146	5,031	5,177	28
40. Kharkow - - -	469	18,482	18,951	25
41. Archangel - - -	70	2,434	2,504	24
42. Witebsk - - -	179	7,819	7,998	23
43. Mohilew - - -	136	6,334	6,470	21
44. Olonetz - - - -	34	1,739	1,773	19
45. Simbirsk - - -	153	8,498	8,651	18
46. Kiew - - - -	214	12,603	12,817	17
47. Stavropol - - -	88	4,954	5,042	17
48. Penza - - - -	172	10,248	10,420	16
49. Tschernigow - - -	131	13,609	13,740	10
50. Poltawa - - - -	124	14,321	14,445	9

From this table it appears, that there are only two governments, namely, Tauride and Kherson, in which the number of stone is greater than that of wooden houses. In Esthonia, the number of stone houses is somewhat below a third; in the government of St. Petersburg it is above a fourth; in that of Moscow, and in the kingdom of Poland, it is somewhat below a fourth; and in Livonia somewhat above a fifth; in six governments, namely, Wilna, Kowno, Ekathérinoslaw, Jaroslaw, Twer, Courland, and the country of the Don Cossacks, it is between 10 and 20 per cent. of the total number of town houses; and in thirty-seven governments it is below 10 per cent.; of these latter, there are nineteen in which it is below 5 per cent.; and, in that of Poltawa, it does not attain even 1 per cent. We would, however, draw erroneous conclusions from this table, if we were to estimate the wealth and prosperity of the inhabitants by the greater or smaller proportion of stone houses in a given government. The value of such an index is but relative. The choice of building materials depends frequently upon local circumstances. In a district where timber is scarce, stone buildings are much less costly than wooden ones; whilst in districts that abound in forests, wooden buildings are, if we may use the expression, indicated by nature, especially if, along with this abundance of timber, there be a scarcity, as often happens, of good materials for stone buildings. It must also be remembered, that in northern countries wooden houses are often preferred, from an opinion that it is easier to keep up a high temperature in them in winter. It is a natural consequence of all this, that we should find the remarkable differences which we perceive in the foregoing table between the relative cipher of stone houses and the degree of wealth of the different governments. Thus, for example, the government of Poltawa, one of the best provided in regard to its productive forces, is the very last in the series; whilst the government of Pskow, one of the poorest, occupies the twenty-first place, and leaves behind it twenty-nine governments, of which the majority belong to the most productive provinces of the empire. There are very populous, wealthy, and commercial towns, in which the greater part of the houses are of wood. In Kiew, for example, which has a population of 50,000 inhabitants, there were, in 1840, only 145 stone houses; in Astrakhan, 294 stone houses for more than 50,000 inhabitants; in Saratow, 382 for a population of 46,000; in Poltawa, 30 for 17,000 or 18,000 inhabitants; in Tambow, 65 for 18,000. Of the whole 733 towns of European Russia, there are but two, namely, Kertsch and Odessa, in which the whole houses are built of stone; and these two exceptions are explained by the scarcity and dearness of building timber in the neighbouring districts.

On consulting official data with regard to the revenues of the towns, we obtain the following results : —

The total revenues of the towns of European Russia, exclusive of Finland and the kingdom of Poland (and also exclusive of the town of Nowotscherkask, in the country of the Don Cossacks, for which we can find no return), amounted in 1848 to 7,797,653 roubles. According to official returns more recent, but not yet completed, these revenues had risen in 1849 to more than nine millions. (See supplementary note, *post*, p. 120.)

In 1840, the population of these towns, not including eight small towns, of which the population is not given in the statistics of the Ministry of the Interior, amounted to 4,578,697. Adding to this figure 3 per cent. for increase of population, we obtain, for the year 1848, an urban population of 4,716,000. Distributing over this population the town revenues for the year 1848 (7,797,653 silver roubles), we have a revenue of 1 rouble 65 kopecks for each inhabitant. Of the total of these revenues, the share belonging to St. Petersburg, Moscow, Odessa, and Riga, the four richest towns, was about 4,000,000 of silver roubles ; so that there was a balance for the whole remaining towns of only 3,798,000 roubles, which, distributed over the population of these towns (3,748,000 inhabitants in 1848), gives only 1 rouble and 1 kopeck for each inhabitant.

In the kingdom of Poland, the revenues of the towns amounted in 1848 to the sum of 1,093,760 roubles, which gave for the urban population of that year (478,418 inhabitants) 2 roubles 28 kopecks for each inhabitant. Setting aside the town of Warsaw, with a population of 140,470 inhabitants, and a revenue of 752,990 silver roubles, there remains, for the whole other towns of the kingdom, with a population of 337,948 inhabitants, a revenue of 340,770 roubles, which is at the rate of 1 rouble and $\frac{3}{4}$ kopeck for each inhabitant. Thus, when we throw aside from our calculation the five wealthiest and most populous towns, namely, St. Petersburg, Moscow, Warsaw, Riga, and Odessa, the revenue of the towns of the empire, and that of the towns of the kingdom of Poland, are found to stand, in proportion to the respective urban populations, on precisely the same level.

In Finland, the revenues of the towns exhibited, in 1840, a total of 119,865 silver roubles for an urban population of 77,559 inhabitants, which gave 1 rouble 55 kopecks for each inhabitant; so that in this province the towns, although possessing a very trifling population, and although situated for most part out of the great highways of communication and of commercial and industrial movement, dispose of a larger revenue than the towns of Russia and Poland. This is owing to circumstances peculiar to the province in question. The greater part of the towns of Finland enjoy a certain quota of the product of the customs, and likewise draw a certain revenue from the fisheries; so that the inhabitants have to contribute to the charges of the towns only enough to cover the difference betwixt the product of those revenues and the amount of expenditure fixed by the budget of each town.

If, to the total revenue of the towns of the empire in 1848, (7,797,653 roubles), we add those of the kingdom of Poland, and of the duchy of Finland, amounting together to 1,213,624 roubles, (cipher of 1840); or, with an augmentation of 5 per cent. for presumed increase during eight years (calculated according to the progress of municipal revenues during preceding periods), to 1,274,300 roubles, we obtain a grand total of the revenues of the towns belonging to European Russia of 9,072,000 silver roubles, which, distributed over the urban population of that year (5,288,000 inhabitants) gives 1 rouble 71 kopecks for each inhabitant.

The following table exhibits the amount of municipal revenues by provinces and governments, together with the average for each inhabitant. The urban population given is that for the year 1847, according to the statistics of the Ministry of the Interior, except for the governments of Podolia and St. Petersburg, the kingdom of Poland, and Finland: for these countries, not possessing more recent statistical data, we have taken the cipher of the urban population of 1840, and added 3 per cent. for its presumed increase during the seven following years: —

Governments arranged according to the Amount of their municipal Revenue.	Revenues of the Towns in 1848.	Urban Population in 1847.	Mean Revenue for each Inhabitant.	
	Silv. Roub.		Rbles.	Kop.
1. St. Petersburg - -	2,143,881	583,900	3	67
2. Moscow - - -	1,193,669	415,462	2	87
3. Kingdom of Poland * -	1,148,000	492,800	2	33
4. Kherson, with the town of				
Odessa - - -	817,800	146,073	5	60
5. Livonia - - - -	444,680	96,653	4	60
6. Kiew - - - -	147,977	158,079		93
Carried forward -	5,896,007	1,892,967		

* Not having before us the amount of revenue of the towns of Finland and the kingdom of Poland for 1848, we have taken that of 1840, and added 5 per cent. for presumed increase of revenue during these eight years.

Governments arranged according to the Amount of their municipal Revenue.	Revenues of the Towns in 1848.	Urban Population in 1847.	Mean Revenue for each Inhabitant.	
	Silv. Roub.		*Rbles.*	*Kop.*
Brought forward -	5,896,007	1,892,967		
7. Nijni-Nowgorod - -	144,214	71,643	2	1
8. Jaroslaw - - -	140,944	76,447	1	83
9. Saratow - - -	135,755	136,087		99
10. Kazan - - - -	133,773	93,393	1	43
11. Orel - - - -	128,779	129,991		99
12. Grand Duchy of Finland *	126,000	79,900	1	58
13. Astrakhan - - -	122,758	55,233	2	22
14. Kharkow - - -	120,907	135,640		89
15. Archangel - - -	109,486	19,263	5	68
16. Ekathérinoslaw (with municipal district of Taganrog) - - -	107,987	112,994		96
17. Twer - - - -	104,803	84,669	1	24
18. Tauride (with municipal district of Kertsch-Enikolsk) - - -	93,358	129,106		72
19. Kalouga - - -	88,421	80,892	1	9
20. Koursk - - -	86,470	95,130		91
21. Tambow - - -	83,061	96,307		86
22. Poltawa - - -	82,842	124,064		67
23. Toula - - - -	80,711	91,190		88
24. Simbirsk - - -	78,320	89,738		87
25. Wilna and Kowno - -	70,386	109,682		64
26. Courland - - -	65,384	55,714	1	17
27. Nowgorod - - -	63,462	34,648	1	83
28. Wladimir - - -	63,388	57,209	1	11
29. Perm - - - -	60,305	65,750		92
30. Orenburg (with the country of the Ural Cossacks) -	59,416	73,503		81
31. Riazan - - - -	57,244	67,154		82
32. Grodno - - -	55,221	97,778		56
33. Podolia - - - -	54,945	84,600		65
34. Tschernigow - - -	54,780	118,155		46
35. Smolensk - - -	53,429	55,804		96
36. Woronèje - - -	50,691	83,393		61
37. Bessarabia (with municipal district of Ismaïl) -	48,753	143,259		34
38. Wologda - - -	48,015	40,148	1	19
39. Kostroma - - -	45,731	47,243		97
40. Wiatka - - - -	45,547	36,228	1	26
41. Esthonia - - -	44,204	20,460	2	16
42. Penza - - - -	41,224	83,649		49
43. Pskow - - - -	40,823	38,814	1	5
44. Witebsk - - -	40,181	66,987		60
45. Stavropol (with country of Black Sea Cossacks) -	34,615	40,658		85
46. Olonetz - - - -	29,805	16,101	1	85
47. Minsk - - - -	28,674	70,476		41
48. Mohilew - - -	26,721	62,050		43
49. Wolhynia - - -	24,111	111,543		21
Total -	9,071,651†	5,275,660	1	72

* See note, page 109.
† For rectification of the figures in this column, in conformity with more recent information, see supplementary note, *post*, p. 120.

From this table it appears that of the total revenues of the towns in European Russia, amounting to 9,071,651 roubles, a sum of 5,748,030 roubles, or nearly two-thirds, belongs to the four governments of St. Petersburg, Moscow, Kherson, and Livonia, and the kingdom of Poland,—provinces of which the urban population in 1847 amounted to 1,734,888, which gives 3 roubles 31 kopecks for each inhabitant; whilst the remaining revenue, amounting to 2,326,621 roubles, distributed over the other forty-four governments, with an urban population of 3,540,000 inhabitants, gives only 66 kopecks for each inhabitant.

On comparing the relative revenue, we perceive great disproportions amongst the various governments. Thus, for example, in the government of Archangel, this revenue gives 5 roubles 68 kopecks for each inhabitant of a town, and in Kherson it gives 5 roubles 60 kopecks; whilst in Bessarabia, the proportion is only 34 kopecks and in Wolhynia 21 kopecks. It is, however, to be observed, that these disproportions are frequently owing to local and special causes quite irrespective of the degree of prosperity of the inhabitants.

The best provided governments, in which the municipal revenues amount to more than two roubles per head, arrange themselves in the following order : —

| | | | | | Per Head. | |
					Roub.	Kop.
Archangel	-	-	-	-	5	68
Kherson	-	-	-	-	5	60
Livonia	-	-	-	-	4	60
St. Petersburg	-	-	-	3	95
Moscow	-	-	-	-	2	87
Kingdom of Poland	-	-	-	2	33
Astrakhan	-	-	-	-	2	22
Esthonia	-	-	-	-	2	16
Nijni-Nowgorod	-	-	-	-	2	1

In twelve governments the relative municipal revenue varies between 1 and 2 roubles, and in twenty-eight it is below 1 rouble per urban inhabitant. Of the latter number there are six in which it does not reach 50 kopecks per head.

The provincial capitals and largest provincial towns arrange themselves in the following order as regards the extent of their municipal revenues :—

Order according to absolute Revenue.	Order according to mean Revenue per Inhab.	Towns arranged according to the Amount of their Revenue.	In 1848.		Mean Revenue per Inhabitant.	
			Amount of Revenue.	Population.*		
			Silver Roub.		Roub.	Kop.
1	4	St. Petersburg - -	2,708,674	487,000	5	36
2	9	Moscow - -	1,128,490	362,000	3	12
3	1	Odessa - - -	939,074	78,100	12	2
4	6	Warsaw † - -	790,600	145,000	5	45
5	5	Riga - - -	343,810	62,000	5	54
6	10	Saratow - -	135,822	44,000	3	9
7	7	Nijni-Nowgorod -	118,475	33,000	3	60
8	14	Astrakhan - -	110,213	48,000	2	30
9	13	Kazan - - -	105,838	43,000	2	46
10	2	Archangel - -	101,813	10,000	10	18
11	16	Kiew - - -	99,089	49,000	2	2
12	12	Kharkow - -	75,030	30,000	2	50
13	25	Orel - - -	48,300	34,000	1	42
14	31	Jaroslaw - -	44,905	36,000	1	25
15	3	Rybinsk (government of Jaroslaw) -	44,323	‡ 6,000	7	38
16	51	Wilna - - -	43,456	56,000		78
17	18	Taganrog - -	43,166	23,000	1	88
18	8	Kalisch (capital of government of same name in the kingdom of Poland) -	40,800	12,500	3	28
19	42	Kalouga - -	39,277	36,500	1	8
20	22	Revel - - -	39,256	25,000	1	57
21	34	Nikolaïew - -	36,740	30,000	1	22
22	39	Koursk - - -	34,270	31,500	1	9
23	19	Simbirsk - -	33,740	18,500	1	82
24	57	Toula - - -	33,627	53,600		63
25	23	Twer - - -	24,881	16,000	1	55
26	21	Lublin (capital of government of same name in the kingdom of Poland) -	24,400	15,000	1	63
27	64	Woronèje - -	24,278	45,500		53
28	27	Krementschouk (government of Poltawa)	23,078	17,000	1	36
29	65	Kischenew - -	22,887	44,000		52
30	45	Mitau - - -	21,300	21,000	1	1
		Carried forward	7,279,612	1,912,200		

* The detailed statistics of all the towns for 1847 not being yet ready, we have taken the cipher of the population in 1840, adding ½ per cent. per annum for the following years.

† In the towns of the kingdom of Poland and the duchy of Finland, we have, for want of more recent data, taken the amount of revenue in 1840, adding 5 per cent. per annum for its presumed increase, calculated from preceding periods.

‡ This figure indicates only the settled population: adding the floating population, the figure would sometimes amount, during the navigation, to 100,000 or more.

Order according to absolute Revenue.	Order according to mean Revenue per Inhab.	Towns arranged according to the Amount of their Revenue.	In 1848.		Mean Revenue per Inhabitant.	
			Amount of Revenue.	Population.		
			Silver Roub.		*Roub.*	*Kop.*
		Brought forward	7,279,612	1,912,200		
31	35	Nowgorod	20,963	17,500	1	20
32	46	Penza	20,264	20,000	1	1
33	47	Kherson	20,227	23,000		86
34	24	Helsingfors	19,950	13,500	1	53
35	36	Tambow	19,845	17,000	1	17
36	44	Oufa (capital of government of Orenburg)	17,873	17,000	1	5
37	30	Kamenetz-Podolski	17,790	14,000	1	27
38	48	Poltawa	17,029	20,000		85
39	49	Lodiz (industrial town in the government of Masovia, in the kingdom of Poland)	16,970	20,500		83
40	20	Stavropol	16,137	9,600	1	68
41	26	Tschernigow	15,840	11,500	1	38
42	56	Minsk	15,748	24,000		65
43	40	Kostroma	15,254	14,000	1	9
44	11	Radom (capital of the government of Sandomir, in the kingdom of Poland)	15,250	6,000	2	54
45	37	Abo	14,900	13,500	1	10
46	32	Plotzk (capital of government of same name in kingdom of Poland)	14,900	12,000	1	14
47	41	Wologda	14,842	13,600	1	9
48	28	Pskow	14,224	10,600	1	34
49	53	Witebsk	14,188	18,600		76
50	66	Eletz (government of Orel)	14,148	27,000		52
51	38	Perm	13,749	12,500	1	10
52	54	Mohilew	13,130	18,500		71
53	43	Wiatka	11,991	11,300	1	6
54	60	Riazan	11,816	19,600		60
55	33	Kowno	11,130	9,000	1	24
56	15	Petrozavodsk (capital of government of Olonetz)	10,516	4,800	2	20
57	67	Kozlow (government of Tambow)	9,976	21,400		47
58	52	Wladimir	9,720	12,500		78
59	61	Grodno	9,545	17,300		55
60	55	Simféropol (capital of the government of Tauride)	9,383	13,400		70
		Carried forward	7,726,910	2,375,400		

Order according to absolute Revenue.	Order according to mean Revenue per Inhab.	Towns arranged according to the Amount of their Revenue.	In 1848.		Mean Revenue per Inhabitant.	
			Amount of Revenue.	Population.		
			Silver Roub.		*Roub.*	*Kop.*
		Brought forward -	7,726,910	2,375,400		
61	17	Kielce (capital of government of same name in kingdom of Poland) -	9,000	4,500	2	
62	62	Jitomir - -	8,820	16,000		55
63	50	Smolensk - -	8,805	11,400		80
64	29	Siedlce (capital of government of Podlachia in the kingdom of Poland) .	8,800	6,700	1	31
65	68	Berditschew - -	7,880	36,500		21
66	63	Kizliar (government of Stavropol) -	5,876	10,700		55
67	59	Ekathérinoslaw -	5,043	8,200		61
68	58	Suwalki (capital of government of Augustow in kingdom of Poland) - -	4,800	7,600		63
69	69	Akermann (in Bessarabia) - -	2,389	26,000		9
		Total -	7,788,323	2,503,000	3	11

In the above table of the principal towns of the empire, we have not included the two maritime towns of Kronstadt and Sevastopol, on account of the conflicting statements we have received as to the amount of their population. Their revenues were in 1848, Kronstadt 48,141, and Sevastopol 18,181 silver roubles.

We perceive from the table that, of the total revenues of sixty-nine towns there given, amounting to 7,788,323 silver roubles, which gives for their population (2,500,000 inhabitants) 3 roubles 11 kopecks a head, the share of the first five towns, St. Petersburg, Moscow, Odessa, Warsaw, and Riga, amounts to 5,910,648 roubles, or more than three-fourths of the whole, giving for the cipher of their population (1,134,000 inhabitants) 5 roubles 21 kopecks per head, so that there remains for the other sixty-four towns, which embrace a population of 1,366,000 inhabitants, a revenue of only 1,877,675 roubles = 1 rouble 37 kopecks for each inhabitant.

Of the sixty-nine towns comprehended in the table, there are six, namely, Odessa, Archangel, Rybinsk, St. Petersburg, Riga, and Warsaw, of which the revenue exceeds the average of

5 roubles per inhabitant; ten, of which it varies between 2 and 3 roubles; thirty, between 1 and 2 roubles; and twenty-four in which it falls short of 1 rouble per inhabitant.

We find striking contrasts in the cipher of the revenue of the towns as compared with that of their population, and the degree of their prosperity and commercial activity. Thus, for example, the town of Archangel, the commerce and prosperity of which are retrograding rather than advancing, occupies the second rank as to mean revenue per inhabitant, which exceeds the proportion of 10 roubles per head; and the little town of Rybinsk, in the government of Jaroslaw, disposes of a revenue of 7 roubles 38 kopecks per head, thus occupying the third place in the list, whilst the relative revenue of the city of Moscow scarcely reaches 3 roubles for each inhabitant. The town of Petrozavodsk, which has only 5,000 inhabitants, occupies the fifth rank in regard to relative revenue, whilst it stands only fifty-sixth on the list in regard to absolute amount. Wilna occupies the sixteenth rank for absolute amount, but only the fifty-first when its revenue is compared with its population. Kiew, with a population of 49,000 inhabitants, has a revenue of only 99,000 roubles, whilst Archangel with its 10,000 inhabitants disposes of an income of 102,000 roubles.

We have already observed that we must not from a comparison of these figures draw too absolute conclusions with regard to the prosperity of the populations of our principal towns. The disproportions which we have noted often proceed from the peculiar situation of the towns of Russia in regard to their sources of revenue. In other countries there are various indirect imposts, as, for example, the *octrois* in France, raised for the benefit of the towns. The product of these indirect imposts, which are laid on upon articles of consumption and luxury, augments with the progress of population, material well-being, and industrial and commercial activity, and balances more or less the increase of wants and expenses which this same progress brings along with it; in this way, there arises no very great disproportion between the revenue of the towns and their population and importance. In Russia, the merchants and inhabitants possessing burgess rights do not generally contribute to the revenues of the towns except by means of the additional centimes to the guildry tax, and to the capitation tax,—the least elastic of any impost, and one which, in order not to exceed the contributionary powers of the poorest inhabitants, must always remain very low. Besides these additional centimes, there are likewise, in some urban communes, other direct impositions, such as the taxes imposed upon certain trades and professions, upon inns, wine-shops, shops, warehouses, public sales, &c.; but the product of these taxes is not always in proportion to the increasing cipher of population, and the increased expenditure which is its result. For a number of our towns, the revenue from the real estate with which they were endowed at the time of their foundation forms the principal part of their communal resources. These endowments have been in certain cases very considerable; thus, for example, the town of Saratow, which is also one of the richest, and occupies from the amount of its revenue (136,000 silver roubles) the sixth place amongst the towns of the first rank, had obtained from Peter I. the gift of 230,000 dessiatines (= 618,000 English acres) of good land. Sure enough not a city of Europe was ever so extensively endowed with real estate. The greater portion of this property was dilapidated by the municipal authorities at a period when the lands were still of small value, so that at the first revision of communal property there was found to remain in possession of the town no more than 57,000 dessiatines; still this formed a handsome property (more than 153,000 English acres in extent) in one of the most fertile districts of the empire, and amounted on the population of the period to about three dessiatines for each inhabitant. Since that date a portion of the land has again been alienated, but the capital realised from the sale still forms a considerable part of the town's funds. Some of the urban communes less liberally provided with real estate enjoy other sources of revenue. Several maritime towns have the privilege of levying a certain percentage upon the produce of the customs; others, of levying certain taxes on the navigation; others draw considerable revenues from the fisheries; and it is these special resources that augment the cipher of their budgets. On the other hand, there are a vast number of urban communes which are poorly enough provided; being without similar accidental sources of revenue, they are reduced to the trifling product of some direct imposts.

On deducting the total revenues of the 69 towns contained in last table (7,788,323 roubles), from the total revenues of the whole 733 towns of European Russia (9,071,651 roubles), there remains for the other 664 towns, with a population of 2,800,000 inhabitants, a revenue of 1,283,328 roubles, which gives only 46 kopecks per inhabitant, whilst the revenue of the other 69 gives an average for each inhabitant of 3 roubles 11 kopecks. This great inequality in the financial position of our towns is a circumstance that merits attention; and it would be very desirable that, in making a general revision of the budgets of all the towns of the empire, some means could be devised for providing assistance to those of which the revenues are in greatest disproportion to their wants, their industrial or commercial importance, and the chances of their future prosperity.

Of all the towns of the empire, Odessa's revenue is the richest. It amounts to the average rate of 12 roubles to each inhabitant, which is but slightly under the relative revenue of Paris, (13 roubles per inhabitant,) whilst that of St. Petersburg is only 5 roubles 56 kopecks, and that of Moscow only 3 roubles 12 kopecks. This proceeds from a cause which we have already adverted to ; the principal branch of the revenue of Odessa has consisted hitherto in a duty levied upon foreign merchandise, amounting to a fifth of the droits fixed by the ancient general tariff of the empire. Thus the increase in the revenues of this town greatly exceeds the progress of its population.

The following is a comparative view of the revenues of our three principal towns with those of the capitals of the three principal continental states : —

Revenue.	Population.	Mean Revenue per Inhab.	
		Roub.	Kop.
Paris (in 1849), 54,376,000 fr. = 13,569,000 silver roubles - - - -	1,027,000 *	13	21
Berlin (in 1848), 3,068,000 thaler = 2,823,000 silver roubles - -	339,000 †	8	33
Vienna (in 1851), 1,021,000 flor. conv. = 643,000 silver roubles - - -	481,800 ‡	1	33
St. Petersburg (1848), 2,708,600 silver roubles - - - -	487,700	5	56
Moscow (1848), 1,128,500 silver roubles -	362,000	3	12
Warsaw (1848), 790,600 silver roubles -	145,000	5	45

Thus we perceive that Paris is greatly in advance of the other capitals in regard as well to the relative as to the absolute cipher of its revenue ; but, for a just appreciation of this fact, it must not be forgotten that its revenue rests principally on the octroi levied on all articles of consumption which pass the barriers of the town, down even to raw building materials. In the total revenues of the city for the year 1849, amounting to 54,376,000 francs, the product of the octroi figures for nearly

* We have taken the population of Paris in 1836, according to the official statistics published by the Minister of Public Works, Agriculture, and Commerce, adding for increase 1 per cent. per annum, or, in all, 13 per cent. The actual increase of the Parisian population, resulting from the excess of births over deaths, is at the average rate of only ½ per cent. ; but in that capital, as in other large towns, the population is recruited likewise by immigration from the country, so that we cannot add less than 1 per cent. per annum.

† The population of Berlin amounted in 1843, according to M. Dieterici, the head of the statistical bureau, to 322,600 inhabitants. To this figure we have added 5 per cent. for increase during 5 years.

‡ At the end of 1850, according to the official report presented to the Municipal Council.

33 millions, or more than three-fifths. This, then, is a very productive branch of revenue which is enjoyed by scarcely any other capital. At Vienna there is levied upon articles of consumption entering the town a certain impost on its behalf, termed the *Städtischer Zuschlag;* but this is a mere supplementary addition to the excise, which is itself much more moderate than the French octrois; and the total of that branch of revenue figures in the budget of 1851, at no more than 410,000 convention florins, (= 41,000*l.* sterling). At Berlin also there is levied an excise upon certain articles for the benefit of the municipal funds; but this revenue is not nearly so productive as the octroi of Paris. In Russia there is no municipal revenue whatever coming from imposts upon articles of consumption. If we deduct the produce of the *octrois* from the revenue of Paris, the latter will only amount to 21,400,000 francs = 5,350,000 roubles, which, on a population of 1,027,000 inhabitants, would give only 5 roubles 20 kopecks for each inhabitant, being less than the relative product of the revenues of St. Petersburg and Warsaw. In the present state of things, the relative revenue of these two towns is equal to nearly two-fifths of that of Paris, and to nearly two-thirds of that of Berlin. The relative revenue of Moscow is more than a third of that of Berlin, and is equal to three-thirteenths of that of Paris; but the revenue of all these towns greatly exceeds that of Vienna, both in absolute amount, and relatively to the population: of the last-mentioned town, however, the budget has been sensibly diminished by the reduction of the excise which took place in 1848.

In the Russian possessions in Asia, there were reckoned, in 1840, seventy-nine towns, with a population of 309,000 inhabitants, and a total revenue of 225,606 roubles; of which twenty-two towns, with 141,164 inhabitants, were in the Trans-Caucasian provinces, and fifty-seven towns, with 167,827 inhabitants, were in Siberia.

Adding 10 per cent. * to the number of inhabitants in 1840 for the increase of the population during ten years, we obtain a total urban population of the Russian possessions in Asia of 340,000 inhabitants; of whom 155,000 belong to the towns of the Trans-Caucasian provinces, and 185,000 to the towns of Siberia. This gives, in the former, one town to 129 square miles, and to each town an average population of 7,045; and, in the latter, one town to 4,186 square miles, with an average population of 3,246 inhabitants to each town.

---

* The population of our principal towns in Asia augments at a rate so rapid that we do not think we run any risk of exaggeration in reckoning its progress at 1 per cent. per annum.

Amongst the twenty-two towns of the Trans-Caucasian provinces, there are five with a population exceeding 10,000, namely, Tiflis, Staraïa-Chemakha, Noukha, Erivan, and Derbent, which, in 1840, contained a joint population of 76,000 inhabitants; and amongst the fifty-seven towns of Siberia there were likewise five in 1840 with a population exceeding 10,000, namely, Irkoutsk, Tobolsk, Tomsk, Omsk, and Tioumen (in the government of Tobolsk), containing a joint population of 65,000 inhabitants. On the other hand, there are in Siberia five towns in none of which did the population in 1840 reach 300 inhabitants; and of these five there were two, namely, Verchojansk and Olekminsk, in the district of Jakoutsk, with populations under 100 inhabitants.

On comparing the numbers of the urban and rural populations, we obtain the following proportions. In the Trans-Caucasian provinces, 7,045, and in Siberia, 6,166 inhabitants of towns out of each 100,000 of the total population; or, in other terms, to 100 inhabitants of towns, in the Trans-Caucasian provinces, 1,419, and in Siberia, 1,622, of a rural population.

From all the foregoing comparisons it results, that the greater part of our towns are still in a very backward condition as regards their prosperity. Still, in this respect, also, we are making way. In a number of small towns favourably situated for home or foreign commerce, the population has considerably augmented; and in this augmentation several of the larger ones have likewise participated. In consequence of reforms introduced in 1842 into the administration of the towns and the management of their funds, the municipal revenues have been considerably augmented. In 1841 they presented a total of 6,795,120 silver roubles, including the towns of Siberia, but exclusive of Finland and the kingdom of Poland: in 1848 they amounted to 7,989,950, which exhibits an increase of 1,194,830 roubles. According to more recent official data they exceeded, in 1849, the sum of $9\frac{1}{2}$ millions; exhibiting an increase, as compared with 1848, of more than $1\frac{1}{2}$ millions, and as compared with 1841, of more than 2,700,000 silver roubles, or of 40 per cent. in the space of eight years (*see* supplementary note, *post.*). This increase has been obtained in most of the towns, without laying any additional burden on the inhabitants, solely by an improved administration of the municipal property.

The twenty-two towns of the Trans-Caucasian provinces disposed, in 1840, of a revenue of 75,851 silver roubles, which, on the urban population of that epoch (141,000 inhabitants), was at the rate of 54 kopecks for each inhabitant. The revenue of the towns in Siberia amounted at the same period to 149,755 silver roubles, or, on an urban population of 168,000, to 89 kopecks *per* inhabitant.　In 1848, the revenue of the towns of the four Siberian governments of Jenisseisk, Irkoutsk, Tobolsk, and Tomsk, amounted in whole to 192,297 silver roubles; in 1840 it had stood only at 142,625 roubles ; so that, during these eight years, there had been an augmentation of 49,672 roubles, or 35 per cent.*

Supplementary Note concerning the Revenue of the Towns.

Whilst this volume was passing through the press, we received statistical information with respect to the revenue of the towns of European Russia for the year 1849.　Although these returns are not quite complete, we present them in the following table as supplementary information with regard to the changes that have occurred since 1848 in the proceeds of the revenues of the towns in forty-seven governments, and the augmentation of their sum total.

Revenue of the Towns of European Russia during the Year 1849.

GOVERNMENTS.	Estimated Revenue.	Actual Revenue.
	Silver Roubles.	*Silver Roubles.*
1. Archangel　-　　-　　-	79,182	70,352
2. Astrakhan　-　　-　　-	128,621	122,393
3. Bessarabia, with the district of Ismail -　　-　　-　　-	48,850	69,865
4. Courland -　　-　　-　　-	65,384	87,523
5. Ekathérinoslaw, with the district of Taganrog　-　　-　　-	117,891	48,852
6. Esthonia -　　-　　-　　-	43,934	48,864
7. Grodno　-　　-　　-　　-	57,734	51,520
8. Jaroslaw -　　-　　-　　-	138,331	131,266
9. Kalouga　-　　-　　-　　-	87,288	99,319
10. Kazan　-　　-　　-　　-	133,773	162,909
11. Kharkow　-　　-　　-　　-	133,938	137,301
12. Kherson, with the town of Odessa	947,668	1,233,636
13. Kiew　-　　-　　-　　-	140,975	169,417
Carried forward　-　　-	2,123,569	2,433,217

REMARKS.

No. 5. The sum in the second column represents the actual revenue of only Taganrog, Marioupol, and Nakhitschevan, estimated in the budget at 66,790 roubles.　We have no returns of the actual revenues of the other 10 towns of this government.

No. 13. We want returns from two small towns in this government, as well as of the actual revenue of the town of Berditschew, which was estimated in the budget at 8,332 roubles.

---

* We are not aware of what the increase may have been in the municipal revenues of the Trans-Caucasian governments.

GOVERNMENTS.	Estimated Revenue.	Actual Revenue.
	Silver Roubles.	*Silver Roubles.*
Brought forward - -	2,123,569	2,433,217
14. Kowno - - - -	20,465	26,967
15. Kostroma - - - -	45,731	49,677
16. Koursk - - - -	89,945	96,752
17. Livonia - - - -	456,221	491,823
18. Minsk - .. - -	34,143	32,999
19. Mohilew - - - -	27,053	26,662
20. Moscow - - - -	1,174,056	1,094,913
21. Nijni-Nowgorod - - -	85,868	83,359
22. Nowgorod - - -	70,582	70,243
23. Olonetz - - - -	29,629	29,795
24. Orel - .. - -	120,003	124,842
25. Orenburg - - -	79,886	91,743
26. Penza - - - -	41,599	50,001
27. Perm - - - -	60,517	75,701
28. Podolia - - - -	54,845	64,907
29. Poltawa - - - -	80,138	98,707
30. Pskow - - - -	39,304	53,364
31. Riazan - - - -	58,145	65,083
32. St. Petersburg - - -	2,175,031	2,861,336
33. Saratow - - - -	138,326	172,795
34. Simbirsk - - - -	79,565	86,618
35. Smolensk - - -	52,811	60,701
36. Tambow - - - -	92,215	134,562
37. Tauride, with the district of Kertch-Enikolsk - -	92,064	90,905
38. Toula - - - -	85,989	96,127
39. Tschernigow - - -	55,914	59,257
40. Twer - - - -	103,628	110,767
41. Wiatka - - - -	45,641	55,128
42. Wilna - - - -	52,321	79,697
43. Witebsk - - - -	41,376	
44. Wladimir - - -	61,752	70,958
45. Wolhynia - - -	24,903	26,715
46. Wologda - - - -	51,762	68,278
47. Woronèje - - -	51,643	60,939
Total - - -	7,896,640	9,095,538

REMARKS.

No. 19. We want returns from two small towns in this government.

No. 21. Without reckoning the taxes raised from the fair at Nijni-Nowgorod, the proceeds of which are estimated in the budget at 56,377 roubles.

No. 24. We want returns for one small town of this government.

No. 26. We are without returns for three small towns of this government.

No. 27. We are without returns for four towns of this government.

No. 28. We are without returns for three small towns of this government.

No. 32. We are without returns for three small towns. We are also without returns of the actual revenue of the towns of Kronstadt and Tzarskoë-Sélo, estimated in the budget at 59,729 roubles.

No. 34. We are without returns for three small towns of this government.

No. 43. We are without returns of the actual revenue of the towns of this government.

No. 45. We are without returns for five small towns of this government.

No. 47. We are without returns for eight small towns of this government.

On deducting from the sum total of the first column of the foregoing table the budgets of those towns which do not figure in the column of actual revenue, viz.,

Roubles.

1. For ten towns of the government of Ekathérinoslaw (see remark to No. 5.) - - - - -   51,101
2. For the town of Berditschew, government of Kiew (see remark to No. 13.) - - - - -   8,332
3. For the towns of Kronstadt and Tzarskoë-Sélo (see remark to No. 32.) - - - - - -   59,729
4. For the towns in the government of Witebsk (see remark to No. 43.) - - - - - -   41,376

Making together   -   -   -   160,538

the total revenue of all the other towns which figure in the table would amount, according to the estimates of the budgets, to 7,736,112 roubles; whilst the actual revenue amounted to 9,095,538 roubles, which exhibits an excess of income over estimate of 1,359,426 roubles, or 17 per cent.

We have further to observe that the government of Stavropol is not included in the preceding table for want of data with respect to the revenue of the towns for the year 1849. For the year 1848 the revenue of these towns amounted, as per table, p. 110., to 34,615 roubles.

Roubles.

Now, taking the sum of the actual revenues for the year 1849, as given in the preceding table, viz. - - - - -   9,095,538
    and adding thereto,
1. The amount estimated in the budget for the towns of the governments of Ekathérinoslaw, Kiew, St. Petersburg, and Witebsk, *ut supra* - - - - - - - -   160,538
2. Revenue of the towns of the government of Stavropol for 1848, *ut supra* - - - - - - - -   34,615

The actual total revenue of the towns of European Russia for the year 1849 would amount (without including 34 small towns, for which we have no returns) to - - - - -   9,290,691

a sum which, as compared with the revenues of the year 1848 (7,797,653), presents an increase of 1,493,000 roubles, or 19 per cent.

Roubles.

The revenues of the towns of Poland amounted in 1848 to - -   1,148,000
Those of the towns of Finland to - - - - -   126,000

Together -   -   -   -   -   -   1,274,000

They have without doubt augmented since; but, assuming the same amount for 1849, and adding it to the revenues of the towns of the empire, as given above, at 9,290,691 roubles, we obtain for total revenue of the whole towns in the European possessions of Russia the amount of 10,564,691 silver roubles.

The revenues of the towns of Siberia and of the Trans-Caucasian provinces amounted, in 1848, to 192,297 roubles; which brings the total revenue of the whole towns of European and Asiatic Russia, inclusive of Finland and the kingdom of Poland, to 10,756,988 roubles.

We here present a view of the differences for the year 1849 betwixt the actual revenues of the towns in forty-six governments and the revenues estimated in their various budgets.

Governments (Thirty-five in number) *in which the actual Revenue of the Towns was in excess of the Estimate.*

	Excess over Estimate.	Proportion per cent.
	Silver Roubles.	
1. Wilna - - - -	27,376	52·3
2. Tambow - - - -	42,347	45·9
3. Bessarabia - - - -	21,015	43
4. Pskow - - - -	14,060	35·8
5. St. Petersburg (without Kronstadt and Tzarskoë-Selo) - -	746,034	35·3
6. Courland - - - -	22,139	33·9
7. Wologda - - - -	16,516	31·9
8. Kowno - - - -	6,502	31·8
9. Kherson - - - -	285,968	30·2
10. Kiew (without Berditschew) -	36,774	27·7
11. Perm - - - -	15,184	25·1
12. Saratow - - - -	34,469	24·9
13. Poltawa - - - -	18,569	23·2
14. Kazan - - - -	29,136	21·8
15. Wiatka - - - -	9,487	20·8
16. Penza - - - -	8,402	20·2
17. Podolia - - - -	10,062	18·3
18. Woronèje - - - -	9,296	18
19. Wladimir - - - -	9,206	14·9
20. Smolensk - - - -	7,890	14·9
21. Orenburg - - - -	11,857	14·8
22. Kalouga - - - -	12,031	13·8
23. Riazan - - - -	6,938	11·9
24. Toula - - - -	10,138	11·8
25. Esthonia- - - -	4,930	11·2
26. Simbirsk - - - -	7,053	8·9
27. Kostroma - - - -	3,946	8·6
28. Livonia - - - -	35,602	7·8
29. Koursk - - - -	6,807	7·6
30. Wolhynia - - - -	1,812	7·3
31. Twer - - - -	7,139	6·9
32. Tschernigow - - -	3,343	6
33. Orel - - - -	4,839	4
34. Kharkow - - - -	3,363	2·5
35. Olonetz - - - -	166	0·6

The total of the town budgets included in the above table amounted to 5,781,678 silver roubles, and the actual revenues amounted to 7,272,074, which presents an excess over estimate of 1,490,396 roubles, or 26 per cent. The chief excesses in absolute amount, which occur in the governments of St. Petersburg and

Kherson, refer principally to the towns of St. Petersburg and
Odessa. The revenue of St. Petersburg was estimated in the
budget at 2,082,842, and the actual revenue amounted to
2,820,768, which exhibits an excess of 737,926 roubles, or
35 per cent. The budget of Odessa amounted to 862,814 roubles,
and the actual revenue yielded 1,191,621; which presents an
excess of 328,807 roubles, or 38 per cent.

Governments (Eleven in number) *in which the actual Revenue of
the Towns fell short of the Estimate.*

	Deficiency as compared with Estimate.	Proportion per cent.
	Silver Roubles.	
1. Ekathérinoslaw, district of Taganrog, comprehending the towns of Taganrog, Marioupol, and Nakhitschewan -	17,938	36·7
2. Archangel - - - -	8,830	11·2
3. Grodno - - - -	6,214	10·8
4. Moscow - - - -	79,143	6·7
5. Jaroslaw - - - -	7,065	5·1
6. Astrakhan - - - -	6,228	4·8
7. Minsk - - - - -	1,144	3·3
8. Nijni-Nowgorod - - -	2,509	2·9
9. Mohilew - - - -	391	1·4
10. Tauride - - - -	4,159	1·3
11. Nowgorod - - - -	339	0·5

The total estimated revenues of these eleven towns amounted
to 2,005,525 roubles, while the actual revenues came to no more
than 1,823,464, which presents a deficiency of 182,061 roubles,
or 9 per cent.

The deficiency in the towns of the government of Moscow is
referable entirely to the capital, as in most of the other towns
the actual revenue rather exceeded the estimate. The budget
of the town of Moscow came to 1,119,885 roubles, and the
actual revenue having amounted to no more than 1,025,544,
there was thus a shortcoming of 94,341 roubles or of 9·2 per cent.

The two following tables present the amount of revenue and
expenditure in the towns of forty-six governments.

Governments in which the Revenue exceeded the Expenditure.	Revenue in 1849.	Expenditure in 1849.	Excess of Revenue.	
			Amount of Excess.	Proportion per cent.
	Silver Roub.	*Silver Roub.*	*Silver Roub.*	
1. Archangel - -	70,352	59,543	10,809	18·2
2. Astrakhan - -	122,393	119,660	2,733	2·3
3. Bessarabia (with district of Ismaïl) - -	69,865	67,256	2,609	3·9
4. Courland - -	87,523	81,037	6,486	8
Carried forward -	350,133	327,496	22,637	

Governments in which the Revenue exceeded the Expenditure.	Revenue in 1849.	Expenditure in 1849.	Excess of Revenue.	
			Amount of Excess.	Proportion per cent.
	Silver Roub.	*Silver Roub.*	*Silver Roub.*	
Brought forward -	350,133	327,496	22,637	
5. Jaroslaw - -	131,266	122,456	8,810	7·2
6. Kharkow - -	137,301	135,380	1,921	4·4
7. Kherson - - -	1,233,637	1,058,019	175,618	16·6
8. Kiew - - -	169,417	148,493	20,924	14·1
9. Kowno - - -	26,967	26,708	259	1
10. Kostroma - - -	49,677	49,120	557	1·1
11. Koursk - - -	96,752	95,128	1,624	1·7
12. Livonia - - -	491,823	480,928	10,895	2·3
13. Minsk - - -	32,999	28,640	4,359	15·1
14. Mohilew - -	26,662	25,174	1,488	5·9
15. Moscow - - -	1,094,913	1,058,458	36,355	3·4
16. Nowgorod - -	70,243	68,153	2,090	3·1
17. Orenburg - -	91,743	76,127	15,616	20·5
18. Perm - - -	75,701	69,328	6,373	9·2
19. Podolia - - -	64,907	56,262	8,645	15·4
20. Riazan - - -	65,083	63,567	1,516	2·4
21. St. Petersburg - -	2,861,336	2,209,630	651,706	29·5
22. Saratow - - -	172,795	133,559	39,236	29·4
23. Smolensk - -	60,701	55,121	5,580	10·1
24. Tambow - -	134,562	132,391	2,171	1·6
25. Tauride - -	90,905	84,568	6,337	7·5
26. Toula - -	96,127	92,873	3,254	3·5
27. Tschernigow - -	59,257	55,040	4,217	7·7
28. Twer - - -	110,767	109,000	1,767	1·6
29. Wiatka - - -	55,128	47,697	7,431	15·6
30. Wilna - - -	79,697	78,332	1,365	1·7
31. Wladimir - -	70,958	69,050	1,908	2·8
32. Wologda - -	68,278	54,135	14,143	26·1
33. Woronèje - -	60,939	56,826	4,113	7·2
Total -	8,130,674	7,067,659	1,063,015	13

Governments in which the Expenditure exceeded the Revenue.	Revenue in 1849.	Expenditure in 1849.	Excess of Expenditure.	
			Amount of Excess.	Proportion per cent.
	Silver Roub.	*Silver Roub.*	*Silver, Roub.*	
1. Ekathérinoslaw, district of Taganrog -	48,852	57,122	8,270	16·9
2. Esthonia - -	48,864	49,697	833	1·7
3. Grodno - -	51,520	51,658	138	0·3
4. Kalouga - -	99,319	104,951	5,632	5·7
5. Kazan -	162,909	166,491	3,582	2·1
6. Nijni-Nowgorod -	83,359	90,859	7,500	9·0
7. Olonetz - -	29,795	30,202	407	1·4
8. Orel - - -	124,842	128,677	3,835	3·1
9. Penza - - -	50,001	50,578	577	1·2
10. Poltawa - -	98,707	98,895	188	0·2
11. Pskow - - -	53,364	54,365	1,001	1·9
12. Simbirsk - -	86,618	97,827	11,209	12·9
13. Volhynia - - -	26,715	27,943	1,228	4·6
Total -	964,865	1,009,265	44,400	4·6

We perceive from the foregoing tables that there are only thirteen governments in which the amount of expenditure exceeded the amount of actual revenue, whilst in the other thirty-three governments the revenues exceeded the amount of the expenditure. This surplus was in the proportion of more than 10 per cent. in eleven governments, amongst which St. Petersburg and Saratow exhibit a surplus of nearly 30 per cent. and Wologda of more than 26 per cent. In the government of St. Petersburg the surplus belongs almost entirely to the capital, the revenue of which amounted to 2,820,768 roubles, and the expenditure to 2,169,892, leaving a surplus of 650,876 roubles, or 30 per cent. In most of the other towns belonging to this government the expenditure exceeded more or less the amount of revenue. In the government of Saratow, the towns which present the largest surplus are Saratow, Khwalynsk, Wolsk, Kamyschine, and Petrowsk. Of the thirteen governments in which the expenditure exceeded the revenues, there are only two, the government of Simbirsk, and the district of Taganrog in the government of Ekathérinoslaw, where the deficiency exceeded 10 per cent.

The sum of the whole forty-six governments gives the following result: —

			Roubles.
Total revenues	-	-	- 9,095,539
Total expenditure	-	-	- 8,076,924
Excess of revenue	-	-	- 1,018,615 or 12·6 per cent.

From all this we may perceive that, with some exceptions originating in local circumstances, the financial position of our towns is improving in consequence of the improvements introduced into their administration.

If we deduct the population of the towns (amounting in 1851, according to the table, p. 96., to 5,413,000 inhabitants) from the total population of European Russia, (amounting to about 62,000,000), there will remain for the population of the rural districts 56,587,000 inhabitants. The cultivated land extending to about 90 millions of dessiatines, we may reckon 1·6 dessiatines for each inhabitant; and if to this we add, according to a slump approximation, 60,000,000 dessiatines of meadow land, we will have 2·6 dessiatines for each inhabitant.

The following table exhibits the number of the rural population and the quantity of productive soil in each province and government.*

---

* Some statists have reproached us with having, in the distribution of the productive soil over the population, unduly separated the population of the towns

Provinces and Governments arranged according to the Extent of their productive Soil in proportion to the Rural Population.	Rural Population.	Arable Land and Meadows.	Number of Dessiatines per Inhabitant.
		Dessiatines.	
1. Country of the Don Cossacks	778,000	11,850,000	15·2
2. *Astrakhan*, without the nomade populations * - -	155,300	950,000	6·1
3. *Saratow* - - - -	1,679,000	9,043,000	5·4
4. Stavropol - - - -	960,800	4,750,000	4·9
5. Minsk - - - -	910,400	4,366,000	4·8
6. Kherson - - - · -	701,300	3,400,000	4·8
7. Tauride - - - -	550,800	2,350,000	4·3
8. *Orenburg* - - - -	2,071,700	8,567,000	4·1
9. *Simbirsk* - - - -	1,097,200	4,100,000	3·7
10. Pskow - - - -	630,800	2,200,000	3·5
11. Woronèje - - - -	1,585,550	5,407,000	3·3
12. Kharkow - - - -	1,048,600	3,450,000	3·3
13. Bessarabia - - - -	755,400	2,500,000	3·3
14. Kowno - - - -	887,300	2,810,000	3·2
15. Tschernigow - - -	1,291,700	3,821,000	3·
16. Ekathérinoslaw - - -	906,600	2,600,000	2·9
17. Tambow - - - -	1,573,900	4,150,000	2·6
18. Mohilew - - - -	783,100	2,000,000	2·6
19. Witebsk - - - -	658,900	1,720,000	2·6
20. Perm - - - -	1,816,900	4,582,000	2·5
21. Grodno - - - -	786,700	1,990,000	2·5
22. Twer - - - -	1,324,600	2,960,000	2·2
23. Orel - - - - -	1,276,400	2,800,000	2·2
24. Smolensk - - - -	1,029,500	2,280,000	2·2
25. Toula - - - -	1,023,800	2,220,000	2·2
26. Poltawa - - - -	1,558,000	3,215,000	2·1
27. Podolia - . - -	1,510,600	3,213,000	2·1
28. Wolhynia - - - -	1,389,800	2,887,000	2·1
29. Nowgorod - - - -	857,500	1,770,000	2·1
30. Kazan - - - -	1,311,100	2,600,000	2·
31. Penza - - - -	990,000	2,050,000	2·
32. Wilna - - - -	743,500	1,505,000	2·
33. Koursk - - - -	1,612,200	3,116,000	1·9
34. Nijni-Nowgorod - -	1,100,700	2,080,000	1·9
35. *Wladimir* - - - -	1,100,600	2,080,000	1·9
36. Kostroma - - - -	1,005,800	1,940,000	1·9
37. Jaroslaw - - - -	881,800	1,692,000	1·9

from that of the rural districts; but this reproach does not seem quite just, for we have first (p. 75.) established the proportion between the productive soil and the total number of the inhabitants, and again we have given (p. 87.) a table of the distribution of the cultivated soil, equally with reference to the total population, by provinces and governments. The next and subsequent tables are therefore to be considered merely as statistical supplements which present the numerical relation of the extent of productive soil to the rural population, properly so called, or that which is more exclusively occupied with agriculture. We do not think these complementary comparisons are out of place in a work of which one of the objects is to analyse our agricultural position in its different relations.

* For those governments the names of which are printed in *italics*, the rural population has been taken from data antecedent to the date of their new boundaries: for all the other governments, it has been taken from the census of 1851.

Provinces and Governments arranged according to the Extent of their productive Soil in proportion to the Rural Population.	Rural Population.	Arable Land and Meadows.	Number of Dessiatines per Inhabitant.
		Dessiatines.	
38. Wiatka - - - -	1,885,100	3,473,000	1·8
39. Kiew - - - -	1,534,200	2,798,000	1·8
40. Esthonia - - - -	273,600	500,000	1·8
41. Olonetz - - - -	261,600	480,000	1·8
42. Kalouga - - - -	882,200	1,493,000	1·7
43. Courland - - - -	465,800	810,000	1·7
44. Kingdom of Poland - -	4,372,000	6,945,000	1·6
45. Riazan - ·· - -	1,294,700	2,100,000	1·6
46. Wologda - - - -	825,300	1,250,000	1·5
47. Moscow - - - -	1,132,500	1,560,000	1·4
48. St. Petersburg - - -	553,000	750,000	1·4
49. Livonia - - - -	740,200	970,000	1·3
50. Grand Duchy of Finland -	1,472,500	1,591,000	1·1
51. Archangel - - - -	224,800	237,000	1·1

We see figuring in this table one province, the country of the Don Cossacks, which is in a very exceptional condition in regard to the extent of its productive soil as compared with the amount of its rural population. In it there are upwards of 15 dessiatines of productive land for each rural inhabitant. Next to this province, it is the governments of Astrakhan, Saratow, Stavropol, Kherson, Minsk, Tauride, and Orenburg, in which the proportion is greatest, the average running from 4 to 6 dessiatines per head. There are seven governments in which it runs between 3 and 4 dessiatines; seventeen in which it is from 2 to 3 ; and nineteen in which the average is under 2. Of the latter, there are only five in which the average does not reach 1½ dessiatines per head.

If we take the extent of the arable lands and that of the meadows separately, the results we obtain will be entirely different, as will be seen from the two following tables.

Provinces and Governments arranged according to the extent of their arable Land in proportion to the Rural Population.	Rural Population.	Arable Land.	Number of Dessiatines per Inhabitant.
		Dessiatines.	
1. Minsk - - · -	910,400	2,820,000	3·1
2. Country of the Don Cossacks - - - -	778,000	2,310,000	3·
3. Tschernigow - ·· -	1,291,700	3,191,000	2·5
4. Witebsk - ·· -	658,900	1,600,000	2·4
5. Simbirsk - - -	1,097,200	2,500,000	2·3
6. Kowno - - - -	887,300	2,060,000	2·3
7. Mohilew - - -	783,100	1,700,000	2·2
8. Pskow - - - -	630,800	1,400,000	2·2
9. Kharkow ·· - -	1,048,600	2,100,000	2·
10. Orenburg - - -	2,071,700	4,115,000	2·

Provinces and Governments arranged according to the extent of their Arable Land in proportion to the rural Population.	Rural Population.	Arable Land.	Number of Dessiatines per Inhabitant.
11. Toula - - - -	1,023,800	2,000,000	2
12. Kherson - - -	701,300	1,400,000	2
13. Woronèje - - -	1,585,550	3,007,000	1·9
14. Orel - - - -	1,276,400	2,400,000	1·9
15. Smolensk - - -	1,029,500	2,000,000	1·9
16. Grodno - - -	786,700	1,470,000	1·9
17. Bessarabia - - -	755,400	1,300,000	1·7
18. Wiatka - - - -	1,885,100	2,973,000	1·6
19. Tambow - - -	1,573,900	2,500,000	1·6
20. Podolia - - -	1,510,600	2,440,000	1·6
21. Kazan - - - -	1,311,100	2,100,000	1·6
22. Nijni-Nowgorod - -	1,100,700	1,800,000	1·6
23. Wladimir - - -	1,100,600	1,800,000	1·6
24. Kostroma - - -	1,005,800	1,600,000	1·6
25. Penza - - - -	990,000	1,600,000	1·6
26. Wilna - - - -	743,500	1,170,000	1·6
27. Saratow - - -	1,679,000	2,530,000	1·5
28. Koursk - - -	1,612,200	2,503,000	1·5
29. Kiew - - - -	1,534,200	2,353,000	1·5
30. Wolhynia - - -	1,389,800	2,110,000	1·5
31. Kalouga - - -	882,200	1,300,000	1·5
32. Nowgorod - - -	857,500	1,300,000	1·5
33. Perm - - - -	1,816,900	2,589,000	1·4
34. Riazan - - - -	1,294,700	1,800,000	1·4
35. Jaroslaw - - -	881,800	1,200,000	1·4
36. Tauride - - -	550,800	750,000	1·4
37. Olonetz - - -	261,600	370,000	1·4
38. Poltawa - - -	1,558,000	2,000,000	1·3
39. Twer - - - -	1,324,600	1,670,000	1·3
40. Ekathérinoslaw -	906,600	1,200,000	1·3
41. Kingdom of Poland -	4,372,000	5,445,000	1·2
42. Moscow - - -	1,132,500	1,300,000	1·2
43. Courland - - -	465,800	496,000	1·1
44. Wologda - - -	825,300	800,000	1
45. St. Petersburg - -	553,000	550,000	1
46. Astrakhan - - -	155,300	150,000	1
47. Esthonia - - -	273,600	240,000	0·9
48. Stavropol - - -	960,800	750,000	0·8
49. Livonia - - -	740,200	415,000	0·6
50. Grand Duchy of Finland -	1,472,500	520,000	0·4
51. Archangel - - -	224,800	80,000	0·4

According to this table, there are eight provinces, namely, the country of the Don Cossacks and the governments of Minsk, Tschernigow, Witebsk, Simbirsk, Kowno, Mohilew, and Pskow, in which there are upwards of 2 dessiatines of arable land for each rural inhabitant; twenty-four governments in which the proportion varies between $1\frac{1}{2}$ and 2 dessiatines; fourteen governments in which it runs from 1 to $1\frac{2}{3}$ per head; and only five provinces, namely, the Grand Duchy of Finland, and the governments of Esthonia, Stavropol, Livonia, and Archangel, where the average is below 1 dessiatine. It is in this last government and in the Grand Duchy of Finland, that the rural population is most poorly provided with arable lands; for there is not so much as ½ dessiatine for each inhabitant.

Still, we perceive that, throughout the greater part of Russia, the arable lands are pretty equally distributed over the rural population. Such is not the case with regard to the distribution of the meadows, as will appear from the following table.

Provinces and Governments arranged according to the extent of their Meadow Land in proportion to the rural Population.	Rural Population.	Meadow Land.	Number of Dessiatines per Inhabitant.
		Dessiatines.	
1. Country of the Don Cossacks - - -	778,000	9,540,000	12·2
2. Astrakhan - - -	155,300	800,000	5·1
3. Stavropol - - -	960,800	4,000,000	4·1
4. Saratow - - -	1,679,000	6,513,000	3·9
5. Tauride - ·· -	550,800	1,600,000	2·9
6. Kherson - - -	701,300	2,000,000	2·8
7. Orenburg - - -	2,071,700	4,452,000	2·1
8. Minsk - - -	910,400	1,546,000	1·7
9. Ekathérinoslaw - -	906,600	1,400,000	1·6
10. Bessarabia - - -	755,400	1,200,000	1·6
11. Woronèje - - -	1,585,550	2,400,000	1·5
12. Simbirsk - - -	1,097,200	1,600,000	1·4
13. Kharkow - - -	1,048,600	1,350,000	1·3
14. Pskow - - - -	630,800	800,000	1·3
15. Perm - - - -	1,816,900	1,993,000	1·1
16. Tambow - - -	1,573,900	1,650,000	1
17. Twer - - - -	1,324,600	1,290,000	1
18. Kowno - - - -	887,300	750,000	0·9
19. Esthonia - - -	273,600	260,000	0·9
20. Poltawa - - -	1,558,000	1,215,000	0·8
21. Grand Duchy of Finland -	1,472,500	1,071,000	0·7
22. Livonia - - -	740,200	555,000	0·7
23. Archangel - - -	224,800	157,000	0·7
24. Wolhynia - - -	1,389,800	777,000	0·6
25. Nowgorod - - -	857,500	470,000	0·6
26. Grodno - - -	786,700	520,000	0·6
27. Courland - - -	465,800	314,000	0·6
28. Podolia - - -	1,510,600	773,000	0·5
29. Tschernigow - - -	1,291,700	630,000	0·5
30. Jaroslaw - - -	881,800	492,000	0·5
31. Wologda - - -	825,300	450,000	0·5
32. Koursk - - -	1,612,200	613,000	0·4
33. Kazan - - -	1,311,000	500,000	0·4
34. Penza - - - -	990,000	450,000	0·4
35. Mohilew - - -	783,100	300,000	0·4
36. Wilna - - - -	743,500	335,000	0·4
37. St. Petersburg - -	553,000	200,000	0·4
38. Olonetz - - -	261,600	110,000	0·4
39. Kingdom of Poland -	4,372,000	1,500,000	0·3
40. Wiatka - - -	1,885,100	500,000	0·3
41. Kiew - - - -	1,534,200	445,000	0·3

Provinces and Governments arranged according to the extent of their Meadow Land in proportion to the rural Population.	Rural Population.	Meadow Land.	Number of Dessiatines per Inhabitant.
		Dessiatines.	
42. Orel - - - -	1,276,400	400,000	0·3
43. Nijni-Nowgorod - -	1,100,700	280,000	0·3
44. Wladimir - - -	1,100,000	280,000	0·3
45. Smolensk - - -	1,029,500	280,000	0·3
46. Kostroma - - -	1,005,800	340,000	0·3
47. Riazan - - -	1,294,700	300,000	0·2
48. Moscow - - -	1,132,500	260,000	0·2
49. Toula - - - -	1,023,800	220,000	0·2
50. Kalouga - - -	882,200	193,000	0·2
51. Witebsk - - -	658,900	120,000	0·2

We perceive from this table, that the country of the Don Cossacks possesses, relatively to its rural population, a superabundance of meadow land which we do not find in any other country,—more than 12 dessiatines per head. Next to this province, it is the governments of Astrakhan and Stavropol which are most liberally supplied. Their average is from 4 to 5 dessiatines for each inhabitant. We may reckon in the same category of abundant supply, the governments of Saratow, Tauride, Kherson, and Orenburg, which average upwards of 2 dessiatines for each rural inhabitant. In ten governments, the average per head varies from 1 to 2 dessiatines, which may still be considered as a very satisfactory proportion. In fourteen governments, which we may regard as indifferently provided, the average per inhabitant runs from $\frac{1}{2}$ to $\frac{9}{10}$ of a dessiatine ; and there are twenty governments in which the average is below $\frac{1}{2}$ dessiatine. Of these twenty, there are thirteen in which the average is below $\frac{1}{3}$ of a dessiatine. The poorest governments in this respect are those of Riazan, Moscow, Toula, Kalouga, and Witebsk, where there is only $\frac{1}{5}$ of a dessiatine for each rural inhabitant.

All these inequalities in the distribution of the different sorts of productive soil necessarily exercise a decisive influence on the occupations of the agricultural class, and in general on the whole system of our rural economy. They are, however, modified in their effects by the *quality* of the land. Thus, for example, in the table, p. 87., the government of Pskow occupies the ninth place in regard to its relative extent of arable land; whilst, in consequence of the bad quality of its soil, it is one of the poorest in regard to its productive forces. On the other hand, the governments of Podolia, Saratow, and Wolhynia, which are the most fertile portions of the empire, occupy a rank far inferior to many others in regard to their extent of cultivated land. We shall have occasion to return to this subject in the course of the following chapters : meantime, we subjoin a table of the distribution of the forests as compared with the population of the different governments, which concludes the present branch of our subject.

Table of the Extent of the Forests, as compared with the Population.

Provinces and Governments arranged according to the extent of their Forest Lands in proportion to the Population.	Population.*	Forest Land.	Number of Dessiatines per . Inhabitant.
		Dessiatines.	
1. Archangel - -	252,000	29,500,000	117
2. Wologda - -	866,000	32,000,000	37
3. Olonetz - -	278,500	9,700,000	35
4. Perm - -	1,879,000	19,927,000	10·6
5. Nowgorod -	890,000	7,000,000	7·9
6. Grand Duchy of Finland - -	1,554,000	7,460,000	4·8
7. Kostroma - -	1,047,000	5,000,000	4·8
8. Wiatka - -	1,929,000	9,000,000	4·7
9. Orenburg - -	2,130,000	10,000,000	4·7
10. Minsk - -	980,000	3,300,000	3·4
11. Livonia - -	836,000	1,928,000	2·3
12. St. Petersburg -	1,145,000	2,400,000	2·1
13. Pskow - -	673,000	1,400,000	2·1
14. Smolensk - -	1,084,000	2,200,000	2
15. Wilna - -	819,000	1,600,000	2
16. Witebsk - -	733,000	1,460,000	2
17. Kazan - -	1,390,000	2,627,000	1·9
18. Mohilew - -	835,000	1,600,000	1·9
19. Courland ·, -	530,000	975,000	1·8
20. Simbirsk - -	1,203,000	2,000,000	1·7
21. Nijni-Nowgorod -	1,175,000	2,000,000	1·7
22. Wolhynia - -	1,395,000	2,400,000	1·6
23. Twer - -	1,411,000	2,300,000	1·6
24. Wladimir - -	1,171,000	1,700,000	1·5
25. Esthonia - -	302,000	460,000	1·5
26. Penza - -	1,066,000	1,100,000	1
27. Tambow - -	1,685,000	1,450,000	0·9
28. Grodno - -	870,000	760,000	0·9
29. Orel - - -	1,408,000	1,100,000	0·8
30. Jaroslaw - -	961,000	805,000	0·8
31. Kingdom of Poland	4,852,000	3,206,000	0·7
32. Moscow - -	1,526,000	1,100,000	0·7
33. Riazan - -	1,372,000	1,000,000	0·7
34. Saratow - -	1,861,000	1,200,000	0·6
35. Kiew - - -	1,701,000	950,000	0·6
36. Tschernigow -	1,392,000	789,000	0·6
37. Kowno - -	935,000	600,000	0·6
38. Astrakhan - -	207,000	120,000	0·6
Carried forward	46,343,500	174,117,000	

* In this table we have taken the entire population without deducting the inhabitants of the towns.

Provinces and Governments arranged according to the extent of their Forest Lands in proportion to the Population.	Population.	Forest Lands.	Number of Dessiatines per Inhabitant.
		Dessiatines.	
Brought forward	46,343,500	174,117,000	
39. Kalouga - -	976,000	454,000	0·5
40. Country of the Don Cossacks - -	798,000	420,000	0·5
41. Kharkow - -	1,184,000	500,000	0·4
42. Toula - -	1,115,000	440,000	0·4
43. Tauride - -	665,000	244,000	0·4
44. Koursk - -	1,728,000	479,000	0·3
45. Woronèje - -	1,669,000	500,000	0·3
46. Podolia - -	1,596,000	470,000	0·3
47. Bessarabia - -	902,000	255,000	0·3
48. Poltawa - -	1,665,000	252,000	0 2
49. Stavropol - -	1,004,000	113,000	0·1
50. Ekathérinoslaw -	994,000	102,000	0·1
51. Kherson - -	919,000	120,000	0·1
Total -	61,558,500	178,466,000	2·9

Taking the general average of the relative extent of the forests to the population, which is at the rate of nearly 3 dessiatines per inhabitant, Russia would be the best wooded country in the world, if the forest land were less unequally distributed. In Austria, one of the countries in which forests are most abundant, the latter occupy an extent of 18,667,000 dessiatines, which, on a population of about 38,000,000, is at the rate of only $\frac{1}{2}$ dessiatine per inhabitant. They occupy in Prussia 5,545,400 dessiatines, which, on a population of about 17,000,000, is at the rate of 0·33 dessiatines per inhabitant; and in France they occupy 8,062,775 dessiatines on a population of 35,782,000 inhabitants, or at the rate of 0·23 dessiatines per inhabitant; so that the proportion in which our population, taken as a whole, is provided with forests, is

to that of France, as 126 to 10
to that of Prussia, „ 88 „ 10]
to that of Austria, „ 58 „ 10

But the preceding table shows us that the proportion falling to the different provinces and governments presents, in reference to the population, much more striking contrasts than the distribution of the cultivated and meadow land: for there are four governments, namely, Perm, Olonetz, Wologda, and Archangel, where the average is from upwards of 10 to as high as 117 dessiatines per inhabitant; and there are twenty-five governments in which the inhabitant's average share falls short of 1 dessiatine. In the number of the latter there are three, namely, Stavropol,

Ekathérinoslaw, and Kherson, in which the average, per inhabitant, is no more than $\frac{1}{10}$ of a dessiatine. The difference between these three governments and that of Archangel is as 1 to 1,170; but even setting aside these two extremes, as resulting from thoroughly exceptional situations, the difference between the government of Wologda and those of Koursk, Woronèje, Podolia, and Bessarabia, is still as 123 to 1. In Austria, where, in consequence of the diversities of the countries of which that monarchy is composed, there are also very great inequalities in regard to the relative extent of the forests, the difference between Transylvania, which is the most largely timbered as compared with its population, and Venice, which is in this respect the least, is only in the proportion of 10 to 1: in Transylvania the average is 1, in the province of Venice $\frac{1}{10}$ dessiatine of forest for each inhabitant.   However, on taking our least richly wooded provinces each apart and by itself, and comparing them with the totality of any other country, we will find that there are only eleven, namely, Kharkow, Toula, Tauride, Koursk, Woronèje, Podolia, Bessarabia, Poltawa, Stavropol, Ekathérinoslaw, and Kherson, in which the average per inhabitant is below that of Austria; and it is only in the four last governments that it descends below that of France. We may consider as very richly wooded all those countries in which we find 1 dessiatine of forest for each inhabitant; and half this proportion is more than amply sufficient for the wants of the inhabitants wherever the forests are properly economised.   Anything beyond the proportion of 1 dessiatine *per* inhabitant may be considered as a superabundance of forest.

According to this rule, there would be in Russia twenty-five governments superabundantly furnished with forests; of which number there are ten, namely, Archangel, Wologda, Olonetz, Perm, Nowgorod, Kostroma, Wiatka, Orenburg, Minsk, and the Grand Duchy of Finland, reckoning more than 3 dessiatines to each inhabitant; thirteen where the extent of forest, exceeding $\frac{1}{2}$ dessiatine per inhabitant, would in other countries be considered sufficient for the ordinary wants of the population; and eleven which may be considered as greatly deficient in timber, not having so much as $\frac{1}{2}$ dessiatine per inhabitant. But it must be borne in mind, that the sufficiency or insufficiency of the forest land depends, *first*, upon the manner in which the population and the forests are distributed over the soil; *secondly*, on the forest economy and management; *thirdly*, on the greater or less facilities of communication.   In an empire so vast as Russia, it may frequently happen that a given district of a province possessing very extensive forests is in absolute want of timber, whilst another district of the same government possesses much more than it requires. Again, in a country where the woods are well economised, a relative extent of forests of less than $\frac{1}{2}$ dessiatine per inhabitant may suffice for the wants of the population. Thus Austria feels no want, although the whole extent of her forest soil does not average $\frac{1}{2}$ dessiatine per inhabitant: and in France the average is not even $\frac{1}{4}$ dessiatine per inhabitant.

CHAP. V.

PRODUCTS OF THE SOIL AND THEIR GROSS VALUE.

A. Products of the Vegetable Kingdom. — *Cereals.* — Cereal Harvest in Russia, France, Austria, and Prussia. — Governments classified according to their relative Produce. — Gross Value of Harvest. — Potatoes. — Beet Root. — The Vine. — Garden Produce. — Meadows. — Flax. — Hemp. — Tobacco. — Tinctorial and Medicinal Plants. — Forests. — Their great Extent and unequal Distribution. — Dearth of Timber in some Districts. — Destruction of Forests. — Building Timber. — Its Exportation. — Future Prospects. — Estimate of gross Produce of Forests. — General Estimates of Products of Soil pertaining to Vegetable Kingdom.

B. Products of the Animal Kingdom. — *Cattle.* — Cattle-rearing general, but badly managed. — Frequency of Murrain. — Number of Head in European Russia. — Number relative to Population in Russia, France, Austria, and Prussia. — Gross Value arising from rearing of Cattle. — Calculations on which Estimate based. — *Horses.* — Various Breeds and their Qualities. — Negligence in the Mode of rearing. — Provinces which produce the best Breeds and largest Numbers. — Number of Horses in European Russia. — Comparisons with France, Austria, and Prussia. — *Sheep.* — Local Circumstances favourable to Sheep-farming. — Breeds. — Number of Sheep. — Comparisons with France, Austria, and Prussia. — Estimate of Produce. — Swine. — Goats. — Camels. — Rein-deer. — Tables of the Number of Domestic Animals. — Observations. — Poultry. — Bees. — Silk-worms. — Products of the Chase. — Fisheries. — General Estimate of Agricultural Products pertaining to the Animal Kingdom. — Recapitulatory Estimate of Agricultural Products in general. — Comparisons with France and Austria.

C. Products of the Mineral Kingdom. — Gold. — Richness of Russian Gold Mines. — Quantity extracted since 1819. — Gross Value. — Comparison with Mines of Central America. — Probable Consequences of Discovery of Gold in California. — Silver. — Platina. — Iron. — Copper. — Lead. — Zinc. — Coal. — Salt. — General Estimate of Products of Mineral Kingdom. — Comparisons with France, Austria, and Prussia. — Total gross Value of the Products of the Soil.

A.

PRODUCTS OF THE VEGETABLE KINGDOM.

We may have already observed, from the classification of the soil in regard to climate and culture, that the agricultural productions of European Russia and of the Trans-Caucasian provinces are numerous and varied.

Our products the most important for their abundance, are :

In the northern provinces, rye, barley, oats, and flax.

In the central provinces and in the kingdom of Poland, wheat, and all the other cereals, vegetables, hemp, and flax.

In the southern provinces, wheat, wine, silk, oleaginous grains, tobacco, and several tinctorial and medicinal plants.

Rye is cultivated with success to the 67th degree of north latitude, wheat to the 60th. The fruits of the garden are found in abundance in the southern and central provinces, in the west of the empire, and in the kingdom of Poland. In this branch of culture there is much room for improvement,— a remark which is indeed equally applicable to our agriculture in every one of its departments.

I. *Cereals.*

The reports of the Ministry of the Interior from 1834 to 1840 assign to Russia, exclusive of Poland and the Grand Duchy of Finland, a mean annual production of 179 millions of tchetwerts, (= 129 million quarters,) but it is added that the data which have served as the basis of this calculation are not exempt from error; and there can be no doubt that the above figure is greatly below the actual average.

Statistical information of this sort is, in almost every country, more or less defective and incorrect, and this incorrectness is almost always on the side of *too little:* an agriculturist who deviates from the truth in his declaration to the local authorities has no interest in magnifying the amount of his harvests, but he may have more than one motive for diminishing it. This defect, inherent in all agricultural statistics, is still more prominent with us than elsewhere, for, setting other circumstances aside, the immensity of the surface over which culture is diffused opposes, of itself, great difficulties to inquiry.

We find in the *Journal du Ministère des Domaines,* (*année* 1842, 3e *livraison,*) a very interesting article upon the corn trade of Russia, which bears upon this question. The writer, M. Protopopoff, after giving the above cipher of the average harvest, as taken from the Reports of the Ministry of the Interior, endeavours to rectify it by means of an approximative calculation based on the numbers of the agricultural population, and on the extent and fertility of the soil employed in the culture of cereals. According to this calculation, which appears to have been made with great knowledge of the subject, the mean harvest of cereals may be estimated at 250 millions of tchetwerts (= 180 millions of imperial quarters). The writer estimates the extent of cultivable land (not including Finland, or the kingdom of

Poland,) at 70 millions of dessiatines: but this figure we cannot adopt as correct unless it be meant to apply exclusively to land employed in the culture of cereals; for, according to more recent official data, which we find in the Statistics of M. Arsénieff and M. Kœppen, the arable lands in forty-six governments, that is to say, without reckoning Ekathérinoslaw, Stavropol, Bessarabia, Tauride, and the country of the Don Cossacks, occupy an extent of 72,386,755 dessiatines. The four last governments, with the lands of the Uralian Cossacks, must contain, according to an approximative calculation, 4,130,000 dessiatines, which gives a total of 76,516,755 dessiatines; and as the official estimates are founded in great part upon old surveys, we will probably not be far wide of the reality in estimating the whole arable lands of European Russia, exclusive of Finland and the kingdom of Poland, at upwards of 80 millions of dessiatines. Deducting a tenth for the culture of potatoes, flax, hemp, oleaginous grains, wine, and other products, there would remain for the land occupied solely in the culture of cereals, about 70 millions of dessiatines. Admitting for mean harvest, according to the writer's calculation, 250 millions of tchetwerts, this would be at the rate of 3·47 tchetwerts per dessiatine, or, deducting about a fourth of the arable land for fallow, it would allow a production of 4·63 tchetwerts per dessiatine of sown land; and, as according to the usual calculation, one tchetwert per dessiatine is required for seed, this would present an average of about four and a half returns.

M. Storch, in his recent interesting work upon the condition of the peasants in Russia, gives tables of the seed and harvests during the years 1840 to 1847, which exhibit a mean annual result of 59,213,691 tchetwerts for seed, and 209,731,974 tchetwerts for crop, (Finland and the kingdom of Poland not included,) thus presenting an average of only three and a-half returns; but these tables are founded upon official data which, for reasons already given, we cannot admit as altogether exact. Adding only 10 per cent.—a small enough addition—for the errors and omissions in the official statistics, we will have a mean crop of 230,705,000 tchetwerts, (= about 166 millions of imperial quarters)—not very wide of the cipher of M. Protopopoff, which we have adopted as founded on the most probable calculations. The average harvest of the kingdom of Poland amounts, according to the official statistics of 1843 and 1846 to 15,843,000 koretz = 8,420,000 tchetwerts; but it must be much larger in reality: that of Finland may be estimated at 1,500,000 tchetwerts at least, which does not allow quite 3 tchetwerts per dessiatine of arable land. Adding these two quantities to the cipher of 250 millions resulting from the calculations of M. Protopopoff, we may estimate the total quantity of cereals reaped throughout the possessions of European Russia at about 260 millions of tchetwerts, (= about 187 millions of imperial quarters). This figure is also much more in harmony with the population of the empire. Deducting from these 260 millions of tchetwerts a fourth for seed, there would be a remainder of 195 millions. But reckoning only 2 tchetwerts per inhabitant for food, as well as for the preparation of *kwass*, a liquor of which there is a large consumption, this would allow for 62 millions of inhabitants a consumption of 124 millions of tchetwerts, without taking into account what is used for the feeding of cattle. The usual calculation is 3 tchetwerts of cereals per inhabitant; but this figure, although it has been confirmed to us by several agricultural writers, appears excessive. A soldier's ration, both for bread and porridge, is fixed at $3\frac{1}{4}$ tchetwerts; but we cannot adopt this proportion for the entire population, including females, children, and aged persons. To avoid, therefore, all exaggeration, and to preserve our calculations within the most moderate limits, we have considered that we may adopt the rate of 2 tchetwerts per head as the mean consumption of grain of every description.

According to this calculation, there would remain but 71 millions of tchetwerts, (= 51 million quarters,) as a reserve for years of scarcity, for the feeding of cattle, which is more numerous in Russia than in any other country, for the distillation of spirits, for the brewing of beer, and for foreign exportation, which amounted, (importation deducted,) on an average of ten years from 1838 to 1848, to 4,110,000 tchetwerts, (= 2,959,000 English quarters,) without reckoning the exportation from the kingdom of Poland.

It will probably be considered that these 71 millions are scarcely sufficient to cover all these various modes of absorption, and that consequently the cipher of our calculations is as low as it can possibly be stated. Of this the reader may be still more thoroughly convinced, if he takes into consideration the large quantity of oats consumed in feeding horses, the number of which in Russia, (without Finland and the kingdom of Poland,) amounts, according to data which will be found in the sequel, to about 17 millions of head.

In the kingdom of Poland, the average crop of oats amounted, according to the official statistics of 1843 and 1846, to 5,103,000 koretz = 3,118,000 tchetwerts. Deducting a fourth for seed, there remain 2,338,000 tchetwerts, of which throwing off 338,000 (about a sixth) for the preparation of beer and for

foreign exportation—which is a very moderate allowance—
there would remain in round numbers 2 millions of tchetwerts,
which gives for 513,000 horses (the number of that period as
appearing from official data,) nearly 4 tchetwerts per head. In
Austria the average annual crop of oats during the years 1841
to 1844 amounted, according to official statistics, to 81,261,000
metzen = 25,678,000 tchetwerts: deducting a fourth for seed,
there remains for home consumption 19,259,000 tchetwerts.*
As the number of horses at that period was officially estimated
at 3 millions, this allows nearly $6\frac{1}{4}$ tchetwerts per horse. But
admitting that with us the horses of the peasants receive less
corn, and that the practice of leaving them to pasture is more
frequent, especially in the southern provinces, we could scarcely
reduce our estimate lower than to the rate of 3 tchetwerts per
head, which, for 17 millions of horses would amount to 51 millions of tchetwerts.† According to this calculation, there would
remain of the whole harvest of cereals, as well for exportation,
—which, without reckoning the exportation from the kingdom of
Poland, amounts at an average to more than 4 millions of tchetwerts—as for the reserve granaries, and for the manufacture
of beer and spirits, 20 millions of tchetwerts, (= 14,400,000
quarters)—a figure which is certainly below rather than above
the reality.

It follows from this analysis of the consumption of our cereals,
that, even reckoning only $1\frac{1}{2}$ tchetwerts per inhabitant for the
aliment of the people properly so called, the figure of 260 millions of tchetwerts, at which we have stated the mean amount
of our harvests, cannot be considered as excessive. It is likewise
to be observed that in this figure we have not comprehended
peas and other dry legumes.

The foregoing calculation coincides in its results pretty
nearly with the following estimate made by M. Protopopoff.

---

* The exportation of this grain is balanced by the importation.

† In the Austrian Empire, and especially in Hungary, there are also a number
of horses which roam over the steppes, and yet the consumption of oats amounted
at an average to nearly $6\frac{1}{2}$ tchetwerts per horse. If we were to deduct from the
total number of horses in Russia about 3 million head, which pasture in the
steppes and consume no oats, there would still be required for the consumption of
the remaining 14 millions, 49,000,000 tchetwerts at the rate of only $3\frac{1}{2}$ tchetwerts
per horse.

Tchetwerts.

Mean harvest of European Russia, exclusive of Finland and the kingdom of Poland - - -	250,000,000
Deduct for seed one fourth, or in round numbers -	60,000,000
Remainder -	190,000,000
Consumption at the rate of 3 tchetwerts per head, food of horses and cattle included, for 55 millions of inhabitants - - - - -	165,000,000
Remain for distillation *, reserve granaries, exportation, and all other purposes - - - -	25,000,000

The whole harvest of cereals in the empire of Austria yielded at an average of the years 1841, 1842, 1843, and 1844, according to the official statistics, 284½ millions of metzen (dry legumes included) = 89,900,000 tchetwerts, from 36,866,762 joch = 19,425,000 dessiatines of arable land, which gives 4·56 tchetwerts per dessiatine, or 1·9 tchetwerts per dessiatine more than the average harvest of Russia according to the calculation we have adopted. The statistical tables of Austria do not give us the extent of land actually sown, but we may probably deduct, without much risk of error, three-tenths of the whole extent of arable land for fallows and other sorts of culture together. There would thus remain for sown corn land 13,597,500 dessiatines, so that the above harvest of 89,900,000 tchetwerts would be at the rate of 6·6 tchetwerts per dessiatine, that is to say, 2 tchetwerts per dessiatine, or 43 per cent. above the average rate of harvest in Russia.

In France the mean annual harvest of six years, from 1830 to 1835, amounted to 196,610,000 hectolitres = 101,056,000 tchetwerts from about 21½ millions of hectares = 19,700,000 dessiatines of cultivable land, which is at the rate of 5·1 tchetwerts per dessiatine. In the official agricultural statistics for 1840 the total harvest, including maize and dry legumes, is put down at 193,757,000 hectolitres = 99,591,000 tchetwerts. The sown land having occupied at the same period an extent of 14,779,000 hectares = 13,534,000 dessiatines, we obtain a mean crop of 7·36 tchetwerts per dessiatine, or 59 per cent. more than the average harvest of Russia. This indicates that our calculations of the latter are not exaggerated.

According to the article on the Russian corn-trade already referred to, Great Britain produces 85 millions of tchetwerts from 6,928,333 dessiatines (= 61,200,000 quarters from 18,640,000 English acres), or at the rate of 12⅐ tchetwerts per dessiatine

---

* M. Protopopoff reckons for distillation 10 million tchetwerts: other statists, as M. Kœppen, reduce the quantity of grain employed for this purpose to 5 millions.

(= 26 bushels per acre), but this cipher for an average harvest appears excessive.

In Prussia, according to the estimate of Professor Dieterici, the wheat and rye harvests, taken together, would amount to from 75 to 80 millions of scheffels. Taking this estimate as our basis we may approximately calculate the whole harvest in the following manner : —

In Austria, the wheat, rye, and maize taken together form 49 per cent. of the total harvest; the barley and oats form 46 per cent., and the other grain and legumes 5 per cent. Assuming the same proportions for Prussia, we would obtain for the total harvest of cereals in that 'country about 150 millions of scheffels = 42,300,000 tchetwerts, which gives for 47,296,000 morgen = 11,055,000 dessiatines of land in culture and in fallow 3·82 tchetwerts per dessiatine, or, deducting a third for other cultures and fallows, 5·74 tchetwerts per dessiatine of sown land.* According to these calculations, the production of cereals in Russia and other countries would present the following proportions : —

			Absolute Cipher of Production.
Russia -	-	-	260,000,000 tchetwerts.
France -	-	-	101,000,000 „
Austria -	-	-	89,900,000 „
Prussia -	-	-	42,300,000 „

Thus Russia's production of cereals is to that of France nearly as 5 to 2, to that of Austria as 20 to 7, and to that of Prussia as 6 to 1.

Returns per Dessiatine of cultivable Land, including Fallows.

| France | - | - | 5·13 tchetwerts. | Prussia | - | - | 3·82 tchetwerts. |
| Austria | - | - | 4·56   „ | Russia | - | - | 3·47   „ |

Thus, the relative cipher of the harvest in Russia is

to that of Prussia, as 10 to 11
to that of Austria, as 10 to 13
to that of France, as 10 to 14

Returns per Dessiatine of sown Land.

| France - | - | 7·36 tchetwerts. | Prussia | - | - | 5·74 tchetwerts. |
| Austria - | - | 6·60   „ | Russia | - | - | 4·63   „ |

These figures give for the harvest in Russia, or the relative fertility of its soil, as compared

with that of Prussia, the proportion of 10 to 12
with that of Austria   „   10 „ 14
with that of France   „   10 „ 16

* In the absence of more complete data for the cereal harvest of Prussia, we have been obliged to have recourse to the above analogical estimate to enable us to place that country on the line of comparison: we give the above figure as merely more or less approximative.

These differences in the product of our harvests arise partly from the quality of our soil and partly from our mode of culture. In the greater part of those Russian provinces where the culture of cereals is most extensively carried on, the soil is generally of great fertility; and there are several governments which may, in this respect, be compared with the most fertile countries of Europe, where the land rarely stands in need of manure; but in regard to our modes of agricultural management we are still sadly in the rear of other countries. To this point we shall afterwards have occasion to recur.

M. Storch, in his work on the condition of the peasantry already referred to, gives the following classification of the governments of European Russia with reference to the relative quantity of grain which they produce.

Governments producing more Grain than they consume.

1. Kharkow.	14. Perm.
2. Kherson.	15. Podolia.
3. Country of the Don Cossacks.	16. Poltawa.
4. Ekathérinoslaw.	17. Riazan.
5. Kazan.	18. Saratow.
6. Kiew.	19. Simbirsk.
7. Kowno.	20. Tambow.
8. Koursk.	21. Tauride.
9. Livonia.	22. Tschernigow.
10. Nijni-Nowgorod.	23. Toula.
11. Orel.	24. Wiatka.
12. Orenburg.	25. Wolhynia.
13. Penza.	26. Woronèje.

Governments producing Grain enough for their own Consumption.

1. Bessarabia.	5. Smolensk.
2. Esthonia.	6. Stavropol.
3. Grodno.	7. Wologda.
4. Courland.	

Governments consuming more Grain than they produce.

1. Archangel.	9. Nowgorod.
2. Astrakhan.	10. Olonetz.
3. Jaroslaw.	11. Pskow.
4. Kalouga.	12. St. Petersburg.
5. Kostroma.	13. Twer.
6. Minsk.	14. Wilna.
7. Mohilew.	15. Witebsk.
8. Moscow.	16. Wladimir.

In regard to the fertility of the soil, the first place is due, as we have already had occasion to remark, to the governments of Saratow, Podolia, Poltawa, Tambow, Bessarabia, Woronèje, Kharkow, Penza, Koursk, and Simbirsk, and to a portion of those of Orel, Toula, Orenburg, Kherson, Ekathérinoslaw, Tauride, Stavropol, Kiew, Wolhynia, and the country of the

Don Cossacks. In these different provinces the harvest returns, on an average, according to M. Protopopoff, from 4 to 8 times, and often from 10 to 15 times, the seed; in the other parts of Russia the returns vary from 2 to 4.   M. Protopopoff considers the average return for the whole empire to be about 4, which is pretty nearly the average which we have ourselves adopted.

The agricultural statistics of the crown domains give the following figures with respect to the return of the harvests in 1847 in forty-seven governments : —

Archangel -	-	4·25	Orenburg -	-	2·85
Astrakhan -	-	2	Penza	-	4·1
Bessarabia -	-	3·8	Perm	-	4·2
Courland -	-	4·45	Podolia	-	3·5
Ekathérinoslaw	-	2·65	Poltawa	-	3·1
Esthonia -	-	3·9	Pskow	-	2·9
Grodno	-	3·7	Riazan	-	4
Jaroslaw	-	1·7	Saratow	-	3·55
Kalouga	-	2·3	Smolensk -	-	2·3
Kazan	-	2·9	St. Petersburg	-	3·85
Kharkow	-	3·2	Stavropol -	-	7·1
Kherson	-	2·3	Tambow	-	2·9
Kiew	-	3·65	Tauride	-	3·75
Kostroma	-	2·7	Toula	-	3·3
Koursk	-	3	Tschernigow	-	3·9
Kowno	-	2·97	Twer	-	2·05
Livonia	-	3·9	Wiatka	-	3·35
Minsk	-	2·85	Wilna	-	3·15
Mohilew	-	2·35	Witebsk	-	2·2
Moscow	-	2·75	Wladimir -	-	2·4
Nijni-Nowgorod	-	3·1	Wolhynia -	-	2·5
Nowgorod	-	2·55	Wologda -	-	3·55
Olonetz	-	4·05	Woronèje -	-	1·9
Orel	-	3·5			

These figures are for most part considerably lower than those which we have adopted; but it is generally considered that official data of this sort are often incomplete, and almost always below the mark. M. Protopopoff, moreover, proves this to be the case by numerous examples; and we shall confine ourselves here to pointing out a few contrasts, which are in themselves sufficient to cast doubts upon their accuracy. For example, in the government of Woronèje, which is one of the most fertile, the harvest is made to yield less than two returns, whilst that of Pskow, which is one of the poorest and most barren, gives nearly three, and that of Witebsk, which is similar to Pskow, gives upwards of two. In the government of Podolia, which is also one of the most fertile, the returns are but $3\frac{1}{2}$, whilst they are 3·85 in the government of St. Petersburg.

Podolia and a part of the kingdom of Poland furnish the finest wheat. Rye is, of all the cereals, that of which the culture is most extensively diffused throughout almost every one of the

Russian governments.   Barley and oats are also cultivated in abundance.   The culture of buck-wheat is widely diffused, and furnishes a wholesome and substantial article of food for the common people ; that of maize begins to extend considerably in the southern provinces of the empire ; rice acclimatises in the Caucasian provinces, where the soil is favourable ; but its cultivation will never acquire importance without a good system of irrigation.

Assuming, according to our calculation, 260 millions of tchetwerts as the mean annual crop of cereals throughout all the European possessions of Russia, and estimating them to be worth 3 roubles 50 kopecks per tchetwert, (= 15s. 4d. per imperial quarter) the mean value of an ordinary harvest would amount to 910 millions of silver roubles, (= 144 millions sterling).

Before fixing our ideas with regard to the price which we ought to adopt for estimating the value of our cereal harvests, we consulted the market lists published in the *Journal du Ministère de l'Intérieur*, and M. Storch's work on the condition of the Russian peasantry.   After comparing the prices of six years, from 1842 to 1847, M. Storch gives the *maximum* and *minimum* prices of rye and oats, from whence he draws the following averages : —

	Rye, per Tchetwert. *Sil. Roub.* *Kop.*		Oats, per Tchetwert. *Sil. Roub.* *Kop.*	
In 1842 -	- 4	99	2	62
In 1843 -	- 4	35	2	10
In 1844 -	- 4	1	2	38
In 1845 -	- 5	39	3	19
In 1846 -	- 5	31	3	29
In 1847 -	- 5	99	4	21
Total -	30	40	17	79
Average of six years -	5		2	96

Average of the two sorts, 3 roubles 98 kopecks per tchetwert.

We have considered that it would be fairer to take, not the mean betwixt the highest and lowest prices, but the mean which would result from the prices in the whole governments of European Russia.   We subjoin first, by way of information, the highest and lowest prices taken from the lists of the Ministry of the Interior for the years 1846, 1847, 1848, and 1849, and referring to four species of grain, namely, rye, wheat, the grit of the buck-wheat, and oats.   The grit is a very important alimentary product for Russia, and enters largely into the total consumption of the people.

Rye.

Governments.	Maximum Price per Tchetwert. Roub.	Kop.	Governments.	Minimum Price per Tchetwert. Roub.	Kop.
1846 Livonia -	7	54	Orenburg -	1	29
1847 Courland -	11	7	Ditto - -	1	16
1848 Livonia -	6	90	Ditto - -	1	7
1849 St. Petersburg	6	49	Koursk and Penza	1	80
Average	8		Average	1	44

Wheat.

1846 Wilna and Grodno	11	12	Saratow - -	2	18
1847 Courland - -	13	82	Orenburg -	2	20
1848 Ditto - -	10	42	Ditto - -	2	40
1849 Wilna - -	11		Ditto - -	3	
Average	11	59		2	44½

Grits.

1846 Wologda - -	11	81	Koursk - -	2	16
1847 Livonia - -	12	12	Orenburg -	2	20
1848 Wologda - -	12	60	Koursk - -	2	6
1849 Livonia - -	11	87	Ditto - -	2	40
Average	12	10	Average	2	20½

Oats.

1846 Livonia - -	5	10	Orenburg -		82
1847 Courland - -	5	70	Ditto - -		84
1848 Ekathérinoslaw -	4	80	Perm - -		79
1849 Ditto - -	4	80	Penza - -		85
Average	5	10	Average		82½

In order to establish as fair an average as possible, and especially to avoid anything like an over-estimate, we have eliminated the highest prices, which depend upon local or accidental circumstances, and especially upon the situation of the maritime governments, which from their export trade are more susceptible of a rise in prices. Accordingly, we have not retained in the scale of market prices for *rye* any prices exceeding 6 silver roubles per tchetwert, nor for *wheat* or *grits* any exceeding 9 roubles, nor for *oats* any exceeding 4 roubles; we have at same time retained all the minimum prices. In this manner we have obtained, on a calculation of the prices of all the governments, an average on the four years from 1846 to 1849 of 3 roubles 33½ kopecks for rye, of 5 roubles 13½ kopecks for wheat, of 5 roubles 28 kopecks for grits, and of 2 roubles 13 kopecks for oats. By adding these four prices we obtain as a general average for grain of every description 3 roubles 97 kopecks per tchetwert; and, if we cast out the grits, we obtain the average price of 3 roubles 53½ kopecks, that is 20 kopecks more than the medium price of rye, the cereal which predominates in the total production. The actual medium price, that is to say, the medium price obtained, without cutting off the highest prices, would be

Rye	-	-	3 roubles	61	kopecks
Wheat	-	-	5 „	67	„
Grits	-	-	5 „	83	„
Oats	-	-	2 „	35	„

which gives a general average price of 4 roubles 35 kopecks per tchetwert.

It may be objected to this calculation that it takes no account of the proportions which exist, in the production of cereals, amongst the different governments; and that the largest quantities being furnished precisely by those countries in which (from the abundance of the harvests) the prices are lowest, this circumstance must produce an influence upon the total value and on the medium price. This objection we have not overlooked; and for this very reason it is, that we have first cut off the highest prices, and then reduced by 47 kopecks, or 12 per cent., the mean result of the whole remaining market quotations; but to do away with all doubts in our own mind upon the subject we have tested our estimate by the following calculations:—

We took the prices of the twenty-five governments which produce more grain than they consume themselves, and from which consequently are drawn the supplies for home and foreign exportation.* These are precisely the countries where local prices are lowest. Now, taking into account the whole quotations of the markets of these governments, we obtain, as average of the four years, the following prices:—

Rye	-	-	2 roubles	65	kopecks
Wheat	-	-	4 „	55	„
Grits	-	-	4 „	92	„
Oats	-	-	1 „	88	„
		together	14 „	0	

giving a general average of 3 roubles 50 kopecks, which is the average we have adopted. Of these twenty-five governments, there are only eight, namely, Kiew, Koursk, Orenburg, Penza, Poltawa, Saratow, Simbirsk, and Woronèje, in which the average is under 3 roubles: on the other hand, there are four, namely, Kherson, Kowno, Livonia, and Tauride, where it exceeds 4 roubles: in the other thirteen governments it varies between 3 and 4 roubles: for example, in the government of Podolia, one of the most fertile, it is 3 roubles 52 kopecks; in that of Perm, it is 3 roubles 55 kopecks; and in that of Riazan, it is 3 roubles 53 kopecks.

* The country of the Don Cossacks is not included in this calculation, the prices of that country not being quoted in the official lists.

In these calculations, oats, it will be perceived, are taken in the proportion of a fourth of the whole; and as it is probable that the actual quantity raised of this grain bears à higher proportion, we have made the following farther calculation. The prices of rye, wheat, and grits, in the twenty-five governments where they are lowest, average 4 roubles 4 kopecks per tchetwert, — the average price of oats being only 1 rouble 88 kopecks. Now suppose that one-third of the entire crop of cereals is composed of oats: according to this proportion—the highest that could reasonably be adopted—we would have to take

Once the average price of oats, or - -	1 rouble	88	kopecks
And twice that of the other sorts of grain, or	8 „	8	„
Total -	9 „	96	„

which, divided by 3, gives an average of 3 roubles 32 kopecks, which is only 18 kopecks or 5 per cent. under the average price adopted in our estimate for all Russia,—an estimate the moderation of which we therefore consider to be justified by a sufficient number of tests.* The reader will pardon us this digression, in

* After the publication of the first edition of this volume, several economists observed to us that the average which we had drawn from the prices current was too high, because the official quotations are almost always from 15 to 20 per cent. higher than the actual market prices; at the same time they were of opinion that our estimate of the quantity of cereals reaped was too low; so that, in the general estimate of the gross value of the cereal harvest, the two errors might compensate each other.

Upon combining all the data which we have been able to procure upon this subject, and comparing them with previous estimates, we find that the mean harvest of all descriptions of cereals throughout the empire, exclusive of the kingdom of Poland, must be something between 250 and 300 millions of tchetwerts, and that in no case can it be brought higher than 300 millions. In order, therefore, to keep our estimate within due bounds, we have adopted the figure of 260 millions, including the kingdom of Poland.

As to the observation concerning the averages, we have not left out of view the difference that may exist between the actual prices of the market and the official quotations; and it may be observed that, by cutting off the highest prices, we have adopted an average of 85 kopecks per tchetwert lower than would result from adopting *simpliciter* the official quotations, collected for the whole empire, which is equivalent to a difference of about 20 per cent.

We find in the *Bibliothèque Russe* (livraison du mois d'Octobre, 1852), statistics of the prices of cereals throughout all the governments during the period from 1847 to 1851. Of these prices the quinquennial average is,

Rye	-	-	3 roubles 21	kopecks per tchetwert.
Wheat	-	- 5	„ 76	„ „
Grits of buck-wheat		5	„ 65	„ „
Oats	-	2	„ 15	„ „
Total		- 16	„ 77	„ „

This gives a general average of 4 roubles 19 kopecks, that is to say, 69 kopecks, or nearly 20 per cent., more than the average which we have adopted in our estimate.

consideration of the importance of the article it refers to, in an estimate of the gross products of our agriculture. When we lay down a statistical figure we consider ourselves bound to justify it.

In France, the mean price resulting from a statistical valuation of the whole crop of rye, wheat, barley, oats, and maize, for a very fertile year (1838) is 11 francs 23 centimes per hectolitre = 5 roubles 46 kopecks per tchetwert, that is to say, 56 per cent. above our rate of valuation. In Prussia, the average prices of wheat, rye, barley, and oats, give a general average of 1 thaler and 9 silbergroschen per scheffel = 4 roubles 15 kopecks per tchetwert, or 18½ per cent. above our rate of valuation. In Austria, the medium price resulting from the official valuations of the harvest of 1844, for every sort of grain, maize, and dry legumes included, was 2 florins 16 kreuzers per metzen = 4 roubles 30 kopecks per tchetwert, or 23 per cent. above the rate of valuation which we have adopted.

To the value of the crop of grain, which we have estimated at 910 millions of roubles, must be added the value of the straw.

In Austria, according to the official statistics of the years 1841 and 1842, the mean crop of cereals amounting to 240,062,000 metzen = 75,860,000 tchetwerts, yielded 187,494,000 Vienna quintals = 642,167,000 poods of straw, which gives 8 poods 18 pounds Russian of straw to 1 tchetwert of grain: but reckoning only 6 poods per tchetwert, there would result for the average crop in Russia, (260 millions of tchetwerts), 1,560 millions of poods. In the estimates of the agricultural statistics of Austria, the average price of straw is set down at 45½ kreutzers per quintal = 14 kopecks per pood: but reckoning only one half of this price, or 7 kopecks per pood, we obtain for 1,560 millions of poods, 109,200,000 silver roubles, which added to the preceding sum, gives a total of 1,019,200,000 silver roubles,(= 160 millions sterling).

II. *Potatoes and Beet-root.*

The culture of the potatoe is not yet very widely diffused in Russia, although the soil is in great part very suitable. The peasant entertains considerable repugnance* to its cultivation, which, however, has for some time back been gradually extend-

---

* This repugnance, however, refers only to a portion of Russia, and especially to the southern and eastern provinces.

ing. There were harvested in 1847, according to the Report of the Ministry of Domains, 19,394,000 tchetwerts*, of which 1,337,000 belonged to the six northern governments of St. Petersburg, Nowgorod, Pskow, Olonetz, Wologda, and Archangel; 8,937,000 to nineteen central governments; 807,000 to the four eastern governments of Kostroma, Perm, Orenburg, and Wiatka; 7,947,000 to twelve western governments; and only 366,000 to the five southern governments of the Tauride, Kherson, Ekathérinoslaw, Bessarabia, and Astrakhan. The largest quantity was gathered in the government of Minsk, and amounted to 1,658,000 tchetwerts. In the kingdom of Poland there was gathered, according to the official statistics, on an average of the years 1843 and 1846, the quantity of 12,790,000 korzetz = 6,797,500 tchetwerts, which quantity, added to the preceding, brings the total crop to 26,191,500 tchetwerts. Adding, farther, the crop of Finland, and making some allowance for progress, we may admit in slump, for the whole European possessions of Russia, an actual crop of 30 millions of tchetwerts, representing, at the average rate of 50 kopecks per tchetwert, a money value of 15 millions of roubles, (= 2,375,000l. sterling).

The culture of beet-root as a sacchariferous plant has acquired considerable importance in Russia within the last few years. The *Journal des Manufactures et du Commerce* gives, in its *livraison* for November and December 1849, very detailed statistics with regard to the manufacture of beet-root sugar in 1848, the numerical results of which are embodied in the following Table, (see p. 150.):—

We have to observe, in the first place, that in the *Journal des Manufactures et du Commerce*, the extent of soil employed in beet-root cultivation is indicated only in so far as the culture is carried on by the sugar manufacturers themselves: but, besides this, there is the land employed in raising 3,843,300 poods purchased by the manufacturers from peasants and other cultivators, and 2,186,291 poods manufactured in the kingdom of Poland. If we deduct these two quantities (amounting together to 6,029,591 poods) from the total quantity of beet-root employed in the manufacture (27,141,541 poods) we have a remainder of 21,111,950 poods raised upon 35,207 dessiatines of land, being at the rate of about 600 poods per dessiatine, which would imply

* Since that period potatoe culture has not been progressive. The following are the returns for the four subsequent years according to the reports of the same Ministry.

1848	-	-	18,787,106	tchetwerts.
1849	-	-	17,814,331	„
1850	-	-	18,168,792	„
1851	-	-	16,406,896	„

an extent of about 45,200 dessiatines employed in the raising
of the 27,141,541 poods.

Governments arranged according to the Quantity of Sugar manufactured.	Number of Establishments.	Extent of Soil employed in Culture of Beet-root.	Quantity of Beet-root employed in the Manufacture of Sugar.	Quantity of Sugar produced.
		Dessiatines.	Poods.	Poods.
1. Kiew - -	72	15,615	12,712,500	382,400
2. Kingdom of Poland	30	*	2,186,291	106,460
3. Podolia - -	37	3,490	2,658,500	91,750
4. Tschernigow -	26	1,461	1,489,800	70,090
5. Kharkow - -	24	2,275	1,599,050	39,900
6. Toula - -	22	1,549	1,159,000	39,550
7. Woronèje - -	16	1,960	1,435,000	38,600
8. Wolhynia - -	14	1,150	700,000	37,300
9. Koursk - -	22	804	569,300	27,310
10. Poltawa - -	18	1,255	823,900	14,000
11. Tambow - -	9	626	409,100	10,980
12. Orel - -	13	3,620	279,000	8,330
13. Kalouga - -	7	164	263,000	6,900
14. Penza - -	7	390	270,000	6,860
15. Nijni-Nowgorod -	3	198	127,500	5,910
16. Riazan - -	4	298	173,400	5,800
17. Kherson - -	1	60	61,000	3,000
18. Mohilew ' - -	3	148	81,000	2,900
19. Smolensk - -	2	34	31,000	1,550
20. Saratow - -	1	*	50,000	1,500
21. Minsk - -	2	60	16,700	850
22. Simbirsk - -	1	25	17,500	500
23. Twer - -	1	15	21,000	400
24. Grodno - -	2	10	7,600	120
Total - -	337	35,207	27,141,541	902,960

We perceive from the table that the government of Kiew
furnishes alone nearly four-ninths of the total quantity of sugar
produced in the empire and in the kingdom of Poland. Adding
the quantities produced in that kingdom, and in the governments
of Podolia and Tschernigow, we find that of the entire 902,960
poods, these four provinces furnish 650,700, or more than two-
thirds. To obtain these 902,960 poods of sugar, there are used
27,141,541 poods of beet-root, which affords a return of $3\frac{1}{3}$ per
cent.—a return very inferior to that obtained in France and
Germany, where the average yield is reckoned to be 5 per cent.
As the manufacture is with us yearly on the increase, and as
moreover we may take it for granted, that, owing to the tax,
the quantities are not always very exactly indicated, the actual
production of sugar may be estimated at 1,200,000 poods at

* The extent of soil is not given in the *Journal des Manufactures et du Commerce.*

least, which, at the rate of yield of $3\frac{1}{3}$ per cent., supposes a production of 36 million poods of beet-root, representing, at the average price of 5 kopecks per pood, a gross value of 1,800,000 silver roubles (= 285,000*l.* sterling).

III. *Wines.*

The culture of the vine extends in Russia to the 49th degree of north latitude. In European Russia it is only in the country of the Don Cossacks, in Bessarabia, and in the governments of Stavrapol, Kherson, and Tauride, that it has attained any great extent. In 1835 it occupied in these countries 12,535 dessiatines = 13,690 hectares, of which the product amounted to 993,275 vedros = 12,609,626 litres of wine, being at the rate of 79 vedros per dessiatine, or 921 litres per hectare. In France the average production is 2000 litres per hectare. There were reckoned farther, at the same period, 268 dessiatines of vineyard in the governments of Astrakhan, Ekathérinoslaw, Kiew, and Podolia, which produced nearly 18,000 vedros. In 1835 the total culture extended to 13,303 dessiatines, which yielded 1,011,209 vedros,[*] thus exceeding the quantity of foreign wines (1,003,800 vedros,) imported during that year. Since then the culture has been considerably extended.

According to the most recent data, which we find in the Report made by the Department of Rural Economy to the Ministry of Domains, and in other statistical publications, the present total production of wine in the southern provinces of European Russia, must be little short of $7\frac{1}{2}$ millions of vedros, (= $20\frac{1}{4}$ millions of gallons, valued at 571,500*l.* sterling), namely :

	Quantity. *Vedros.*	Value. *Silver Roubles.*
1. In the government of Stavropol -	3,200,000 †	1,120,000
2. In Bessarabia - - -	3,000,000	1,500,000
3. In the Crimea - - -	850,000	500,000
4. In the country of the Don Cossacks	250,000	375,000
5. In the government of Kherson -	150,000	90,000
6. In the government of Podolia -	15,000	15,000
7. In the government of Astrakhan -	10,000	10,000
Total	7,475,000	3,610,000

From this we may perceive the enormous increase which the cultivation of the vine in Southern Russia has attained during the last fifteen years.

The Trans-Caucasian provinces produce, according to the latest information, more than 8 millions of vedros : the following

[*] See the work of M. Kœppen on the culture of the vine in Russia.
† Product of the vintage of 1846, as given in the Journal of an Economical Society, published under the title of *Mittheilungen der freien œconomischen Gesellschaft zu Sanct Petersburg* (*Lieferung* of second trimester of year 1849).

exhibits the result of official returns collected on the spot in 1850, by order of the superior authorities: —

		Quantity. Vedros.	Value. Silver Roubles.
In the government of Tiflis	-	3,101,500	2,661,000
„ Contaïs	-	4,648,000 *	1,159,000
„ Erivan	-	83,130	73,000
„ Schemakha	-	514,290	188,000
„ Derbent	-	7,500	5,000
Total		8,354,420	4,086,000†

Adding to this the 7,475,000 vedros produced by European Russia, and representing, according to an average struck from the local prices, a value of 3,610,000 roubles, we obtain a total production of 15,830,000 vedros ($=$ 42,741,000 gallons,) representing in round numbers a value of 7,700,000 roubles ($=$ 1,219,000l. sterling) — almost fifteen times the quantity (136,000 to 137,000 hectolitres,) and more than the total value (6,896,000 roubles) of the foreign wines now imported into Russia.

The wines of the Trans-Caucasian provinces are consumed almost entirely on the spot; very little is transported into the interior of the empire. They are, with few exceptions, of but very middling quality; the best are in general heavy and heating, which is owing, not only to the nature of the soil and climate, and to negligence in the culture, but likewise to the excessive carelessness which prevails throughout every process of the manufacture. Still, the Hakhetian wine of good growths is in fair repute; it is heady, and to some extent resembles Burgundy. The wines of the southern provinces of European Russia, especially those of Bessarabia, the Crimea, the country of the Don Cossacks, and Stavropol, are exported in pretty considerable quantities to the other provinces. The quantity exported from the Crimea to St. Petersburg has considerably augmented of late. The wine of Kizliar, in the government of Stavropol, reputed the best, figures almost always at the fair of Nijni-Nowgorod, to which 100,000 vedros or more are annually sent; but the price it fetches is often very low. According to data contained in the *Journal du Ministère de l'Intérieur*, for the year 1835, there were sent in 1833 to the fair of Nijni 150,000 vedros of Kizliar wine; but having been

* The total production of this government is given at 6,488,000 vedros, of which 5,540,000 are referred to Mingrelia; but as the returns from this province are founded merely on approximative data, which are suspected of exaggeration, we have reduced the amount by one-third.

† We have obtained these figures by taking the average prices of each vinicultural district apart.

somewhat late of arriving, it fetched only 3½ roubles paper
(= 97 kopecks silver) per vedro,—a very trifling price indeed if
we take into account the costs of carriage. The country in the
neighbourhood of the Don produces a good deal of sparkling
wine of an agreeable flavour.

IV. *Garden Produce.*

In all the southern provinces of the empire, as far north as
the fiftieth degree of latitude, and in the western to a still
higher latitude, the climate and soil, with the exception of the
steppes, are exceedingly favourable to the culture of garden
fruits. The southern coasts of the Crimea and the Trans-Caucasian provinces are especially favoured in this respect. In the
latter, there are whole forests of fruit-trees. The inhabitants
set aside a portion by means of an enclosure, by way of appropriating the fruits; "and this," says the traveller Jevetski, "is
what is termed in that country employing themselves in gardening." The backward condition of this culture must undoubtedly be attributed chiefly to the carelessness of the
natives, but a deficiency of rain and river-water is also one of
the causes. Amongst the fruits which come to maturity
beyond the Caucasus, those most deserving of mention are the
peach, the apricot, the orange, the lemon, the date, the plum,
the pear, the pomegranate, the almond, and the chestnut.

The Crimea is one of the provinces that furnish the best
fruits, and it possesses the principal olive plantations. The
apples of the Crimea are sent into every part of Russia, and
fetch on the spot from 50 to 60 kopecks (silver) per pood.
The governments of Kharkow, Tauride, Poltawa, Kiew,
Podolia, Bessarabia, Astrakhan, Saratow, Simbirsk, Penza,
Wladimir, Nijni-Nowgorod, a part of Lithuania, and the kingdom of Poland, are the provinces most advanced in the culture
of fruit-trees. In some parts of Southern Russia there are
orchards where the produce, in a good year, brings in as much
as 700 roubles per dessiatine.

The culture of the kitchen-garden has in Russia made much
less progress than that of the orchard; it is mostly concentrated
about the capitals and large towns, where there is a ready sale
for this sort of produce. In the neighbourhood of St. Petersburg and Moscow good profits are made from the culture of
early vegetables, which has there been brought to considerable
perfection. The best kitchen-gardens are found in the governments of Moscow and Jaroslaw ; but the culture is also extensive in several governments of the west and south of the
empire, as well as in the kingdom of Poland.

The fruit and kitchen-gardens attached to dwellings occupy, according to Androssow, without including Finland or the kingdom of Poland, an extent of 2,205,000 dessiatines, of which 46,676 are in the five northern governments; 569,360 are in fourteen governments situated between 55° and 60° north latitude; 1,393,136 in twenty governments situated between 50° and 55°; and 196,113 in eight southern governments.

Reckoning only at 25 roubles the gross produce of a dessiatine thus cultivated, we would find the yearly value from gardens attached to dwellings alone to amount to more than 55 millions of roubles.* Adding the gardens of the kingdom of Poland and of Finland, and the vegetables cultivated in the open field, such as cabbage, carrots, turnips, &c., we may carry the value of the whole produce to 60 millions of roubles as the minimum.

V. *Meadow Produce.*

The cultivation of plants for fodder has hitherto been practised on but a very small scale in Russia, although in most of the governments there is nothing, either in the soil or in the climate, to prevent it; it will probably extend with the improvement of our agriculture. Its want has been supplied hitherto by the natural meadows and pastures, which are of immense extent, especially in the steppes of the south; but there, as we have already had occasion to observe, the culture of artificial forage has little chance of being permanently introduced, on account of the frequent droughts.

With regard to the produce of our meadows, not being possessed of any statistical data on the subject, we can only attempt to form a more or less approximative estimate.

In France, the natural meadows yield at an average (according to the official agricultural statistics published in 1840 and 1841), a crop of 25 metrical quintals of hay per hectare = 167 poods per dessiatine. In Austria, the medium crop, according to the official statistics, is nearly 19 quintals per joch = 120 poods per dessiatine. As in a considerable part of Russia the mowings are more rarely repeated on account of the shortness of the summer and the frequent droughts, and as in general our crops of hay are lighter, we will assume a dessiatine to yield at an average no more than 60 poods, that is to say, somewhat more than a third of the yield in France, and half the yield in

---

* In France the produce of gardens is valued in the agricultural statistics at the average rate of 435 francs per hectare = 120 roubles 83 kopecks per dessiatine, which is almost five times the rate of valuation which we have adopted.

Austria; and this is certainly as moderate a proportion as could well be adopted. On comparing the market quotations of all the governments of European Russia, for the years 1846, 1847, 1848, and 1849, we find that the highest prices of hay were, in 1846, 31 kopecks per pood (in the government of Esthonia); in 1847, 55 kopecks (in the same government); in 1848, 45 kopecks (in the government of Ekathérinoslaw); and, in 1849, 45 kopecks (in the governments of Ekathérinoslaw and Kharkow); whilst the lowest prices were in 1846, 1847, and 1848 (in the government of Orenburg) 6 kopecks, and in 1849 also 6 kopecks (in the government of Koursk and Simbirsk). Taking the prices of all these governments we obtain as average,

In 1846	-	-	-	14 kopecks per pood.
In 1847	-	-	-	15 „ „
In 1848	-	-	-	17 „ „
In 1849	-	-	-	20 „ „

Together 66

which gives a general average of 16$\frac{1}{2}$ kopecks.

In order to reduce our estimate to the most moderate possible terms, we assume an average value of only 10 kopecks, or five-eighths of the average price resulting from the market quotations of the whole governments.* Adopting this estimate, 60 poods of hay would give 6 silver roubles as the gross money produce of a dessiatine, less than a fifth of the average resulting from the statistical estimates adopted in France, which bring the gross money produce of the natural meadows to 111 francs per hectare = 30 roubles 25 kopecks per dessiatine. In Austria, the gross money produce of a joch of meadow is reckoned, in the official estimates, at 24 florins, which is equal to 28 roubles 65 kopecks per dessiatine.

Thus an extent of 60 millions of dessiatines (= 161 millions of acres) of meadow land in European Russia would, according to a minimised estimate, yield a gross money produce of 360 millions of silver roubles (= 57,000,000*l*.).

VI. *Oleaginous Grains and Textile Plants.*

Oleaginous grains are raised in Russia in large quantities, and form, along with our textile plants, flax and hemp, one of

---

* We request, once for all, the reader to observe, that wishing to avoid the reproach of having attempted to·exaggerate the productive forces of Russia, we have laid down the rule of reducing our estimates to the most moderate possible standard, especially in those cases where there exists a deficiency of positive information.

the principal articles of our export commerce. Flax is cultivated, as well for the seed as for the fibre, in the governments
of Pskow, Livonia, Courland, Witebsk, Kowno, and Wilna.
The grains coming from these provinces bear the highest character, and are used for seed in England, France, and the
Netherlands. In the governments of Jaroslaw, Kostroma,
Wologda, Wiatka, and in part of the government of Olonetz,
eastward of Lake Onega, flax is cultivated chiefly as a textile
plant. On the other hand, in the governments of Kherson
and Ekathérinoslaw, in the northern part of the government of
Tauride, and in the country of the Don Cossacks, it is cultivated solely as an oleaginous grain, the stalk being used only
for manure or fuel.

Hemp grows, throughout a great part of Russia, as far north
as the latitude of 66°; but, as an article of commerce, it is cultivated chiefly in the governments of Kalouga, Toula, Orel,
Koursk, Riazan, Tambow, Mohilew, Smolensk, and in part of
the governments of Witebsk, Minsk, Wilna, and Tschernigow.
The best sorts come from the Ukraine and White Russia. It
is found growing wild on the banks of the Volga, the Ural,
and the Terek. The culture of these two textile plants is still
susceptible of great extension and improvement.

The total production of flax in Russia has been estimated at
10 millions of poods, and that of hemp at 6 millions, an estimate which seems perfectly moderate when we consider the
large exportation of these articles and their extensive home
consumption. There were exported during the years 1847,
1848, and 1849, 12,512,443 poods of flax, and 8,462,311 poods
of hemp, in all 20,974,754 poods, which gives an annual average of 6,991,581 poods, representing, according to official estimates founded on the prices current, a value of 17,223,000
roubles (= 2,346,000l.). Adding to this an average export of
linen cloth and cordage to the extent of from 350,000 to
400,000 poods, we obtain a total exportation of flax and hemp,
raw and manufactured, of nearly 7,350,000 poods. In 1849,
this exportation attained the cipher of 8,229,000 poods. Now,
if we take into view the large quantities of cordage and sail-
cloth destined for the fleet and the commercial navy, as well as
for the coasting trade, and inland navigation, the quantities of
coarse linen cloth employed in the army, as well for the soldiers'
equipment, as in barracks and hospitals, the cordage employed
in the transport, packing, and tying-up of merchandise, and for
harness, and the linen and hempen manufactures and cordage
which must be consumed in domestic use by a population of
more than 60 millions, we may, without exaggeration, estimate

the home consumption at double the quantity exported. This would give for these two articles a total production of about 22 millions of poods, but we adhere to the figure of 16 millions already given, admitting it as *minimum*. The production of flax and hemp in the kingdom of Poland may be estimated at 1 million poods at least, making a total production of 17 millions. If we subtract the average annual exportation during the three years, from 1847 to 1849, which, including an exportation of about 500,000 poods from the kingdom of Poland, amounted to 7,350,000 poods, there remains for home consumption 9,650,000 poods[*], representing, at the minimum price of 2 roubles per pood, 19,300,000 roubles. The average value of the flax and hemp exported in their raw state amounting to 17,233,000 roubles, there results as the total value of these two articles the sum of 36,523,000 silver roubles.

To these two textile plants we must add the cotton grown in the Trans-Caucasian provinces. This culture is there beginning to assume some degree of importance. In his last statistical work, M. Hagmeister estimated the production at 60,000 poods ; but according to more recent data collected on occasion of the last exhibition of the products of the Trans-Caucasian provinces, it is now calculated at 130,000 poods, representing, at the price of 4 roubles per pood, a value of 520,000 roubles.

The average annual exportation of oleaginous grains during the same triennium was 1,320,400 tchetwerts, representing a value of 8,386,100 roubles, without reckoning the exportation of oil, which sometimes amounts to 200,000 poods and upwards. Taking into account the large consumption of oil, as well in the food of the population during the long lents, as in lighting and various technical uses, we may admit for these various purposes a home consumption of at least double the quantity exported, which would come to 2,640,800 tchetwerts, and bring the total production to 3,961,000 tchetwerts; but, in order to keep our estimate within bounds, we shall reckon for the entire home consumption only 2 millions of tchetwerts, representing, at the medium price of 5 roubles per tchetwert, 10 millions of roubles. This sum, added to the average value of the exports, gives for the total value of oleaginous grains the amount of 18,386,000 roubles (= 2,911,000*l.* sterling).

Besides flax, hemp, and rape, the helianthus is also cultivated as an oleaginous plant, principally in the governments of Sara-

---

[*] The 9,650,000 poods, distributed over a population of 67 millions of inhabitants, afford but 5·8 Russian pounds, exhibiting a value of 53 kopecks per head, which may show that the figure we have adopted for the total production is as low as it could well be.

tow and Woronèje, where this culture has already attained some importance.

According to the foregoing calculations, the production of textile plants and oleaginous seeds represents a gross value of 55,429,000 roubles (8,776,000*l*. sterling).

VII. *Tobacco.*

The culture of tobacco has likewise attained some degree of importance in Russia, principally in the governments of Tschernigow, Saratow, and Poltawa. The following are the official returns of the production in those governments where numerical data on the subject have been collected : —

Governments.	Poods.	Governments.	Poods.
1. Tschernigow -	500,000	Brought forward -	1,066,750
2. Saratow - -	250,000	10. Nijni-Nowgorod -	5,400
3. Poltawa - -	200,000	11. Kherson - -	4,412
4. Bessarabia -	30,500	12. Stavropol - -	3,585
5. Woronèje - -	22,000	13. Ekathérinoslaw -	1,854
6. Podolia - -	21,000	14. Astrakhan -	1,000
7. Toula - -	16,600	15. Minsk - -	1,000
8. Tauride - -	15,650	16 Koursk - -	800
9. Kharkow - -	11,000	17. Penza - -	600
Carried forward -	1,066,750	Total - -	1,085,401

We must observe that this table is far from complete, and that the greater number of the figures are considerably below the mark. In the Report of the Department of Economy to the Ministry of Domains, published in 1849, the total production of tobacco in Russia, inclusive, probably, of the Trans-Caucasian provinces, is estimated at upwards of 3,000,000 of poods, — a figure which accords with information which we have procured from other sources. This quantity, estimated at the minimum price of 70 kopecks per pood, represents a gross value of 2,100,000 roubles. The most ordinary tobacco is sold on the place of production at from 60 to 80 kopecks per pood, and sometimes as high as at from 1 rouble to 1 rouble 50 kopecks. The superior qualities, which grow principally in the governments of Kherson, Tauride, and Tschernigow, fetch from 2, 3, 5, to 15 roubles per pood.

VIII. *Dye and Medicinal Plants.*

Amongst the dye plants, madder holds the principal place. It is found wild in the provinces of the Caucasus. It is only, however, in the province of Derbent that its culture has attained much importance. M. Hagmeister estimated its production at 75,000 poods; but, from more recent information published on the occasion of the exposition of Trans-Caucasian products, it would appear that the actual production amounts to

120,000 poods, representing a value of 1,200,000 silver roubles. Saffron is also found wild in several districts of South Russia; but it is only in the province of Bakou that it has been cultivated hitherto. Shumac grows in the Crimea, and is much used in giving a yellow dye to morocco. The Trans-Caucasian provinces also produce indigo (which is extracted from an indigenous plant called *Krassilnaia gretshka*), cochineal, and Avignon grains.*

Amongst medicinal plants, liquorice holds the chief place. It is found principally in the Caucasian provinces. Opium, likewise, is gathered in the environs of Taganrog.

We pass over, on account of their small importance, various other tinctorial and medicinal plants which Russia produces. We shall merely mention anise and cummin, which are found in the Ukraine; and mustard, which is cultivated chiefly in the government of Saratow. Sarepta mustard has even acquired a certain character in the market. According to the most moderate calculation, we may estimate in slump the value of the dye and medicinal plants produced in Russia at $2\frac{1}{2}$ millions of silver roubles.

IX. *Forest Products.*

Our forests contain a great variety of timber suitable for ship-building, for carpentry, for cart-making, cabinet-making, fire-wood, and other purposes. The forests of the northern regions contain only pines and firs, intermixed sometimes with birch. In proportion as we advance towards the east, we find, also, a mixture of larches, and sometimes even of cedars. In the more temperate regions, the pine forests are almost always intermixed with birch, aspen, and alders. In the southern regions, we find also forests of oak, elm, maple (which grow especially in marshy districts), ash, and lime. The predominant species are the pine, the fir, the birch, the oak, the ash, and the larch. The principal oak forests are found in the government of Kazan; and the lime forests in the governments of Kostroma, Perm, and Wiatka, and in general in the countries of the Ural. In the forests which border the banks of the Siberian rivers, we find almost everywhere lofty cedars, which are used as building material by the nomade populations. Cedar-nuts, from which oil is extracted, are also gathered in abundance. The forests of the Trans-Caucasian provinces abound in oak and beech. Taking the extent of her forests as a whole, and comparing it with the whole extent of her area, European Russia is, as we have already had occasion to observe, one of the best

* The berry of the *Rhamnus infectorius.*

timbered countries in the world; and yet nowhere else do we find such immense tracts of treeless, timberless country. In the steppes of the south, such is the scarcity of wood, that straw and dried dung are used for fuel. Nature has been unequal in her distribution : in some districts the soil is unfavourable to forest vegetation; in some, the forests have been laid waste by cuttings, undertaken without plan and conducted without economy, so that where timber formerly existed in lavish profusion, building timber is no longer to be had, and even fire-wood is scarce and dear. To this destruction of forests have been attributed changes noxious to culture, alleged to have taken place in certain districts, and to affect the condition of the large rivers to such an extent as to interfere with their navigation. It has been observed, that forest clearances, when unsystematic and excessive, have rendered inundations more frequent, by occasioning a more rapid melting of the snows, and affording a readier course to the rain-water. To the same cause have been attributed the great droughts, by which several countries are so frequently ravaged. Some meteorologists, however, are probably inclined to lay too much stress upon these influences; for both droughts and inundations must mainly depend upon geographical position, elevation, and the direction of the prevailing winds.

Without contesting the partial devastation of our forests, which is an open and acknowledged fact, we may observe that the complaints and apprehensions so frequently manifested with regard to a scarcity of timber, however well founded they may be in the case of some individual districts, are at least exaggerated in their generality. A good proof of this is afforded by the circumstance, that these complaints are of very long standing, having attracted the attention of government before the middle of the seventeenth century. In the collection of laws (*Oulojenié zakonoff*) of 1649, we find regulations upon the subject. M. Baer, in an interesting article which precedes M. Koeppen's Report on the Waters and Forests of the Basin of the Volga[*], very justly observes, that, if the destruction of the forests has been able to proceed for such a length of time, we may draw from this fact the re-assuring inference that a large store of forest vegetation still remains, and that the interest of Russia in this respect may be amply secured by good administrative measures for the future. " In Livonia," proceeds this writer, " where complaints on this subject were heard more than a century ago, and where thirty or forty years

* Beiträge zur Kenntniss des Russischen Reiches, vol. iv.

ago these complaints began to bring forth their fruits, I know estates on which, in my childhood, the dearth of timber gave rise to the introduction of very strict measures for the preservation of the forests; and which, in consequence of these measures, are now become some of the most richly timbered districts that are anywhere to be met with."

The information which we have been able to procure, as to the reserve of timber suitable for building purposes still contained in the recesses of our immense forests, is exceedingly incomplete and contradictory. Thus, for example, when the Admiralty, at the end of last century, alarmed at the diminution of naval timber, dispatched naval officers to investigate the state of the forests in thirty-three governments, it appeared from their report that, taking as their basis only those forest districts which were in the vicinity of river communication with the naval dockyards, there would be an abundant supply for the latter, — 1st, for the Baltic fleet, of mast wood for fifty-five years, and of building timber for ever; 2nd, for Archangel, of mast wood for fifteen years, and of larch wood for four years only, supposing there should be built at that arsenal three ships of the line and five frigates yearly; 3d, for the ports of the Black Sea, both masts and planks for an indefinite period. On the other hand, according to a report, likewise official, of Count Kouscheleff, dated about the same period, the districts in the neighbourhood of rivers emptying into the Black Sea were already almost entirely stripped of their naval timber.* The incorrectness of the latter report has been demonstrated by experience; for since that date a large number of vessels, both men-of-war and merchantmen, have been constructed, and are still in course of construction, in the dockyards of the Black Sea—a fact which proves that there is no want of timber. As for the docks of Archangel, M. Baer observes that few men-of-war have been built there for the last several years, from the difficulty of procuring good timber; and yet the government of Archangel, taken as a whole, is one of the most richly timbered in the whole country, the forests there covering an area of 29,500,000 dessiatines, or more than 48 per cent. of the surface (Nova Zembla deducted). Still there are annually built at that port one ship of the line and several small vessels.

We export building timber of every description to the annual value of 3,000,000 of silver roubles, of which about 200,000 roubles worth is from the ports of the White Sea, and principally from Archangel. It may, perhaps, excite surprise that, notwithstanding the reiterated complaints about the want

---

* See M. Baer's article, just cited.

of building timber, the export of this article, far from falling off, has been going on augmenting.

*Triennial average Value of Timber exported.**

					Silv. Roubles.
1828 to 1830	-	-	-	-	2,387,000
1831 to 1833	-	-	-	-	1,938,000
1834 to 1836	-	-	-	-	2,693,000
1837 to 1839	-	-	-	-	2,749,000
1840 to 1842	-	-	-	-	2,378,000
1843 to 1845	-	-	-	-	2,951,000
1846 to 1848	-	-	-	-	3,308,000
1849 to 1851	-	-	-	-	3,301,000

Thus, on comparing the average exportation during the years 1849—51 with that of 1828—30, we perceive an increase of 914,000 roubles, or more than 38 per cent.; and on comparing the first-mentioned triennium with the period 1831—33, there is an increase of 1,363,000 roubles, or more than 70 per cent. It must, however, be observed that this augmentation is mostly in the department of battens and deals. It is chiefly the districts bordering on the Dwina, the Düna, the Niemen, and the Vistula, with their affluents, that furnish the timber for exportation; and it is principally by the Niemen and the Vistula that the larger kinds of wood for ship building, as beams, masts, &c., are exported.

According to the abstract of the state forests in 47 governments, founded on official returns, which we find in Professor Ziabloffsky's Statistics, their total extent in European Russia amounted in 1831 to 123,486,000 dessiatines, of which 967,000 dessiatines, or about $\frac{4}{5}$ per cent., were composed of naval timber. Adopting the same proportion for the whole forests of that part of Russia (about 180,000,000 of dessiatines), the naval timber would occupy an extent of 1,355,000 dessiatines, nearly one-sixth of the extent of the whole forests of France.

According to the report of the Ministry of Domains for the year 1848, the state forests, which are now under that administration, occupy an extent of 115,638,000 dessiatines, deduction being made of that portion of the forest land which has passed into the administration of the appanages and the Admiralty.

The transcaucasian provinces and the districts of Siberia bordering on the rivers Obi, Jenisseï, Lena, and their affluents, abound in forests which produce good building timber. M. Karniloff maintains that the country lying along the banks of the Obi could supply all Europe with mast timber.

Combining the general information above given with all that

---

* The exportation from the kingdom of Poland is not here included.

we have been able to procure for ourselves upon the subject, we consider that we may legitimately draw the following conclusions : —

That the apprehensions which have been manifested amongst us with regard to a deficiency of timber are, taken in their generality, exaggerated :

That, notwithstanding the partial destruction of our forests, which has sensibly impoverished some districts, we still possess immense resources for present supply, and a fund of forest vegetation which only requires to be properly economised in order to dissipate all danger for the future for our own demands, and even to admit of a considerable exportation :

That the waste of our forests has occurred chiefly in the vicinity of some of our largest, at any rate, of our navigable rivers; and that the description of trees wasted has been mostly building timber:

That, on the other hand, in districts at a distance from such means of communication, there are forests which are still nearly intact, and which may in the course of time be rendered available for home consumption :

That the dearth of fire-wood in some governments, especially those of St. Petersburg, Moscow, and Wladimir, arising from the extension of various branches of industry which require a large consumption of fuel, can afford no index to the resources which we have still in reserve :

That, necessity being the best teacher, the dearness of wood which has been felt in some districts will, in the course of time, induce our proprietors to manage their forests with more economy, and thus the evil will work out its own remedy:

That the working of peat-mosses and coal-pits, formerly greatly neglected, but to which more attention has begun to be paid of late, will likewise contribute to the preservation of our forests * :

That the Steppes of Southern Russia are the only districts which are almost entirely destitute of wood; but that even there, where both soil and climate are generally unfavourable to forest vegetation, partial re-timbering is not impossible, and may remedy the inconvenience, at least partially, in future; to which we may add the resource of coals, of which some rich mines have already been discovered :

* According to M. Kœppen, there are already, in the government of Moscow alone, and only on the state domains of that government, 22 peat mosses in operation, which occupy an extent of 4,187 dessiatines, and are capable of yielding 5,850,000 cubic *sagènes* (= 74,300,000 cubic yards) of peat. Two sagènes of good peat will replace three of fire-wood.

That the introduction of regular cuttings will augment the natural fertility of the forest vegetation, and may double its profit:

Lastly, that for all these reasons, there is no cause for anxiety about the future prospects of Russia in regard to her supplies of wood of every description.

In estimating the present produce of a dessiatine of forest at the average rate of only 75 kopecks, we would obtain for 180 millions of dessiatines, a revenue of 135 millions of roubles, leaving out of account the produce from the forests of Siberia and the transcaucasian provinces.

However moderate this estimate may be—and it is nearly as 1 to 9 compared with the estimates in the agricultural statistics of France, where the average value of the annual product of a hectare of forest is set down at 23 francs 48 centimes = 6 roubles 41 kopecks per dessiatine—it might be considered excessive if it were compared with the revenue which the state and individuals actually derive from their forests, and with the selling price of the latter in the best timbered districts; but such a comparison is here inadmissible, because we have to do at present only with the gross value of the materials which the forest land furnishes to the various wants of consumers. Now, in this branch of agricultural economy, the gross produce stands, more than in any other branch, in great disproportion to the net revenue, which is composed solely of the proceeds of sale. A forest, for example, in consequence of being locally situated at a distance from populous towns, or the great arteries of communication, may return its proprietor no farther benefit than that of furnishing fire-wood and building timber to himself and his peasants: it brings him in consequently no positive revenue; its value is merely negative. There are with us immense forests which are thus situated, and yet these cannot be classed as entirely unproductive property.

Deducting the value of the building timber exported[*], the sum at which we have estimated the gross produce of our forests affords, for the home consumption of 62 millions of inhabitants, an average of only 2 roubles 15 kopecks per head. If we take into view the immense quantity of wood consumed in Russia for fuel, both in dwelling houses and in various sorts of industrial establishments, as well as its extensive employment as a building material, and in the manufacture of household furniture, waggons, and implements, we will perceive that this estimate is quite as moderate as it could possibly be made.

[*] The value of the building timber exported from Russia and the kingdom of Poland comes, at an average, to about 4,500,000 silver roubles.

A very large proportion of the products of the soil being transported in the interior of Russia by water, the construction of flat boats, which are used only for a single voyage, absorbs every year no small quantity of timber. M. Kœppen, in his interesting statistical work on the waters and forests of the basin of the Volga*, calculates that there are built every year in the seven governments of Nowgorod, Twer, Moscow, Wladimir, Jaroslaw, Kostroma, and Nijni-Nowgorod, nearly 9,000 barks, and that there are employed in the construction of one of these barks, according to their dimensions, from 150 to 1,500 trees, of which more than a seventh are full-grown.† These constructions represent but a part of the river navigation of the empire. The greater portion of our dwellings, moreover, both in town and country, are built of wood, and must therefore be frequently renewed. These various causes, together with the severity of our climate, render the consumption of wood, both for fuel and for building purposes, much greater with us than it is in any other country. In Austria, where a much more temperate climate than ours does not render requisite so large a consumption of combustibles, the value of the wood consumed *for fuel alone* is estimated in the official statistics of 1841 and 1842 at about 84 millions of florins = 52,900,000 silver roubles, which gives for the population of that period (36 millions) 1 rouble 47 kopecks per inhabitant, or more than two-thirds of our average estimate *for uses of every description*, whether fuel, furniture, implements, buildings, or ships and vessels, large and small.

The approximative estimates which we have adopted in this chapter for the principal products of our soil belonging to the vegetable kingdom give a total of 1,658,729,000 silver roubles (262,632,000*l.* sterling).

B.

PRODUCTS OF THE ANIMAL KINGDOM.

I. *Cattle.*

Although cattle are reared in almost every part of Russia, this branch of agricultural industry, taken as a whole, is but carelessly carried on, and does not prosper well except in localities where it is specially favoured by nature.

---

* Beiträge zur Kenntniss des Russischen Reiches, vol. iv. p. 216.

† M. Kœppen, following M. Stuckenberg, reckons for one of the large barks of the Volga of a burden of 45,000 poods, or 735,000 kilogrammes (720 tons), 238 trees of full growth, and 1,300 of from five to ten years' growth; but this calculation seems rather beyond the mark.

With very few exceptions, the proprietors give themselves little trouble about the improvement of their breeds. The government frequently imports cows and bulls from the Tyrol, Holland, and other countries of which the breeds easily acclimatise in Russia, with a view to their propagation in the country; but its measures frequently remain fruitless for want of being seconded by the country population, who are not generally sufficiently enlightened to perceive their utility. The breed of cattle is, however, very fine in some districts, particularly in the country of the Black Sea Cossacks, in Wolhynia, Podolia, Bessarabia, the Ukraine, and the district of Cholmogory, in the government of Archangel. It is to Peter the Great that we owe the introduction of good breeds into the last-named government, several districts of which contain excellent pastures, and are well suited for cattle rearing, notwithstanding the severity of the climate. In many other provinces the cattle are generally small and puny, owing in great part to the neglect in the cultivation of artificial fodder. The want of good pasture gives rise to frequent murrains, which are so much the more fatal from the extreme difficulty of enforcing upon our country population the strict observance of the sanitary measures recommended by the authorities to prevent the extension of the disaster.

M. Reden, in his work upon Russia, published in 1843, estimates the number of horned cattle in Russia, exclusive of the kingdom of Poland, at 19 millions. This figure is evidently below the mark. According to the statistics of M. Arsénieff, who gives an estimate of the cattle in each government for the year 1846, founded upon official returns, the total number of cattle in forty-nine governments would amount to 23,160,000 head. In the kingdom of Poland there was reckoned for the same year, in the official statistics, 1,540,000 head, which would give a total of 24,700,000. Adding Finland, which is not included in the foregoing estimate, the total number of horned cattle in all European Russia, as officially ascertained, would exceed the cipher of 25 millions. Considering that this department of statistics is still more or less incomplete in every country, —that with us, in most of the governments, data of the sort are not collected with a sufficient degree of carefulness,—that the local authorities frequently find it difficult to acquit themselves of their task with precision,—and that the errors which creep into the official reports are almost always errors of diminution,— we consider that we should obtain a result nearer the reality if we were to add about 10 per cent. to the above figure. This would bring the total number of horned cattle up to $27\frac{1}{2}$ millions; but we shall hold by the official number of 25 millions, which would give on a population of $61\frac{1}{2}$ millions, nearly 5 head of cattle to every 12 inhabitants. In Austria there were reckoned in 1846, according to the official statistics, 11,957,500 head for a population of about $36\frac{1}{4}$ millions, or nearly 3 head of cattle to every 10 inhabitants. In Prussia in 1843 there were reckoned 5,042,000 head of cattle for a population of 15,472,000, or nearly one head of cattle to 3 inhabitants. In France there were in 1838, according to the official statistics, 7,823,894 head, without reckoning the calves *, which would give on the population of that epoch (34,226,000) 23 head of cattle to 100 inhabitants, or less than 1 head of the former to 4 of the latter.

The product of 25 million head of cattle, estimated at the average rate of 4 roubles per head, represents a value of 100 millions. In France there is reckoned, in the official statistics, from 7,823,894 head of cattle, a product of 311,127,629 francs, (including 25,072,852 francs for 2,057,156 calves,) which gives 41 francs = 10 roubles 25 kopecks per head, so that our rate of estimate is less than two-fifths of that which we find in the French official estimates. Our estimate is justified moreover by the following calculation:—

We export at an average 3,810,000 poods of tallow, representing a value of 13,871,000 roubles (average of triennium 1846—48). We may admit at least an equal quantity of tallow for home consumption,—in the manufacture of soap, stearine, candles, and every other industrial purpose: but considering that mutton tallow comes likewise into play in considerable quantities, although in less quantities than beef tallow, we will reckon for the whole production of this article no more than 5 millions of poods; so that—deducting the 3,810,000 poods exported, there would remain for home consumption only 1,190,000 poods, giving for a population of $61\frac{1}{2}$ millions an average consumption of only three quarters of a pound per head.

Let us now determine what number of cattle must be slaughtered in order to furnish these 5 million poods of tallow.

In France there has been reckoned at an average, for an ox 275 kilogrammes (= 672 Russian pounds) of meat, and 26 kilogrammes (= $63\frac{1}{2}$ Russian pounds) of tallow; and for a cow 165 kilogrammes (= 403 Russian pounds) of meat, and 15 kilogrammes (= 37 Russian pounds) of tallow.† But the offi-

---

* The calves not being included in the agricultural statistics of other countries, we have required to withdraw them from the comparison. They were reckoned in France, in 1840, to amount to 2,057,156 head.

† See Schnitzler's Statistics of France, vol. iii. p. 370.

cial agricultural statistics for 1840 exhibit a smaller result than this as regards the meat. There were slaughtered during that year 492,905 oxen, which yielded 122,446,618 kilogrammes of meat (mean weight 248 kilogrammes), and 718,956 cows, which yielded 103,567,986 kilogrammes (mean weight 144 kilogrammes), in all 1,211,861 head of cattle, yielding 226,014,604 kilogrammes of meat, or, on a general average, 187 kilogrammes = 457 pounds Russian per head.

In Prussia, taking the weight as appearing from the impost levied at the town slaughter-houses, an ox yields at an average 570 (= 650 Russian) pounds of meat, and a cow or heifer 357 (= 407 Russian) pounds*; but as in the country a much larger proportion of small beasts are slaughtered than in the towns, M. Dieterici, in his statistical estimates, reckons only 500 (= 570 Russian) pounds for an ox, and 300 (= 342 Russian) pounds for a cow or heifer.

We have been unable to procure positive data with respect to the weight of either meat or tallow of the cattle slaughtered in Russia. The following is the most authentic information we could obtain with respect to the slaughter-houses of St. Petersburg. We find in the *Journal du Ministère de l'Intérieur*, that a well fattened ox of the largest size yields as much as 1,000 pounds of meat and 200 pounds of tallow: the smallest and leanest yields 305 pounds of meat and only 10 pounds of tallow. Between these two extremes there exists such a disparity that it is difficult to draw from them any probable estimate whatever. The numerical mean of the two quantities would be 652½ pounds of meat and 105 pounds of tallow; but it is evident that the instances of such an enormous weight as 1,200 pounds, of which 200 pounds are tallow, can be but rare and exceptional, requiring oxen both of very large size and of very full feeding. This latter quality is with us of less frequent occurrence than in other countries where feeding is more in use, and where the cattle have not so far to travel before arriving at the slaughter-house.† Lean beasts, weighing from 350 to 400 pounds, must arrive at the shambles much more frequently, especially when we take the cows into account.

In order to obtain more positive information we had recourse to the experience of the parties who have charge of the slaughter-house at St. Petersburg; and, from information thus obtained, it results that the oxen which arrive under the name of Cir-

---

* The weight of the tallow is not indicated in the statistical returns.

† Six sevenths of the cattle slaughtered at St. Petersburg arrive from the south-eastern provinces, under the name of Circassian cattle, after a journey of 200 German (= 920 English) miles and upwards.

cassian cattle give at an average 580 pounds of meat and 60 pounds of tallow, and the oxen which arrive under the name of Russian cattle, give 260 pounds of meat and 40 pounds of tallow. As oxen of the latter breed form no more than a seventh of the total quantity slaughtered at St. Petersburg, we obtain for this total an average of 534 pounds of meat and 57 pounds of tallow. But then we must consider, *first*, that it is generally animals of prime quality that are sent to the capital, and that the proportion of tallow to meat almost always diminishes with the weight of the carcase; and *secondly*, that cows are sent only in very small numbers to the abattoir of the capital, and are slaughtered chiefly in the small towns and in the country. In France cows form 59 per cent. of the cattle slaughtered: in cattle statistics they form, in France, 70 per cent.; in Austria 67 per cent.; in Prussia 57 per cent. of the total number. But, admitting that in Russia there are reared proportionally more oxen and fewer cows than in other countries, we do not think that we can estimate the latter at less than a third of the total number slaughtered.

For all these reasons, we do not think that we can reckon at an average for all Russia, more than 400 to 450 pounds of meat and 50 pounds of tallow per beast, cows included: but in order not to run any risk of over-estimating the number of cattle slaughtered, in calculating it according to the quantity of tallow produced, we shall reckon 60 pounds of tallow per beast. According to this average, the production of 5 millions of poods of tallow for exportation and home consumption, would indicate a slaughter of 3,333,333 head of cattle, affording, at the mean weight of 425 Russian pounds, 1,416,666,525 pounds of meat, or, for a population of $61\frac{1}{2}$ millions, about 23 pounds per inhabitant, —a proportion which will surely not be considered as excessive.

In Prussia, where butcher's meat is generally much dearer than in Russia, the consumption is, in towns subject to the excise, at the rate of 83 (= 95 Russian) pounds per head, and in the country and in small towns at a very moderate calculation, at the rate of about 35 to 40 (Russian) pounds per head, of which about 45 per cent. is ox-beef and veal.[*]

In France, according to the official agricultural statistics prepared in 1839, the total annual consumption of meat of every sort amounts, at an average, to 20 kilogrammes =48·9 lbs. Russian for each inhabitant, of which only 6·74 kilogr. =16·47 lbs. Russian consists of ox-beef and cow-beef.

Having thus approximately determined the quantities of meat

---

[*] See Dieterici's Statistics of the Zollverein, second continuation, p. 214.

and tallow annually furnished for consumption, we may estimate the gross revenue arising from cattle-rearing as follows: —

		Silver Roubles.
Meat, 1,416,667,000 lbs., @ 2½ kopecks per lb. - -		35,416,000
Tallow, 5,000,000 poods, @ 3 roubles 50 kopecks - -		17,500,000
Hides, 3,333,000, @ 1 rouble - - - - -		3,333,000
Total - - - - - - - -		56,249,000

without reckoning the calves or dairy produce.

In France, the total number of horned cattle, estimated in the agricultural statistics at 7,869,689 head, furnished to the slaughter-house 2,487,362 calves, which is at the rate of 31·6 per cent. According to this proportion, the 25 million head of cattle in Russia would furnish 7,900,000 calves; but we will reckon them instead at only 4 millions, or little more than the half, and we will rate this number at no more than 3 roubles per head, being less than half the average price (26 francs = 6 roubles 50 kopecks) adopted in the official statistics of France. At this rate, the 4 millions of calves would yield a gross revenue of 12 millions of roubles.

In regard to the products of the dairy, M. Chaptal, one of the best informed economists in France, reckoned in 1818 from less than 7 million head of cattle, a return of 78,199,000 francs = 19,550,000 roubles. According to this estimate, 25 million beasts ought to give a return of 69,821,000 roubles, but, taking into consideration the difference of prices, we will reckon only 30 millions of roubles, or three sevenths of the value resulting from the French official estimates, which would give as the mean value of consumption, on a population of 61½ millions, less than 50 kopecks per head.

In Austria, for 11,479,604 head of cattle, there was reckoned in the official statistics of 1844 a product of 1,563,472 centners of cheese, which quantity, estimated at the price of 20 florins per centner = 3 roubles 70 kopecks per pood (the official value at the Austrian custom-house of cheese exported is 50 fl. per centner = 9 roub. 25 kop. per pood), represented a value of 31,269,440 florins = 19,749,000 roubles. Thus, this single article, independently of milk and butter, produced nearly two-thirds of the amount which we have estimated for the whole products of the dairy arising from more than twice the number of cattle,—a proof more of the moderation of our figures.

Adding the value of the two last-mentioned articles, veal and dairy produce, making together 42 millions of roubles, to the value of the meat, tallow, and hides, amounting to 56,249,000 roubles, we obtain a total gross produce of 98,249,000 roubles, to which fall to be added from 700,000 to 800,000 roubles for the value of cattle exported.

M. Chaptal reckons, moreover, on less than 7 million head of cattle, a sum of 22,140,000 francs = 5,503,000 roubles for the benefit of the increase of the bulls and heifers, which would give for 25 million head a sum of about 20 millions of roubles. This item we entirely leave out of our estimate.

Having thus reduced our figures to the most moderate possible terms, we think it reasonable to conclude that the gross produce arising from cattle must considerably exceed in value the sum of 100 millions of silver roubles, (= 15,833,000*l*.), which we have adopted as *minimum*.

II. *Horses.*

We possess various breeds of horses of great excellence. We do not raise many of those huge heavy animals, fit only for heavy draughts, which may be seen in Normandy, Picardy, and some parts of Germany; a breed of that sort would be unsuitable for our present roads, which would be mostly impracticable for those massive waggons used in some foreign countries with loads weighing hundreds of quintals; but we have good draught horses of medium size, excellent cavalry horses, and a justly celebrated breed of riding horses; all the breeds have this good quality in common, that they long preserve their vigour, and are able to go through an immense deal of fatigue. No cavalry, except the English, is so well mounted as ours; nor could any country in the world mount such a numerous cavalry, or horse such an artillery train as we can, without having recourse to foreign purchases, even if we required to put our army on the most thorough war establishment.

In several countries, however, and especially in the Polish provinces, in Lithuania, in Samogitia, and in some governments of the north and centre of the empire, the horse has degenerated; the horses of the peasants are very small and of little vigour. This is owing to the circumstance that the peasantry bestow little care on the rearing of their horses, and employ them too soon in hard work; in Poland, for example, they are put in harness in their third year, and foals a fortnight old, may often be seen following their dams in long and fatiguing journeys, thus losing their strength in the very first period of their growth. It is evident that under a system like this the race must ever more and more degenerate. This carelessness in horse-rearing has been always observable amongst the Slavonic populations. Wherever there is a settlement of German colonists, we are at once struck with the difference between their horses and those of the native peasantry; the same difference is observable in Bohemia between the German and the Tschech villages.

Government has always been anxious to improve the breed; but the chief measures adopted for this purpose, to which we shall have occasion to recur in the sequel, such as the organisation of imperial studs, the establishment of depôts of stallions, the awarding of prizes to the best breeders, are still too recent to have been able to bring forth the good fruits that may in time be expected from them. It is also to be regretted that the lower officials connected with the crown studs have not always conscientiously observed the rules prescribed for the management of the stallions, and the precautions necessary in copulation; reforms have been recently introduced into this branch of the service which promise the most favourable results.

The best horses are reared in the provinces of New Russia, and especially in the governments of Ekathérinoslaw, Tauride, Kherson, and Bessarabia, the country of the Don and Black Sea Cossacks, the governments of Saratow, Woronèje, Orel, Tambow, and Simbirsk. The Kirghiz and the Kalmucks, who possess very extensive pastures, rear them in great numbers, not very elegant in form but indefatigable in action. The mildness of the climate admits of their being generally allowed to roam over the steppes without being placed under cover; and this inures them to fatigue of every description; but, on the other hand, they are exposed to frequent mortalities on the occurrence of *chasse-neige* and winters of extraordinary severity. In the Caucasian provinces and in Georgia, there are numerous herds of horses of an excellent breed, very suitable for light cavalry; in the southern provinces, there is a stock of excellent breeds of Asiatic origin, Arab, Persian, Tscherkessian, Anatolian, and Chivan, which might be greatly improved if more care were bestowed upon their breeding. In the north-western provinces, the Finnish breed predominates. The governments of Perm, Wiatka, and Kazan possess a breed peculiar to themselves, of very small stature, but well proportioned, indefatigable, and excellent for light draught. The horses of the government of Woronèje, which are also a peculiar race, are reckoned amongst the handsomest and best.

M. Reden estimates the number of horses in European Russia at 9,500,000,—an estimate far below the actual number; there are reckoned to be 7 millions in the eight governments of Saratow, Tambow, Koursk, Orel, Riazan, Simbirsk, Perm, and Orenburg; and the last-named government alone possesses about 1,900,000. According to the official statistics (see the work of M. Arsénieff), the total number in forty-nine governments of European Russia amounted in 1846 to 16,500,000 head; and in the kingdom of Poland there were reckoned at the same period 513,000 head; this brings the grand total to

17 millions, without reckoning Finland; and this figure must be considerably below the mark, seeing that, as we have already had occasion to observe, in these official surveys the numeral errors have such a constant tendency to be errors of diminution. We shall cite a single recent example in support of this observation. In the statistics of 1846, the number of horses in the government of Kiew is set down at 107,000 only, whilst, according to a statistical notice which has just been published in the gazette of that government, the number amounts to 120,000. Now this difference of about 12 per cent. is too considerable to be put to the account of ordinary increase during a period of three years; it shows rather that, with the progress of statistical labours, the more recent returns are improving in correctness. We, therefore, think that we may set down the total number of horses at 18 millions as *minimum*,—a number which allows 9 horses for every 31 inhabitants. In Austria, there were reckoned in 1846, 2,850,397 horses, or 1 horse for every 13 inhabitants. In Prussia, according to the returns of the statistical bureau of Berlin, there were 1,565,000, or 1 horse for 10 inhabitants. In France, according to the agricultural statistics of 1840, there were 2,818,496, or 1 horse for every 12 inhabitants. Thus, we have nearly seven times as many horses as France or Austria taken separately, eleven and a half times as many as Prussia, and two and a half times as many as the whole three put together. At the same time we have to observe, that the immensity of the distances renders necessary a larger supply of draught horses for Russia than for any other country.

The 18 millions of horses would represent at the *minimum* average of 15 roubles ($=47s.\ 6d.$) per head[*], a value of 270 millions of silver roubles (42,750,000*l.* sterling).

The gross revenue, reckoned at 8 roubles per horse[†], which is only about two-fifths of the rate of valuation adopted in the agricultural statistics of France[‡], would amount to 144 millions

[*] The price of horses exhibits a wider range with us than anywhere else. To say nothing of saddle horses, which sell for from 300 to 1,000 roubles and upwards, there are to be found, in the governments of Orel, Woronèje, and many others, draught and saddle horses of ordinary breeds, which cost from 100 to 200 roubles, whilst the horses of the steppes are sometimes sold for ten roubles or less. On exportation, horses are valued at an average in the official estimates, if for Europe, at 44 roubles, and if for Asia, at between five and six roubles. These two prices give a mean average of 25 roubles. In France, the estimates adopted in the agricultural statistics give, for the mean price of a horse or mare, 148 francs ($=37$ roubles). We cannot be charged with exaggeration in adopting the price of 15 roubles.

[†] The gross produce of horses represents, in statistical estimates, the value of their motive force, and the produce of the sales of foals and colts.

[‡] The mean revenue taken from the official estimates in France is 78 francs ($=19$ roubles 50 kopecks) per head of horses, mares, and foals taken in slump.

of silver roubles.   If from this amount we deduct 15 millions
of roubles for about 3 millions of horses which roam over the
steppes, and which, not being occupied in labour, yield no
return, beyond what is derived from the sale of the colts and
foals, there still remains a gross revenue of 129 millions of
roubles (20,425,000*l.*).

III. *Sheep.*

In the opinion of the most distinguished agricultural authorities, Russia, from the great extent of her pastures, and from
other local circumstances, is one of the most suitable countries
in the world for sheep-farming; the propagation of this race of
animals is extending more and more throughout the empire,
especially in the steppes of Southern Russia; and this branch
of rural economy is unquestionably that which has of late
made most progress, and attracted most attention from our
great landed proprietors.

We possess a great variety of ordinary breeds, of which the
best known are, the original native sheep which passes by the
name of *Romanoff*, the sheep of the Don, of the Ukraine, of
the Crimea, together with those of Wallachian, Kirghiz,
Tscherkessian, and Bohemian origin.   Several of these breeds,
especially that of Kirghiz origin, require but little care; the
animal easily supports the inclemency of the seasons, and is
satisfied with a very slender pasture; it gets very lean in
winter, for want of proper food, but comes soon into condition
upon the return of spring; they multiply rapidly, giving birth
ordinarily to two lambs at a time.

Their flocks of sheep constitute the principal wealth of the
Kirghiz, several of whom have as many as from 10,000 to
20,000 head.   Their wool is so inferior that it cannot be employed in the manufacture of even the most ordinary cloths,
and is used solely in the preparation of felt; on the other hand
they yield upwards of a pood, sometimes as much as two, of
tallow.   This breed is of very large size, and is distinguished
by a broad tail containing a large quantity of fat, a distinctive
quality which it soon loses when removed from its natal soil.
The number of sheep which annually arrive in Russia from the
steppes of the Khirghiz, and which are purchased solely for the
skin and tallow, is estimated at about a million.

All the breeds of sheep which are reared on the left bank of
the Volga, as well as those of the Ukraine and the Crimea,
yield a very coarse wool which is good for nothing but the
manufacture of common felts.   In the governments of the
Tauride and Ekathérinoslaw, there is a peculiar species un-

known throughout the rest of Europe, called *tchoundouki;* it is distinguished by a forked tail, and by the irregularity of the tup's horns. In the Crimea there is a peculiar breed, found nowhere else, covered with a sort of grey hair.

Amongst the breeds which yield a wool somewhat less coarse, suitable for the fabrication of cloth for soldiers' apparel, and even cloths of medium quality, the sheep of Tscherkessian and Bohemian origin seem the most susceptible of improvement; but they degenerate upon being mixed with the more ordinary breeds. These two breeds are extensively diffused over Southern Russia.

The rearing of fine-woolled sheep has been gradually extending with us for the last twenty years. It is principally carried on in the south of Russia, in the Baltic governments, in some parts of Little Russia, in Wolhynia, and in the kingdom of Poland. In 1832 there were reckoned in the governments of Esthonia and Livonia no more than 66 sheep-walks with 29,115 sheep; in 1836, there were already 169 walks with 84,869 sheep; and in 1846, the number of sheep had increased to 400,000 head. At the latter period there were reckoned in the six governments of Tauride, Ekathérinoslaw, Poltawa, Kherson, Saratow, and Bessarabia, more than 12 millions of sheep, of which more than 4 millions were of the finer breed. The government of Saratow alone reckons nearly 3 millions, of which nearly 360,000 are fine-woolled animals. According to the most recent official accounts published in the *Gazette du Commerce de Saint Petersburg,* with regard to the number of fine-woolled animals in 1846 and 1848 in a portion of Russia, we perceive that, in eight governments, namely, Tauride, Poltawa, Kherson, Kharkow, Woronèje, Kiew, Grodno, and Tschernigow, their number had augmented in the space of two years by 478,000 or nearly 13 per cent. A circumstance which may serve to give an idea of the progress we have been making in sheep-farming, is the rapid increase which took place in the quantity of wool exported. Previously to 1830, our export of this article scarcely exceeded 30,000 or 40,000 poods; in 1844 it amounted to 842,000 poods, representing a value of 9,152,000 roubles, without including the exportation from the kingdom of Poland, amounting to at least 100,000 poods; so that we may estimate the total exports of that year at about a million of poods. Since that date the exportation has considerably diminished; but this has been owing to the unfavourable state of the foreign wool market.

The accounts given in foreign publications with regard to the number of our sheep are very contradictory. Balbi and

Martini have within a recent period estimated the number for all Russia at 36,000,000, whilst Hassel, so long ago as 1829, estimated the number for European Russia alone at 60,000,000, justly adding, that it is impossible to form an estimate of the numerous flocks belonging to the nomadic populations which wander about over the Russian territories in Asia. Hassel's estimate is excessive with reference to the time when it was made; but at present, it would probably not vary widely from the reality. According to M. Arsénieff's statistics, there were in 1846, in European Russia, exclusive of Finland and the kingdom of Poland, 41,654,000 sheep, of which about $7\frac{1}{2}$ millions belonged to fine-woolled breeds; in the kingdom of Poland there were reckoned for the same year, according to the official statistics, 3,192,000 head, of which 588,000 were of fine breeds, and 1,624,000 crossed and improved, making a total of 44,846,000 head. As Finland is not included in this calculation, and as statistical enumerations of the sort are always more or less incomplete, we may, without exaggeration, estimate the total number of sheep in European Russia at about 55,000,000; but, admitting 50,000,000 as *minimum*, we obtain a result of 25 sheep for every 31 inhabitants.*

In Austria there were reckoned in 1844, according to the official statistics, 27,197,000 sheep; but M. Czoernig, the director of the statistical bureau, calculated, from the quantity of wool produced, that the total number must amount to 33,767,000, including lambs, which, for a population of 36,369,000 souls, is at the rate of nearly 17 sheep to 18 inhabitants. In Prussia there were reckoned in 1843, according to the returns of the statistical bureau, 16,236,000 head; that is to say, for the population of that period (15,471,000 souls), somewhat more than 1 sheep for each inhabitant, or, more exactly, 16 sheep to 15 inhabitants. In France there were reckoned, according to the agricultural statistics of 1840, 32,151,430 sheep for 33,541,000 inhabitants, which gives 32 sheep for 33 inhabitants. Thus we perceive that, notwithstanding the immense extent of our pastures, we rear, in proportion to our population, fewer sheep than either Austria, Prussia, or France; so that this branch of agricultural industry is still susceptible of very great extension, especially as there must be a greater demand for warm clothing in our climate than in any of the others.

Reckoning the annual return from our flocks, in wool, skins, tallow, and butcher's meat, at the average rate of 50 kopecks

* In the transcaucasian provinces there were reckoned in 1850, according to official data, 2,732,000 head, or 17 sheep to 10 inhabitants.

per head, we would obtain from 50,000,000 head, which we have adopted as their minimum number, a return of 25,000,000 roubles per annum. The fine-woolled sheep, where they are properly managed, bring in to the farmer a net return of 1 rouble per head.

IV. *Swine.*

The rearing of swine is pretty general in Russia, especially in the governments of Mohilew, Kowno, Tschernigow, Kharkow, Saratow, Tambow, Woronèje, Orel, and Koursk. In the latter government there were reckoned in 1846 nearly 600,000 head, and in each of the others from 400,000 to 500,000. The total number in 48 governments, according to M. Arsénieff's statistics, amounts to 10,053,500 head. In the kingdom of Poland there were reckoned in 1846 more than 800,000. Adding Finland and the governments in which the numbers have not been officially ascertained, we may carry the total number to about 12,000,000, or 1 swine for every 5 inhabitants.

In Austria there were reckoned in 1842, according to the official statistics, without including the Arch-duchy of Austria, Styria, the Littoral, or Gallicia, from which there were no official returns, 5,990,436 head, which gave, as compared with the population (27,146,000 souls), 2 swine for every 9 inhabitants. Of the above number of 5,990,436 head, Hungary with the Military Frontier furnished more than 4,600,000. In Prussia the number of swine in 1843 amounted, according to returns of the statistical bureau, to 2,115,000 head, which gave for the population of that period (15,471,000 souls), 3 swine for every 22 inhabitants. In France, according to the agricultural statistics of 1840, there were reckoned 4,910,721 head, which gave for the population of that period (33,541,000 souls) nearly 1 swine to every 7 inhabitants.

As the swine is reared only for fattening, we may assume that the race is renewed every two years, which, for the number of 12,000,000, supposes an annual production of 6,000,000 head, representing, at the average price of 3 roubles 50 kopecks, 21,000,000 roubles. This includes the value of the bristles, which form in Russia no inconsiderable article of commerce. Most of the bristles for exportation are supplied by Little Russia.

Besides the four races of domestic animals of which we have just given a general abstract, there were reckoned in 1846, from official statistics, in European Russia (Finland not included) and in the kingdom of Poland, 650,000 goats, of which the gross produce may be estimated (at the minimum rate of 20 kopecks per head) at 130,000 silver roubles. Camels are also reared in the governments of Astrakhan, Tauride, and Orenburg, and in the country of the Don Cossacks : they are set down in M. Arsénieff's statistics at the number of 33,000 head : their number must be much more considerable in the Asiatic possessions, from whence there is an annual export of 600 or 700 head. Asses and mules, which are found in small numbers in some of the south-eastern provinces, are included amongst the horses : the buffaloes, which also exist in small numbers, are reckoned in with the cattle. In the north of Russia there are reared a number of rein-deer : there were reckoned in 1846, in the government of Archangel, more than 250,000 head, of which the product, estimated at 1 rouble per head, would represent a value of 250,000 roubles.

According to the foregoing calculations, reduced to their minimum, the rearing of the four principal races of domestic animals, with the addition of the goats and rein-deer, would, in European Russia, bring in a gross return of 275,380,000 silver roubles (43,600,000l. sterling).

On comparing the numbers of cattle, sheep, and horses, with the extent of productive soil, we obtain the following results :

Cattle.

	Extent of Productive Soil * in Sq. Miles.	Number of Animals.	Number of Head per Sq. Mile of Productive Soil.
Austria	6,553	11,657,500	1,779
Prussia	3,705	5,042,000	1,361
France	7,635	7,824,000	1,025
Russia	39,676	25,000,000	630

Sheep.

Austria	6,553	33,767,000	5,153
Prussia	3,705	16,236,000	4,382
France	7,635	32,151,000	4,211
Russia	39,676	50,000,000	1,260

Horses.

Russia	39,676	18,000,000	454
Austria	6,553	2,850,000	435
Prussia	3,705	1,565,000	422
France	7,635	2,818,000	369

The three races together.

Austria	6,553	48,274,500	7,367
Prussia	3,705	22,843,000	6,165
France	7,635	42,793,000	5,605
Russia	39,676	93,000,000	2,344

* Under the term *productive soil* we here comprehend arable land, vineyards, gardens, meadows, and pastures.

From these figures we perceive that, in proportion to the extent of our productive soil, the rearing of sheep and cattle is with us much more susceptible of extension than it is in any other country. It must farther be considered that, in the above cipher of the extent of productive soil in an agricultural point of view, we have, in the absence of authentic data, slumped the pastures at a tenth of the total area, whilst, taking into consideration the immense extent of pasture land in the southern and eastern provinces, the actual extent of surface utilised as pasture must be much larger. But the development of this branch of rural economy depends essentially on the progress of our agriculture, and especially on the culture of artificial provender. At present, it is only in the relative number of the horses as compared with the extent of productive land, that we are ahead of other countries.

On distributing the domestic animals over the extent of cultivated land and of meadow land in the four principal states of continental Europe, we obtain the following results:

To 100 *Dessiatines of cultivable Soil, Fallows included.*

				Cattle.	Sheep.	Horses.	Total.
In Austria	-	-	-	56	161	14	231
Prussia	-	-	-	44	141	14	199
France	-	-	-	33	135	12	180
Russia	-	-	-	28	56	20	104

To 100 *Dessiatines of Meadow.*

				Cattle.	Sheep.	Horses.	Total.
In Austria	-	-	-	209	605	51	865
France	-	-	-	148	608	53	809
Prussia	-	-	-	151	486	47	684
Russia	-	-	-	42	83	30	155

Setting aside the sheep, the number of head of cattle and horses taken together would be distributed as follows:

To 100 *Dessiatines of cultivable Land.*

In Austria	-	-	70 head.	In Russia	-	-	48 head.
Prussia	-	-	56 „	France	-	-	45 „

To 100 *Dessiatines of Meadow.*

In Austria	-	-	260 head.	In Prussia	-	-	198 head.
France	-	-	201 „	Russia	-	-	72 „

From these collocations it results that, in proportion to the cultivable soil, there are reared in Russia somewhat more horses and cattle than in France, a seventh less than in Prussia, and nearly a third less than in Austria; but the difference in favour of the other countries is very great in the relative number of these domestic animals to the extent of meadow land: it may be expressed in the following proportions:

In relation to Prussia, it is as	-	-	-	10 to 27·5
„ France, „	-	-	-	10 to 28
„ Austria, „	-	-	-	10 to 36

In other terms, there is reckoned for one head of horses and cattle taken together:

	Dessiatines of Meadow.			Dessiatines of Meadow.
In Russia	- - 1·4	In France	- -	0·5
Prussia	- - 0·5	Austria	- -	0·4

If we take into consideration the quantity of hay reaped in Russia, in France, and in Austria*, we obtain the following results:

For Russia, we have reckoned 60 poods of hay to 1 dessiatine of meadow, which gives for 60 millions of dessiatines 3,600 millions of poods: this quantity, distributed over 43 million head of horses and cattle, gives nearly 84 poods per head; but if to the cattle and horses we add 50 millions of sheep, we will obtain only $38\frac{2}{3}$ poods per head.

In France, the hay harvest is estimated in the agricultural statistics at 152 millions of metrical quintals = 929,100,000 poods, which gives for 7,824,000 head of cattle and 2,818,000 head of horses, 87 poods per head; but if to these we add 32,151,000 head of sheep, we will obtain an average of about 22 poods per head.

In Austria, the hay harvest is set down in the official statistics at 209,990,000 quintals = 718,666,000 poods, which gives for 14,312,000 head of cattle and horses nearly 50 poods per head; or, adding to these 33,767,000 head of sheep, we have an average of about 15 poods per head.

The fact that so much less hay is consumed in Austria than in Russia or France may be partly explained by the more extensive culture in the former country of artificial provender; and it indicates a more advanced system of rural economy in some of the provinces of that empire. It is, however, understood that the value of calculations of this description can only be more or less approximative, and with the view of serving as points of comparison.

We subjoin a statistical table of the three principal races of domestic animals in forty-nine governments, founded upon M. Arsénieff's statistics, which we have occasionally rectified from more recent information, and with the addition of the kingdom of Poland.

---

* Having no data for the hay harvest of Prussia, we have been obliged to leave that country out of our comparison.

Governments arranged in the order of their absolute Number of Domestic Animals.	Horses.	Cattle.	Sheep (Goats not included).		Total.
				Of which fine	
1. Orenburg -	1,913,800	1,284,080	2,372,790	20,590	5,570,670
2. Kingdom of Po-land - -	513,000	1,540,000	3,192,000	587,700	5,245,000
3. Saratow - -	871,230	884,650	2,911,750	358,990	4,667,630
4. Country of the Don Cossacks	372,640	*1,168,740	2,431,570		3,972,950
5. Simbirsk -	863,340	622,820	2,111,420	71,080	3,597,580
6. Tauride -	156,990	694,150	2,440,420	978,360	3,291,560
7. Woronèje -	552,130	784,800	1,707,320	342,260	3,044,250
8. Kherson -	300,500	765,620	1,624,250	627,390	2,690,370
9. Ekathérinoslaw	102,560	495,680	2,059,730	1,389,110	2,657,970
10. Poltawa - -	159,585	691,130	1,684,180	657,360	2,534,895
11. Kharkow -	191,750	584,050	1,462,770	614,150	2,238,570
12. Wiatka - -	494,910	741,170	923,730	540	2,159,810
13. Perm - -	697,990	615,150	828,940	1,650	2,142,080
14. Bessarabia -	89,950	570,510	1,439,380	717,320	2,099,840
15. Tambow -	643,060	501,090	926,750	80,570	2,070,900
16. Stavropol -	252,190	631,200	1,182,480	24,220	2,065,870
17. Koursk - -	739,960	428,550	777,300	74,220	1,945,810
18 Orel - -	551,820	427,620	937,300	16,430	1,916,740
19. Smolensk -	484,730	667,560	561,190	1,875	1,713,480
20. Wolhynia -	282,630	412,400	996,920	461,580	1,691,950
21. Riazan - -	565,670	338,370	758,300	8,690	1,662,340
22. Twer - -	499,530	670,550	447,850	260	1,617,930
23. Kazan - -	389,610	361,980	770,330	4,950	1,521,920
24. Kiew - -	120,000	567,390	820,740	273,560	1,508,130
25. Kostroma -	309,790	591,990	569,620	2,190	1,471,400
26. Mohilew -	395,280	587,370	457,630	30,200	1,440,280
27. Toula -	452,940	314,380	506,670	17,640	1,273,990
28. Tschernigow -	356,630	254,150	633,330	90,955	1,244,110
29. Jaroslaw -	288,950	502,250	445,450		1,236,650
30. Penza - -	331,330	256,380	612,490	42,490	1,200,000
31. Podolia -	100,470	406,660	682,980	300,320	1,190,110
32. Kalouga -	334,670	361,900	445,570	280	1,142,140
33. Astrakhan -	87,400	231,780	810,450	3,420	1,129,630
34. Wladimir -	298,890	439.745	398,950		1,137,585
35. Wologda -	193,090	479,250	434,350		1,106,690
36. Kowno -	211,350	458,420	390,490	8,830	1,060,260
37. Nijni-Nowgorod	266,780	235,000	500,550	10,020	1,002,330
38. Moscow -	307,700	292,940	339,300	1,000	939,940
39. Nowgorod -	208,720	517,920	207,390		934,130
40. Minsk - -	117,620	450,610	302,040	96,425	870,270
41. Grodno - -	78,290	247,600	507,230	260,000	833,120
42. Wilna - -	185,070	369,640	251,940	26,970	806,650
43. Livonia - -	142,650	324,070	256,930	54,545	723,650
44. Courland -	110,200	231,700	167,700	17,500	509,600
45. Witebsk -	170,460	245,880	87,830	1,090	504,170
46. Pskow - -	114,790	191,250	92,080	1,500	398,120
47. St. Petersburg -	93,800	162,830	57,400		314,030
48. Esthonia -	39,380	126,480	142,770	55,880	308,630
49. Archangel -	37,000	95,200	100,000		232,200
50. Olonetz -	49,510	93,150	75,610		218,270
Total -	17,092,335	24,917,805	44,846,160	8,334,110	86,856,300

* The figures printed in a stronger type are taken from the *Atlas Sttaistique Agricole*, prepared by the Ministry of Domains, department of Economy.

From the foregoing table we perceive that the largest number of domestic animals is found in the first ten governments, each of which contains more than $2\frac{1}{2}$ millions of them, and which, taken together, reckon upwards of 37 millions, or more than two-fifths of the whole. The governments of Orenburg and Saratow and the kingdom of Poland alone reckon nearly $15\frac{1}{2}$ millions.

Horses are found in greatest numbers in the governments of Orenburg, Saratow, Simbirsk, Koursk, Perm, Tambow, Riazan, Woronèje, Orel, and the kingdom of Poland. Each of these governments reckoned in 1846 more than half a million, and the whole together more than 7,900,000, or upwards of two-fifths of the total number. In the government of Orenburg, there are reckoned more than 1,900,000 head[*], or upwards of a ninth of the number which we have admitted for all European Russia.

For cattle, the first rank is occupied by the kingdom of Poland, the government of Orenburg, the country of the Don Cossacks, the governments of Saratow, Woronèje, Tauride, Twer, Smolensk, Kherson, Wiatka, Poltawa, Simbirsk, Stavropol, and Perm. Each of these governments contains upwards of 600,000 head, and the whole fourteen taken together reckoned in 1846 upwards of $11\frac{1}{2}$ millions, or nearly a moiety of the whole. Next to these fourteen governments come those of Kostroma, Mohilew, Kharkow, Bessarabia, Kiew, and Tambow, each of which reckoned in 1846 upwards of 500,000 head.

In regard to the number of sheep the following provinces and governments stand first, namely, the kingdom of Poland, Saratow, Tauride, country of the Don Cossacks, Orenburg, Simbirsk, Ekathérinoslaw, Woronèje, Poltawa, Kherson, Kharkow, Bessarabia, and Stavropol. Each of these governments possesses more than a million, and the whole together reckoned in 1846 upwards of 26,600,000 head, or more than half of the entire flocks of European Russia. The total cipher of our fine-woolled sheep officially ascertained, amounted in 1846 to 8,334,000 head, of which nearly 5 millions were in the five southern governments, Ekathérinoslaw, Tauride, Bessarabia, Poltawa, Kharkow, and in the kingdom of Poland.

The following -table exhibits the relation of the number of horses and cattle to the extent of productive soil in the various governments, with the exception of the Grand-Duchy of Finland, as to which we do not possess complete information.

---

[*] According to M. Arsénieff's statistics. The number given in the *Atlas Statistique Agricole* is only 1,663,229 head.

Provinces and Governments arranged according to the absolute Number of Cattle and Horses which they contain.	Extent in Dessiatines.		Number of Horses and Cattle in each Government.	Number of Horses and Cattle to 100 Dessiatines	
	Arable Land.	Meadow.		of Arable Land.	of Meadow.
1. Orenburg - -	4,115,000	4,452,000	3,197,880	78	72
2. Kingdom of Poland	5,445,000	1,500,000	2,053,000	38	132
3. Saratow - - -	2,530,000	6,513,000	1,755,880	69	27
4. Simbirsk - -	2,500,000	1,600,000	1,486,160	59	93
5. Country of the Don Cossacks - -	2,310,000	9,540,000	1,341,380	58	14
6. Woronèje - -	3,007,000	2,400,000	1,336,930	44	56
7. Perm - - -	2,589,000	1,993,000	1,313,140	51	66
8. Wiatka - -	2,973,000	500,000	1,236,080	45	247
9. Twer - - -	1,670,000	1,290,000	1,170,080	70	91
10. Koursk - - -	2,503,000	613,000	1,168,510	47	191
11. Smolensk - -	2,000,000	340,000	1,152,290	58	339
12. Tambow - -	2,500,000	1,650,000	1,144,150	46	69
13. Kherson - - -	1,400,000	2,000,000	1,066,120	76	53
14. Mohilew - - -	1,700,000	300,000	982,650	58	328
15. Orel - - -	2,400,000	400,000	979,440	41	240
16. Riazan - - -	1,800,000	300,000	904,040	50	301
17. Kostroma - -	1,600,000	340,000	901,780	56	295
18. Stavropol - -	750,000	4,000,000	883,390	118	22
19. Tauride - - -	750,000	1,600,000	851,140	113	53
20. Poltawa - -	2,000,000	1,215,000	850,715	43	70
21. Jaroslaw - -	1,200,000	492,000	791,200	66	161
22. Kharkow - -	2,100,000	1,350,000	775,800	37	57
23. Toula - - -	2,000,000	220,000	767,320	38	349
24. Kazan - - -	2,100,000	500,000	751,590	36	150
25. Wladimir - -	1,800,000	280,000	738,635	41	264
26. Nowgorod - -	1,300,000	470,000	726,640	56	155
27. Kalouga - -	1,300,000	193,000	696,570	54	361
28. Wolhynia - -	2,110,000	777,000	695,030	33	89
29. Kiew - - -	2,353,000	445,000	687,390	29	154
30. Wologda - -	800,000	450,000	672,340	84	149
31. Kowno - - -	2,060,000	750,000	669,770	33	89
32. Bessarabia - -	1,300,000	1,200,000	660,460	51	55
33. Tschernigow -	3,191,000	630,000	610,780	19	97
34. Moscow - - -	1,300,000	260,000	600,640	46	231
35. Ekathérinoslaw -	1,200,000	1,400,000	598,240	50	43
36. Penza - - -	1,600,000	450,000	587,710	37	131
37. Minsk - -	2,820,000	1,546,000	568,230	20	37
38. Wilna - - -	1,170,000	335,000	554,710	47	166
39. Podolia - - -	2,440,000	773,000	507,130	21	64
40. Nijni-Nowgorod	1,800,000	280,000	501,780	28	179
41. Livonia - - -	415,000	555,000	466,720	112	84
42. Witebsk - -	1,600,000	120,000	416,340	26	347
43. Courland - -	496,000	314,000	341,900	69	109
44. Grodno - - ··	1,470,000	520,000	325,890	22	63
45. Astrakhan - -	150,000	800,000	319,180	213	40
46. Pskow - - -	1,400,000	800,000	306,040	22	38
47. St. Petersburg -	550,000	200,000	256,630	47	128
48. Esthonia - -	240,000	260,000	165,860	69	64
49. Olonetz - -	370,000	110,000	142,660	39	130
50. Archangel - -	80,000	157,000	132,200	165	84

From this table we perceive that the number of cattle and horses taken together varies, in relation to the extent of cultivated soil, from 19 to 213 head per 100 dessiatines.

The government of Astrakhan, which reckons 213 head per 100 dessiatines of arable land, is precisely one of those in which the extent of cultivated soil is smallest in proportion to the total area: its cultivated land occupies but the hundredth part of its surface, the meadows occupying upwards of $5\frac{1}{2}$ per cent., or more than five times as much as the land in culture: on the other hand this government possesses immense tracts of pasture. The governments which have fewest horses and cattle compared with the extent of their cultivated land are those of Tschernigow, Minsk, Podolia, Pskow, and Grodno, where the number is under 25 head per 100 dessiatines. Those governments which have an average of from 25 to 50 head are twenty-three in number, namely, Woronèje, Wiatka, Koursk, Tambow, Orel, Riazan, Poltawa, Kharkow, Toula, Kazan, Wladimir, Wolhynia, Kiew, Kowno, Moscow, Ekathérinoslaw, Penza, Wilna, Nijni-Nowgorod, Witebsk, St. Petersburg, Olonetz, and the kingdom of Poland. In these governments, as in those of the preceding category, rotations are difficult in consequence of the want of manure: in several of them, however, as Wolhynia, Podolia, Poltawa, and Kharkow, the soil is of itself eminently fertile. The governments most favoured in regard to rotation, which reckon from 50 to 100 head of cattle and horses per 100 dessiatines of cultivated land, are seventeen in number, namely, Orenburg, Saratow, Simbirsk, the country of the Don Cossacks, the governments of Perm, Twer, Smolensk, Kherson, Mohilew, Kostroma, Jaroslaw, Nowgorod, Kalouga, Wologda, Bessarabia, Courland, and Esthonia. In some of these governments, for example in Saratow and Simbirsk, we likewise find districts in which the soil is so fertile as to be independent of manure. The governments in which the number of cattle and horses exceeds the number of dessiatines of arable land are those of Livonia, Astrakhan, and Archangel. Cattle-rearing is favoured in the government of Livonia by the skilful management of the meadow land, and a generally more advanced system of rural economy; it is favoured in Astrakhan by the abundance of the pastures; and in Archangel by the good quality of the herbage in the neighbourhood of the rivers.

The differences amongst the governments in the relative number of cattle, as compared with the extent of meadow land, is still more considerable. The number varies from 14 to 361 head per 100 dessiatines. The governments in which this proportion is smallest are those of Saratow, the country of the

Don Cossacks, Stavropol, Ekathérinoslaw, Minsk, Astrakhan, and Pskow, where the numbers are under 50 head per 100 dessiatines. In the country of the Don Cossacks the number is only 14 head per 100 dessiatines, which is the more remarkable as the province abounds in good pastures: it is evident that the rearing of cattle and horses might there be greatly extended; and the same remark is applicable to the governments of Saratow, Stavropol, Ekathérinoslaw, and Astrakhan: in Pskow progress is impeded by the bad quality of the meadows and pastures. Those governments which present the medium figure of from 50 to 100 head per 100 dessiatines of meadow, are nineteen in number, namely, Orenburg, Simbirsk, Woronèje, Perm, Twer, Tambow, Kherson, Tauride, Poltawa, Kharkow, Wolhynia, Kowno, Bessarabia, Tschernigow, Podolia, Livonia, Grodno, Esthonia, and Archangel. In all the other governments the number of cattle and horses taken together exceeds the number of dessiatines of meadow; and there are eleven, namely, Wiatka, Smolensk, Mohilew, Orel, Riazan, Kostroma, Toula, Wladimir, Kalouga, Moscow, and Witebsk, which count from 2 to 3 head, or even more, per dessiatine.

Such large disproportions in the relative number of cattle and horses as compared with the cultivated land or with the meadow land, and such great differences amongst the different provinces of the empire, are not found in any other country. Austria is undoubtedly one of the European states which presents most variety in this respect. But on comparing with each other the different provinces of that empire, according to the official statistics of 1846, we perceive that in Moravia and Silesia, which raise the smallest number of bestial in proportion to the extent of their cultivated soil, there were reckoned 43 head per 100 dessiatines, and in the Tyrol, where the relative cipher of the bestial is largest, there are reckoned 250 head per 100 dessiatines, so that the difference between the minimum and maximum is only in the proportion of 10 to 58; whereas in Russia the difference between Tschernigow and Astrakhan is as 10 to 112.

There are 18 governments with us in which the relative number of horses and cattle to the land in cultivation is below the relative cipher of Moravia and Silesia; and there is not one in which the relative cipher with us is equal to that of the Tyrol. The *minimum*, which in Austria is 43 head to 100 dessiatines of cultivated land, descends in Russia, in the governments of Grodno and Pskow, to 22; in that of Podolia, to 21; in that of Tschernigow so low as 19 head per 100 dessiatines. In regard to the numerical relation of this class of

animals to the extent of meadow land in Austria, it is the
Adriatic Littoral which presents the lowest cipher, namely, 121
head to 100 dessiatines. The highest figure, namely, 955 head
to 100 dessiatines, is found in Dalmatia; but that province, the
soil of which is almost entirely volcanic and rocky, possesses
scarcely any meadow land — not so much as a hundredth part
of its surface being thus occupied. Next to Dalmatia the
highest relative figure is found in Transylvania, where the proportion is 352 head to 100 dessiatines. Thus, laying Dalmatia
out of view, on account of its exceptional position, topographical and geological, the difference between the *minimum* and
maximum in Austria is only in the proportion of 10 to 29;
whilst in Russia it is, between the country of the Don Cossacks
(14 head per 100 dessiatines) and the government of Kalouga
(361 head per 100 dessiatines), in the proportion of 10 to
258. There are 27 governments with us in which the relative
number of horses and cattle to the extent of meadow land is inferior to that of the Austrian Littoral: the *minimum* per 100
dessiatines, which is there 121 head, descends with us as low as
14 head.

The opposite table exhibits a recapitulation of the numerical
relations which exist in European Russia betwixt the extent of
productive soil, the population, and the number of domestic
animals in the various provinces and governments. The statistical results of this table having been already analysed in
our commentaries upon the different special tables here re-
capitulated, it only remains for us to add one or two observations on the proportion betwixt the number of domestic animals
and the population of the several governments.

There are 15 governments where the number of head of
cattle attains or exceeds half the number of the population. Of
these 15 there are 3, namely, the country of the Don Cossacks
and the governments of Stavropol and Tauride, in which the
number of cattle exceeds the number of the inhabitants. Of
the 35 provinces and governments in which this number does
not attain half the cipher of the population, there are 5,
namely, Penza, Moscow, Nijni-Nowgorod, Tschernigow, and
St. Petersburg, in which the number is less than a fourth of
the population.

In France there are reckoned 23 head of cattle to every 100
inhabitants; in Austria, 31; and in Prussia, 33. Comparing
these ciphers with the preceding table, we perceive that there
are in Russia only 4 governments in which the relative number
is inferior to that of France, and 16 in which it does not reach
that of Prussia and Austria.

GOVERNMENTS.	Mean Extent of productive Soil per Inhabitant, expressed in Dessiatines.				Mean extent of Forests, per Inhabitant, for the entire Population.	Number of domestic Animals per 100 Inhabitants.				Number of Heads of Cattle and Horses per 100 Dessiatines		
	For the entire Population.		For the rural Population.							of arable Land.	of Meadow.	of the two Sorts of land together
	Arable	Meadow	Arable	Meadow		Cattle	Horses	Sheep	Total			
					Dess.							
1. Archangel -	0·32	0·62	0·36	0·70	117·6	38	15	40	93	165	84	56
2. Astrakhan -	0·72	3·86	0·97	5·15	0·6	112	42	392	546	213	40	34
3. Bessarabia -	1·44	1·33	1·72	1·59	0·3	63	10	160	233	51	55	26
4. Kharkow -	1·77	1·14	2·10	1·29	0·4	49	16	124	189	37	57	22
5. Kherson -	1·52	2·19	2·00	2·85	0·1	83	33	177	293	76	53	31
6. Country of the Don Cossacks -	2·89	10·20	2·97	12·26	0·5	146	47	305	498	58	14	11
7. Courland -	0·94	0·59	1·06	0·67	1·8	44	21	31	96	69	109	42
8. Ekathérinoslaw -	1·21	1·41	1·32	1·54	0·1	50	10	207	267	50	43	23
9. Esthonia -	0·79	0·86	0·88	0·95	1·5	42	13	47	102	69	64	33
10. Grodno -	1·69	0·60	1·87	0·66	0·9	28	9	58	95	22	63	16
11. Taroslaw -	1·25	0·51	1·36	0·56	0·8	52	30	46	128	66	161	47
12. Kalouga -	1·33	0·20	1·57	0·22	0·5	37	34	46	117	54	361	47
13. Kazan -	1·51	0·36	1·60	0·38	1·9	26	28	55	109	36	150	29
14. Kiew -	1·38	0·26	1·53	0·29	0·6	33	7	48	88	29	154	25
15. Kostroma -	1·53	0·32	1·59	0·34	4·8	57	30	54	141	56	295	46
16. Koursk -	1·45	0·35	1·55	0·38	0·3	25	43	45	113	47	191	38
17. Kowno -	2·20	0·80	2·32	0·85	0·6	49	23	42	114	33	89	24
18. Livonia -	0·50	0·66	0·56	0·75	2·3	39	17	31	87	112	84	48
19. Minsk -	2·88	1·58	3·10	1·70	3·4	46	12	31	89	20	37	13
20. Mohilew -	2·04	0·36	2·17	0·38	1·9	70	47	55	172	58	328	49
21. Moscow -	0·86	0·17	1·15	0·23	0·7	19	20	22	61	46	231	39
22. Nijni-Nowgorod -	1·53	0·24	1·63	0·25	1·7	20	23	43	86	28	179	24
23. Nowgorod -	1·46	0·53	1·52	0·55	7·9	58	23	23	104	56	155	41
24. Olonetz -	1·33	0·40	1·41	0·42	34·8	33	18	27	78	39	130	30
25. Orel -	1·70	0·28	1·81	0·31	0·8	30	39	67	136	41	240	35
26. Orenburg -	1·93	2·09	1·99	2·15	4·7	60	90	111	261	78	72	37
27. Penza -	1·50	0·42	1·61	0·45	1·0	24	31	57	112	37	131	29
28. Perm -	1·38	1·06	1·42	1·10	10·6	33	37	44	114	51	66	29
29. Podolia -	1·56	0·48	1·61	0·51	0·3	25	6	43	74	21	64	16
30. Kingdom of Poland -	1·12	0·31	1·25	0·34	0·7	32	11	66	109	38	132	30
31. Poltawa -	1·20	0·73	1·28	0·78	0·2	42	10	101	153	43	70	26
32. Pskow -	2·08	1·19	2·22	1·27	2·1	28	17	14	59	22	38	14
33. Riazan -	1·31	0·22	1·39	0·23	0·7	25	41	55	121	50	301	43
34. Saratow -	1·36	3·50	1·51	3·88	0·6	48	47	156	251	69	27	19
35. Simbirsk -	2·08	1·33	2·28	1·46	1·7	52	72	176	300	59	93	36
36. Smolensk -	1·85	0·26	1·94	0·27	2·0	62	45	52	159	58	339	49
37. St. Petersburg -	0·48	0·17	0·99	0·36	2·1	14	8	5	27	47	128	34
38. Stavropol -	0·75	4·00	0·78	4·16	0·1	63	25	118	206	118	22	19
39. Tambow -	1·48	0·98	1·59	1·05	0·9	30	38	55	123	46	69	28
40. Tauride -	1·13	2·41	1·36	2·90	0·4	104	24	367	495	113	53	36
41. Tschernigow -	2·29	0·45	2·47	0·49	0·6	18	26	45	89	19	97	16
42. Toula -	1·79	0·20	1·95	0·21	0·4	28	41	45	114	38	349	35
43. Twer -	1·18	0·85	1·27	0·97	1·6	48	35	32	115	70	91	40
44. Wiatka -	1·54	0·21	1·58	0·26	4·7	38	26	48	112	45	247	36
45. Wilna -	1·43	0·41	1·57	0·45	2·0	45	23	31	99	47	166	37
46. Witebsk -	2·18	0·16	2·42	0·18	2·0	34	23	12	69	26	347	24
47. Wladimir -	1·53	0·24	1·64	0·25	1·5	38	26	34	98	41	264	36
48. Wolhynia -	1·41	0·54	1·52	0·56	1·6	28	19	67	114	33	89	24
49. Wologda -	0·92	0·52	0·97	0·55	37·0	55	22	50	127	84	149	54
50. Woronèje -	1·80	1·44	1·90	1·51	0·3	47	33	102	182	44	56	25

In regard to the distribution of horses, we find 24 governments in which the number exceeds a fourth of the population, and 16 in which it is under the proportion of 1 to 5. Of these 16 there are 4, namely, Grodno, Kiew, Podolia, and St. Petersburg, in which there is not 1 horse for every 10 inhabitants. The governments in which the relative number of horses is greatest are Orenburg and Simbirsk, where the number exceeds half the number of the inhabitants.

In France and Austria there are reckoned 8 horses to 100 inhabitants, and in Prussia 11. From our table it appears that there are only two governments, namely, Kiew and Podolia, in which the relative number of horses is inferior to that of Austria and France; and seven, namely, the two just named, and Bessarabia, Ekathérinoslaw, Grodno, Poltawa, and St. Petersburg, in which it is inferior to that of Prussia.

In regard to sheep, there are 13 governments, namely, Astrakhan, Bessarabia, Kharkow, Kherson, Ekathérinoslaw, Orenburg, Poltawa, Saratow, Simbirsk, Stavropol, Tauride, Woronèje, and the country of the Don Cossacks, in which their number exceeds that of the population. The figure is highest in the governments of Astrakhan, Ekathérinoslaw, Stavropol, Tauride, and the country of the Don Cossacks. In the two latter, and in Astrakhan, the number of sheep is more than triple that of the population. The governments in which there are less than 1 sheep for every 2 inhabitants are 25 in number, and of these the cipher is lowest in Pskow, Witebsk, and St. Petersburg. In the first of these governments there are but 14; in the second, 12; and in the third, only 5 sheep to every 100 inhabitants.

We shall have occasion to recur to this table in the sequel: meantime we proceed with our estimates.

V. *Poultry.*

Although the proper fattening of poultry is still very much neglected with us, fowls are reared in considerable numbers. There are not many peasant families whose yard is unprovided with a few hens, or ducks, or perhaps a few geese or turkeys; and in villages not very remote from populous towns, this branch of rural economy is found very remunerative.

If we were to reckon but a single fowl for each inhabitant, or 62,000,000 in all, and to estimate the gross product in flesh, eggs, feathers, and down at 10 kopecks per head, we would obtain a result of 6,200,000 roubles; but we consider that we may, without exaggeration, admit a gross product of 10,000,000 of roubles. In France, M. Chaptal estimated the product of the poultry at 64,700,000 francs = 16,175,000 roubles; and other statists have carried it very much beyond this amount. In the remarks accompanying the agricultural statistics of France for 1838, the product of eggs alone is estimated at 120,000,000 francs = 30,000,000 roubles.

VI. *Bees.*

The bee acclimatises up to a very high latitude, not only in European Russia, but in Siberia. It was long thought that the climate of Siberia was utterly unsuitable for the rearing of bees; but experiments made at the commencement of the present century in the governments of Tomsk, Omsk, and Jenisseisk, have proved the contrary. The religious ceremonies of the Greek Church, requiring a large consumption of wax candles, greatly favour this branch of rural economy in Russia, and preserve it from the decline to which it is exposed in other countries from the increasing use of stearine and oil for lighting. We produce wax so cheaply, that, notwithstanding the consumption of that article has greatly diminished abroad, it still continues to form an important item of our commerce; but the exportation of honey has considerably decreased, in consequence of the increasing use of potatoe syrup, which has also injured the honey trade in the interior of Russia.

The rearing of bees is extensively carried on in several parts of European Russia, especially in Little Russia, in the southern governments, in some governments of Central Russia, in the Polish and in the transcaucasian provinces. In 1832, there were reckoned in the single government of Poltawa 360,069 hives. The government of Moscow likewise occupies a high rank in this branch of rural economy. The product of preparations of honey and wax in this government is valued by M. Arsénieff, from quantities officially ascertained, at 970,000 roubles; but it is more than probable that the whole raw material was not produced in this government alone, and that, considering the large consumption of wax in religious ceremonies at Moscow, a good deal of it is imported from the neighbouring governments and from Little Russia.

Taking into consideration the quantities of wax candles that are employed in the ceremonies of the Greek and Romish churches, we may form some estimate of the importance of apiarian economy in Russia. There are in the empire, without including Finland or the kingdom of Poland, 46,741 churches and chapels of the orthodox Greek Church, 2,264 Catholic churches, 52 Armenian Catholic, and 1,048 Armenian Grego-

rian.   In the kingdom of Poland there are about 3,500 Catholic
and Greek churches, which brings the total number of churches
of the two communions to 53,605.

The revenues from the sale of wax-candles for 46,741 churches
and chapels of the Greek rite amount, according to official returns, to 799,066 roubles.   Assuming the value of the actual
consumption of wax-candles not to exceed the amount of net
revenue which the clergy derive from the sale, and reckoning
the wax at the average price of 12 roubles per pood, this would
indicate a consumption of only 66,589 poods, or an average of
57 lbs. for each church ; but we think we cannot fairly estimate
the average consumption of each church at less than 2 poods,
which for the total number of 53,605 churches of the two communions, would give a consumption of 107,210 poods.   Adding
to this the wax employed in various industrial and technical
uses, the wax-candles burned in the synagogues, in the religious
ceremonies of various sects, and in private houses, and the quantity exported, (11,000 to 12,000 poods), we may estimate the total
production of wax at 150,000 poods; and, as the usual calculation is 3 poods of honey to 1 pood of wax, this supposes a production of 450,000 poods of honey.   Reckoning the wax at 12
roubles and the honey at 2 roubles per pood, we obtain for the
total production a gross value of 2,700,000 roubles; but we do
not think it would be an excessive estimate if we were to carry
the figure up to 3 millions.   In France the product from bees
is estimated at 13 millions of francs = 3,250,000 roubles.

VII. *Silk-worms.*

The climate of Southern Russia has long been recognised as
favourable for the rearing of silk-worms.   The first attempts at
the cultivation of the mulberry date from the reign of Peter the
Great, since which period it has been the object of numerous
encouragements on the part of the state.   We possess no very
exact or complete data with respect to the production of silk in
Russia.   According to information collected by the Ministry of
the Interior, there should have been produced in the governments of Astrakhan, Saratow, Kiew, Podolia, Kharkow, Ekathérinoslow, Kherson, and Tauride, during three years from
1833 to 1835, a mean annual quantity of about 300 poods.
Since that period little progress seems to have been made in the
southern provinces, if we may judge from the information contained in the Report by the Department of Economy to the Ministry of Domains, published in 1849, where it appears that the
production of silk in the governments of Tauride, Bessarabia,
Podolia, Kherson, Astrakhan, and Ekathérinoslaw, during the

five preceding years, had yielded at an average only about 180 poods per annum.

Independently of the provinces which we have just named, this branch of agricultural industry begins to assume some importance in the governments of Poltawa and Tschernigow; but its principal seat is the transcaucasian provinces, where M. Hagmeister estimates the production at about 30,000 poods.* The information which we have obtained directly from the local authorities exhibits the production of Caucasian silk as follows:—

Governments.				Poods.	Roubles.
Tiflis	-	-	-	560	40,000
Koutaïs	-	-	-	920	42,000
Erivan	-	-	-	569	29,000
Shemakha	-	-	-	11,425	640,000
Derbent	-	-	-	4,668	295,000
Total	-	-		18,142	1,046,000 †

But this information is not complete; the production of some districts of Mingrelia is not included at all, and that of some other districts is estimated far below the actual quantity. Altogether, combining the most recent data which we have been able to procure, we consider that we may estimate the production of silk in the transcaucasian provinces at 25,000 poods as *minimum*, which quantity, along with the silk produced in the southern provinces of European Russia, we value at the slump sum of 1,500,000 roubles.

The silk of the Caucasus is generally of very inferior quality; it is sold on the spot at from 40 to 50 roubles, and the better qualities at from 80 to 100 roubles per pood: the district of Chekhime produces the best, and these sorts sell at from 100 to 200 roubles per pood; but this latter price is very rare.

VIII. *Products of the Chase.*

Our chase of furred animals may be divided into three branches, namely, that of the Russo-American Company, founded at the end of last century; that of Siberia; and that of European Russia.

The following, according to authentic returns which we owe to the kindness of Rear-Admiral Wrangel, is a general summary of the products of the chase of the Russo-American Company from 1798 to 1848 inclusive:—

* See the pamphlet published by this author in 1848, under the title of " Novijia Otscherki Zakavkazïa " (New Sketches of the transcaucasian Provinces). |

† We have obtained this sum by valuing the product of each district at the prices current on the spot.

		Skins.
Furred seals (*phoca ursina*) - - - -		1,775,132
Sea otters - - - - - -		118,225
Fresh-water beavers - - - - -		246,162
Otters - - - - - -		88,554
Norki (a sort of marsh otter) - - -		20,283
Black, grey, and red foxes - - -		187,101
Blue and white foxes of the Polar regions - -		39,251
Lynxes - - - - - -		10,313
Sables - - - - - -		38,018
Musk-rats - - - - -		4,491
Gluttons - - - - - -		2,725
Wolves - - - - - -		221
Bears - - - - - -		8,441
Otter and seal tails - - - -		91,855
Total - - - - -		2,630,772

or, at an average, 43,745 pieces per annum.

We perceive from the above summary that the principal produce of this chase consists of seals, which represent, as regards number, 71 per cent. of the whole. The present produce is by no means so large as it was formerly,—the numbers of various species having considerably diminished. Thus, for example, during the quinquennial period from 1806 to 1810, there were brought in 18,525 beaver and sea-otter skins, and from 1844 to 1848 only 7,056, being a decrease of 11,469 skins, or 62 per cent.; of seals there were brought in during the period from 1806 to 1810, 379,236 skins, and from 1844 to 1848 only 61,222, showing a falling off to such an extent that the produce was only one-sixth of its former amount. On the other hand, the number of skins of the fresh-water beaver, which the Company receives from the Americans by way of barter, has considerably augmented. During the period from 1806 to 1810, the number received was only 2,267, and during the period from 1844 to 1848, it amounted to upwards of 40,000. A comparison of the total product during these two quinquennia gives the following result : —

		Skins.
From 1806 to 1810 - - - -		447,887
From 1844 to 1848 - - - -		186,346
Decrease - - - -		261,541

or 58 per cent., which exhibits a fall in the number of skins to about two-fifths of what it was eight-and-thirty years ago.

The fur products of the Russo-American Company, imported into Russia, or sold to the Americans and Chinese, during the twenty-one years from 1817 to 1838, represented a value of about 20,000,000 of paper roubles, equivalent, at the average value of paper currency during the period in question (47 per cent.), to 9,400,000 silver roubles. The value of the present produce, taking an average of the five years from 1843 to 1847, is about 194,000 silver roubles per annum.

The product of the chase in Siberia consists principally of the skins of the sable, the ermine, the squirrel, the fox, and the musk-rat. The finest species are found in the countries inhabited by the Jakoutes, who exterminate the furred animals without the least consideration, so that they are becoming rarer and rarer, and the produce of the chase is visibly declining. The following comparative summary of the number of animals killed in the country of the Jakoutes in 1825 and 1830 respectively is borrowed from the statistics of M. Boulgarine.

	Number in 1825.	Number in 1830.	Decrease.
Sables -	18,600	6,000	12,600
Foxes -	32,750	16,485	16,265
Squirrels	455,000	332,500	122,500
Ermines	25,000	18,500	6,500
Musk-rats	15,000	8,000	7,000
Total -	546,350	381,485 *	164,865

Besides the species above mentioned, the bear, the wolf, the hare, and the wild rein-deer, are hunted by the colonised peasants, and the nomade populations of Siberia. In regard to the present produce of the chase there we possess no positive data; but we think it can scarcely be estimated at a higher value than from 200,000 to 250,000 silver roubles. A large proportion of the Siberian and American furs are sold at Kiachta for China.

In European Russia the principal fur hunting-grounds are in the Ural mountains, and in the north of the empire, especially in the governments of Archangel, Olonetz, and Wologda, and in Nova-Zembla. The animals hunted in this part of Russia are the bear, the wolf, the badger, the fox, the hare, the squirrel, the lynx, and many others. The chase in the government of Archangel brings in upwards of 200,000 silver roubles: the produce of the year 1846 was 231,000 roubles.

Game of every sort, which might, except in the steppes and some northern districts, be easily propagated throughout Russia, especially in the western governments and in the kingdom of Poland, is very far from plentiful: this is owing to its not being properly preserved, and also to the large numbers of wolves and foxes. The hazel hen (gelinotte) is the principal game of the northern governments.

This single item brings in to the inhabitants of the government of Archangel and Wologda from 35,000 to 40,000 silver roubles.

* This produce of the chase in 1830 represented, according to an approximative estimate, a gross value of about 200,000 silver roubles.

We may approximatively estimate the annual product of the chase throughout the whole empire at 2 millions of silver, roubles as *minimum*.

IX.   *Fisheries.*

It is well known that Russia abounds in fish of every description, and that in some districts fishing forms one of the principal occupations of the people. Of all the maritime fisheries, that of the Caspian Sea is the most important. Its principal products are the sturgeon, with the caviar which is prepared from it, the beluga or large sturgeon, the seal, and the sevriouga. M. Arsénieff estimates the value at 5 millions of silver roubles— an amount which does not seem excessive, if we consider the enormous quantities of fish of every sort which are captured. The Volga and its affluents abound in caviar sturgeon, the best fresh-water fish known. The Black Sea and the Sea of Azow likewise abound in fish of the greatest variety. We find, amongst others, the tunny, the salmon, the sea-trout, anchovies, and herrings weighing as much as a pound and a half.

In 1843, the fisheries of the government of Ekathérinoslaw produced, according to official data which we find in the statistics of M. Arsénieff, 1,010,000 poods of large fish and caviar, and 27 millions of herrings and other fish which are sold by tale,— quantities which would represent, at the very moderate rate of 50 kopecks the pood for large fish, and $\frac{1}{2}$ kopeck a-piece for the herrings, &c., a value of 640,000 silver roubles. In the country of the Don Cossacks, the fishery produced in 1834, likewise according to official data, 5,172,000 poods, representing, at the average price of 50 kopecks, 2,586,000 silver roubles. The product of the principal fisheries of the governments of Kherson, Tauride, and Stavropol, is estimated by M. Arsénieff at 250,000 roubles.

The Baltic furnishes cod, salmon, and halibut, lampreys, and several sorts of small fish. In the White Sea are found herrings, cod, salmon, and halibut. This fishery is almost the sole resource of the inhabitants along the coasts of the government of Archangel. The product which it yields to commerce is estimated at more than 200,000 silver roubles; and it only requires a more numerous population to augment this value. In 1846, the sea fishery produced 200,000 poods of cod and 129,000 poods of other fish, representing together, at the local prices, a value of 211,000 silver roubles.

The principal fishing rivers are the Volga with its affluents, the Emba, the Don, the Ural, the Terek, the Düna, the Neva, the Dniester, the Bug, the Dnieper, the Couban, the Vistula, and the Danube. A traveller, whose narrative will be found in the *Archives du Nord* for 1827, No. 14, asserts that the Danube fisheries may bring in to Russia, in the course of time, as much as 10 millions of roubles: but this estimate we consider somewhat beyond the mark. The rivers of Siberia likewise abound in fish of different sorts.

The best fish lakes are, in European Russia, Ladoga, Onega, Ilmen, and the White Lake: in Siberia, lakes Baïcal, Korin, Taïmour, Bistrouchine, and Barabine.

The proceeds of the different fisheries which we have cited, representing a total value of about 8,700,000 silver roubles, comprehend only the officially ascertained quantities of some of our principal sea fisheries: adding the quantities which escape the control of authority, together with the products of the Baltic and Danube fisheries, which are not included in those estimates, and of the whole lake and river fisheries of the interior, we think we may carry the total proceeds of the fisheries of European Russia, Finland, and the kingdom of Poland, to 15 millions of roubles as *minimum*, which gives, for a population of more than 62 millions, only 24 kopecks per inhabitant.

This estimate will undoubtedly be considered very moderate, when it is observed that during the long lents of the Greek Church a large portion of the population in a good many governments subsist principally upon fish, either fresh, or salted, dried, or smoked.

According to the preceding calculations, the products of the animal kingdom, in so far as they are susceptible of a valuation more or less approximative, would represent in round numbers a gross value of about 307 millions of silver roubles.

Recapitulatory Estimate of Agricultural Products.

	Silver Roubles.
Cereals, including straw - - -	1,019,200,000
Potatoes - - - - -	15,000,000
Culture of beet-root for sugar - -	1,800,000
Product of vineyards - - -	7,700,000
Product of gardens - - - -	60,000,000
Product of meadows - - -	360,000,000
Flax and hemp - - - -	36,523,000
Cotton - - - - -	520,000
Oleaginous grains - - - -	18,386,000
Tobacco - - - - -	2,100,000
Tinctorial and medicinal plants - -	2,500,000
Forest products - - - -	135,000,000
Products of domestic animals - -	275,380,000
Poultry - - - - -	10,000,000
Bees - - - - -	3,000,000
Silk - - - - - -	1,500,000
Chase - - - - -	2,000,000
Fisheries - - - - -	15,000,000
Total (=£311,221,000 sterling) -	1,965,609,000

In this estimate the agricultural products of the Russian possessions in Asia are not included. Our calculations embrace only the wine, the silk, the cotton, and the tinctorial plants of the transcaucasian provinces, and the product of the chase in Siberia; but these items taken together amount to no more than 8 or 9 millions of roubles. Adding, then, to the above cipher, 4 per cent. only, or $78\frac{1}{2}$ millions for the whole other agricultural produce of that part of Russia, which reckons more than four millions of inhabitants, or about 8 per cent. of the population of the entire empire, we obtain for the gross product of our rural economy a grand total of, in round numbers, 2,044 millions of roubles, ($= 323\frac{1}{2}$ millions sterling).

It might perhaps be objected, and not without some show of reason, that in our estimates are included products which figure twice over—as, for example, that the hay, which is employed in feeding the cattle and horses, is virtually counted over again in the gross revenue arising from these animals. In answer to this objection, if raised, we must observe, *first*, that in statistical calculations, of which the object is to represent the gross value of the whole productions of a country, it is impossible to proceed otherwise: we cannot estimate and subtract every thing that is consumed in the course of production, for this is precisely what constitutes the difference between gross value and net value; and *secondly*, that, wishing to form a comparison betwixt the productive forces of our own and those of other countries, by means of which comparison alone can statistical figures of the sort assume their proper signification, we have been obliged to follow the system adopted in the agricultural statistics of France and Austria. Now, in these two countries, this double estimate of values is employed in the same manner as it has been employed by us; and in France it has been so to a comparatively greater extent; for, independently of the hay harvest, there is likewise taken into account the produce of the pastures and fallows, and afterwards the produce of the domestic animals. In regard to the latter, we find the following remark in M. Schnitzler's General Statistics of France, (vol. iii. p. 276, in note):

"The agricultural statistics leave us in uncertainty with regard to what they mean by the term *income from domestic animals;* for the consumption of meat is subsequently given apart by itself; and in the Report to the King, which is prefixed to the body of the work, we read (page xxxi.), ' Domestic animals add to the wealth of Eastern France '" (the half of the country of which the statistics were then finished),

	Francs.
' 1st, an annual revenue amounting to - -	350,000,000
2nd, a consumption of meat reckoned at - -	260,000,000
Total -	610,000,000 '

"What is the meaning of this? Was the meat not included in the annual revenue? Of what, then, was the latter composed? Was it of the hides and the wool — the dung and the motory forces? We do not think the author of the Statistics meant to include in his estimate the two latter articles; he has stated the first apart by itself, and the second does not amount to 20,000,000 of francs. What is most probable, and is indeed rendered almost certain by the circumstance that the horses are included in the table, is, that he meant to speak of the value of the annual reproduction. But this reproduction takes place at the expense of existences which partly compose the capital of that branch; and its value, therefore, cannot properly be reckoned as true income. We think there is some confusion here; but it is only fair to bear in mind that the author himself admits (tome i. p. xxxix.) that the figures relating to this income are to be regarded as mere hints, in respect that the materials were not so satisfactory as could have been wished."

Our estimates are not liable to a similar objection, and they appear to be fairer; for, eliminating entirely the value of the motory force furnished by the cattle employed in the plough, and in the transport of agricultural produce and merchandise, we have taken into account merely the meat and tallow consumed or exported, together with the hides and dairy produce. Our estimates will also be found very moderate on a comparison with the French statistics, which give as the mean product of the cattle, 36 francs 48 centimes = 9 roubles 12 kopecks per head, independently of the value of the meat, whilst we have reckoned the same product only at 4 roubles per head, the value of the meat included.

In France, the gross returns from agriculture were estimated in 1819 by Count Chaptal at 4,678,708,000 francs; in 1826, by M. Charles Dupin, at 5,313,163,755 francs; M. Lullin de Chateauvieux restricts their value to 5,020,510,000 francs; M. Dutens carries it for 1836 to 6,728,760,000 francs, and M. Royer arrives at 7,543,023,000 francs. M. Dombasle considers the cipher of 6 milliards as below the reality, and M. Schnitzler is of the same opinion with that celebrated agronomist.

The official agricultural statistics prepared in 1840 give the following estimate :—

		Francs.
Product of cultivated land, including crops of every sort		3,558,014,132
„ of pasture lands - - - -		762,482,433
„ of woods and forests - - -		206,600,525
„ of domestic animals - - -		767,251,851
Value of meat consumed - - - -		543,180,518
	Total -	5,837,529,459

In his Report to the King, and in the observations which accompany the official statistics, the Minister of Agriculture and Commerce calls attention to the omissions which lessen the sum total of agricultural production, arising from the want of exact data for the valuation of some items, as bees, straw, orchards, willow and alder plantations, the gleanage and maraudage of forests, poultry and eggs, hides and leather, tallow and offals. To meet these omissions, the minister adds to the foregoing estimate a slump sum of 240 millions, and brings the total cipher of agricultural production to 6,077,000,000 francs. Comparing with this cipher the result of our estimate of the gross produce of agriculture in Russia, it will be found that the latter exceeds the former by more than 2 milliards of francs. But in order to appreciate at their just value the results of these two estimates, it must be borne in mind, that not being possessed of such exact data as the official statists of France had at command, we have been obliged, in order to avoid laying ourselves open to the charge of exaggeration, to reduce our figures to the lowest possible standard, in regard both to the quantities of gross produce, and to the rate of money valuation of the same. It is only necessary to make a few comparisons between our estimative prices and those adopted in the French official statistics, in order to perceive how easy it would have been for us to have attained a much higher figure, if we had not confined our estimates within such narrow limits:

The following are a few examples:—

	Estimates adopted in the Official Statistics of France.	Estimates adopted by us.
Average price of cereals, viz. wheat, rye, barley, and oats, taken in slump -	11 frs. 23 cent. per hectol. = 5 roub. 46 kop. per tchetw.	3 roubles 50 kopecks per tchetwert.
Garden produce - -	435 frs. 55 cent. per hec. = 118 roub. 90 kop. per dessiatine	25 roub. per dessiatine.
Produce of natural medows	110 frs. 20 cent. per hect. = 30 roub. 8 kop. per dessiat.	6 roub. per dessiatine.
Flax - - - -	1 fr. 15 cent. per kilo. = 4 roub. 70 kop. per pood -	2 roub. per pood.
Hemp - - - -	90 centimes per kilogr. = 3 roub. 70 kop. per pood -	
Linseed and Hempseed -	18 fr. 46 cent. per hectol. = 8 roub. 98 kop. per tchetw. -	5 roub. per tchetwert.
Produce of forests - -	23 fr. 46 cent. per hect. = 6 roub. 40 kop. per dessiatine	75 kopecks per dessiatine.

	Estimates adopted in the Official Statistics of France.	Estimates adopted by us.
Produce of cattle - -	40 fr. = 10 roub. per head *	4 roub. per head.†
Produce of sheep - -	3 fr. 73 cent. = 93 kops. per head * - - - -	50 kops. per head.†
Produce of horses - -	78 fr. 44 cent. = 19 roub. 61 kops. per head - -	8 roub. per head.

We have further to add, that in the absence of sufficient data for even an approximative estimate, we have entirely omitted several articles which occupy an important place in the agricultural statistics of France, as, for example, the produce of the pasture lands. The average annual produce from pastures in France is estimated at 8 francs 95 centimes per hectare, and the average annual produce from fallows used as pasture is estimated at 13 francs 65 centimes per hectare, which gives, for 6,763,000 hectares of fallow, and 9,191,000 hectares of pasture land, nearly 175 millions of francs. To what an enormous sum would the produce of our immense area of fallow and pasture amount at this rate, occupying as it does, according to an approximative estimate, at least 80 millions of dessiatines = 87 millions of hectares. Reckoning the produce from a hectare at only 5 francs, or less than half the estimate adopted in France, we would have a product of 435 millions,—a value which is entirely eliminated from our calculations. In the agricultural statistics of France, there is taken into account the value of beer and brandy, representing together a sum of more than 117 millions of francs: the value of these articles with us will be taken into account in the second part of this work, designed to treat of the different branches of industry immediately connected with agriculture. These collocations prove irrefragably that if we were to adopt, in estimating the productive forces of Russia, the plan pursued in the agricultural statistics of France, even whilst reducing for some articles by a third or by a half the rate of estimate adopted in the latter country, we would obtain for total value of the gross products of our agriculture more than 3 milliards of silver roubles, or 12 milliards of francs: but as this work is only a statistical study or essay which we submit to the criticism of the public, we have confined ourselves to taking an account of the elements of our national wealth, and ascertaining approximatively the *minimum* gross value of the products of our soil as based upon the most moderate calculations which it is possible to adopt.

That the reader may judge still better of this comparison, we exhibit in parallel columns the quantities of the principal raw

* Value of the meat *not* included.
† Value of the meat *included*.

products of our agriculture and of that of France, together with the extent of our respective forests, meadows, and pastures.

	France.			European Russia.
Cereals, including dry legumes	200,000,000 hect. =	102,800,000	tchetw.	260,000,000 tchetw.
Flax and hemp	84,380,000 kilog. =	5,128,000	poods.	20,000,000 poods.*
Oleaginous grains	2,409,000 hect. =	1,238,000	tchetw.	4,865,000 tchetw.*
Cattle (calves not included)	- - - - -	7,870,000	head	25,000,000 head
Sheep - -	- - - -	32,000,000	„	50,000,000 „
Swine -	- - - -	4,910,000	„	12,000,000 „
Horses -	- - - -	2,818,000	„	18,000,000 „
Meadows -	5,775,000 hect. =	5,288,000	dessiat.	60,000,000 dessiat.
Fallows and pastures	15,954,000 hect. =	14,700,000	„	80,000,000 „ *
Forests - -	8,804,550 hect. =	8,063,000	„	180,000,000 „

From this summary we perceive what an immense fund of production Russia already possesses, independently of the extension and improvement of which our agriculture is still susceptible; with increased facilities of communication, and a more active commerce, the value of this mass of production will be prodigiously augmented.

In Austria the gross value of agricultural produce is estimated in the official statistics for 1842 at 1,375,024,000 florins = 866,265,000 silver roubles, without including the produce from horses, from cattle slaughtered, from gardens, tinctorial and medicinal plants, poultry, fisheries, and the chase. Deducting from the total gross value of our agricultural products, (amounting in our estimate to 2,048,500,000 silver roubles,) $317\frac{1}{2}$ millions representing the value of the last-named articles, the gross value of our remaining produce will amount to 1,731,000,000 roubles, that is to say, to about double the sum resulting from the estimate of the agricultural produce of Austria, although in that country the official valuations, based on the market prices, are for most articles very much higher than those which we have adopted. Thus, for example, whilst we have reckoned hay at 10 kopecks per pood, the average market prices in Austria give that article a value equal, in our weight and money, to 23 kopecks per pood; and we have reckoned straw at 7 kopecks per pood, whilst the medium Austrian price is 14 kopecks.

The great difference in our favour which results from an estimate of the agricultural produce of the two countries, notwithstanding the much lower rate of valuation which we have adopted, is justified by the difference in quantity. It is sufficient to remember that we produce of cereals more than thrice the average

* According to a very moderate approximative estimate.

quantity reaped in Austria, and that this article forms the most important item in the agricultural production of both countries. The number of head of cattle officially ascertained in Russia exceeds double the quantity raised in Austria, and there are reared in the European possessions of Russia six times as many horses as are counted in the whole Austrian empire. These three articles, which form the basis of rural economy, necessarily infer with us, independently of the differences of price, a gross value of more than double the product of agriculture in Austria.*

If it be not easy in general to estimate with much precision the gross produce of a country's agriculture, it is still more difficult to determine, even approximatively, its net returns. We will, however, attempt a sketch of ours, which may possibly, after all, be not very far wide of the reality.

	Francs.
In France, Count Chaptal estimated the value of the	
gross agricultural produce at - - -	4,678,288,884
And the expenses of production † at - -	3,334,005,515
Leaving a net return of - -	1,344,283,369

or 29 per cent.; so that the expenses of production amounted to 71 per cent.

Some years afterwards M. Charles Dupin estimated the value of the

	Francs.
Gross produce at - - - - -	5,313,163,735
And the expenses of culture at - - -	3,687,163,735
Leaving a net return of - -	1,626,000,000

or 31 per cent.; so that the expenses of production amounted to 69 per cent. We will assume the average cost of production to be 70 per cent.; and this high figure is justified by a circumstance we have already adverted to, namely, that in the French estimates of gross produce, values are taken into account which are afterwards reproduced under another form, and which therefore require to be added to the producers' charges.

To render our calculation as fair and as clear as possible, we shall subtract from the estimate of our own gross produce (amounting to 2,044 millions of roubles) the value of the produce of the domestic animals, as being already represented in the value of the corn and meadow produce employed in the

---

* It is proper, however, to observe that for the empire of Austria, and parcularly for Hungary, the numerical estimates with regard both to cattle and to cereals, adopted in the official statistics, are, in our opinion, too low.

† Which we think he rather over-estimates.

feeding of these animals; and this we do, notwithstanding that the product of the pastures, which forms no inconsiderable part of their food, is not included in our calculations.   As the item in question amounts in our calculations to 275,380,000 roubles, the total gross value of our agricultural products is thus reduced to 1,768,620,000 roubles.   Taking into consideration this reduction, and taking into consideration, further, that under the system of rural economy pursued in Russia, the expenses of management are considerably less than in France, we do not think that we need deduct from the gross produce (already reduced by upwards of 275 millions of roubles) more than 40 per cent., or, in round numbers, 707½ millions, which affords a net return of 1,061 millions of silver roubles, (= 168 millions sterling), or nearly 52 per cent. of the gross return.   If we deduct 70 per cent. from the gross return in France, amounting, by the most recent official estimates, to 6,077,000,000 francs, there remains a net return from agriculture of 1,823,000,000 francs, which is much less than half the amount of what we have estimated for Russia; but we have to observe that in France the general income is augmented in a high proportion by the products of industry and commerce, which do and must occupy with us a much more secondary rank, owing to the different geographical positions of the two countries, and to a number of other special circumstances, to which we shall have occasion to advert in the sequel.

C.

PRODUCTS OF THE MINERAL KINGDOM.

Our mineral wealth is concentrated chiefly in the Ural Mountains and in the eastern part of Siberia; it is still far from being known in its whole extent.

It was only under Peter the Great, the stamp of whose creative genius is found on whatever bore the germ of Russia's prosperity and grandeur, that the working of our mines began to attain some importance; but it has been especially under the Emperor Alexander, of glorious memory, and under the present reign, that the administration of this branch of our products has been reduced to system, and that a larger extent and higher degree of scientific attainment has been introduced amongst the corps of our mining officials.   A matter so intimately connected with our financial administration could not fail to occupy the earnest attention of government, and the progress made and making in this important department is continuous and considerable.

Our chief mineral products are gold, silver, iron, copper, and salt. Less important as regards the product hitherto are platina, lead, saltpetre, naphtha, and coal. Tin mines have also been recently discovered in Finland.

I. *Gold.*

The gold mines of the Ural and of Eastern Siberia have within the last twelve or fifteen years attained great importance and celebrity. The latter are by far the richer and more extensive, and produce six times as much gold as the former. The explorations hitherto made in the Ural Mountains have shown more and more that it is along their eastern slopes that the most considerable auriferous strata are to be met with. In their alluvial deposits native gold has been found in larger lumps than any known hitherto. There is preserved in the Museum of Mines at St. Petersburg a lump of gold of remarkable purity, found in 1842 in the district of Zlatooust in the Ural, which weighs 87 lbs. 92 zolotnik Russian. The largest lump found in the mines of Eastern Siberia weighs 24 lbs. Russian. The richest returns are yielded by the washings of the auriferous sands; the extent of these has been hitherto but partially ascertained, and new strata continue to be discovered. The auriferous sands of Biroussa, in Eastern Siberia, are, according to the estimate of M. Hoffman, 47 versts, or nearly 7 geographical miles in length by 100 toises in breadth. The returns from these are very different according to the richness of the strata, and partly, also, perhaps, according to the more or less careful system of washing pursued. Some strata yield as much as 7 or 8, or even 11 zolotnik to 100 poods of sand, which is in the proportion of 1 to 34,900. M. Hoffmann, in his account of his travels to the gold washings of Eastern Siberia* cites cases of much greater returns than this: for example, in the Miass washings, (southern part of the Ural), there was found on one occasion a layer which yielded 1 lb. 1 zolotnik of gold to 3 poods of sand, that is, $\frac{1}{119}$ of the mass. In a washing near Oktolik there was found in 1842 one stratum,—a very thin one, it is true, being of the thickness of only half an inch,—which contained $2\frac{1}{2}$ lbs. of gold to 10 lbs. of sand, or at the rate of 25 per cent.; but such cases are only very rare exceptions. On the other hand, there are washings which yield no more than $\frac{1}{2}$ zolotnik to 100 poods of sand, or $\frac{1}{768000}$, or even less. Those strata which do not

---

* See Beiträge zur Kenntniss des russischen Reiches, vol. xii.

yield more than $\frac{2}{3}$ zolotnik are not usually worked, except experimentally : they are reserved for a period when the richer
strata shall have become exhausted; yet in the government
mines of the Ural, strata not yielding more than $\frac{1}{2}$ zolotnik per
100 poods are, with the help of improved machinery, worked at
a profit.

The usual returns, considered good, are from 2 to 3 zolotnik
to 100 poods of sand, that is to say, from $\frac{1}{192000}$ to $\frac{1}{128000}$ of
the mass. In the richer strata, which give from 5 to 6 zolotnik
or more per 100 poods, the yield generally diminishes as the
working advances. The opposite case is of much more rare
occurrence.

The winning of gold in the Ural dates only from 1819, and,
in Eastern Siberia, from 1829. There was extracted from the
Uralian mines of

Gold alloyed with a little Silver.

	Poods.	Lbs.		Poods.	Lbs.
In 1823 - - -	89	17	In 1832 - - -	351	23
1824 - - -	165	5	1833 - - -	327	8
1825 - - -	232	34	1834 - - -	301	22
1826 - - -	235	24	1835 - - -	278	28
1827 - - -	260	35	1836 - - -	270	34
1828 - - -	274	38	1837 - - -	283	37
1829 - - -	309	29	1838 - - -	299	39
1830 - - -	332	38	1839 - - -	313	8
1831 - - -	368	13			

Thus the production of gold from these mines, progressing
rapidly from 1823, more than quadrupled within the short space
of eight years. Commencing with 1832, the cipher of production decreases during the next five years, till the decrease attains
about 26 per cent.: after this, it resumes an ascending movement, and the last triennial period, from 1837 to 1839, compared
with the three years preceding, exhibits an augmentation of 46
poods, or 5 per cent.

The product of pure gold from all the Russian mines, whether
crown or private property, was

	Poods.		Poods.
In 1840 - - -	554	In 1845 - - -	1,372
1841 - - -	655	1846 - - -	1,657
1842 - - -	908	1847 - - -	1,826
1843 - - -	1,295	1848 - - -	1,731
1844 - - -	1,342		

Thus, in the space of eight years, the production increased in
the proportion of 229 per cent.; that is to say, it more than trebled.
But since that period the product of the principal washings in
Siberia has fallen off. The total during the three years from
1849 to 1851 gives an average of only 1523 poods, that is to

say, 303 poods, or about $16\frac{1}{2}$ per cent., less than in 1847, the year in which it reached its culminating point.

Beds of auriferous sand have been recently discovered in Georgia, in the vicinity of Elizabethpol; but we are not yet possessed of sufficient information regarding them to be able to judge whether, and to what extent, they are likely to be profitably worked.

The total quantity of gold extracted from the mines of Russia from the year 1819 down to the end of the year 1851 amounted to 22,831 poods, representing, at the rate of 12,500 roubles per pood*, a value of 281,012,500 silver roubles (= 44,493,645*l.* sterling). The mean annual product during the years 1849-51 (1523 poods) represented a value of 19,037,500 roubles (= 3,014,270*l.* sterling).

Before the discovery of the gold beds of California, the product of the whole mines of America amounted, according to the most authentic data, compiled by M. Michel Chevalier, to 15,215 kilogrammes. The mines of Europe yielded at that period†, 2151 kilogrammes: those of Siberia yielded in 1847 the quantity of 1826 poods = 29,873 kilogrammes. Thus the whole gold mines of America, Europe, and Northern Asia, yielded at that period 47,239 kilogrammes, of which Russia contributed upwards of three-fifths, or, more exactly, 63 per cent.

The year 1848 announced the commencement of a new era in the annals of gold-mining, by the discovery of the gold sands of California, the richness of which, if the first accounts be completely justified in the long run, will surpass any thing of the kind that has been witnessed since the discovery of Mexico and Peru. The accounts which we possess hitherto, either as to the quantity actually won, or as to the richness of the yield in California, are too vague and contradictory to enable us to form a just idea of the influence which this new discovery may exercise on the value of the metal. All is still disorder and confusion; and some years must elapse before sufficient regularity shall have been attained to allow us to estimate scope and limits. It is clear that, at the outset, discoveries of this sort are almost always exaggerated; and interested parties are apt to propagate such reports as they consider favourable to their specu-

* The mint price of 1 zolotnik of pure gold is 3 roubles 55$\frac{5}{8}$ kopecks, which comes to 341 roubles 33 kopecks per lb. = 13,653 roubles 20 kopecks per pood ; but as in the above figures the quantities of pure gold are sometimes confounded with gold not yet refined, and alloyed with a little silver, we have thought it best to adopt the medium price of 12,500 roubles per pood.

† See the author's pamphlet, *Essai sur les conséquences éventuelles de la découverte des gîtes aurifères en Californie et en Australie*, pp. 19. and 145.

lations, without very nice inquiry into their truth or falsehood. Experience has also shown that, during the first years that succeed the discovery, the quantities won are more considerable than afterwards, in consequence of the vast numbers of individuals who flock to the spot, and who, once engaged in the adventure, continue to work on, even at a loss, in hopes of better luck in future,—which of course always helps to augment the absolute mass of metal recovered. Afterwards, when illusions get dissipated, and the work gets into a natural and normal condition,—when it is restricted to strata of which the richness has been sufficiently ascertained to insure a profitable return, the absolute product will diminish along with the number of adventurers. This anticipation seems exceedingly applicable to the mines of California,—the discovery of which took place during a period of excessive excitement, when men were ready to embark upon every new element of speculation. Never was there an age so rich in adventurers of every sort,—sometimes plunging into the abyss of politics and sociology, and sometimes invading the domains of material interests: accordingly, we see flocking to California by thousands, from all ends of the earth, people ready to risk the little that they have, and their lives to the bargain, in hopes of making their fortune at a stroke, and who, for the most part improvident of the future, and deceived by fantastic or exaggerated recitals, arrive without the means of even temporary subsistence on the spot, or of purchasing their return home in case of unsuccess: they therefore dig amongst the golden sands with the vigour of despair, that they may earn by the sweat of their brow a morsel of bread. To appreciate the discovery at its true value, we would require to know what the extraction of the gold costs at present, and what it is likely to cost in future. Upon these points we possess as yet no certain data; but we are daily hearing more and more complaints of failure; and one fact at least is clear, namely, that of the few who have succeeded in making a fortune, a large proportion have done so, not by digging for gold, but by speculating in food and raiment, and the other necessaries of the new colony. We may foresee, even at present, that the paucity of resources offered by the country itself, in regard to aliment, and even the most elementary branches of industry, will sensibly augment the working expenses for a long time to come. Thus the richness of the return is partially balanced. On the other hand, we know by experience what enormous masses of gold can, from the endless variety of its uses, monetary and industrial, be absorbed into the circulation without producing a sensible permanent fall in the value of the metal: the Uralian and Siberian mines, together with those of America, have furnished, during several years, 50,000 kilogrammes and more per annum—representing an annual value of more than 150 millions of francs, without producing a perceptible difference on its exchangeable value. The same observation applies to the working of silver mines. The silver mines of America and Europe, without reckoning those of Asia, send annually into the market a value of upwards of 200 millions of francs (8 millions sterling), without producing any depreciation of this metal. The prices of some products of the soil, and of almost every production of industry, far from augmenting, have, on the contrary, (with a few exceptions arising from special causes) undergone a considerable fall within the last thirty years. The precious metals represent so small a proportion of the mass of fixed and moveable property which constitutes public and private wealth, that they become absorbed or transmuted, as it were, into mere agents of circulation.

Since the discovery of the gold mines of the Ural and Eastern Siberia, Russia has become the richest country of Europe as regards production of the precious metals, whilst in regard to her national wealth, she is still, in proportion to her population, one of the poorest and least industrial; and yet the value of the gold and silver she produces does not constitute one hundredth part of the value which is created every year by her soil and her industry.

The employment of the precious metals in the different technical purposes to which they are applied, necessarily augments with the progress of population and material wealth, just as the demand for them as agents of circulation augments with the progress of commerce and the extension of industry : and this explains how the excess of production of these metals, which is undoubtedly very large, beyond what is lost by waste and friction, by shipwreck, conflagrations, and buried treasure, exercises so small an influence on their pecuniary value.

Before the discovery of the gold mines of the Ural and Eastern Siberia, the value of the gold produced from the whole mines of Europe and America was to that of the silver produced nearly as 3 to 10. After our mines had been extensively worked, this proportion had become latterly, before the discovery of the auriferous sands of California, nearly as 5 to 6 ; that is to say, the production of gold represented a value of 151 millions, and that of silver about 186½ millions of francs. This great alteration in the proportions of the value of gold and silver thrown into circulation, taking place, as it did, within a very short space of time, remained, notwithstanding, without influence upon the relative exchangeable value of the two metals; and we think we are entitled to conclude that, even admitting—a bold enough assumption—that the mines of California are capable of furnishing twice or thrice the quantity of gold now supplied by our Uralian and East-Siberian washings, a long period of time must still elapse before this discovery shall have produced a sensible depreciation. Were that case to arrive, England would be the first country to feel it, and it is by no means impossible that she might feel herself obliged in the end to alter her monetary system, which is based on the value of gold, and regulates the operations of the bank and of all commercial transactions. This change would produce a great revolution in the whole financial system of that country, and will of course only be adopted in case of the most extreme necessity.

To these observations we may add, that if the gold produced by California shall in effect bring about a depreciation in the value of that metal, this very fall in value will react upon its production by reducing the profits—a diminution which would be doubly felt by the undertakers, if at the same time the expenses of working should increase, either from decreased fertility of the auriferous strata, or from their having to be sought at a greater depth, or from a rise in the price of labour and necessaries. These circumstances might very possibly in the long run re-establish the equilibrium in the exchangeable value of gold.*

II. *Silver.*

The quantity of silver produced is much less important. The principal silver mines are situated in the Altaï Mountains and at Nertschinsk. Their product in 1834 was 1,262 poods 38 zolotnik. From 1840 to 1848 inclusive, their average production was only 1,196 poods, representing, at the legal mint price of 100 silver roubles for 5 lbs. 6 zolotnik, a value of 944,988 roubles. In 1848, the quantity produced was only 1,135 poods, containing $42\frac{1}{2}$ poods of pure gold; and during the years 1849—1851, the mean production fell to 1,090 poods, representing a value of 861,200 silver roubles.

---

* Since the above was written (in 1851), the discovery of gold in Australia has thrown a new weight into the balance, and the production of that metal has augmented in still larger proportions, without depreciating its market price. In regard to the future consequences of this production, we have stated our views at greater length in the pamphlet already referred to, which was published at Paris in the beginning of the year 1853.

III. *Platina.*

Platina is found in the Ural mines, sometimes in perfectly pure lumps of from 10 to 20 lbs. weight Russian. The production of platina has greatly diminished since the coin composed of this metal was withdrawn from circulation. In 1834 there were produced from crown and private mines 103 poods 24 lbs. 29 zolotnik; and, in the following years, still larger quantities; but in 1847 the production had fallen to 18 lb. 92 zolotnik, representing at the old price (1 rouble 23⅗ kopecks per zolotnik) a value of 2,250 roubles.

IV. *Iron.*

Iron ore is diffused over a great part of Russia; but the principal iron mines are in the governments of Perm, Orenburg, and Wiatka. The first named of these governments furnishes nearly three-fourths of the total production. There are a few mines in Finland, and in the governments of Wladimir, Tambow, Kalouga, Olonetz*, and Nijni-Nowgorod; but they are only of secondary importance. The whole of these provinces taken together do not furnish above 3 per cent. of the total production. Some mines have been recently discovered and worked in the government of Wilna; but it is still very doubtful if anything considerable is to be expected from them. There were reckoned in 1844 (Finland included) 107 working mines, of which 66 were in the single government of Perm.

The following was, according to official returns, the total production during 11 years from 1838 to 1848: —

				Pig Iron.		Bar Iron.	
1838	-	-	-	10,655,034	poods.	7,175,093	poods.
1839	-	-	-	10,802,933	„	6,772,329	„
1840	-	-	-	10,331,510	„	6,925,927	„
1841	-	-	-	10,552,636	„	6,665,588	„
1842	-	-	-	11,172,706	„	7,319,121	„
1843	-	-	-	11,580,931	„	8,277,058	„
1844	-	-	-	11,291,816	„	8,189,878	„
1845	-	-	-	11,432,645	„	7,716,106	„
1846	-	-	-	11,601,916	„	8,211,239	„
1847	-	-	-	11,880,692	„	8,513,637	„
1848	-	-	-	12,080,273	„	8,397,644	„

The production of the years 1846, 1847, and 1848 gives an average of 11,854,294 poods of cast iron, and 8,374,173 poods

---

* In the government of Olonetz the marshes contain iron ore in great abundance; but there are no mines properly so called.

of malleable iron, of which about 6 per cent. was the production of crown mines.*

We perceive by this abstract that the production of iron augments very slowly, when compared with the increasing demand for this metal in every branch of industry. The mean production of the three years from 1846 to 1848, as compared with that of the three years from 1838 to 1840, exhibits an increase of only 1,257,800 poods, or about 12 per cent. on the cast iron, and of 1,416,390 poods, or about 20 per cent., on the malleable iron.†

In the kingdom of Poland the produce in 1843 amounted, according to official data, to 1,341,580 quintals‡ = 3,320,410 poods.

We may, therefore, estimate the total annual production, in round numbers, at about 15,000,000 poods (= 240,000 tons) of cast iron, representing, at the average price of 30 kopecks per pood, a gross value of 4½ million silver roubles.

Although this production, considered apart and by itself, is by no means inconsiderable, it is exceedingly small for such an immense empire as Russia, and for the wants of a population of 67,000,000 of inhabitants. Our iron is excellent, and suitable for every purpose; but its high price renders it inaccessible to the poorer classes of the population, and prohibitory for ordinary purposes. That which most contributes to the dearness of our iron, independently of other causes to which we will have occasion to recur, is the concentration of our mines at the extremity of European Russia, and the great distances by which they are separated from the principal markets of the interior. This article of prime necessity, the low price of which is one of the main conditions of industrial progress, is, for our agricultural population, almost an article of luxury. We may admit, without the least exaggeration, that in Russia and Poland more than nine-tenths of the cart and waggon wheels of every description are without iron hoops, and that, except in equipages of luxury, all the axles are of wood. This adds greatly to the difficulty of our means of transport and communication, not to speak of the other grave inconveniences, in a technical and agricultural point of view, which result from the dearness of iron.

---

* The three following years, 1849—51, gave an average of 12,638,540 poods of cast iron, and 9,141,845 of malleable iron.

† In several other countries the employment of iron in the different branches of industry has doubled within the same space of time.

‡ Since that period the production in the kingdom of Poland has considerably fallen off; but, as it has augmented in the mines of the empire, our total estimate remains unaffected by this circumstance.

Many persons are of opinion that because Russia exports iron, this is a proof that she produces more than is requisite for the wants of her internal consumption. But this is a very superficial mode of judging. *First*, the exportation was never very large, and it has of late been falling off: at present it does not amount to more than 700,000 or 800,000 poods, representing a value of about 1,000,000 silver roubles. And, *secondly*, this exportation consists of certain sorts of iron of a very superior quality, which are greatly in demand for some special purposes. Instead of the wants of our internal consumption being satisfied, if the article were cheaper, more than double our actual production would be consumed.

V. *Copper.*

The production of copper in Russia exceeds the demand for home consumption, and it is exported to the value of more than 1,000,000 of roubles. The principal copper mines are situated in the Ural and Altaï mountains, in Finland, and in Georgia; but the first place is again occupied by the government of Perm, the principal seat of our mineral wealth. The total production during the last five years was as follows: —

In 1847	254,568	poods.
1848	292,525	„
1849	323,556	„
1850 and 1851	724,026	„
Total -	1,594,675	„

giving an average for the five years of 318,935 poods, of which about a ninth was from crown mines. The average production of the last three years (349,194 poods) represented, at the medium price of 9 roubles per pood, a value of 3,142,750 silver roubles.

VI. *Lead.*

Lead is found in small quantities in the crown mines of the Altaï mountains and at Nertschinsk. During the years 1830 to 1833 the mean annual production was 44,200 poods, and it has but slightly increased since that period. In 1847 and 1848 the average production was 54,350 poods (representing, at 2 roubles per pood, a value of 108,700 roubles), which does not supply more than about a seventh part of the demand for the use of the army and industrial purposes.

VII. *Zinc.*

The production of zinc in the kingdom of Poland amounts at an average to 85,000 quintals Polish=210,396 poods, representing, at the rate of $2\frac{1}{2}$ roubles per pood, a value of 525,990 roubles.

VIII. *Coal.*

In consequence of researches made or encouraged by government, beds of coal and anthracite have recently been discovered on the coast of the Sea of Azow, between the Dnieper and the Donetz, in the governments of Kharkow, Kalouga, and Perm, in the Caucasus, and in Siberia.* These discoveries, and especially the discovery of the mines situated between the Dnieper and the Donetz, are of the utmost importance both for the steam navigation of the Don, the Wolga, the Black Sea, and the Sea of Azow, and for the future prospects of a great portion of New Russia, which has hitherto been unprovided with fuel. The beds of anthracite are of immense extent, and the fuel of superior quality to any hitherto known; it is almost pure carbon, leaving a residue of only 2 to 3 per cent. It is to be regretted that this important discovery has not yet been sufficiently worked. There also exist old coal mines in the crown domains situated within the government of Ekathérinoslaw; but they are naturally barren, and the mode in which they are worked by the crown peasants is very defective.

The present production of this combustible in Russia is estimated at only 2 million poods, representing, at the average price of 5 kopecks per pood, a value of 100,000 silver roubles.

IX. *Salt.*

Russia abounds in salt of every description, and could furnish supplies of that article to more than double its present population; but from the geographical position of the places where it is produced, which renders its transport too expensive for some provinces, recourse must be had to importation. The kingdom of Poland and the Baltic provinces are almost entirely supplied with foreign salt, of which the mean importation during the years 1846—1848 amounted, in the empire to 4,934,555 poods, and in the kingdom of Poland to about 2,200,000 poods, in all 7,134,555 poods, or more than 20 per cent. of the total consumption.

The mines of rock-salt known and worked are situated in the governments of Orenburg, Astrakhan, Irkoutsk, and in Armenia. The most important is that of Iletsk on the frontier of the government of Orenburg, towards the steppes of the Kirghiz. The salt lakes are situated in Bessarabia and the

---

* See the report of M. Woskresenski, presented to the Academy of Sciences in 1845.

Crimea, in the steppes lying betwixt the Volga, the Don, and the Emba, in Georgia, and in Siberia. Lake Elton, in the government of Saratow, is the largest of the whole. A number of small salt lakes have also been recently discovered near the mouth of the Volga, along its banks, in the government of Astrakhan. The establishments in which salt is extracted from salt springs by evaporation are situated in the governments of Perm, Nowgorod, Wologda, Nijni-Nowgorod, and in Siberia. At present those of Perm are the most important. Sea-salt is prepared, but only in very small quantities, in the government of Archangel and at Okhotsk in Siberia.

The greater part of the salt mines and salt lakes belong to the state. Only the establishments in the government of Perm for precipitating salt by evaporation, and some salt lakes in the Crimea, belong to individuals. The establishments in the government of Perm produce about 5 millions of poods, which are sold to the magazines of the fisk under old contracts.

The working and preparation of salt is of course regulated by the demand. In 1846, there were sold from the crown magazines 26,250,000 poods, and as the sale is increasing at the rate of about 400,000 poods per annum, we may estimate the present amount at about 30 millions. Adding to this about 7 millions of poods imported into Russia and the kingdom of Poland, and about 1 million of poods produced from salt lakes belonging to individuals, and disposed of by free sale, we may estimate the total consumption at 38 millions.

The 31 million poods produced in the country, reckoned at the medium price of 20 kopecks the pood, would represent a gross value of 6,200,000 roubles.*

The principal products of our mines which we have just enumerated, represent together a value of 34,478,000 silver roubles (= 5,460,000*l.* sterling), of which more than 55 per cent. is composed of the value of gold alone. We have left out of calculation the accessory products of our mines, the quarries of granite and of other building stone, the malachite, the gems and precious stones which are found in the mountains of Siberia. Several savans, especially M. de Humboldt and Professor Engelhardt, have found indications of diamonds in the Ural, and some fragments have actually been found in con-

* In this estimate we have taken the average price at which the salt could be sold at the place of production, without taking into account the benefit of the fisk, which, of course, does not form any portion of the value.

sequence of researches undertaken agreeably to Humboldt's advice.

With the addition of those secondary articles of our mines and quarries, which are not included in the foregoing estimates, we may carry the gross value of the whole productions of the mineral kingdom to 40 millions of silver roubles (= 6,333,333*l.* sterling).

In Austria, the whole products of mines, salt excepted, on an average of the years 1841—1844 inclusive, represented a value of 22,102,000 florins. Adding the gross value of 5,500,000 quintals of salt, at 1 florin per quintal, the total gross product of the mines will amount to 27,602,000 florins = 17,389,000 roubles. Taking into account the progress of production during preceding years we may estimate the present production at about 20 million roubles.

In Prussia, according to statistical information published in the Berlin newspapers, the total produce of the mines amounted in 1848 to the value of 32,950,000 thalers = 29,655,000 roubles (nearly 5,000,000*l.* sterling).

In France, according to M. Schnitzler's statistics founded on official returns, the total produce of the mines represented, in 1843, a value of 411,057,000 francs, and according to the progress of production assigned by this author, it may now be carried to about 420 millions of francs = 105 millions of roubles (= 16,600,000*l.* sterling): but we have to observe that in the French estimates, the produce of quarries and peat bogs, to the amount of 40 millions of francs, is included.

It would thus appear that the value of the produce of mines in Russia exceeds that of Austria in the proportion of 2 to 1, and that of Prussia by more than a third; but attains only two-fifths of that of France. We have, however, to observe that M. Schnitzler's rates of valuation are much higher than ours; thus, for example, in the principal article of iron, he reckons pig iron at 19 francs 75 centimes per metrical quintal, and bar iron at 43 francs 96 centimes, which gives an average of 31 francs 85 centimes per metrical quintal = 1 rouble 30 kopecks per pood, whilst we have carried to the account merely the gross value of the pig iron at the rate of 30 kopecks per pood.

On adding to the gross produce of our agriculture (2,044 millions) the value of the produce of our mines (40 millions), we obtain as the total gross value of the products of our soil, the sum of 2,084 millions of silver roubles (330 millions sterling), an estimate which we think we have sufficiently demonstrated to be considerably within the mark.

From this general sketch of the extent and natural fertility of our soil, of its culture, and of the variety of its productions, we perceive that Russia occupies an independent position in everything that regards the material well-being of her inhabitants; that she yields in abundance every object of aliment, as corn and wine, cattle and horses, the raw material for every sort of textile manufacture, dye-stuffs, gold, silver, copper, and all sorts of building-materials; that she furnishes several of these objects in considerable quantities for exportation, and that she is capable of producing more than would be requisite for the subsistence of twice her present population.

This first part of our work having been dedicated solely to an estimate of the *material* forces of Russia, we have confined ourselves, in treating of our agriculture, to a statistical analysis of its elements: everything relating to its progress by the concurrence of *intellectual* forces, of which the development depends on the institutions of the country, on the genius of its inhabitants, and on the circumstances which may exert a more or less direct influence on the national labour, is reserved for the following chapter.

PART II.

INTELLECTUAL PRODUCTIVE FORCES.

WE comprehend under the above term those forces which. consist in the application of the human intellect to the creation of values, and which produce their results in the three departments of agriculture, industry, and commerce, which embrace the whole elements of national wealth.

CHAPTER I.

AGRICULTURE.

HAVING exhibited in the first part of this work a general outline of the gross products of our agriculture, and given an exposition, if we may be allowed the expression, of its material situation, we shall here examine, under a more comprehensive aspect, its present condition and its future prospects. The questions pertaining to this subject are so much the more important, as with us, more than in most other countries, the welfare of the inhabitants and the national wealth are dependent, above all, on the prosperity and progress of this branch of our social economy.

Russia, from the extent, the quality, and the configuration of her soil, as well as from her geographical position, is an eminently agricultural country. All the other elements of prosperity occupy but a secondary rank, and can play but a more or less subordinate part in the mechanism of her productive forces. We are far from sharing the errors of those economists who will concede a real value only to the productions of the soil, and consider as merely fictitious those values which proceed from industry, and are created by the transformation of these same products into others more suitable for the various wants and usages of civilised society. On the contrary, we are fully persuaded of the high importance of industry, not only in regard to national wealth taken as a whole, but in regard to the influence which it directly exerts upon agriculture itself, the nursing mother of the nations: but we are of opinion, that on a superficial estimate of the public wealth, there are prevailing errors in the degree of importance attributed to these respective branches of social economy. Such error is natural enough. The infinite variety of industrial products, the unheard-of progress which industry has made within the last half century, the tribute so largely paid to it by the exact and natural sciences, the ingenious inventions which augment its productive forces, the wonderful mechanisms by means of which it has rendered tributary the physical forces of nature to spare the labour of man,—all these prodigies are apt at once to strike the intellect and the imagination, whilst agriculture, more simple and uniform in its gait and procedure, is much less susceptible of exciting similar admiration. When, however, industry is stripped of its brilliant prestige, and we descend to the reality of facts, we perceive that the plough, after all, in its modest guise, plays the principal part in the creation of values, even in countries the most commercial and industrial. Of this England furnishes a notable example. Of all nations England is without dispute the most industrial and the most mercantile—the weaving factory of the universe — the commercial centre of all the ends of the earth: it is notorious that her trade and her industry form the main basis of her power; and yet it appears from her income-tax returns that the net revenue of all the industry, of all the commerce, and of all the personal capital of the country, does not come up to two-thirds of the net revenue derived from agriculture alone. From this single fact we may infer the degree of pre-eminence that ought to be attributed to the agricultural element of national wealth in a country like Russia.

We frequently hear complaints of the precarious and backward condition of our agriculture: similar complaints are heard in other countries, as France and Austria, and some parts of Germany: as regards ourselves they are certainly not unfounded, but we believe they are often exaggerated; and the causes to which our agricultural backwardness is referred are no less frequently erroneous. Several of the causes of this backwardness are obvious enough; but we will fall into inevitable error with regard to the intensity of their operation if we view them out of connexion with the complex antecedents of our rural economy. Our agriculturists are often reproached with remaining strangers to all improvement, and with persevering in an antiquated routine which has long been condemned by experience; but in making this too often merited reproach, the various circumstances, independent of their own will, which contribute to keep them on the old beaten track, are frequently overlooked.

It is well known, that with the exception of the Baltic provinces, (where agriculture is in an advanced condition,) and of the region of the Steppes, (where a mode of culture is required suitable to their peculiarities of soil and climate,) the old three-field system of husbandry, or *Dreifelderwirthschaft** as it is termed by the Germans, is usually followed throughout Russia. But it is generally agreed that this mode of culture is open to many objections: by exhausting the soil it requires large supplies of manure, whilst at same time, by excluding the culture of artificial fodder, it is unfavourable to cattle-rearing, and thus cuts off the source from which manure is to be obtained: the feeding of cattle upon straw and hay alone produces very mediocre fattening, and gives rise moreover to frequent cattle epidemics: it is alleged that the extirpation of forests, so injurious in its consequences, is inherent in this system; and that under it the destruction of weeds, which so greatly contribute to the exhaustion of the soil, becomes impossible. It is also to this system of husbandry that some agriculturists, both native and foreign, attribute the great irregularities in the product of our harvests and their frequent failures,—an opinion to which we cannot give an unqualified assent. The main causes of these inequalities and failures are referable to the geographical position of the country, and the configuration of its soil; in some districts, also, to local atmospheric influences, of which a more careful culture might perhaps moderate, though it could not entirely remove, the effects. Russia being one of the vastest plains of Europe, frequently swept by the east wind and the north wind, the effects of drought or of superabundant moisture

---

* Under this system the land is divided into three shifts, namely 1. Fallow, 2. Winter Corn, 3. Summer Corn. The forage is drawn from permanent meadows and pastures not included under the rotation. The advantages of the system consist in this, that in the fallow year there is the best possible opportunity for thoroughly cleaning, and loosening the ground, which can then be dunged and sown without impediment with winter corn whenever the favourable moment arrives ; that two-thirds of the arable land bear white crop, which, in affording a large quantity of straw, yields good material for manure ; and that the mode of management is exceedingly simple, and generally known. But, on the other hand, one-third of the cultivable land is always lying idle, and the production of the whole stock of forage is limited to that arising from the permanent meadow and pasture land, where a dry soil, combined with a dry summer, often gives occasion to a bad hay harvest, so that there is then a deficiency of forage and the stock is weakened. This three-field rotation with clean fallow is, therefore, suitable only for farms which are provided with moist, fertile meadows, whence a supply of the requisite quantity of fodder may be calculated on with certainty, and where the farm is large enough to raise a sufficiency of corn and straw upon two-thirds of the arable land ; or for those cases in which the object in view is to produce a surplus rather by saving expenses in dung and labour, than by insuring the largest possible amount of production. See Veit's *Lehrbuch der Landwirthschaft*, 2nd edition, p. 540.—TRANSLATOR.

are there felt with a generality unknown in countries where the
atmospheric influences vary from one district to another,—where
shady valleys, sheltered from parching winds, suffer less from
the absence of rain,—where the hills and elevated plateaus are
less subject to inundations, and, by their natural drainage, are
sooner freed from any excess of humidity which might prove
injurious to vegetation. It is especially the frequent droughts
that constitute one of the severest scourges of our agriculture*;
and the most scientific system of culture could not destroy their
pernicious influences. It would certainly be very desirable to
see our agriculturists entering on the path of improvement,
especially in districts where improvements are facilitated by
local circumstances : but it must not be disguised that the three-
shift system, defective as it undoubtedly is, is nevertheless the
one most appropriate on the whole to our present position, and
that it will long remain predominant in those governments at
least which have much land to till, and few hands to till it.
This system, requiring as it does, less care and less capital than
a more scientific one, is too deeply-rooted both in the habits of
our people, and in the condition of our rural economy, to be
capable of undergoing a rapid and general reform. Improvement can be but slow and gradual, and must be the result of
successive imitations of isolated examples. There are even
districts, as, for instance, the greater portion of the Southern
Steppes, in which (as we have already observed) it is the opinion
of experienced agriculturists who have studied the soil and
climate during a long series of years, that a rational system is
impossible, because the land is incapable of bearing more than
one sort of crop†; and it has long been remarked that all the
Slavonic populations have a special predilection for the three-
shift system : in the German provinces of Austria it is rapidly

---

* It has been proved by meteorological observations that there falls in Russia,
under the form of rain and snow, much less water than in most other countries.
See the information collected on this subject by M. Gasparin in his *Cours d'Agriculture* (tome ii., p. 255.)

	Mean Quantity of Water that falls in shape of Rain and Snow expressed in Paris Inches.
In England, western part	37·59
Ditto eastern part	26·56
On the coast of western Europe	26·12
In the southern parts of Spain and France	34·43
In Northern Italy	44·76
In the northern parts of France and Germany	25·64
In the Scandinavian Peninsula	20·41
In Russia	15·88

† See M. Teetzmann's article in the *Beiträge zur Kenntniss des russischen
Reiches*, vol. xi. p. 89.

disappearing, whilst it predominates in all the Slavonic provinces of that empire, as well as in Hungary, where the mode of culture pursued by the Slavonic populations served as a model to the Magyars.

Independently of the obstinate perseverance in the old routine displayed by our cultivators, even in districts where a better mode of culture is indicated by local circumstances, and of their almost invincible prejudices on the score of innovations, there are many other circumstances which help to retard the progress of our agriculture. Let us endeavour to give some account of these, so that we may be enabled to form an impartial judgment on our position, without being led astray by the erroneous or exaggerated views which are so frequently put forth upon the subject. Of course we do not pretend to discuss the matter in its whole bearings. An exhaustive treatise of the sort would far exceed the limits of this general survey, and imply a profundity of special knowledge of the subject to which we dare not lay claim. All we venture is a few summary observations on the principal questions connected with it.

In consequence of the disproportion which exists in a great part of the empire between the number of the population and the extent of the soil, we find ourselves, as respects the relative values of land and labour, in a totally different position from any other country. Elsewhere, the land is usually more valuable than the labour; with us, the labour is usually more valuable than the land. In valuations of real estate, it is not the extent of productive soil, but the number of peasants, that serves as the basis of calculation. The fertility of the soil enters, no doubt, into the estimate; it is this which renders the peasant in one government more valuable than the peasant in another; but it is always a secondary, never the primary, element of the price. As a natural consequence of this state of things, it becomes much less an object to derive the greatest possible advantage from the land, to maintain or increase its fertility, than to turn to the most profitable account the hands which the owner has at his disposal. This relation betwixt the value of the land and the value of labour is now beginning to be somewhat modified in some districts; lands without peasants astricted to the glebe which, twenty or thirty years ago, were almost valueless, and sold at 5 paper roubles the dessiatine, now fetch five or even ten times that amount. It is in New Russia that this favourable change in the value of land has been going on with the greatest rapidity. In the government of Kherson, a dessiatine of good land sold in 1810 for 1 paper rouble, or even less. About 1815, the price had risen to 5 or 6 paper roubles; at present, it is

10 silver roubles, and there are not many districts in which it can be purchased for less than 4 silver roubles per dessiatine. This progress will of course extend with the increase of the population; but it is nevertheless true that the abnormal condition which we have just described is now, and will probably for a long time to come continue to be, the characteristic feature of our agricultural situation throughout a great part of Russia.

Several economists, native as well as foreign, attribute almost exclusively to our system of serfage the little care which the peasant bestows either on the cultivation of the soil which he labours on his own account, (not considering it as his property,) or on the work which he performs on account of his master. Now, here we must observe that people are very apt to fall into error with regard to the ideas which the Russian peasant attaches to his serfage and state of dependence : the feeling of indifference about his possession is very far indeed from being so marked as many persons are disposed to believe; everybody that has come into frequent contact with our peasants must have had occasion to perceive that, though they, no doubt, consider *themselves* as the property of *their masters,* yet each of them at same time regards *the land* laboured for himself as *his own,* or rather as part and parcel of the property of his community which has fallen to his own share *by right;* he, therefore, cannot be indifferent to its culture on the ground of its *not* being his own. If the Russian peasant is often a negligent cultivator, this proceeds from other causes which we shall afterwards have occasion to advert to. The system of serfage may, and undoubtedly must, exercise an unfavourable influence upon the culture of the soil, inasmuch as thirled labour is always less productive than free labour; this it is, not always as regards the interest of the employer,—for there are many cases in which the substitution of paid labour for the corvée would not, by its increased productiveness, compensate the proprietor for his increased working expenses,—but as regards the total amount of value created by the employment of labour; for, the obligatory task being always executed with more or less negligence, the result is a loss of time and of productive force, and consequently a waste of the elements of national wealth. It is, moreover, undeniable that the prestation of villenage services, where they are too onerous, frequently deprives the serf of the means of doing justice to the land; but the influence of this cause upon the condition of our agriculture is by no means so predominant as is generally supposed.

To judge of the degree of influence which the corvée exercises upon the complex of our agricultural economy, we must, in the first place, take into consideration the relative numbers of that class of our peasants which is still subject to this régime, and of those who dispose freely of their labour. The following is the information which we find in the Reports of the Ministry of Domains, and in the statistical works of M. Koeppen, with regard to the male population of our different classes of cultivators. According to last census, finished in 1851, there were reckoned on the state domains, (without including Siberia or the transcaucasian provinces,) 8,850,324 crown peasants, 188,456 foreign colonists, and 17,700 colonised Israelites,—in all, a male population of 9,056,480 cultivators, of whom not more than 221,000 male individuals were subject to the corvée.* The remaining male population of our cultivators in European Russia has been classed by M. Koeppen, for the year 1838† as follows:—

		Souls.
1. Free peasants - - - - -		72,844
2. *Odnodvortsy* (possessors of a single farm) -	-	1,361,833
3. Peasants attached to the lands possessed by the *Od-nodvortsy* - - - - -		10,978
4. Post peasants (*Jemschetschki*) - - -		41,696
5. Forest peasants (*Laschmany*) - - -		115,235
6. Appanage peasants - - - - -		700,987
7. Serfs attached to estates belonging to private owners		10,796,461

13,100,034 ‡

The free peasants designated under number 1. were formerly serfs, who have been enfranchised and at same time invested with a certain portion of land, or who have acquired land by purchase. This class of cultivators increases from year to year by new affranchisements. In 1839 their numbers were reckoned at 84,413 instead of the 72,844 inscribed in the population list of 1838: in the course of the year 1844 there were reckoned 12,500 peasant serfs who passed into the condition of free cultivators: their present number must be somewhere about 230,000 male individuals. The *Odnodvortsy* are also free peasants: the lands which they cultivate are of two descriptions: the one sort belongs to them in absolute property; the other sort constitutes a state property of which the usufruct had been conceded to

* The corvée no longer exists for the peasants of the crown domains, except in some of the western governments, where it remains a relic of the ancient economical condition of these provinces. It is being gradually converted into a quit-rent, and in 1852 there were reckoned to be no more than 121,450 crown peasants subject to the corvée.

† See his *Mémoire sur la population de la Russie divisée par classes*, published in 1847.

‡ In this classification the governments of Esthonia, Livonia, and Courland are not included. The peasants of these provinces are gradually passing from the *régime* of the corvée into the class of copyholders.

their ancestors as a recompense for old services, or in room of other emoluments. This class of our cultivators is most numerous in the governments of Koursk, Tambow, Woronèje, Orel, Penza, Orenburg, and Saratow. In 1838 there were reckoned in the three first of these governments 741,663, or considerably more than half the total number. The *Odnodvortsy* formed, in the government of Koursk, more than a third; in that of Tambow, 30 per cent.; and in that of Woronèje, 32 per cent. of the total male population. As for the serfs attached to the lands belonging to the *Odnodvortsy*, their number (which in 1838 was under 11,000 males) is gradually diminishing in consequence of the humane measures successfully pursued by government for bringing them into the class of crown peasants. The peasants belonging to the Administration of the Post are bound to furnish for that service a certain number of carts and horses with their drivers. On the other hand, they are freed from all personal services or quit-rents for the lands held by them, and they receive for each journey a certain fare fixed by regulation. The distribution of this postal service is so arranged as that every twenty-eight individuals of the male population have to furnish a cart and three horses with a driver. The number of these post peasants is also gradually decreasing. Government affranchises them, on their own request, from their postal obligations, and they then become subject to the same imposts as other peasants who are not serfs. There are thirty-two governments in which peasants of this class do not exist. The peasants belonging to the Administration of the Woods and Forests (*Laschmany*) are now found only in the seven governments of Kazan, Nijni-Nowgorod, Orenburg, Simbirsk, Tambow, Wiatka, and Penza: they are descendants of the ancient Tartars who formerly executed various services on account of the government, and of the Mordwins who were formerly subject to a tribute of furs: in exchange for these prestations, from which they were released, they are employed at various works in the forests which furnish timber for the navy, and they receive a certain remuneration fixed by regulation. Three hundred families of these peasants do the work of forest bailiffs; a certain number are employed as guides; others carry on the trade of carpenters in the service of the crown. At the census of 1811, the male population of these peasants amounted to 943,000 individuals; but by a regulation concerning the management of forests appropriated to the service of the navy, the number of peasants employed in these different services has been reduced to 120,000. The appanage peasants are assimilated by law to the free cultivators: they are not subject to personal service (corvée), but they pay a rent termed *Obrok*, the amount of which is determined by the extent and quality of the lands conceded to them. They have the right of passing into another class upon payment of a certain tax. An appanage peasant who wishes to become a simple burgess has to pay 600 silver roubles, and one who wishes to become a merchant has to pay 1,500. These taxes are raised for the benefit of a fund instituted for discharged soldiers who have been recruited from this class of peasants and returned home after serving out their time.

According to this short analysis, and taking into account the increase of population since 1838, we may class our cultivators in the two following categories:—

I. *Peasants subject to Personal Service* (à corvée).

	Male Population.
Peasants belonging to individuals in all the governments of European Russia, according to the census of 1851 -	11,451,200
Peasants attached to the lands pertaining to the *Odnordvortsy*	11,000
Peasants of the crown domains not yet freed from the corvée in some of the western governments - - - -	221,000
Total -	11,683,200

II. *Cultivators not subject to Personal Service.*

	Male Population.
Peasants of the state domains paying a quit-rent - -	8,629,300
Foreign colonists on the state domains - -	188,500
Colonised Israelites - - - - - -	17,700
Free peasants - - - - - - -	230,000
Odnodvortsy - - - - - - -	1,500,000
Appanage peasants and other cultivators not subject to the corvée - - - - - - -	1,122,000
Total -	11,687,500

On comparing these two totals, we find that the number of peasants still subject to the corvée is equal to that of the cultivators who dispose freely of their labour; but if we consider that, in many of the domains belonging to individuals, the corvée has been converted into a pecuniary quit-rent, we may admit that more than two-thirds of the productive soil are now no longer worked under the corvée system. This system, therefore, cannot exert so general an influence as is supposed on the condition of our agriculture.

M. Koeppen, in his memoir already referred to, gives a table of the proprietors of real estates and of their serfs in forty-six governments, from which it appears that the number of these peasants amounts to somewhat more than 46 per cent. of the male population. The governments taken separately present results worthy of observation, and we reproduce them here in the following table.

Governments.	Total Male Population.	Male Population of Serf Cultivators.	Number of Serf Cultivators to 100,000 Male Inhabitants.
1. Archangel - - - -	110,800	72	65
2. Bessarabia - - -	353,000	7,271	2,060
3. Wiatka - - - -	721,700	18,404	2,550
4. Province on this side Cauca- sus - - - - -	244,200	7,668	3,140
5. Astrakhan - - - -	143,600	5,256	3,660
6. Olonetz - - - -	112,700	6,117	5,430
7. Tauride - - - -	265,200	17,425	6,570
8. Orenburg - - - -	865,300	115,775	13,380
9. Kazan - - - -	583,300	97,467	16,710
10. Wologda - - - -	359,200	94,836	26,400
11. Perm - - - -	707,900	218,664	30,890
12. Country of the Don Cossacks	320,100	103,500	32,330
13. Kharkow - - - -	659,100	226,136	34,310
14. Woronèje - - - -	734,300	258,244	35,170
15. Kherson - - - -	392,400	151,430	38,590
16. Ekathérinoslaw - - -	396,200	155,827	39,330
17. Poltawa - - - -	809,400	337,027	41,640
18. Saratow - - - -	774,700	328,297	42,380
19. Kowno - - - -	409,250	175,773	42,950
20. Simbirsk - - - -	589,900	262,336	44,470
21. Tschernigow - - -	647,000	290,390	44,880
22. Koursk - - - -	769,200	356,812	46,390
23. Tambow - - - -	779,800	372,066	47,710
24. Nowgorod - - - -	403,500	194,158	48,120
25. Grodno - - - -	405,500	196,403	48,430
26. Moscow - - - -	616,500	318,608	51,680
27. Wilna - - - -	386,100	201,407	52,160
28. Penza - - - -	485,600	259,798	53,500
29. St. Petersburg * - - -	253,100	135,531	53,540
30. Orel - - - -	670,300	377,085	56,260
31. Twer - - - -	618,000	357,500	57,850
32. Pskow - - - -	342,200	206,269	60,280
33. Podolia - - - -	753,200	462,750	61,440
34. Wladimir - - - -	535,800	335,495	62,610
35. Minsk - - - -	467,800	293,054	62,650
36. Riazan - - - -	615,800	390,738	63,450
37. Witebsk - - - -	375,100	238,539	63,600
38. Wolhynia - - - -	705,700	451,498	63,980
39. Kostroma - - - -	456,500	298,716	65,430
40. Nijni-Nowgorod - - -	509,700	340,752	66,850
41. Jaroslaw - - - -	429,100	287,026	66,890
42. Kiew - - - -	733,100	504,589	68,830
43. Kalouga - - - -	455,500	314,185	68,970
44. Mohilew - - - -	423,300	299,130	70,670
45. Smolensk - - - -	517,400	379,603	73,370
46. Toula - - - -	552,300	416,366	75,390
Total - - - -	23,459,350	10,865,993	46,318

* Without the floating population.

From this table we perceive that there are twenty-five governments in which the number of serfs attached to estates belonging to individuals does not amount to half the male population, and twenty-one governments in which it exceeds that proportion. Of the governments belonging to the former class, there are seven where their number does not attain a tenth of the male population, and five in which there are not 4 serf peasants to 100 male inhabitants. In the government of Archangel there are not 1 to 1000. Of the twenty-one governments in which the number of these peasants exceeds half the male population, there are seven, namely, Nijni-Nowgorod, Jaroslaw, Kiew, Kalouga, Mohilew, Smolensk, and Toula, in which it exceeds two-thirds, and, in the last-named government, it attains three-fourths of the male population.

However defective the corvée system may be in itself, in a general agricultural point of view, it is for the moment, for a great part of Russia, a necessity of our agricultural position; for, *first*, the amount of disposable capital requisite to be invested in agriculture, in order to establish a rational system of culture in conjunction with paid labour, does not exist in proportion to the immense extent of the arable lands; *secondly*, in many districts, the value of the products of the land would not afford a sufficient return to cover the working expenses; *thirdly*, in those provinces which are little favoured in regard to commerce and industry, and where money circulation is trifling, it is much easier for the peasant to discharge his quit-rent in the shape of labour, than to pay any rent whatever in the shape of money. Thus it happens that sometimes those peasants who have become quit-renters, or, as it is termed in Russia, have come under the *Obrok* régime, are in less easy circumstances than the peasants in the same district who are under the corvée régime ; and they occasionally return of their own accord to their former prestation in kind. This has been remarked by M. Haxthausen during his journey in the government of Simbirsk. It has also been frequently observed that peasants who have been freed from the corvée and become quit-renters have neglected the culture of their fields, and quitted their homes in quest of some easier mode of gaining a living. On the other hand there are districts where we may observe the conversion of the corvée into *Obrok* attended with quite different effects. Wherever the workman readily finds employment, as, for example, in most of the districts situated along the banks of the Volga, the peasants have found their advantage in this conversion. But this proves that these changes can be successfully introduced only where they are favoured,

and, if we may use the expression, indicated, by local circumstances. In general, the manifestation of a desire for this
conversion may be regarded as a certain indication of the progress of national wealth and comfort. Whatever bad influence
upon the condition of our agriculture may be attributed to the
corvée on one hand, or to causes inherent in the character of
our population on the other, it is, nevertheless, a fact, that, in
the most of those districts which have a fertile soil, ready
outlets, and a certain amount of commercial and industrial
activity, we find, as well amongst the different classes of free
cultivators as amongst the serf-peasants who have become quit-
renters, and those likewise who remain under the corvée régime,
fields tolerably well cultivated, stalls and stables well replenished
with stock, and a degree of fulness and general comfort not
often to be met with in many of the countries of central
Europe. M. Haxthausen cites various examples of the sort
that came under his own observation. This distinguished
savant passed a portion of his life in studying the agricultural
condition, the communal institutions, and the state of the peasantry in various countries, and of late he has been making the
manners and social condition of the Slavonic populations the
object of his special inquiries. We attach too much weight
to his opinion to omit citing it, in confirmation of our own
views in regard to the corvée. After calculating what would
be the cost, in the government of Jaroslaw, of working
without corvée a domain of a certain extent, and estimating the
loss of interest upon capital which would remain idle during
great part of the long winter season, for want of any productive
employment for the working stock and farm servants, and on
a comparison of these expenses with the income from such a
property in Russia, in France, and in Germany, M. Haxthausen
draws the following conclusions : " If any one were offered, in
a present, the fee-simple of a domain near Jaroslaw on condition
of converting it into a farm on the model of those which
are found in the countries of central Europe, with the whole
inventory and appurtenances of such an establishment, bestial,
agricultural implements, &c., and of labouring it in the manner
practised in those countries, he would be a fool if he were to
accept it ; for not only would he draw no return, but he would
be obliged to incur additional outlay every year if the establishment were to be kept going. We see, therefore, that in those
districts a large estate cannot be cultivated by the proprietor on
his own account ; and yet he cannot abandon it. Agriculture
is here not a speculation to be entered on in hopes of profit,
but a task imposed by the most imperative necessity (*eine*

eiserne Nothwendigkeit).   In the present state of things, I must
give it as my opinion of the rural economy of these Russian
districts that farming on a large scale (*grosse Grundwirth-
schaften*) can be carried on only in one or other of these two
modes; either upon the corvée system, so that the proprietor
does not himself require to supply the farm-servants, cattle, and
implements employed in the labour, or, in other words, that he
has not himself to defray the expense of culture; or else by
establishing a system of labour in combination with some industrial enterprise which would furnish the means of turning to
some useful account the productive forces — the labour of
man and beast — which would otherwise lie idle during the
long intervals when the works of the field are interrupted.
That there should, in these districts, be a certain number of
large landed estates, I regard as a matter of prime necessity;
for without these we need never dream of agricultural improvement, which in Russia is much more required than has hitherto
been generally supposed.   Russia, therefore, requires a nobility
in the country just as she requires a burgess class in the towns;
and agriculture could not improve if the nobility did not possess
estates and establishments which render a country life agreeable and desirable.   But, if the existence of these large properties is necessary for agricultural improvement and national
well-being, it follows that serfage cannot be at present abolished;
it may, however, be regulated, and placed under a normal
régime, determining with precision what the obligations of the
corvée are, so as to remove abuses and arbitrary conduct; this is
the object of the ukase of 2d September, 1842." *

To these judicious observations we have to add, that the
Russian peasant is not what was formerly termed in France
taillable et corvéable à volonté † ; and that, if he is sometimes
exposed to unjust exactions, this can only happen by abuse,
and is contrary to existing laws.   An ukase of the Emperor
Paul dated in 1797 fixed the *maximum* of the corvée at three
days' work per week; and subsequent laws have constantly
had in view to introduce greater definiteness and regularity in
everything relating to the prestation.   Nor can we fail to perceive that time and the progress of manners are exercising a
gradual influence in softening its rigours, and giving rise more
and more to voluntary arrangements.   These lead by degrees
to the conversion of prestations in kind into a personal rent,
which may in its turn be converted into a ground rent,—a

* *Studien über die inneren Zustände Russlands*, vol. i. p. 174.
† Or, as it has been translated, *cutable and carveable at pleasure*.

commutation which has already begun to come into operation on the Crown domains. But an attentive observation of the very different results of these isolated arrangements, according to the localities in which they have come into operation, must convince us of the difficulties that are opposed to any general measure which should have in view a systematic and uniform regulation of the relations betwixt peasants and their proprietors. A measure which would be successful in one place might be productive of most pernicious consequences in another; and M. Haxthausen observes, with perfect justness, that the emancipation of the peasants in Russia ought to be regarded rather as a local question than as a general and political one.

In districts where the soil is of small fertility or difficult of culture, where the production does not suffice for the wants of the cultivator, where the latter is obliged to seek in some other employment of his time and labour for some secondary means of providing for his subsistence and discharging his obligations, the conversion of the corvée into a personal rent is a measure for the interest equally of peasant and proprietor ; but it cannot operate advantageously either for the one or for the other, except in localities where man's labour is in constant requisition. Similar motives lead to similar arrangements in localities where the quantity of cultivable land is limited, and where the superfluous hands easily find employment in other branches of industry. On the other hand, in districts where a large quantity of the land is arable, where the soil is fertile, where the harvests exceed the wants of the population, and where, at the same time, there are ready outlets for agricultural produce, it is often more advantageous for the proprietor to work his estate by means of the corvée. Still the corvée does not exclude the well-being of the cultivators ; and its commutation into *obrok*, when such takes place, is then rather the result of mutual convenience than a measure imperiously called for by circumstances. It is therefore exceedingly difficult to regulate the matter by any previous enactment of general rules.

Independently of the measures adopted by government for the regulation of the corvée, there are others which might render the latter more productive, and, at the same time, less burdensome to those who are subject to it. These depend principally upon the proprietors themselves. One of them would consist in the conversion of the day's work into piecework ; so that, for example, to plough a field, or to cut down a meadow of a certain extent, should be considered equivalent to so many days' labour. In this way a diligent labourer would discharge his corvée sooner, and have more time to employ usefully on his own behalf. This might take place by mutual agreement, just as arrangements are now made between communities and proprietors for converting the corvée into *Obrok*. Arrangements of this sort are met with here and there; and M. Haxthausen cites a case which came under his own notice on an estate belonging to M. Bonine, in the government of Tambow. It would be well that such examples should find many imitators. Modifications of the sort, arranged upon equitable principles, would be a real improvement on the system of culture; but we must abstain from offering an opinion as to how far such a change would be generally practicable. We will add that, whatever reforms the system may, and doubtless will, undergo in the course of time, they will exert but a secondary influence on the condition of our agriculture, so long as certain other conditions are not more or less modified.

One of these conditions, and it is one which probably impedes much more than serfage does the progress of agricultural improvement, is the manner in which the land is distributed amongst the peasants, that is, its distribution by *hearths* (*tièglo*). The whole land, of which the use and possession is conceded to the peasants of a village, is divided into as many lots as there are hearths or families. As the community is liable *in solidum* for the rents and prestations affecting each of its members, it is it that makes the distribution. The extent of the different allotments is proportioned to the number of members in a family, regard being had to its wants and to its strength in working hands. When a son marries in his father's lifetime, he has right to an allotment to be laboured by himself for his own behoof. Where there are marked inequalities in the fertility of the land, the division is equalised by assigning to every hearth a portion of land of each different quality. Where the extent of the lands exceeds the strict wants of the population, that is to say, the normal proportion considered requisite for the subsistence of each family, it is to the peasants who are in the best circumstances,—who have the greatest number of good hands at their disposal,—who have the most stock,—and, in general, who have the best means of cultivating, that the surplus is adjudged,—often against the will of the receivers, whose contribution to the charges of the community is then proportionally augmented. This distribution is generally made with great equity and discretion; and the surplus, thus distributed, forms a reserve for future distributions, which may be rendered necessary by the progress of population. When, on the other hand, there is not land enough to assign each family an allotment proportioned to its wants, the surplus population emigrates to other localities, sometimes in the neighbourhood, sometimes in distant governments, in quest of work and a living.

However equitable this system of distribution may be in itself, it is easy to see how thoroughly it must cut up the land, and what frequent changes of possession must be the consequence, according as the population of a village varies — as the hearths increase or diminish in number. Now, such a state of matters cannot be favourable to agricultural progress ; for, *first*, the uncertainty of long retaining, or of leaving as an inheritance to his children, the land which he cultivates, renders the peasant indifferent to any improvement of which the fruits are not to be immediate ; and, *secondly*, the formation of a peasant's allotment out of several detached fractions, in order to equalise the productive value, has also an unfavourable influence upon the culture. These are inconveniences to which it is very difficult to apply a remedy. This system of distribution is inherent in the patriarchal organisation of our communes, which it would be dangerous to meddle with. It is based on the fundamental idea of the unity of the community, and of the equality of right possessed by every one of its members to an aliquot part of the land pertaining to the community. It thus consolidates and strengthens that communal spirit which is one of the most conservative elements of social organisation, and one of the best preservatives against the invasion of proletarianism and of communistic notions ; the latter at least can have little room for taking hold of a set of agriculturists who are already enjoying in common, by means of an equitable distribution, the usufruct of the lands which they cultivate. One remarkable feature of the case is the practical good sense with which our peasants themselves frequently modify the inconveniences of the system according to circumstances, — the facility with which they make arrangements amongst one another for compensating the inequalities which arise from the different degrees of fertility of the soil, — and the cheerfulness with which every one submits to the awards of the elders of the commune. One would think that those agrarian distributions, so frequently renewed, would give rise to numerous disputes ; and yet it is but rarely that the parties interested have recourse to the intervention of authority. This fact, surprising enough in itself, is explicable by a single cause, namely, that the system, however vicious it may be in other respects, is so identified with the manners and ideas of our peasantry, that they cheerfully submit to all its inconveniences as a matter of course. We cannot do better than refer to what has been said upon this subject by M. Haxthausen;

and we shall confine ourselves to quoting two remarkable examples adduced by that author, which go to show that this system of distribution, with all its imperfections, is still the system which, under the present state of things, is most suitable, both to the manners and to the real wants of our agricultural population.

On arriving at the village of Gorapiatnitzkaïa, in the government of Jaroslaw, M. Haxthausen collected on the spot the following information in regard to the economy of that commune. The village, composed of 23 hearths, with a population of 82 individuals, formerly belonged to Prince Kozlowski. The peasants purchased their freedom by paying to the proprietor the sum of 14,280 silver roubles, three-fifths of which were paid down in cash, and payment of the remainder distributed over a period of seven years. They have now no other charges than the poll-tax and the imposts laid on for the requirements of the commune. The land was distributed amongst the peasants, not according to the usual custom, that is to say, according to the number of families and the number of members in each family, but in proportion to the sum contributed by each to the purchase of their freedom. This arrangement seemed both just and natural : and yet the peasants found it so inconvenient and so little conformable to their habits, that they resolved to distribute amongst themselves the amount of the purchase-money as a simple debt of the community, and to proceed to a redistribution of the lands according to the system generally adopted.

The second example is more striking still. The German colonists established in the government of Saratow brought along with them the principle of the transmission of the property of the soil by inheritance, according to the law and practice of their old country. The government not only authorised the observance of this principle, but even adopted it as obligatory for the colonists in the statute of their communal organisation. After the experience of some years, however, they solicited a change in this provision of the statute, and permission to adopt the system of distribution in use amongst the Russian peasants, which they considered much more favourable to the preservation of their welfare : after persevering in their application for a considerable time, the permission was accorded them.

All this goes to prove that, whatever impediments the system may oppose to the progress of agricultural improvement, it would be imprudent to lay a rash hand upon an order of things so identified with local traditions, and with the wants and habits of the peasantry: one modification, however, might, we think, be gradually introduced, without altering the principle of equal partition per tièglo, namely, to proportion the extent of the allotments to the fertility of the soil, instead of assigning to each family a small bit of each parcel of land classed according to its quality. Those who came worst off in this distribution might obtain a proportional alleviation in the distribution of the communal assessments, and every one would obtain the advantage of possessing his allotment in a single piece, which would greatly facilitate its culture. Of course, such a change could not take place in the way of compulsion, and under the form of a general measure: but it might be brought about in the way of encouragement and by the influence of example. Government might perhaps be able to exercise some influence by making grants of its unoccupied lands, attaching to the grant certain conditions limiting the subdivision of the portions brought under cultivation.

To the inconveniences inherent in the distribution of the lands by tièglo, as one of the causes of negligence in their culture, we must add the marked inclination of our peasants for a wandering life, which leads them to roam abroad in quest of work, when they could employ their time usefully without quitting their native village. This tendency has moreover been favoured for the last thirty years by the impulse which the prohibitory system has given to the development of manufacturing industry,—a subject to which we shall have occasion to return in the sequel. But, for a just appreciation of the fact, we must also bear in mind, that this inclination for a nomadic life, derived from an epoch which can scarcely yet be termed remote in the history of a large portion of our population, is stimulated throughout all the northern regions of Russia by the influence which the rigour of the climate exerts upon field labour. In more temperate regions, the labours of husbandry are more conveniently distributed, occupying the cultivator during a larger portion of the year: the winters being shorter, it is easier for the inhabitants of the country to employ themselves usefully during the interval between harvest and seed-time; they can bring home their fire-wood; they can carry their produce to market; they can pursue some of those accessory labours which are more or less connected with their main avocation. They have also more scope for varying their culture. Nor can we deny that, independently of the natural inclination of our population for this wandering mode of life, it has become, in many districts, a real necessity. There are provinces where many of the peasants would never be able to pay their taxes if they did not go elsewhere in search of the money. In one government the cause of this penury is the want of land for culture, in another it is the want of markets for produce.

The manner in which our agricultural population is distributed with reference to the productive soil also exercises a certain amount of impeding influence. In the greater part of Russia the rural population is grouped in large villages, in which the houses are crowded together just as in towns. The consequence is, that a large number of the inhabitants thus reside at considerable distances from the lands which they cultivate; and thus, independently of the loss of time in going and returning, there arises a moral cause of negligence in culture; for it is impossible that the man who has to travel several versts in order to reach his field should cultivate it with the same interest, and bestow upon it the same care, as the man who has it constantly under his eye, and who can turn every favourable minute to account, whether it be for dunging or for labouring, for sowing or for reaping, for watering his meadow or for cutting his hay. This is one of the causes of the greater prosperity of the German colonies, where the dwellings are so distributed that each colonist has the land that he cultivates, if we may use the expression, under his thumb. This also partly explains the progress of agriculture in the Baltic provinces, where the rural population is much more scattered than in other parts of Russia. Such an agglomeration of the peasantry into numerous groupes predominates amongst nations which were formerly exposed to the incursions of barbarians or to the devastations of wild animals, and thus felt the want of residing in each other's neighbourhood for mutual protection. In no country, for example, are populous villages so numerous as in Hungary, where, according to the official statistics, there existed, in 1843, 21 villages with between 5,000 and 10,000 inhabitants, and 324 with between 2,000 and 5,000. In 1823, there existed in the county of Bekesch, a village named Tschaba, of more than 17,000 inhabitants, which has since been erected into a burgh, and now reckons a population of 25,000. The system of grouped populations, if not in general favourable to the progress of culture, presents on the other hand the advantage of keeping up the communal spirit, whilst isolation tends to destroy it. And thus it is, that in this respect, as in so many others, every system has its advantages and disadvantages; and it is in vain to hope to profit by the one without experiencing somewhat of the other. But it cannot be denied, that in Russia this aggregation of the peasantry in large villages frequently exceeds the limits necessary for the purpose in question. In several governments — in Simbirsk and Saratow for example — we have villages of 3,000 and 4,000 inhabitants, which, from the great extent of their territory, are so distant from each other, that we may travel a whole post without casting our eyes upon a human being, and where the fields are 10 or 15 versts or more from the dwellings of their cultivators. In these districts the labours of the field are executed *en masse :* a great part of the village population moves twice a year — at seed-time and at harvest — to the distant fields, and remains there bivouacking till the work is brought to a conclusion. The same course is followed in the vast plains of Hungary. It may be conceived that, under such a nomadic system of husbandry, a culture even moderately careful is out of the question. The breaking down of these large villages would powerfully contribute to agricultural progress; and this, in the opinion of M. Haxthausen, might be accomplished in a very simple and natural manner. " It may be taken for granted," says he, " that in Russia, in the course of 30 years every village is either wholly or in part consumed by a conflagration. Now, it would be sufficient to ordain that, after each fire, the peasants whose houses had been burned, or at least a portion of them, instead of rebuilding upon the same site, should remove to another part of the village territory. In this way there would be formed, in the course of thirty years, twice or thrice the present number of villages." Although we do not regard this measure as totally impracticable, we believe that its execution would frequently be prevented by local difficulties; and that in many cases a struggle would have to be undergone with the habits and prejudices of the people. We happen to be acquainted with an enlightened and benevolent proprietor, who undertook a subdivision of this sort upon his lands, solely with a view to the benefit of his peasants, and with their own consent; but he did not succeed in carrying it through without a great deal of difficulty, and at the expense of considerable sacrifices incurred in order to render his experiment as advantageous as possible to the parties interested, and to conquer their repugnance to the innovation. He was, moreover, obliged to undertake formally that, in case the parties removing were not satisfied with the change at the end of three years, he would restore the old order of things, and rebuild their houses at his own expense upon their former foundations. As the new arrangements were admirably appropriate to local circumstances, the people felt their benefit; and, when the three years were out, not a man amongst them desired to get back to his ancient quarters: the difficulty consisted in getting them to comprehend the benefits of the change before they saw it in operation. It is true, on the other hand, that with the spirit of submission which our peasantry entertain for whatever emanates from authority, an arrangement of the sort undertaken by order of government would probably meet with fewer obstacles. For this reason it seems to us that M. Haxthausen's idea is deserving of consideration ; but his estimate of the period required to carry it through generally is based on the somewhat exaggerated assumption, that a 30th part of the villages of all Russia is yearly consumed by fire. The annual calamity from this source is probably not quite so large; but, in our prospective view of the matter, it is of less importance to calculate whether the result would arrive 10 or 20 years sooner or later, than it is to ascertain the possibility of carrying through the measure. In some localities, where the old houses are in a state of decay, and there is at same time an abundance of building materials, the breaking up of the large villages might be undertaken without waiting for the occurrence of a conflagration.

However favourable the division of extensive rural communes would be for agriculture, no less noxious would be the frittering down of the soil beyond certain limits. We witness the consequences of this in France, where the class of petty proprietors whose material position approximates to proletarianism is continuously augmenting. It results from statistical documents published in 1834 by the Minister of Commerce that the rateable extent of the territory of France at that period amounted to 49,363,609 hectares, divided into 10,896,682 quotas of impost, which comprehended 125,360,338 parcels, giving at an average 4 hectares and 53 ares $= 4\frac{3}{20}$ dessiatines for each quota, and 39 ares $= \frac{36}{100}$ dessiatine for each parcel. The number of proprietors is endless ; but few of them possess more than portions of scattered properties, situated often at considerable distances from each other.* From such a state of matters, we ourselves are still far remote : but it is nevertheless true that the subdivision of villages in consequence of partition on succession has, in some governments, especially in districts where the corvée system is predominant, been carried to an extent which is not favourable to the progress of agriculture. M. Haxthausen's work contains observations upon this subject which, in a prospective point of view, are well entitled to consideration.

We have now before us a statistical table of M. Koeppen, exhibiting the number of landed proprietors and their peasants,

* See the *Revue des Deux Mondes* for the year 1836, vol. viii.

Statistical Table of Landed Proprietors and their Peasants.

GOVERNMENTS.	Number of Landed Proprietors.	of their Peasants.	of small Proprietors possessing not more than 20 Peasants.	of Peasants belonging to Proprietors of this Class.	Proportion per Cent. of small Proprietors, possessing not more than 20 Peasants to total Number of landed Proprietors.	Number of Peasants belonging to small Proprietors out of every 1,000 Serfs.	Average Number of Peasants per Proprietor of Class possessing not more than 20 Peasants.
1. Olonetz - -	293	6,005	230	1,940	78·5	323	8·4
2. Bessarabia -	259	6,894	194	1,289	74·9	187	6·6
3. Tschernigow -	5,411	289,119	4,036	22,315	74·6	77	5·5
4. Poltawa - -	7,538	335,944	5,457	33,548	72·4	100	6·2
5. Orel - -	2,937	375,992	2,117	18,106	72·1	48	8·6
6. Koursk - -	6,536	355,115	4,680	30,800	71·6	87	6·6
7. Woronèje -	2,825	256,165	1,933	12,751	68·4	50	6·6
8. Tauride - -	320	16,335	218	1,533	68·1	94	7·0
9. Smolensk -	5,645	378,858	3,650	30,134	64·7	80	8·3
10. Kharkow - -	3,316	223,587	2,014	15,232	60·7	68	7·6
11. Riazan - -	5,392	389,728	3,233	24,721	60·0	63	7·7
12. Nowgorod -	3,823	193,791	2,263	20,368	59·2	105	9·0
13. Wilna - -	3,115	201,057	1,799	8,017	57·8	40	4·5
14. Kostroma -	4,010	298,706	2,208	17,349	55·1	58	7·9
15. Province on this side Caucasus -	78	5,836	42	287	53·8	49	6·8
16. Tambow - -	4,180	370,462	2,189	18,124	52·4	49	8·3
17. Orenburg -	1,233	116,875	640	4,791	51·9	41	7·5
18. Wologda - -	1,520	94,650	787	7,822	51·8	83	9·9
19. Jaroslaw - -	3,395	286,751	1,652	16,386	48·7	57	9·9
20. Twer - -	4,344	357,069	2,077	19,072	47·8	53	9·2
21. Simbirsk - -	2,224	261,639	1,057	8,793	[47·5	34	8·3
22. Penza - -	2,036	258,937	935	7,400	45·9	29	7·9
23. Kherson - -	2,606	148,882	1,169	10,524	44·9	71	9·0
24. Saratow - -	2,390	327,276	1,071	9,169	44·8	28	8·6
25. Mohilew - -	2,037	298,173	912	6,228	44·8	21	6·8
26. St. Petersburg -	1,402	129,471	624	6,401	44·5	49	10·3
27. Grodno - -	1,821	196,227	808	5,569	44·4	28	6·9
28. Toula - -	4,152	415,578	1,840	14,863	44·3	36	8·1
29. Minsk - -	2,021	292,348	896	6,175	44·3	21	6·9
30. Pskow - -	2,253	206,032	956	8,404	42·4	41	8·8
31. Kowno - -	1,923	175,733	784	7,773	40·8	44	9·9
32. Wladimir -	2,778	335,178	1,078	12,469	38·8	37	11·6
33. Kalouga - -	2,636	313,759	1,005	8,879	38·1	28	8·8
34. Wiatka - -	99	18,018	36	219	36·4	12	6·1
35. Kazan - -	898	96,605	313	2,738	34·9	28	8·8
36. Witebsk - -	1,667	237,869	570	3,908	34·2	16	6·9
37. Wolhynia -	1,949	451,088	638	4,363	32·7	10	6·8
38. Nijni-Nowgorod	1,686	340,245	529	5,460	31·4	16	10·3
39. Moscow - -	2,450	314,521	742	7,087	30·3	23	9·6
40. Ekathérinoslaw	1,360	141,939	409	4,112	30·1	29	10·1
41. Podolia - -	1,449	461,755	398	2,950	27·5	6	7·4
42. Perm - -	49	217,725	12	64	24·5	0·3	5·3
43. Kiew - -	1,262	501,834	256	1,904	20·3	4	7·4
Total - -	109,318	10,699,791	58,457	450,037	53·5	42	7·7

in forty-five governments. From this table it appears that, of 109,340 landed proprietors who possessed in 1838 a male population of 10,704,378 peasants, there were 58,457, or more than half, of whom none possessed more than 20 peasants. The male population belonging to these proprietors amounted at that period to 450,037 individuals, giving an average of only 7 peasants to each proprietor. The largest number of those small proprietors is found in the governments of Kharkow, Kostroma, Koursk, Nowgorod, Orel, Poltawa, Riazan, Smolensk, Tambow, Tschernigow, and Twer. There were upwards of 2000 in each of these eleven governments, and, in the eleven together, 33,924, or nearly three-fifths of the entire number of this class. The table on page 237. exhibits the statistics of these small proprietors in forty-three governments*: it appears from it that there are eighteen governments in which the number of proprietors, possessing not more than 20 peasants, exceeds half the total number of landed proprietors, and that there is only a single government, namely Kiew, where their number does not exceed the proportion of one-fifth. The number of peasants possessed by proprietors of this class does not attain in any government the average of 12 per each proprietor; and there are thirteen governments, namely, — Bessarabia, Tschernigow, Poltawa, Koursk, Woronèje, Stavropol, Mohilew, Grodno, Minsk, Wiatka, Witebsk, Wolhynia, and Perm, in which the average is only 5 or 6 peasants per proprietor, whilst in the government of Wilna the average is only 4.

The whole landed proprietors were classed in 1834, according to the number of their peasants, as follows:

Number of Proprietors.		Absolute Number of Peasants. Male Population.	Average Number of Peasants for each Proprietor.
58,457	with fewer than 21 peasants -	450,037	7·7
30,417	with from 21 to 100 -	1,500,357	49·3
16,740	„ „ 101 „ 500 -	3,634,194	217·1
2,273	„ „ 501 „ 1000 -	1,562,831	687·6
1,454	„ 1000 and upwards -	3,556,959	2448·
109,340		10,704,378	98·

Thus, of 1000 proprietors, there were

535	who did not possess more than	-	-				20	peasants
278	who possessed from -	-	-	-	-	21	to 100	„
153	„ „ „ -	-	-	-	-	101	„ 500	„
21	„ „ „ -	-	-	-	-	501	„ 1000	„
13	„ „ upwards of	-	-	-		1000		„

* In the governments of Archangel and Astrakhan there were no proprietors of this class.

so that more than four-fifths of the proprietors possessed not more than 100 peasants. As, amongst the large proprietors, there are some who possess lands in more governments than one, and who consequently figure twice or thrice in the statistics from which we have derived the foregoing figures, their actual number must be in reality below what we find in M. Koeppen's table; and, *per contra*, the proportional number of small proprietors must be larger. According to the same table, the number of peasants was distributed amongst the different classes of proprietors as follows:

Of 100,000 peasants

4,204 belonged to small proprietors having not more than							20
14,016 belonged to proprietors having from			-	-	21	to	100
33,951 ,,	,,	,, ,,		-	-	101	,, 500
14,600 ,,	,,	,, ,,		-	-	501	,, 1000
33,229 ,,	,,	,, ,,		-	-	1000 and upwards.	

Thus about a third of the peasants belonged to proprietors of the largest class, and more than a third to the easy class owning from 100 to 500; more than 15 per cent. belonged to wealthy proprietors, owning from 500 to 1000, and more than a fifth to proprietors possessing not more than 100,—whilst of the latter proportion, 4 per cent. were held in vassalage by small proprietors not owning more than 20.

On examining the column of the table which indicates the proportion of peasants belonging to the class of small proprietors, as compared with the total numbers of the former, we perceive that there are only three governments, namely, Olonetz, Bessarabia, and Nowgorod, in which more than 10 per cent. belong to small proprietors owning, at an average, from 6 to 9 peasants: in the first of these governments, however, their number nearly attains the proportion of a third; and in Bessarabia it approaches a fifth of the entire serf population: in the government of Poltawa, there are exactly 10 peasants per 100 belonging to small proprietors who own 6 at an average: in the government of Tauride, the proportion is nearly 10 per cent.: in thirty-one governments it varies between 2 and 8 per cent.: in four governments, namely Wiatka, Witebsk, Wolhynia, and Nijni-Nowgorod, it is a fraction above 1 per cent.: and there are only three governments, namely, Podolia, Perm, and Kiew, where it does not attain 1 per cent. of the total number.

The greatest number of large proprietors, possessing more than 500 peasants, is found in the governments of Kalouga, Kiew, Kostroma, Minsk, Mohilew, Moscow, Nijni-Nowgorod, Orel, Penza, Podolia, Riazan, Saratow, Simbirsk, Smolensk, Tambow, Tschernigow, Toula, Twer, Wladimir, and Wolhynia.

These twenty governments contained 2,634 proprietors of this class, with 3,540,691 peasants, giving, at an average, 1344 peasants to 1 proprietor, and composing about seven-tenths of this class of proprietors and their peasants. In the other twenty-four governments there were reckoned only 1092 large proprietors with 1,579,099 peasants, making 1446 peasants to 1 proprietor.

As to the relative extent of large properties,—large, that is, in regard to the number of their peasants,—the first rank is held by the governments of Kiew, Minsk, Mohilew, Nijni-Nowgorod, Penza, Podolia, Saratow, Simbirsk, Tschernigow, and Wolhynia. In each of these the number of peasants belonging to proprietors who possessed 500 and upwards exceeded the half of the entire number of serfs. In the governments of Kiew and Podolia there were 403 large proprietors with 673,614 peasants, giving an average of 1671 peasants to 1 proprietor. In the former of these governments, the large properties of 500 peasants and upwards embraced more than seven-tenths, and in the latter, they embraced more than two-thirds, of the total serf population.

The medium properties of from 100 to 500 peasants do not, in any government, attain the half of the total number of serf cultivators. The largest number of these properties is found in the governments of Jaroslaw, Kalouga, Kiew, Kostroma, Koursk, Moscow, Poltawa, Riazan, Smolensk, Tambow, Toula, Twer, Wladimir, and Wolhynia. There were reckoned in these fourteen governments 8,504 proprietors of this class, with 1,809,921 peasants, which gives an average of 213 peasants to 1 proprietor. As the total number of these proprietors amounted to 16,740, with 3,634,194 peasants, it follows that more than half of the proprietors, and nearly the half of their peasants, were concentrated in the governments in question.

Another circumstance which may also be considered a great obstacle to culture is insecurity of possession, resulting from a want of precise determination of the boundaries of estates, and the numerous *enclaves* which form matter of litigation. These are termed *tcherespolosnyià zemli ;* and there are some governments in which they occupy more than a third of the whole arable lands. To remedy the inconveniences thence arising, government has established in all the provinces special commissions for the regulation of boundaries and the termination of this state of contentious possession, and has instituted a department in the senate to adjudicate in the last resort all disputes which cannot be brought to an amicable settlement. The labours of these commissions are in a very advanced state in those governments where fewest local obstacles have had to be encountered. The following are the results in a few governments.

Extent of Enclaves in Litigation.

					In 1836. Dessiatines.	In 1846. Dessiatines.
In the government of Wologdà	-	-	-	- 2,232,762	709,898
„ „	St. Petersburg	-	-	- 1,338,277	613,331
„ „	Nowgorod -	-	-	- 4,220,753	2,249,260
„ „	Twer -	-	-	- 2,183,161	650,811
„ „	Smolensk, upwards of	-	- 2,000,000	1,175,997
„ „	Pskow, about	-	-	- 1,200,000	309,237
„ „	Kalouga	-	-	- 1,125,711	643,938
„ „	Toula -	-	-	- 1,421,881	495,748

We perceive from these examples that, in some governments, the extent of the lands in litigation has been reduced, in the space of ten years, by a half, by two-thirds, or even by three-fourths. In the government of Wiatka, the enclaves in litigation, which in 1836 had occupied a very considerable extent, were reduced in 1846 to 33,000 dessiatines. On the other hand, in some other governments, where there is a deficiency of land surveyors, the operation proceeds at a very slow pace indeed; in the government of Koursk, for example, out of 2,906,424 dessiatines of land which were in litigation in the year 1836, there had been determined in the space of 10 years no more than 189,878, leaving 2,716,546 dessiatines still in litigation in the year 1846.

Adding to the governments above mentioned, those of Jaroslaw, Kostroma, Nijni-Nowgorod, Orel, Riazan, Simbirsk, and Kazan, there remained in 1846, according to the statistics of M. Arsénieff, in these seventeen governments, 16,915,772 dessiatines of enclaves in litigation, making nearly 14 per cent., or about a seventh part of the total area of these governments.

In the governments of Nowgorod, Kostroma, and Kalouga, the enclaves still in litigation in 1846 occupied more than a fifth of the area; in that of Smolensk, nearly a fourth; in that of Jaroslaw, a third; in those of Orel and Riazan, considerably more than a third; and, in that of Koursk, nearly two-thirds of the entire territorial extent. These figures show how important it would be to hasten definitive settlements of these boundary questions by means of amicable arrangements.

Another cause which has been, and to some extent rightly, assigned for the backward state of our agriculture, is the want of capital for the necessary improvements and the absence of credit upon real as well as upon personal security. The error is on the side of those only who attribute to this cause a too general and too exclusive influence. The system of real security, properly so called, exists with us only in the kingdom of

Poland and in the Baltic provinces. The only real security which the legislation of the empire recognises, is that of the lender's taking into his actual possession in pawn the land of the party to whom he advances money on loan; a sort of security which the Russian law terms *zakladnyïa*. But a credit of this description is not favourable to the progress of agriculture, and those who have recourse to it are rather spendthrifts and ruined landowners than prudent men desirous of improving their estates. Personal credit is also in a loose state with us; the rate of interest on loans amongst individuals is very high; to give from 10 to 12 per cent. is nothing unusual even for very solvent borrowers. Where credit is so costly, improvements to be paid for with borrowed money will not be undertaken. This precarious state of personal credit is attributable to two main causes: on the one hand, to want of economy, a taste for luxury and ostentation, and a too general inclination to live beyond one's means, which diminishes the confidence of lenders; and, on the other hand, to the mechanism of our judicial system and forms of process. In the recovery of a simple debt, duly constituted and vouched by legal documents, the creditor is exposed to long and vexatious delays, if he happen to have a litigious and unscrupulous debtor; happily, however, these two causes are gradually wearing out: the taste for dissipation is diminishing, and economy and good management prevail amongst the proprietors to a much greater extent now than formerly; at the same time, improvements are continually being introduced into the administration of justice; legislation is amended; doubts and ambiguities in the law are cleared up; and deficiencies are supplied. But all these reforms require time for their completion. In every other country have not centuries elapsed before a tolerably satisfactory legislation has been attained? At this day even, and in the countries the most advanced in civilisation, do we not, in spite of all the reforms that have been introduced into legislation both civil and criminal, hear numerous complaints, well or ill-founded, regarding the defectiveness of existing laws and forms of procedure? In England, for example, it is matter of general complaint that justice is sacrificed to form and to the letter of the law, — that it is too expensive, and often inaccessible to the poor; whilst in France they complain, and with reason, of the defectiveness of the hypothecary system, which does not afford sufficient security to the lender, in consequence of the latent mortgages which may, without his knowledge, prejudice his right of priority. We cite these examples merely to remind the reader that legislation ripens but slowly, that it is the growth of long experience, and that it can never be very much in advance of a country's manners and uses, of its customs, and material wants. As regards the hypothecary system, or system of real security, which would undoubtedly be of immense benefit from the favourable influence which it would exert upon the credit of landowners, its introduction, so desirable in every respect, finds more difficulty in Russia than elsewhere, on account of the collision which it presents with the organisation of our banks *; still, it has occupied, and it deserves to occupy, in a very high degree, the attention and solicitude of the government. Meantime it cannot be maintained as a general fact that our proprietors are void of the resource of credit, because our banks take the place of the hypothecary system up to a certain point, a proprietor being able to obtain from them a loan at the, for us very moderate, rate of 5 per cent. If the banking system in Russia have not done so much for the progress of agriculture as might have been expected, if the loans have been rather squandered on luxury or thrown away in hazardous speculations than usefully applied, this has been the fault, not of the institution itself, but of the parties who had recourse to it. But we must observe that it is only to the class of landed proprietors that the institution is open; the bank can be of no direct use to the peasants, the numerous class, upon the welfare of whom the welfare of our agriculture in general essentially depends. For these small cultivators, the credit that would be useful would be personal credit, retail credit if we may use the expression, credit from day to day and for sums of small amount. But this sort of credit is very little developed amongst us, because, with the exception of some specially favoured districts, commercial movement and money circulation are still exceedingly insignificant in the country. This want of petty credit and smallness of money circulation, to which is joined in some districts the absence of markets for agricultural produce, deprives the small cultivator of the means of improvement, and makes him find it difficult, unless he has some subsidiary means of earning a little money, to pay his quit-rent; so that he is often obliged to part with his crop for a trifle, in order to find the means of discharging the pecuniary demands upon him and providing for his most urgent wants.

We now touch upon a question which more nearly concerns our agricultural interests, and which may exert upon the condi-

---

* The organisation of the banks being one of the most important subjects in the financial economy of a country, we shall reserve a chapter for it in the sequel. We here allude to it only under the general aspect of the influence which these establishments exercise on our agricultural situation.

tion of our cultivators a much more direct influence, than any of the circumstances which we have hitherto adverted to; we mean the question of markets for our grain, and its selling price in the interior of the empire. The frequent complaints which we hear on this point from our agriculturists relate to the great instability of the market prices of cereals,—their successive depreciation upon the whole,—and the want of outlets for their produce in those governments which are most productive. The statistical data carefully collected by M. Wesselowski, and reproduced by him in an interesting article upon the price of grain in Russia, inserted in the Journal of the Ministry of Domains for 1845, prove by the irrefragable testimony of figures, that one part of these complaints is unfounded, —that the price of grain, far from undergoing a reduction, has almost constantly followed an ascending movement. M. Wesselowski, amongst other proofs, exhibits a scale of prices in the maritime towns from which our grain is exported, commencing with 1824 and ending with 1843. This scale is reproduced in a recent publication of M. Storch on the condition of the peasants in Russia, and brought down by him to the year 1847 inclusive. It gives the decennial averages in silver roubles; and we insert it here, with the addition of the four subsequent decennial periods, bringing it down to the year 1851 inclusive.

				Wheat per Tchetwert.		Rye per Tchetwert.	
				Roubles.	Kopecks.	Roubles.	Kopecks.
From 1824 to 1833	-	-	-	4	34	3	3
1825 „ 1834	-	-	-	4	60	3	17
1826 „ 1835	-	-	-	4	60	3	27
1827 „ 1836	-	-	-	4	80	3	18
1828 „ 1837	-	-	-	4	94	3	12
1829 „ 1838	-	-	-	5	1	3	21
1830 „ 1839	-	-	-	5	21	3	31
1831 „ 1840	-	-	-	5	29	3	41
1832 „ 1841	-	-	-	5	23	3	72
1833 „ 1842	-	-	-	5	31	3	73
1834 „ 1843	-	-	-	5	29	3	71
1835 „ 1844	-	-	-	5	10	3	37
1836 „ 1845	-	-	-	5	14	3	32
1837 „ 1846	-	-	-	5	26	3	58
1838 „ 1847	-	-	-	5	49	3	94
1839 „ 1848	-	-	-	6	87	4	57
1840 „ 1849	-	-	-	6	77	4	58
1841 „ 1850	-	-	-	6	62	4	46
1842 „ 1851	-	-	-	6	52	4	33
General average	-	-		5	39	3	63

Thus, in the space of twenty-seven years, from 1824 to 1851, the average price of wheat at our sea-ports has augmented 218 kopecks per tchetwert, or 50 per cent., and the average price of rye, 130 kopecks or 42 per cent.

The statistics of the exportation of grain exhibit no less favourable results. The following is a summary of the triennial exportations of the four principal sorts of grain during the same period from 1824 to 1851, according to the official tables, to which we have subjoined the value of the whole quantity of cereals exported, flour included : —

				Triennial Average of Exportation of Wheat, Rye, Barley, and Oats, taken in cumulo.		Value of whole Grain exported, including dry Legumes, Grits, and Flour.
				Tchetwerts.		Silver Roubles.
1824 to 1826	-	-	-	1,136,022	-	3,971,700
1827 „ 1829	-	-	-	2,451,611	-	8,240,600
1830 „ 1832	-	-	-	3,749,531	-	16,622,400
1833 „ 1835	-	-	-	761,660	-	3,689,000
1836 „ 1838	-	-	-	2,532,531	-	10,847,000
1839 „ 1841	-	-	-	2,966,467	-	16,521,000
1842 „ 1844	-	-	-	2,913,731	-	13,810,500
1845 „ 1847	-	-	-	6,397,000	-	38,927,400
1848 „ 1850	-	-	-	3,764,984	-	19,908,000
1851	-	-	-	4,409,471	-	20,963,000

The total exportation of the four sorts of grain during this period of twenty-eight years amounted to 84,430,000 tchetwerts (= 60,789,000 English quarters), representing (together with flour and legumes) a value of 418,575,700 silver roubles (= 66,270,000l. sterling).

We perceive from this summary that, even setting aside the most brilliant period of our corn trade, that, namely, of 1845 to 1847, which presents an exceptional case, from the failure of the harvest of 1846 in France and England, whilst it was abundant in Russia,—the exportation of the four principal sorts of grain taken in cumulo has almost quadrupled, whilst the value of cereals and flour exported has more than quintupled. The difference between the increase of quantity and of value exported is occasioned, *first*, by the general rise of prices ; *secondly*, by the increased quantity of exported grain falling chiefly upon the most valuable sort, namely, wheat; and *thirdly*, by grits and flour being included in the value column.

If these figures show that the complaints as to the general fall of prices are unfounded, it cannot, on the other hand, be denied that the complaints of great fluctuations of price in the home market, and of a decline of prices in the most productive governments, are, unhappily, but too well founded. To justify the rate of valuation which we adopted in our estimate of the entire harvest of Russia, we have already given some indications with regard to the prices of wheat, rye, grits, and oats throughout European Russia. We complete these general indications by inserting the table of prices (p. 247.)

in the several governments during the years 1846, 1847, 1848, and 1849. This table, prepared from the prices current which are published monthly in the "Journal du Ministère de l'Intérieur," contains the highest and lowest prices quoted during this period, together with the average of the whole. It is to be regretted that, in these prices current, the price of barley is not given, and that for some governments there are likewise no quotations of the prices of other sorts of grain. Still, notwithstanding these defects, the table does not fail to throw some light upon the question.[*]

We perceive that prices have varied according to locality or harvest : —

For *rye*, from 98 kopecks to 11 roubles 7 kopecks per tchetwert.

For *wheat*, from 2 roubles 19 kopecks to 13 roubles.

For *grits*, from 1 rouble 60 kopecks to 12 roubles 60 kopecks.

For *oats*, from 79 kopecks to 5 roubles 70 kopecks.

Thus, the greatest difference of prices was, for rye, as 1 to 11 ; for wheat, as 1 to 6 ; for grits, as 1 to 8 ; and, for oats, as 1 to 7.

Such extraordinary variations are met with in no other country ; and it is to be observed that the greatest difference of prices takes place upon rye, which is the grain most extensively cultivated in Russia and constituting the principal food of the people ; so that a fall in the price of this article is very ruinous for the producer, whilst an excessive rise is a calamity for the largest number of consumers.

The lowest prices are observed : —

For rye, in the governments of Kharkow, Courland, Ekathérinoslaw, Kiew, Koursk, Orenburg, Penza, Perm, Poltawa, Saratow, Simbirsk, Tambow, Toula, and Woronèje. In these fourteen governments, the price fell, for a certain time, under 2 roubles ; in seven of them, namely Courland, Ekathérinoslaw, Kiew, Koursk, Orenburg, Saratow, and Woronèje, it fell below 1 rouble 50 kopecks ; and in the government of Saratow it was, in 1846, below even one rouble per tchetwert.

For wheat, in the governments of Kazan, Kiew, Orenburg, Poltawa, Saratow, Simbirsk, Tambow, and Woronèje ; in these eight governments it fell below 3 roubles.

The highest prices were : —

For rye, (above 6 roubles), in the governments of Archangel,

---

[*] The reader will observe that the *average* price is obtained, not from a comparison of the *highest* and *lowest* prices, but from a calculation of *the whole* market prices during a period of four years.

Table of the Prices of Rye, Wheat, Grits, and Oats.

Governments.	Rye.			Wheat.			Grits.			Oats.		
	Lowest Price.	Highest Price.	Mean Price.	Lowest Price.	Highest Price.	Mean Price.	Lowest Price.	Highest Price.	Mean Price.	Lowest Price.	Highest Price.	Mean Price.
	Rbs.Kp.	Rbs. Kp.	Rbs.Kp.	Rbs.Kp.	Rbs. Kp.	Rbs.Kp.	Rbs.Kp.	Rbs. Kp.	Rbs. Kp.	Rbs.Kp.	Rbs.Kp.	Rbs.Kp.
1. Archangel	3 50	6 90	4 75	6	6 50	6 12	7 20	10 80	7 87	1 97	3 75	2 82
2. Astrakhan	*	*	*	*	*	*	4	6 50	5 14	1 63	3 8	2 9
3. Bessarabia	2 80	4 64	3 75	3 95	6 8	5 13	5	7 84	6 40	2 3	3 75	2 74
4. Kharkow	1 80	4 25	2 90	3 50	6 75	4 80	3	5	4 23	1 20	3 28	2 2
5. Kherson	2 50	4 60	3 44	*	*	*	5 66	9 45	6 85	2 2	4 20	2 85
6. Courland	1 17	11 7	6 26	5 35	14	9 45	5 23	12 5	7 79	2 20	5 70	3 46
7. Ekathérinoslaw	1 30	5 20	2 95	3	7	4 42	3 25	7	5 10	1 20	4 80	2 5
8. Esthonia	4 23	9	5 43	3 85	13	8 95	*	*	*	2 10	4 16	2 66
9. Grodno	2 30	6 75	4 19	5 60	8 50	6 95	5 80	7 50	6 63	2 5	3 20	2 55
10. Jaroslaw	2 97	4 7	3 27	6	7 20	6 45	4 62	6 12	4 33	1 77	2 66	2 18
11. Kalouga	2 81	4 30	3 19	5 9	7 30	5 98	3 15	6 2	4 70	1 2	2 39	1 81
12. Kazan	2 2	4 10	2 86	2 89	6 55	3 89	3 12	4 97	4 11	1 20	3 83	1 52
13. Kiew	1 30	2 98	1 96	2 65	3 97	3 41	2 95	5 25	4 9	1 30	2 76	1 66
14. Kowno	3 25	8 35	5 12	*	*	*	*	*	*	1 87	4 8	2 93
15. Kostroma	3 25	3 90	3 60	5 40	6 80	6 36	3 90	6 5	4 95	1 38	2 15	1 76
16. Koursk	1 35	3 80	2 44	3 94	6 50	4 74	1 60	3 90	2 94	80	1 70	1 20
17. Livonia	4 10	7 44	5 92	6 62	12 34	9 46	8 62	12 30	10 65	2 35	5 10	3 60
18. Minsk	2 20	6 93	4 11	5	8	6 51	5 50	8 91	6 88	1 85	3	2 18
19. Mohilew	3 44	5 35	4 22	5 40	7 5	6 8	5 20	6 70	6 10	2 22	3 28	2 74
20. Moscow	3 6	5 9	3 91	5 33	7 62	6 49	4 23	7 14	5 64	2 6	2 77	2 43
21. Nijni-Nowgorod	2 5	5 66	3 16	4 2	6 7	5 5	4 3	7 50	5 46	1 20	2 62	1 99
22. Nowgorod	4 28	6 6	5 13	5 63	8 81	7 30	6	7 79	6 94	2	3 67	2 72
23. Olonetz	*	*	*	*	*	*	*	*	*	2 75	4 9	3 45
24. Orel	2	3 45	2 58	4 50	7 65	5 75	2 65	5 10	3 74	1 25	2	1 52
25. Orenburg	1 7	2 24	1 53	2 49	3 24	2 62	2 29	3 65	2 92	82	1 47	1 7
26. Penza	1 50	3 80	2 52	*	*	*	2 45	5	3 33	85	2 30	1 34
27. Perm	1 88	2 44	2 14	4 25	4 25	4 25	5 36	7 27	6 41	79	1 74	1 43
28. Podolia	2 35	3 86	2 98	3	4 80	4 8	3 70	5 5	4 54	1 75	3 30	2 47
29. Poltawa	1 60	3 75	2 29	2 40	4 95	3 49	3 10	5 70	3 94	1 20	3	1 82
30. Pskow	4	7 25	5 34	6 42	9 88	7 92	7 37	9 13	8 23	2 19	4 28	3 1
31. Riazan	2	4 17	2 80	4 56	6 1	5 7	3 29	6 64	4 51	1 20	2 32	1 75
32. Saratow	98	3 56	1 96	2 18	5 9	3 29	2 40	5 13	3 33	1 14	2 70	1 61
33. Simbirsk	1 65	4 30	2 69	2 75	5 25	3 78	2 90	6 10	3 89	1	2	1 43
34. Smolensk	3 45	4 60	4 18	6	7	6 31	4 30	6 66	5 91	1 70	3 17	2 33
35. St. Petersburg	5 94	6 88	6 34	*	*	*	6 97	8 75	7 97	3 33	4 79	3 84
36. Stavropol	2 70	5 11	4 14	*	*	*	6 60	8 45	4 87	2 60	4 23	3 65
37. Tambow	1 60	3 81	2 58	2 45	7 12	4 90	2 68	6 7	3 95	99	2 19	1 50
38. Tauride	2 12	5 35	3 52	3 92	7 17	5 48	4 60	7 75	6 24	1 33	4 56	2 76
39. Tschernigow	2 10	3 19	2 59	3 30	5 14	3 98	3	4 96	4 1	1 30	2 43	1 92
40. Toula	1 88	3 85	2 57	4	6 33	4 77	2 86	5 47	4 15	1 16	2 19	1 50
41. Twer	*	*	*	*	*	*	*	*	*	1 50	3 25	2 30
42. Wiatka	2 4	3 40	2 69	4 20	6 40	4 72	6 40	7	6 45	1 26	1 98	1 57
43. Wilna	2 25	10	4 78	7 50	12	9 14	4 15	10	7 69	1 50	3 75	2 50
44. Witebsk	3 80	7	4 81	6 50	10	7 64	5 10	7 10	6 17	1 80	3 30	2 44
45. Wladimir	3	4 90	3 85	4 18	8 34	6 5	4 21	7 69	5 72	1 62	3 12	2 29
46. Wolhynia	2 15	3 50	2 74	3 23	4 25	3 97	4 25	6	4 95	1 50	2 50	1 97
47. Wologda	3 60	5 1	4 13	5 4	6 52	5 73	8 46	12 60	10 11	1 93	3 75	2 37
48. Woronèje	1 37	4 21	2 49	2 75	6 40	4 15	2 55	5 90	3 44	94	2 59	1 51

* The prices replaced by this mark have not been quoted.

Courland, Esthonia, Grodno, Kowno, Livonia, Minsk, Now-gorod, Pskow, St. Petersburg, Wilna, and Witebsk, twelve governments in all. In the government of Wilna, the price attained the amount of 10 roubles; and in Courland, it reached as much as 11 roubles 7 kopecks.

For wheat (8 roubles and upwards), in the governments of Esthonia, Grodno, Livonia, Minsk, Nowgorod, Pskow, Wilna, Witebsk, and Wladimir,—nine in all. The greatest rise,—to 10 roubles and upwards,—took place in the governments of Esthonia, Livonia, Wilna, and Witebsk: in the first of these, the price rose as high as 13 roubles per tchetwert.

The medium prices were : —

For rye, under 3 roubles, in the governments of Kharkow, Ekathérinoslaw, Kazan, Kiew, Koursk, Orel, Orenburg, Penza, Perm, Podolia, Poltawa, Riazan, Saratow, Simbirsk, Tambow, Tschernigow, Toula, Wiatka, Wolhynia, and Woronèje,—twenty governments in all. It did not reach 2 roubles in the governments of Kiew, Orenburg, and Saratow; and it exceeded 5 roubles in the governments of Courland, Esthonia, Kowno, Livonia, Nowgorod, Pskow, and St. Petersburg.

For wheat, under 5 roubles, in the seventeen governments of Kharkow, Ekathérinoslaw, Kazan, Kiew, Koursk, Orenburg, Perm, Podolia, Poltawa, Saratow, Simbirsk, Tambow, Tscher-nigow, Toula, Wiatka, Wolhynia, and Woronèje; in one of these governments, namely, Orenburg, the average price was under 3 roubles (2 roubles 62 kopecks), and it exceeded 7 roubles in the seven governments of Courland, Esthonia, Livonia, Nowgorod, Pskow, Wilna, and Witebsk. The highest average (upwards of 9 roubles) is found in the governments of Courland, Livonia, and Wilna.

The greatest fluctuations of price took place : —

For rye, in the governments of Courland, from 1 rouble 17 kopecks to 11 roubles 7 kopecks; Ekathérinoslaw, from 1 rouble 30 kopecks to 5 roubles 20 kopecks; Kowno, from 3 roubles 25 kopecks to 8 roubles 35 kopecks; Minsk, from 2 roubles 20 kopecks to 6 roubles 93 kopecks; Saratow, from 98 kopecks to 3 roubles 56 kopecks; Wilna, from 2 roubles 25 kopecks to 10 roubles ; Woronèje from 1 rouble 37 kopecks to 4 roubles 21 kopecks. The governments in which the fluctu-ations in the price of rye have been less considerable, that is, in which they have not attained the proportion of 50 per cent., are those of Jaroslaw, Kostroma, Nowgorod, Orel, Perm, Smolensk and St. Petersburg,—seven in all.

For wheat, in the governments of Courland, from 5 roubles 35 kopecks to 14 roubles; Ekathérinoslaw, from 3 roubles to 7 roubles ; Esthonia, from 3 roubles 85 kopecks to 13 roubles; Kazan, from 2 roubles 89 kopecks to 6 roubles 55 kopecks; Poltawa, from 2 roubles 40 kopecks to 4 roubles 95 kopecks ; Saratow, from 2 roubles 18 kopecks to 5 roubles 9 kopecks ; Tambow, from 2 roubles 45 kopecks to 7 roubles 12 kopecks ; and Woronèje, from 2 roubles 75 kopecks to 6 roubles 40 kopecks. The least variable prices, that is to say, where the difference during the four years did not exceed 50 per cent., were maintained in the governments of Archangel, Jaroslaw, Kalouga, Kiew, Kostroma, Mohilew, Moscow, Orenburg, Perm, Riazan, Smolensk, Wolhynia, and Wologda,—thirteen governments in all.

It is evident that with such rapid rises and falls, when the prices of the chief productions of the soil vary within a short space of time in the proportion of 1 to 5 and even more, agriculture must necessarily be in an abnormal condition; such fluctuations of price cannot be otherwise than exceedingly prejudicial to it; they render it impossible for the cultivator to estimate, even approximatively, his chances of loss or gain. Everybody is agreed as to the evil; the only difference of opinion is as to the source from whence it proceeds, and the remedy that ought to be provided.

Amongst the publicists who have directed their attention to this important subject, M. Zablotski is distinguished by the profoundness with which he has treated it in an article inserted in the national ephimerides (Otetchesivennyïa zapiski, vol. 42, year 1847,) equally remarkable and instructive from the lucidity with which the author analyses the question under its different aspects. As any attempt to treat the subject in a manner so detailed and scientific would carry us beyond the limits of the present work, we must refer those desirous of studying it more specially to the article itself. There is also much interesting and instructive information to be found in M. Protopopoff's article on the Russian corn trade, inserted in the " Journal du Ministère des Domaines " for the year 1842, and in M. Wesselowski's article on the price of grain published in the same journal for the year 1845. Referring to these three articles, we here confine ourselves to the reproduction in substance of some of the ideas enunciated by M. Zablotski on the causes of the fluctuations in the price of grain in Russia.

M. Zablotski considers our system of rural economy to be one of the primary causes of this fluctuation ; for, under this system, which substitutes for a determinate rent under a voluntary agreement, an obligatory rent (termed by M. Zablotski *obïazatelna renta*) represented by gratuitous labour, that is to

say, the corvée, anything like a moderately precise estimate of
the expense of production becomes impossible ; and thus there
is no index supplied to the principal regulator of the market
price.   The author explains and supports his opinion by an
analysis of the circumstances which determine the selling prices
of commodities, and of the elements which concur in working
up the products of the soil, and determine what is called the
prime cost, represented by the total expenses of production.

The selling price of commodities is determined by three
elements which require to be taken into consideration :

1st, the cost of production ;

2ndly, The intrinsic value of the commodity :

3rdly, The relation which subsists between supply and
demand.

The influence of the two latter constituents of the selling
price is more or less variable, whilst the first is the prime
regulator ; it is the centre of gravity which the current price
of each commodity must always be approaching, more or less
nearly according to circumstances, but from which it can never
widely deviate for any considerable length of time.   When, in
consequence of a disproportion between the supply and the
demand, favourable to the vendor, the price rises to an amount
greatly exceeding the cost of production, the supply augments,
and causes the price to descend to its natural level ; when, by
a contrary effect, the price falls below the amount of the cost of
production, including the producer's profit (which constitutes
the recompense for his trouble), the production will necessarily
fall off ; this re-establishes the equilibrium between supply and
demand, and causes the selling price to rise to its natural level.
The manufacturer or producer of a given commodity may sometimes find himself necessitated to sell below prime cost, but production cannot long go on under such conditions.   Thus, in the
natural order of exchanges, the cost of production, bating accidental and temporary variations, always forms the main element of the selling price of a commodity.

For the products of the soil the cost of production consists ;
first, of the rent of the land, representing in some sort the
interest of the fixed capital ; *secondly*, of the interest of floating
capital employed in the purchase and support of the objects
constituting the inventory of the farm, in the maintenance of
the buildings, in the purchase of agricultural implements, in
the necessary ameliorations, &c. ; *thirdly*, of the cost of the
labour employed in cultivation.   These three agents of production, land, capital, and labour, are sometimes divided amongst
three parties, who are interested and participate in some way

or other in the cultivation of the soil, and sometimes concentrated in the hands of a single party. The latter case does not usually occur, except for small patches of ground, which the proprietor labours himself with the means at his own disposal, without having recourse to the labour or capital of others.

In those countries where the cultivation of the land is based upon voluntary contracts, where every one disposes freely of his landed property, labour, and capital, the participation of these three agents of production and their respective values can be determined with precision; and it is therefore easy enough to calculate the cost of production. The proprietor of the land, if he be at the same time the undertaker of its culture, that is to say, if he labour it on his own account, knows beforehand the price at which he must sell his produce to cover, *first*, his advances for wages to his workpeople; *secondly*, the interest of his floating capital; and, *thirdly*, the rent, which he ought to draw from his land, constituting what, in industrial enterprises, is termed the fixed capital. In the same manner, if the land is let to a tenant, the farmer, who becomes the undertaker of its cultivation, must find in the selling price of his products, *first*, the rent which he pays to the owner; *secondly*, the wages of the servants and labourers whom he employs; and, *thirdly*, the interest of his capital, and a reasonable remuneration for his own trouble. This is the limit below which the price of agricultural produce cannot fall, without putting a stop to its production; and it is this limit which serves principally to regulate the market price. On the other hand, in a country where one portion of the soil is under servitude to obligatory labour, and another portion is cultivated on the proprietor's account by means of this same obligatory labour, capital, labour, and rent become so confounded, that a calculation of the cost of production, or of the prime cost of the produce of the soil, becomes impossible. This centre of gravity being lost, the market price floats at the will of chance or of local circumstances. It undergoes a rapid fall when the harvest is abundant; or, in the opposite case, it as rapidly rises to an exorbitant amount. Under such circumstances, the proprietor can never say, " Such a year I sold my corn at a loss; such another year I sold it at a profit." For him *profit* and *loss* are meaningless terms. He can only say, " Such a year I had a good income; such another year I had a bad one." Whether prices rise or fall, he must go on sowing and reaping, in order that he may draw *some* advantage, however small, from the compulsory labour of his peasants; and he must sell his produce often for a trifle, in order that he may have at least *some* revenue, unless he be possessed of means enough to enable him to hold on with his produce for a year or two, waiting for better times. But when a large number of cultivators are not in this favourable condition, every one hastens to sell before another at such price as can be got; and the result is an excessive depreciation of agricultural produce, especially in those districts which generally produce more grain than they consume, and have not sufficient outlets for their surplus production. In this explanation of one of the principal causes of the great fluctuations in the price of corn in Russia, which seems reasonable enough, we think we have substantially reproduced the ideas of M. Zablotski. But we would probably be carrying the consequences too far, if we were to attribute a very exclusive influence on the present state of our corn trade to the cause in question. A cause so peremptory and so decisive must needs be productive of the same results wherever it is in operation, and this extreme variability of price would therefore require to be manifested in the same degree in every country where the corvée exists. This, however, is not the case. In the empire of Austria, for example, all the provinces of which, with the exception of the Italian, were under the corvée régime until 1848, the fluctuations in price have never been so excessive as in Russia*; and we see, even amongst ourselves, precisely the same system of agricultural labour attended with totally different results. The statistical data carefully collected by M. Protopopoff prove that within the space of nine years, from 1832 to 1841, prices varied in some governments only in the proportion of from 10 to 22 or 25, which is nothing extraordinary in a trade which by its nature is so hazardous as the corn trade, whilst in others they fluctuated in the proportion of 10 to 82, or even 111, that is to say, more than from single to decuple. There must, therefore, independently of our system of agriculture, be other causes, local and particular, in operation, which contribute more or less to these fluctuations. These causes, we think, may be referred to the following circumstances: —

1. The inequality of our harvests, which the climate with us renders much more variable than they are in other countries.

2. The difficulty of our communications, in consequence of the bad state of the main roads in a great part of the empire, and of the cross roads everywhere.

3. The immense distances between the principal corn-markets.

4. The narrow limits within which our internal corn trade is confined. But few merchants invest their capital in it, and

---

* We shall see by and by, that, with the exception of some provinces peculiarly situated, the price of grain varies in Austria nearly in the same proportion as in Prussia.

these few monopolise the great outlets in those directions where, favoured in respect of river communication, this commerce has attained a certain standing. Some governments do not produce, even in the best years, grain enough for their own consumption, and others generally produce much more than is necessary for that purpose. Between some of the governments of these two classes there has been established, owing to certain facilities of communication, a sustained and regular corn trade which is not susceptible of extensive variation. The corn-market of St. Petersburg furnishes a striking example of the happy influence which this regular march of commerce exerts on the stability of prices. The government of St. Petersburg being united by a good system of river communication with the most fertile central provinces of the empire, its supplies of grain are perfectly certain. They are provided with regularity and uniformity, being based upon previous calculations of what will be required: and the trade is carried on by a certain number of individuals whose mutual competition tends to prevent excessive rises and falls; accordingly, we find that in this government the price of rye did not vary in the space of four years, from 1845 to 1849, in the proportion of more than from 5 to 6, whilst in many other districts, it varied in the proportion of 1 to 3, 4, or more. The increased scale of variation proceeds in part from the circumstance that those small branches of the corn trade, which, though they do not come within the limits of the great lines of communication or of larger speculation, are yet so important in their sum, are for the most part neglected, either on account of the difficulties of transport, or from an indisposition to undertake smaller speculations. There are in general with us few speculators disposed to run the risk of purchasing in years of plenty in order to sell in years of scarcity; this is owing in part to the prejudice which exists in Russia (as in many other countries) amongst the less enlightened classes, against those who engage in speculations of the sort; they are accused of forestalling and of producing artificial scarcities; in times of real scarcity, the people who suffer from the dearness of bread throw the blame upon the corn-merchants, without ever dreaming that this very dearness often becomes a preventive against absolute famine. That it does so, however, might be shown them by a very simple example. Let us suppose that in a country of a million of inhabitants there occurs a bad harvest, which yields only the ordinary year's supply for 500,000 mouths; it is not surprising that in such a case the prices should rise to double or treble their ordinary amount; in consequence of this rise, the most numerous classes will find themselves obliged to restrict their consumption of bread, and to supplement it as much as possible by other articles of food; at the same time, the high price of corn will stimulate importation; and it is in this way alone that the inhabitants will be able to rub on till the ensuing harvest without suffering a complete famine. But what would be the case, if, in the absence of all spirit of speculation, the producers and merchants were to go on selling at the ordinary prices? It it is evident that, bread fetching only the same price as formerly, every family would go on consuming its usual quantity, so that, the whole provision being exhausted at the end of six months, and the moderation of prices having hindered arrivals from abroad, famine would be the inevitable consequence. The corn trade, like every other, may become a business of jobbing and fraudulent speculation hurtful to the general weal; but, taken in its natural condition, it is precisely the sort of speculation founded on a calculation of probabilities which re-establishes equilibrium of price in the grand article of consumption by preventing too excessive depreciation in years of abundance, and excessive scarcity of grain in years of defective harvest. The greater the competition of these speculators, the more do prices become equalised. But with us, whether from want of capital or from want of enterprise, this commerce is much less active in its different ramifications than it is in other countries, and the administration is obliged to supplement it by imposing on the communes the obligation of establishing magazines of reserve. This absence of enterprise, which necessitates direct intervention on the part of government with the vast means at its disposal, is found in many other branches of our social economy. We must bear in mind that in other countries, the large number of small towns, which are so many markets and entrepôts for the produce of the land, greatly facilitates exchange, by putting the surrounding districts in communication with each other, and thus equalises prices. We have already seen that in European Russia there is reckoned only 1 town to $130\frac{1}{2}$ square miles, whilst in Austria there is reckoned 1 town or burgh to $3\frac{3}{4}$ square miles; in Prussia, 1 town to $5\frac{1}{3}$ square miles; and in France, 1 town or burgh to 7 square miles. We may easily conceive how troublesome, slow, and difficult, the operations of internal commerce must be in a country where the centres and intermediate points of those operations are so scattered, and separated by such great distances. From all these circumstances our internal commerce is placed in an exceptional position, and, presenting peculiarities to be met with nowhere else, it is not to be judged of by theories applicable to other countries. The effects of this absence of competition, and the difficulty of intermediate communication, are, we think, sufficiently exhibited in the great differences which are found in the prices of grain in the various governments. We see, amongst other instances, from the data furnished us by M. Zablotski, that in 1843, a year which presented no peculiarity in regard to the harvest, the medium price of rye was 6 roubles 21 kopecks per tchetwert in the government of St. Petersburg, and 1 rouble 35 kopecks in the government of Koursk,—which represents the difference of 10 to 46. Alongside of this, M. Zablotski cites the case of Prussia, where, during the period from 1822 to 1835, the difference between the lowest average price ($47\frac{5}{6}$ silbergroschen the scheffel of wheat, and $30\frac{1}{2}$ silbergroschen the scheffel of rye, in the province of Prussia) and the highest average price ($59\frac{3}{4}$ silbergroschen the scheffel of wheat and $43\frac{1}{6}$ silbergroschen the scheffel of rye, in the province of the Rhine) presents the proportion of no more than 10 to 12 for wheat and 10 to 14 for rye. The writer from whom we borrow these figures is of opinion that the enormous difference in the prices of grain in the two Russian governments above mentioned cannot be attributed to their geographical situation; and in support of this opinion he cites, amongst others, the following examples: that in the government of Archangel, situated at the northern extremity of the empire, the price of grain was nearly 19 per cent. lower than in the government of Pskow; more than 4 per cent. lower than in the government of Nowgorod; and 15 per cent. lower than in that of Livonia;—that in New Russia, in the most southern governments, grain was dearer, during the year in question, than in governments nearer the centre, and even than in some of the northern governments: in the government of Tauride, for example, the price was more than 4 per cent. higher than in that of Kalouga;—that the difference is still more striking when we compare the price of grain in neighbouring governments: thus, in 1843, the price of rye was 1 rouble $42\frac{1}{2}$ kopecks per tchetwert in the government of Tschernigow; 1 rouble 90 kopecks in the government of Kiew; 2 roubles 46 kopecks, in that of Minsk; 2 roubles 98 kopecks in that of Mohilew; 3 roubles 4 kopecks in that of Smolensk; and 4 roubles 34 kopecks in that of Witebsk. We, too, are of opinion that the geographical position of the governments, and the distances by which they are separated, are not the sole cause of these great differences of price; but that other circumstances, which we have already indicated, also contribute to that effect. The greater or less amount of commercial intercourse subsisting between two given districts, and their greater or less facilities for intercommunication, will aggravate or counteract the influence of distance : but that the latter must necessarily exercise a preponderating influence on the commerce of cereals is a point about which we apprehend there can be no dispute whatever. It, therefore, seems to us that, in an empire which occupies more than half the surface of Europe, the prices of grain—though their tendency will be towards equalisation, as a natural consequence of the progress of commerce, population, and prosperity—will probably never attain the same degree of uniformity and steadiness that they will in countries of more limited extent.

The influence of geographical position on the corn trade is as incontestable as the influence of distance. Of this we may find a proof in the empire of Austria : in Gallicia, a province which produces large quantities of corn, and which, being surrounded by countries similarly situated, has little external outlet, the average prices during the years 1840 to 1843 were for wheat 114 kreutzers, and for rye 83 kreutzers, per metzen ; in the Tyrol, which does not produce grain enough for its own consumption, and where transport is costly, owing to the chains of mountains which everywhere intersect the country, and to the interruption of river communication by rapids and cataracts, the average price of wheat during the same period was 285 kreutzers per metzen, and that of rye 192 kreutzers : thus the difference in prices between these two provinces was, for wheat, as 10 to 25, and for rye as 10 to 23 ; in 1843 the difference for both species of grain was as 1 to 4 ; whilst in none of the other provinces, German or Slavonian, did the lowest average differ from the highest in the proportion of more than 10 to 12 for wheat and 10 to 14 for rye. It is somewhat remarkable that the two last proportions are exactly the same as the markets of Prussia presented, according to M. Zablotski, during the period from 1822 to 1835 : and yet, down to 1848, the situation of the two countries in regard to agricultural labour was very different : in Austria the corvée system still subsisted in all its integrity, whilst in Prussia it had long previously been abolished. This affords one proof more that the great difference and fluctuations in the prices of grain in Russia cannot be attributed solely to our system of agricultural labour : and indeed we may observe in general, that, in matters touching the social condition of a country, where effects and their causes are linked together by a complicated and often imperceptible chain-work, it is well to be cautious of referring too many phenomena to a single cause : for, if we once give way to this tempting but unprofitable habit, it will be found, that, instead of patiently noting and collating the facts that come before us, we are almost sure to distort them into a sort of Procrustean conformity with certain foregone conclusions. Russia, moreover, differs in such a multitude of respects from every other country under the sun, that similar causes often produce results which are very far indeed from being exactly analogous to what we find them producing elsewhere; and there exists so copious a diversity in the economical relations of her various provinces, that similar antecedents are often attended by very divergent consequences, even from one province to another.

In regard to the examples cited by M. Zablotski, relative to the prices of grain in the north as compared with the south of Russia, we shall permit ourselves the following observations: The lowness of the price of rye in the government of Archangel compared with the prices quoted for the governments of Pskow, Nowgorod, and Livonia, may, we think, be explained, at least in part, by the commercial situation of the different governments. Traversed by the Dwina, the government of Archangel is situated in the highway of one of our outlets for the exportation of our cereals. Its population being very limited (about 240,000 inhabitants), it is only a small quantity of grain which, in addition to its own scanty harvests, it requires for its own consumption: this supply forms part of the quantities arriving by the river, and destined mainly for exportation, so that the market price is determined much less by the home demand of this government, than by the state of the foreign corn trade: now the port of Archangel is during a long period of the year closed by ice, and is, moreover, very remote from its ports of destination, so that if during the short period of navigation there be but little demand from abroad, it is likely enough that a considerable fall of prices may be the result. The government of Livonia is in a much more favourable position: the port of Riga lies much nearer to foreign ports: the navigation opens sooner and closes later than at Archangel, and commerce is very much brisker: during the year 1843, for example—the very year of which the average prices have served M. Zablotski for his term of comparison—there were exported from the port of Riga 104,627 tchetwerts of rye, and from that of Archangel only 8,374. It is moreover to be observed that in Livonia a large quantity of rye is employed in distillation, and that that province finds it very easy to dispose of any surplus it may have on hand after the closing of the navigation, being surrounded by governments which do not generally produce grain sufficient for their own consumption. These are the causes which render prices in Livonia so much higher than in the government of Archangel, notwithstanding its better geographical position.   During the period from 1846 to 1849, average prices were, *for rye,* in the government of Archangel, 4 roubles 75 kopecks, and in Livonia 5 roubles 92 kopecks per tchetwert, being a difference of 25 per cent. ; and *for wheat,* in the former, 6 roubles 12 kopecks, and in the latter 9 roubles 46 kopecks, being a difference of 55 per cent.   As regards the governments of Pskow and Nowgorod, they do not produce grain enough for their own consumption, and are at same time in the most unfavourable position for procuring it, being surrounded by seven governments, namely, Smolensk, Wologda, Jaroslaw, Olonetz, St. Petersburg, Twer, and Witebsk, of which the two former scarcely produce sufficient grain for themselves, and the five others always require to draw supplies from their neighbours.   Taking all these circumstances into account, we perceive that the lowness of price in the government of Archangel as compared with the prices of Livonia, Pskow, and Nowgorod, presents no extraordinary feature, and is referable to local causes.   The higher average price in the government of Tauride (the most southern of European Russia) as compared with that of Kalouga,—a difference, however, of only 10 kopecks per tchetwert, or about 4 per cent., is referable to causes of the like sort.   Tauride is at the door of our South-European corn ports ; and it is well known that in all maritime districts prices are higher than in the interior, especially when a brisk export trade is going on.   Now in this very year 1843, there were exported from Odessa and Taganrog 1,511,434 tchetwerts of wheat and 32,428 tchetwerts of rye, — in all, 1,543,862 tchetwerts, or 60 per cent. of the total exportation of that year.

The differences in the average prices of rye in 1843 in the neighbouring governments of Tschernigow, Kiew, Minsk, Mohilew, Smolensk, and Witebsk, is undoubtedly much more striking ; but, to form a right appreciation of the cause of these, we require to take into consideration the particular position of each of these governments.   For the sake of distinctness, we reproduce here the prices of rye in these governments in 1843 :

			Rye per Tchetwert.		
Tschernigow	-	-	1 rouble	42½	kopecks.
Kiew -	-	-	1 ,,	90	,,
Minsk	.	-	2 ,,	46	,,
Mohilew	-	-	2 ,,	98	,,
Smolensk	-	-	3 ,,	4	,,
Witebsk	-	-	4 ,,	34	,,

It is to be observed, in the first place, that, of these six governments, it is only the two first, namely, Tschernigow and Kiew, which produce more grain than they consume: the government of Smolensk belongs to the category of those that generally produce enough for their own consumption: the other three governments, Minsk, Mohilew, and Witebsk, draw a portion of their supplies from their neighbours. The government of Tschernigow, one of those which produce the largest quantities of rye, has for its neighbours, on the east and south, the governments of Orel, Koursk, Kiew, and Poltawa, which abound in grain; on the west and north, the governments of Minsk and Mohilew, which do not produce grain enough for their own population. It has thus for rivals four governments producing abundance of the same article, and for customers two governments standing in want of it, one of which, however, (Minsk) can also draw direct supplies from the governments of Kiew and Wolhynia. The government of Kiew has for neighbours, on the east, south, and west, the governments of Tschernigow, Poltawa, Kherson, Podolia, and Wolhynia, which are the chief granaries of the empire, and on the north Minsk, the only neighbouring government that can stand in want of its grain, but which, however, can draw its supplies directly from Tschernigow and Wolhynia. The government of Minsk has for its neighbours, on the east and south, three governments, Tschernigow, Kiew, and Wolhynia, from which it can draw what supplies it may require: on the west is Grodno, which produces grain enough for its own population, but which has rarely any surplus for export: on the north-west and north are Wilna and Witebsk, which do not produce grain enough for their own consumption. The government of Mohilew is bounded on the east by the government of Smolensk, which ordinarily produces enough for its own consumption, but has seldom any surplus; on the south, by the government of Tschernigow, which is able to supply it; on the west and north by the governments of Minsk and Witebsk, which do not produce a sufficiency of grain for themselves. The government of Smolensk is bounded on the south by the governments of Orel and Tschernigow, which abound in grain; on the east, west, and north, by the governments of Moscow, Kalouga, Mohilew, Witebsk, Pskow, and Twer, all of which require to draw additional supplies from other governments. The government of Witebsk has for neighbours, on the east and south, Smolensk and Mohilew, which, like itself, require supplies of grain in addition to what they raise themselves; on the west, the government of Wilna, which is not one of the most fertile, and Courland, which seldom produces more than is strictly necessary for its own consumption; on the north, Livonia, which frequently produces more than it can consume, and the government of Pskow, one of the poorest and least productive in cereals.

Upon examining in what relation prices stand to the geographical situation of these six governments, we perceive that the lowest prices are found in the two governments which abound in grain, and have for their neighbours, along a considerable portion of their frontiers, governments belonging to the most fertile countries of the empire. Medium prices are found in the governments of Minsk and Mohilew, of which the former does not produce grain enough for its own population, but which, having three fertile governments for its neighbours, is favourably situated for drawing its supplies; and the latter generally produces grain enough for its own internal consumption. The highest prices are quoted in the two governments of Smolensk and Witebsk, the harvests of which are generally insufficient for their own consumption, and which are moreover disadvantageously situated for drawing their supplies, being surrounded, along a considerable portion of their frontier, by governments which are poor in cereals, and obliged to be themselves importers of these commodities. Thus the progressive scale of prices seems to stand in a natural enough relation to the geographical position of the respective governments, the degree of fertility of their soil, and their facilities for receiving supplies.

Let us now see in what relation the difference of prices stands to geographical situation and distance. To facilitate our view and enable us to take into consideration the expense of transport, we reduce the grain measure into poods, reckoning 9 poods to a tchetwert of rye. At this rate, the difference of prices per pood presents the following figures : —

In the government of Witebsk, $+ 14\frac{1}{2}$ kopecks as compared with the government of Smolensk, $+ 15$ kopecks as compared with Mohilew, $+ 21$ kopecks as compared with Minsk, $+ 27$ kopecks as compared with Kiew, and $+ 32\frac{1}{2}$ kopecks as compared with Tschernigow.

If, taking into consideration the bad roads at certain seasons and in certain localities, we assume, at an average, for the expense of transport the rate of 1 kopeck per pood for 10 versts, the greatest difference betwixt the price of the government of Tschernigow and that of Witebsk will correspond to the amount of the expense of transport for 325 versts. This is pretty nearly the distance between the capitals of the two governments. Of course this calculation cannot be strictly applied to the commercial relations between these two governments: the governments of Wilna and Livonia, which bound with the government of Witebsk, can more readily supply it than the government of Tschernigow can. We, therefore, merely exhibit this comparison as a more or less approximative indication of the influence which distance may exert upon price. But the comparison of price and distance will be more conclusive if we apply it to two contiguous governments which carry on with each other a direct corn trade. Thus, for example, the price of rye, in 1843, being in the government of Tschernigow, 1 rouble 42½ kopecks, and in that of Mohilew 2 roubles 98 kopecks; the difference is 155½ kopecks per tchetwert, or 17¼ kopecks per pood, which corresponds in expense of transport, at the above-mentioned rate, to a distance of 172½ versts only, whilst the distance between the centre of the government of Mohilew and that of the government of Tschernigow, taken in a straight line, is about 300 versts; so that if we were even to reckon only 1 kopeck per pood for 20 versts, the difference of price would hardly cover the expense of transport, taking into account the sinuosities of the ordinary road. The same comparison applied to the government of Minsk, and to the neighbouring governments from which it might draw its supplies, gives the following results: —

From its geographical situation, the government of Minsk can draw in a direct way its supplies of grain only from the governments of Tschernigow, Kiew, and Wolhynia. Between these three governments and that of Minsk, the proportion of the difference of prices to the distances which separate them, taken in a direct line, is as follows: —

Average prices in 1843. — Tschernigow, 1 rouble 42½ kopecks; Minsk, 2 roubles 46 kopecks; difference 103½ kopecks per tchetwert = 11½ kopecks per pood; distance in a direct line between the centres of the two governments, about 350 versts: thus the difference of price distributed over the distance gives but 1 kopeck per pood for 30 versts transport; Kiew, 1 rouble 90 kopecks; Minsk, 2 roubles 46 kopecks; difference 56 kopecks per tchetwert = 6¼ kopecks per pood; distance 400 versts; this gives 1 kopeck per pood for 64 versts transport.

Average prices during four years 1846—49 * — Wolhynia, 2 roubles 74 kopecks; Minsk, 4 roubles 11 kopecks; difference, 137 kopecks per tchetwert = 15¼ kopecks per pood; distance 270 versts; this gives 1 kopeck for 17½ versts transport, always taking the distances in a straight line.

These comparisons seem to us to establish that the differences of price amongst these neighbouring governments, however great they may seem at the first glance, are nowise dis-

---

* Not having at hand the average price for 1843 of the government of Wolhynia, we have been obliged to take the average of 1846 to 1849.

proportionate to their geographical position; but even if examples should be found of cases in which the difference of price exceeded the ordinary cost of transport, that might still be explained by the nature of the commercial relations between the respective governments, and by other local circumstances. And it is beyond all doubt that the geographical position and degree of fertility of the different governments must exert a very direct and sensible influence upon the price of grain.

M. Zablotski observes that, according to the statistical data collected by M. Protopopoff, prices are much less variable in those governments which do not raise a sufficiency of grain for their own consumption, than in those which produce a surplus. Thus, for example, during the period from 1833 to 1841, prices varied at Petrozavodsk, St. Petersburg, Nowgorod, Kostroma, Jaroslaw, Wladimir, and Moscow, only between the proportions of 10 to 22 minimum difference (at Petrozavodsk), and 10 to 42 maximum difference (at Moscow); whilst at Simbirsk, Woronèje, Penza, Ekathérinoslow, Riazan, Tambow, Saratow, Koursk, Toula, and Stavropol, they varied between the proportions of 10 to 48 minimum difference (at Simbirsk,) and 10 to 111 maximum difference (at Stavropol). This difference in the fluctuation of prices he explains in the following manner:—In those governments which habitually require an importation of grain, a considerable mass of cereals is always in the hands of the wholesale merchants, and the commodity assumes the character of a current article of merchandise, of which the prime cost, transport and warehousing included, is perfectly well known to the merchant: of course, this prime cost (*perwonatchalnaïa tsiena*) depends upon the price at which he has purchased the grain from the producer; but the selling price, which includes the merchant's profit, is always more or less equalised by the competition of speculators; this proves that when, to one of the elements which determine the selling price, namely, the proportion betwixt supply and demand, there comes to be added another regulative element, namely, the price which is determined by an exact calculation of the whole expenses, fluctuations in the market price decrease, and the latter has a tendency to become steadier and steadier. The justness of this reasoning is incontestable: it supports also an observation we have already had occasion to make, namely, that one of the causes of the extreme fluctuation of prices in certain districts is the narrow limits within which the wholesale speculations of our internal corn trade are confined. But to this explanation of the greater stability of prices in those governments which do not produce grain enough for their own requirements, we may add the following observations: — In governments which produce a surplus of grain, the price of that commodity depends principally upon the demand there may be for it either for home consumption or for exportation. When the demand ceases, or is not in proportion to the quantity of provision stored — when a considerable part of last crop remains unsold, and there is the prospect of a new one equally abundant with no prospect of additional markets, — the producers become discouraged, and prices fall to a figure to which they never can sink in those governments which are regularly dependent upon external sources for a portion of their supplies, and in which the cost of transport alone maintains prices at a higher quotation. The lower the price has fallen, the greater and more rapid must be the rise when the state of the foreign market presents a prospect of disposing of the stock on hand at a large profit. In every sort of trade, and especially in the corn-trade, great falls are almost always followed by great rises, for the one is a natural consequence of the other; and this, in our opinion, is one of the chief causes of the great fluctuation of prices in our fertile districts.

If we have here gone into explanatory details which may seem too minute, we have been led away by the importance of the subject; for the question of the instability of prices is one of the most vital that affect our agriculture.

In examining some of the opinions broached by M. Zablotski, we have been far from wishing to depreciate the merit of an author who has treated the question in a manner at once lucid and profound; we have considered that an amicable discussion could only contribute to the farther elucidation of a subject on which we often meet with erroneous opinions which this writer has triumphantly refuted. On the whole, we agree with him, that the present system of our rural economy excludes the possibility of ascertaining the costs of production with anything like accuracy; that it thus eliminates one of the regulative elements of the market price, and becomes one of the main causes of its instability. But it seems to us that M. Zablotski does not assign a due share of influence to several other causes, moral and physical, which are at least concurring ones. Of these, some are merely temporary, and may be gradually removed with the progress of wealth and the successive improvements in our social economy; of this description are the causes connected with the present condition of our internal commerce and our defective means of communication: but others may be regarded as permanent, being referable to the uncertainty of our harvests, the physical and geographical situation of vast tracts of country, and the immense distances which separate the localities of production from those of consumption.

The corn trade is, by its very nature, one of the most hazardous and variable that can have an existence.   In articles of secondary importance to man,—articles of pleasure or luxury, in food or apparel for example,—increase of production and diminution of price contribute to extend their consumption; and thus the price is prevented from falling excessively low; or, conversely, when production decreases, and they become dearer, people restrict their consumption or use cheaper substitutes; so that, in this manner, the price is hindered from rising excessively high.   But this is not the case with regard to man's prime necessity,—corn.   In fertile agricultural countries, each individual, in ordinary seasons, has his ration of bread; and when a harvest of extraordinary abundance is greatly in excess of the habitual wants of the community, consumption does not augment in such proportion as to hinder a depreciation in value, unless there be some foreign outlet; the consequence is, that an excessive fall in prices is inevitable if such outlets are wanting; and this is precisely the case with several of our most productive districts.   On the other hand, if, in consequence of a bad harvest, the supply be insufficient for the home consumption, or if, along with an average harvest, there be a brisk demand from abroad, prices rise, as we have already observed, no less rapidly than they had formerly fallen. These extraordinary fluctuations are most marked and frequent with us in the southern governments, which having, in years of abundance, no sufficient outlets in the interior, are essentially dependent for their market price on the conjunctures of foreign commerce, and in some of the most fertile central governments which are dependent on the home demand, and must suffer from a cereal plethora when the harvest is generally good, and the districts which usually draw their supplies from them have themselves produced more grain than usual.   Change the system of husbandry as you may, and let the new one be as rational as you please, you will not put an end to this fluctuation of prices, which is inherent in the nature of things, and proceeds in great part from the geographical position of these countries. The most that can be expected is, that the inconvenience, though it will never be entirely removed, may yet in the course of time be gradually diminished by the improvement and extension of our means of communication.   Our fertile southern provinces will always be exposed to suffer more or less from a redundancy of grain in years of abundance, when the chances of foreign commerce turn against them,—the more so, that their topographical position is very ill-suited for commerce with the interior; for all the great rivers that traverse them, together with their tributaries, flow in a southerly direction; so that, to transport their grain into the provinces of the north or west, they have only the alternative of land carriage or up-stream navigation. And then we have to bear in mind the very great inequality of the harvests. We have seen, in the first part of this work, that on the estates of the Duke of Anhalt Koethen, in the government of Tauride, during the space of ten years, from 1832 to 1841, there were wheat harvests which yielded fifteen returns, others which scarcely returned the seed, and one which was a total failure. Such inequality, such uncertainty in the products of agriculture, easily explains the immense fluctuation of prices without going farther in quest of a cause.

As regards lines of communication, M. Zablotski, while recognising their utility and importance, attributes to them only a secondary influence on the stability of prices, citing the following examples in support of his opinion: 1, the government of Kostroma is no more favourably situated in this respect than those of Simbirsk and Saratow, where the fluctuations are twice and thrice as great as in the former; 2, the government of Toula is much more favourably situated in this respect than those of Woronèje and Penza: yet the difference between the minimum and maximum price in the first named government is as 1 to 10, whilst in the two others it is only as 1 to 5 and as 1 to 6. Now it is incontestable that, notwithstanding all the importance of lines of communication, we cannot claim for them an exclusive influence on the stability of prices: but as for the examples here cited, we must observe that the government of Kostroma belongs to the category of those which do not produce grain enough for their own consumption, whilst Simbirsk and Saratow abound in cereals, and furnish large quantities for home or foreign export; and we have shown that in countries of the latter class prices must necessarily be much more variable than in the former. The government of Toula is also one of those which have a large surplus for exportation: its market price greatly depends on its relations with other governments, especially the contiguous one of Moscow; and such is the extent of speculation which thence prevails, that it sometimes happens that in Moscow, which receives the grain of Toula, the price of grain is lower than in Toula itself.

Before concluding this digression, which many of our readers may perhaps consider as already too long, we should wish to add a word or two in regard to the excess of our production, and the influence of the foreign corn trade upon the fluctuation of prices in the interior of Russia.

M. Zablotski refutes in a very logical manner the opinion of those who maintain that Russia, possessing a boundless extent of cultivable land, produces grain in far too great a quantity, and who attribute to this cause the excessive lowness in the price of that commodity. He refers to the statistical researches of M. Protopopoff as proving that the excess of grain which can be furnished for exportation does not exceed 12,500,000 tchetwerts (9 million quarters), which does not amount to 5 per cent. of the average harvest. The average of exportation in the commerce with Europe during the decennial period of 1839 to 1848, amounts (exclusive of the kingdom of Poland) to about 4,400,000 tchetwerts, so that there remains only a floating quantity of about 8 millions of tchetwerts, or $3\frac{1}{3}$ per cent. of the whole production. M. Zablotski cites the example of the United States, which likewise possess an immense extent of arable land, and produce in proportion to their population (according to M. Z.'s statistics, twice as much grain as Russia*, yet the price has not there been reduced to a trifle: in August, 1844, the price of wheat in Carolina and Virginia was equivalent to 6 roubles 84 kopecks per tchetwert; and in 1845, when there had been a fine harvest, the price at New York in the month of October was equal to 7 roubles 18 kopecks, and at Philadelphia, in the month of September, to 7 roubles 40 ko-

---

* According to the general census, (taken every ten years,) the population of the United States amounted in 1840 to 17,063,000 individuals, and the harvest of cereals and dry leguminous plants of every sort to 615,525,673 bushels = 103,450,000 tchetwerts, which gave 6·06 tchetwerts per head. In 1847, a year of a very abundant harvest, the total production amounted, according to statistical data published in the "Gazette du Commerce de Saint Petersburg (No. 101 of year 1848), to 848,132,000 bushels = 142,543,000 tchetwerts, dry legumes included, and the population of that year was estimated at 20,746,000 inhabitants, giving 6·87 tchetwerts per inhabitant. In Russia, the average harvest, estimated at 250 millions of tchetwerts, gives, for a population of 55 millions (without Finland and the kingdom of Poland) 4·55 tchetwerts per head. The difference of the relative harvests of the two countries, therefore, is not as 1 to 2, but as 100 to 151. We have also to observe, *first*, that we take here as our point of comparison for the United States, one of their most abundant harvests, and, for Russia, the average harvest according to a very moderate estimate ; and, *secondly*, that the population of the United States for the year 1847, given in the "Gazette du Commerce de Saint Petersburg," seems to be under-rated, since, from the partial results already known of the census of 1850, the total population must now amount to $23\frac{1}{2}$ millions, which would imply an increase during the last three years of about a million per annum, if we were to admit the correctness of the data given by the "Gazette du Commerce." We therefore think that we cannot estimate the ordinary cereal harvest of the United States at more than 6 tchetwerts per inhabitant, which would present, as compared with the production in Russia, (4·55 tchetwerts per head) a difference in the proportion of only 132 to 100.

pecks; whilst at Odessa it stood at about 6 roubles per tchetwert.

We agree with M. Zablotski in thinking that the amount of our surplus production, and the degree of influence which it exerts in rendering our corn trade precarious, are generally exaggerated; but, in order to judge of the effect upon prices which may be produced in certain cases by the excess of our harvests, we must not confine our attention to the total amount of production and of home consumption. In even the most fertile countries, the larger portion of the harvest is consumed by the cultivators themselves, and does not enter into commerce at all. We have already seen that the male population of our cultivators in the various governments of European Russia may be taken to amount to upwards of 24,000,000, including the Cossacks and the other military colonies; and, as we have farther seen that the female population exceeds the male by 2·1 per cent., we may estimate the agricultural population of both sexes in European Russia, exclusive of Finland and the kingdom of Poland, at about 49,000,000, from which we deduct 1,000,000 for that part of the country population which is not stationary, but passes a portion of its life in manufactories and cities; thus reducing the settled rural population to about 48,000,000. Reckoning for the subsistence of this population 3 tchetwerts per head (including the aliment of domestic animals), we have 144,000,000 tchetwerts consumed upon the spot by the producers, and therefore not entering into commerce at all. To this cipher we must further add a fourth of the crop, or 60,000,000 tchetwerts, for seed, and, at a very moderate estimate, 5,000,000 tchetwerts for brandy distillation by landed proprietors*, making in all 209,000,000 tchetwerts. Going rigorously to work, we would subtract from this total about 9,000,000 tchetwerts, representing the quantities which pass from the most fertile districts to those which do not raise grain enough for their own agricultural populations, which would reduce the quantity consumed on the spot of production to 200,000,000 tchetwerts. The average crop being estimated at 250,000,000, there remains for internal commerce, that is to say, for the supply of the towns, of the army, of the industrial

---

* M. Protopopoff estimates the quantity of grain consumed in distillation at 10,000,000 tchetwerts, whilst M. Kœppen reckons it at only 5,000,000. We consider the latter figure much below the mark ; but we have adopted it in the above calculation, because the proprietors of large distilleries sometimes use grain purchased at the market or from their neighbours when they do not raise enough themselves, and consequently this part of the grain ought to be included in the movement of internal commerce.

establishments, and of the ambulatory population, 50,000,000 tchetwerts. Of this quantity, the excess, estimated by M. Protopopoff at 12,500,000 tchetwerts, amounts to a fourth, for which the only outlet is exportation, the extent of which must, therefore, necessarily exercise a very strong reaction on the home corn trade and on the market price. A stagnation in export, therefore, especially in years of abundance, cannot fail to produce a very considerable fall of prices in the home market, nor can the opposite case of a favourable demand abroad fail to produce the contrary effect. It is evident that these oscillations of the corn-trade barometer must be greatest in the most fertile provinces, where an extensive fall is the inevitable consequence of an abundant harvest, when the demand, home or foreign, is not in proportion to the supply. In this situation we find especially — as respects rye, the governments of Kharkow, Eka-thérinoslaw, Kiew, Koursk, Orenburg, Penza, Perm, Poltawa, Saratow, Simbirsk, Tambow, Toula, and Woronèje, in all of which governments prices sometimes fall below two roubles, and in the government of Saratow, below even one rouble; and as respects wheat, the governments of Kazan, Kiew, Orenburg, Poltawa, Saratow, Simbirsk, Tambow, and Woronèje, in all of which governments prices often fall below three roubles : to these we might add the following, in which it sometimes falls below four roubles the tchetwert, namely — Bessarabia, Kharkow, Ekathérinoslaw, Koursk, Podolia, Tauride, Tschernigow, and Wolhynia.

In the southern governments, and in several of those where grain is abundant, and which have river communication with the Baltic and White Sea, prices can be supported at their natural level only in so far as there is a demand at the sea ports. The provinces of New Russia are thus situated, and, whatever may be the progress of their internal welfare, the prosperity of their agriculture will always in great measure depend upon the activity of the Black Sea commerce.

As regards the example of the United States, which produce in proportion to their population much more grain than Russia, without experiencing such great falls in the price, we think this fact may be attributed in great part to their facilities of communication, to the great activity of their internal commerce, and to the rapid extension of their maritime commerce with all parts of the world. During the triennial period of 1846 to 1848, their imports and exports represented a value of 283,000,000 dollars = 377,000,000 roubles, whilst our commercial exchanges with foreign countries did not attain during the same period a value of more than 232,000,000. These values, distributed over the population of the two countries, give in America an amount of about 17 roubles, and in Russia an amount of 4 roubles 30 kopecks per head. In 1850, there entered the single port of New York 3,500 large vessels; that is to say, more than the number entered in 1848 in our whole Baltic and White Sea ports (3,422); and much more than double the number entered the same year in the port of Kronstadt (1,517). It is evident that such a prodigious maritime commerce must exceedingly facilitate the exchange of the products of the soil. In the export commerce of the United States cereals are now forming an article of great and increasing importance. It is but a short time since the quantity of grain exported from thence scarcely amounted to a third or fourth of that exported from Russia; now their exports almost equal ours, and will probably soon exceed them. During the year 1847, a very favourable year for the corn trade of both countries, the value of our cereal exports amounted to 71,000,000 silver roubles, and that of those of the United States to 51,000,000 dollars = 68,000,000 roubles, giving us only the trifling difference of $4\frac{1}{2}$ per cent. upon the value. If we consider at the same time that the quantities exported were taken in Russia from an annual production of 250,000,000 tchetwerts, and in the United States from a harvest of from 130,000,000 to 140,000,000 tchetwerts at the utmost, and that the selling price was distributed with us over an agricultural population of about 50,000,000, whilst in the United States it fell to the lot of about 15,000,000 or 16,000,000 cultivators, it cannot but appear natural that in the latter country the excess of production should not bring about a great fall in the price of a commodity which is so rapidly absorbed in foreign commerce. The difference of price observed by M. Zablotski between our markets and those of the United States is sufficiently explained by the difference which subsists between the two countries in regard to manual labour and the expenses of cultivation: these are in North America much greater than in Russia; and it is precisely this difference in the cost of production that enables us to support the competition of the United States in foreign markets — a competition which is daily becoming more menacing to our cereal exports.

On recapitulating the circumstances which exercise a more or less direct influence on the state of our agriculture, of which we think we have enumerated the more important, we perceive that there are some which may be regarded as temporary, and which will disappear with the gradual development of the material and intellectual resources of the country, and others

which we regard as permanent, having their seat, partly, in
physical causes, such as soil, climate, and geographical position,
our frequent droughts, the length of our winters, the disproportion,
in some governments, between the relative extent of our several
sorts of land, arable, meadow, or forest, and partly in the
character and manners of the people, which are identified with
the basis of our social organisation.

In all these respects the situation of our country differs from
that of most others, and it cannot be fairly judged of according
to generally received theories. A system of rational husbandry,
as practised in some countries of central and western Europe,
will never be applicable to all the vast countries of our immense
empire. Those who might imagine that, by dint of successive
changes and improvements such as are practised elsewhere,
agriculture might be brought throughout Russia to that state of
perfection which it has attained in England, Holland, Belgium,
and some parts of Germany, would in our opinion be cherishing
a singular illusion. We have already seen, that, in a great
part of the region of the Steppes, embracing an extent of
17,728 geographical square miles, or nearly a fifth of the whole
area of European Russia, the alternate culture of cereals and
fodder as practised in other countries is almost impossible, and
that those regions require a peculiar system of husbandry appropriate to their climate and soil. In several other parts of
the empire, where, along with a large extent of arable land,
there is only a scattered population, the three-shift system,
with all its imperfections, will remain best adapted to local circumstances. In regard to improvements, we ought to adopt
those which harmonise best with our entire system of husbandry,
and avoid, as tending generally to disappointment, those which
require a radical transformation of everything that exists. We
know more than one instance of the failure of reforms of this
sort. It is only after careful study of the whole conditions of
our agriculture in general, of its peculiarities in each district,—
for these differ immensely,—and of the character and manners
of our people, that it is possible to judge how far systems or
proceedings which have been advantageously introduced elsewhere are likely to thrive with us. It is not long since several
distinguished pupils of our agricultural institutes, who had
finished their studies abroad at the expense of government,
were sent to New Russia in the capacity of registrators of the
State domains, to put their theoretical knowledge into practice.
A sojourn of a couple of years in their place of destination
served to convince these gentlemen that most of their knowledge was of but little practical use, and that the rural economy

of those countries required a totally different procedure applicable to their own local circumstances. This, however, does not exclude very essential improvements; many of these are applicable to any agronomic system : such are, the introduction of better agricultural implements, better modes of feeding and fattening, mechanical improvements for various subsidiary processes, a better distribution of the labours of the field. Unfortunately the dearness of our iron has hitherto contributed to retard ameliorations of this sort; but to this subject we shall afterwards have occasion to revert.

Those who feel annoyed—perhaps to an unnecessary degree —that the antiquated three-shift system still so extensively predominates in our agriculture, may find some consolation upon turning their eyes to the other countries which are more or less analogously situated. In France, out of 26,078,000 hectares of arable land, there were reckoned in 1840 no less than 6,763,000, or 26 per cent., lying fallow; and, in the Austrian empire, Hungary with its dependencies, Gallicia, Buckowina, Bohemia, great part of Moravia and Silesia, and a portion of the German provinces, are, down to this date, tributary to the same system. These examples show, that, if we are still far in the rear of those countries in which agriculture is at its best, our position is, after all, not so far as might be imagined behind that of others, of which the productive forces and national wealth are already largely developed. A rational system of alternate cultures can be introduced amongst us only very gradually and very slowly, even in those districts which are best adapted for it. It would be useful chiefly in provinces where the quantity of arable land is small in proportion to the population,—in those where the soil is of no great fertility, and requires large quantities of manure,—and in those where the relative extent of meadow land as compared with arable is below the proportion necessary for supporting a sufficient quantity of cattle. In this respect, also, we have been making some progress of late, as the following indications, which we borrow from M. Arsénieff, will show : —

In the western part of the government of Wologda, a system of rational husbandry has, notwithstanding the rigour of the climate, been introduced by several proprietors. Different sorts of grain and fodder are sowed in rotation, and some traces of improvement are already seen even on the lands of the peasantry. In the government of Nowgorod, the mode of cultivation in the military colonies is visibly improved. In the government of Twer, a rational system of husbandry is pursued by the small number of proprietors who are possessed of the necessary capital. In the government of Smolensk, some proprietors are beginning to improve their cultivation by the introduction of the four-shift system and the employment of better agricultural implements. In the governments of Esthonia, Livonia, and Courland, the rational system predominates; and, in some districts, the three-shift system is met with only exceptionally. In the government of Kiew, rural economy is making visible progress. The cultivation of beet-root for the manufacture of sugar is extending more and more. In the governments of Wladimir, Penza, and Kalouga, the amelioration of their culture is beginning to attract the serious attention of the land owners. In the government of Moscow, the transition from the three-shift to a rational system is successfully proceeding with a number of proprietors. In the government of Toula these good examples are less frequent, but on the increase. In the government of Simbirsk, an improved mode of culture and the use of better implements of husbandry are making visible progress, not only upon the estates of proprietors, but also on the lands of the peasantry. With many proprietors we find a system of culture that might serve as a model. In the government of Kazan, the practice of a rational system is still confined to a small number of isolated examples. Still, improvement is visible even on some of the lands of the peasants, especially the appanage peasants; it is, however, still in its infancy amongst the Tschuwasches and the Tscheremisses.

The governments in which agriculture, as regards the mode in which it is conducted, is most backward, are: In the region of the north, Archangel: in the Aloune region, St. Petersburg: in the lower region, Witebsk, Wilna, and Minsk: in the Carpathian region, Wolhynia and Tschernigow: in the central region, Kostroma, Nijni-Nowgorod, Tambow, Woronèje, Koursk, and Orel; and in the region of the Ural, Wiatka and Orenburg.

If we attentively examine the particular situation of each government in regard to its productive forces, its means of communication and its commerce, we will perceive that cultivation is improved, and a more rational system of husbandry pursued and propagated, wherever such progress is favoured by local circumstances, and especially where the price of grain is maintained at a figure sufficiently high to cover the expense of agricultural improvements. On the other hand, culture is most neglected in those countries which are rich in grain and poor in outlets for the surplus. There are also governments where, notwithstanding comparative scarcity and high prices, which, one would say, ought to stimulate cultivation, the latter is still in a very backward state. This is owing to special causes. In some of these governments, agricultural enterprise is checked by the frequent recurrence of cattle epidemics and bad harvests: in others, it is negligence and want of capital among the proprietors that are at fault. But what is most remarkable is the very backward state of agriculture in the government of St. Petersburg, where local circumstances would seem to favour the introduction of a system of husbandry more adapted to augment the very moderate fertility of the soil: the price of grain is high, rising sometimes for rye to about 7 roubles: the average price during the years 1846—1849 was 6 roubles 34 kopecks: the outlet is ready either for exportation or for home consumption: this government, moreover, possesses an Agricultural Institute, well organised both for theory and for practice, and well adapted to the wants of the country; and some well-meaning agriculturists have established a model farm in the vicinity of the metropolis: but the good examples thus placed before the eyes of the public have met with few imitators; and we still find, in the immediate vicinity of St. Petersburg lands in a state of uncultivation, which, from their proximity to the town, and the command of manure thus afforded them, might very easily be rendered productive. The chief cause of this, in our opinion, must lie in the carelessness of the cultivating class, and the facilities which they find for gaining their bread as carters, artisans, or by means of some branch of petty industry. It is also frequently observed that peasants who reside in the neighbourhood of large cities are apt to be bad husbandmen, as they often lead an irregular life, and are addicted to sloth and drunkenness.*

Apart from the sporadic ameliorations undertaken by our more enlightened agriculturists, which are undoubtedly deserving of encouragement and will bring forth their fruits in due season, it is the state which, as the great landed proprietor, is destined in Russia to give the chief impulse to agricultural improvement. Reserving for the end of this chapter an outline of the measures, general and special, which have been adopted with this view, and which compose the labours of the Administration of Domains, we shall here confine ourselves to the exhibition of some statistical information with regard to these state properties.

According to the Report of the Ministry of Domains for the

---

* We see, for example, in the neighbourhood of Vienna, lands that might be fertilised and converted into market gardens, but which still remain in a state of nature, notwithstanding the ever increasing dearness of vegetables.

year 1849, the lands belonging to the crown occupied at that period an extent of 79,169,400 dessiatines* (=212,965,600 English acres) = 15,705 geographical square miles, which is equivalent to more than a fourth of the area of the whole Austrian Empire. In regard to possession, these lands were distributed as follows : —

	Dessiatines.
Domains vacant and uncultivated - - -	10,298,703
Communal lands in litigation and boundaries not ascertained - - . - - -	10,226,684
Lands conceded to crown peasants - - -	39,496,733
Ditto to foreign colonists - - -	2,308,613
Ditto to colonised Israelites in New Russia -	156,709
Ditto to Calmucks in the governments of Astrakhan and Stavropol -	10,248,556
Ditto to Kirghiz in the governments of Orenburg and Saratow - -	6,400,000
Lands dependent on the department of rural economy -	33,413
Total -	79,169,411

Of the 39,496,733 dessiatines of land conceded to peasants, there were estimated, in 1848, of productive soil (arable, meadow, and pasture), 33,993,137 dessiatines, distributed over a male population of 9,353,516 individuals, which gives an average of 3·6 dessiatines for each male individual, or, taking the population of both sexes (18,873,069), and allowing 5 individuals to a family, it gives an average of 9·1 dessiatines (= 24·5 English acres) for each family.† This exceeds the average amount of land enjoyed by peasants in other countries‡; but, as the productive soil is very unequally distributed, there are several governments in which, with the progress of population, there begins to be a deficiency of arable land, and the Administration of Domains is obliged to provide for this deficiency either by new concessions of vacant land, or by removing from time to time a certain number of families into districts where the extent of the cultivable soil exceeds the wants of the local population. Still, the situation of the peasants of the domains may be pronounced satisfactory on the whole (though with some exceptions) as regards the size of their concessions; but they have too often

* Without reckoning the appanage lands, and 608,833 dessiatines belonging to the Administration of Studs.

† The peasants belonging to private proprietors possess, in most governments, more land than those belonging to the crown domains.

‡ In Austria, the peasants are classed, in regard to their prestations, according to the extent of land conceded to them, into entire peasants, half peasants, and quarter peasants. There is generally reckoned, for an entire peasant, 28 joch =14¾ dessiatines ; for a half peasant, 14 joch=7⅜ dessiatines ; and for a quarter peasant, 7 joch=3¾ dessiatines ; but, as in most districts the class of entire peasants is the least numerous, it is seldom that the average is more than from 6 to 7 dessiatines per family.

to suffer, in common with the other cultivators, from droughts and cattle epidemics, and, in the more fertile governments, from the want of outlets for their produce. The following table, taken from a Report of the Ministry of Domains, exhibits the extent of arable land, meadows, and pastures, as compared with the number of the male population of the peasants of the domains in each government, in 1851.

Governments arranged according to the relative Extent of Land conceded to the Crown Peasants.	Male Population of Peasants of the Domains.	Extent of Arable Lands, Meadows, and Pastures conceded to them.	Average Extent of Land for each Male Individual.
		Dessiatines.	*Dessiatines.*
I. Governments in which all the Crown Peasants pay a Money Rent.			
1. Stavropol - - -	76,181	1,498,191	19·7
2. Astrakhan - - -	71,370	837,354	11·7
3. Orenburg - - -	186,611	1,818,279	9·7
4. Bessarabia - - -	36,677	329,225	9·0
5. Kherson - - -	48,482	398,920	8·2
6. Samara - - -	338,690	2,701,333	8·0
7. Ekathérinoslaw - -	215,052	1,544,163	7·2
8. Tauride - - -	229,111	1,605,395	7·0
9. Saratow - - -	253,181	1,133,358	4·5
10. Perm - - - -	443,300	1,944,676	4·4
11. Pskow - - -	105,747	468,581	4·4
12. St. Petersburg - -	34,157	145,828	4·3
13. Woronèje - - -	533,893	2,183,881	4·1
14. Kazan - - -	502,183	1,988,231	4·0
15. Smolensk - - -	97,621	386,680	4·0
16. Tambow - - -	394,474	1,526,440	3·9
17. Wiatka - - -	730,701	2,739,099	3·7
18. Nowgorod - - -	103,169	377,682	3·7
19. Nijni-Nowgorod - -	127,806	463,317	3·6
20. Kalouga - - -	97,490	351,431	3·6
21. Olonetz - - -	82,468	286,276	3·5
22. Wladimir - - -	132,906	440,857	3·3
23. Twèr - - - -	214,948	677,636	3·2
24. Kostroma - - -	86,099	273,104	3·2
25. Penza - - - -	230,621	716,623	3·1
26. Jaroslaw - - -	116,482	362,392	3·1
27. Toula - - - -	87,167	240,039	2·8
28. Moscow - - -	165,092	444,121	2·7
29. Kharkow - - -	315,906	824,594	2·6
30. Orel - - - -	218,211	574,930	2·6
31. Riazan - - -	202,137	521,731	2·6
32. Wologda - - -	239,895	605,339	2·5
33. Tschernigow - -	301,914	667,533	2·2
34. Archangel - - -	79,025	160,874	2·0
35. Koursk - - -	400,084	337,126	0·8
36. Poltawa - - -	424,205	210,035	0·5
Total - - -	7,923,156	31,785,274	4·0

Governments arranged according to the relative Extent of Land conceded to the Crown Peasants.	Male Population of Peasants of the Domains.	Extent of Arable Lands, Meadows, and Pastures conceded to them.	Average Extent of Land for each Male Individual.
		Dessiatines.	*Dessiatines.*
Brought forward -	7,923,156	31,785,274	4·0
II. Governments in which part of the Crown Peasants are still under the Corvée.			
37. Minsk - - -	72,776	431,698	5·9
38. Kowno - - -	101,151	548,015	5·4
39. Livonia - - -	53,884	291,763	5·4
40. Esthonia - - -	2,286	11,095	4·9
41. Grodno - - -	134,418	557,562	4·1
42. Wilna - - -	109,514	449,519	4·1
43. Mohilew - - -	34,580	129,271	3·7
44. Kiew - - - -	104,622	362,744	3·5
45. Witebsk - - -	67,762	226,788	3·3
46. Wolhynia - - -	103,934	297,824	2·9
47. Podolia - - -	71,614	209,437	2·9
48. Courland - - -	70,727	108,143	1·5
Total - - -	927,268	3,623,859	3·9
Foreign Colonists * -	188,456	1,676,693	8·9
Grand Total - -	9,038,880	37,085,826	4·1

In reference to this table we have to observe, in the first place, that the waste land partly utilised as pasture is not included in it. Land of this description pertaining to the concessions of the crown peasants and foreign colonists occupied, in 1851, an extent of 6,048,722 dessiatines, to which fall to be added 9,932,554 dessiatines of enclaves in litigation and communal lands: these two added to the grand total of the preceding table give an extent of 53,067,102 dessiatines, or, for the male population of the state domains (9,038,880 individuals) 5·9 dessiatines per head.

On comparing the governments with each other, we perceive that there are great inequalities in the distribution of the productive lands. In two governments, Koursk and Poltawa, there is less than a dessiatine to each male inhabitant; and in seven, namely, Stavropol, Astrakhan, Orenburg, Bessarabia, Kherson, Samara, and Ekathérinoslaw, there are more than 7 dessiatines,—in the two first even between 12 and 20. The difference between the *minimum* (half a dessiatine in the govern-

---

* The foreign colonies are established in the governments of Saratow and St. Petersburg, and in the provinces of New Russia, in which there is a large quantity of arable land belonging to the state.

ment of Poltawa) and the *maximum* concession (19·7 dessiatines in the government of Stavropol), is as 1 to 39. These inequali-- ties are a natural result of the great disproportions which exist in several governments in the relative extent of arable land, meadows, forests, and unproductive soil.

The peasants best provided with productive land belong mostly to the eastern and southern governments, which abound in meadows and pastures, and where the domestic animals form the chief branch of rural economy. We may consider all those governments abundantly provided with productive land where the average is above 4 dessiatines per head of the male popula- tion. The proportion of from 3 to 4 dessiatines, which gives from $7\frac{1}{2}$ to 10 dessiatines per family, may be regarded as suffi- cient, but below 3 dessiatines it is narrow.

According to this classification, and saving modifications which may arise from the degree of fertility of the soil, there are nineteen governments, namely, Stavropol, Astrakhan, Oren- burg, Bessarabia, Kherson, Samara, Ekathérinoslaw, Tauride, Saratow, Perm, Pskow, St. Petersburg, Woronèje, Minsk, Kowno, Livonia, Esthonia, Grodno, and Wilna, containing 3,046,481 peasants of the domains, in which the latter are amply provided with productive land; sixteen governments, with 3,123,932 peasants, in which the provision may be consi- dered as sufficient, namely, Kazan, Smolensk, Tambow, Wiatka, Nowgorod, Nijni-Nowgorod, Kalouga, Olonetz, Wladimir, Twer, Kostroma, Penza, Jaroslaw, Mohilew, Kiew, and Witebsk; and thirteen governments, namely, Toula, Moscow, Kharkow, Orel, Riazan, Wologda, Tschernigow, Archangel, Koursk, Poltawa, Wolhynia, Podolia, and Courland, containing 2,680,000 crown peasants, in which the allowance of productive land is scanty. In the last named governments, the peasants eke out their means by various branches of petty industry or retail commerce, or they move off elsewhere in quest of work.

The crown woods and forests (without reckoning the forests belonging to the appanages, or those depending on the Admiralty and the Administration of Studs) occupy an extent of 115,342,411 dessiatines = 22,881 geographical square miles, or more than the entire area of France and the Empire of Austria put together, and form nearly two-thirds of the whole forests of European Russia. A portion of these forests, containing 13,060,000 dessia- tines, more than one-and-a-half times the extent of the whole forest area of France, is attached to the concessions of the crown peasants, giving an average of 1·6 dessiatines per head of the male population.

The principal state forests are situated in the following go- vernments : —

Dessiatines.

Wologda	-	-	-	32,976,249
Archangel	-	-	-	30,283,020
Perm	-	-	-	16,641,843
Wiatka	-	-	-	8,861,282
Olonetz	-	-	-	8,627,289
Kazan	-	-	-	2,174,196

Together	-	99,563,879

or 86 per cent. of the whole extent of the state forests.

The crown lands and forests taken together occupy an extent of 194,511,822 dessiatines = 38,587 geographical square miles, or nearly two-fifths of the area of European Russia. The following table, from the Report of the Ministry of Domains for 1849, exhibits the statistics of the state lands and forests in the sixteen governments in which these possessions are most extensive.

Governments.	Total Area.	Crown Domains.			Proportion per cent. of Extent of State Domains as compared with total Surface.
		Lands.	Woods and Forests.	Total State Property.	
	Dessiatines.	*Dessiatines.*	*Dessiatines.*	*Dessiatines.*	
1. Wologda - -	35,113,680	1,044,935	32,976,249	34,021,184	96·9
2. Archangel - -	78,215,760	161,137	30,283,020	30,444,157	38·8
3. Perm - -	30,607,920	4,853,917	16,641,843	21,495,760	70·2
4. Stavropol and Astrakhan * -	27,770,400	13,375,056	75,207	13,450,263	48·4
5. Orenburg †	28,128,240	11,616,859	1,760,542	13,377,401	47·6
6. Wiatka - -	12,600,000	3,288,794	8,861,282	12,150,076	96·4
7. Saratow † - -	17,766,000	10,744,693	668,470	11,413,163	64·2
8. Olonetz - -	14,026,320	852,225	8,627,289	9,479,514	67·6
9. Kazan - -	5,685,120	2,232,544	2,174,196	4,406,740	77·5
10. Woronèje - -	6,093,360	3,504,506	338,144	3,842,650	63·0
11. Kostroma - -	7,539,840	1,654,668	1,510,450	3,165,118	42·0
12. Tambow - -	6,058,030	2,020,869	694,181	2,715,050	44·8
13. Tauride - -	5,861,520	2,296,967	116,778	2,413,745	41·2
14. Ekathérinoslaw -	6,078,240	1,840,237	36,745	1,876,982	30·9
15. Kharkow - -	4,964,400	1,306,572	262,322	1,568,894	31·6
Total in these 16 governments -	286,508,830	60,793,979	105,026,718	165,820,697	57·9

We perceive from this table, that in two governments, Wiatka and Wologda, the state property covers more than 96 per cent. of the entire area; and in five, namely, Perm, Saratow, Olonetz, Kazan, and Woronèje, the relative extent of these domains varies between three-fifths and three-fourths of

* Including the lands conceded to the Calmucks.
† Including the lands conceded to the Kirghiz.

the area. It amounts to nearly three-fifths in the sixteen governments taken together.

These slight hints suffice to indicate the degree of influence which every improvement in the rural economy of the state domains must exert upon the prospects of our agriculture in general; but with the domains of the state, as with the estates of individuals, the effect, more or less slow, of the cumulative measures adopted for improving the condition of the peasants and the culture of the soil, will always depend upon the various circumstances peculiar to Russia which we have already adverted to, and especially on the greater or less facilities that we may enjoy for the disposal of our agricultural produce. All our meditations upon this subject confirm us in the persuasion, that the future fate and progress of our agriculture depend essentially on the extension and perfecting of our means of communication and transport. Compared with this grand lever of national wealth, all the other circumstances which may affect the welfare of our cultivators are, in our opinion, of very secondary moment. When our provincial capitals, our sea-ports, and our chief commercial towns, have been brought into a state of steady communication by railways and good ordinary roads,— when the cross-roads have been rendered more practicable,— when our fluvial system has been completed by canals and by the improvement of navigable rivers,—all the other improvements will follow in their train. The undertaking is a gigantic one; we do not seek to dissemble its difficulties. We are aware that its progress must be slow and gradual, and that the sacrifices involved in it are great; but we know, also, that every inch of territory conquered upon this domain is another step in advance on the path of progress and prosperity. We shall have occasion to occupy ourselves more at large with this important question in a future chapter; meantime, we resume our observations on the different branches of our husbandry.

REARING OF DOMESTIC ANIMALS.

I. *Cattle.*

The rearing of domestic animals forms an integral part of agriculture properly so called; it goes hand in hand with the raising of corn. If the one branch of husbandry pines, the other suffers; and their prosperity greatly depends on a good distribution of the productive soil, or, in other words, on the arable lands, meadows, and pastures being duly proportioned to each other.   In this respect the situation of Russia is peculiar.

As, in the statistical tables given in the first part of this work, the classification of the productive soil in Bessarabia and in the governments of Ekathérinoslaw, Stavropol, and Tauride, rests upon data more or less approximative, we shall place these governments out of view in the following comparisons.   The whole remaining possessions of Russia in Europe, taken together, contain 85,677,000 dessiatines of cultivable land, and 51,994,000 dessiatines of meadow.   In France there are reckoned 26,078,000 hectares of cultivable land, and 5,775,000 hectares of meadow; in Austria, 39,710,000 joch of cultivable land, and 10,595,000 joch of meadow; in Prussia, 48,320,000 morgen of cultivable land, and 14,326,000 morgen of meadow. These figures give out the following proportions between meadow and soil dedicated to culture of every sort.

Russia	-	-	-	-	in the proportion of 100 to	165
Prussia	-	-	-	-	„ 100 „	337
Austria	-	-	-	-	„ 100 „	375
France	-	-	-	-	„ 100 „	452

Thus the meadows occupy in Russia, in proportion to the cultivable land, a much more considerable extent than in the other countries which we have taken as points of comparison.*

The length and severity of our winters, which abridge the period during which cattle can remain out at pasture,—the frequent droughts, which render the hay harvests less abundant, —and the want of artificial fodder, which in many other countries supplements the inadequacy of the natural pasture, whilst in Russia it is very little used,—all these circumstances combined place our husbandry in an exceptional position, which requires a larger extent of meadow land than is elsewhere necessary to place the rearing of cattle in a normal relation with the culture of the soil.   Still, the average proportion of 3 dessiatines of meadow to 4 of cultivated land, resulting from the above calculation, might be considered as satisfactory, if the meadows were less unequally distributed.   But we have already seen that there are twenty-seven governments where they do not attain half the extent of the arable lands; and of this number there are sixteen where they do not extend to even one-fourth of these.   In the government of Witebsk there is not 1 dessiatine of meadow to 10 of cultivated land.   On the other hand, in the governments of Esthonia, Livonia, Kherson, Tau-

---

* We are here repeating some of the comparisons and observations which accompany the table, page 49.   Such repetitions are sometimes unavoidable in a work of this nature, for the sake of distinctness of exposition.

ride, Ekathérinoslaw, Orenburg, Archangel, Saratow, Stavropol, and Astrakhan, in Finland, and in the country of the Don Cossacks — twelve provinces in all — the extent of meadow exceeds that of cultivated land.   In the country of the Don Cossacks, there are more than 4, and in Astrakhan and Stavropol there are more than 5 dessiatines of meadow to 1 of cultivable land.   From such a distribution of cultivated land and meadows, there results a variety in the agricultural situation of the different parts of the empire which is not found, in the same degree, in any other country.

In the empire of Austria, composed at it is of countries so different from each other in regard to climate, soil, and culture, we do not find any thing like the same disparities between the extent of meadows and of corn land.   There is only a single province, the Tyrol, a mountainous country, poor incultivable soil, in which the extent of meadow exceeds that of corn land and vineyard together in so large a proportion as 10 to 7.   In Carinthia and Carniola, the extent of meadow equals that of the cultivated land: in the other provinces, it varies between the proportions of 10 to 14 (*minimum* difference, in Lower Austria), and 10 to 58 (*maximum* difference, in Moravia and Silesia).   Dalmatia, with its volcanic and rocky soil, forms the only exception : it is almost destitute of meadows : they occupy an extent of only 11,236 dessiatines, whilst there are 191,315 dessiatines of arable land and vineyards, thus giving the proportion of 1 to 17.   In France, out of 86 departments, there is but a single one, namely, that of Cantal, in which the extent of meadows exceeds that of cultivable land in the proportion of 4 to 3.   On the other hand, there are twenty-eight departments in which the meadows occupy less than a tenth of the extent of the corn land and vineyards taken together ; but in that country the territory is so minutely parcelled out in administrative divisions, that these disproportions refer to districts of trifling extent, and cannot consequently serve as points of comparison with the huge areas of our governments and provinces.   The largest French department, that of the Dordogne, has an area of only 166 geographical square miles—not half the extent of our smallest province, Esthonia ; and there are 70 departments in which the area is less than 100 square miles.

It is very difficult, as we have already had occasion to observe, to determine what proportion of meadow to corn land is most suitable, as well for the rearing of domestic animals as for agriculture proper, so that they may render each other mutual support and go along hand in hand : this depends greatly upon the system of agricultural economy pursued, on the abundance of the hay harvest, and on the extent and quality of the pasture. In countries where agriculture is in an advanced condition, it is generally considered that the proportion of 1 acre of meadow to 3 of corn land is fair enough, especially if there be good pasture land over and above. In Russia, and especially in the central and northern districts of the empire, a larger proportion of meadow land is required, for reasons which have been already explained: we have therefore adopted half the extent of arable land as the *minimum* proportion of meadow land required. M. Arsénieff goes greatly beyond this in his estimates, considering as disadvantageously situated for the rearing of domestic animals, even those provinces where the extent of meadow land is equal to three-fourths of the arable. "In Courland," says he "the meadows occupy an extent equivalent to only three-" fourths* of that of the arable land. It is evident that with " such a small extent of mowable land, the hay harvest cannot " be great." This opinion coincides with that of the department of Husbandry at the Ministry of Domains, which considers that for each dessiatine of arable land there ought to be at least another of meadow land yielding 150 poods of hay; but in this opinion, for reasons already given (*antè*, p. 50, *et seq.*) we do not coincide. We perceive, moreover, that in several governments where there is but a small extent of meadow land as compared with arable, there is raised a very fair quantity of cattle. Thus, in Courland, a province considered by M. Arsénieff to be a very poor one as regards its hay crop, there are reckoned 62 head of cattle and horses to every 100 inhabitants, whilst in the governments of Esthonia, Livonia, and Archangel, where the extent of meadow greatly exceeds that of cultivable land, there are reckoned only 53 to 58 head for every 100 inhabitants. In this respect also there are great inequalities to be found in Russia and nowhere else. We have seen by the table given at page 183. that there are governments in which the average does not amount to 30 head of cattle and horses for 100 dessiatines of meadow land, that is to say, less than 1 head for 3 dessiatines, whilst in others there are reckoned from 2 to 3 head per dessiatine. The same dissimilarities are observable in the proportion between the number of domestic animals and the extent of cultivable land. Thus, in the table which has just been referred to, we find some governments in which there is not 1 head of cattle and horses to 4 dessiatines of cultivable soil, and others in which the number of these animals exceeds

---

* According to this writer's statistics, the meadows in Courland occupy an extent of 313,877 dessiatines, and the arable land, of 489,710; this would be in the proportion of 100 to 156, or 2 to 3, not 3 to 4.

the number of dessiatines of soil in cultivation. But what is still more remarkable is this, that there are governments in which the soil is in great part of very indifferent quality, and where agriculture is exceedingly backward, but which, nevertheless, are much more abundant in horses and cattle than the greater number of those governments which occupy the highest rank in reference to their productive forces. Thus, for example, in the government of Mohilew, one of the least fertile and worst cultivated in the empire, there are reckoned 328 head of cattle and horses to 100 dessiatines of meadow, and 58 head of the same description of animals for 100 dessiatines of arable land, whilst in the governments of Simbirsk, Tambow, Wolhynia, Woronèje, Podolia, Poltawa, and Kharkow, the number of head varies from 56 to 93 per hundred dessiatines of meadow, and from 21 to 59 per 100 dessiatines of arable land. If we take into view the number of head of cattle as compared with the total population, we find (see table, page 187.), that in the government of Mohilew the average is 117 head of cattle to 100 inhabitants, whilst in the government of Tschernigow it is but 44; in that of Kharkow, 65; in that of Tambow, 68; in Wolhynia, 47; in Poltawa, 52; in Orel, 69; in Toula, 69; and in Podolia, only 31 per 100 inhabitants; and yet these eight governments are ranked in the number of the richest and most fertile.

From a comparison of these figures we may infer that in Russia the rearing of domestic animals is not always in proportion to the advanced state of the culture of the soil, — that the proportion of meadow to arable land cannot be admitted without reserve as a criterion for judging of the more or less favourable condition of our rural economy, — and that the large number of horses and cattle reared in some provinces is far from being a proof of the flourishing state of their agriculture. In many of those provinces where, in proportion to the extent of the meadow and corn land, the *number* of cattle and horses raised is large, the *quality* is very inferior, small of size, and small in production of milk, flesh, or working muscle. It is only in districts where cultivation is considerably advanced, that the two branches of rural economy, agriculture proper and the rearing of domestic animals, are rationally combined, and advance at an equal pace. With agronomic progress, pasture lands are gradually converted into meadow lands, whilst natural meadows give place to artificial meadows, and to the culture of artificial fodder. With us there are boundless districts where the soil is of itself so fertile as not to require a spadeful of manure, and its culture is often so easy that the plough scarcely requires to scratch its surface.* To this category belong all the provinces where the black humus (*tschernozième*) predominates, which occupy nearly a fifth, or, more exactly, 18 per cent., of the total area of European Russia. Manure there runs to waste; in the country of the steppes it is used for fuel. In none of those districts where the soil is of great fertility, and the harvests greatly exceed the wants of the population, can the rearing of domestic animals be combined with the culture and melioration of the soil in the same rational manner as in the countries of central and western Europe. It is based upon other principles and other elements; it is carried on at much less cost, but at the same time with much less care; it often follows a march totally independent of the course of agriculture proper; in many provinces, horses and cattle are used in agriculture merely as a motive power, and their number, in those districts which are richer in meadows and pasture than in cultivable land, being beyond what is requisite for this purpose, a great part of this power runs to waste. In a large portion of the steppes, the oxen and horses remain at pasture the whole year round. In this respect there are such prodigious differences between different parts of the empire, — between north and south, — between the countries of the steppes and the provinces of the centre, — between the latter and the governments of the west, — that we cannot consider their systems of rural economy under one point of view, nor apply to them, in a general manner, the agronomic principles derived from the experience of other countries. In adopting, therefore, a certain proportion for the relative extent of meadow and cultivable land, as the normal one, we have had in view only those provinces of which the agricultural situation is more or less similar — climate apart — to that of the countries of central Europe. In assuming as *minimum* 1 dessiatine of meadow to 2 of arable land, there would be, according to the

---

* M. Haxthausen mentions a village in the government of Saratow near Petrowsk, where, for 4,528 dessiatines of arable land, there were kept only 400 horses and nearly as many head of cattle, so that there were more than 11 dessiatines for one horse; whilst in Germany, in the neighbourhood of Magdeburg, there is required a yoke of 4 horses for from 70 to 90 morgen = 4 to 5 dessiatines for one horse, though the horses there are much larger and stronger than those employed in the yoke in Russia, and the land is by no means so stiff and heavy. To render the comparison more exact, the author ought to have taken into account the number of oxen engaged in labour at the village in question. But at all events it is abundantly true that in many districts of Russia the soil is so fertile that, to obtain abundant harvests, no more labour is necessary than slightly stirring a very thin slice of the surface; and this fertility, which is in itself a precious gift of Nature, does, alas! but encourage the indolence of our peasants, whose mode of culture is as negligent as their implements are defective.

table, page 49., twenty-seven provinces, embracing an extent of nearly 149 millions of dessiatines, or about 30 per cent. of the total area of the Russian possessions in Europe, which might be considered as poor in meadows, since the latter are not equal in extent to one half of the soil in culture ; but of these, there are nine, namely, Kazan, Toula, Penza, Riazan, Orel, Tschernigow, Kiew, Wolhynia, and Podolia, embracing an extent of 40 millions of dessiatines, that belong in whole or in part to the region of humus which requires no manure ; so that the number of provinces where there may be a sensible want of meadows is reduced to eighteen, occupying an extent of 109 million dessiatines, or somewhat more than a fifth of the total area of European Russia. To this category belong, *in the central region*, the governments of Moscow, Wladimir, Kalouga, Nijni-Nowgorod, Jaroslaw, Koursk and Kostroma; *in the northern region*, the government of Olonetz ; all the governments of the *region of the Alaoune mountains*, St. Petersburg, Nowgorod, and Smolensk ; *in the lower region*, the governments of Witebsk, Mohilew, Kowno, Wilna, Grodno, and the kingdom of Poland; and in the *Uralian region*, the government of Wiatka. It is in these provinces, and especially in those of the lower and Alaoune regions, which embrace the larger portion of the less fertile districts, that agricultural improvement is most required, and that the landed proprietors ought to combine their exertions to introduce the culture of artificial fodder,—a culture of which we already find amongst them a few isolated examples.

If we compare the number of cattle with the extent of cultivated land, we shall find that of these 18 provinces there are 12, namely, Moscow, Wladimir, Nijni-Nowgorod, Koursk, Wiatka, Olonetz, St. Petersburg, Witebsk, Kowno, Wilna, Grodno, and the kingdom of Poland, which do not possess one head of the one to two dessiatines of the other. Three of these, namely, Witebsk, Grodno, and Nijni-Nowgorod, do not possess one head for four dessiatines. Deducting the horses employed in the towns, there remain very few indeed for agriculture. It is evident that in all these provinces there must be a great deficiency of manure ; and they are precisely the districts which, from the very inferior fertility of their soil, require it the most.

As to the proportion between the number of cattle and the extent of meadow land, we have already seen from the table, p. 183., that there are 11 governments, namely, Kalouga, Kostroma, Mohilew, Moscow, Orel, Riazan, Smolensk, Toula, Wiatka, Witebsk, and Wladimir, which possess more than two head of cattle and horses to a dessiatine of meadow. In the greater part of those districts, where there are few meadows and the culture of artificial provender is neglected, it is usual to leave the bestial upon open pasture till the ground becomes covered with snow, or the cold excessive : often it is necessary to feed them upon straw. In the steppes, where meadows and good pasturage abound, the rearing of these animals is left to the care of Providence: in these forestless regions the want of building timber renders it impossible to house them, so they remain in the open air, summer and winter. In the neighbourhood of rivers, the herds sometimes construct sorts of cane sheds ; in other districts they put piles of hay around the spot where the cattle are feeding, to be some little protection to them against frost and drift. It is evident that under such rough husbandry as this, improvements in feeding or breeding, and sanitary precautions against epizoötic diseases, are alike out of the question.

The unsatisfactory condition in which this important branch of rural economy is found in some parts of Russia has long attracted the attention of government, and several inquests have been made with the view of ascertaining on the spot the cause of this state of matters, and devising a remedy. The causes may be summed up as follows:—Degeneration of breeds resulting from want of care about copulation; in some countries, the want of good herbage ; frequent cattle epidemics, which, again, are themselves the result, sometimes of bad nourishment, sometimes of the state of abandonment in which the cattle are left during winter ; the want of good veterinary surgeons; and, finally, the little profit that can be derived in some provinces from cattle-rearing, in consequence of the want of markets for either meat or dairy produce. We consider the last-mentioned cause as the main one: it carries, indeed, the others in its train; for if the rearing of cattle were found to be a profitable branch of husbandry, more care would be bestowed on it as a matter of course. In the south of Russia and in the eastern provinces, especially in the governments of Kherson, Tauride, Ekathérinoslaw, Saratow, Stavropol, Astrakhan, Orenburg, and the country of the Don Cossacks, where meadows and pastures abound, where the population is thin, and where there is little land in cultivation, the rearing of domestic animals costs almost nothing, but it also brings in very little more. It is not long since, in some of the southern provinces, the ox was killed for the sake of the hide and tallow, and the carcase buried for want of consumers. Even at present the price there is but a perfect bagatelle. It is natural enough, then, that in those countries the rearing of cattle should not be carried on with much system: the number augments, but the breed remains unimproved. In countries where this forms a profitable branch of husbandry, the race is renewed in a short space of time, say in four, five, or six years*; and from the improvement of breeds, which gain in weight as feeding becomes better understood, the number of head sometimes remains the same, though the consumption of meat has augmented. M. Zablotski cites the example of Würtemberg, where, in 1834, there were reckoned 503 head of cattle to 1,000 inhabitants; whilst in 1840 there were reckoned only 491, which, however, yielded more dairy produce and more flesh than the 503 had done in 1834. With us, there is a vast field open for improvements of this sort. In some of our southern provinces, owing to the want of market for butcher's meat, the race of cattle is not entirely renewed oftener than once in eight or ten years, that is, after the age at which the cow has ceased to yield milk in abundance, and the horse to be fit for the labour of the fields. Thus, for example, in the country of the Don Cossacks, the number of animals killed for home consumption and exportation did not, according to the data collected by M. Zablotski, amount to more than a 14th of the total number; so that, if a portion did not succumb to epidemics and the inclemency of the seasons, the bovine race would not be entirely renewed oftener than once in 14 years.

We have always found it matter of surprise that no native or foreign speculators or joint-stock companies have hitherto attempted to organise on a large scale a salt-provision trade through the ports of the Black Sea, by establishing slaughter and salting-houses either in the vicinity of these ports or in the interior of the provinces of New Russia. Every circumstance would seem to be favourable for such an undertaking ; both the flesh and the salt are to be had for next to nothing ; and even if the salt of the country should turn out to be unsuitable, Setubal salt might be had on very easy terms, as it could be brought as ballast by the ships arriving at Odessa and the other ports of the Black Sea and the Sea of Azow. The import duty might be levied when the provision came to be exported.

The large quantity of cattle raised in Russia and the comparatively small consumption of flesh leave a broad margin for exportation. We have already seen, in the first part of this

---

* In France, it is renewed in less than six years, and in some parts of Germany in four or five. M. Zablotski, in his article on the Russian corn trade, cites the case of Belgium, where, according to him, the number of head annually consigned to the shambles amounts to half the total number of animals. It is evident that the former number must include the calves, otherwise the race would require to be renewed every two years, which is not in nature.

work, that the number of cattle must exceed 27 million head; but we have reduced this number to a *minimum* of 25 millions in conformity with figures officially ascertained. In France, a total number of 7,869,689 head furnished to the slaughter-houses, according to the official agricultural statistics, 226 million kilogrammes = 552,570,000 Russian lbs. of meat, without reckoning the calves. According to the same proportion, 25 million head ought to furnish 1,755,400,000 lbs.; but as in Russia there are killed much fewer cows than in France, a circumstance which augments the average weight per head, we may set down at 2,000 millions of pounds, or 50 millions of poods at least, the quantity of meat which the present number of cattle in Russia might annually furnish to the slaughter-house. In our calculations with regard to the produce from cattle-rearing, page 169., we have estimated the consumption of ox and cow flesh at 23 lbs. per inhabitant; and it cannot well be carried beyond 25 lbs., which gives for 62 million inhabitants a consumption of 38,750,000 poods. The exportation of live meat amounts to about 450,000 poods, (40,000 head estimated at 450 lbs. nett,) making in all 39,200,000 poods; so that there would still remain for export 10,800,000 poods of meat, which, at the price of 2 roubles per pood, would represent a value of 21,600,000 roubles, whilst our whole exportation of smoked and salted meat amounts to only 30,000 or 40,000 poods. In 1848 we exported to the value of only 54,000 roubles for meat of every description, whilst the value exported during the same year from Prussia, which reckons only 5 million head of cattle, and where the relative consumption of flesh is much greater than with us, amounted to upwards of 90,000 roubles. In our trifling exportation, the whole ports of the Black Sea and the Sea of Azow figure for a value of no more than 2,600 roubles, and yet it is in the provinces lying contiguous to these two seas,—in Bessarabia, Tauride, the country of the Don Cossacks, and the governments of Kherson and Stavropol,—that cattle are to be found in greatest profusion. In these five provinces there were reckoned in 1846, according to the official statistics, of which the figures are always below the reality, 3,620,000 head for a population of 3,437,000 inhabitants, or more than 1 head of cattle for each inhabitant, whilst in Prussia and Austria the average is below 1 head of cattle for 3 inhabitants.

The present nullity of this branch of commerce, which might become so very important, is for us a manifest proof of a want of industry and enterprising spirit, for we cannot persuade ourselves that there are insurmountable difficulties opposed to its development. If some partial attempts have been unsuccessful, this, we think, can have been owing only to insufficiency of means for carrying them out, or to an absence of practical knowledge on the part of the undertakers. At any rate, it is a question which deserves to be probed to the bottom, and the possibility of execution being once demonstrated and recognised, it is one of those enterprises that deserve every sort of encouragement on the part of government.

The products of the dairy might also become important as articles of commerce, if more care were employed in their preparation, if they were made to keep better, and to be more conformable to the taste of foreign consumers. The quality of cheese depends greatly, not only on the mode of preparation, but also on the quality of the pasture and of the cows' food in general, and the manufacture of this article cannot be equally successful everywhere. Of course, there are many districts in Russia where local circumstances are not favourable to cheese-making, but there are also many others where the sole impediment consists in the carelessness of the farmer. Of this no better proof need be sought than the fact that several proprietors who have bestowed on the dairy the attention it deserves, have been perfectly successful. M. Haxthausen cites, amongst other cases, a proprietor in the government of Wologda who brought Swiss dairy-people to organise the manufacture of cheese upon his estate, and now draws an income from that source of between 5,000 and 6,000 silver roubles. It is desirable that such experiments should find many imitators. In the Baltic provinces and in Finland, the manufacture of cheese has for some time past been sensibly progressive. Such is also the case in some other districts. We find amongst the provision dealers of St. Petersburg and Moscow imitations of foreign cheese of different sorts, inferior no doubt in quality to the genuine article, but yet resembling it sufficiently to be sold under the name of Gruyère or double Gloucester. These examples go to prove that this branch of industry is very susceptible of development amongst us, the one thing needful being a little more skill and painstaking on the part of our rural economists. This is also patent from the profits drawn by the German colonists from the products of the dairy in districts where it is left by the natives in total neglect. The preparation of salted butter is less dependent than that of cheese upon local circumstances : requiring only care and cleanliness, it might more or less succeed anywhere, and yet it is very backward in Russia. We export only about 25,000 or 30,000 poods, representing a value of from 100,000 to 120,000 roubles — scarcely equal to the foreign export of this article from the little kingdom of Bavaria *; and this export is with us quite stationary: that of cheese is almost *nil*: it does not appear in our list of exports at all, being slumped along with various other trifling articles under the general head of " provisions."

Our trade in dairy produce, as well as in salted and smoked meat, was for a long period more or less impeded by the high duties imposed upon these articles in foreign countries; but now there is everywhere a tendency to lower duties upon alimentary substances. England has been the first to set an example which is very encouraging to our cattle breeders, and it is to be hoped that the encouragement may not be lost upon us. It is a new era which has opened for this branch of our commerce, and the results may be important if we but know how to turn them to account.

As for the cattle epidemics—that great scourge of our husbandry—their most frequent cause is undoubtedly the want of proper nourishment; they generally make their appearance after great droughts; but the degree of intensity which they attain, almost unknown in other countries, must be attributed chiefly to the carelessness of our peasantry, and to their disregard of sanitary precautions — faults sufficiently common amongst all the Slavonic populations. The animals that die are not buried deeply enough in the earth; and no care is taken to separate the healthy cattle from the sick.

Government has devoted its most anxious attention to this subject. On the proposal of the Minister of Domains, there was formed in 1845, a special commission composed of this minister, of the President of the Committee of Studs, and of the Ministers of the Interior and of Public Instruction, in compliance with whose recommendation, distinguished professors and savans were invited from Prussia, Saxony, and Denmark to examine upon the spot the ravages of this scourge, and to ascertain its causes and its remedies. These learned foreigners, accompanied by veterinary surgeons delegated by the Ministry of Domains and the Ministry of the Interior, were despatched to the provinces where such epidemics are most frequent, and in consequence of their investigations a series of measures of sanitary police were decreed and put in execution; but such measures cannot have their full effect except in so far as they are seconded by the population; and this, again, will only take place when the latter have acquired a conviction of their utility. Such cooperation by the country people in the

---

* Bavaria exports from 9000 to 10,000 quintals = 27,000 to 30,000 poods.

measures taken by the authorities is so much the more necessary with us, because, in consequence of the immense distances, the action of the rural police can be but exceedingly limited. Of these measures, one of the most important, in our opinion, would be the organisation of good veterinary schools. We must also refer to the wishes more than once expressed by our agriculturists to be able to procure salt for their cattle at a cheap rate. This question has often been agitated in other countries, and especially in France; but the proposed arrangements have almost always succumbed to the difficulty of reconciling the interests of agriculture with the financial interests of the state. The desideratum mainly consists in the discovery of some cheap and certain means of rendering the salt destined for cattle unsuitable as a condiment for man. It would seem, that in Prussia and some other German states, such a discovery has been made; for the government magazines in those countries furnish at prime cost to every landowner that applies for it, upon obtaining certain securities against abuse, a salt prepared for the consumption of cattle, known by the name of *Viehsalz.* This is the case also in some provinces of Austria. With us, no doubt, salt, being but lightly taxed, is cheaper than in most other countries; but it would be desirable that it should be made still cheaper for cattle, at least in those districts where the rearing of domestic animals forms one of the main branches of production, and where cattle epidemics are most destructive.

Independently of the frequent epidemics, the great droughts sometimes carry off numerous herds by depriving them of their food. Such cases occur much more rarely in other countries; and when they do occur, the proprietors may escape at least a part of their loss by selling their cattle at a reduced price to the butchers, whilst in Russia that resource is frequently cut off by the want of a market. This is an evil resulting from our climate and geographical position to which no thorough remedy can be applied: but the progress of population, of material well-being, and of commerce, will doubtless diminish its intensity. With improvements in breeding and feeding (which essentially depend upon the facility of effecting sales), a herd of 1000 head of cattle renewed every five or six years, would produce more meat and more profit than are now derived from a herd of 2000, which annually furnish to the butcher not more than an eighth or tenth of their total number. By replacing quantity with quality, proprietors might also contrive to have more fodder in reserve for a year of calamity.

In the southern provinces, in spite of the little care bestowed on their rearing, the breed of cattle, thanks to the fine pastures, is a handsome one.   The oxen are in general of large size, but, in some districts, of a constitution more bony than muscular, and less suitable for fattening than middle-sized, thick-set, broad-chested animals.   In the governments of the west, and in great part of the north, the breed is very poor : in order to improve it, amongst the peasants, the plan was tried of crossing their cows with bulls of a better breed ; but these experiments were not attended with the desired result ; the cows, being small and weak, continued to give birth to a puny progeny.   In the north, the government of Archangel is almost the only one which is distinguished by a handsome breed of cattle.   The cattle of the Cholmogory district, of Dutch origin, enjoy a deserved reputation ; but attempts made in this government to acclimatise some English breeds have been unsuccessful.   The best herbage is found on the banks of the Dwina, the Mezena, and the Pinega.   Fine fattening cattle, however, are found in the Baltic provinces, especially in the government of Esthonia.

According to the opinions expressed in a Report made by the Department of Rural Economy to the Ministry of Domains, published in 1849, the best breeds of cattle in European Russia are the following : —

The Cholmogory breed, of Dutch origin, already mentioned ; it is distinguished by its fine form and good milking qualities ; it is found pure only in the district from which it takes its name, in the government of Archangel.

A cross between the Cholmogory and native breeds, found in some districts of the governments of Archangel, in the governments of Wologda, Kalouga, Twer, Kostroma, and Jaroslaw, and in the districts near the capitals.

The Tyrolese, Scotch, and English breeds, acclimatised in the Baltic provinces.

These are the principal breeds of the northern provinces.

The Circassian breed, often confounded with the Hungarian, distinguished by its length of horn.   It is of large size, but the cows are indifferent milkers ; it is fitter for fattening than for field work ; it is diffused chiefly in the south, especially in the governments of Ekathérinoslaw, Kherson, Poltawa, and Kharkow.

The Ukraine, or Wallach breed, yields little milk ; it is robust and well suited for field labour.   It is to be found from Podolia to the Ural.   The finest type of this breed is found at Karlowka, in the government of Poltawa, an estate belonging formerly to the Countess Razoumoffsky, and now to Her Imperial Highness the Grand Duchess Helena.

The Don and Black Sea breeds, extensively diffused over the southern provinces.

The Swiss breed, extensively diffused, as is also the Tyrolese, in the kingdom of Poland.

Lastly, the Lithuanian breed, of middle size, but well built, are good milkers.

The crossing of foreign breeds with each other, and especially of the English, Tyrolese, and Swiss breeds, has been often attempted, but seldom with success. As a general rule, cattle of foreign origin do not acclimatise well with us, except in those districts where there is good herbage. These breeds require more care and better food, and likewise succumb more readily to epidemics than the native cattle. The Dutch and Tyrolese breeds seem to succeed best, and the English cattle seem to be those which are worst adapted to our climate and mode of nourishment.

From the information which we find in M. Arsénieff's statistics, and in the recent Report, already referred to, by the Department of Rural Economy to the Ministry of Domains, it would appear that, for some little time back, landed proprietors have been beginning to pay more attention to the improvement of their breeds of cattle and to the management of their dairies. These attempts have hitherto, no doubt, been rather exceptional; but they cannot fail to bring forth good fruits, in proportion as improved communications, the progress of well-being amongst the lower classes, and increased activity of commerce, open more outlets for this branch of rural economy, and render it more profitable. The principal improvements have taken place amongst some proprietors in the Baltic provinces, and in the governments of Archangel, Wologda, Twer, Smolensk, Mohilew, Minsk, Grodno, Kowno, Kiew, Wolhynia, Podolia, Poltawa, Kharkow, Bessarabia, Ekathérinoslaw, Saratow, Nijni-Nowgorod, Tambow, Woronèje, Koursk, Moscow, Toula, Riazan, and Simbirsk.

It is principally the southern provinces, especially Bessarabia, the country of the Don Cossacks, Wolhynia, Podolia, Poltawa, Tschernigow, Kharkow, Kherson, Ekathérinoslaw, and Stavropol, from which the two capitals and several governments of the centre of the empire draw their supplies of cattle. The government of Orenburg likewise furnishes its contingent. In the north it is only the governments of Archangel and Esthonia which furnish supplies to the city of St. Petersburg and to some other governments.

According to the statistics of the number of cattle as compared with the number of the population (see table, page 187.), the provinces of European Russia will be arranged in the following order as regards their relative abundance in cattle: —

To 100 Inhabitants.

	Head of Cattle.			Head of Cattle.
1. Country of the Don Cossacks	146	26. Livonia - - -	39
2. Astrakhan - - -	112	27. Wiatka - - -	38
3. Tauride - - -	104	28. Wladimir - - -	38
4. Kherson - - -	83	29. Archangel - - -	38
5. Mohilew - - -	70	30. Kalouga - - -	37
6. Stavropol - - -	63	31. Witebsk - - -	34
7. Bessarabia - - -	63	32. Perm - - -	33
8. Smolensk - - -	62	33. Kiew - - -	33
9. Orenburg - - -	60	34. Olonetz - - -	33
10. Nowgorod - - -	58	35. Kingdom of Poland - -	32
11. Kostroma - - -	57	36. Tambow - - -	30
12. Wologda - - -	55	37. Orel - - -	30
13. Simbirsk - - -	52	38. Wolhynia - - -	28
14. Jaroslaw - - -	52	39. Toula - - -	28
15. Ekathérinoslaw - -	50	40. Grodno - - -	28
16. Kharkow - - -	49	41. Pskow - - -	28
17. Kowno - - -	49	42. Kazan - - -	26
18. Saratow - - -	48	43. Koursk - - -	25
19. Twer - - -	48	44. Podolia - - -	25
20. Woronèje - - -	47	45. Riazan - - -	25
21. Minsk - - -	46	46. Penza - - -	24
22. Wilna - - -	45	47. Nijni-Nowgorod - -	20
23. Courland - - -	44	48. Moscow - - -	19
24. Poltawa - - -	42	49. Tschernigow - -	18
25. Esthonia - - -	42	50. St. Petersburg - -	14

We perceive from this table that the number of cattle relative to the population differs, in different provinces of the empire, in the usual extraordinary proportions as compared with other countries. In Prussia, in 1843, the highest relative cipher (in East and West Prussia) was 40 head of cattle to 100 inhabitants, and the lowest (in the province of Saxony) was 25 to 100. In the Austrian empire, in the province most abundant in cattle, namely, Upper Austria, there was reckoned, in 1846, to 100 inhabitants 60 head of cattle; and in Lombardy, where the relative cipher is lowest, the proportion was 16 head to 100 inhabitants; whilst in Russia, in the country of the Don Cossacks, there are 146 head of cattle to 100 inhabitants, in the government of Tschernigow only 18, and in that of St. Petersburg only 14. Thus, the difference between *minimum* and *maximum* is

In Prussia	-	-	as 10 to 16
In Austria	-	-	as 10 to 38
In Russia	-	-	as 10 to 104

This great variety in the numerical relations of cattle to population presents a vast field for the cattle trade, which must be more and more developed with the progress of national wealth, since that progress is sure to be followed by increased consumption of meat and dairy produce. Following the example of other countries, we may class as rich in cattle all those provinces in which their total number exceeds two-fifths of the population. In Austria, there are only three provinces, namely, Upper Austria, the Tyrol, and the Military Frontier, in which this proportion is exceeded. In Prussia not one province exceeds this proportion, and only one attains it. In Russia there are twenty-five governments in which are reckoned more than 40 head of cattle to 100 inhabitants; twelve in which the cipher varies between 30 and 40, which is still a very satisfactory proportion; and thirteen in which there are less than 30 head to 100 inhabitants. A great impediment to the cattle trade in Russia consists in this, that the provinces which contain most, as the country of the Don Cossacks, Bessarabia, the Tauride, and the governments of Stavropol, Kherson, Astrakhan, and Orenburg, are precisely those which are most remote from those districts which do not produce a sufficiency of meat for their own consumption. A large portion of the cattle that supply the abattoirs of St. Petersburg arrive from the southern provinces after a journey of from 200 to 250 German (900—1000 English) miles. The cost of transport is considerable, and the cattle lose a great deal of weight upon the journey. Meat sells at St. Petersburg for 10 kopecks per lb., whilst in the southern and eastern provinces it fetches but 2 or 3 kopecks, or sometimes less. Prices, no doubt, may become more equal in the course of time, when, with the progress of wealth amongst the most numerous classes, the consumption of meat becomes larger in the interior of the empire, and the districts where most cattle are produced acquire more extensive markets in the districts that surround them. Still, there is little probability that the consumption of this article should reach the extent necessary to absorb the whole surplus production of the provinces of New Russia, unless new outlets are opened up in the way of foreign commerce.

II. *Horses.*

More attention has always been paid, in a great part of Russia, to the rearing of horses than to that of cattle. The warlike and nomade habits of the ancient population, the increasing demands for the supply of the numerous cavalry and artillery of a large army, the immense distances, which require a large amount of motive power as well for the conveyance of produce and merchandise as of locomotion; all these circum-

stances combined have stimulated the development of this
branch of rural economy, favoured as it is over a large portion
of the empire by the great extent of good pasture lands. Accordingly, we possess excellent horses for all uses. The statistical tables of the domestic animals already given exhibit a
number of horses greatly exceeding, even relatively to the
population, that of those countries which possess the most; for
whilst in Russia there are nearly 3 horses to every 10 inhabitants, in Austria there is but 1 for every 13; in France, 1 for
every 12; and in Prussia, 1 for every 10 inhabitants. Still,
in some provinces, there is much room for improvement, and
several observations which we have made in regard to cattle
rearing are no less applicable to the rearing of horses. The
same causes which produce degeneracy in the one sort of stock
are also in operation upon the other. In the western and
northern governments and in the kingdom of Poland, the
horses of the peasantry are generally small of size and void of
vigour, which proceeds from too early copulation, from their
being set prematurely to work, and from the insufficient attention paid to the brood mares; in some districts also from bad
pasture and general carelessness. In the southern and eastern
provinces, the steppes, with their abundant pastures, are well
suited for horse-rearing; but during their severe winters, the
frost and drifting snow often occasion great mortalities amongst
the numerous herds which roam about exposed to all the inclemency of the sky. In some districts, especially in the governments of Orenburg, Stavropol, and Astrakhan, and in the
country of the Don Cossacks, horse-breeders consider themselves lucky if, after a severe winter, they have not lost more
than a tenth of their stock. The animals, however, which
have passed through the ordeal are found indomitable in the
endurance of fatigue. What is chiefly wanting for the encouragement of breeders is a market: amongst the nomades of
Orenburg and Astrakhan, and the Don Cossacks, a good three-
year old horse can sometimes be bought for 8 or 10 roubles.
The horses exported to Asia from some of the eastern districts
are valued in the official estimates at 5 or 6 roubles per head;
but we must not take these figures as indicating the value of
all our steppe horses; many of them fetch from 80 to 100
roubles, or even more. The horses which figure in our export
commerce with Europe are valued in the official estimates at
from 45 to 50 roubles per head; but this trade has greatly
fallen off of late, and during the three years 1847—1849, the
average yearly export was but 1,950 head. In the government
of Astrakhan the horse trade, which used formerly to be very

actively carried on, has fallen off within the last twenty or five-and-twenty years in consequence of some severe winters having caused a great mortality among the animals; purchasers lost the habit of frequenting the fairs, and now, although several hundreds are brought to market, scarcely 40 or 50 find purchasers.

In a statistical work published in 1847 by the Administration of Studs, there is given a historical exposition of the circumstances which, both in earlier and in more recent times have mainly influenced the fortunes of horse-rearing, — embracing the causes of its progress and of its recent partial decline. From this we learn that in proportion as Russia, after having thrown off the yoke of the Tartars, recovered from their devastations, the rearing of horses became more and more extensively practised throughout the country. The obligation which the nobility lay under to furnish in case of war a contingent of cavalry to the Tsar's army contributed greatly to extend both the want and the liking; but the horse trade long remained almost exclusively in the hands of the Tartars. It was not until towards the end of the seventeenth century that Russia became more independent in this respect, both from the progress made in breeding in the interior of the empire, and from the annexation of several portions of Little Russia and especially of the Ukraine. At the commencement of Peter the Great's reign the state of the equine breed was quite satisfactory both as to quality and as to quantity; but the gigantic works undertaken by that monarch in order to lay the foundation of Russia's future grandeur and prosperity, and executed in the midst of bloody and obstinate wars, required extraordinary efforts of every sort. The financial resources of the state were then so limited that the cavalry and artillery could be remounted only by means of forced requisitions, which often robbed the cultivators of their best stallions; for it was just the largest and strongest horses that the army required; and the numbers became in consequence so much reduced that it was necessary to have recourse to foreign markets in order to remount the cuirassier regiments, for which purpose an extraordinary contribution required to be levied. According to the writer's opinion, it is from this epoch of crisis and extraordinary effort, prolonged through a period of fifty years, that dates the deterioration of the peasants' horses throughout a great part of the empire; but it is also from the same period that the rearing of horses by means of studs began to be developed and extended. The first part of this assertion seems to be open to question. We possess no certain data with respect to the condition of horses in Russia at the commencement of Peter the Great's reign; but we cannot attribute to this reign the ruin of the horses of the peasantry, for several measures specially favourable to the rearing of common horses were adopted by order of that sovereign. A large number of stallions were distributed over several districts, and got stock of a remarkably good quality and of a sort which is still greatly in request, as the horses of Obva, Wiatka, Kazan, Mezen and others. This proves that even at that period the improvement of horse flesh occupied the serious attention of government; but it is to the reign of the Empress Anne Joannovna that belongs more especially the idea of introducing into Russia a system of horse-rearing founded upon rational principles. It was under this reign that the first regulation appeared for the organisation of studs, and that the resolution was formed to found 105 crown studs. This magnificent plan was not carried into execution; but it drew the attention of private landowners to the subject: the requirements of the army held out the certainty of a market, and government was always more and more ready with its encouragement. A ukase published in 1756, in the reign of the Empress Elizabeth, enjoined the landed proprietors to pay special attention to the rearing of horses for the heavy cavalry, and indicated the crosses most suitable for that purpose. The price was fixed at 60 roubles for cuirassier horses, and 50 roubles for dragoon horses, very high prices for the time. Since that period, and especially since the memorable reign of the Empress Catherine, the rearing of horses has been carried on upon a very important scale; several of the most renowned studs were founded, and their numbers were multiplied more and more. At the beginning of the present century, the idea was formed of improving the breed by the introduction of English stallions; but though many of these were bought at extravagant prices, it was only a few studmasters that attained the object of their pecuniary sacrifices. Many of them, from want of skill, were cheated by the jockeys, who pocketed the money, but palmed off upon the purchasers degenerate animals for pure blood horses. The author of the work we are quoting is of opinion that these English acquisitions, far from improving the native breeds, greatly deteriorated the quality of the smaller studs; but we apprehend that in this remark he generalises too extensively; we now possess pure English blood horses of the first order; the Russian stud-book contains the names of 925 brood mares of the best breeds; amongst the English stallions purchased both for government and for individuals we find several names of renown both for their pedigree and the trophies of the racing-course; and the race-horses which we now possess are fit to run against the best racers in England.

Still, it cannot be denied that, for the last twenty or five-and-twenty years, horse breeding in Russia has been labouring under the influence of unfavourable circumstances. In consequence of the impulse given by the prohibitory system to manufacturing industry, the large proprietors have preferred directing their attention to sheep-farming, and many of them have either sold or neglected their studs, either to increase the number of their flocks of sheep, or to embark their capital in other industrial enterprises, which held out the prospect of larger and more immediate returns. Several establishments have fallen into decay on the death of their owners: others have been entirely disorganised by the division of a deceased party's succession; and a heavy tax laid upon the export of horses (which during a period of some years was converted into an absolute prohibition), may have also contributed to the discouragement of some stud-masters.

But, however this may be, we have still in reserve a large fund of excellent breeds; and government perceived that in order to restore this branch of rural economy from its temporary decline, the great requisite was to convey an impulse which should guide into a proper path the isolated efforts of the stud-masters. Accordingly the crown studs, which formerly were conducted with a purely military object—the remounting of the cavalry—were, in 1843, converted into imperial studs destined for the public benefit; and in order to place these establishments upon a better footing, government acquired, in 1844, the two most celebrated studs in the empire, that of Count Rostoptchine and that of the Countess Orloff. In a very short time twenty-four dépots of stallions were organised under the title of "rural mews" (*ziemskia sloutshnyia koniouschni*), with the view of propagating good breeds in every part of Russia. In order to afford the proprietors of private studs facilities for procuring good stock-getters, there were instituted periodical sales of the surplus mares and stallions belonging to the crown studs: the value and number of the imperial premiums were augmented, and various other measures were taken to encourage the rearing of good stock. The whole of this branch of the service was incorporated in 1848 with the Ministry of Domains, and in 1850 it received a new organisation based upon rational principles derived from the experience of other countries. The relative regulations contain the necessary rules with regard to the crossing of breeds,—the choice of stallions appropriate to the wants of the various localities and to the breeds predominating in the different districts,—the selection of mares for being covered,—the frequency of copulations, to be determined by the age and vigour of the stallion,—the rests to be allowed, &c., &c.: measures of superintendence were also devised to prevent the recurrence of certain irregularities which had slipped into the service through the negligence of some of the subalterns. In regard to encouragements held out for the rearing of horses, the new administration has laid it down as a rule that these are to be extended to whatever is good in the different kinds, from the pure blood horse down to the working garron. The Minister of Domains is the head of this administration, of which the special guidance is entrusted to a committee. The execution of all measures is entrusted to an inspector, under whose orders are placed all the imperial studs and stallion depôts: this inspector and all employés are guided in the discharge of their duty by precise and detailed instructions, in addition to which the depôts established in the different governments are superintended by committees presided over by the respective governors.

The influence of these wise and beneficial measures will become more and more manifest in proportion as the officials acquire more experience and aptitude, and the people learn to appreciate the advantages to be derived from them. The improvement of the breeds amongst the peasantry is undoubtedly a great desideratum, and the establishment of the rural mews is a means to this end, of which the experience of other countries has already demonstrated the appropriateness.

The imperial studs are now seven in number, namely, two in the government of Woronèje, four in that of Kharkow, and one in that of Nijni-Nowgorod. Being destined to raise stallions for different services, they have been arranged accordingly, and each of them has a type peculiar to itself:—1. The *Tsches-menka* stud is a nursery of pure blood horses, and is divided into two sections, one devoted to English racers, the other to Arabs;—2. The *Khrénovoïé* stud is composed of three departments: (a) saddle horses of the old Orloff breed, uncrossed; (b) saddle horses, cross breeds, including the Rostoptschine breed; and (c) trotters;—3. The *Dérkhoul* stud, for large framed cuirassier horses;—4. The *Streletz* stud, for light cavalry;—5. The *Novoalexandroff* stud, for carriage horses of large frame;—6. The *Limareff* stud, for draught horses, medium size;—7. The *Potchinki* stud, for heavy draught horses of large size, and peasants' horses. In 1850 the total number of horses amounted to 6,291, of which 149 were stallions, and 1,553 brood mares, being about 10 mares to 1 stallion.

The rural mews, 24 in number, serve twenty-nine governments, and in 1850 reckoned 1440 stallions. The following table presents a summary of their labours:

		Number of Depots.		Number of Mares covered.
In 1844	-	-	9	6,523
„ 1845	-	-	16	15,629
„ 1846	-	-	18	19,311
„ 1847	-	-	21	24,748
„ 1848	-	-	23	25,903
„ 1849	-	-	23	23,569
„ 1850	-	-	24	25,189
„ 1851	-	-	24	20,919
„ 1852	-	-	24	21,171
			Total -	182,962

The number of mares covered in 1850 (25,189), compared with the number of stallions (1,440), gives an average of 17 or 18 mares for each stallion. The number of horses sold during the year 1848 amounted to 684, of which 595 came from the studs, and 89 were discharged from the rural mews. The proceeds of sale amounted to 82,665 silver roubles, which gives an average price of 120 roubles per horse; but this average gives no fair idea of the value of some of the animals, in consequence of the differences amongst the sorts. The horses included in the annual sale of surplus stock are divided into three classes, viz.: 1st. Superior quality sold at Moscow, which is the centre of the horse trade, where all the principal stud-masters meet. Horses of this class put up to public competition fetch prices of 1,000, 2,000, or even as much as 3,000 silver roubles; 2nd. Quality inferior to the preceding but suitable for rearing stock, sold in the interior at the principal fairs in order to supply breeders with mares and stallions of a good stock at reasonable prices; 3rdly. Discharged horses considered as of trifling value. The proceeds of sale are applied to the reduction of the debt contracted by the administration for the acquisition of the Khrénovoïe land and stud. The official staff of the studs is composed of 1,186 individuals. In order to provide instruction for the children of the officials, the administration has founded schools, to which private boarders are also admitted. The studies are divided into two courses,— one elementary, destined to form subjects for the subaltern employments; the other superior, for the preparatory instruction of veterinary surgeons. In 1848 the total number of pupils amounted to 646, of whom 611 were state bursars, and 35 were private pupils.

The lands belonging to this administration contain 714,427 dessiatines, of which 105,594 consist of forest. In 1848 the population of the cultivators of these lands amounted to 176,521 individuals of both sexes. The

	Roubles.
revenues during 1848, a calamitous year, both from cholera and bad harvest, amounted to - - - -	402,173
and the expenses to - - - - -	432,984
leaving an excess of expenditure over revenue of - -	30,811
taken from the reserved capital, which, at the end of 1847, amounted to - - - - - -	108,297
If, from the total expenses, amounting, *ut suprà*, to - -	432,984
we deduct :	

	Roubles.	
1. Annual payment to bank for interest and reduction of principal of loan contracted for the purchase of Khrénovoïe land and stud -	95,849	
2. Prizes for horse-racing - - -	30,000	
3. Purchase of horses and other expenses not belonging to the support of the studs -	35,000	
		160,849
there will remain for the support of the studs an expense of - - - -		272,135

which, distributed over 4,837 horses, the number contained in the studs that year, gives 56 roubles 26 kopecks as the average expense per horse. In 1850, in consequence of reforms which had then been introduced, this expense amounted to no more than 37 roubles per horse.

The expenses for the support of the rural mews amounted in 1848 to 237,028 roubles, which for 1,337 stallions, the number of that year, gives an expense of 177 roubles per head. Distributing the amount over 25,903 mares covered that year, we have an expense of 9 roubles 15 kopecks for each copulation.

Comparing the preceding figures with the statistics of the state studs in Austria, we find some matter worthy of observation.

In Austria there are two court studs and five military studs, besides which there are depôts of stallions, called stations of copulation (*Beleg-Stationen*), established in every province of the empire with the exception of Dalmatia and the military frontier. The number of the latter is very considerable. In 1846, (the latest year for which we have returns), it amounted to 444.

The statistics of all these establishments exhibit, for the year 1846, the following figures :—

A. *In the Court Studs.*

Stallions	-	-	-	24
Mares	-	-	-	203
Saddle and coach horses		-	-	32
Young horses and foals		-	-	595

Total - 854

B. *In the Military Studs.*

Stallions	-	-	-	236
Young ditto	-	-	-	371
Brood mares	-	-	-	1,540
Young mares	-	-	-	640
Foals	-	-	-	2,715
Cavalry horses	-	-	-	689

Total - 6,191

C. *In the Stations of Copulation.*

Stallions	-	-	-	1,730
Young ditto	-	-	-	44
Cavalry horses	-	-	-	913

Total - 2,687

This presents a grand total of 9,732 horses and foals, (a fourth more than the number belonging to the crown studs in Russia in 1850), of which 1,990 are stallions and 1,743 are brood mares. The proportion of the number of full-grown stallions to that of brood mares in the studs was:

In Russia	-	-	as 10 to 104
In Austria	-	-	as 10 to 65

so that the relative number of mares in the studs was in Russia nearly two-thirds larger than in Austria. But when we compare the number of stallions in the stations of copulation with the number of mares covered, the result which we obtain is totally opposite. In Russia there were, in 1850, in the copulation stables, 1,440 stallions which covered 25,189 mares, giving 175 mares for 10 stallions. In Austria there were set to cover, in 1846, in the 444 stations, 1,859 stallions, which covered 106,955 mares, giving 575 mares for 10 stallions. From this it appears that the Austrian stallions performed more than thrice as much work as the Russian.

This inferiority in the number of mares covered by a stallion is explained by the difference of opinion which exists with regard to a horse's reproductive powers. Abroad, the calculation is 50, or even 60 mares to a stallion; but this proportion cannot be admitted into practice without detriment to the animal's powers. In Russia, especially where the climate does not admit of the covering season being prolonged beyond four months, it would be impossible to allow a stallion such a large number of mares, for, each mare requiring two or even three leaps, the number of the latter would amount to from 120 to 180 ; the stallion therefore would not have a single day's rest, and would often have to cover twice in one day.   This system would infallibly ruin our stallions, and be hurtful to their progeny ; whilst by economising the strength of the generator we are surer of attaining the end proposed.   Forced and too frequently repeated leaps are often null, and at any rate afford no security for the vigour of the get.

As regards the number of mares admitted to cover in the stables of copulation as compared with the total number of horses in the two countries, we obtain the following results.

In Austria, in the provinces where there are copulation stations, — that is to say, in the whole empire with the exception of Dalmatia and the Military Frontier,—the number of horses, in 1846, amounted to 2,618,885, and the number of mares covered amounted to 106,955, which gives 4,084 copulations to 100,000 head.   In Russia there were reckoned at the same period, in 28 governments served by 23 rural mews, 12,104,465 horses, and there were admitted to cover in 1848, only 25,903 mares, which gives the proportion of 214 copulations to 100,000 head. Thus, the absolute cipher of the copulations of mares belonging to private parties with the crown stallions in Russia is to that of Austria nearly as 1 to 4, and the relative cipher, in proportion to the number of horses in the two countries, is as 1 to 19.

This great difference in the results hitherto obtained in the two countries proceeds from the following causes : 1st. The difference between the principles (appropriate to the different situations of the two countries) upon which the organisation of these establishments is founded in Russia and Austria respectively.   In Russia, the private studs are much larger and more numerous than in Austria ; in the latter country, the depôts of crown stallions are intended to make up for the insufficiency of the private studs, whilst in Russia these establishments are intended solely to assist private enterprise, without making any pretensions to over-ride or to replace it.   Far from entering into competition with the private studs, they are meant to encourage them, and to offer a material assistance, which for some of the breeders is in fact indispensable.   The sale of stallions and mares of the best stock from the crown studs, the purchase of select horses from their proprietors, the distribution of premiums and medals, are the means of encouragement had recourse to, and the copulation stables are meant principally for the benefit of the peasantry who find in them stallions of such descriptions as they require. 2ndly. 'The novelty of the institution of depôts of crown stallions in Russia, whence their utility is not yet so generally appreciated as it is in other countries; our agricultural population, however, is now beginning to understand it; half the number of the mares covered belong to peasants. 3rdly. The great distances by which, in Russia, the copulation mews are separated, and the great extent of territory requiring to be served by a single stable. In Austria there were, in 1846, for an area of 11,117 geographical square miles (without Dalmatia and the Military Frontier), 22 central mews and 444 copulation stations, with 1859 stallions, which gives 1 central stable for 508 square miles, 1 copulation station for 25 square miles, and 1 stallion for 6 square miles; whilst in Russia 24 copulation stables with 1,440 stallions have to serve 29 governments embracing a territory of more than 43,000 geographical square miles. The number of copulation stations was fixed at 4 for each government. Thus there were on an average 1 stable for 1,792 square miles, 1 copulation station for 371 square miles, and 1 stallion for 30 square miles; in the government of Orenburg there was one copulation stable for a territory of 6,773 square miles, and in that of Wologda, 1 for 6,967 square miles. The Administration of Studs has latterly extended the number of stations to 6 for each government, of which 1 is permanent at the provincial capital, and the other 5 change their site every two years, so that each district may be served in its turn. A greater subdivision of the depôts of stallions, however desirable in one point of view, namely, as bringing them within the reach of a larger number of horse-owners, would render superintendence more difficult, and probably give rise to abuses which it is of importance to prevent as much as possible. We thus perceive that, in this branch of service as in many others, it is the great distances which chiefly contribute to impede the operation and diminish the advantage of the most patriotic measures. 4thly. The degeneracy of the breed of horses amongst our cultivators, owing to which there are in many districts but few mares fit for copulation with stallions of a superior breed. We perceive from the reports of the Administration of Studs that, in 1848, out of 40,673 mares presented for cover, 14,720, or 36 per cent. were rejected. This inconvenience must disappear in the course of time; for, after the institution of the stallion depôts, and of special examinations of the horses of the peasantry, we may justly expect a marked improvement in the breed. According to the official reports, several horses got by crown stallions upon peasants' mares, have been sold at the rate of 100 and even 200 silver roubles; some of them have been admitted for cavalry remounts. The trials of speed exhibit for peasants' horses a celerity of 6 versts (= 4 English miles) in from 9 to 12 minutes: in those of large draught, the weight has never been less than 100 poods, and has often amounted to 200 and upwards. These are palpable proofs of the care which is now being bestowed on the rearing of horses, and of the progress making in it. The competitors in these trials are numerous; the peasants' horse-races in the government of Samara, for example, presented in 1850 the remarkable spectacle of 106 horses running at once, a thing which never happened even in England. All this shows that the intentions of government are now beginning to be understood, and that we are warranted in expecting very satisfactory results. It is farther to be observed that the stallion has often to be refused not only on account of disease in the mares offered for covering, but also from want of vacancies; for in some districts applications are very numerous, whilst the number of admissions is fixed by the regulations at 25 mares per stallion, each mare being entitled to be offered until fecundation has taken place.

The lands belonging to the military studs in Austria occupy an extent of 339,092 joch = 178,700 dessiatines. This is a fourth of the extent of the lands belonging to the Administration of Crown Studs in Russia. The expenses in Austria of the military studs, including the Veterinary Institute, amounted in 1846 to the sum of 1,002,082 florins = 632,894 roubles; and, for the remounting department, including maintenance of stallions in the copulation stations, to the sum of 292,065 florins = 184,462 roubles; in all 1,294,147 florins = 817,356 silver roubles. The revenue from the funds belonging to this administration amounted to 654,799 florins; and the remaining expense, amounting to 639,348 florins, was carried to the budget of the war department. Distributing the expenses of administration and maintenance over the number of horses maintained, the expense amounts in the studs to 102 roubles 23 kopecks, and in the remounting department, including the copulation stations, to 68 roubles 65 kopecks per horse.

In Russia, the expense of the studs does not now come to more than 37 roubles per horse; but for the rural mews, it amounted in 1848 to 177 roubles per stallion. Thus the expenses of administration and maintenance of the horses in the military studs of Austria are, in proportion to the number of horses maintained, almost thrice as high as in the imperial studs of Russia; but it is to be observed, that in these expenses there are included, in Austria, the price of horses purchased and other extraordinary expenditure, whilst for the imperial studs we have taken into account only the maintenance of the horses and the ordinary expenses of management: farther, the Russian crown studs possess four times as much land as the Austrian military studs, and this affords them greater facilities for provender. On the other hand, the costs of maintenance and management of the rural mews are, in Russia, nearly two and a half times as high as in the copulation stations of Austria, in proportion to the number of stallions. This difference is partly explained by the novelty of this institution in Russia, considerable expenses being incurred for buildings and other purposes incidental to the first outset. There are, moreover, in these depôts, stallions of very distinguished breeds, for a copulation from which the proprietors of mares willingly pay as much as 25 roubles.

Distributed over the number of mares covered in the copulation stations, the expense of this branch of the service amounts in Austria to 1 rouble 72 kopecks per covered mare; and in Russia to 9 roubles 15 kopecks. This disproportion in Russia between expenses and hitherto obtained results proceeds from causes which we have already adverted to; and these sacrifices may be recompensed in no distant future, if the regulations concerning the establishments are strictly observed, and the measures of government are as faithfully carried out as they have been patriotically devised.

But, notwithstanding the importance of the crown studs and their dependent establishments, the progress of horse-rearing will always depend principally upon the private studs, the number of which, in Russia, is very considerable. According to the statistics published in 1847 by the Administration of Studs, there were at that period in European Russia, exclusive of Finland, the kingdom of Poland, and the country of the Don Cossacks, 2,107 private studs, of which 1,672 were of the first class, 365 of the second class, and 70 of less importance. For more than 1,200 of these studs the number of horses has not been officially ascertained. The following table, prepared from data furnished by the above-mentioned publication, exhibits the number of studs in 37 governments, indicating also the number of horses in 831 studs, of which the statistics have been more or less completely ascertained: —

Statistical Table of Studs belonging to private Parties.

Governments.	Total Number of Studs.	Studs more specially denoted in the Official Statistics.		Observations.
		Their Number.	Number of Horses.	
1. Kherson -	46	38	2,750	This is only the number of brood mares.
2. Ekathérinoslaw	257	28	3,932	Stallions and foals of only 8 studs included.
3. Poltawa - -	463	37	4,099	Stallions and foals of 6 studs not included.
4. Kharkow -	112	19	925	Brood mares.
5. Podolia - -	28	5	695	
6. Tschernigow -	91	18	735	Brood mares.
7. Woronèje - {	- -	-	600	Brood mares amongst the German colonists
	100	96	9,498	Stallions and foals of 10 studs not included.
8. Tambow -	134	134	6,871	Stallions and foals of only 57 studs included.
9. Riazan - -	46	18	420	Stallions and foals of only 2 studs included.
10. Penza - -	23	16	533	Brood mares.
11. Simbirsk -	70	39	1,166	Brood mares.
12. Orel - -	51	49	1,921	Stallions and foals of 33 studs not included.
13. Toula - -	56	14	396	Brood mares.
14. Koursk - -	78	78	4,748	Whereof 263 stallions and 1976 brood mares.
15. Saratow -	35	33	1,546	Brood mares.
16. Orenburg -	16	9	365	Brood mares; besides which there are in this government 402 herds (*Tabouny*), with 82,000 horses. [mares.
17. Wiatka - -	2	2	146	Whereof 15 stallions and 131 brood
18. Perm - -	9	6	516	
19. Wologda -	4	3	130	
20. Tauride -	115	22	3,677	Brood mares.
21. Astrakhan -	1			Besides the studs of the Cossacks and the *Tabouni.*
22. Bessarabia -	52	52	8,152	
24. Kiew - -	9	7	652	Brood mares.
23. Wolhynia -	22	1	180	Brood mares.
25. Nijni-Nowgor-od - -	12	9	417	
26. Kazan - -	5	5	232	
27. Jaroslaw -	44	9	190	Brood mares.
28. Twer - -	20	20	326	Stallions and foals of 1 stud not included.
29. Smolensk -	9	5	161	Foals not included.
30. Mohilew -	3			
31. Grodno - -	10			
32. Minsk - -	2	2	226	Stallions and foals of 1 stud not included.
33. Moscow -	9	9	641	
34. Wladimir -	10	9	394	
35. Kalouga -	14	14	252	Foals not included.
36. Kostroma -	24	24	691	Stallions and foals of 17 studs not included.
37. Pskow - -	3	1	75	
Total - -	1,985	831	58,258	

The statistical information recently collected by the new Administration of Crown Studs, with regard to the studs of private parties, makes the total number of the latter in European Russia, without Finland and the kingdom of Poland, amount to 2,166.

In regard to progress in the rearing of horses and the reputation of studs, European Russia may be divided into five classes, in which the governments will be arranged in the following order: —

			Number of Studs.					Number of Studs.
CLASS I.					Brought forward			243
Woronèje*	-	-	97		Simbirsk	-	-	70
Tambow*	-	-	123		Jaroslaw*	-	-	25
Kharkow	-	-	109		Riazan	-	-	47
	Total		329			Total		385
CLASS II.					**CLASS IV.**			
Ekathérinoslaw*	-		269		Esthonia	-	-	2
Poltawa	-	-	463		Grodno*	-	-	8
Orel -	-	-	103		Kazan*	-	-	7
Toula	-	-	86		Kalouga*	-	-	17
Koursk	-	-	78		Kostroma*	-	-	45
Kherson	-	-	46		Livonia	-	-	6
Tschernigow*	-		81		Minsk	-	-	2
Tauride*	-	-	112		Mohilew*	-	-	5
	Total		1,238		Nijni-Nowgorod	-		11
CLASS III.					St. Petersburg	-		2
Bessarabia	-	-	62		Smolensk*	-	-	17
Wolhynia*	-	-	14		Twer*	-	.	15
Kiew*	-	-	20		Wladimir*	-	.	7
Moscow*	-	-	15		Wologda*	-	-	3
Penza*	-	-	27		Wiatka*	-	-	4
Perm*	-	-	12		Astrakhan	-	-	1
Podolia	-	-	28			Total		152
Orenburg	-	-	16		**CLASS V.**			
Saratow*	-	-	49		Pskow*	-	-	2
Carried forward -			243					

Grand Total 2,106

Considering that the preceding table gives the number of horses for only 831 studs—that of this number there are 425 containing no indication of the number of stallions and foals—and that for 1,335 studs we are totally destitute of data for the

* In those governments to which an asterisk is attached, the number of studs according to the most recent information, differs from the information for 1847 given in the preceding table.   The differences, sometimes plus, sometimes minus, proceed partly from changes that have taken place in the actual numbers during the interval, and partly from rectifications of the numbers formerly given.

number of horses maintained, it will not be too much to assume
that the total number of horses maintained in the 2,106 studs
enumerated in the last official statistics, must, with the addition
of the *Tabouny** amount to about 200,000 head.

In this number there are undoubtedly many studs in which
the breeds have degenerated; but there are also a large number in which the noblest breeds, Arabian, Persian, Turkish,
English, Danish, German, as well as Russians of good old
family pretensions, are well represented. Amongst the Russian horses, the best breeds trace their origin to the studs of the
Countess Orloff and Count Rostoptschine, and there are few
studs of much reputation which do not possess some mares and
stallions issuing from these sources. Here, then, we possess a
fund of reproduction which only requires a little care on the
part of breeders to insure a large development for this branch
of rural economy. It is a vast field open for the progress of
national wealth, of which the rearing of domestic animals is
one of the principal elements. The degree of benefit that may
be drawn from a horse in the different purposes to which he is
applied depends especially upon the care bestowed upon his
rearing. England supplies us with the best example of the
perfection that may be attained in this department. It has been
calculated that the motive power of an English horse is equal
to that of three German horses; and if we compare the quantity
of labour in the fields executed by an English horse and by a
Russian horse respectively, we shall attain a similar result.
With us, in most districts, the peasants' horses are smaller and
weaker than they are even in Germany, and we may assume without
exaggeration that by regenerating the breed, we would obtain
from the same number of horses, triple the motive power which
is now obtained from them,—an immense increase of productive
forces gained to the country! There are reckoned to be in the
European possessions of Russia about 18 millions of horses, of
which at least 12 millions belong to the class of cultivators.
Now, if we estimate at an average of only 12 roubles—certainly
the most moderate estimate that can be adopted—the annual
value of the motive power of a peasant's horse in Russia, the
mere duplication of this power by improvement of the breed,
would give a yearly increase to the national wealth of 144
millions of roubles.

In the countries of central and western Europe, the future
prospects of improvement in the breeds of horses may in the

---

* This term is applied to the herds of horses in the country of the steppes,
where the reproduction of the race is left in a manner to take care of itself,
without that special superintendence which is practised in the studs proper.

course of time be more or less compromised by the immense extension of railways. In Russia this casualty is still exceedingly remote. The epoch at which the whole empire may be traversed by means of steam from east to west and from north to south is a very distant one; and even when the gigantic labours of which this implies the undertaking shall have been accomplished, there will remain a vast network of intermediate roads over this immense space; and these new facilities of communication, by giving a strong impulse to the industry and commerce of the country, will multiply the demands for motive power both for the locomotion of the inhabitants and for the transport of goods along the thousand railway feeders; so that this prospect, distant as it is, encourages instead of threatening the interests of our horse-rearers.

We have seen at page 309, that the largest number of studs is found in the governments of Tambow, Kharkow, Ekathérinoslaw, Poltawa, Orel, and Tauride, each of which contains upwards of 100, and the whole of them together upwards of 1,179, or much more than half the whole number of studs of the existence of which we have official evidence. There are 732, or nearly a third, in the two governments of Ekathérinoslaw and Poltawa. The most important private studs for pure blood-horses are in the governments of Poltawa, Kherson, Tambow, Woronèje, Koursk, Orel, Riazan, Toula, Penza, and Moscow; and for saddle-horses proceeding from a cross of different breeds, in the governments of Poltawa, Kharkow, Tambow. Woronèje, Toula, Penza, Moscow, Wladimir, and Wiatka. The oldest studs and the best breeds are found in the districts lying along the banks of the Bitiouga, which flows through the governments of Tambow and Woronèje, and empties itself into the Don. Besides the two fine crown studs of Khrénowoïé and Tschessmenka, and 234 private studs, some of them very large ones, which are situated within these two governments, a number of the peasants rear excellent horses, which fetch prices of from 100 to 200 roubles.

The *Journal de Saint Petersbourg*, in its number for 20th April (2nd May), 1850, gives a historical sketch of horse-rearing in Russia containing some interesting details which we shall insert here by way of supplement to what we have already said upon the subject.

" As far back as our historical accounts of Russia extend, the rearing of horses seems always to have formed a notable branch of the national industry. The cause must be sought as much in the vast extent of its territory as in the fertility of the country and the variety of its products. The financial history of

Russia shows us the importance which the commerce derived from this branch of industry anciently possessed. Thus, amongst the fiscal revenues, one of the principal, along with the octroi upon fermented liquors, arose from the tax levied upon the sale of horses by means of a stamp duty. The following are some facts relative to the commerce itself, as it appeared during the reign of the czar Alexis Mikhaïlowitch. The exclusive objects of importation being the Tartar and Nogay breeds, the cities of Astrakhan and Kazan became the principal centres of commercial operations, and annually supplied the markets of Moscow with from 30,000 to 50,000 horses. Of these, from 5,000 to 6,000 were selected on the spot for the service of the court; and, after being marked and registered, were entrusted to guides who had the charge of escorting them to the capital. On their arrival, the intendants of the royal mews made an inspection of them, agreed upon a price which was paid out of the czar's privy purse, and abandoned the sale of the remainder to the Tartar and Nogay subjects who had come along with them, by whom they were disposed of at the current rate of from 5 to 15 roubles per head. The first Russian purchasers, after feeding and petting their purchases for a month or two, resold them at a considerable rise of price. Government did everything in its power to promote this trade. When it was over for a season, the foreign merchants, to the number of 200 and upwards, were regularly invited to a court repast, received a present of rich vestments taken from the royal treasury, and returned by water to Kazan at the expense of the state. The superintendence and direction of the commerce were confided to a special administration—the Chamber of the Palace of Kazan. It kept registers in the different towns of Russia, in which all the bargains contracted between horse-dealers and purchasers required to be inserted by the parties concerned under the penalty of a rouble. The registration fees, levied at the rate of three *diengas* per rouble, formed a fiscal revenue of the mean yearly value of about 10,000 roubles.

" But the introduction of a regular and rational system of horse-rearing into Russia dates only from the reign of Peter the Great, who opened a new era for this branch of industry. Government peopled the steppes in the neighbourhood of Woronèje with Dutch stallions, to which the famous Bitioughine draught horses owe their origin; whilst Prince Menschikoff established at Bronnitsy and on the Pakhra no less celebrated studs, which furnished horses for the service even of the czar. Under the reign of the Empress Anna Joannovna, the Duc de Biron, by the acquisition of first-rate animals selected from every European breed, powerfully contributed to the development of the hippic establishments of the crown; whilst the fashion of keeping splendid sets of carriage horses, which was maintained throughout the reigns of the Empress Catharine II. and the Emperor Paul I., induced individuals to found similar establishments, and gave rise, towards the end of last century, to the studs of Counts Orloff, Razoumovsky, Goudovitch, and Koutouzoff. These, from the smallness of their number, could of course exercise but little influence on the rearing of horses in general. Still, by introducing into Russia the Mecklenburg, Danish, and Dutch breeds, they contributed to the production of coach horses of a superior quality, distinguished by their frame, their strength, and the beauty of their shape, although the type, unfortunately, has since been lost.

" At the beginning of the present century, the exigencies of war giving rise to an exclusive demand for cavalry horses,—the abolition of the old massive vehicles which were replaced by the more modest equipages then used in the rest of Europe,— and especially the formidable competition of the crown establishments,— all these circumstances combined had an unfavourable effect upon the studs of individuals, and caused their rapid decrease. Only a few of them were maintained; but it was these which furnished the best horses to the generals of our army, as well as to the artillery, the rapid development of which is referable to the glorious years 1812, 1813, 1814. On the re-establishment of peace in Europe, the decay of this branch of industry became complete. The inconsiderate admission into the studs of old cavalry horses ruined by service, and still more of English horses, furnished no doubt with pompous certificates but in reality full of faults, contributed in a short time, with the help of jockey-greed, to inundate the country with brutes of the most degenerate description; so that after paying as much as 7,000 roubles for the pair, the breeders were glad to get 75 for the progeny.

" The Hungarian trotters of the Orloff stud were then, no doubt, in existence, and in the enjoyment of a just celebrity; but they were confined to a limited number of owners, belonging almost entirely to a few rich Moscow merchants. As for the mares of that breed, which were sold by auction, they nowise contributed to the improvement of the species, because they were usually covered by the mediocre descendants of the English horses.

" About this time was founded the Hippic Society of Moscow, to which belongs without contradiction the honour of having given a new and vivifying impulse to the rearing of horses in Russia. It gained from the outset the patronage of government and the attention of the public by the institution of horse-races, which brought prominently into notice the eminent qualities of the trotters. The brilliant success of the first experiment had for its immediate result an augmentation of the number of private studs, of which the greater part were employed in the production of the horses that appeared at the Moscow races. · These races thus acquired, in the opinion of breeders, the reputation of an infallible criterion to guide them in the selection of good animals. The supreme authority, on its part, has not failed to second the useful efforts of the society by putting at its disposition annual prizes, which it justly considers the best and most suitable stimulants.

" Such are the most important historical data with regard to the rearing of the equine race in Russia; and when we consider the very favourable conditions for its development presented by the natural richness of the country, and the encouragements held out to it by government, it must be obvious that its ulterior progress must depend entirely upon the judgment with which it is pursued. Russia especially requires strong horses. Breeders, therefore, ought to make it their object to obtain in their establishments animals possessed of that essential quality, and to study the improvement of three distinct breeds,—the sort commonly called trotters,—racers or cavalry horses,—and the common horses employed by the peasants in the labours of agriculture: all they require is to follow the path so brilliantly opened up by Count Alexis Orloff, who has enriched his country with the two former varieties. The new breed of trotters, formerly unknown, and still peculiar to Russia, was created in the studs of the Counts Orloff by the fusion of the most opposite types: it possesses the massive but regular stature of the Danish breed, the strength of the Dutch, and the fire and velocity of the Arab and English: it is now distributed over the whole empire, and furnishes excellent horses for the heavy cavalry and the artillery. The eminent qualities by which it is distinguished render it particularly suitable for the production, 1st. Of horses, for private coaches and carriages; 2ndly. Of draught horses, which may be attained by crossing the pure breed with a more common sort; 3rd. Of horses intended for the post service and for heavy waggons. This latter class is exceedingly deserving of attention: the post recruits its horses for most part in the studs of South Russia, and there is little doubt but that a cross betwixt the breed peculiar to the steppes and that of the trotters would give progeny of a superior quality, principally in regard to frame. As for the horses employed in carriers' waggons, they generally present certain vicious characteristics which render them exceedingly unsuitable for the purpose for which they are destined: a lymphatic temperament, and fleshy legs very apt to founder, render these horses weak and ineffective as workers: the annoyance thence resulting for the carriers is incessant: every now and then in the course of their journey, they are obliged to make forced halts, and to provide themselves with relays; they are thus involved in useless expenses, which, by enhancing the cost of transport, fall ultimately upon the consumer. We see then what large interests are concerned in the improvement of this description of horses — an improvement which might be easily attained by crossing these horses with the trotters.

" The studs founded in Russia with the object of rearing race or cavalry horses are divisible into two classes: the first comprehends the establishments destined solely for rearing animals of the English breed, imported into the country by the breeder Massaloff, whose efforts to preserve the purity of the blood and to prevent the degeneracy of the species have been crowned with success. His example has found many imitators,—amongst others, Messieurs Voeïkoff and Petrovsky: but, strange as it may appear, the influence of these attempts upon horse-breeding in general has been but little felt. At present the demand for race horses is so trifling that the operations of the studs is pretty nearly confined to furnishing champions for the racing-course. This is explained by two circumstances: on the one hand, those horses which by their frame and structure would seem peculiarly suitable for the army do not form one per cent. of the cavalry remounts, owing to their too mettlesome temperament and the stiffness of their necks, to which it is difficult to communicate the requisite degree of suppleness; on the other hand, the value of the prizes of the racing-course induces the breeders to train the best animals in their establishments to that end, and many of them fall a premature sacrifice to the regimen to which with this view they are subjected. The second class comprehends those studs which are destined to the rearing of horses of Arabian origin : such are those of the counts Rostoptschine, Zavadovski, Radzoumovski, Goudovitch, of the Passeks, and, in part, of the counts Orloff, who furnish the cavalry with its finest chargers. The horses from these establishments are distinguished by qualities not always possessed by racers, and not considered indispensable for these. It follows that the breeders of saddle horses, properly so called, ought to operate directly upon animals of the Arab breed, the parent stock of all the varieties of the racer, and endeavour to procure the points required by the nature of the animal's destination, as strength of croup, elasticity and suppleness of chest and shoulder, flexibility of knee, delicacy of mouth.

" In the breed of agricultural horses, two varieties are to be distinguished. The common or native breed possesses every proper quality both as to strength and energy of temperament: but although it leaves nothing to be wished for in either of these respects, it is unfortunately in the present day subject to degeneracy, in consequence of precocious copulations between animals of only two or three years old. The evil indicates the remedy. The second, or improved breed, ought to have been principally placed at the disposal of those agriculturists who engage in the rearing of horses. Numerous examples show how easy it would be to improve this breed by crossing it with trotters."

As respects the number of horses in proportion to the population, the provinces and governments range in the following order:

	Number of Horses per 100 Inhabitants.			Number of Horses per 100 Inhabitants.
1. *Orenburg** -	- 90	26. Tauride -	-	- 24
2. Simbirsk -	- 72	27. Nijni-Nowgorod -		- 23
3. *Saratow* -	- 47	28. *Kowno* -	-	- 23
4. Mohilew -	- 47	29. *Nowgorod*	-	- 23
5. Country of Don Cossacks -	47	30. Wilna -		- 23
6. Smolensk -	- 45	31. *Witebsk* -	-	- 23
7. *Koursk* -	- 43	32. Wologda -	-	- 22
8. *Astrakhan* -	- 42	33. *Courland* -	-	- 21
9. *Riazan* -	- 41	34. Moscow -	-	- 20
10. Toula -	- 41	35. Wolhynia -	-	- 19
11. *Orel* -	- 39	36. Olonetz -	-	- 18
12. Tambow -	- 38	37. Livonia -	-	- 17
13. Perm -	- 37	38. *Pskow* -	-	- 17
14. Twer -	- 35	39. *Kharkow* -	-	- 16
15. Kalouga -	- 34	40. Archangel -	-	- 15
16. Woronèje	- 33	41. *Esthonia* -	-	- 13
17. Kherson -	- 33	42. Minsk -	-	- 12
18. Penza -	- 31	43. Kingdom of Poland	- 11
19. Kostroma -	- 30	44. Poltawa -	-	- 10
20. *Jaroslaw* -	- 30	45. Ekathérinoslaw -		- 10
21. Kazan -	- 28	46. Bessarabia -		- 10
22. *Wiatka* -	- 26	47. Grodno -	-	- 9
23. *Tschernigow* -	- 26	48. *St. Petersburg* -	-	- 8
24. Wladimir -	- 26	49. Kiew -	-	- 7
25. Stavropol -	- 25	50. Podolia -	-	- 6

* In the information which we have obtained from the Administration of Imperial Studs, the relative number of horses differs, for some governments, from the cipher which we have adopted; but as our figures are founded upon data collected by M. Arsénieff, the head of the statistical bureau at the Ministry of the Interior, and as these data have hitherto been considered the most authentic of any, we

From the foregoing table we perceive that, in this respect also, there exist very large disproportions. Thus, there are four governments which do not reckon 1 horse to 10 inhabitants, and two in which the number of horses exceeds half the population. The difference between the government of Podolia, which reckons the smallest number of horses in proportion to its population, and that of Orenburg, which possesses the largest relative number, is as 1 to 15. Such divergent numerical relations are not met with in any other country. In Austria, in the Military Frontiers, the provinces which have comparatively the largest number of horses, there are reckoned only 17 horses to 100 inhabitants, and in the Italian provinces, which possess the fewest, there are 3 to 100. Thus the proportion between *minimum* and *maximum* is:

In Austria	- -	as 10 to 51
In Russia	- -	as 10 to 150

There are in European Russia thirty-six governments in which the relative number of horses exceeds that of those Austrian provinces which possess the most, and only twelve which do not attain as high a proportion as the latter. Those great differences between the numbers of horses in the two countries is partly explained by the immense extent of Russia, which requires a greater mass of forces for the locomotion of its inhabitants, for the labours of the field, for the transport of the products of the land, and of foreign merchandise.

The following table exhibits for each government, the relative population, the number of horses per geographical square mile

have preferred adhering to them, all the more that, with the exception of the government of St. Petersburg, the differences presented by the figures of the Administration of Studs are all differences of diminution. It is well known that the errors found in this part of statistics, as well in other countries as in Russia, are almost always errors of diminution, the official figures being generally under the real number; when, therefore, there is a divergence between two official figures, the probability is that we will approach nearest the truth by taking the higher one. We subjoin, however, the relative number of horses as fixed by the Administration of Studs for all those governments where the difference between their figures and those of the above table exceeds the proportion of 1 horse to 1000 inhabitants.

	Number of Horses to 1000 Inhabitants.			Number of Horses to 1000 Inhabitants.
Orenburg	- - 853	Kowno -	-	- 194
Saratow	- - 483	Nowgorod	-	- 207
Koursk -	- - 397	Witebsk	-	- 204
Riazan -	- - 259	Courland	-	- 183
Orel -	- - 336	Pskow -	-	- 117
Astrakhan	- - 269	Kharkow	-	- 105
Wiatka -	- - 252	Esthonia	-	- 118
Jaroslaw	- - 225	St. Petersburg -		- 147
Tschernigow	- - 208			

The names of all these governments are, in the table, printed in *italics.*

of area, and the numerical relation of the latter to the absolute cipher of the population.

Governments.	Population per Square Mile.	Number of Horses per Square Mile.	Number of Horses per 100 Inhabitants.
1. Moscow - - - -	2,591	522	20
2. Koursk - - - -	2,112	905	43
3. Kingdom of Poland - -	2,111	224	11
4. Podolia - - - -	2,062	130	6
5. Toula - - - -	2,009	816	41
6. Kiew - - - -	1,861	131	7
7. Poltawa - - - -	1,856	178	10
8. Riazan - - - -	1,791	738	41
9. Kalouga - - - -	1,703	584	34
10. Orel - - - - -	1,639	642	39
11. Penza - - - -	1,545	480	31
12. Jaroslaw - - - -	1,456	438	30
13. Tambow - - - -	1,402	535	38
14. Tschernigow - - -	1,392	357	26
15. Woronèje - - - -	1,381	457	33
16. Wladimir - - - -	1,358	347	26
17. Nijni-Nowgorod - - -	1,340	304	23
18. Grodno - - - -	1,255	113	9
19. Kowno - - - -	1,234	279	23
20. Kazan - - - -	1,223	345	28
21. Kharkow - - - -	1,202	195	16
22. St. Petersburg - - -	1,180	97	8
23. Wolhynia - - - -	1,154	218	19
24. Twer - - - -	1,154	408	35
25. Courland - - - -	1,069	222	21
26. Wilna - - - -	1,066	241	23
27. Smolensk - - - -	1,064	476	45
28. Bessarabia - - - -	1,049	105	10
29. Livonia - - - -	980	167	17
30. Mohilew - - - -	944	447	47
31. Simbirsk - - - -	915	657	72
32. Witebsk - - - -	908	210	23
33. Pskow - - - -	832	142	17
34. Ekathérinoslaw - - -	824	85	10
35. Esthonia - - - -	803	105	13
36. Wiatka - - - -	772	198	26
37. Kostroma - - - -	700	207	30
38. Kherson - - - -	690	226	33
39. Minsk - - - -	604	73	12
40. Tauride - - - -	572	135	24
41. Saratow - - - -	528	247	47
42. Nowgorod - - -	402	94	23
43. Stavropol - - - -	379	95	25
44. Orenburg - - -	314	283	90
45. Perm - - - -	309	115	37
46. Country of the Don Cossacks - - - -	271	126	47
47. Wologda - - - -	124	28	22
48. Olonetz - - - -	100	18	18
49. Astrakhan - - -	72	30	42
50. Archangel * - - -	21	3	15

* In this province there are reared a number of reindeer, which partly supply the place of horses.

The first thing that strikes us in the preceding table is the great variety of numerical relations between the extent of area, relative population, and number of horses. We perceive that provinces situated almost entirely alike in regard to the density of their population differ essentially in regard to the number of horses which they possess. Thus, for example, the relative population of Toula and Podolia are nearly alike; but the former reckons 41 horses to 100 inhabitants, and the latter only 6. In the government of Koursk, the population is denser than in that of Poltawa, and yet the relative number of horses in the former is 43 and in the latter only 10 to 100 inhabitants. The government of Riazan reckons 1791 inhabitants to the square mile, and 41 horses to 100 inhabitants; the government of Kiew reckons 1861 inhabitants to the square mile, and only 7 horses to 100 inhabitants. The government of Nijni-Nowgorod has 1340 inhabitants to the square mile, and 23 horses to 100 inhabitants; that of Grodno has 1255 inhabitants to the square mile, and 9 horses to 100 inhabitants. The government of Simbirsk 915 inhabitants to the square mile, and 72 horses to 100 inhabitants; and that of St. Petersburg 1180 inhabitants to the square mile, and 8 horses to 100 inhabitants. These deviations from the general law, which requires a larger number of horses for the same number of inhabitants when the latter are scattered over a more extensive territory, are so much the more remarkable, because in most cases we find no explanation of them either in the proportional extent of meadow land, which ought to exercise a great influence on the numbers reared, nor in that of the arable land, which determines the numbers employed in the plough. Thus, for example, in the government of Toula, which reckons 41 horses to 100 inhabitants, there is but two-tenths of a dessiatine of meadow to each inhabitant, whilst in that of Podolia, where there are 6 horses to 100 inhabitants, the relative extent of meadow land is forty-eight hundredths to an inhabitant. In the government of Poltawa, the relative extent of meadows compared with the population is more than twice as great as in that of Koursk, whilst the relative number of horses is, in the latter government, more than four times as large as in the former. The government of Kiew presents an extent of meadow for each inhabitant somewhat larger than that of Riazan, and the relative number of horses is, in the latter government, six times as large as it is in the former.

On comparing the relative number of horses with the relative extent of arable land, we find that most of the examples we have cited present a larger proportion of cultivated land per inhabitant in those governments where the relative number of horses is also larger; but the difference in extent of land is very trifling when compared with the difference in the number of horses. Thus between the governments of Poltawa and Koursk, the difference in regard to the relative extent of arable land is nearly as 10 to 12, and in regard to the relative number of horses, it is as 10 to 43. The governments of Riazan and Kiew even present an opposite numerical relation. In the former of these two governments there are but 1·31 dessiatines of land in culture for 1 inhabitant, and in the latter 1·38, whilst the relative number of horses in the former is more than six times as large as it is in the latter. In some governments, as, for example, in that of Poltawa as compared with Koursk, in that of Kiew as compared with Riazan, and in that of Grodno as compared with Nijni-Nowgorod, the difference in the number of horses is, to a certain but very trifling extent, balanced by the comparatively larger number of cattle, part of which is employed in the plough and in drawing waggons.

Independently of the extent of territory and of the agricultural situation of the country, which determine the quantity of motive power required for the wants of the population, and independently, likewise, of the abundance of forage in each district, which has an influence on the relation between the number of horses and that of the inhabitants, there are frequently other local causes which may exercise a greater or less degree of influence on this branch of agricultural statistics; as, for example, industrial activity, which aliments the circulation both of goods and merchandise and of human beings,— the direction of the great commercial routes, which concentrate in this or that district the demand for the motive power of domestic animals,—and the frame and strength of the animals themselves, which differ from one province to another. In all these respects, Russia presents a great variety of local peculiarities which partly explain the disproportions expressed in figures in the preceding table.

Of all the states of Europe the empire of Austria is one of those of which the component parts are most heterogeneous, as well in regard to the nationality of the inhabitants, their customs, and degree of material well-being, as in regard to their agricultural situation, and yet we do not find in that country such great differences in the statistics of the equine race as exist with us. The different provinces of that monarchy may be arranged, in that respect, in the following order : —

		Population per Sq. Mile.	Number of Horses per 100 Inhab.	Average.
Lombardy	- - -	6,895	3	3
Province of Venice	-	5,290	3	
Bohemia	- - -	4,666	3	
Moravia and Silesia	-	4,609	6	5
Lower Austria	-	4,229	5	
Littoral	- - -	3,503	4	
Gallicia	- - -	3,203	11	8·7
Hungary	- - -	2,671	9	
Upper Austria	-	2,502	6	
Styria	- - -	2,502	6	9·3
Transylvania	-	2,198	16	
Carniola and Carinthia	-	2,158	6	
Dalmatia	- - -	1,802	5	11
Military Frontiers	- -	1,796	17	

We perceive at once that, with few exceptions, upon taking the provinces by groups, the relative number of horses augments in inverse proportion to the density of the population, so that the statistical law which requires, under given circumstances, for the same number of inhabitants a greater number of horses in proportion to the greater extent of territory, here finds its application, and the exceptional cases are explained sometimes by the agricultural situation of particular provinces, sometimes by other causes quite as natural. Thus, for example, in Gallicia, the peasants' horses are much smaller and less robust than in the other provinces, and a comparatively larger number of them is required for the labours of the fields; the meadow and pasture lands likewise are much more extensive than in most of the other countries; and these two circumstances explain the higher figure in this province. In Transylvania the large number is explained by the quality and relative extent of the meadows and pastures. In the Military Frontiers, horse-rearing is favoured at once by the extent and quality of the meadows and pastures, and by the military organisation of the provinces.

On directing our attention to the statistical table page 316, we will perceive that the great differences which exist between many of our provinces in regard to their supply of horses,— several of them rearing these in numbers far beyond the wants of the population, and others possessing very few relatively to the extent of their territory — open up a vast field for the horse trade of the interior.

III. *Sheep.*

The rapid extension of sheep-farming which has taken place in Russia within the last thirty years, in consequence of the progress of the woollen manufacture, both at home and abroad, affords a striking proof of the development of which our husbandry is susceptible under the stimulus of a fair market for its products. Having, in the first part of this volume, given a sketch of its material progress, we will now confine our attention to its present position and future prospects.

Sheep-farming is dependent, with us, first on the fabrication of woollen tissues in the country, and secondly on the demand for our wool in foreign markets; it prospers only so long as its extension goes hand in hand with increased demand for this raw material of industry either at home or abroad; the moment that production gets ahead of this demand is also the moment at which the sheep-farming interest begins to languish.

Since the commencement of the present century, and especially since the peace, the increase of the woollen manufacture with a rapidity formerly unknown gave a strong impetus to the rearing of sheep, especially of the fine-woolled sorts. Formerly Spain and a small part of Germany were almost the only continental countries which furnished wool suitable for the manufacture of the finer fabrics; and, even for fabrics of medium quality, the production of the raw material being scarcely sufficient for the wants of the manufacturer, either in England or on the continent, the price of wool was maintained at a figure which insured a good profit to the sheep-farmer, at a time when many other agricultural products exhibited a tendency to fall. Such powerful encouragement drew the attention of agriculturists in every country to this department of husbandry; and, notwithstanding the enormous increase in flocks of sheep, the wool trade remained in a very satisfactory condition until the period, still recent, when the wools of Australia made their appearance, first in the markets of Great Britain, and subsequently in those of the continent. This competition becomes more and more threatening for the future prospects of the continental sheep-farmer; and we may form some idea of its extent from the quantities of wool imported into England. During the years 1839 to 1841 the quantity of wool imported into the United Kingdom from the whole English colonies amounted only to about 11,500,000 lbs., forming 21 per cent. of the total importation of that article; whilst during the period from 1846 to 1849 the mean importation from Australia alone amounted to 28,440,000 lbs., or more than 48 per cent. of the total quantity imported. The following was the progress of the importation during the latter period.

	Total Importation into United Kingdom. lbs.	Of which coming from Australia. lbs.	Proportion from Australia. per cent.
In 1846 -	65,255,000	21,789,000	33·4
,, 1847 -	62,593,000	26,057,000	41·6
,, 1848 -	70,865,000	30,034,000	42·4
,, 1849 -	76,769,000	35,879,000	46·7

Thus there was imported into England from Australia in 1849 more than thrice the quantity of wool which had been imported from the whole English possessions during the period from 1839 to 1841; and the wools from that source amounted to nearly the half of the entire quantity imported, whereas during the former period those from the whole British colonies had amounted to little more than a fifth. This is a prodigious increase for so short a space of time, and affords matter of serious reflection for all who are concerned in sheep-farming. It is becoming more and more probable that the importation of wool from the English colonies will so thoroughly invade the markets of the mother-country as to leave very little room for the wools of the continent, and that in the course of time they will formidably compete with the latter even in their own home markets: the wools of Australia are already finding their way into the markets of Germany.

Russia is one of those countries whose direct wool trade with England has most keenly felt the competition of Australia. This branch of commerce first began to acquire importance with us about 1830. Previously to then, the exportation, as we have already observed, amounted to only about 30,000 or 40,000 poods; since then it has amounted, without reckoning the exportation of Poland, to 842,000 poods: this was its culminating point, which it attained in 1844: from that date it followed a decreasing movement down to 1848, when it had fallen to 238,000 poods: in 1849 it rallied, the exportation of that year being 601,000 poods, of which two-fifths went to England; but the quantity retained there for home consumption during that year amounted only to 159,822 poods. On comparing the statistical tables of the four preceding years, 1845 to 1848, we perceive the importation of wools from Russia following a steadily decreasing movement. In 1845 it occupied in importance the third rank, and in 1848 it had descended to the seventh. The following are the figures:—

	Quantity imported from Russia. lbs.			Proportion of total Importation. per cent.
In 1845	-	8,709,000	- - -	11·3
„ 1846	-	4,766,000	- - -	7·3
„ 1847	-	2,950,000	- - -	4·7
„ 1848	-	2,349,000	- - -	3·3

In 1849 there were imported in all 76,768,647 lbs., of which 5,764,539 lbs., or 7½ per cent., were from Russia, so that the cipher, both absolute and relative, of our importation of wool into the British market during that year considerably exceeds that of the three preceding years, and attains nearly two-thirds of the importation of 1845. This sudden increase would be a very satisfactory symptom if it were to be supported, but it may have proceeded from temporary causes: in commerce a single year can never form a basis for the estimation of future probabilities. At any rate, the great and increasing preponderance of Australian wool in the English market is a fact about which there can be no doubt whatever; and, what is perhaps of more importance in a prospective point of view, is the appearance of wool from those distant regions in the continental markets, and especially in Germany. But, however this may be, we are far from losing all hope for the future for this important branch of our foreign commerce: on the contrary, we are persuaded that its fate will chiefly depend upon the care which may be applied to the rearing of our stock and the manipulation of our wools. If proprietors continue to direct their attention, as they have done hitherto, rather to increasing the numbers of their flocks than to the improvement of their breeds, and if the wool trade in the interior be allowed to remain upon its present unsatisfactory footing, we may indeed safely predict that our foreign wool trade will fall off more and more. It is notorious that the washing and assorting of the wool—operations of great importance—are, with a few laudable exceptions, performed amongst us with such consummate slovenliness as to be elsewhere unparalleled; and what is more, such is the ignorance and absurdity of some flock-masters, that they speculate on the increment of weight from dirt, and wash their sheep in muddy water in expectation that the fleece will thus bring in more money,—the fact being that the price offered by the merchant, who is quite alive to the trick, is in consequence so small, that the advantage redounds to him, and not to the farmer. In sorting the wool there is no separation made of the different parts of a fleece: sometimes the wool of dead animals is thrown in along with that shorn from the living one: and, for ordinary wools, the product of different breeds is mixed up together. This negligence is detrimental not only to the sale of our wools abroad, but also to the fabric of our home manufactured cloths, especially in regard to their dye. Their great want, next to equality and softness of texture, is pureness of dye. The latter defect is most manifest in light and lively colours—the shades being unequal and ·always presenting small spots, which is owing to the circumstance that ill-assorted wools do not equally absorb the colour. The fault disappears to a certain extent in black or very dark shades, which are more mordant. In the packing and transporting of the wool the negligence exhibited is as great as in every other department, and forms a striking contrast with the care bestowed upon these processes in foreign countries: the wool is often found to contain a mixture of heterogeneous trash, such as waste of straw and hay, fragments of torn bags, grain, husks, &c.: it is packed in coarse bags of bad quality, which are easily torn; and as the packing is bad and the bales are exposed to the weather during transport, nothing is easier than for humidity to penetrate.

On observing such gross carelessness, we cannot but be painfully struck with the difference which it exhibits from the well-organised routine of Germany and other countries, where there exists a healthy emulation amongst the larger flockmasters. Every one takes care to have his wool well washed and well sorted, well packed, and ticketed, and carefully protected from mixture. Every one endeavours to acquire a good character for his flock, and to maintain it: this causes the wool of the best producers to be in demand and always sure of finding purchasers: often the very name of the master inspires confidence, and makes his goods go off: amongst us very few flock-masters possess this advantage, and very few give themselves the trouble to deserve it. Accordingly, our foreign wool-trade is based not upon quality but upon cheapness: in the official estimates the value of wool exported during the years 1847, 1848, and 1849, amounts at an average to only 10 roubles 20 kopecks per pood ($= 10\frac{3}{4}d.$ per lb.), whilst the wool exported from the states of the German Zollverein is estimated in slump at 24 roubles per pood.

The rearing of fine-woolled sheep, which about thirty years ago was carried on but to a very trifling extent, has since then been proceeding so rapidly, that in 1846 the official statistics exhibited, as the number of merinos within the empire (including Poland), 8,300,000 head. In many of the flocks, however, the breed has degenerated in consequence of the bad selection of tups and for want of the proper crossings. These points require very continuous attention; for it has been proved by experience that even the best breeds lose a portion of their good qualities and their productive powers, if the necessary crossings are not timely undertaken. There are celebrated sheep-stocks in Silesia and Moravia where these precautions are observed with a degree of punctuality and order which, to the superficial observer, would appear uselessly minute. In this respect the establishments of Count Larich might serve as a model. The separation of the flocks into sections or families is strictly observed. The product of each animal is carefully controlled, weighed, and registered from generation to generation; and, as soon as it is perceived that the fleece is diminish-

ing in weight or deteriorating in quality, there is a change
made on the tup or the ewe according as the degeneracy is
manifested in the whole family or only in the progeny of some
ewes; and experience has proved that very frequently the same
tup and the same ewe, of which the progeny had begun to degenerate, have resumed their whole reproductive powers solely
by the effect of these crossings amongst families of the same
flock. We have to observe, that the stock subjected to this
careful régime consists, not of a small number of animals, but
of flocks of from 10,000 to 20,000 head.

The support of sheep-farms organised with such thorough
regularity as this, requires, no doubt, a large amount of care and
expense; but for these the results obtained afford a handsome
return. Of course such a perfect system is inapplicable to the
countless flocks which pasture on our steppes: but between a
system so refined on the one hand, and the negligence which
pervades the greater part of Russia on the other, there is surely
a broad margin for gradual improvement.

Deterioration of breeds has been manifested with us for some
time back, not only amongst the merinos, but also amongst the
indigenous breeds which furnish wool for our common cloths.
We possess several sorts of these common breeds, some of which
yield, as we have already mentioned, such coarse wool that it
can be used only for the manufacture of common felts, or in the
calking of ships; but there are also others of which the wool is
employed for several sorts of common cloths, and might be improved, at least up to a certain point, by judicious crossing and
more careful management, but which nevertheless go on deteriorating. Instead of being regenerated by copulations with
tups of a better breed, they are allowed to mix with races more
inferior still; and their pining nurture in winter, joined to the
inclemency of the seasons, likewise helps to make their wool
coarser. It has been observed that the wool of the common
steppe sheep, which are exposed without shelter to all the
inclemency of the atmosphere, becomes sensibly improved when
they are removed into the central or western provinces of the
empire, where they can be placed under shelter during a part
of the year.

The valuable work of M. Nebolsine on the foreign commerce
of Russia, published in 1850, contains, in regard to the rearing
of sheep—to their various breeds—and to the present condition
of our wool-trade, ideas both interesting and instructive, which
can scarcely be too often repeated, until they become the property of all who are interested in this important branch of
rural economy. Would that our sheep-farmers would lay to

heart the useful advice contained in this book, and turn it to account.

Observing that the fine-woolled sheep require a temperate climate, together with more care and better food than the common sheep, M. Nebolsine considers that there are but few parts of Russia in which these conditions are found combined; and that the southern provinces especially are but little propitious to the rearing of fine breeds, which are there very apt to degenerate, and yield but little wool. He attributes this deterioration to the bad food during winter, to the quality of the pastures in the steppes where the base is saline, to the want of good water, the frequent droughts, the heavy dews, and other circumstances peculiar to these countries. We are far from contesting the pernicious influence of any of these causes; but several of them are, as M. Nebolsine himself observes, purely local and peculiar to certain parts of the steppes. In these vast plains there are many districts abounding in good pasturage, and furnishing a sufficiency of winter food: we cannot then consider all the southern provinces of the empire as unsuitable for the rearing of fine-woolled sheep: the degeneracy of these breeds in the south of Russia, which is an ascertained fact, proceeds in great part, in our opinion, from the rapid and often inconsiderate extension of this branch of rural economy within the last twenty years. Encouraged by the good markets, many of the proprietors in these districts have augmented beyond bounds their stock of merinos, without calculating their means of supporting them during winter: others have introduced this breed into districts subject to all the disadvantages noted by M. Nebolsine: others, again, having an eye to quantity rather than to quality, have not paid sufficient attention to keeping the breed up to the mark—a matter demanding the most continuous care and attention; for the merino sheep, not being pure blood, readily degenerates unless this tendency be obviated in time by new crossings. We are therefore of opinion that its deterioration in the south of Russia does not proceed solely from disadvantages inherent in the soil and climate—disadvantages inherent only in certain portions of this vast country—but likewise, and probably in a greater degree, from want of care and foresight on the part of a number of our flock-masters. This is proved by the circumstance that those who manage their sheep-farms well, and avoid over-stocking, succeed in raising fine wool, which perfectly stands competition in the foreign market. If, again, these breeds have generally succeeded better in the Baltic provinces,—if they do not there degenerate, and if the wool which they furnish is larger in quantity and better in quality than in the south,—this, in our opinion, is owing less to the peculiar situation of these provinces, than to the system of management adopted, and the assiduity with which it is pursued: for the climate is cold, the soil of little natural fertility, and undoubtedly there are in Russia many other districts which are in this respect much more advantageously situated.

We agree entirely with M. Nebolsine in regard to the following points:—1. That the system pursued in the pasturing of large flocks of sheep in our steppes is in general little applicable to the rearing of fine-woolled animals, which requires an amount of care incompatible with the system in question; 2ndly. That the rearing of merinos has been practised in the south of Russia to an extent disproportioned to the demand for fine wool for home manufacture, and for any outlet which that article can find at present in foreign markets; 3rd. That our proprietors, especially those in the steppes, instead of augmenting their merino stock, ought in future to direct their attention rather to the rearing of sheep which yield wool suitable to the fabrication of ordinary stuffs of medium quality, which find an easier outlet in foreign commerce, and of which the prices have risen considerably during the last twenty or five-and-twenty years, whilst the price of fine wool has had a constant downward tendency[*]; lastly, That much more attention ought to be paid than has been paid hitherto to the rearing of common sheep with long combing wool, called in German *Kammwolle*, which serves for the manufacture of worsted fabrics that do not pass the fulling mill: this sort of wool would find a ready market both at home and abroad.

We have to add a single observation, which seems to us of some importance. It is notorious, as we have repeatedly had occasion to observe, that the frequent droughts which occur in the South of Russia, and especially in the countries of the steppes, form one of the greatest scourges of our agriculture in general, and of the rearing of domestic animals in particular. Of this we have lately had a melancholy example. In consequence of the want of forage occasioned by the bad hay-harvest of 1848, the mortality was so great amongst the finer breeds of sheep, that, according to the calculations of the Economical Society of Moscow, the total number of merinos throughout

---

[*] In 1825, fine wools sold, according to their quality, at from 26 to 60 paper roubles per pood, and from 1830 to 1840 they fetched only from 18 to 35 ; whilst common wools from the Bohemian breed of sheep which, in 1825, fetched only from 6 to 8 roubles, sold from 1830 to 1840 at from 8 to 17 roubles per pood ; so that the former fell, in the course of fifteen years (compared with the highest prices) in the proportion of 42 per cent., whilst the price of the latter rose in the proportion of 112 per cent. See M. Nebolsine's work on the Foreign Trade of Russia, vol. ii., p. 47.

Russia has fallen off about one-third. This is a sort of calamity to which no perfect remedy can be applied, because it proceeds from the climate and geographical position of a great part of the empire, and forethought alone can mitigate its deplorable results. The surest means towards this end would be to avoid too great an increase in the quantity of stock, to economise the forage in good years, and endeavour to have always in reserve at least several months' stock of aliment. This is especially necessary for the fine breeds, which do not stand bad food. We have more than one proof that such precautions are both possible and efficacious. We know proprietors possessing large stocks of merinos, who during the calamitous year 1849—having a reserve of forage—did not lose a single sheep from famine, whilst some of their neighbours lost two-thirds or three-fourths of their stock, and some did not even save a tenth: such are the natural consequences of over-stocking; for it is obvious that those who charge their land with as many sheep as they can contrive to pasture in a good year, leave nothing in reserve against the occurrence of a bad one.

It has been seen from the statistical data contained in the first part of this work, in what proportion the ovine race has augmented in Russia within the last twenty years. The number of sheep officially ascertained in European Russia, without reckoning Finland and the kingdom of Poland, amounted in 1846 to 41,654,000 head, of which about $7\frac{1}{2}$ millions were merinos. According to official data subsequently collected in eighteen governments * the number of fine-woolled sheep had augmented in these, during the two following years, by 555,000 head, or nearly 10 per cent.; in some other governments the number of merinos had fallen off, but not in any thing like the same proportion; so that we may safely assume that in 1848 the total number of sheep of this breed must have amounted to fully 8 millions. Deducting, according to the estimate of the Economical Society of Moscow, for the losses of 1849, about a third, or 2,600,000 head—a fourth of which must have been made up by the reproduction of 1850—we may estimate the present number of fine-woolled sheep at about 6,000,000 head.

In Germany, in the statistical estimates of the production of wool, there is reckoned at an average 22 lbs. for 10 sheep † = 2·69 lbs. Russian per fleece. In Russia the calculation is 4 lbs.

* These governments, arranged in the order of their importance in regard to merinos, are Tauride, Poltawa, Kherson, Kharkow, Woronèje, Kiew, Grodno, Tschernigow, Esthonia, Mohilew, Wilna, Orenburg, Toula, Courland, Kowno, Astrakhan, Kalouga, and St. Petersburg.

† See Dieterici, *Statistische Uebersicht*, part ii., p. 348.

per fleece for the native breeds, which can be admitted only for very common animals of a very large size. M. Nebolsine reckons for the south-raised merinos $2\frac{3}{4}$ lbs. per fleece washed on the living animal. He considers this quantity very small, and infers from its smallness the degeneration of the breed in these countries. But if this calculation were correct, it would prove rather the contrary; for in Silesia, on the best sheep farms, the yield is not more than $1\frac{1}{4}$ or $1\frac{1}{2}$ lbs. Viennese $= 1\cdot71$ or $2\cdot05$ lbs. Russian, per fleece, lambs included. The stock of Count Larisch, which bears the highest character for the quality and richness of its fleeces, yields only $1\frac{3}{4}$ to 2 lbs. Viennese $= 2\cdot39$ to $2\cdot74$ lbs. Russian. It is then more than probable that either M. Nebolsine's figure is erroneous, or else that the wool is so badly washed with us that the waste which it contains adds very considerably to its weight. The latter supposition is confirmed by what we find stated in M. Nebolsine's work with regard to the negligent manner in which the washing is performed. For these reasons, and in conformity with the statistical estimates adopted in Germany as the result of long experience, we do not think we can reckon for the production of wools in Russia more than $2\frac{3}{4}$ lbs. per fleece without distinction of breeds, which, for the number of animals officially ascertained in 1846, namely 41,654,000 head, would give a production of 2,863,700 poods. But we must here repeat the observation already made, that in Russia the statistics of domestic animals are still very incomplete — that the official are almost always far below the actual numbers — and that we will be very safe in adding for the latter ten per cent. to the former; this would bring the total number of sheep, for 1846, in European Russia, exclusive of Finland and the kingdom of Poland, to 45,820,000, and the quantity of wool to 3,150,125 poods, or, for a population of 55 millions, $2\cdot29$ lbs. Russian per head. Deducting from this quantity about 500,000 poods for that year's exportation, there would remain for home consumption 2,650,125 poods, or $1\cdot93$ lbs. Russian per head.

In the states of the German Zollverein the production of native wool was estimated in 1842 at 48,315,419 lbs. $= 59,087,757$ lbs. Russian, which gives for the population of that epoch ($27\frac{1}{2}$ millions) $1\cdot76$ lbs. $= 2\cdot15$ lbs. Russian per head. Adding the excess of importation over exportation of wool (2,113,100 lbs.) the consumption of this article in these states amounted to $1\cdot84$ lbs. $= 2\cdot25$ lbs. Russian per head.

In Austria there were reckoned in 1846, according to official estimates, 34,500,000 sheep, including ewes, wedders, tups, and lambs, which, reckoning $2\frac{3}{4}$ lbs. Russian per fleece, supposes a production of 94,875,000 lbs., being, for a population of 36 millions (in 1846) at the rate of 2·64 lbs. Russian per inhabitant. Deducting the excess of exportation, which amounted to 36,131 quintals = 4,946,000 lbs. Russian, there remained for home consumption 89,929,000 lbs. Russian, or 2·5 lbs. per head. Thus, the relative production of wool in Russia, compared to the population, exceeds that of the Zollverein in the proportion of 10 to 9, and is to that of Austria as 10 to 11½; and the consumption per head is to that of the Zollverein nearly as 10 to 12, and to that of Austria as 10 to 13.

It might be supposed that owing to the severity of our climate, which necessitates a large supply of warm clothing, the consumption of wool ought to be much greater in Russia than in Germany; but there are other circumstances which modify this influence. In Germany the peasants generally wear cloth garments, winter and summer; their habiliments are more complete; and they change them more frequently: in Russia, especially in the northern provinces, the peasants wear in winter a sort of great coat of sheep-skin, which lasts for several years, and often forms, along with a pair of coarse pantaloons, their sole garment. In other districts their only habiliment consists of a sort of cassock or *bourka* of felt or some other very coarse fabric, which lasts equally long: in summer they generally wear a calico blouse, and a pair of coarse canvass pantaloons: thus our production of wool, although moderate enough in comparison with the population and the severity of the climate, exceeds what is requisite for home consumption; and this excess is principally upon the finer sorts. M. Nebolsine's work contains, according to a more or less approximative calculation, the following data with respect to the consumption of wool in the home manufacture: laying out of account the manufacture of coarse fabrics for the use of the peasantry, the home manufactures consume about 300,000 poods of common wool for clothing the army, and as much fine or improved wool for the manufacture of all other fabrics, in all 600,000 poods, that is to say, less than three-fourths of the quantity exported, which in 1844 amounted to 840,000 poods. M. Nebolsine approximatively estimates the production of improved wools at 800,000 poods; and as he estimates the quantity of wool of this description worked up in the home factories at no more than 300,000 poods, he takes the excess of production at 500,000 poods: this excess has no other outlet than the foreign market. Without wishing to contest the correctness of this calculation, which the author himself regards as merely approximative, we may be permitted to observe that the quantity of 800,000 poods appears too high for the production of improved wools, if M. Nebolsine comprehends under that term merino wool alone. We have seen, that according to the most recent calculations, the total number of merinos in European Russia, exclusive of Finland and the kingdom of Poland, might be estimated at about 8 million heads in 1848; and the experience of other countries shows us that we cannot reckon on an average, including ewes and wedders, tups and lambs, more than $2\frac{1}{2}$ lbs. Russian per fleece, which for 8 million head would give only 500,000 poods. Even, therefore, if native wool should form as much as one-half of the 300,000 poods worked up, according to M. Nebolsine, in the home factories in the manufacture of fabrics of fine and middling qualities, there would remain for exportation, of merino wool, only 350,000 poods. This calculation is justified moreover by the figures of our actual exports, and by the valuation in the custom-house registers founded on the prices current. There was exported in all during the triennial period from 1847 to 1849, the quantity of 1,275,262 poods, representing, at the official estimate, a value of 12,947,595 roubles, or, at an annual average, 425,087 poods, worth 4,315,865 silver roubles, which gives an average price of 10 roubles 15 kopecks per pood. In the total of this triennial exportation the inferior qualities figured in the following proportions:

	Poods.	Per cent. of total Exportation.
Wools exported by the Baltic ports, valued at 9 roubles 2 kopecks per pood - - -	84,714	$6\frac{2}{3}$
Wools exported by dry frontier, valued at 7 roubles 45 kopecks per pood - - - -	311,258	$24\frac{1}{2}$
Wools exported by same frontier, valued at 5 roubles 22 kopecks per pood - - -	60,424	$4\frac{3}{4}$
Wools exported by the Asiatic frontier, valued at 2 roubles 33 kopecks per pood - -	8,027	$\frac{2}{3}$

We perceive from these figures that the wools of inferior quality, below the price of 10 roubles, figure for more than 36 per cent. of the total exportation, which reduces the exportation of wools valued at 10 roubles and upwards to 810,838 poods, or 270,279 poods per annum. It is the wools exported by the ports of the Black Sea and the Sea of Azow which present the highest prices in the official estimates. The quantities exported in this way during the years 1847, 1848, and 1849, amounted to 757,973 poods, representing a value of 8,977,828 roubles, which gives as the average price of a pood 11 roubles 84 kopecks. This price is still very moderate compared to that of foreign markets. The wools exported from Germany are valued in the statistical estimates at 24 roubles per pood. At Breslau, one of the principal wool markets, the prices of fine and medium wools vary between 50 and 125 thalers per quintal = 15 to $37\frac{1}{2}$ roubles per pood. The exportation by the ports of the Black Sea and the Sea of Azow during the three years from 1847 to 1849, gives an average of 252,658 poods, representing a value of 2,992,609 roubles, and forms nearly 60 per cent. of the total quantity exported during that period. In consequence of the great mortality of fine-woolled sheep during the year 1849, the total number of that breed must now be reduced to 6,000,000, which, at the rate of $2\frac{3}{4}$ lbs. per fleece, would yield 375,000 poods of washed wool. If we admit, agreeably to the foregoing calculations, that 150,000 poods are employed in the home manufacture, there remain only 225,000 poods of fine wool for exportation. Still, it is an incontestable fact that this trade is an important one for us, and that its complete decay would be very severely felt, especially by our southern provinces, to whose prosperity it would deal a heavy blow. The increasing competition in regard to this article, with which we will henceforth have to struggle in foreign markets, ought to stimulate our flock-masters to more care and exertion, that they may prevent the quality of their stock from falling off, and have their wools better washed and assorted. We are persuaded that, in spite of all the inconveniences arising from climate and other local circumstances, our wools, from the lowness of their price, will not be evicted from foreign markets; and that their exportation may even augment in the course of time, notwithstanding Australian competition, if the germs of the decline of this trade, namely, the carelessness of stockmasters on the one hand, and the vicious manner in which its home department is carried on upon the other, were to be stifled. These causes of decline are more fully entered into in the work of M. Nebolsine.

Nothing, in our opinion, could exert a more favourable influence upon the improvement of the breeds than well organised associations of proprietors and merchants, established with the view of introducing more regularity into this branch of business, and in particular the necessary improvements in the way of washing and assortment. The society of wool-growers established at Moscow, and the joint-stock company founded at Kharkow, are already doing something in this way; but their means are still too limited to warrant the expectation of great results. Still, it is a step in the right direction, and may lead to future improvements. The special object of the Kharkow joint-stock company is to keep up the price of wool by making advances to producers on the security of their goods when the trade is in a state of stagnation.

The following figures derived from custom-house returns for the years 1847, 1848, and 1849, indicate the direction of our wool trade during that period.

Countries to which exported.	Quantity exported during Three Years. *Poods.*	Proportion of total Exportation. *per cent.*
Great Britain - -	429,477	33·7
Austria - - -	372,562	29·2
France - - -	144,062	11·3
Prussia - - -	76,005	6
Turkey - - -	72,602	5·7
Belgium - - -	68,859	5·4
All other countries - -	111,695	8·7
Total	1,275,262	

According to the official estimates, the finest wools are exported to France and Belgium, and the commonest sorts to Turkey and Austria.

The prices are:

		Roubles.	Kopecks.
For the wools exported to Belgium - -	19	
,, ,, France - -	13	
,, ,, England - -	11	40
,, ,, Prussia - -	9	36
,, ,, Austria - -	7	
,, ,, Turkey - -	3	56

As regards the importance of this commerce, the countries which have the largest share of it are England, Austria, and France. It appears from the preceding figures that the wool exported to these three countries during the above period amounted to three-fourths of the entire quantity exported. The trade with England is still the most important, for it absorbs a third of the total export; but it has the drawn sword of Australian competition hanging over its head: the trade with Austria, which comes next in point of importance, may gain in extension in consequence of the reduction of import duty adopted in the new tariff: the trade with France might be much more important if the import duties in that country were not so high, namely, 20 per cent. upon uncombed, and 30 per cent. upon combed wools,—an exorbitant duty on a raw material which plays such an important part in the national industry; but it seems impossible that an import system so superannuated, and the defects of which are so generally recognised, can be maintained much longer; and it is more than probable that the French tariff, which is now the highest and most prohibitive in the world, will soon undergo some reforms, the first of which will, no doubt, be the exemption of raw materials. The trade with Prussia, which comes fourth in order, has for some years back been decreasing: the exportation to that country, which amounted during the triennium 1841-43 to 171,700 poods, had fallen during the triennium 1847-49 to 76,000. The rearing of sheep has of late been greatly extended in almost all the states of the Zollverein, which themselves export 100,000 to 150,000 quintals of wool: still, the production of this article does not suffice for their own internal consumption, for their importation of wool usually exceeds their exportation: in the year 1849 this excess amounted to 40,998 quintals = 123,351 poods. The trade with Turkey is increasing: it augmented during the years 1847-49 in the proportion of 2 to 5; but it is only for very coarse wools that it holds out a prospect. The fine wool trade with Belgium seems capable of coming to something in the course of time, considering the immense progress of the woollen manufacture in that country, and the low price at which we are able to furnish it with the raw material.

Although we have already in the general table of the agricultural situation of European Russia (page 187.) exhibited the numerical relation between the number of domestic animals and the population of each province, we do not think there will be any harm in reproducing here the result of this calculation as regards sheep alone, arranging the governments inthe order of the relative number of these animals contained in them respectively.

	Number of Sheep to 100 Inhabitants.			Number of Sheep to 100 Inhabitants.
1. Astrakhan	392	26. Wiatka		48
2. Tauride	367	27. Kiew		48
3. Country of the Don Cossacks	305	28. Esthonia		47
4. Ekathérinoslaw	207	29. Kalouga		46
5. Kherson	177	30. Jaroslaw		46
6. Simbirsk	176	31. Koursk		45
7. Bessarabia	160	32. Tschernigow		45
8. Saratow	156	33. Toula		45
9. Kharkow	124	34. Perm		44
10. Stavropol	118	35. Podolia		43
11. Orenburg	111	36. Nijni-Nowgorod		43
12. Woronèje	102	37. Kowno		42
13. Poltawa	101	38. Archangel		40
14. Wolhynia	67	39. Wladimir		34
15. Orel	67	40. Twer		32
16. Kingdom of Poland	66	41. Minsk		31
17. Grodno	58	42. Livonia		31
18. Penza	57	43. Wilna		31
19. Tambow	55	44. Courland		31
20. Kazan	55	45. Olonetz		27
21. Riazan	55	46. Nowgorod		23
22. Mohilew	55	47. Moscow		22
23. Kostroma	54	48. Pskow		14
24. Smolensk	52	49. Witebsk		12
25. Wologda	50	50. St. Petersburg		5

We perceive from this table the disproportions which exist between the different provinces in regard to the number of sheep contained in them. The difference between the two extremities of the scale is as 1 to 78. These disproportions are explained in part by climate and local circumstances (as relative extent and quality of meadows and pastures), and in part by the greater or smaller number of large proprietors who have the means of supporting numerous flocks. The thirteen governments which figure at the head of the table belong partly to the country of the steppes, which abound in meadows and pastures, and partly to the eminently fertile region of black humus. In all these the number of sheep exceeds the cipher of the population. In each of the four first, there are more than 2, and in the governments of Astrakhan and the Tauride there are nearly 4 sheep to 1 inhabitant. The governments where the relative number of those animals is smallest are mostly countries in which meadows and good pasture lands are scarce; in the governments of Moscow and St. Petersburg the small relative number of sheep is explained by the large population of the two capitals. The governments in which the ovine race exists in largest numbers are precisely those in which its proper rearing is most neglected. No doubt, the more numerous that flocks become, the more difficult does it become to bestow upon them the necessary amount of care and attention. The abundance of summer pasture leads the proprietors to augment the number of their stock beyond what they are able to support during a severe or premature winter; and the want of sufficient food causes a deterioration of the breed and in the quality of the wool. This difficulty of alimenting is aggravated in the south of Russia by the frequent droughts. The common native sheep of the steppe countries supports pretty well the privation of good food; but this privation tells very severely on the fine breeds, which dwindle and degenerate if the forage with which they are supplied during winter is not good enough to replace, at least to a certain point, the substantial nourishment of good pasture land.

In mild and temperate climates the rearing of sheep depends entirely on the extent and quality of the pasture. Thus, for example, in Austria, we see that the poorest province in regard to productive soil, Dalmatia, the arable land of which does not occupy more than 11 per cent. of the whole area, and which is almost entirely destitute of meadow land, possesses a comparatively larger number of sheep than any other province of the monarchy. But in countries in which the winters are long and severe, it is impossible to maintain very large stocks without exposing them,—especially the finer breeds,—to great and frequent losses, unless there be a well-secured supply of fodder for the whole period that they are unable to remain at pasture. This is a fact which our proprietors seem constantly to forget.

IV. *Swine.*

We have already seen, that the rearing of swine is carried on in Russia to a considerable extent, the relative number of these animals to the population being nearly the same as in Austria, and much larger than in Prussia and France; but it is still greatly behind what it might be, considering our means of feeding them. In general our agriculturists bestow too little care on this department, although it is very profitable and very suitable to the country. It is especially neglected in the provinces of New Russia, where, in the opinion of M. Skalkowski*, they might raise ten times the quantity of pigs now reared. It results from statistical data published by this economist that in the governments of Kherson, Ekathérinoslaw, Tauride, and Bessarabia, the number of these animals has scarcely augmented in the course of forty or fifty years, notwithstanding the encouraging example of the German colonists, who derive great profits from this source. As a proof of the negligence with which they are treated in some districts, we cite the following observation from M. Haxthausen during his sojourn in the government of Nijni-Nowgorod. "We have seen herds of long-bristled swine wandering about in the forests during summer, like deer, without the least superintendence. In autumn they catch as many as they can, and make an equal distribution of them amongst all the families of the village, so that in regard to these animals there is no distinction of individual property."

When we consider what large quantities of swine have for some time past been sent from Hungary and Servia by railway to Hamburg, and thence to England, notwithstanding the enormous expenses of such a long inland journey, we may conceive the importance which this trade might attain in a very short time in those provinces of Russia which are not remote from the sea coast; and it is to be hoped that our agricultural population and our capitalists will not long remain indifferent to such encouraging examples.

* See the article of this economist on the rearing of domestic animals in New Russia, *Journal du Ministère de l'Intérieur* (*livraison* of July, 1850).

Culture of Meadows and of Fodder Plants.

Under the three-field system which prevails in the greater part of Russia, and under the difficulties which attend the transition from this to a more rational system of husbandry, the cultivation of fodder-plants must necessarily have been with us very limited hitherto. Still, the necessity of having recourse to this subsidiary source of aliment has been felt. In the Baltic governments it has been pretty generally adopted; in many other districts the proprietors are beginning to alternate this culture with that of cereals; and in some it is getting gradually introduced amongst the peasants, especially in the vicinity of St. Petersburg, in some of the central and northern governments, and amongst the colonists of New Russia. In the Report by the Department of Rural Economy to the Ministry of Domains published in 1849, it is stated, amongst other proofs of the progress of this culture, that in Courland there were reaped, in 1847, upon 40 estates belonging to the crown and 108 belonging to private proprietors, 604,000 poods of hay, from artificial meadows;—that in the government of St. Petersburg, in which a few years before the peasants had not paid the slightest attention to this species of culture, they sold in 1846 more than 65,000 poods of hay, and in 1847 and 1848 more than 86,000, in like manner proceeding from artificial meadows;—that during the last ten years, from a single depôt of fodder-plant seeds established by the Agronomic Society of Moscow, there was sold of these to the value of 75,000 silver roubles. The Ministry of Domains encourages this culture by premiums, by the distribution of seeds amongst the peasants, and by introducing the system into some farms belonging to the state. Upon one farm in the government of Tambow the experiment was made of sowing rye and oats to be cut as fodder, and there was obtained from the former 340 and from the latter 160 poods of hay per dessiatine. However satisfactory these beginnings may be, the system of artificial meadows can play but a secondary part in the present condition of our agriculture. In the south of Russia, and even in several of the central governments, the climate is unsuitable for it in consequence of the frequent droughts; and in the more fertile districts the fodder-plants, requiring a clayey soil, rarely succeed well upon the black humus (*tschernozième*).

Much more valuable results might be obtained by the improvement of our natural meadows. We have already seen that Russia, taken as a whole, is in nowise deficient in meadow land,—12 per cent. of her total area (a larger proportion than is the case in France or Austria) being occupied in this manner, and the extent of meadow to cultivable land being as 2 to 3, whilst in Austria the proportion is about 2 to 7 ; in Prussia, about 3 to 10 ; and in France, about 2 to 9. Still, there are some governments in which the meadows do not occupy above 1 or 2 per cent. of the area, or even less, and others in which they stand to the extent of cultivable land in the proportion of no more than 1 to 10 or less. Besides this inequality of distribution, the scantiness of the hay harvest is a frequent cause of the scarcity of fodder ; in some districts the mean produce per dessiatine does not exceed, or perhaps amount to, from 40 to 60 poods, whilst in France it is 167, and in Austria 120. This shows the necessity of attending to the improvement of our natural meadows, and the important consequences which might result from it. We may pretty safely assume that by the general introduction of improvements adapted to local circumstances, the present hay harvest might be augmented by at least 50 per cent., and this would add a value of 180 millions of roubles to the gross value of our agriculture (see calculations *antè*, p. 155.). There are, no doubt, many portions of the empire, as, for example, the country of the Don Cossacks and the governments of Stavropol, Saratow, Orenburg, Tauride, Kherson, and Bessarabia, which possess a superabundance of fodder, and in which, consequently, meadow culture does not, under existing circumstances, present itself as a measure of general utility,—though even in these districts a deficiency of fodder not unfrequently results from drought; but there are many others in which an improved system of meadow culture is an indispensable condition to the progress of cattle-rearing.

In the present state of our rural economy it is not easy, especially for the peasants, to improve the meadow land by the application of labour and manure; improvement of this sort can be but rare and exceptional. But great results might be anticipated from draining and irrigation. Hitherto it has been only in the Baltic provinces,—and in these it has been only within the last ten years,—that these two processes have been undertaken and regularly carried out. In irrigated meadows the harvest amounts to 260 or 270, and in some cases to as much as 700 poods of hay per dessiatine; the rent has quintupled; and the capital expended in the improvements has been returned in from two to four years. Yet those examples, notwithstanding such astonishing results, have not hitherto found many imitators even in the neighbouring provinces, whilst in the other parts of the empire there have been but a few partial attempts in this direction, some of them not of recent date. It is to be hoped that the measures taken by government for the encouragement of this branch of rural economy will bring forth fruits in their season. The Scientific Committee of the Ministry of Domains occupied itself upon this question from the first years of its organisation, and made the amelioration of meadow culture one of the earliest subjects of a prize-essay. Several treatises upon the same subject appeared in the journal of this ministry and in the *Gazette Agronomique.* Agents were sent abroad to acquire the necessary information in regard to the best systems of drainage and irrigation—to examine the works of this nature which had been executed in the Baltic provinces, and the arrangements used for irrigation in the horticultural establishments of the Crimea—and to select in the different governments the districts most suitable for works of the sort. More favourable terms for working the lands belonging to the state domains are granted to those farmers who undertake to irrigate them; and amongst other encouragements we must not forget to cite that of freedom from military service,—a privilege enjoyed by the pupils who successfully pass through a course of special study upon this subject at the Agronomic School of Livonia.

This brief outline of the measures taken by government to encourage the improvement of meadow culture shows the high importance which it attaches to this branch of rural affairs.

Culture of Flax and Hemp.

Next to the culture of cereals and the rearing of domestic animals, the culture of flax and hemp, both as textile plants and as oleaginous grains, is the most important branch of Russian husbandry. The gross value of these products amounts, at a very moderate estimate, to about 55½ millions of silver roubles, (8,700,000*l.* sterling); and both soil and climate are exceedingly favourable to their culture throughout a great part of the empire. As their production greatly exceeds the wants of the home manufacture, the extension of their culture essentially depends on the facility with which they find an outlet in the foreign market. Flax and hemp have always formed two of our principal exports; and if to these we add oleaginous grains — a product depending on the two former—we will find that the export of these three articles taken as a whole exceeds in value that of any other article. In the course of twenty-nine years, from 1822 to 1850 inclusive, there were but four, namely, 1830, 1831, 1846, and 1847, in which the value of exported cereals was greater than that of these.

From the custom-house returns we find that during the period in question the total value of exports for European commerce amounted to 1,903,448,300 silver roubles; of which,—

Flax - - -	S. R. 243,482,000 or 12·8 per cent.
Hemp - - -	195,031,000 or 10·2 „
Oleaginous grains * -	163,991,000 or 8·6 „
The 3 articles together -	602,504,000 or 31·6 „

These figures sufficiently show the importance of the culture of textile plants for our foreign commerce. In this branch we have hitherto met with no serious competition. The other countries of the European continent in which these articles are cultivated not having much land to spare for that purpose, and finding it, from their greater relative population, more profitable to cultivate corn and potatoes, do not raise enough for any considerable exportation; nowhere in Europe can they be raised in such abundance or so cheaply as in Russia. Of extra-European countries, it is the East Indies that furnish the largest supplies,—200,000 to 250,000 English cwt. The exportation from the United States—25,000 to 30,000 cwt. of hemp—is insignificant.

In his work on the foreign commerce of Russia, M. Nebolsine estimates the exportation of flax and hemp from all countries of their production at 9,300,000 poods, distributed as follows:

Russia	-	-	-	-	6,600,000
States of the German Zollverein†			-		350,000
Austria	-	-	-	-	200,000
Holland and Belgium -		-		-	850,000
France	-	-	-	-	160,000
Italy -	-	-	-	•	500,000
East Indies	-	-	-	-	400,000
Philippine Islands		-		-	240,000
		Total	-	-	9,300,000

Thus our flax and hemp composed more than two-thirds of the whole.

But there are, in the above estimate, a few figures to correct. The exportation from the East Indies is at least double what is here given. England alone imported from thence for her own consumption during the five years 1845—1849, 1,272,000 cwt., which gives an annual average of 254,400 cwt. = 789,900 poods. England, moreover, imports about 300,000 poods of flax and hemp from Egypt and the English possessions in Africa, and about 90,000 poods of hemp from the United States of America, which are not included in the above estimate,

* This exportation consists almost entirely of lint-seed, and a very small quantity of hemp-seed. The other sorts of oleaginous grains do not exceed 2 per cent.

† These states export 500,000 to 600,000 poods of flax and hemp; but nearly the half of this is Russian produce shipped at Prussian ports.

so that we may reckon the total exportation of these articles from the countries of production at about 10,300,000 poods, of which Russia exports 64 per cent., or somewhat more than three-fifths.

The imports of flax and hemp into England amounted during the quinquennial period 1845—49 to 11,421,811 cwt., of which 7,659,394 cwt., or 68·4 per cent., were from Russia. The annual imports during the period in question were as follows:

	Total Importation. cwt.	Importation from Russia. cwt.	Proportion per cent.
In 1845 -	2,350,173	1,462,913	62·2
„ 1846 -	2,029,986	1,361,052	67
„ 1847 -	1,863,654	1,224,024	65·7
„ 1848 -	2,309,432	1,622,132	70·2
„ 1849 -	2,868,566	1,989,273	69·4
Total -	11,421,811	7,659,394	68·4*

We perceive from these figures, derived from official sources, that the imports from Russia exceed those from all other countries put together, and that in the commerce of those articles we enjoy a great and increasing preeminence in the British market. Our general exportation of them is also rapidly and steadily increasing. The following is the average annual exportation given by quinquennial periods:

			Flax. Poods.	Hemp. Poods.	Total.
From	1822 to 1826	-	1,906,641	2,938,673	4,845,314
„	1827 „ 1831	-	2,539,978	2,526,095	5,066,073
„	1832 „ 1836	-	2,499,922	3,065,420	5,565,342
„	1837 „ 1841	-	3,125,507	3,260,817	6,386,324
„	1842 „ 1846	-	3,663,766	2,802,419	6,466,175
Quadrennium	1847 „ 1850	-	4,616,755	2,819,781	7,436,536

Thus, in the space of twenty-nine years, the export of flax has augmented in the proportion of 242 to 100, that of hemp has declined about 4 per cent., and that of the two together has increased 53½ per cent.

The export of our flax and hemp taken together during the quinquennial period 1846—1850 was distributed amongst the countries of destination as follows:

				Poods.	Per cent.
To Great Britain	-	-		21,909,197	61·3
„ France	-	-	-	2,696,225	7·5
„ Denmark	-	-	-	1,553,916	4·3
„ Prussia	-	-	-	1,458,810	4·1
„ Sweden and Norway	-	-		1,113,722	3·1
„ Spain and Portugal	-	-		731,118	2

* Without reckoning the Russian produce shipped at Prussian ports, which figure as imports from Germany.

			Poods.	Per cent.
To Netherlands	-	-	608,223	1·7
„ Belgium	-	-	374,547	1·1
„ United States	-	-	351,419	1
„ Other countries	-	-	4,959,399	13·9*

Thus it is in England that we find a market for these two articles to the extent of three-fifths of the entire quantity exported, without reckoning the quantities exported to that country by the foreign Baltic ports and by Elsineur,—a fact which proves that the progress of this branch of commerce, so important for our agriculture, depends essentially upon the quantity which England may be able to consume for its various industrial wants. It may therefore, perhaps, not be superfluous to inquire a little into the chances which this market holds out for the future.

It is well known that the immense increase in the use of cotton fabrics was of the utmost prejudice to the linen manufacture in every country of Europe; whilst the cotton manufacture assumed gigantic proportions, the fabrication of linens was arrested in its progress, and in many countries fell into a state of decay. England alone formed an exception,—a circumstance which she owed to the invention of flax-spinning machinery. With its characteristic enterprise and foresight, English industry, seconded by abundance of capital, speedily appropriated and improved the French invention; and, applying it upon a large scale, it succeeded in turning the depressed condition of the linen manufacture in other countries to its own advantage. English linens, which thirty years ago were an article of secondary importance in the markets of the European continent and in most transatlantic countries, have since acquired an importance menacing for the linen industry of Germany and of every other country. During the triennial period, 1827-29, the average annual export of linen manufactures from Great Britain amounted to 57,706,125 English yards, representing a value of 2,043,745l. sterling; and during the period 1847-49, the mean annual export amounted to 96,530,308 yards, representing a value of 2,855,402l. sterling, which exhibits an increase of 67 per cent. in quantity and 40 per cent. in value. In 1850 the exportation amounted to the enormous quantity of 122,397,457 yards, or double the mean exportation of the triennium 1827-29; and this immense exportation from England followed the largest exportation of flax from Russia that ever

* Of this quantity, 4,219,280 poods, or nearly 12 per cent. of the whole quantity exported, were shipped "for the Sound," without farther designation. These shipments are despatched to Elsineur, where they receive their final destination, which is usually England.

took place, namely, that of 1849, which amounted to 5,323,409 poods (tow included); of which there were sent to England 3,700,097 poods, or 70 per cent., without reckoning the exportation thither by way of Elsineur and the Prussian ports; so that our exportation to Great Britain may be taken at upwards of three-fourths of the whole. This important branch of our commerce has generally followed step by step the progress of the linen manufacture in England, and it has more than tripled since 1822. The average of the three years 1822-24 was only 1,575,632 poods, whilst that of 1848-50 amounted to 4,809,296 poods, being an increase of 205 per cent., which corresponds with the increased exportation of English and Irish linens.

During the quinquennial period 1845-49, there were imported into England for home consumption 6,887,838 cwt. of flax, tow included, of which 4,719,257 cwt., or 68½ per cent., came direct from Russia; and, if to this quantity we add what arrives through foreign ports, we may admit that three-fourths of the flax imported into England comes, directly or indirectly, from Russia. The following was the annual importation during the period in question: —

	Total Importation. cwt.	Importation from Russia. cwt.	Proportion per cent.
In 1845 -	1,418,323	859,627	66·3
„ 1846 -	1,147,092	740,396	64·6
„ 1847 -	1,052,089	681,167	64·7
„ 1848 -	1,463,661	1,085,732	74·2
„ 1849 -	1,806,673	1,352,335	74·9
Total -	6,887,838	4,719,257	68·5

The only competition of any importance which we have in that country is the flax imported from Germany, Holland, Belgium, and Egypt: the importation from these countries during the above-mentioned quinquennium was as follows: —

	Cwt.	Per cent.
From Prussia and other German countries -	837,141	12
[About half of this comes from Russia]		
„ Holland - - - - -	527,545	7¾
„ Belgium - - - - -	234,956	4½
„ Egypt - - - - -	318,500	5⅓

But it is to be observed that the Dutch and Belgian flax is much dearer than ours, and is employed only in the manufacture of very fine fabrics, whilst the Egyptian flax is inferior to the most ordinary Russian sorts.

All this goes to prove that the linen manufacture of England and the flax-culture of Russia are intimately dependent upon each other. The former could not maintain, and still less

increase, its present prosperity without being sure of receiving
from us an abundant supply of the raw material at a very
moderate price; and we, on the other hand, would be at a loss
for the disposal of our surplus produce, if we were not assured
of an outlet in the British market.

Some parties are of opinion that the progress of flax-culture
in Ireland may one day close the markets of Great Britain
against us. Without quite participating in this opinion, we
consider it at any rate worth examination. It is certain that
the soil and climate of Ireland are well adapted to this culture,
and that, seconded latterly by a return of favourable circumstances, it has of late been making rapid progress. In a country
so thickly peopled (about 4,300 inhabitants to the geographical
square mile) the culture of esculent products required for home
consumption must in the general case leave but a limited
amount of land available for the culture of flax. Accordingly,
down to 1840, the latter occupied no more than 83,000 acres;
and in 1848, in consequence of the fall in the price of linen
yarn, the quantity of land employed in this culture had fallen
to 53,000 acres: but the fall in the price of grain which accompanied the reform of the import duties, together with the potato
disease brought about, from the last-mentioned year, a change
in the rural economy of Ireland favourable to flax-culture; and
accordingly, in 1850, the quantity of land under flax amounted
to 140,000 acres, producing at an average 16 poods ($=5\cdot14$ cwt.)
per acre, which gives a total production of 2,240,000 poods
($=720,000$ cwt.). During the triennial period 1847—49,
when Ireland produced from about 60,000 acres 960,000 poods
($=308,500$ cwt.) of flax, the mean annual importation of this
article into the United Kingdom amounted to 2,350,000 cwt.
$=7,285,000$ poods. Now, to replace that quantity, there
would require to be devoted to the culture of flax, at the rate
of 16 poods ($5\cdot14$ cwt.) per acre, 455,000 acres. This, added to
the 60,000 acres already employed in this culture in 1849,
would give for that purpose a total extent of 515,000 acres, so
that to the 140,000 acres now under flax there would require
to be added 375,000 more. Ireland has an extent of about
1500 geographical square miles: assuming the arable land to
occupy about 40 per cent. of the entire area, or 600 square
miles $=8,150,000$ acres, the culture of flax, carried to the
extent of 515,000 acres, would occupy nearly $6\frac{1}{2}$ per cent. of
the whole extent of arable land. But we scarcely know any
country in which so large a proportion of land is thus occupied;
and at any rate the proportion would be exceedingly high in a
country reckoning only 8,150,000 arable acres for a population

of $6\frac{1}{2}$ millions of inhabitants *, which does not allow more than
1·25 acres per head.   Nor must it be forgotten that the higher
value of land in Ireland must always render the cost of production higher there than in Russia,—a circumstance that must
render our competition easier.   But however this may be, the
rapid extension of the culture of flax during the last three years
in that part of Great Britain, where it occupies an area almost
thrice as large as in 1848, is unquestionably a fact worthy the
attention of our agriculturists.   Hitherto, however, there seems
to be little cause for alarm.   During the quinquennial period
1846—50 our exportation was as follows:—

In 1846	-	-	-	3,182,266 poods
„ 1847	-	-	-	3,038,834 „
„ 1848	-	-	-	4,150,200 „
	Total of the three years			10,371,300 „
	Average	-	-	3,457,100 „
In 1849	-	-	-	5,523,409 poods
„ 1840	-	-	-	4,954,277 „
	Total of the two years	-	-	10,477,686 „
	Average	-	-	5,238,843 „

Thus the average of the two years which correspond to the
great increase of Irish production exceeds by 1,781,743 poods,
or 51 per cent., that of the three preceding years, during which the
Irish culture was decreasing.   This comparison cannot of course
be considered as decisive in regard to future consequences;
but it proves at least that this important branch of our commerce
is in no imminent danger, and that a very considerable increase
in the produce of Irish flax may be absorbed by the continued
progress of the British linen manufacture.   It is unquestionably
difficult, in matters of this sort, to prejudge the future ; all that
we can do is to estimate the value of probabilities, taking into
view the respective conditions of the two countries.

The lower value of land in Russia, and the very moderate
returns which, in our rural economy, secure us against producing at a loss, compared with the high price of land and
labour in Ireland, afford us, of course, considerable advantage in

---

* Ireland reckoned in 1841 a population of 8,175,000 inhabitants.   Adding 10
per cent., or 817,000 inhabitants, for increase during ten years by the excess of
births over deaths, there ought in 1851 to be a population of about 9 millions: but
during the last several years the emigration has been so great that the actual
number of the population is only $6\frac{1}{4}$ millions.   Thus $2\frac{1}{2}$ millions, or more than a
quarter of the population, has been expelled from its natal soil by famine and
misery within the short space of seven or eight years.   This example, unique in
the annals of humanity, reveals a deep and bleeding sore in the social condition
of a great country, which holds itself up to the admiration of the civilised world.

regard to competition. In those districts with us which are most suitable for this culture, it is generally more profitable than the culture of cereals. A produce of 5 tchetwerts of rye (the common grain of the districts in question) per dessiatine is generally considered an excellent return; and in many places 3 tchetwerts per dessiatine is regarded as a passable crop. Estimating the average price upon the spot to be 3 roubles per tchetwert, a crop of 5 tchetwerts represents a gross value of 15 roubles, and a crop of 3 tchetwerts, 9 roubles,—a value which is sometimes reduced by a fall of prices to 6 roubles, and even less; whilst a dessiatine of land employed in the culture of flax affords an average return of 25 poods, representing on the spot, at the average price of 2 roubles, a gross value of 50 silver roubles. In some districts, from 15 to 16 poods, representing a value of 30 to 32 roubles, is considered as a tolerable harvest. Notwithstanding that the culture and preparation of flax require much more care and labour than the culture of cereals, and exhaust the soil more, the difference of the value produced, even with a mediocre harvest, amply compensates the increased cost of production. But it is evident that in Ireland, with its highly rented land, a much larger return is absolutely necessary to enable the farmer to live and pay his rent. Accordingly, it is only by dint of a more rational and careful culture than is usually to be met with amongst us, that the Irish producers can stand the competition of foreign flax, especially ours, in consequence of its low price. A dessiatine of land in that country yields at an average about 43 poods of flax, representing, at the average price of 5 roubles per pood, a gross value of 215 roubles; and in good years there is obtained a return of 63 poods, with a gross value of more than 400 roubles[*], whilst our cultivator considers himself exceedingly fortunate if he obtain a return of 20 to 25 poods[†], bringing him in a gross revenue of from 40 to 50 roubles. Yet, notwithstanding this superiority of the gross return in Ireland, we find that a fall in the price of linen yarn during the years 1840 to 1848 was enough to reduce that culture from 83,000 to 53,000

---

[*] The Agricultural Society of Ireland in its Report for the year 1847, cites as an encouraging instance, that 3 acres of land had yielded 70 poods (22½ cwt.) of flax, which fetched 75*l.* sterling, = 63 poods per dessiatine, sold for 435 roubles. That this was flax of a very superior quality is proved, first, by its high price (6 roubles 91 kopecks per pood), and, secondly, by the purpose to which it was applied. We learn that it was manufactured into 1050 dozens of pocket-handkerchiefs, which sold for 50 shillings = 16 roubles 15 kopecks per dozen.

[†] In some districts, especially in the government of Kostroma, the return is as high as 40 poods: but such cases are exceptional, and 25 poods per dessiatine is generally considered a good average return.

acres,—a fact which proves that the cost of production must be very high. The only manner in which the Irish cultivators can struggle against this difficulty is by making constant efforts to improve the culture and preparation of the flax, which, since the repeal of the corn laws, has become a favourite object of encouragement with the agricultural societies. As it is an ascertained fact that this culture exhausts the soil, science has been had recourse to for the application of a remedy; and the quality of the fertilising salts which the plant absorbs during the period of its growth having been ascertained by the analysis of organic chemistry, it has been found that they can be restored to the soil by an artificial manure composed of bone-dust, sulphate of lime, muriate of soda, chloride of lime, and sulphate of manganese. The Agricultural Society of Ireland has farther rendered great service to this culture by introducing the method of maceration in hot water invented by Schenk, the American, and a new system of scutching, by which a great saving of manual labour and expense is effected. On the whole, we think we may conclude, *first,* that if Ireland possesses over us the advantage of more abundant harvests, greater proximity to her market, and a better preparation of the raw material, we, on the other hand, even after adding the cost of transport and all other expenses, can supply our article at a price below the cost of production in Ireland,—a circumstance which prevents the successful competition of that country except for certain qualities paid for at a high price; and, *secondly,* that the extension of that culture in the United Kingdom may be balanced, at least to a considerable extent, by the progress of the linen manufacture; so that the British market is likely to be open to us for a long series of years. Moreover, we may preserve the chances in our favour by improving, in our turn, the culture and preparation of our flax, which would augment the produce of the harvest in regard both to quality and to quantity. We do not yet know if in our climate we shall ever attain the rich harvests of Ireland; but there are certain districts in which the return is as high as 40 poods — pretty nearly the Irish average; and it is certain that, through a more rational system of culture, the natural fertility of the soil might be augmented, and thus more favourable results obtained. Nor must it be forgotten that in Russia the fibre is sometimes partly sacrificed for the sake of the seed. But the experiments made in Ireland have shown, that when the plan of hot water retting is adopted, the seeds may be allowed to ripen without injury to the fibre.*

---

* When the common mode of cold water retting or steeping is employed, the gluten does not separate so easily after the seed has been allowed to ripen, as if the stalk had been cut while still green.

The introduction of this process into Russia, where local circumstances admit its application, might also augment the gross value of our harvests, and thus assist our competition in the British market.

As for the outlets presented by other countries, they are but limited and of slender promise. The linen manufacture of Germany finds its raw material in the country, and is retrograding rather than advancing. During the triennial period from 1840—42 the mean annual export from the states of the Zollverein of linen, bleached and unbleached, was 101,447 centners, and during the years 1847—49 it had fallen to 66,126 centners, presenting a diminution of 35,321 centners, or 35 per cent. The consumption of linens having been every where supplanted by that of cottons, and being now restricted to certain uses, cannot be expected to augment with the progress of wealth and population in the same proportion as that of other fabrics, and the linen manufacture seems condemned to play a secondary part in the gradual development of the productive forces of manufacturing countries; but in the struggle which most of the industries of the continent have to support with England, that country possesses, for the fabrication of its linens as well as for many other branches of national labour, the advantages of abundance of capital, cheap fuel, and perfection in its mechanical appliances. So long as the linen manufacture depended upon the produce of the spinning-wheel plied by the wives and children of the peasantry, when not engaged in the labours of the field, and required little machinery and little capital, Germany, from the cheapness of its fabrics, occupied the first rank in that branch of industry : but the introduction of flax-spinning by machinery soon turned the tables in favour of England. To the mechanical and financial advantages which that country possesses must be added the facilities for a market which it finds in its colonies, and its immense commerce with transatlantic countries ; and the larger the British manufacturer's market for his linens, the more constant is likely to be the demand in Britain for our flax. Our exportation of this article during the five years from 1846—50, which amounted to 21,648,987 poods, was distributed amongst the countries of destination as follows :

				Poods.			
England (direct)	-	-	-	14,226,043	or	65·7	per cent.
France	-	-	-	1,845,626	„	8·5	„
Prussia	-	-	-	787,345	„	3·7	„
Denmark	-	-	-	668,134	„	3·1	„
Spain and Portugal	-	-	-	519,080	„	2·4	„
Belgium	-	-	-	284,367	„	1·3	„
Other countries*	-	-	-	3,318,392	„	15·3	„
	Total -	-		21,648,987			

* See note, p. 343.

Next to England, France is our best customer, and could take off more if our flax were better prepared and sorted. Our exportation to Prussia and other German countries (of which a portion finds its way to England) presents, as we have already observed, no great prospects for the future; and the remaining exports are of very secondary importance.

The influence of the home linen manufacture upon the culture of flax is not likely to be great. In Russia, as elsewhere, this branch of industry has been supplanted by cotton; our exports of linen manufactures are rather falling off than increasing; and, as regards the home market, the present fabrication of ordinary linens is quite sufficient for the wants of the most numerous classes, whilst the quantity of fine linen imported, representing an average value of about 500,000 roubles, is so small that if the whole were to be replaced by the home manufacture the result upon the culture of flax would be imperceptible. The foreign market, as we have already seen, is secure to us for an indefinite period; but the trade might be rendered at once more extensive and more lucrative by improving, first, the culture, and then the preparation and assortment. It is well known that the various qualities of flax, — its colour, elasticity, length, flexibility, the strength and equality of its filaments,—greatly depend on seed, soil, and culture, as well as on careful reaping and retting. But in all these respects Russian practice is very careless. A commission of inquiry appointed by the Minister of Domains examined the condition of this culture in those districts where it is most widely diffused; and its defects are pointed out in an interesting and instructive report, which was published in 1847. But of still more importance than any improvement in the culture would be an improvement in the processes adopted for preparing the flax for sale,— that is in beating, cleaning, sorting, and heckling. All these operations are generally performed in a very slovenly manner, and with very imperfect instruments. The experiments made in the adoption of the Flemish system have not hitherto been successful in a commercial point of view. There are but two establishments, the one in Livonia and the other in the government of Jaroslaw, in which that method has been tried; and the higher price obtained for the flax has not been in proportion to the increased cost of production: but a closer examination of the matter will show that this want of success hitherto is anything but decisive of the general question. It does not seem to be the necessary result either of our soil and climate or of the general situation of our rural economy, but to be due to a combination of circumstances which time may remove. When the Flemish system was first tried in the government of Jaroslaw, it was observed that the seed obtained was smaller in quantity and inferior in quality, whilst the new mode of preparing the fibre was much more expensive; but it was observed also that the loss of time, and corresponding enhancement of expense, proceeded partly from the small aptitude of our cultivators for the sort of manual labour required by the new process; and this is a difficulty which time may overcome. One thing is clear, that where the Flemish method has been employed, *better* flax has been obtained, and the only question is, Can such an enhancement of price be obtained as to repay the increased cost of production? That such prices have not been obtained hitherto is, in our opinion, in great measure owing to the present condition of our flax trade, and the course which it has followed from a very early date. England, as we have seen, has always been our principal customer; and as Russia has been the source from which England has been accustomed to draw her raw material, the English merchants and manufacturers, long habituated to receive our flax dressed in a very inferior manner, have made their mechanical arrangements to suit this state of circumstances. They find their account in the low prices at which they purchase from us; and it is only for the manufacture of very fine fabrics that they purchase the better dressed flax of France and Belgium. It is this that has accustomed our cultivators and merchants to go on in the old routine, and to regard improvements with indifference. A confirmation of our opinion will be found in an article by M. Zablotski, on the introduction of the Flemish method into Russia, inserted in the eighth *livraison* of the *Journal du Ministère des Domaines* for 1851. After giving an account of the shipment to England, by way of experiment, of a certain quantity of flax dressed in the Flemish manner, on the property of M. Karnowitch, and of the unsatisfactory result in a pecuniary point of view, the author gives a summary of M. Karnowitch's practical notions on the subject. This enlightened agriculturist, who introduced the Flemish method into the government of Jaroslaw, and who still laudably perseveres in his enterprise notwithstanding his pecuniary discouragements hitherto, indicates as one of the causes which now impede the more general introduction of this method into Russia, the circumstance that the merchants and brokers who purchase flax for exportation inquire only for low prices, and give no marked preference to a superior article. " If you question," says he, " the principal merchants of Velikoïe-Selo*,

---

* Principal mart for flax and linen in the government of Jaroslaw.

they will tell you that flax distinguished by the equality of its filaments is better than that which is cottony, and of which the filaments are always weaker and more ravelled — that it is better to bind the bundles with flax than with straw — that the fineness of the filaments indicates superiority of quality — that the flax of which the points are equal is better than that in which they are not, and so on; but when it comes to making a bargain, they apparently attach very little value to all these advantages, and purchase by preference flax much less carefully prepared, provided only they can get it a little cheaper."

M. Karnowitch attributes this circumstance to the mode of sorting adopted by the merchants of Archangel, who distinguish only three qualities, and look much more to consistence of fibre and lowness of price than to good dressing. He finds likewise that those who purchase the flax for spinning in the country much better appreciate goodness of quality; and gives it as his opinion—in which we entirely coincide—that the establishment of spinning mills in the districts where flax is cultivated would be the best means of encouraging improvement in its cultivation and dressing.

With all this we must not shut our eyes to the circumstance that so perfect a system as the Flemish is not yet generally practicable amongst us, but would in many districts encounter difficulties, inherent partly in the climate and soil, and partly in our present agricultural and economical condition. In Belgium we often find that every thing which regards the preparation of the flax, beginning with the harvest, is concentrated in the hands of a few capitalists, who purchase the crops upon the ground, so that the landowner has only to concern himself with the culture properly so called, whilst the retting, scutching, &c., form a separate branch of industry. This division of labour has greatly contributed to bring about the degree of perfection which Belgian flax-dressing has attained. But, with few exceptions, such a system would be inapplicable amongst us. For an improved culture, also, much care and a considerable command of manure are requisite, so that where agriculture in general is backward, improvement need scarcely be looked for in this department alone. It would therefore seem that, without excluding the Flemish method where it is favoured by local circumstances, our agriculturists should rather endeavour to introduce into the processes commonly in use such improvements as they are susceptible of. This is what several proprietors in Livonia are now doing; and they have of late been succeeding so well that their flax fetches at Pernau and Riga from 40 to 50 per cent. above the current price. M. Nebolsine also cites in his work on the foreign commerce of Russia, examples of flax prepared in Livonia by the Flemish method, which, on being shipped to England fetched 1 rouble per pood, or 33 per cent. more than flax dressed in the ordinary manner.[*]

We should not omit to mention the persevering efforts of M. Mouravieff to improve the mechanical preparation of flax upon his estate situated in the government of Moscow. The perseverance is so much the more meritorious inasmuch as it is disinterested; for the prices which he has hitherto been offered upon the St. Petersburg exchange for his improved flax have not corresponded to the increased cost of production, which is another instance of the truth of M. Karnowitch's observations.

The introduction of the flax-dressing machines used in other countries has also experienced some difficulties. The late Count Cancrin, Minister of Finance, sent in 1842 for some of Garnier's scutching machines, with which various experiments were made at Riga, Dorpat, Pskow, and Jaroslaw, under the superintendence of the inventor himself. It was generally acknowledged that the machine performed very well, but as to the practical benefit to be derived from its introduction into Russia no very favourable impression was formed either amongst the cultivators or amongst the merchants. It was observed that the tow which remained after scutching by this machine was less suitable for exportation, and that the loss falling upon this article would more than counterbalance any gain upon the flax. The inventor himself acknowledged, as the result of some experiments made at Pskow, that his machine would require some changes to render it suitable for the Russian flax, which is neither so equal nor so continuous as that of France and Belgium. The quality of the flax may, no doubt, affect the application of improved instruments to the different operations it has to undergo previous to sale; but independently of this, we find on the part of our cultivators and merchants ingrained prejudices against every thing having the aspect of novelty; and the observations we have made in regard to culture upon the Flemish system are no less applicable to the introduction of new scutching and heckling machinery. When the Riga merchants were consulted at the

---

[*] During the three years 1847—49, there were exported from Riga 6,074,131 poods of flax, (exclusive of tow), representing at the official estimate a value of 14,403,868 silver roubles, which gives an average price of only 2 roubles 37 kopecks per pood. But as the improved dressing applied chiefly to the superior qualities, which fetched during the same period from 2 roubles 40 kopecks to 3 roubles 80 kopecks, we have adopted 3 roubles as the medium price, upon which there was a rise of 1 rouble, or 33 per cent.

time the first experiments were made with Garnier's machine, they declared that the flax prepared with it would scarcely fetch a higher price in England than was received for what they were in the habit of then sending, and that the only advantage to be hoped for was in the French market: this would not be a sufficient reason for rejecting its use, since France, next to England, is our best customer. On the other hand, after the experiments made at Dorpat, the Economic Society of Livonia acknowledged that satisfactory results were obtained from breaking the flax by Garnier's machine, and hand-cleaning it in the usual manner, and that even flax of a very inferior quality, when thus prepared, became very supple and silky. The opinion expressed by the Riga merchants can only mean that the augmented cost of preparation would not be met by a corresponding increase of price: but it is also connected with a notion prevalent enough amongst our merchants, that even though the flax were to be better dressed they would not obtain a better price for it. This idea is founded more upon old habits and traditions than on facts, and seems likely to be erroneous for this reason, that every additional degree of preparation produces a saving to the manufacturer of time, labour, and expense in the operations to which he requires to subject the raw material before it is ready for the spinning mill; and,—what is perhaps of more importance—in purchasing flax better dressed and assorted, he can form a better estimate of the probable waste and quantity of yarn likely to be turned out. It is possible enough that the English merchants, who have long been accustomed to purchase our flax at a very low figure, and to enjoy in this branch of our commerce a sort of purchasers' monopoly, might not be inclined at first to raise their prices in proportion to the improvement in the dressing; but as England cannot do without our flax, seeing that no other country is able to supply her in sufficient quantities, it is impossible for prices to remain very long below their natural level. As for the loss arising upon the tow, we apprehend that this would soon be amply compensated by the higher price received for the flax itself. Such a result is indicated by the ciphers of exportation of the two articles. During the three years 1847—49 there were exported *in toto* 10,765,921 poods of flax, representing a value of 27,180,669 silver roubles, and 1,746,522 poods of tow, representing a value of 2,884,064 roubles, making together a value of 30,064,733 silver roubles, of which the proportion of the latter article is only 9·6 per cent. Thus an increase of 5 per cent. only upon the price of the flax will counterbalance a reduction of about 50 per cent. on the price of the tow.

Since the experiments with Garnier's machine were made, another, the invention of Kouté, has been used to some extent in Livonia, and appears to be more suitable for our flax than the first named instrument. When its advantages have been proved by experience it will probably be introduced into other provinces. The system of steeping in hot water, which we have already adverted to, may also in course of time contribute to improvement, as well as to reconcile the two conflicting interests — the production of flax as a textile plant and the production of linseed for seed. The introduction of this method would also be attended with the additional advantage of promoting the division of labour, the good consequences of which are so observable in Belgium; the cultivator would have only to sow and reap, and then deliver his flax at the steam-retting establishments, where the dressing would be carried on with care and intelligence; instead of which the whole processes are now very carelessly carried on by the peasants themselves, who seldom possess the knowledge or the means necessary for carrying out the improved processes. This division of labour is one of the essential conditions of progress; and if, from want of capital, it cannot be introduced all at once, its partial introduction is always a great step gained with a view to the future.

On considering the various improvements that have hitherto been attempted, and the various opinions that have been expressed concerning them, we are of opinion that ill success has frequently proceeded, not merely from material difficulties inherent in soil, climate, and other local circumstances, but also from a certain degree of inexperience in manual operations, and from the repugnance of our peasantry to innovation. The experience of all countries has shown that improvements of the sort are never introduced without the expense of repeated failures, of time, and of money. The good results are slow to manifest themselves; the manufacturer will not pay a higher price for the raw material till he ascertains that it is really worth more to him; and this takes some time. The experiments undertaken with us, moreover, have been upon too small a scale to have any effect upon our foreign commerce. When a trade is carried on in the old groove to the extent of hundreds of thousands of poods, a small parcel—perhaps 100 poods—of superior quality is not easily disposed of at a price proportioned to the intrinsic value of the merchandise. But one fact is clear, and that is, that with a few trifling exceptions our very best flax sells at a low price owing to the bad condition in which it comes to market. M. Nebolsine gives a table of the prices of flax in England, with reference to the countries from whence

it was imported, from 1830 to 1847, inclusive, in pounds sterling per ton of 63 poods, of which the mean result is as
follows: —

Courtray flax	-	-	-	£117 per ton
Flemish ditto	-	-	-	99 „
Dutch ditto	-	-	-	79 „
Irish ditto	-	-	-	$70\frac{1}{3}$ „
Riga ditto	-	-	-	43 „

Thus the price of Riga flax is to Irish, as 10 to 16·3 ; to
Dutch, as 10 to 18·4 ; to Flemish, as 10 to 23 ; and to Courtray,
as 10 to 27 : — in other words, our flax fetches 38 per cent.
less than the next lower quality, namely, Irish.   We thus
perceive what an increase of value it might attain if the culture
and preparation were carried on in a more rational manner.
Without aiming at the perfection of Belgium, if we only came
up to the average of Ireland, that alone would be an increase of
more than 27l. sterling per ton, or 2 roubles 76 kopecks per
pood, amounting on 3,588,640 poods (the mean exportation of
the three years 1847—49 without reckoning the tow) to
9,904,000 silver roubles.   A prospective gain of even half the
amount would be worth some exertion and sacrifice on the part
of our producers.

Government, having long recognised the importance of the
flax and hemp trade, has established a system of official inspection (*brak*), under which these articles cannot be exported until
they have been examined by skilful sworn inspectors, who
classify the merchandise according to its qualities, and reject what is bad; but this measure, which is recognised as
necessary to prevent fraud and the shipment of trash, which
would give our article a bad character in the foreign market, is
not sufficient to insure such an amount of dressing as would
enhance its value ; if the inspection were too severe, it would
become an impediment to commerce ; all, therefore, that the
inspectors can do is to make a sort of wholesale survey, and reject
what appears to be really bad or damaged goods.   Even restricted
within these limits, the control is sometimes found troublesome
and inconvenient.   The St. Petersburg merchants, finding
themselves, in a measure, at the mercy of the inspectors, made
complaints of the delays and expense which the system occasioned ; and in consequence of their complaints, government,
in 1844, abolished inspection at the port of St. Petersburg
in all cases where such was the mutual wish of both buyer
and seller, retaining it only in those cases where one or
other of the parties should require it.   From that date the
custom fell gradually into disuse ; the whole flax and hemp

exported from St. Petersburg is now shipped without the formality in question; and government intends extending the same freedom to the other ports when such a desire is manifested by the local commerce. Compulsory inspection naturally becomes superfluous from the moment merchants recognise that it is for their own interest to earn the confidence of purchasers, and to supply them with a good article in order to maintain their character; the optional inspection, however, accorded to the port of St. Petersburg, has not hitherto induced any of the other ports to apply for the same franchise; the control of authority, however troublesome it may be in certain cases, will continue necessary until the honesty of sellers and the confidence of buyers have become consolidated. M. Nebolsine shows that the flax-trade of Archangel fell into decay in consequence of a laxness which had crept into the practice of inspection there, and only began to look up after efficient steps had been taken to restore the system to its former integrity. Government desiring to reconcile the necessity of preventing fraud and of maintaining the credit of our flax trade, with the liberty of commercial transactions, no doubt took the wisest course in rendering the inspection optional; but it is desirable that where it still remains imperative, the practice should be carefully watched by the local authorities, to prevent parties from being exposed to the caprice or extortion of the inspectors, and to insure the execution of their duties in a proper and legal manner. Any modification of the system, or its total suppression, ought to be naturally and gradually brought about by the establishment of confidence on the part of purchasers, instead of arising from the necessity of putting a stop to its abuses.

Everything we have said relative to the improvements desirable in the culture, dressing, and assortment of our flax, is likewise applicable in a great measure to our hemp, — the more especially that this branch of our commerce is under the influence of less favourable conjunctures than the former. It is again England that is our principal outlet for this article. The prodigious development of the naval constructions of this power presents a vast field for the employment of hemp in the equipment of its numerous fleets and mercantile navy; but the increasing use of cotton sail-cloth and iron cables, joined to the extension of steam navigation, and the construction of iron ships, has considerably diminished the use of hemp for naval purposes; and we have already seen that whilst the exportation of our flax has been following an ascending movement since 1822, our exportation of hemp has of late been diminishing. This decrease, however, is also partly owing to the competition of other countries with us in the British market. The following figures exhibit the quantities of this article imported into England from 1831 to 1849 inclusive, and the proportion which our hemp forms of the whole.

Mean Annual Importation.

	Total. cwt.	From Russia. cwt.	Proportion per cent.
From 1831 to 1835	602,642	532,695	88·4
„ 1836 „ 1840	753,958	581,797	77·1
„ 1841 „ 1845	763,779	536,126	70·2
„ 1846 „ 1849	900,530	584,213	64·9

Thus, notwithstanding the increasing competition of other countries, two-thirds of the hemp imported into England is supplied by us, (without reckoning what we send indirectly), and the absolute quantity supplied has not fallen off. Our chief competitors are the East Indies, the annual importation from which during the five years 1845—49, amounted at an average to 124,605 cwt. or $13\frac{2}{3}$ per cent. of the total importation. What partly contributes to support this branch of our commerce notwithstanding the unfavourable changes that have occurred in regard to the different uses of hemp, and also notwithstanding the increasing competition of other countries, is the manufacture of cables and cordage in England for trans-marine commerce, and especially for the English colonies in America.

The quantity of hemp exported by us during the five years 1846—50 amounted to 14,107,610 poods, distributed as follows:—

England (directly)	7,683,154 poods, or 54·5 per cent.
Sweden and Norway	1,027,409 „ „ 7·3 „
Denmark	772,895 „ „ 5·5 „
Prussia	671,465 „ „ 4·8 „
Holland	518,818 „ „ 3·7 „
United States	379,898 „ „ 2·6 „
Hanse towns	378,666 „ „ 2·6 „
Other countries (of which 2,237,517 poods for "the Sound")	2,675,305 „ „ 19 „
Total	14,107,610

Thus, next to England, Sweden and Denmark are our best customers. The exportation to Sweden followed an ascending movement during the period in question, rising from 188,000 to 260,000 poods. The exportation to Denmark has kept between 108,000 and 167,000 poods: that to Prussia has rather fallen off; that to Holland has risen from 92,000 to 152,000. The other countries hold out little chance of extension for the future.

As connected with the culture of flax and hemp, oleaginous grains form an important part of our products for European commerce. The exportation of this article has rapidly increased within the last five-and-twenty years. The mean annual exportation was

From 1824 to 1833	-	-	-	544,947 tchetwerts
„ 1834 „ 1843	-	-	-	905,370 „
„ 1844 „ 1846	-	-	-	1,237,873 „
„ 1847 „ 1849	-	-	-	1,320,385 „
In 1850	-	-	-	1,124,978 „

Thus the triennial average of 1847 — 49 compared with the decennial average of 1824 — 33 presents an increase of 242 for 100. The value exported, taken by triennial periods, was as follows:—

1823 — 1825	-	-	-	2,108,000 silver roubles
1826 — 1828	-	-	-	2,821,000 „ „
1829 — 1831	-	-	-	3,966,000 „ „
1832 — 1834	-	-	-	3,726,000 „ „
1835 — 1837	-	-	-	5,683,000 „ „
1838 — 1840	-	-	-	7,164,000 „ „
1841 — 1843	-	-	-	9,047,000 „ „
1844 — 1846	-	-	-	8,365,000 „ „
1847 — 1849	-	-	-	8,720,000 „ „
In 1850	-	-	-	7,555,000 „ „

From these figures we perceive that during twenty years commencing with 1823, the value of the exports followed a very rapidly ascending movement, augmenting nearly in the proportion of 2 to 9. In the period 1844—46, it declined about $4\frac{1}{2}$ per cent.; but the last period 1847—1849 again presents an increase of upwards of 4 per cent. This article now occupies in point of importance the fourth rank in our commerce with Europe: the rapid increase in its exportation during a period when in most large towns the use of oil for lighting has been superseded by gas, whilst at same time the culture of oleaginous plants has been becoming more or less diffused over every district, is an advantage due not only to the great extent to which flax and hemp are cultivated in Russia, whereby we are enabled to supply the seed cheaply, but also to the mode of cultivation. In those foreign countries where rape and other oleaginous plants are extensively cultivated, the great object in the cultivation of lint and hemp as textile plants is to obtain the longest stalks and the finest filaments: for this purpose the seed is sown as thick as possible, so that the plant, finding no room for development in breadth, attains considerable height and produces finer filaments, but, on the other hand, yields much less seed. In Russia, again, where these plants are cultivated for the sake of the seed as well as of the filament, the opposite mode of sowing is pursued. In Germany, France, and Belgium, about two tchetwerts of linseed are taken to sow a dessiatine, whilst in Russia it is rare that more than one tchetwert is used for that quantity of land. In the government of Jaroslaw the quantity is from 6 to 7 tchetweriks (8 tchetweriks=1 tchetwert) per dessiatine; in the government of Pskow it is from $3\frac{1}{2}$ to $5\frac{1}{2}$; and in New Russia, where the flax is cultivated solely for the sake of the seed, there is sown only $2\frac{1}{2}$ to 3 tchetweriks. But would it not be better to sacrifice the seed harvest a little for the sake of obtaining more and better flax? This is a question of which we must leave the solution to the agriculturists themselves,—believing at the same time that it cannot receive a general answer.

Hemp-seed is consumed almost entirely in the country in the preparation of oil, and of the oleaginous grains exported about $\frac{19}{20}$ are linseed. The best seed linseed is raised in the governments of Pskow and Livonia. The quantity of linseed exported during the five years 1846—50 amounted to 5,811,448 tchetwerts, distributed as follows:

To England (direct) - -	3,343,000 tchetwerts,	or 57·5 per cent.
„ Prussia - - -	527,000 „	„ 9·1 „
„ Holland - - -	513,000 „	„ 8·8 „
„ France - - -	411,000 „	„ 7·1 „
„ Belgium - - -	353,000 „	„ 6·1 „
„ Denmark - - -	185,000 „	„ 3·2 „
„ Other countries - -	479,448 „	„ 8·2 „
Total - -	5,811,448	

Thus England takes about $\frac{3}{5}$ of our exports of this article and receives also the chief part of its supplies from us, as appears from the following abstract of its average annual importation during the eighteen years 1831—49:—

	Total. Quarters.	From Russia. Quarters.	Proportion from Russia.
1831—1835 - -	251,903 - -	188,222 -	or 74 per cent.
1836—1840 - -	394,339 - -	291,465 -	„ 74 „
1841—1845 - -	441,843 - -	333,517 -	„ 75 „
1846—1849 - -	557,235 - -	441,106 -	„ 79 „

France for a while occupied the next place to England as a customer for this article, but since it raised the duty on oleaginous grains our exports thither have greatly diminished. From 1841 to 1844 they amounted at an average to 216,613 tchetwerts yearly; of late they have fallen to 70,000 or 80,000.

The culture of flax for commerce is most extensively carried on in the governments of Wologda, Wiatka, Jaroslaw, Wladimir, Nowgorod, Pskow, Livonia, Courland, Smolensk, Wilna, and Witebsk, and that of hemp in the governments of Tschernigow, Koursk, Orel, Toula, and Tambow. This important branch of rural economy has attracted the special attention of government, and we will mention a few of the steps that have recently been taken by the Ministry of Domains with the view of promoting its progress: —

1. After having appointed special commissioners to examine and report upon the present state of flax culture and the linen manufacture at home and abroad, the Ministry published the results of its researches.

2. They published 6,000 copies of a treatise on the preparation of flax.

3. The Flemish method was introduced on the farms of Gorigoretsk and Wologda, which serve as practical schools.

4. Models of improved heckling machines have been sent into various districts.

5. Premiums have been distributed for the best qualities of flax exhibited at shows.

6. To give facilities for the home trade, flax fairs have been established in Livonia.

7. Constant efforts are made to facilitate for the western provinces the means of procuring good seed from the government of Pskow.

8. Persuaded that the introduction of mill-spinning would afford the most effective stimulus to the improvement of flax cultivation, government has held out encouragements to the first undertakers of that branch of industry; and accordingly three establishments of this description have been founded within the last two or three years,— two in the government of Wologda, and one in the government of Moscow.

In regard to the culture of hemp, a commission was also appointed to examine into the subject, and its report, which is now in the press, points out the defects in the system of culture, and the remedies which ought to be applied.

Rearing of Silk-worms.

The mulberry, as is well known, acclimatises up to a certain point in pretty high latitudes, and the facility with which silkworms can be reared wherever the leaves of this tree can be procured has been the cause of frequent mistakes with regard to the chances of sericultural industry. It is not enough that a mulberry plantation should partially succeed; it must be so favourably situated in regard to soil and climate as to possess that copiousness and vigour of vegetation by which it is distinguished in all countries where the production of silk has attained any degree of importance; for it is upon these conditions that both the quantity and the quality of the silk depend. To acquire vigour of vegetation the mulberry requires a considerable depth of good vegetable soil and a temperate climate—warm at certain seasons, and rather somewhat humid than dry, as for example the climate of the north of Italy or the south of France. A light soil is more suitable than stiff clayey soils, or òthers which present difficulties to the spreading of the roots. Where these conditions exist, the success of sericultural industry will depend on the care and judgment with which the worms are reared and the various processes conducted.

It is difficult to estimate the degree of importance which this culture may in course of time acquire in the southern provinces of European Russia. If we were to judge from the little progress which it has made hitherto notwithstanding the numerous encouragements it has received from government since the beginning of last century, we should be disposed to think that local circumstances were unfavourable ; but recent experiments would seem to lead to a contrary conclusion, in regard at least to certain localities, and various measures of encouragement have been adopted by government. Mulberry culture and the rearing of silk-worms have been introduced into the horticultural establishments of the crown domains, and the pupils receive practical instruction in everything that regards the subject. This measure has already produced good consequences ; mulberry plantations are getting more and more diffused in these establishments, and the silk produced in that of Constantinograd in the government of Poltawa, of which a sample was sent to France in 1848, united, in the opinion of competent judges, all the qualities peculiar to the best sorts. Several elementary works on the culture of silk have been published under the auspices of the Department of Rural Economy ; and the prompt sale which they have found attests the interest which is now taken on the subject. One of those works published by Mr. Steven, Inspector of Rural Economy in South Russia, was reprinted in 1848 at the expense of government, and 1,500 copies distributed gratis. The old mulberry plantations situated within the crown domains have been reinclosed, and the Ministry of Domains has given instructions that, wherever the communities of crown peasants are not desirous of turning them to account, they shall be conceded gratuitously to private parties for ten or five-and-twenty years on condition of their maintaining them in good order and augmenting the number of trees. As impediments have often arisen from the want of a market for the cocoons, and the difficulty of procuring good reeling apparatus, the Department of Rural Economy, with the view of removing these, has caused factories to be opened in various localities where the cocoons are purchased on account of the establishments of the crown. In these establishments improved reeling machines have been introduced, measures have been taken for diffusing these amongst the peasants, and premiums awarded to the best cultivators. These encouragements are seconded by the efforts of the economic societies of Moscow and of South Russia, which endeavour to propagate an acquaintance with sericulture in the agronomic schools; make gratuitous distributions of mulberry-trees and silk-worms' eggs; take steps for improving the reeling; and invoke the influence of the curés for the extension of mulberry culture amongst the peasantry. It is to be hoped that these measures will bring forth fruits in their season, and indeed in some quarters their effects are already beginning to be felt. The governments in which most progress has been made hitherto are the Tauride, Bessarabia, Podolia, Kherson, Astrakhan, and Ekathérinoslaw. The total production of silk in these six governments is about 180 to 200 poods. This culture is also beginning to get more extensive in the governments of Stavropol, Kharkow, Poltawa, Tschernigow, and Kiew, but its principal seat is in the trans-caucasian provinces, which now produce about 30,000 poods, representing, at the average price of 60 roubles, a value of 1,800,000 silver roubles.* The climate of these provinces is exceedingly favourable to the silk-worm; but the process is in the hands of ignorant Tartars who carry it on with excessive carelessness. Their hand-winding is so defective that the floss attached to the cocoons gets mixed up with the silk, and thus deteriorates the quality, rendering it unequal and knotty: the reel is far too large, being 9 to 10 archines (= 7 to 8 yards) in circumference; the thread, in consequence, breaks very often; and the silk thus prepared in long skeins is not well suited for the throwing-mill. From this bad manipulation there results, first, a considerable amount of waste in the twisting—being as much as 20 to 25 per cent., instead of the 2 to 3 per cent. which occurs in silk wound in the European manner—and secondly a great loss of time and labour. Owing to all this, the Caucasian silk is not in great repute: it can seldom find its way into foreign commerce, and fetches only a trifling price. The best sorts fetch only from 80 to 100, and the inferior sorts from 40 to 60 roubles per pood. It is used by the Russian manufacturers almost solely for the weft—very rarely for the warp. In order to get over the bad winding, the experiment has lately been tried of sending the cocoons themselves, compressed, from the Caucasus to Moscow.

The quantity of silk annually manufactured in Russia is

* This estimate is higher than the one we have given at p. 191. More recent information which we have procured since that part of the work was in the printer's hands, have satisfied us that M. Hagmeister's estimate was within the mark.

estimated by M. Nebolsine at 30,000 poods: more recent statistical information enables us to form a higher and, we believe, a
more correct estimate. The production of silk in the transcaucasian provinces amounts, as we have already seen, to 30,000
poods annually. The mean exportation of raw silk during the
three years 1848—50 amounted to 3,566 poods, and the mean
importation was, of raw silk, 8,731 poods, and of thrown silk
9,653, together, 18,324. These figures present, in regard to
home consumption, the following results:

Poods.

Silk produced in the transcaucasian provinces and in the southern provinces of European Russia, about - - - -	30,000
Deduct exportation - - - -	3,566
Remainder - - -	26,434
Add importation - - - - -	18,384
Total consumption - - - - -	44,818

of which about 6,000 or 7,000 poods of Caucasian silk are employed in the place of production in the manufacture of fabrics
used in these countries, and the remainder is worked up in the
manufactories of Moscow. This quantity is referable to the
different countries in the following proportions:

	Quantity.		Value.	
	Poods.	= *p. cent.*	*Silver Roub.*	= *p. cent.*
Native silk, export deducted - -	26,434	= 59	1,586,000	= 29·2
Silk imported from Europe - -	10,142	= 22·6	3,247,000	= 60·
Silk imported from Persia and Asiatic Turkey - - - - -	8,242	= 18·4	589,200	= 10·8
	44,818		5,422,200	

From these figures we perceive that the silk of the transcaucasian provinces used in the home manufacture represents
nearly $\frac{3}{5}$ of the quantity and less than $\frac{5}{10}$ of the value, whilst
the silk imported from Europe represents little more than $\frac{1}{5}$ of
the quantity and about $\frac{3}{5}$ of the value. The Persian and
Turkish silk amounts to less than $\frac{1}{5}$ of the Russian consumption
and represents about $\frac{1}{9}$ of the value—which shows the great
superiority of the European over the Asiatic silk.[*]
It is very difficult to foresee to what extent the Caucasian

* It must, however, be remembered that a large proportion of the importation
from Europe consists of thrown silk, which, of course, greatly enhances its value.
Taking raw silks for our comparison, we obtain from the official estimates the
following results:—

European	per pood	172 silver roubles
Persian and Turkish „	73 „ „
Caucasian - „	47 „ „

silk may in time replace the silk which we now obtain from Italy and other European countries: it is probable that the best qualities of Italian silk will never be entirely superseded; but undoubtedly the Caucasian, if prepared with a little more care, might entirely replace the Persian and Turkish, which are still imported in considerable quantities from Ghilan and Broussa: it might also, if it were better prepared, become an article of export, as its cheapness would cause it to be in demand for ordinary fabrics. With care in the preparation and a good demand, the present production might be doubled in a few years, and we might export 25,000 to 30,000 poods, which at the average price of 100 roubles per pood would bring in from 2,500,000 to 3,000,000 silver roubles, whereas the present exportation of about 3,500 poods, mostly of floss silk, represents, at the official prices, a value of only 164,000 roubles.

Sericulture in the transcaucasian provinces forms a constant object of solicitude with the administration: no means of encouragement have been spared: a society specially instituted for the purpose occupies itself with the introduction of improvements; and the measures which have been adopted have begun in some districts to exhibit their good effects: but the progress of improvement in these countries can be but slow, having to struggle against the ignorance and apathy of the natives. The following are a few of the measures which have recently been adopted by the orders of Prince Woronzoff, His Imperial Majesty's Lieutenant in these provinces:

1. New reeling machines have been brought from Odessa, distributed amongst the principal producers, and sent as patterns to the local authorities;

2. Bursars selected from the various classes of the population are admitted into the practical school of mulberry culture and silk-worm rearing at Tsar-Abad, and on finishing their studies are presented with a reeling machine gratis. Premiums of from 50 to 100 roubles are also granted to those who prepare the largest quantities of silk in the European manner.

3. As the Treasury receives from some cultivators the silk in kind, in payment of their taxes, discounts are allowed to those who furnish it reeled in short hanks, in the European manner;

4. Silk-worms' eggs of the best description, and mulberry seed, are sent into various districts, and elementary treatises on the rearing of silk-worms are gratuitously distributed.

Viticulture.

According to the historical researches of M. Kœppen, the culture of the vine in Russia dates from the middle of the sixteenth century: some ancient chronicles make mention of it as early as the fourteenth; but vinicultural industry properly so called—the preparation of wine—was not introduced till towards the middle of the seventeenth century, in the neighbourhood of Astrakhan, from whence it spread in succession along the banks of the Terek, the Don, and the Kouma, and through several other countries of Southern Russia. Since the time of Peter the Great, government has constantly encouraged this culture in all those provinces for which it seems to be adapted. Lands have been conceded for that purpose to colonists and other cultivators: plants have been imported at various intervals from Hungary, Germany, France, Spain, and Italy: numerous vineyards have been planted in the horticultural establishments of the crown, and vine-dressers and wine-pressers brought over from abroad. These administrative measures, seconded by the efforts of some large proprietors, laid the foundation of vinicultural industry in Russia; but it is only since the commencement of the present century, and especially within the last twenty or thirty years, that any great progress has been made. Government, persuaded that, independently of all other encouragement, it was indispensable to diffuse amongst the wine growers the knowledge suitable to their occupation, instituted two schools for that special purpose, one of which was founded in the Crimea in 1804, and the other near Kizliar in the government of Stavropol in 1807. For these establishments master vine dressers and wine brewers were brought over from France, together with cuttings of different sorts and models of improved presses: besides the crown bursars, private pupils of every class are received into these establishments. Nor have other measures of encouragement been wanting. New concessions of land have been made—new vinicultural colonies founded—slips have been distributed gratuitously to the new colonists — money contributions awarded to new establishments and to districts which had suffered from inundations—funds have been appropriated to the construction of cellars; and a capital of 120,000 roubles arising from the sale of the crown horticultural and vinicultural establishments in Bessarabia has been appropriated to the encouragement of vineyard and orchard cultivation in New Russia.

Favoured by all these measures, and by an additional duty laid upon foreign wines, the culture of the vine has of late rapidly extended. We have already seen (*antè*, p. 152.) that the present production amounts to 15,830,000 vedros. This is nearly $\frac{1}{22}$ of the production of France, estimated by M. Schnitzler at 45,000,000 of hectolitres, and $\frac{1}{11}$ of the production of the whole

Austrian monarchy, which is estimated in the official statistics of 1846 at 39,492,900 eimers. The rapid progress of this culture in the southern provinces of European Russia within the last five-and-twenty years may give some idea of the importance which it may acquire in the course of time. The present production is distributed as follows:—

	Vedros.		Proportion per cent.
Transcaucasian provinces - - -	8,354,420	-	52·8
Ciscaucasian province (government of Stavropol)	3,200,000	-	20
Bessarabia - - - - -	3,000,000	-	19
Other provinces - - - -	1,275,000	-	8·2
Total - -	15,829,420		

Thus the cis- and transcaucasian provinces yield more than $\frac{7}{10}$ of the total production. In these provinces the climate is so favourable and the culture so easy, that nothing but hands and markets are wanting to double or triple the present product in a very few years. On the whole southern declivity of the Caucasus the vine grows wild with a vigour of vegetation which is rarely found paralleled elsewhere. Its stem is sometimes half a foot in diameter; and its shoots, which twist themselves about the large trees, attain a length of from 50 to 60 feet. From a single plant it is no uncommon thing to obtain a vedro (= 2·7 imp. or $3\frac{1}{4}$ wine gallons) of wine, or more.

The culture of the vine extends in Russia to the 49th degree of north latitude; but the vinicultural districts, properly so called, do not extend beyond the 48th. Beyond this parallel, in the opinion of Pallas and Fribé, the vine can only be cultivated as a garden plant. Its natural limit in European Russia is generally considered to be the line of the Ukraine, extending a distance of 268 versts from the confluence of the Chorel with the Dnieper above Verkhnodnieprowsk, up the line of the little river Berestovaïa, and on from the right bank of that river to the confluence of the Bereka with the Donetz, a few leagues to the westward of the town of Jzium. Experience has shown, says Pallas in his Memoirs, that the vine can be cultivated on the banks of the Volga, as far as Tsaritzine; on the banks of the Don, as far as the mouth of the Miedviednitza; on the banks of the Donetz, as far as Tschougouïew, a few leagues to the south-east of Kharkow; on the banks of the Dnieper, as far as Kiew; and on the banks of the Bug, as far as Olviopol. But, to make good wine, this culture must not be extended northward of the parallel of Tsaritzine; on the banks of the Don and the Donetz, not higher up than the confluence of the Lougane with the latter; and, on the banks of the Dnieper, not beyond the line of the Ukraine. Following the first of these lines of demarcation in a westerly direction, the region more or less suitable for the culture of the grape would embrace the whole of Bessarabia and Podolia, the greater part of the government of Kiew, the southern portion of the governments of Kharkow and Poltawa, the governments of Kherson, Ekathérinoslaw, Tauride, and Stavropol, the greater part of the government of Astrakhan, and nearly three-fourths of the country of the Don Cossacks — in all, a territory of from 13,000 to 14,000 geographical (275,000 to 295,000 English) square miles. Of course the whole arable land comprehended within this territory cannot be considered suitable for viniculture. This culture is dependent not merely on geographical, but on topographical position, as well as on soil. The culture of the vine is frequently unsuccessful in very southern latitudes at a certain height above the level of the sea, or where the locality is not well defended from the north, or where the quality of the soil is not suitable; whilst it is successfully cultivated at much higher latitudes, where these conditions are favourable. We must also take into view the continental position of Russia and the longitudinal position of the countries comprehended within the foregoing limit, as we have already seen (*antè*, Chap. II.) that the temperature diminishes under the same parallel in proportion as we proceed eastward; so that we must expect the vine to succeed, *cæteris paribus*, at a much higher latitude on the Dnieper than on the Volga. Accordingly, we find that the government of Astrakhan, where the culture of the vine dates from a much more remote period than in the other provinces of European Russia*, produces only from 8,000 to 10,000 vedros; whilst the government of Podolia, where the culture is much more recent, and of which the vinicultural districts are situated in a much higher latitude, produces about 15,000.

The districts most favourably situated are undoubtedly the transcaucasian provinces and the southern portion of the Crimea, which are capable of producing not only good table wines but also wines of considerable strength and body. Next to these may be ranked the government of Stavropol, the country of the Don Cossacks, and Bessarabia. In the Crimea as well as in the Caucasian provinces the vine thrives vigorously without cultivation; it is derived probably from old plantations formed by the Greek colonists; during the Turkish domination

---

* Peter the Great, with the view of improving the culture of the vine, which already existed in that government, introduced cuttings from Hungary and the Rhine, and brought over foreign vine-dressers: this was about the beginning of the eighteenth century.

viticulture remained nearly in abeyance; after our acquisition of that province, government directed its attention to the means of extending and improving it. Prince Potemkin imported cuttings from Tokay; but this first experiment was unsuccessful, the plantations having been made in ill-chosen localities exposed to the northerly winds, which at the time gave rise to the opinion that the Tokay vine would not acclimatise in the Crimea. Shortly after the foundation of the viticultural school at Soudak (in 1804), which was afterwards suppressed and replaced by that of Magaratch, established in a better locality in 1828, M. Rouvier, Counsellor of Commerce, introduced for that establishment cuttings and two vine-dressers from Malaga; but experience having demonstrated that the Malaga vine required a warmer climate than that of the valley of Soudak, Rouvier undertook to establish on the southern declivity of the peninsula a plantation of vines proceeding from warm climates, and received for this purpose from government an advance of 12,000 roubles on condition of importing foreign cuttings of the best description, of selling every year at least 20,000 plants to private growers at a very moderate price, and of gratuitously instructing a certain number of pupils in viticulture and wine-brewing. At a subsequent period (in 1826), German colonists from the banks of the Rhine, who were already familiar with viticulture, established new plantations in the district of Melitopol, government of Tauride, and their example has been followed by others. By degrees this branch of economy attracted the attention of some wealthy proprietors, who acquired lands in the Crimea and established large plantations, introducing cuttings from the most renowned vinicultural countries. But it is especially since 1823, the date at which Prince, then Count, Woronzoff was appointed governor-general of New Russia, that viticulture has made most marked progress both in the Crimea and in the other southern countries of the empire. Independently of the model establishments founded on the estates which he himself acquired in the Crimea, the enlightened and indefatigable activity of this statesman in every matter regarding the well-being of the provinces entrusted to his administration, gave a very strong impulse to vinicultural industry both extensive and intensive. Amongst a number of other useful measures, government made at his suggestion in 1830, within a radius of the old village of Magaratch, a distribution of more than 200 dessiatines of land divided into small lots, which were conceded for the culture of the vine free of all land-tax, on condition that the cessionaries should plant at least 2,400 cuttings upon each dessiatine. In consequence of these concessions, the village of Magaratch, inhabited by Greek shepherds who had established themselves there in the eighteenth century, was converted into a colony of laborious and intelligent vine-dressers. These encouragements, seconded by the persevering activity of an enlightened administration, operated both by their material results and their moral influence on the extension and improvement of vinicultural industry both in the Crimea and in other parts of the government of Tauride. New establishments sprung up by the hundred, and this branch of husbandry is now in a condition so satisfactory as to warrant the most favourable anticipations for the future. There are already within this government more than 2,800 vineyards yielding nearly a million vedros of wine; and the progress of this culture during the last five-and-twenty years permits us to hope that in a short time hence this production will amount to 2 or 3 millions. In 1832 there were reckoned to be in the whole government 5,846,000 vines; in 1848 the number amounted to 35,577,000, so that it had augmented more than six-fold in the course of 16 years. The Crimea produces every sort of table wine, both white and red, sparkling wines, and even full-bodied wines.   M. Kœppen, in his work on the wine trade, published in 1832, gives the nomenclature of the different sorts of wines cultivated there, and brings the total number to more than fifty.   These different sorts proceed from the plants of Burgundy, Champagne, Spain, Portugal, Greece, Italy, the Rhine, and Hungary. The best red wines of the Crimea resemble those of Burgundy in flavour, and the white resemble the wines of Hungary and the Rhine. Several sorts of them possess the quality of good foreign wines, and are mixed with the wines of the other Russian provinces to correct their flavour and give them additional body.   The wines of the southern declivity are in general heady, and consequently cannot be used as light table wines.   It requires habit to appreciate their quality ; those who are not accustomed to them find that they " smack of the soil." The prices vary according to quality and sort from 25 kopecks to 10 roubles per vedro (= 3d. to 10s. per gallon). At Magaratch the best liqueur wines sell at 15 roubles per vedro, and 1 rouble per bottle, and even higher; we have to observe, however, that in this establishment the sale of wine forms but a secondary object, the main object being to raise good plants for distribution amongst the wine growers, to experiment upon mixtures of the various sorts, to ascertain their qualities in regard to keeping and ripening, and to train pupils for viticulture and wine-making.

According to the official report of the Inspector of Rural Economy in Southern Russia, the prices stood to the quantities produced in the following proportions : —

	Vedros.
Liqueur wines fetching 8 to 10 roubles per vedro (= 7s. 10d. to 9s. 9d. per gallon), about - - - - - - -	100
Wines of the southern declivity fetching 2 to 3 roubles per vedro (= 1s. 11d. to 2s. 10d. per gallon), about - - - - - -	120,000
Wines of medium quality fetching 70 kopecks to 1 rouble per vedro (= 8d. to 11¾d. per gallon), about - - - - -	200,000
The remaining vintage, amounting to about - - - -	700,000

is sold at from 25 to 40 kopecks per vedro (= $2\frac{3}{4}d.$ to $4\frac{1}{2}d.$ per gallon), so that the whole represents a value of about 700,000 roubles (= 110,800l. sterling).

The wines in most repute are those of Aloupka, Marsanda, and Aï-Danil, belonging to Prince Woronzoff; those of the vineyards belonging to General Schatiloff and M. Hartwiss; and the dessert wines from the vinicultural establishment of Magaratch already mentioned. All these vineyards are situated on the southern slope of the Crimea. The sparkling wine from Prince Woronzoff's vineyards prepared like Champagne sells at Petersburg and Moscow for 1 rouble, and sometimes as high as 1 rouble 25 kopecks per bottle.

As a part of the population of the Crimea is Mussulman, the home consumption of the province is but limited. The progress of vinicultural industry, therefore, in that province, depends upon its commercial relations with the other parts of the empire. The wine trade of the Crimea having formerly been very limited, the wine growers were in a hurry to get rid of their vintages, and sold their wines very new and at very trifling prices to the merchants from the interior of the country, who resold them as foreign wines. The vines grown in the valleys of the interior of the Crimea were transported in winter, and sold, frozen, at so much per pood; they thence received the name of *vymorozki* (which have passed through the condition of being frozen). With the view of regulating and promoting this commerce by means of familiarising consumers with the flavour of the wines of the Crimea and letting them be known under their true names, the Department of Economy at the Ministry of Domains have undertaken since 1843 the establishment in the principal cities of the empire of entrepôts of these wines, the growth of crown vineyards. The first parcel of 188 vedros of Magaratch wine, which was forwarded to St. Petersburg in 1843, found so prompt a sale that the following year the quantity was doubled, and in 1845 the quantity of 875 vedros was invoiced; but this latter quantity being found insufficient to meet the demand, the commissioner charged with the sale imported on his own account 4000 vedros, purchased partly from the crown magazines, and partly from private proprietors.   In 1846 the quantity of wine dispatched from the Crimea to St. Petersburg amounted to 5,287 vedros, and the following year to nearly as much, without taking into account 1000 bottles of sparkling wine grown by Prince Wo-ronzoff.   In 1848 the quantity did not exceed 2000 vedros.

Notwithstanding the success of these first experiments, there is in our opinion but slight chance of an extensive market for the wines of the Crimea being found at St. Petersburg; being subject to the expense of a long land journey, it is difficult for them to compete with the foreign wines to which the inhabitants of the capital and of all the Baltic ports have long been accustomed, and of which the inferior qualities, although subject to a tolerably heavy duty, can, owing to their maritime mode of transport, be sold at a reasonable price.   For some time past there have been arrivals by sea also from the Crimea; in 1851 a merchant of St. Petersburg received an entire cargo. This direct communication with the Crimea has rendered the intervention of the commissioners superfluous, and may give this commerce a better direction.   At any rate the most natural outlet for the wines of the Crimea is to be found in the eastern governments, more remote from the seaports and the European confines of the empire.   This fact the Administration of Domains was not slow to recognise, and it has directed towards these countries its commercial operations for the sale of the crown wines.   The first parcels dispatched in 1845 to Nijni-Nowgorod, Kazan, and Saratow, had a very rapid sale, and produced such a considerable demand that, in order to supply it, the Department of Rural Economy was obliged to make purchases from private parties.   In 1848 parcels of these wines were dispatched to Oufa and Orenburg; and, in order to facilitate the sale in all the eastern governments, entrepôts were established at Taganrog and Kazan.   The example of these fortunate speculations gave an impulse to the exertions of private proprietors; and from the year 1847 considerable quantities of wine began to be exported from the Crimea to Rostow on the Don, whence they are forwarded to different governments.   This commerce is gradually extending, and at present about 300,000 vedros are exported to the different cities in the interior of the empire.

In the government of Stavropol viticulture anciently prevailed to a considerable extent in the environs of Kizliar and Mozdok, on the Terek, the banks of which are well adapted for that purpose.   In the time of the Emperor Paul there were reckoned to be 1,100 vineyards producing more than 200,000 vedros. Since that period different measures of encouragement have been adopted by government, of which unquestionably one of the most important was the institution of the school of vine-dressers near Kizliar, where the growth of various sorts of wine has been introduced along with foreign vine-dressers and wine-brewers, and plants from the Rhine, Burgundy, and other countries. Assistance was granted to the colony of Armenians from Derbent, who towards the end of the eighteenth century came and settled in the district of Kizliar and devoted themselves to the culture of the vine. In consequence of these encouragements this culture gradually extended, and we have seen that the production now amounts to about 3,200,000 vedros (10,400,000 gallons) of various sorts; but the greater part is of very inferior quality, and is used chiefly in the distillation of brandy, which forms one of the principal sources of income for the population. The district of Kizliar is the centre of this fabrication, and the brandy is known in commerce by the name of Kizliar brandy; it is also sold as French brandy; the annual production was estimated in 1830 at 200,000 vedros (650,000 gallons), and it must now be much larger. Some of the Terek red table wines are, however, tolerably good, and sparkling wines of average quality are also produced in the neighbourhood of Kizliar. From 150,000 to 200,000 vedros of wine are annually sent from the government of Stavropol into the interior of the empire, and particularly to Nijni-Nowgorod, from whence it is distributed to several of the eastern governments; but it usually sells at a very low price. The merchants of Moscow and Jaroslaw, who purchase it at the fair of Nijni, prepare from it, by means of various mixtures, imitations of certain foreign wines, and the greater portion of the cheap wines sold in the towns of the interior under the name of Madeira, Sauterne and St. Julien is manufactured from the wines of Kizliar. The inferiority of the Terek wines is attributed to the following causes :—the grapes are not well assorted; different species are mixed together without regard to their various degrees of maturity, and often without rejecting those that are half rotten; sometimes old casks are employed which formerly contained other liquids. * There is also a want of good cellarage for keeping, so that the growers are in a hurry to get quit of their wine for

* Negligences of this sort, the latter of which proceeded from the difficulty formerly met with in procuring casks, were noted at the end of last century in consequence of a government inquiry; but they recur frequently at the present day. At the period of the inquiry the Terek wines were sold at from 10 to 20 kopecks per vedro ($\frac{3}{4}d$. to $1\frac{1}{2}d$. per gallon), and the price of an old cask was its fill of new wine.

whatever it will fetch, and it is thus sold too new. These inconveniences will disappear only in the course of time, and with the progress of that knowledge which it is the object of the Vinicultural Institution to diffuse.

In Bessarabia, and particularly in the southern parts of the province, the culture of the vine is continually gaining ground. We perceive from the Report of the department of Rural Economy to the Ministry of Domains published in 1849 that the number of plantations is greatly augmenting. The German and Bulgarian colonists plant every year about 200,000 new cuttings; in the environs of Akermann there are planted nearly 100,000, and in the environs of Kischenew 50,000, so that we may reckon in all about 400,000 new plants added annually to the old plantations. There are now reckoned amongst the Bulgarian colonists more than 4,000,000 of vines, producing about 500,000 vedros, and the total vintage of Bessarabia is estimated at 3,000,000 vedros, being nearly equal to that of Stavropol. But the progress in the way of improvement is not so satisfactory as the progress in the way of extension; the quality of the Bessarabian wines is in general very mediocre; the best sorts, grown in the neighbourhood of Soroki and Akermann, sell at from 70 kopecks to 1½ roubles per vedro (=8d. to 1s. 5d. per gallon); on the other hand, the vintage is so abundant, that a dessiatine of vineyard in the neighbourhood of Akermann yields 750 vedros, and in some other districts as much as 1,200. Reckoning the wines of Akermann at 40 kopecks and the others at 30 kopecks only, this gives a gross return per dessiatine of 300 roubles in the first case, and of 360 in the second: the expense of cultivation amounting to only about 30 roubles per dessiatine, there remains a nett return of from 270 to 330 roubles per dessiatine (=15l. 15s. to 20l. per acre). This explains the rapid progress of viticulture; moreover the soil and climate are so favourable that the quality of the wine might readily be improved by the expenditure of a little trouble, as was proved by some samples forwarded in 1847 to the show of agricultural products at Kischenew by some improving proprietors; but, unluckily, persons of this description form but rare exceptions. There are now exported from Bessarabia into the other provinces of the empire about 500,000 vedros, of which the greater part goes to Odessa and the governments of Podolia and Ekathérinoslaw; some parcels are also sent to the government of Kiew. This exportation might be doubled or tripled, and much higher prices obtained, if more care were employed in the manufacture. The observation we have made as to the cause of the backward state of vinicultural industry in the government of Stavropol are partly applicable to Bessarabia. A great evil for the wine grower is that, for want of cellarage and want of capital, he is obliged to send his commodity immediately into the market to fetch what price it may, and to be drunk before it is ripe. From the great abundance of the vintage, a good portion might be converted into brandy, and thus a productive branch of commerce might be created ; at present there is only a very small quantity distilled for local consumption, and to correct the wines which are beginning to spoil. Upon the whole, the product of the vineyards of Bessarabia, which represent a value of about 1,500,000 roubles, might, with a little more industry on the part of the growers, be soon raised to 3,000,000 or 4,000,000.

Next to the three provinces which we have just named, we must rank the country of the Don Cossacks, where this culture dates from about the middle of the eighteenth century, though it is only within the last five-and-thirty years that it has begun to acquire much importance. There are now cultivated from 15 to 20 different species of grapes, having most affinity with those of Champagne and Burgundy : the average vintage is estimated at 100,000 vedros : the wines are mostly sparkling : the best sorts, which are grown in the military district of Symlansk, fetch from $1\frac{1}{2}$ to 3 roubles per vedro (1s. 6d. to 3s. per gallon), and the others from 80 kopecks to 2 roubles per vedro ($9\frac{1}{2}d.$ to 2s. per gallon): the average export is 60,000 vedros, which are sold in the governments of Kharkow, Woronèje, Poltawa, Koursk, and Nijni-Nowgorod, and in the two capitals. About 175,000 bottles of Don wine are annually sold at the fair of Nijni. The product of the whole wines and grapes sold is estimated to amount to 380,000 roubles, being more than a fifth of the money value of the whole productions of the province.

In the government of Kherson, the first plantations took place about the end of last century, in the environs of Odessa on the Moldawanka, in the environs of Kherson, and in general on the banks of the Dnieper, the Ingoul, and the Ingouletz. They have considerably extended in the eastern part of the province, especially amongst the German and Bulgarian colonists in the districts of Odessa and Tiraspol, and amongst the crown peasants in several villages situated upon the Dniester. The wines are mostly of very inferior quality, fetching from 30 kopecks to 1 rouble per vedro ($3\frac{1}{2}d.$ to 1s. per gallon), and are almost entirely consumed on the spot. A few better sorts are, however, to be met with : on the estates of General Narischkine, near Odessa, there are made about 80,000 bottles of sparkling wine of tolerable quality. The total production amounts to about 150,000 vedros, of which 100,000 are grown by the colonists and 30,000 by the crown peasants: besides this about 3,000 vedros of brandy are distilled.

In the government of Astrakhan, but little progress has been made in this branch of industry notwithstanding that the culture of the vine dates here from an era more remote — the middle of the seventeenth century — than in any other province of European Russia. In 1640 several inhabitants of Astrakhan brought over a German wine-grower to introduce this culture, and since then it has gradually extended in the neighbourhood of that town. In 1669 the traveller Strauss found a good number of vineyards, which furnished for the court of the Tsar about 200 tuns of wine and 50 vedros of brandy. The vinicultural capacity of the country attracted the attention of Peter the Great, who brought over a vine-dresser from Hungary and plants from Tokay and the Rhine; he gave the first impulse to the development of the crown horticultural and vinicultural establishments on the Volga, which were afterwards ceded to the city of Astrakhan on condition of its supplying the table of the court with fruit, and subsequently passed, in the way of sale, into the hands of private parties. The vineyards of Astrakhan produce an abundance of excellent raisins, which are sent, in considerable quantities, to almost every part of the empire. Large parcels used to come to St. Petersburg; but the greater facility of sea carriage has of late caused them to be supplanted by the raisins of Malaga. The manufacture of wine has made but little progress. The wine is generally mediocre, fetching on the spot from 1 rouble 25 kopecks to 1 rouble 55 kopecks per vedro (= 1s. 3d. to 1s. 6d. per gallon). The total vintage does not exceed 10,000 vedros.*

In the government of Podolia, viticulture has hitherto acquired little importance, except in the environs of Mohilew on the Dniester and on the crown domain of Tarouga, situated between Jampol and Mohilew; but it might succeed in many other places, especially along the Dniester. The estate of

* "Nowhere in the world," says Alexander v. Humboldt, "not even in Italy or the Canary Islands, have I seen ripen such fine clusters of grapes as at Astrakhan on the shores of the Caspian Sea, (mean temperature of the year only 52° Fahrenheit); and yet upon this same spot, and even farther south, at Kizliar, at the mouth of the Terek (in the latitude of Avignon and Rimini), we frequently see the thermometer descending in winter to 15° to 20° below zero Fahrenheit. At Astrakhan, where, during summers as hot as those of Provence and Lombardy, the force of vegetation is excited by the artificial irrigation of a soil impregnated with muriate of soda, the vine plants must be inserted at a considerable depth."—*Asie centrale, par A. de Humboldt*, vol. iii. pp. 32, 33.

Kaminka, belonging to the Princess Wittgenstein, in the district of Jampol, produces good table wine which fetches 50 kopecks, and sparkling wine which fetches 1 rouble, per bottle. This province produces in all 15,000 vedros.

In the governments of Kiew and Ekathérinoslaw the vine is cultivated rather for the sake of the grapes as a dessert fruit than with a view to wine-making.

It results from the foregoing data, that, in regard to vinicultural industry, there exists in the southern provinces of European Russia a fund of production susceptible of great development; and that this development depends, *first*, upon the progress of population and industry amongst the peasantry, and, *secondly*, on their commercial relations and facilities of intercourse with the provinces of the interior. Improvements in the manufacture of the wine leading to the production of a better article, would facilitate its sale in the other parts of the empire; and, conversely, a ready sale would encourage production and improvement. These improvements are especially desirable for the weak table wines, which can be sold at from $1\frac{1}{2}$ to 2 roubles per vedro (1*s.* 6*d.* to 2*s.* per gallon); for, however profitable the preparation of finer and stronger wines might be for a few proprietors, the prosperity of viticulture in these provinces will depend much more on the sale of those wines of medium quality, of which the consumption is large when they are placed within the reach of the less wealthy classes of the population.

In the transcaucasian provinces this culture is already very extensive. They produce upwards of 8,000,000 vedros (28,000,000 gallons),—more than all the provinces of European Russia put together. The greater part are of very inferior quality, and will not bear a long carriage. The wines of the Colchide, in the government of Coutaïs, fetch on the spot from 15 to 50 kopecks per vedro ($= 1\frac{3}{4}d.$ to 6*d.* per gallon); and those of the district of Samourzakane sell as low as 10 kopecks per vedro ($= 1\frac{1}{5}d.$ per gallon); but in these there is much room for improvement. Still, all that is required is more care in culture, more pains in brewing. As it is, the grapes are badly assorted; they are often pressed in brick troughs, the cement of which introduces calcareous substances into the wine; and the wine is kept and transported in leather skins. Some winegrowers in Kakhetia, however, are beginning to improve their qualities; and we find in the government of Tiflis several wines, both white and red, of good quality and great strength, which fetch on the spot 1 to 2 roubles per vedro ($= 1s.$ to 2*s.* per gallon), and upwards. The vintages of the Caucasus are abundant.

There are generally planted upon a dessiatine 5,000 vines, which yield about 400 vedros (= 4649 litres per hectare). This is equivalent to nearly the highest product of the vintage in France, where the minimum of production is 500 to 700 litres, and the maximum 4,500 to 5,500 litres per hectare. The 400 vedros, estimated at the moderate rate of from 25 to 50 kopecks per vedro, give a gross return of from 100 to 200 silver roubles per dessiatine (5*l*. 18*s*. to 11*l*. 16*s*. per acre); which is a very profitable culture, especially in the neighbourhood of towns where there is a ready sale.

The historical information carefully collected by M. Kœppen shows, that as far back as the time of Peter the Great government took steps to improve the culture of the vine in the transcaucasian possessions, and especially in the Derbent. In the beginning of the eighteenth century, plants were brought over from Hungary and the environs of Schiraz, which in some places have been preserved to the present day; and the wines from them are considered the best. Of all the transcaucasian provinces, it is the governments of Tiflis and Coutaïs that produce the largest quantities of wine,—furnishing more than seven-eighths of the whole. The culture might be very much extended, were it not that the outlets for production are still so limited, owing to geographical position and local circumstances. The quantity of wine already produced suffices for the wants of the Christian population. Amongst the Mussulmen, who are numerous in these provinces, there is of course no demand for it. Asia, for the same reason, offers no better chance of a market. The sole hope, therefore, must be in European Russia. But the difficulties of communication and the quality of the wines, which will not bear transport, throw great impediments in the way of such a commerce at present.

M. Kœppen, in his work on the production and commerce of wine in Russia, to which we have repeatedly referred, has indicated the following measures which he considers necessary to promote viticulture in Russia:

1. The institution—were it only temporary—of two or three viticultural schools, especially in the transcaucasian and southwestern provinces, in Bessarabia, or at Odessa, and on the Don;

2. The establishment in various localities of good vine nurseries, especially of the earlier sorts of vine, for distribution amongst intending growers;

3. The publication of treatises on vine culture and wine brewing in the Russian, German, Tartar, Armenian, Georgian, and modern Greek languages;

4. The propagation of cork plantations on the south coast of the Crimea and in the transcaucasian provinces;

5. To encourage the establishment of glass-houses, especially in the last named countries;

6. To encourage the establishment of verdigris manufactories in the vinicultural districts;

7. To propose premiums for introducing the use of the residue of the grapes instead of oak bark in tanneries;

8. To do away entirely with the system of brandy farming, which exercises a noxious influence on the sale of wine both wholesale and retail;

9. To grant every possible relief to those engaged in brandy distillation;

10. To establish cellars of entrepôt for wines intended for sale in the interior, especially at Kiew, Kharkow, Astrakhan, Nijni-Nowgorod, and in the trauscaucasian provinces near the Black Sea or the Caspian * ;

11. To give high premiums to wine growers and coopers who may distinguish themselves, the former, by raising fine grapes and manufacturing superior wines, and the latter, by the good construction of their casks;

12. To augment the import duties on foreign wines, especially those arriving by the ports of the Black Sea, the Sea of Azow, and the Caspian Sea †, and by the dry frontier of the south and west.

The majority of these proposals are founded upon very just notions. Some, as for example those mentioned in numbers 2, 3, 10, and 12, have been already put in execution, at least in part, since M. Kœppen's book was published. The application of some of the others, as for example those concerning the manufacture of verdigris and the employment of the grape refuse in tanneries, depends more on private industry than on administrative measures. The establishment of cellars of entrepôt, to which a beginning has been made by the Department of Economy, seems to be one of the most urgent measures of the whole. As for protection to native wines, it is now more than ample. Our tariff for that article when imported in wood is the highest of all Europe, Great Britain alone excepted. For champagne it exceeds even the English tariff in the proportion

---

* After passing the winter in these entrepôts, the wines of the southern provinces could, says M. Kœppen, easily be exported to other districts—even to the northern provinces; whilst at present, owing to the want of good cellarage, great part of the wines destined for the interior of Russia are spoiled during the intense heats or the strong frosts.

† There are no wines imported by the Caspian Sea. (*Author's note.*)

of 3 to 1, and for other bottled wines in the proportion of 5 to 3. The present duty of 48 roubles per *oxhoft* of 240 bottles amounts on table wines of medium quality to cent. per cent. of their value, and on ordinary qualities to 200 per cent. : the duty of 90 kopecks per bottle for sparkling wines, and of 50 kopecks for all other bottled wines, comes also to about 100 per cent. and upwards. The wines of Moldavia, Wallachia, and Greece (with the exception of those of the Isle of Cyprus) are subject, it is true, on their entry by the ports of the Black Sea and the Sea of Azow, as well as by the Bessarabian frontier, to a duty of only 24 roubles per oxhoft, but their quality is so inferior that even this amounts to 75 per cent. or upwards on their value. The Austrian and Hungarian wines pay, on their importation by the dry frontier, 15 roubles per oxhoft, which comes, for the weak table wines of medium quality, to about 50 per cent. of their value.

To judge of the influence which these duties must exert upon foreign competition with native wine-growing, we must take into consideration the price at which native wines are sold in Russia, the quantities of foreign wines imported, and the quantity of wine furnished by the southern provinces for the consumption of the interior. Let us first establish the numerical relation which exists between the duties levied on foreign wines and the selling prices of native wines on the spot.

1. The duty of 15 roubles per oxhoft levied on Austrian and Hungarian wines imported by the dry frontier is equivalent to 83 kopecks per vedro :

			Average Prices of Native Wines per Vedro.			Proportion of Duty to these Prices.
			Roubles.	Kopecks.		
Crimea wines	1st quality	-	2	50	-	33 per cent.
Ditto	2nd ,,	-	0	85	-	98 ,,
Ditto	3rd ,,	-	0	33	-	251 ,,
Terek wines	1st ,,	-	1	0	-	83 ,,
Ditto	2nd ,,	-	0	50	-	166 ,,
Ditto	3rd ,,	-	0	25	-	332 ,,
Bessarabian wines	1st ,,	-	1	10	-	75½ ,,
Ditto	2nd ,,	-	0	50	-	166 ,,
Ditto	3rd ,,	-	0	25	-	332 ,,
Don wines	1st ,,	-	2	25	-	37 ,,
Ditto	2nd ,,	-	1	40	-	59 ,,
Kherson wines	1st ,,	-	1	0	-	83 ,,
Ditto	2nd ,,	-	0	60	-	138 ,,
Ditto	3rd ,,	-	0	30	-	277 ,,

2. The duty of 24 roubles per oxhoft levied on the wines of Moldavia, Wallachia, and Greece imported by the Black Sea, the Sea of Azow, and the Bessarabian frontier, amounts to 1 rouble 33 kopecks per vedro :

			Average Prices of Native Wines per Vedro.			Proportion of Duty to these Prices.
Crimea wines	1st quality	-	2	50	-	53 per cent.
Ditto	2nd ,,	..	0	85	-	156 ,,
Ditto	3rd ,,	-	0	33	-	403 ,,
Terek wines	1st ,,	-	1	0	-	133 ,,
Ditto	2nd ,,	-	0	50	-	266 ,,
Ditto	3rd ,,	-	0	25	-	532 ,,
Bessarabian wines	1st ,,	-	1	10	-	121 ,,
Ditto	2nd ,,	-	0	50	-	266 ,,
Ditto	3rd ,,	-	0	25	-	532 ,,
Don wines	1st ,,	-	2	25	-	59 ,,
Ditto	2nd ,,	-	1	40	-	95 ,,
Kherson wines	1st ,,	-	1	0	-	133 ,,
Ditto	2nd ,,	-	0	60	-	222 ,,
Ditto	3rd ,,	-	0	30	-	443 ,,

3. The duty of 48 roubles per exhoft levied upon foreign wines other than those designated under numbers 1 and 2 amounts to 2 roubles 66 kopecks per vedro:

			Average Prices of Native Wines per Vedro.			Proportion of Duty to these Prices.
Crimea wines	1st quality	-	2	50	-	106 per cent.
Ditto	2nd ,,	-	0	85	-	312 ,,
Ditto	3rd ,,	-	0	33	-	806 ,,
Terek wines	1st ,,	-	1	0	-	266 ,,
Ditto	2nd ,,	-	0	50	-	532 ,,
Ditto	3rd ,,	-	0	25	-	1064 ,,
Bessarabian wines	1st ,,	-	1	10	-	242 ,,
Ditto	2nd ,,	-	0	50	-	532 ,,
Ditto	3rd ,,	-	0	25	-	1064 ,,
Don wines	1st ,,	-	2	25	-	118 ,,
Ditto	2nd ,,	-	1	40	-	190 ,,
Kherson wines	1st ,,	-	1	0	⌐	266 ,,
Ditto	2nd ,,	-	0	60	-	443 ,,
Ditto	3rd ,,	-	0	30	-	886 ,,

Thus the duties which protect the home manufacture amount at their minimum to 33 per cent., and at their maximum to more than 1,000 per cent. on the foreign article. It clearly results from the whole of these figures that competition is possible only for foreign wines of superior quality, which can fetch much higher prices than the best country wines. It is only the Austrian and Hungarian wines imported by the dry frontier that can compete at equal prices with the best wines of the Crimea and the Don, which sell at the average prices of 2 roubles 50 kopecks and 2 roubles 25 kopecks per vedro. Deducting from these prices the duty of 83 kopecks, there would remain for the seller only 1 rouble 67 kopecks or 1 rouble 42 kopecks per vedro, cost of transport included. It is evident that under such a duty the competition of Austrian and Hungarian wines, the most favoured of any, is null as regards those home wines which are sold at the rate of 1½ roubles per vedro; and as regards the wines of Wallachia, Moldavia, and Greece, which pay a duty of 1 rouble 33 kopecks, competition must cease (prices being equal) as soon as the price of the home article stands at as low a figure as 1 rouble 75 kopecks.   But there are not manufactured in all Russia more than 200,000 vedros which attain such a high price as this.   In the Crimea, where the best wines are grown, out of a million vedros vintaged, there are reckoned only about 120,000 which fetch more than 1 rouble.   For all the other foreign wines, which are subject to a duty of 2 roubles 66 kopecks per vedro, the duty alone exceeds the medium price of the best home wines.   The sparkling wines imported in bottle, being subject to a duty of 90 kopecks per bottle, can scarcely be sold for less than 2 roubles, all expenses included, whilst the best sparkling wines of the Don and Crimea are sold at the rate of 1 rouble per bottle.   It seems to us that a competition thus moderated by protective duties, and limited to the superior qualities of foreign wines, which can be sold only at much higher prices than the best country wines, can neither impede the development of vinicultural industry, nor discourage its improvement: it ought, on the contrary, to stimulate both.   Of the $7\frac{1}{2}$ millions of vedros produced in the south of Russia, more than 7 millions are sold at less than a rouble, and much more than three-fourths at less than 50 or 60 kopecks per vedro.   But, by improvements in culture and preparation, the selling price might be raised to $1\frac{1}{2}$ or 2 roubles, without incurring danger of foreign competition—which would triple or quadruple the gross value of the present production.   Thus we see what a vast field for improvement is still open to our wine-growers.

There is imported into Russia in an average year from 1,100,000 to 1,200,000 vedros of wine, bottled wines included; and the home production, including that of the transcaucasian provinces, amounts to 15,830,000 vedros, giving a total consumption of about 17,000,000 vedros, of which foreign wines form about $6\frac{1}{2}$ per cent.   If we take the production of the southern provinces only ($7\frac{1}{2}$ millions), it is to the importation as 66 to 10.   The mean importation during the three years 1847—49 amounted to 1,136,376 vedros, of which the favoured wines formed the following proportions:

Austrian and Hungarian, 10,332 vedros, or less than 1 per cent.

Greek, 224,658 vedros, or $19\frac{1}{2}$ per cent.

Wallachian, including Cyprus*, which is not favoured, 234,360 vedros, or $20\frac{1}{2}$ per cent. of the total importation.

* The wines of Wallachia and Moldavia are not separately entered in the custom-house returns.   They are included in the importations from Turkey.

We thus perceive that the competition of the wines of Austria and Hungary is quite insignificant: moreover their importation for some time back has been rather decreasing: that of the Wallachian, Moldavian, and Greek wines has for the last twenty years been pretty stationary.

In the official returns of foreign commerce, the wines of Austria and Hungary are estimated at an average value (derived from the prices current) of 3 roubles 55 kopecks per vedro; those of Greece at 1 rouble 79 kopecks; and those of Moldavia and Wallachia at 1 rouble 14 kopecks per vedro. Adding to these prices the import duties on the respective wines, we find that they cannot be sold in Russia below the following prices: the wines of Austria and Hungary for 4 roubles 38 kopecks per vedro, or far beyond the price of the best wines of the Crimea: the wines of Greece for 3 roubles 12 kopecks per vedro,—a price which still exceeds that of the best home wines: the wines of Moldavia and Wallachia for 2 roubles 47 kopecks per vedro, which is about the average price of the best Crimea wines. Thus the competition of these wines is limited by their selling prices, at least as concerns the weak country wines of inferior qualities.

The importation of all other wines—not favoured—has progressed in the following proportions:

Wines in Wood subject to a Duty of 48 Roubles per Oxhoft (=18 Vedros).

Mean annual importation from	1832 to 1834 -	-	-	27,999 oxhoft.
Ditto	„	1835 „ 1837 -	-	-	27,701	„
Ditto	„	1838 „ 1840 -	-	-	26,185	„
Ditto	„	1841 „ 1843 -	-	-	30,035	„
Ditto	„	1844 „ 1846 -	-	-	23,618	„
Ditto	„	1847 „ 1849 -	-	-	32,788	„

Champagne, subject to Duty of 90 Kopecks per Bottle.

Mean annual importation from	1832 to 1834 -	-	-	482,956 bottles
Ditto	„	1835 „ 1837 -	-	-	574,803	„
Ditto	„	1838 „ 1840 -	-	-	694,182	„
Ditto	„	1841 „ 1843 -	-	-	786,445	„
Ditto	„	1844 „ 1846 -	-	-	807,750	„
Ditto	„	1847 „ 1849 -	-	-	888,587	.,

Still Wines in Bottle, subject to Duty of 50 Kopecks per Bottle.

Mean annual importation from	1832 to 1834 -	-	-	107,000 bottles
Ditto	„	1835 „ 1837 -	-	-	131,350	„
Ditto	„	1838 „ 1840 -	-	-	96,592	„
Ditto	„	1841 „ 1843 -	-	-	117,087	„
Ditto	„	1844 „ 1846 -	-	-	93,630	„
Ditto	„	1847 „ 1849 -	-	-	142,718

It results from these figures that importation has augmented during this period of 18 years, for the wines of France, Spain, and Portugal, (non-favoured countries), imported in wood, in the proportion of 17 per cent. ; for sparkling wines in bottle, in the proportion of 84 per cent. ; and for other wines in bottle, in the proportion of 33 per cent.   Thus the sparkling wines, especially those of Champagne, alone present any considerable increase of importation.   In regard to all the others this increase is insignificant compared with the increased consumption of country wine, of which the production has more than tripled during the same period.   It is scarcely twenty-five years since the wines of the southern provinces of European Russia formed only about a-half of the total consumption: now they form about 87 per cent. of it.   All this goes to prove that without too greatly restricting the consumption of foreign wines, or depriving the state of a large revenue from that article, the present tariff offers more than ample guarantees to our vinicultural industry, which has already made such rapid progress.   It will unquestionably become more and more extended and improved as the material welfare of the inhabitants increases, and in proportion as the knowledge necessary for the cultivation of the grape and the manufacture of wine becomes more and more diffused amongst the peasantry.   On this branch of rural economy also, as on others, improved means of communication will exert a most favourable influence.

Horticulture.

We have already (page 153. *et seq.*) given a few hints that may serve to indicate the importance which orchard cultivation has already attained in some parts of Russia, and the much greater importance which it is susceptible of attaining, especially in the southern and western provinces, and in some of the central districts.   We have seen that in Russia—exclusive of Finland and the kingdom of Poland—there are more than 2,000,000 dessiatines employed in horticulture.   In France garden produce is estimated in the official agricultural statistics at 435 fr. per hectare = 120 roubles 80 kopecks per dessiatine.   With us, with a little care, this culture might be made to return at least 75 roubles per dessiatine[*], which would bring the total produce to more than 150 millions of silver roubles,—an estimate which will not appear too large if we remember that in the south of Russia there are orchards which bring in as much as 700 roubles

---

[*] In our estimate of the gross produce of the soil, we have set down the produce from horticulture at only 25 roubles per dessiatine.

per dessiatine. The culture is still susceptible of great extension. Fruit-trees are seldom cultivated but by landed proprietors, or in gardens belonging to the inhabitants of the larger towns, and in the horticultural establishments of the crown. They are cultivated but rarely by the peasants — a circumstance arising partly from want of the requisite taste and skill, and partly from the difficulty of procuring young trees. Government has of late taken various steps for removing these impediments. The horticultural establishments of the crown have been reorganised upon a wider basis; orchards have been established in connexion with the communal schools in fifteen governments; new horticultural schools and nurseries of fruit-trees have been founded in various parts of the empire with the view of instructing pupils in gardening, and supplying individuals with young trees and grafts of superior quality gratis, or at a very moderate price. A popular manual of gardening, published in 1832, has been reprinted and extensively distributed, nor has the institution of suitable premiums been forgotten. Thus, a taste for horticulture will be gradually diffused amongst the peasantry. Its prosperity, however, as a branch of agricultural industry must of course depend on the extent of outlet for its produce. Its principal seat is in the southern provinces, and it can be maintained on a large scale only by a fruit-trade with the north. But here an impediment arises from the difficulty of transport, which for fresh fruits is seldom practicable except for short distances, unless it be by water. Accordingly, those districts where horticulture is most largely carried on, and especially the Crimea, have often experienced great difficulty in procuring a market for their produce. This circumstance did not escape the enlightened attention of government. Persuaded of the benefits which would result from encouraging a trade in dried fruits, the Administration of Domains despatched in 1847 an employé of the Department of Rural Economy to the south of France, Italy, and the islands of the Archipelago to learn the best methods of drying and curing. Premiums have been awarded to those private proprietors whose prepared fruits, exhibited at agricultural shows, appeared deserving of [this encouragement; and, to familiarise the inhabitants of the north with the dried fruits of the south of Russia, the Department of Rural Economy has imported into Petersburg at various intervals the best sorts of dried fruit from Simféropol and Kischenew.

These measures are no doubt well devised, and cannot fail to be attended with excellent consequences; but it must not be disguised that, though some partial progress may be made in the curing of fruits for commerce, this branch of industry will never be duly developed so long as sugar remains so dear as it now is in Russia in consequence of the high duty on colonial sugar. For this article our tariff goes beyond the very highest in Europe,—imposing upon raw sugar an average duty of 3 roubles 50 kopecks per pood (= 34s. 4d. per cwt.), which is more than foreign sugar pays in the maritime states most interested in protecting their colonial plantations. In England foreign sugar pays at an average 1 rouble 96 kopecks per pood; in France, 2 roubles 94½ kopecks; in Holland, 1 rouble 17 kopecks; in Denmark, 63½ kopecks; in Portugal, 1 rouble 18½ kopecks; in Spain, 1 rouble 37½ kopecks. Thus, the duty levied in Russia exceeds by from 56 kopecks to 1 rouble 54 kopecks per pood, or from 20 to 80 per cent., the tariffs of the maritime states which impose the highest protective duties upon foreign sugar. In Austria, colonial sugar imported for the home refineries pays 1 rouble 45 kopecks per pood, or less than $\frac{5}{7}$, and in the states of the Zollverein, 1 rouble 50 kopecks, or just $\frac{3}{7}$ of the average duty levied in Russia. Thus, nowhere is sugar so dear as it is with us, and as to cure a pound of fruit, from ½ to ¾ lb. of sugar is required, it is obvious that the high price of the latter article must stand greatly in the way of the preparation and consumption of dried fruits.

In regard to the trade in fresh fruits with the other parts of the empire, the Crimea occupies the first place. Crimea apples are renowned, and are found on sale in almost every part of Russia. The quantity of pears sent to Petersburg has considerably augmented within the last few years; but their principal market is Moscow, where they have not to stand such a competition with foreign fruit as in the Baltic ports. *

Amongst private proprietors the culture of fruit-trees has made more or less progress even in the northern provinces. For a long time past trees that do not thrive in the open air, as cherry, plum, peach, and apricot, have been cultivated in hothouses in the neighbourhood of Petersburg and Moscow : and this mode of cultivation, troublesome and expensive as it is, returns a good profit from the exorbitant price that fruit fetches in the early part of the season.

Upon the whole, this branch of rural economy is in a state of progress; but its farther progress will greatly depend on the improvement of land and water communication. We subjoin some special information on the subject abridged from a report

---

* There arrive annually in the Baltic ports from abroad, fresh apples and pears to the value of 70,000 or 80,000,—sometimes even 100,000 roubles. The average value during the three years 1847—49 amounted to 74,244 roubles.

by the Department of Rural Economy to the Ministry of Domains, published in 1849.

In the northern region, besides the orchards in the neighbourhood of the capital, there are a good many in the government of Pskow and in a part of that of Nowgorod. In the governments of Twer and Smolensk, it is the apple-tree that is chiefly cultivated. In the environs of St. Petersburg the peasants derive considerable profit from the cultivation of rasps and gooseberries. In the centre of Russia, and especially in the governments of Moscow, Toula, Kalouga, and Orel, the fruit-trees suffered greatly from drought and frost in 1839 and 1840; but matters are now getting better. The government of Koursk abounds in orchards; in the cities of Koursk and Toula fruit-tree nurseries form a rather important branch of occupation. In the government of Wladimir apples and cherries are raised; the latter have a considerable reputation. In the government of Nijni-Nowgorod, orchard cultivation has been greatly extended on the banks of the Volga. In the government of Penza there are a number of orchards known for the abundance and variety of their fruits. In the governments of Tambow and Woronèje this culture is tolerably productive, and has of late been getting introduced amongst the crown peasants. In the government of Saratow, gardening forms a very productive branch of rural economy, especially in the environs of the towns of Saratow, Wolsk, Khvalynsk, and Kamychine, where there is a command of water for irrigation. Some orchards in this government bring in as much as from 4,000 to 7,000 roubles per annum. In the government of Astrakhan, the culture of fruit-trees, which formerly existed only in the neighbourhood of the city of Astrakhan, has for some time past been extending in the district of Krasnoïarsk, where there are now considerable orchards producing fruits superior to those of Astrakhan itself. In Little Russia, this culture is of ancient date and much diffused; but it has lately decreased in importance in consequence of its progress in the governments nearer Moscow, which have greater facilities for supplying the capital. In the government of Poltawa, there are a considerable number of orchards, some of them of a good size; in the government of Kiew they are innumerable. In this latter government the culture of fruit-trees is diffused even amongst the peasantry, of whom almost all have their little gardens. In Podolia horticulture has so greatly extended that there is a felt want of nurseries, and the proprietors must often have recourse for their young trees to the school of horticulture at Kischineff. In the provinces of New Russia, especially in

the Crimea and in Bessarabia, progress is more marked than in
Little Russia.   In the government of Tauride, horticulture is
diffused not only in the Crimea, but also in the northern parts
of the government.   Amongst the Mennonite colonists alone
there are planted yearly from 25 to 50,000 fruit-trees; the
total number owned by them is now more than 375,000, and
new establishments are daily arising; some orchards contain
50,000 fruit-trees and upwards.   Amongst the largest and best
known we distinguish those of Prince Woronzoff at Marsanda;
of Count Potocki at Livadia; and of Narischkine's heirs at
Myskhora.   Amongst apples, the rennet, and amongst pears,
the St. Germain and virgouleuse (a winter pear) are greatly
cultivated in the Crimea.   A single tree of the latter sort will
sometimes yield a return of 30 silver roubles.   The best cherries are those of Spain and Anatolia.   The Simféropol show in
1846 furnished the best proofs of the abundance and variety of
fruits in the Crimea.   One orchard proprietor sent an assortment of 45 species of apples, all of good quality.   The fruit
sent from the Crimea to Moscow represents an annual value of
about 43,000 roubles, which might be greatly increased but for
the high cost of transport.   The return is from 50 kopecks to
1 rouble per pood.   In 1846 there were sent from the Crimea
to Moscow about 1000 carts of apples, and 500 cases (= 2,500
poods) of pears; and into the government of Kharkow nearly
500 carts of different sorts of fruit.   This culture is also progressive in the government of Kherson, both amongst the colonists and amongst the proprietors, whose lands are situated
along the Dnieper, the Bug, the Teligoul, the Ingoul, and
the Ingouletz, as well as in the military colonies near Woss-
nossensk, and the neighbourhood of Odessa.   At Tiraspol there
is an orchard of 20 dessiatines (= 54 acres) in extent, which in
good years brings in as much as 15,000 silver roubles, being at
the rate of 750 roubles per dessiatine (= 44l. per acre).
Amongst the orchards of this government, the first place, in
every respect, belongs to those of M. Skarzynski, and of M.
Garoutt, a merchant near Kherson.   In the latter, established
in 1840, the apricot-trees alone give a produce of 700 poods.
In the district of Tiraspol there are gathered from 10,000 to
20,000 poods of plums, and about 20,000 poods of other
sorts of fruit.   Since 1845 they have begun sending fruit from
this government to Moscow.   In Bessarabia, horticulture is
widely diffused, both amongst the proprietors and amongst the
colonists and crown peasants.   The culture of fruit-trees makes
most progress in the villages near the Dniester and the Pruth.
In the wooded parts of the districts of Kischenew, Orgouew,

Soroki, and Choczim (Khotin), especially where there are beech forests, and in some villages of the district of Bender, gardening constitutes the chief source of income. Of late it has extended chiefly amongst the colonists of the district of Akermann. In the communal gardens of that district there were planted in 1846 nearly 150,000 fruit-trees. The plums of Bessarabia, which, from their great abundance, are the most important fruit raised in the province, are sold in several other provinces *, and the Kischenew show in 1847 furnished proof that several species of delicate fruit might there be cultivated with success. In the government of Ekathérinoslaw horticulture makes most progress amongst the German colonists. In ten villages, the most remarkable in this respect, there are reckoned 300,000 fruit-trees, and from 20,000 to 30,000 are annually planted. In the south of Russia wild pears and nuts form also an object of commerce. The pears are dried and used as food during Lent; they replace in the south the use of dried mushrooms, which form in the north an important article of diet, especially during Lent.

This great and rapid progress of horticulture in the provinces of New Russia, due in great measure to the horticultural establishments of the crown, is the more remarkable and satisfactory because the climate of these countries cannot be considered as particularly favourable to the culture of fruit-trees. The frequent droughts and hurricanes which take place in spring when the trees are in blossom, are the great scourge of this culture in the south of Russia.

We pass over unnoticed the numerous fruit gardens found in large towns and their environs; for it would be difficult to enumerate all those deserving of special mention. As for botanic gardens, besides those attached to universities and other educational establishments, there exist some belonging to private amateurs. There are also physic gardens, the foundation of which dates from the time of Peter the Great. See the work of E. R. Trautvetter, *Grundriss einer Geschichte der Botanik in Bezug auf Russland*, published at St. Petersburg in 1837.

The culture of vegetables is not nearly so advanced as that of fruit-trees. It is only in the neighbourhood of the large

---

* The culture of plums in the south of Russia might become much more important were it not that, from the system of farming out the sale of liquors, proprietors are deprived of an opportunity of distilling the plum brandy known under the name of *slivianka* or *slivovitzer*. For want of this, in good years, great part of the crop is allowed to rot.

towns that it prospers: in the country, the inhabitants generally confine themselves to planting, here and there, a few cabbages and turnips, with a handful of onions and cucumbers. The reason is natural enough: vegetable gardens compared with orchards require much more pains, and bring in much smaller gains. Vegetables will not bear the cost of a long transport: in order to pay, their market must be at the door. Yet this culture is exceedingly deserving of encouragement, on hygienic grounds, no less than on agricultural. A mixture of vegetables with an animal and farinaceous diet is generally recognised as a sound alimentary regimen; but it becomes indispensable where the people is frequently unable to procure fresh animal food, or where it abstains from it upon religious grounds. It has, accordingly, been often observed in Russia that scurvy and epidemics are most severe in those districts where vegetables are scarce.

Except in the villages near the capitals, and a few of the larger towns, and in some districts of Little Russia where the culture of vegetables and their preservation during summer is favoured by the abundance of water, the poverty of the peasant's cabbage garden is nearly universal. Amongst the chief moral impediments to this branch of culture the Department of Rural Economy places, on the one hand, the little care which our peasants have for varying their diet, and, on the other, the want of horticultural knowledge: to this may be added that our female peasantry seldom pay any attention to it: but in no branch of rural economy is their assistance so indispensable as in this:— in every country where it thrives, it is almost always the women and children that do the work of planting, watering, and weeding.*

In order to encourage this branch of culture, the Administration of Domains directs the officers at the head of the crown farms and horticultural establishments to use every effort for the extension of kitchen-gardens—for the introduction into these of the culture of different sorts of herbs—and for the instruction of pupils in the necessary practical knowledge. In consequence of these instructions various sorts of vegetables are already cultivated in several of the crown establishments; and, with a view to variety, the Department of Rural Economy has imported seeds of various vegetables formerly unknown in

* In those districts where the male population exercised some branch of industry which calls them from their homes, the women employ themselves in the labours of the field : such cases, however, are merely exceptions caused by some local necessity. With us the females amongst the common people lead in general much less active and industrious lives than they do in other countries.

Russia, and caused them to be distributed amongst the agronomic schools and the best cultivators amongst the peasantry.

Market vegetable gardens exist in Russia only in the neighbourhood of the two capitals and a few other large towns — in some parts of the government of Jaroslaw, especially in the district of Rostow — in the government of Nijni-Nowgorod, especially in the villages lying along the Volga — in some districts of the government of Kalouga — in some villages of the governments of Kherson and Tauride, lying along the banks of the Dnieper — and in Courland, along the banks of the river Aa, from Mitau to the coast. There also some — and not inconsiderable ones — in the islands of the Dwina, near Archangel. The best are found in the district of Rostow, in the government of Jaroslaw (which also furnishes the best gardeners), and in the villages within a radius of 14 versts from the city of Moscow: in both these districts gardening brings in considerable profit to the peasants. In the neighbourhood of Rostow, a dessiatine of land employed in the culture of green peas will give a return of 400 to 480 silver roubles (= 23*l.* to 28*l.* per acre). This article forms no unimportant item of home commerce, and, since 1844 it has even been an article of export. In the environs of Petersburg and Moscow the culture of early vegetables is both extensive and lucrative. The principal occupation in some of the crown villages in the environs of Nijni-Nowgorod is raising and curing cucumbers, which are sent to Petersburg and other places. Around the cities of Kazan, Saratow, Astrakhan, and Penza, gardening has also acquired a certain degree of importance: in the vicinity of the first of these towns and in the district of Rostow (government of Jaroslaw), besides kitchen vegetables, mint is extensively cultivated for use in the manufacture of Kazan soap. In the Penza market, asparagus, fresh cucumbers, and mushrooms, are to be had almost the whole year round. There is a village called Bessonowka, situated about 12 versts from Penza, in which about 2,000 individuals are engaged in the culture of onions, which are sent into all the neighbouring governments, and even as far as Kiew and Astrakhan.

The raising of cucumbers in the open field is extensively practised in a great part of Russia: quantities of melons and pumpkins are likewise raised in the open field in the southern provinces. A melonry sometimes gives a return of 80 to 100 roubles per dessiatine (= 4·14*l.* to 5·17*l.* per acre). Pumpkins, in those districts, are often used by the people as common vegetable food; they are boiled with a mixture of grits. In the northern governments, quantities of turnips are raised in the open fields; a fermented liquor, called *repitza*, is prepared from them. In Little Russia and the Polish provinces the culture of beetroot as an alimentary substance is greatly diffused, and is of ancient date; there is prepared from it a sweetish acid soup which is well known under the name of *borschtch*.

We must not omit to mention the culture of mustard, which is extensively grown in the colony of Sarepta (government of Saratow); nor that of chicory, which for a short time past has been extending in the governments of Jaroslaw and Wladimir.

The shows of agricultural products at which kitchen garden stuffs made a considerable figure, have been those of Simféropol, in the government of Tauride (1846), of Lebediane, in the government of Tambow (1845,1846, and 1847), of Wologda and of Elizabetgrade, in the government of Kherson (1848).

Floriculture, in its larger sense, is hitherto but little diffused in Russia. A felt want on the part of the inhabitants to adorn their dwellings and their gardens with flowers — denoting, as it does, a certain refinement of taste and softness of manners — has not yet penetrated with us beneath the upper classes of society. The culture of flowers, accordingly, has not been hitherto developed except in the environs of large towns and in the gardens of some wealthy proprietors, where, indeed it is often carried the length of luxury. At Petersburg and Moscow floricultural luxury is much greater than in any other European capital, though it is also much more expensive; for a nosegay or a pot of flowers costs at Petersburg as many roubles (3s. 2d.) as it would cost francs (9¾d.) at Paris or Vienna, and often more. Nevertheless, it is rare to see an apartment with any pretensions to ornament in which flowers do not come in for their share. They abound in the country houses, parks, and gardens belonging to proprietors in easy circumstances; though the taste has not descended to their inferiors. In the northern provinces this might perhaps be attributed to the severity of the climate rendering the culture more troublesome and expensive, were it not equally observable in milder regions. Abroad, we often see before the humblest cottages little garden plots adorned with flowers; but this is seldom to be met with amongst ourselves. The poppy is almost the sole embellishment of the peasant's garden, except in the provinces of Little Russia; for the Little Russian has an innate love of flowers, and a taste for their culture descends to the lowest classes of the population. It is not that the

Russian peasant is in general indifferent to ornament; on the contrary, he is fond of glitter and liveliness of colour, and likes to adorn the roof, the doors, the gable of his dwelling with carvings in wood, which often strike the eye of the traveller by the originality of the design and the carefulness of the execution. This taste for ornament leads us to hope that, in temperate districts at least, a taste for floriculture will in time be acquired by our country population in proportion as the appropriate knowledge becomes diffused amongst the rising generations. One of the most potent means to this end will be the influence of floricultural societies and the stimulating of emulation by public shows. As yet there is but one society of this sort, which has been instituted at Moscow under the exalted patronage of Her Majesty the Empress; it is called the Society of Amateurs of Gardening, and its object is to encourage horticulture in general, and the culture of flowers in particular. It has organised annual shows of flowers and other garden products; at several of these, which have been held in regular succession since 1844, there have been exhibited as many as 5000 samples of plants and flowers of various species. The Department of Rural Economy has also introduced floriculture into the horticultural establishments under its control; so that a supply of flowers can be furnished to private amateurs, the pupils of the establishments may become familiarised with their culture, and a taste for them be propagated amongst the agricultural classes.

Culture of Potatoes.

This culture, to which our rural population has displayed a certain amount of repugnance, required for some time to be propped up by measures of encouragement. It has now become pretty generally naturalised, except in the southern provinces, and in some governments of the eastern part of the empire, where the soil and climate seem less adapted for it, though there likewise the main impediment seems to lie rather in the prejudices of the natives.

In those provinces, which do not usually produce grain enough for the subsistence of the population, the potatoe is a useful and almost indispensable surrogate. In those where grain is abundant, it is a reserve to fall back upon in a bad year; but, to keep up its cultivation in countries of the latter class, there must be found some profitable mode of employing it when not required for food, as brandy distillation, or the preparation of syrups or starch. It is in this way that government has sought to encourage its cultivation.

The principal measures of encouragement date from the years 1839 and 1840,—years of bad harvest and scarcity throughout a great part of the empire; and it is from this same epoch that the culture has made most progress. The first measures decreed by government were as follows. Potatoes were ordered to be planted in all the communal lands of the state domains, in order to afford a supply of seed for the peasants; practical instructions were published on their culture, preservation, and use; and premiums were allowed to such cultivators as should raise the largest quantities and best qualities. The consequence was, that the quantity of potatoes planted, which had formerly scarce amounted to 1,000,000 tchetwerts, was increased in 1841 to 3,874,000 tchetwerts. In 1843 the planting of the communal lands was left off as superfluous in all those villages where the quantity planted by the peasants themselves amounted to 1 tchetwerik ($=\frac{1}{8}$ tchetwert) per soul. In 1844 it was considered unnecessary to keep up the premiums, except in the eastern and southern governments, where the culture continued backward.

As in many districts the peasants, little disposed to use the potatoe as an article of food, were at a loss what to do with their crop after they had gathered it in, government perceived the necessity of encouraging its use in the distillation of brandy and the preparation of flour, starch, and syrup. Accordingly, besides other measures of encouragement, they awarded gold and silver medals to parties who should establish manufactories of starch, syrup, and other products from potatoes, and keep them going for a certain number of years. These measures, seconded by the good-will of the private proprietors, produced the desired effect. The quantity of potatoes planted increased from year to year. In 1844 it already amounted to 5,909,000 tchetwerts; manufactories of starch and syrup were established in various districts; and the price of these two articles was reduced by more than a half. Various processes have also been invented and tried for preserving potatoes, both fresh and dried, for preparing bread from them, and for converting them to some useful purpose after they have been attacked by frost. Their culture has penetrated of late into districts where, eight or ten years ago, it was totally unknown; it has even found its way into some districts of Siberia. In the western provinces it has so greatly increased, that in 1844 it exceeded the wants of the population; and from that period the quantity planted in these districts has fallen off. All that could now be wished for is to see the tubercle more extensively used in the feeding of cattle, — which would be a very desirable improvement, especially in those provinces where fodder is scarce. In some districts the return of the potatoe crop is ten or twelve times the seed; but the general average for Russia is only three or four times the seed. The following are the quantities sown and reaped during the ten years 1841 to 1850 in forty-six governments: —

	Seed. Tchetwerts.	Harvest. Tchetwerts.	Return. Times the Seed.
In 1841 - - -	3,920,479	18,540,759	4·7
1842 - - -	4,964,629	23,270,372	4·7
1843 - - -	5,488,098	26,889,566	4·9
1844 - - -	5,904,521	21,621,466	3·7
1845 - - -	5,535,674	21,270,801	3·8
1846 - - -	6,724,657	18,142,453	2·7
1847 - - -	5,872,850	19,257,212	3·3
1848 - - -	6,082,627	18,787,106	3·1
1849 - - -	5,835,630	17,814,331	3·1
1850 - - -	5,399,326	15,168,792	2·8
Total -	55,728,491	200,762,858	
Annual average -	5,572,849	20,076,285	3·6

We perceive from these figures that, during the first four years, the quantity of seed followed an ascending movement. After that year it varies up and down, but, upon the whole, rather augmenting; whilst the harvest, after considerably augmenting during the first three years, follows, after 1844, a constantly decreasing movement, with the exception of the year 1847, which presents an augmentation of 6 per cent. over the preceding year. The largest quantity of seed used was in 1846, and the best harvest was that of 1843, which returned the seed nearly five-fold. The triennial averages present the following results : —

	Seed. Tchetwerts.	Harvest. Tchetwerts.	Return. Times the Seed.
In 1841—43 - -	4,791,069	22,900,232	4·8
1844—46 - -	6,054,951	20,344,907	3·4
1847—49 - -	5,930,369	18,619,550	3·1

Thus, as ultimate result, the quantity sown during the last triennial period had increased, as compared with the first, by 1,139,300 tchetwerts, or nearly 24 per cent. ; whilst the quantity harvested had decreased by 4,280,682 tchetwerts, or more than 19 per cent. This unfavourable result is a consequence of the potatoe disease, which in 1846 appeared in the Baltic provinces, in 1847 extended to the governments of the west and north, and in 1848 penetrated, although with less severity, to the governments of the centre. The apprehensions awakened by this disease contributed also to slacken the progress of the culture during the latter years. To remedy this evil, the Department of Rural Economy, and the Agronomic Society of St. Petersburg, attempted to renovate the species by propagating it from the seed. The results of their experiments are given in various periodical publications. The following table, prepared from data contained in the report of the Ministry of Domains, exhibits the statistics of potatoe culture in forty-six governments during the year 1847, being the year of greatest abundance during the last triennial period.

Table exhibiting the Quantities of Potatoes planted in Forty-six Governments during the Year 1847.

Governments.	Population in 1846.	Quantity of Potatoes planted in 1847.	Quantity of Seed per 100 Inhabitants.
I. Western Governments.		*Tchetwerts.*	*Tchetwerts.*
1. Kowno - - - -	915,500	398,310	43·5
2. Wilna - - - -	863,700	370,358	42·9
3. Minsk - - - -	1,046,400	440,107	42
4. Esthonia - - - -	310,400	123,198	39·7
5. Grodno - - - -	907,100	333,569	36·8
6. Courland - - - -	553,300	141,401	25·6
7. Mohilew - - - -	931,300	223,568	24
8. Witebsk - - - -	789,500	187,829	23·8
9. Wolhynia - - -	1,445,500	292,156	20·2
10. Livonia - - - -	814,100	128,540	15·8
11. Kiew - - - -	1,605,800	160,621	10
12. Podolia - - - -	1,703,000	153,762	9
Total -	10,885,600	2,953,419	27·1
II. Northern Governments.			
13. Pskow - - - -	775,800	119,494	15·4
14. St. Petersburg - - -	971,500	120,316	12·4
15. Nowgorod - - -	907,900	108,894	12
16. Archangel - - -	253,000	14,065	5·6
17. Olonetz - - - -	263,100	13,550	5·1
18. Wologda - - - -	822,200	23,877	2·9
Total -	3,993,500	400,196	10
III. Central Governments.			
19. Twer - - - -	1,327,700	258,097	19·4
20. Smolensk - - - -	1,170,600	177,693	15·2
21. Kalouga - - - -	1,006,400	130,676	13
22. Tschernigow - - -	1,430,000	159,173	11·1
23. Orel - - - -	1,502,900	164,198	10·9
24. Toula - - - -	1,227,000	132,308	10·8
25. Jaroslaw - - - -	1,008,100	103,225	10·2
26. Moscow - - - -	1,374,700	138,213	10
27. Koursk - - - -	1,680,000	167,790	10
28. Poltawa - - - -	1,783,800	172,334	9·7
Carried forward -	13,511,200	1,603,707	

Governments.	Population in 1846.	Quantity of Potatoes planted in 1847.	Quantity of Seed per 100 Inhabitants.
		Tchetwerts.	*Tchetwerts.*
Brought forward -	13,511,200	1,603,707	
29. Saratow - - - -	1,718,600	116,733	6·8
30. Riazan - - - -	1,365,900	90,888	6·7
31. Woronèje - - - -	1,657,900	100,536	6·1
32. Wladimir - - - -	1,246,500	71,330	5·7
33. Tambow - - - -	1,750,900	100,662	5·7
34. Kharkow - - - -	1,467,400	77,501	5·3
35. Penza - - - -	1,087,200	45,890	4·2
36. Kazan - - - -	1,342,900	54,041	4
37. Nijni-Nowgorod - -	1,178,200	45,918	3·9
Total -	26,326,700	2,307,206	8·8
IV. Eastern Governments.			
38. Kostroma - - -	1,054,600	68,811	6·5
39. Wiatka - - - -	1,662,800	63,619	3·8
40. Perm - - - -	1,637,700	45,159	2·8
41. Orenburg - - -	1,948,500	33,180	1·7
Total -	6,303,600	210,769	3·3
V. Southern Governments.			
42. Ekathérinoslaw - -	870,100	48,043	5·5
43. Bessarabia - - -	792,000	12,940	1·6
44. Tauride - - - -	572,200	8,764	1·5
45. Kherson - - - -	842,000	11,315	1·3
46. Astrakhan - - -	284,400	1,650	0·6
Total -	3,361,100	82,712	2·5
Abstract.			
I. Western Governments -	10,885,600	2,953,419	27·1
II. Northern do. - -	3,993,500	400,196	10
III. Central do. - -	26,326,700	2,307,206	8·8
IV. Eastern do. - -	6,303,600	210,769	3·3
V. Southern do. - -	3,361,100	82,712	2·5
Grand Total -	50,870,500	5,954,302	11·7

From this table we perceive that potatoe culture is most diffused in the western governments, where the average quantity planted in 1847 is equivalent to $\frac{1}{4}$ tchetwert per inhabitant; and in the northern governments, where we have an average of $\frac{1}{10}$ tchetwert per head. The minimum quantity planted in any of the former was somewhat less than $\frac{1}{10}$ tchetwert, and the maximum somewhat more than $\frac{2}{5}$ tchetwert per head: the minimum in the latter was $\frac{3}{100}$ and the maximum nearly $\frac{1}{6}$ tchetwert per head. In the central governments it has already become tolerably diffused, since the mean quantity planted gives nearly $\frac{9}{100}$, the maximum nearly $\frac{1}{5}$, and the minimum nearly $\frac{4}{100}$ tchetwerts per inhabitant. But it is still very backward in the eastern and southern governments; in the former of which the average quantity planted per inhabitant is only about $\frac{3}{100}$, and in the latter only $\frac{1}{40}$ tchetwert. The harvest of the year in question yielded —

In the northern governments	-	$3\frac{1}{3}$ returns $=\frac{13}{100}$	tchetw. per inhab.	
In the central	do.	nearly - 4	„	$=\frac{35}{100}$ „
In the eastern	do.	nearly - 4	„	$=\frac{12}{100}$ „
In the western	do.	nearly - 3	„	$=\frac{3}{4}$ „
In the southern	do.	nearly - $4\frac{2}{3}$	„	$=\frac{1}{10}$ „

Culture of Maize.

This culture is very suitable for the soil and climate of southern Russia, but hitherto it has acquired little importance except in Bessarabia, where this article forms a main item of the food of the common people. It is now, however, beginning to extend in the other provinces of New Russia, and is encouraged by government.

The following, according to data collected by the Department of Rural Economy, were the quantities of seed maize required for the crown domains in the governments of Kherson, Tauride, and Ekathérinoslaw during the years 1844—1848.

In 1844	-	-	-	2,059 tchetwerts.
1845	-	•	-	2,493 „
1846	-	-	-	2,628 „
1847	-	-	-	2,716 „
1848	-	-	-	2,720 „

Assuming that nearly similar quantities were required for the domains of private parties, we may estimate the total quantity now sown at about 5,000 or 6,000 tchetwerts. However trifling this quantity may be, compared with the extent of these three provinces, it may become greatly increased in the course of time, if it goes on at the slow but steady rate of progress which it has been following during these four years.

Culture of Beet-root.

The culture of beet-root as a sacchariferous plant has been introduced into Russia within the last twenty-five or thirty years. Previously to that, it was cultivated only in small quantities, chiefly in Little Russia and the western provinces, as an esculent vegetable, and in some districts as an article of food for cattle. In 1825 there existed in the whole empire only two sugar-manufactories, which did not produce above 1,500 poods of raw sugar: in 1848 there were reckoned 337 manufactories, consuming 30 millions of poods (= 483,000 tons) of beet-root, and producing upwards of a million poods (= 322,000 cwt.) of raw sugar. This is $2\frac{1}{2}$ times the product of the whole sugar manufactories of the Austrian monarchy (about 400,000 poods), $1\frac{1}{2}$ times the product of the states of the Zollverein (about 700,000 poods) and somewhat more than $\frac{1}{4}$ of the product of France in 1850 (65 millions of kilogrammes).

Reserving for next chapter a detailed discussion of the important question of the sugar manufacture, we shall here confine ourselves to exhibiting a summary of the advantages derived from this manufacture by agriculture,—having in view especially the agricultural position of Russia,—as the same are set forth in a Report of the Department of Rural Economy to the Ministry of Domains.

Serving as the raw material of a high-priced commodity, beet-root puts into circulation a considerable amount of capital; it furnishes an article of food for cattle: and, by the application of a new process, the cellular membrane, after the extraction of the saccharine matter, can serve, on being mixed with rye-meal, for the preparation of a very wholesome and palatable sort of bread: it is not an exhausting crop, and is well adapted for the system of alternate culture so desirable for Russia: it is also favourable to the cleaning of the land, and the leaves serve for manure: it augments the return from the land, and the value of manual labour, especially in districts where grain is low-priced: it generally brings in from 50 to 100 per cent. more than the culture of cereals: it finds a readier and more certain market: it is generally sold at the time when the land-owner has to pay his taxes, before the corn is threshed out, or its market-price determined: the deliveries of bones—the use of which was formerly almost unknown in the interior of Russia, —the transport of wood, charcoal, and peat, as well as of the raw sugar, and the labour carried on within the manufactory itself, set money in circulation all around these establishments, and diffuse comfort amongst the agricultural classes by giving them the means of turning their time and labour to account: the peasants of the State Domains derive also a large share of the advantages of this industry, by selling to the sugar establishments bones, wood, lime, and charcoal, and by labouring in the beet-root fields.

Without disputing any one of these advantages, we shall only observe that, important as they undoubtedly are for certain localities, their influence upon our agriculture in general is but very limited. The sugar manufacture is dependent upon certain conditions which are not always to be found in combination; it requires, first of all, a soil suitable for the cultivation of beet-root—a light soil of average quality, or what the Germans term good barley land—and a locality sufficiently populous to be able to furnish, at certain seasons and for a moderate hire, the requisite number of hands for cleaning and gathering in the crop. We see that wherever this branch of industry has made considerable progress, as in France and Germany, it has chiefly concentrated itself in those districts where these advantages are found combined. It is much the same thing in Russia. Of the whole 27,141,541 poods of beet-root which, according to the official statistics, were furnished in 1848 to the sugar manufactories of the empire and of the kingdom of Poland, 12,712,500, or nearly half, were grown in the government of Kiew alone. A circumstance, moreover, which must prevent the extension of this culture in a great part of Russia, is the frequent droughts already alluded to, which usually extend over a surface of fifteen or twenty governments at a time; but assuming for it any amount of extension which it is possible to conceive, we apprehended that it can never exercise any material influence on the *ensemble* of our rural economy. According to official data already commented on (*ante*, p. 150. *et seq.*), the mean crop of beet-root is at the rate of 600 poods per dessiatine, and the mean yield of raw sugar $3\frac{1}{3}$ per cent.; this latter rate must be under the actual yield; and with the progress of improvement —seeing that in France 6 per cent. and upwards is obtained in the best organised establishments—an average return of at least $4\frac{1}{2}$ per cent. may be looked for; which would be at the rate of 27 poods of raw sugar per dessiatine. The actual production is about 1,000,000 poods, and the mean importation during the triennial period 1847-49 was 1,926,260 poods, giving a total consumption (when we add the importation of raw sugar into the kingdom of Poland) of about 3,100,000 poods. Let us suppose that indigenous takes the place of colonial sugar entirely, and that the consumption rises to 10,000,000 poods, or more than treble its present amount. Upon this supposition—the most favourable that can possibly be conceived—the culture of beet-root would occupy, at the rate of 27 poods of sugar per dessiatine, 307,000 dessiatines, or $\frac{2}{3}$ per cent. of the cultivable land of European Russia. In the government of Kiew, where it is most extensively carried on, it occupies less than 1 per cent. of the arable soil. But, notwithstanding this, the benefits which it confers upon those districts where it is favoured by local circumstances are real and incontestable, and it deserves protection and encouragement within proper limits; that is to say, within those bounds beyond which it cannot be carried without being prejudicial to other interests no less important. We will have occasion to return to this subject in the following chapter; at present we have merely endeavoured to assign to the culture of beet-root the place which properly belongs to it in a general estimate of the productive forces of the country.

In proportion as the manufacture of indigenous sugar becomes more extensive, so much the more desirable does it become to propagate the cultivation of beet-root amongst the peasants; our rural populations still entertain a certain degree of repugnance for this culture, the advantages of which they are unable to appreciate, and most of the sugar manufactories are supplied by their own plantations; but in consequence of the measures of encouragement adopted by the Administration of Domains, it now begins to make way amongst the peasants of the State Domains, especially in the vicinity of the manufactories in the governments of Smolensk, Tschernigow, Podolia, and Penza. The profits which they make and the prompt sale which they find will serve as a stimulus; and there is room to expect that this culture will extend itself under favourable circumstances of soil and demand, as for example in Little Russia, Lithuania, and Poland, where beet-roots were long ago raised in considerable quantities as esculent vegetables, and especially for the preparation of a sour soup called *borschtsch*.

Culture of Hops.

This culture can prosper only in those countries where beer is extensively brewed; accordingly it has acquired little importance except in the kingdom of Poland, in some of the western, and in some of the central provinces of the empire.   It requires a great deal of care and the crop is very uncertain. In countries where the culture of cereals is successful, hops are raised only where they find a very ready and profitable sale. In Russia their cultivation is more hazardous than in many other countries; the harvests fail more frequently on account of the great variability of the climate, and when an abundant one arrives the very limited demand for the article (which does not admit of being long stored to wait for better markets) causes an excessive fall of price. The domestic culture of hops for the wants of the family is common enough; but as an article of commerce its cultivation in hop-plantations is chiefly confined to the governments of Moscow, Riazan, Wladimir, Nijni-Nowgorod, the south-western part of the government of Kostroma, and the north-western part of the government of Kazan. In the latter government it is almost exclusively Tschuwasches that occupy themselves with this culture. The principal hop-plantations are found in the governments of Moscow and Riazan along the little rivers Gousslitza and Nerskaïa and their affluents, where a light and sandy soil watered by an infinity of small streams seems to be particularly favourable to this culture; to this we must add that these are well wooded countries—a circumstance which secures the hops against the malignant influences of the north and easterly winds, and affords a supply of poles at small cost. As the culture requires unintermitting care and a great deal of manual labour, it is rarely undertaken on a large scale by the proprietors themselves: it is carried on almost exclusively by the peasants on their own account; and, as they are for most part unskilled in the process of drying, that operation is left to certain individuals who make a trade of it. Formerly wood was employed for drying, but this was found to impart a smoky smell to the hops and a disagreeable taste to the beer, so that latterly charcoal has come into general use; this is an important improvement, but it has been attended with one abuse, namely, the employment of sulphur, which is mixed with the charcoal during the drying. In England sulphur is used only for hops of bad quality with the view of removing a certain nauseous odour, but in the hop-grounds in the neighbourhood of Gousslitza, the mixture of sulphur has been generally adopted. In this locality the average crop is about 70 poods, and in other districts about 50 poods per dessiatine. Good hops fetch 5 roubles and 5 roubles 10 kopecks per pood. In Bohemia the average crop is 55 to 56 poods, in France 80 poods, and in England about 60 poods per dessiatine (=805 lbs. per acre). We have taken these figures from a little work on the culture of the hop in Central Russia published at Moscow in 1851 by M. Jeleznow: it contains very interesting information both agronomic and statistical; as the result of a detailed estimate of the costs of culture in the vicinity of Gousslitza, and a comparison of the return there and in other countries it would appear that the nett return of a dessiatine is

				Roub.	Kop.
In Bohemia	-	-	-	- 92	58
In France	-	-	-	- 300	0
In England	-	-	-	- 254	68
And in the environs of Gousslitza			-	122	94

This shows that hop cultivation is very profitable under favourable local circumstances, and that it might become important in Russia if the use of beer were more general.

The foreign commerce in this article is but trifling, though its importation has of late considerably augmented, namely from 495 poods in 1844 to 1763 poods in 1849, whilst its exportation has fallen off from 1369 poods in the former year to 349 in the latter. Fifteen or twenty years ago more than 20,000 poods were exported for the kingdom of Poland; but this exportation has successively diminished by two-thirds, although the manufacture of beer has there considerably augmented, which would seem to indicate an extension of hop cultivation in that kingdom.

Culture of Tobacco.

However incomplete the returns we possess regarding the progress of tobacco culture (see *antè*, p. 158.), it is evident that it has now attained considerable importance, especially in the governments of Tschernigow, Saratow, and Poltawa. It has also of late begun to extend itself in several provinces of New Russia, in the government of Stavropol, in Podoliä, in some of the central governments, and even in some parts of Siberia. In the transcaucasian provinces, notwithstanding the favourable nature of the climate, the tobacco plantations are but inconsiderable, the quantity grown not exceeding 25 to 26,000 poods. The greater part of the tobacco raised in Russia is of very ordinary quality, selling at from 40 to 80 kopecks per pood; but this cheapness has diffused a taste for it throughout the lower classes of the population, including even the nomadic tribes of Astrakhan and Siberia, and the natives of the Aléoutic islands. Down to the year 1842, the culture of tobacco of a better quality was confined to a few isolated experiments, which however served to afford an indication of the species most suitable for the different districts. By way of encouraging and promoting these attempts, the Department of Rural Economy periodically imports tobacco seed from the Havannah, Virginia, Persia, and Turkey, which it distributes gratuitously in every district where the inhabitants testify a desire to introduce plantations, and especially amongst the best known planters and colonists of New Russia. In the space of five years there have been distributed upwards of 600 lbs., a quantity sufficient to sow 12,000 dessiatines. Works and hints on tobacco culture have likewise been published and distributed in considerable numbers with a view to the instruction of the cultivators. In order to facilitate sales, the Department of Rural Economy has, by its own intervention, put the producers in communication with the principal manufacturers; it has also very recently dispatched a distinguished agriculturist with a commission to visit Turkey, Egypt, the south of Europe, the United States of America, and the Island of Cuba, to study the culture of tobacco in those countries, and, upon his return, to visit Holland, the countries of the Rhine, and the central parts of Germany, in order to examine the various modes of manufacturing tobacco and snuff. This agent is charged at the same time to engage in Germany an experienced cultivator who will assist in introducing the best modes of culture, both into the agricultural schools and amongst private planters. Meantime experimental plantations have been introduced into all the model farms and horticultural establishments of the crown; particular attention is paid to these on the Kharkow farm, which is intended to propagate sound notions on the subject of tobacco culture in Little Russia, where there are already raised about 2 millions of poods: the greater part of this, no doubt, is of a very ordinary description at present; but in the course of time the better sorts will be more extensively raised. The good effect of these measures has already been felt, especially during the last five or six years, in New Russia, Bessarabia, and the governments of Podolia, Kiew, and Poltawa. In Podolia some proprietors have obtained seed from America of a good sort, suitable for the manufacture of cigars; and in Bessarabia the crown peasants of the district of Khotin have begun cultivating the better sorts. In regard to quantity, the first place is due to the government of Tschernigow, where from 800,000 to 1,000,000 poods are raised. Next comes the government of Saratow, where the culture is carried on exclusively in the German colonies near the Volga, and in some Little Russian villages; the quantity raised is about 500,000 poods. Tobacco culture has no doubt the disadvantage of exhausting the soil more than many other plants; but this disadvantage is counterbalanced by the abundance of the crop. A dessiatine yields commonly from 80 to 100 poods, which, reckoning only 60 kopecks per pood,—the average price of the commonest sort—affords a gross return of from 48 to 60 roubles per dessiatine (= 56s. 6d. to 70s. 6d. per acre). This culture is particularly advantageous for those districts which abound in good arable land, and have at the same time little outlet for cereals; in those districts it withdraws from cereal cultivation a very trifling proportion of the productive soil. For example, in the government of Tschernigow, the tobacco plantations would occupy—reckoning 80 poods per dessiatine—not more than 12,500 dessiatines, or less than $\frac{2}{5}$ per cent. of the whole arable land. Assuming that the production in all European Russia should be raised to 10 million poods, or thrice its present amount, the culture would not occupy at the utmost more than 125,000 dessiatines or $\frac{1}{7000}$ per cent., or thereby of the entire productive soil (90 millions of dessiatines). We apprehend that its chances for the future are good in regard both to its extension and to its improvement. The total produce of Russia is now about 3 millions of poods, being a fifth more than the total produce of the Austrian dominions (about 2,500,000 poods), and more than double the production of the whole states of the Zollverein, which amounted in 1847 to 1,586,023 poods. The exportation is trifling, and has considerably fallen off within the last fifteen years; the following are the triennial averages: —

From 1835 to 1837	-	-	- 56,939 poods.
1838 to 1840	-	-	- 44,877
1841 to 1843	-	-	- 39,311
1844 to 1846	-	-	- 27,812
1847 to 1849	-	-	- 19,867

These figures exhibit a diminution of two-thirds in the quantity exported; during the same period importation has augmented more than 45 per cent., as appears from the following figures : —

From 1835 to 1837	-	- 101,831 poods.
1838 to 1840	-	- 90,010
1841 to 1843	-	- 120,936
1844 to 1846	-	- 131,281
1847 to 1849	-	- 147,052

An exportation so largely and steadily decreasing side by side with a so considerably augmented import shows that the fate of tobacco culture in Russia is entirely dependent on the home consumption. The total quantity raised throughout the empire being estimated, according to the best and most recent returns, at upwards of 3 millions of poods, and the exportation being now under 20,000, we may safely estimate the home consumption of indigenous tobacco at about 3 millions of poods; and if to this we add the foreign tobacco entered at the custom-house (nearly 150,000 poods) besides what comes in by smuggling, we may estimate the total consumption in round numbers at 3,200,000 poods, which gives for a population of 65,500,000 inhabitants nearly 2 lbs. per head. In Austria the total consumption gives $2\frac{1}{2}$ lbs., and in the Zollverein $3\frac{1}{3}$ lbs. Russian per head; thus the consumption per head in Russia is to that of Austria nearly as 10 to $12\frac{1}{2}$, and to that of the Zollverein as 10 to $16\frac{1}{2}$.

Foreign tobacco forms in Russia only $6\frac{1}{4}$ per cent. of the total quantity consumed; but the 147,000 poods represent, at the official estimate, a value of 2,385,000 silver roubles; whilst the 3 million poods of indigenous tobacco, reckoned at the average price of 70 kopecks per pood, give a value of only 2,100,000 roubles, being 285,000 roubles, or 12 per cent. less than the value of the foreign import. In Austria foreign tobacco forms only 6 or 7 per cent. of the total consumption, but in the Zollverein it forms more than $\frac{2}{3}$.

For all the inferior qualities which sell under 1 rouble per pood, and which make up the great part of the consumption, the home market is secured to the home grower, since no foreign tobacco can compete at the price, and since, moreover, the duty of 6 roubles per pood is absolutely prohibitory even for tobacco of medium quality; the consumption must necessarily augment with the progress of wealth and population, especially as the extensive use of tobacco amongst the lower classes is rather of recent origin. Assuming for the development of this culture an increase at the rate of only 5 per cent. per annum — certainly no very hazardous estimate considering the rapidly increasing consumption of the article in other countries and the recent progress of plantations amongst ourselves — the present production of 3 million poods will be doubled by the end of twenty years. As for the superior qualities, there seems little chance that ours will be able entirely to supersede the sorts we now receive from America and Turkey; but the experiments already made have shown that the culture of these sorts of tobacco may succeed up to a certain point in several districts of Little Russia and the Southern provinces, if the culture be rationally pursued and care taken to renew the seed. The best plantations of the Crimea and of the governments of Kherson, Tschernigow, and Saratow already produce tobaccos of good quality which fetch from 6 to 12 and even 15 roubles per pood. Such examples show that, seconded and encouraged by government, there is a vast field for improvement which cannot be allowed to lie waste. The circumstances of other countries are also favourable to this culture with us. The increase in the consumption of tobacco, and especially of cigars, is becoming so rapid in every country of Europe, that the transatlantic plantations have difficulty in supplying the demand of the continent. Good Havannah cigars are becoming rarer and rarer, and their place is supplied by cigars manufactured in Germany, of a mixture of Havannah with leaves of a more ordinary description, foreign or native; this facilitates competition on the part of continental tobacco, in the production of which Russia holds the first place in so far as quantity is concerned. To benefit by this state of matters, we must endeavour to improve the quality. If the progress recently made in this respect in some of our plantations be maintained, and if it do not remain an isolated exception, it may be anticipated that indigenous tobacco will replace the importations of the medium sorts at least; and it is not impossible that the now declining exportation may resume an ascending movement; with better management we could afford to sell much better qualities at a very moderate price. If of the 3 million poods which we now produce, and which represent a value of little more than 2 millions of roubles, the planters succeeded in raising only $\frac{1}{10}$, or 300,000 poods of a better quality, worth 5 or 6 roubles, this of itself would augment the product by 1,300,000 or 1,600,000 roubles, independently of what might be gained by extension of the culture.

Rearing of Poultry.

This is a branch of rural economy which in Russia is naturally capable of much extension, especially in those governments which abound in grain. It depends greatly on the progress of wealth amongst certain classes of the inhabitants and on the facilities of communication. It is in the towns that the chief markets for poultry must be sought. When, along the roads— the radii, as we may term them, converging to these great centres of consumption, the means of transport are easy, the circle of supply becomes widened, and the cheapness which is the result of a wide circle of supply widens also the circle of the consumers, just as conversely the circle of the latter is narrowed when the commodity becomes dear. But in Russia, in regard to this article, as in regard to so many others, the means of turning production to account are not always found in a satisfactory ratio to the elements of production themselves. In a number of districts where the rearing and fattening of poultry might be advantageously carried on from the abundance of the materials for feeding them, there are not sufficient markets to render it profitable; but besides this, there is another impediment in the way of its extension; it requires a considerable amount of care, which is in all countries confided to the females; it is essentially a branch of female industry, and constitutes one great occupation of good country housewives. Now in a great many districts, with us, the country women attend only to their most indispensable household concerns; and a number of little branches of rural industry—the rearing of poultry among the rest—are either entirely neglected or very negligently gone about. One has often occasion to observe the difference manifested in this respect between foreign colonists and the native population by whom they are surrounded; in the very same district the rearing of poultry is found an important and profitable branch of industry amongst the one, whilst amongst the other it is totally neglected,— often even when every local circumstance is favourable. With a few isolated exceptions, the rearing and fattening of poultry as an object of commerce exists only in the vicinity of the large towns, and even in these localities it is carried on to such a limited extent, that poultry, from its high price, has become an article of luxury reserved for the wealthier classes. Amongst the rural populations which devote most attention to it, the Mennonites of the government of Ekathérinoslaw deserve special mention; they raise it in large quantities and carry on a considerable trade in it. This branch of rural economy would greatly gain by the increase and improvement of our means of communication.

Rearing of Bees.

We have already (*antè*, p. 189., *et seq.*) presented some statistical data regarding the present state of apiarian economy. It has greatly suffered in some provinces from the destruction of forests, for the bee prefers well wooded districts, where it is protected from the wind. It has also, as we have already observed, suffered from some influences of a general nature, especially the fall in price of wax and honey, which have been to a great extent supplanted by stearine and potato syrup,— a circumstance which has caused the decline of our foreign commerce in the two former articles. The rearing of bees is now dependent almost exclusively on the manufacture of candles for religious ceremonies and on the consumption of honey during lent,— it being then used instead of sugar by the strict observers of the fasts. Government encourages this branch of rural industry as affording to the peasant an extra source of income, and has adopted various measures with a view to that end. With the view of diffusing the necessary knowledge amongst the peasants of the state domains, bee-hives and a course of practical instruction upon the subject have been established at several of the crown farms, and pupils are sent every year at the expense of government to the special school founded for that purpose in 1828 by Lieutenant Prokopowitsch in the government of Tschernigow. After having finished their studies, the pupils quitting this establishment may become teachers in the schools dependent on the Ministry of Domains, or carry on the business of teacher on their own account. They enjoy a temporary exemption from military service; and such of them as wish to establish hives for themselves obtain loans for the purpose from the Department of Rural Economy. By way of farther encouragement, the Ministry of Domains has granted permission to the peasants to establish hives in the crown forests, under the precautions necessary to prevent the occurrence of conflagrations. Instructive articles on apiarian subjects are inserted in the Agricultural Gazette, and the Journal of the Ministry of Domains, under the auspices of the Department of Rural Economy, which also encourages the culture of melliferous plants, and distributes their seed gratis among the rural population. These encouragements will no doubt promote the progress of apiarian industry in so far as improvement is concerned ; but it has no great chance of future extension, since, from the causes already indicated, the demand for wax and honey has fallen off both at home and abroad.

Sylviculture.

We have seen from the classification of the soil contained in an earlier part of this volume, that, in regard to forest vegetation, Russia is peculiarly and exceptionally situated.   Taken as a whole, it is the best timbered country in Europe, if we except some of the smaller German States, such as the Duchy of Nassau and the Grand Duchies of Baden and Hesse-Darmstadt; and yet there is no country in which such vast treeless plains are to be found.   The table which we have given at page 53. exhibits in detail the extreme inequality with which forest vegetation is distributed over the different provinces.   We perceive at the head of this table seven northern governments, namely, Wologda, Wiatka, Olonetz, Kostroma, Perm, Nowgorod, and St. Petersburg, embracing an extent of 115,924,500 dessiatines $=22,997$ geographical square miles, or nearly a fourth of the total area of European Russia, in which the forest soil occupies more than the half, or, taking all these governments in a lump, 74 per cent. of their territorial extent; in one, namely, Wologda, forests occupy more than $\frac{9}{10}$ of the surface.   On the other hand, in nine southern governments, namely, Saratow, Woronèje, Bessarabia, Stavropol, Tauride, Ekathérinoslaw, Kherson, Astrakhan, and the country of the Don Cossacks, embracing an extent of 89,434,800 dessiatines $=17,742$ geographical square miles, or nearly a fifth of the area of European Russia, the forest land does not occupy so much as 7 per cent., and in the whole nine taken together it occupies only $3\frac{1}{3}$ per cent. of their entire superficies: of this number there are five, namely, Stavropol, Tauride, Ekathérinoslaw, Kherson, and Astrakhan, embracing an extent of 46,423,440 dessiatines $=9,210$ geographical square miles, which are almost entirely bare of timber— the forest land occupying less than 2 per cent. of the surface. In the other governments, thirty-six in number, the relative extent

of the forests varies between 10 and 50 per cent. The relative
extent of forest land and population (see table, p. 132.) presents
no less remarkable disproportions. There are four northern
governments, namely, Archangel, Wologda, Olonetz, and Perm,
embracing an extent of about 28,000 square miles, with a population of 1,365,000 inhabitants, in each of which there are estimated to be more than 10 dessiatines of forest per head, or,
taking them all together, with an average of 67 dessiatines per
inhabitant; and ten southern governments, namely, Kharkow,
Stavropol, Tauride, Poltawa, Koursk, Bessarabia, Podolia,
Woronèje, Ekathérinoslaw, and Kherson, embracing an extent
of 11,892 square miles, with a population of 12,133,000 inhabitants, where we do not find $\frac{1}{3}$ dessiatine of forest per inhabitant. The forest land of these ten governments, taken together, gives an average of $\frac{1}{4}$ dessiatine per inhabitant, and there
are two of the number where the average quantity is only $\frac{1}{10}$
dessiatine per head. In all the other governments, twenty-
seven in number, the relative extent of forest land varies be-
tween $\frac{2}{3}$ and $7\frac{3}{5}$ dessiatines per inhabitant. No less striking
disproportions are frequently found between different parts of
the same government, so that there are pretty extensive districts
suffering from a scarcity of wood in provinces which, taken as a
whole, may be regarded as very richly timbered.

These natural inequalities in the distribution of forest vegetation have been augmented in many districts by the devastations
arising from conflagrations and from cuttings carried on without
system or foresight. These devastations have chiefly occurred,
1st, in the vicinity of towns and factories, where a large quantity
of fuel is consumed; 2ndly, in countries lying along the banks
of navigable rivers, especially the Volga and its tributaries,
where quantities of timber have been cut down for sale and for
boat-building. The number of boats which descend the Volga
for the purpose of transporting to the south of the empire the
products of the north, and which never make more than the
single voyage, is estimated by M. Brinken at 10,000 as the
minimum; 3rdly, in districts where, from the rapid increase of
population, the want of arable land has induced numerous
clearings — principally of oak forests, the soil of which is generally fertile and well adapted for cereal culture.* The immense
consumption of fire-wood required in our climate to feed the

---

* "In 1785," says M. Storch in his work, *Russland unter Alexander I.,* vol. ii.
p. 426, " the traveller Sauer, who accompanied Billing's expedition, traversed the
most magnificent forests of oak in the government of Kazan, and on his return
from Siberia by the same route in 1794, he found these forests so completely destroyed that not a vestige of them remained."

enormous stoves with which every cottage is furnished — the consumption for house-building both in villages and towns, the houses being usually built of logs — the preparation of tar and of potash — the manufacture of shoes and mats from lime-tree bark * — all these circumstances contribute greatly to the destruction of the forests. The result has been that in many districts formerly remarkably well timbered, a number of towns, villages, and factories, are now obliged to fetch their supply of wood from a distance of 6 or 8 miles and upwards. The rebuilding of the city of Moscow, after the fire of 1812, occasioned the destruction of a great part of the forests in the neighbourhood of that capital.

It is only the governments of Archangel, Wologda, Olonetz, Wiatka, Perm, and Kostroma, and part of the governments of Nowgorod, Minsk, Wilna, Grodno, and Volhynia, which can still be considered as very richly timbered. Besides these governments, in which the most extensive forests are concentrated, a partial superabundance of wood is found only in some districts of the Baltic provinces, of the government of St. Petersburg, of White Russia, of Little Russia, and of the governments of Riazan, Nijni-Nowgorod, and Penza. In the governments of Moscow, Wladimir, and Tambow, there is a general scarcity of timber, along with a superabundance in some particular districts. In the northern part of the steppes, anciently very populous, the most beautiful forests of oak, beech, and maple, have been destroyed by clearances which have penetrated from thence to the centre of the empire. The following observations are copied from an article in the *Journal de Saint Pétersbourg* of 10-22 March, 1850 :

" The forests with which Russia is so abundantly provided render her unquestionably one of the most richly timbered countries in the world. In this respect her wealth is greatly beyond her wants. Such at least is the general opinion; and speaking in a general sense, the opinion seems to be correct: to convince ourselves of this, we need only compare the total area of her forests with the number of her inhabitants, or the annual growth of ligneous vegetation with the mass annually consumed throughout the empire. But if we examine the different portions of the country apart and by themselves, we will at once perceive that there is great irregularity of distribution: in certain districts timber is superabundant, in others it is scarce, in others it is entirely wanting. Thus, in the north, eight govern-

---

* The number of mats annually manufactured in Russia is estimated at about 40,000,000 ; and as the bark of one tree affords materials for only fifteen or twenty mats, this implies the cutting down of 2,000,000 to 2,666,000 trees.

ments, namely, Olonetz, Wologda, Kostroma, Wiatka, Perm, and part of Kazan and Nowgorod, form, as it were, one immense continuous forest, intersected at intervals by narrow plains, like gaps, in which the population is concentrated. Again, at the opposite extremity — towards the south and south-east — we perceive countries of vast extent, peopled at certain points, desert at others, but almost every where totally naked of trees: these occupy the governments of Poltawa, Kherson, Ekathéri-noslaw, the northern parts of the Tauride and Bessarabia, the country of the Don Cossacks, the government of Astrakhan, the greater part of the government of Saratow, that of Oren-burg on the south-west, and, partially, the government of Simbirsk. It is rare to find timbered land in these countries; and, when we do, it is simple masses of forest trees, generally young. The country included between these extreme limits partakes of the character of its two border regions, and presents a graduated transition from the one to the other. Taking for our point of departure the countries of the north-east, which contain the greatest mass of forests, and directing our course across the central and western portions of the empire, we will perceive, as we descend towards the south, that the timber progressively decreases, — the forests giving place to cultivated land. We are struck by the irregularity with which they are disseminated over the soil: thus the surface of the governments of Kostroma and Wologda is covered with immense forests; these suddenly decrease in the adjacent government of Jaroslaw, to re-assume new vigour in the governments of Wladimir, Moscow, and Toula. Here the district of Wéniew still contains woods of considerable extent, but they diminish as soon as we reach the district of Bogorodsk, and almost entirely disappear in those of Jéfrémow, Novosil, and Tscherne. At no great distance, in the government of Kalouga (districts of Jizdra and Kozelsk), they are again abundant. The same contrast is repeated on the western thinly timbered boundaries of the governments of Poltawa and Kiew: to the former succeed the forests of the government of Tschernigow, situated between the Desna and the Dnieper (district of Oster); to the second are contiguous the vast forests of Wolhynia. Sometimes we find in provinces richly provided with forest land certain localities in which they are totally wanting, such as the district of Nolinsk in the government of Wiatka, and the district of Wologda. The latter is obliged to draw its supplies either from the neighbour-ing district of Kadnikow, or from the district of Kirilow in the government of Nowgorod.

" Facts prove generally that the diminution of forests corresponds directly to the increase of the population. Thus in the district of Tétuschi, (government of Kazan), at the period of the general survey, the forests covered an area of 113,205 dessiatines, whilst at present they do not occupy above 80,000: the population of this district in the interval between the seventh and eighth census had increased from 32,581 to 42,808. It is scarcely twenty or thirty years since the city of Wiatka, a provincial capital, was everywhere surrounded by dense forests which covered the entire district, and in the midst of which the cleared lands occupied a very trifling space. At the present day these forests do not suffice for the wants of the locality: the inhabitants are obliged to provide themselves with timber in the district of Slobodsk. The population has simultaneously augmented to the point of exuberance, a circumstance which occasions frequent migrations of the peasantry into the neighbouring districts.

" To arrive at the same conclusion, it is sufficient to compare the various governments of European Russia under the double aspect of their population and their relative importance in the forest economy of the empire. These governments, according to the cipher of their population as ascertained by the academician Kœppen, are grouped in the following order:

" Fourteen contain from 16 to 700 individuals per square mile. Of this number the governments of Archangel, Olonetz, Orenburg (partly), Perm, Wologda, Wiatka, Nowgorod, Kostroma, and Minsk, belong to the region of forests; those of Astrakhan, Saratow, Kherson, certain parts of Orenburg, and the Tauride, together with the country of the Don Cossacks, belong to the region of the steppes. Fifteen contain from 700 to 1,200 inhabitants to the square mile, namely, Ekathérinoslaw, St. Petersburg, Esthonia, Pskow, Witebsk, Livonia, Simbirsk, Mohilew, Twer, Wolhynia, Courland, Wilna, Smolensk, Kazan, and Bessarabia. Eight contain from 1,200 to 1,500 inhabitants per square mile, namely, Kowno, Grodno, Nijni-Nowgorod, Woronèje, Tauride, Wladimir, Tambow, and Kharkow. Seven contain from 1,500 to 2,000 inhabitants per square mile, namely, Jaroslaw, Penza, Orel, Kalouga, Kiew, Riazan, and Poltawa. Lastly, four contain from 2,000 to 2,323 inhabitants per square mile, namely, Koursk, Podolia, Toula, and Moscow. Thus almost the totality of the forests are concentrated in the most thinly peopled districts of the empire,—the only exceptions being the governments of Kowno, Grodno, and Nijni-Nowgorod. It is impossible not to recognise that the forests have been preserved solely in those localities which, owing either to their distance from the centre of the empire, or to certain influences of soil and climate, presented less favourable conditions for the increase of population.

" This unequal distribution over the Russian territory induces us to believe that the forest régime cannot be established everywhere upon the same uniform basis. Whilst in certain localities the superabundance of wood authorises, and often renders necessary for the sake of agriculture, more or less irregular cuttings, there are other districts in which besides necessary superintendence, the introduction of an improved system of management is absolutely necessary for the purpose of carrying on new plantations, as well as preserving the timber that is still standing."

The author's observation with respect to the forest régime is perfectly just: it cannot be rendered uniform, but must necessarily be adapted, in its principles and in their application, to local circumstances and predominating interests.

Of the total extent of the forests, amounting to about 180 millions of dessiatines (*antè*, p. 35.), those belonging to the state domains occupy more than 115 millions *, without reckoning those belonging to the appanages and those under the special administration of the Admiralty, so that nearly two-thirds of the forest land belongs to the state. It is obvious, then, that the administration of the state forests must have the greatest influence on the whole forest economy of the country. The duties of this administration are certainly not light, even if we consider nothing more than the immense area over which its action and superintendence must extend, independently of other difficulties to which we will advert in the sequel. Its task may, in our opinion, be summed up as follows:

1. To a certain extent, and according to a regular plan, to encourage clearances in the most thickly timbered districts, and where there is not arable land enough for the wants of the population. Such clearances, if judiciously conducted, may gradually open a way to the working of the still virgin forests in the north of the empire: but this is a question which belongs to the subject of colonisation, already treated of (*antè*, p. 77., *et seq.*).

2. To regulate the cuttings in all those districts where the forests are worked, and to prevent waste in the neighbourhood of towns and manufactories, and along the banks of rivers, especially the Volga and its tributaries;

3. To re-timber the countries of the south wherever the soil is not totally unsuitable for sylviculture.

---

* According to the Report of the Ministry of Domains for 1849 the extent was 115,342,411 dessiatines.

Government has long recognised the importance of this branch of rural economy for Russia's future, and has given the subject its serious attention. There existed very anciently severe penal laws against the wasting of forests; but it was not till under Peter the Great that the foundation of a system of forest-polity was laid. There were laid down certain districts in the vicinity of navigable rivers, and certain descriptions of timber of which the cutting was forbid, except by virtue of special authority, both in the forests of the state and in those of individuals. The forest land became thus divided into reserved forest and free forest. In the latter, including the non-reserved forests of the crown, the liberty of felling timber was granted without restriction. The prohibition established in the reserved forests had originally for its object the preservation of naval timber; but it was afterwards extended not only to several other species of wood required in various establishments of the crown, but also to building timber for common houses, and even wood for agricultural implements and household furniture. The wood required for government purposes was felled without distinction in the crown forests or in those of individuals, without any compensation to the latter. Commissaries and inspectors were appointed for the management of the reserved forests. In 1722, a new organisation, based on these principles was given to the forest service, and all the woods and forests of the empire were placed under the direction of the admiralty. Shortly afterwards the new regulations being recognised as too onerous for the proprietors, were modified by an ukase of the Empress Catherine I., which appeared in 1726, mitigating considerably the stringent regulations concerning the reserved forests, and at same time suppressing the forest-masters, and entrusting the superintendence of these forests to the landed proprietors, the elders of the villages or heads of the district, (*Starosty,*) and the ordinary administrative authorities. But in consequence of this relaxation, the destruction of forests assumed such large proportions that in 1729 an ukase of the Emperor Peter III. directed the resumption of more stringent measures, especially in regard to the cutting of oak. From this date, also, the crown began to pay proprietors for the timber cut in their forests for the exigencies of the state, and to derive a certain revenue from its own forests, by levying a tax upon the timber exported.

In 1730 and 1732 the topographical description of the forests in the governments of central Russia which had been begun at a preceding period was brought to a conclusion: this document showed the unsatisfactory condition of the forest administration, and induced the resumption, with some modifications, of the instructions drawn up by Peter I. for the grand-master of the woods and forests. Towards the middle of the eighteenth century there was undertaken and finished in a few years a description of a portion of the northern forests from the banks of the Dwina and its affluents on to the town of Oustioug. About the same period forest-overseers were brought over from Germany for the purpose of training apprentice foresters and forming plantations of timber, especially oak, in suitable localities : but complaints were made that the principles of German forestry pursued by these strangers were inapplicable to the climate, soil, and local circumstances of Russia, and that in general the measures adopted by government to stop the waste had not answered their purpose. Under the Empress Catherine II., several important changes took place in the *personnel* of the employés, and in 1780 the whole system was placed upon a new basis. Hitherto the main object had been to assure a sufficient supply of timber for the imperial navy, but from this date government thought seriously of deriving a revenue from this source, and began levying a certain tax upon the timber felled in the state forests and in those of the peasants of the domains. On the other hand there was restored to private proprietors the right of freely disposing of their timber, so that the crown could no longer order cuttings in private forests, except under special agreement with their owners. M. Hermann remarks, in his work on the Forest Economy of Russia, that the private proprietors, abusing this unlimited liberty, have entirely devastated their forests or allowed them to go to decay.

The Emperor Paul I. issued several ukases with a view to the improvement of forest-polity and to the completion of the topographical description of the forests. Private forests suitable for a supply of naval timber were placed under the superintendence of the Admiralty ; the different sorts and qualities of wood proper for the purpose were determined ; and the taxes to be levied on timber cut in the state forests for the use of private parties were regulated. An ukase fixed at 25 trees for each house the quantity of building timber to be delivered gratuitously to the peasants. This ordinance is still in vigour in this sense, that peasants, whose houses have been burned, receive 25 trees in those districts where forests are not abundant, 50 trees in well-timbered districts, and in the richest-timbered districts as many as they require.

Under the Emperor Alexander I. the administration of forests was united in 1802 to the Ministry of Finance, and in 1803 three commissions were appointed in the governments of

St. Petersburg, Olonetz, and Kazan with instructions to make particular examination, and to separate the forests belonging to the state from those of the peasants and private proprietors, to concede a certain extent of forest land to peasants who had not land enough, and to reserve, on the other hand, a fifth part of the forests belonging to the peasants as timber set apart for the buildings of the state. The woods reserved in those governments which are in the vicinity of sea-ports have been placed at the disposal of the imperial marine; in the other governments they have been appropriated partly to various departments of the public service, and partly to the subvention in certain cases of the peasantry of the domains. In consequence of the separation of the estates appropriated to the support of the members of the imperial family from other crown property, the forests belonging to the former were placed under the charge of the department of Appanages, instituted in 1808. The department of Domains, then forming part of the Ministry of Finance, received in 1811 its definitive organisation, and the administration of Forests was incorporated with it. In 1828 a separate department was created at the Ministry of Marine for the administration of forests appropriated to the purpose of ship-building. In 1837 the administration of the state forests (with the exception of those belonging to the Appanages and the Marine) and of those belonging to the towns and the clergy was transferred to the Ministry of Domains, which was instituted at that epoch, and in 1843 it received a new organisation. It now forms a department of that ministry, and the whole *personnel* is placed under the orders of a chief inspector, who is at same time the director of the department. The whole forest land is divided into six districts, each under the direction of a vice-inspector. The department is also divided into six sections, of which the first attends to everything connected with the inspection of the forests; the second, to the administration properly so called; the third, to the working of the forests; the fourth, to the introduction of a rational system of forest economy; the fifth to the commercial department; and the sixth, to the control of the entire administration. There is besides an *auditoriate* for conducting inquiries and settling differences, and a special committee for everything that concerns projects of improvement. To this committee are referred all communications which arrive from the scientific committee instituted at the Ministry of Domains. In the provinces, the administration of the forests is entrusted to the chambers of Domains appointed for each government, which are divided into two sections,— one for rural economy properly so called, and the other for forest economy. This second section is under the direction of the master of forests in each government, who also takes part in the deliberations of the Chamber of Domains. Under his orders are placed all the officers and sub-officers belonging to the districts, as well as the forest guard, which is a corps possessing a special organisation.

In regard to forest economy, European Russia, together with the Caucasian provinces, is divided into four regions. In the northern district, the principal object of administration consists in utilising as much as possible the immense forests with which it is covered. In the second, which extends in the direction north and south from Kostroma to Penza, and which comprehends on the west the Baltic provinces with a portion of Lithuania, it is required not only to regulate the working of the forests, but also to turn them to account commercially, and to introduce improvements in sylviculture. In the third, which also extends from north to south, but somewhat more towards the east, comprehending the governments of Simbirsk and Saratow, and where the forest vegetation scarcely supplies the requisite quantity of fuel for the local population, it becomes indispensable, not only to introduce a better system of managing the old, but also to plant new ones. In the fourth region — the south of European Russia — the great problem is to apply some remedy to the pernicious influences which the want of timber exerts upon the climate, soil, and rural economy of the district. Accordingly, there is required from the forest employés destined for this region, besides a special acquaintance with sylviculture, some notion of meteorology and vegetable physiology, and of the different methods of forest culture suitable for fixing the moving sands and retimbering the steppes, as well as of the means for facilitating the transport of wood.*

Ever since the general survey of the empire, government has been endeavouring to ascertain, by special geometrical surveys and topographical descriptions, the situation of every district of the empire in regard to its forests. These operations were formerly executed by parties who did not possess the requisite knowledge of sylviculture. But now that a corps of well-trained officials is yearly recruited from the pupils leaving the Forest Institute, the administration has found itself in a position to proceed in a more regular manner ; it is enabled to procure the preparation of inventories and plans for working by regular cuttings ; so

---

* The preparatory works on the re-timbering of the steppes were terminated partially in 1843, and their execution is now being proceeded with in the steppes of the government of Ekathérinoslaw.

that a rational forest economy will henceforth be more and more propagated throughout the empire.*

Of all the recent economical institutions in Russia, the Forest Institute of St. Petersburg has been one of the happiest in its conception, and of the most useful in its results. This institute, which received in 1837 a new organisation, includes an academy of sylviculture and a school of land surveyors and topographers. This organisation is exceedingly appropriate to the situation of our forest economy. The establishment of a school of land surveyors and topographers corresponds to one of our most urgent wants, that of a good statistical topography of the forests. Besides the theoretical instruction, which is the main object of this institution, a course of practical instruction has been organised; and there have been assigned for the purpose a nursery and plantation of forest trees, together with a piece of land destined for agricultural experiments. Attached to the establishment is a workroom, and geometrical instruments for the school of land surveying and topography. In this institution forest employés are educated; and those pupils who are destined to become teachers of sylviculture themselves, or to become directors of the model establishments of forest economy, are sent abroad at the expense of government to finish their studies. The forest school established at Lissino, in the neighbourhood of Tsarskoïe-Selo, is a succursal of the institute of St. Petersburg, more especially destined for practical instruction, and attached to it is a school of wood-keepers, the pupils of which are chosen from amongst the peasants of the state domains, and form a company d'élite. There is, besides, a forest school near Moscow, and another in the government of Grodno. In several parts of the empire there have been founded model establishments of forest economy, where experiments are made in different systems of culture. The pupils of the Forest Institute of St. Petersburg admitted into these establishments receive a task, which consists in forming a survey and valuation of a certain extent of forest land (perhaps as much as 10,000 dessiatines), and preparing an economic inventory of the same.

Government has often been criticised for not having located the Forest Institute in the interior of the empire, in one of the best timbered districts of Wologda, Olonetz, Wiatka, or Kazan, instead of at St. Petersburg. These criticisms have been disposed of by M. Haxthausen, an impartial observer, in the following manner: " Forest economy in Russia is still in its infancy; Russian foresters or Russian professors of sylviculture

---

* See Haxthausen, " Studien über Russland," vol. i. p. 26. *et seq.*

have no existence. To fill the professors' chairs they have been obliged to have recourse to Germany. Now, though distinguished foreigners may make up their minds to remove to Petersburg or Moscow, it is quite a different thing to accept a situation in the interior of the empire. It would even be difficult to find in the provinces the necessary number of pupils. This institute cannot be regarded as destined to furnish the necessary number of subjects for the practical service of the forests; it is rather a nursery of professors and higher employés for those forest institutes which may hereafter be established in the interior of the empire."* We have to observe, that M. Haxthausen's opinion as to the want of well-instructed Russian foresters is applicable only to a period anterior to the establishment of the institute in question; for now we have a considerable number of distinguished officers in this part of the service; but his observations are none the less just as to the choice of the capital for the foundation of this establishment.

To complete the preceding general hints regarding our forest economy, we insert here a notice on the same subject, which originally appeared in the "Northern Bee," and was copied into the St. Petersburg Journal of 26 January, 7 February 1850:—
"The introduction of a regular and uniform system of management of the crown forests dates from 1843, when the department of Woods and Forests was instituted at the Ministry of Domains. Since then, that important branch of national economy has rapidly developed, and its organisation progresses towards a state of perfection which authorises the fairest hopes for the future.

"The following are the principal steps which have been taken by this department since its formation.

"In order to establish its ulterior labours on a solid basis, it proceeded, in the first instance, to a survey of the forests of the domains, estimated to cover an area of 115 millions of dessiatines. For this purpose it ordered the preparation in different governments of plans of the forest lands belonging to the domains — of economic inventories of each of these separate territories — and of exact information with regard to the geographical position of the forests, and their proximity to the centres of population and to river communication. These preparatory labours having been accomplished, it directed its attention to other particulars.

"In order to make effectual provision for the preservation of the forests, the latter were divided into three categories, accord-

* Studien über Russland, vol. i. p. 10.

ing to their value and relative importance. Those of the first class are now entrusted to the care of a permanent forest guard composed of peasants who are established with their families along the borders, where they are provided with allotments of land sufficient for their subsistence. Nevertheless, as the extension of this system to the whole forest domains would have been attended with considerable difficulty, both from the expenses attending the removal of the agriculturists from their old and installing them in their new localities, and from the repugnance felt by the inhabitants to submit to an unoptional change of domicile, government found it necessary to create for forests of the second class a corps of keepers recruited exclusively from the discharged military. These guards, besides their fixed salary, have each the use of a cottage and kitchen garden. Lastly, in forests of the third category, or those which, in consequence of their remoteness from rivers capable of floating timber, and the small revenue consequently derived from them, cannot be subjected to a strict régime, the old mode of supervision has been retained; this is effected by means of individuals selected from amongst the inhabitants of the neighbouring rural communes, who, under the denomination of patrol, are required to make their rounds either on foot or on horseback over a certain extent of territory. To afford facilities in the discharge of their duty to the individuals thus employed, the administration has undertaken the task of building habitations for them in the interior of the forests, instead of leaving them to reside, as formerly, in the neighbouring towns and villages.

"In the measures having for their object the economical management of the forests agreeably to the principles of good forestry, the administration has constantly kept in view the local conditions depending upon soil, climate, geographical position, and established custom. The first attempts at the introduction of an improved mode of management, such as the preparation of plans, division of the forests into regular cuttings, determination of the periodicity of the same, estimates of their value, &c., were made in those forests which their local position and the readiness of their outlets indicated as most suitable for that purpose. Every forest territory managed in this manner is subjected to a plan of administration, based upon the wants of the locality, and there is periodical inquisition made into the strict execution of the orders given. These improvements, by augmenting the pecuniary returns, have covered their own expenses, and consequently cost the treasury nothing.

" The re-timbering of the forests cleared by working, and the plantation and sowing of forest trees in those districts where they are required, have necessarily attracted the special attention of the central administration ; on this subject detailed instructions have been published for the use of the officials ; and, as in some localities it is difficult to procure good seed, kilns for drying the cones have been established at various points, and from these the other districts are supplied.

" The labours undertaken with a view to the cultivation of forest trees in provinces where no forests existed are especially worthy of notice. Experience has proved that the success of this sort of culture depends very much on the choice of the parties selected to superintend the plantations ; and that the first requisite is a thorough acquaintance with the nature of the soil of the southern steppes, with the influence of climate on vegetation, and with the care indispensably necessary for the young plants during the three first years of their growth. With the view of training good managers, model plantations designed to afford practical instruction for pupils have been established in the governments of Ekathérinoslaw, Kherson, Tauride, and Bessarabia. The pupils, who belong exclusively to the agricultural class, return home after passing through their course of study, and are usually employed in the direction of plantations in the neighbourhood of their native villages. This at least is the practice amongst the foreign colonists of South Russia. The number of those pupils recently amounted to 68. In the government of Ekathérinoslaw they have proceeded to the organisation, on the same plan but on a larger scale, of a forest school remarkable for its meteorological observatory, which has been established principally with the view of resolving the question of the influence of forests on climate and the humidity of the atmosphere. We may remark that the observatory is placed in conditions exceedingly favourable for the interests of science ; the neighbouring country being totally destitute of wood, it is conceived that the atmospheric changes which may be produced by the successive increase of plantations will be more sensible than they would be anywhere else. Besides these improvements, very important experiments in culture have been made in the governments of Tauride and Astrakhan. Thus in the shifting sands of Aleschki, an extent of 2,456 dessiatines has been converted into plantations, which now contain nearly 5 millions of trees. In the steppes of the Kirghiz the administration has provisionally fixed upon an area of 700 dessiatines for the projected plantations, reserving to extend them afterwards according to the wants of the population. Between 1846 and 1849 an area of 154 dessiatines has thus been covered with plantations.

" To complete the improvements introduced into the forest department, the general direction has endeavoured to augment the number of officers specially destined for that branch of the administration; and for this purpose it has improved the instruction given in its educational establishments. Previously to 1842, these establishments turned out annually not more than a dozen officers capable of filling the superior charges in their own department. At present they regularly turn out as many as thirty, and the total number of active functionaries possessed of the requisite special knowledge now amounts to 275. Every forest officer, before being admitted to active service, is obliged to go through one year's course of study at the practical forest school of Lissino, where there is also an industrial establishment for affording instruction in the best methods of manufacturing various forest products, as pitch, rosin, tar, charcoal, turpentine, &c.

" Besides the secondary schools established in the plantations of the southern provinces, there are others in the neighbourhood of the two capitals and near Grodno, destined for the training of forest inspectors. The branches of instruction taught are, Russian language, arithmetic, forest economy, mathematics applied to land surveying, and the drawing of plans. Each school possesses nursery grounds for the purpose of affording practical instruction to the pupils. These, of whom the number at present amounts to 150, are divided into two classes, government bursars and private boarders; the latter pay an annual sum of 100 roubles.

" The administration has also found it advisable to publish a manual for the use of its officers. This manual contains, 1. An abridgment of forest economy, in regard to the culture, management, valuation, and working of forests, and the regulations relative to these different subjects. 2. An exposition of the regulations in force with regard to the functions of the various classes of forest employés. 3. Instructions for the guidance of functionaries in matters of correctional and penal procedure.

" The general results of the labours of this department may be summed up as follows :

" *Forest surveys.* Plans have been drawn and inventories prepared in 1,490 forest districts embracing 12,227,758 dessiatines; boundaries have been ascertained over an extent of 24,446,823 dessiatines and 308 sagènes.

" *Management and Organisation.* The number of forest districts managed upon scientific principles amounts to 115, comprising an area of 2,138,341 dessiatines. The draining of marshes in the interior of forests has been carried out over a surface of 15,000 dessiatines.

"*Plantations and sowings.* The quantity of seed sown amounts to 55 poods; the number of trees planted, to 5,208,580; the quantity of seed gathered, to 13,336 poods and 36½ lbs.

"*Preservation of Forests.* In different forest districts there have been established as permanent guards 1,057 families; 1,853 individuals have been placed as superintendents or military guards.

"*Loss and Damage.* In 1842 there were 4,911 cases of fraudulent cuttings and 790 fires, which occasioned losses to the extent of 386,000 and 423,000 roubles respectively. In 1847, the losses in this way amounted only to 135,825 roubles of the former, and 47,652 of the latter.

"*Schools.* The number of pupils who, after special preparation for forest employment, have been admitted to the service, has increased to 183."

The whole facts mentioned in this article prove that government is seriously occupied with the improvement of our forest economy, and that it proceeds on its path with prudent foresight; but, to be able to appreciate at their true value the progress already made, and that which may be hoped for in future, we must take into account the difficulties against which the Administration of Forests has had to contend in the immense task entrusted to it. We shall point out a few of these difficulties with reference to the different branches of our forest economy, merely observing that in our climates the forest service is so severe that it is apt to occasion premature infirmities, and that for this reason the period of active service, which gives a right to a full retiring allowance, is limited to twenty-five years, being the same period as for the department of mines.

Working of the immense Forests of the North.

It would, unquestionably, be an incalculable advantage, as well for the financial interests of the state as for our national wealth in general, if we could succeed in turning to account those immense virgin forests to which the axe has never yet penetrated. But this is an enterprise reserved for a remote futurity, and all that can be done at present is to pave the way. The opposing difficulties consist in the climate, the soil, and the want of population. (See *ante*, p. 77, *et seq.*) To these may be added topographical position. The land carriage of wood is too costly to admit of its transport in this manner, except for short distances; say ten German miles at the utmost. In mountainous countries the streams, swollen by the rains, often furnish a network of little natural canals, by means of which wood can be floated down even long distances at a trifling expense.   In Russia no such facility exists: the greater part of the countries of the northern region are flat; and, if we except some reservoirs of water which, with the assistance of art, may be turned to account at some future period, the only substitutes now available are wooden trams and sledges.

Confining ourselves here to the mere mention of the forest-clearings of the north, as an idea which may be eventually more or less realisable, we may add that M. Petersen, Member of the Scientific Committee at the Ministry of Domains, who has made the subject his special study, considers M. Haxthausen's plan of colonisation to be, in the sense which he himself attaches to it, namely, as an agricultural project, impracticable, even as a question of the future.   M. Petersen considers that, on several points of these regions, agriculture has already attained its maximum; that their climate and character are exceedingly similar to the plateaux of the Alps, which lie near the regions of eternal snow *; and that, with the exception of the chase, the fishery, and some small branches of local and forest industry, the only practicable department of rural economy is cattle-grazing.

Preservation and Management of the Forests.

It would be useless to dwell upon the importance of preserving the woods by the introduction of a rational system of forest economy; but here we are beset by a double difficulty, arising from the great distances which impede supervision on the one hand, and the genius of our population on the other. How is waste to be prevented, or strict surveillance executed, over a forest twice as large as the united territories of half a dozen German potentates?   And, à fortiori, how is this to be done with a peasantry who neither see any necessity for the measures adopted nor feel anywise disposed to second them? The total absence of a conservative spirit, in regard to trees, amongst the Russian populations has been remarked on by various savans and economists — by Pallas, Hermann, Georgi, Storch, Güldenstadt, Lapoukhine, Brinken, and others.†   This

* This resemblance to the climate of the Alps is exhibited to a surprising extent in their flora.

† As a proof of the long enduring influence of traditionary ideas, M. Storch cites the example of the Mordvines, in the districts inhabited by whom, the forests

observation is indeed applicable, more or less, to all Slavonic populations. We have often had occasion to be struck with it in Poland, where the waste of forests is as general as in Russia : whatever comes in the way is cut down without economy and without distinction : a fine tree is felled for some trumpery purpose for which a shrub would have answered equally well, or a portion is lopped off and the remainder left to decay ; whilst in one quarter everything is levelled before the axe ; in another, quite in the vicinity, the trees stand so crowded together, that over square miles of area, not a decent sized one is to be met with for want of thinning. In all these northern regions this tendency to waste has been fostered by the notion that the forests are inexhaustible. Moreover, both in Russia and in Poland, the common people have but loose notions on the subject of sylvan property : they have been accustomed to regard the wood as the common good of the inhabitants; and this convenient belief has been strengthened by the absence of efficacious measures for protecting the forests of the crown. With the exception of the reserves for naval timber, peasant and private owner used to go in with his axe in his hand, and cut down as many trees as he pleased without leave, without price, and without control. It was not till the year 1730 that government attempted to derive the slightest revenue from the crown forests ; and even then it was only in the way of a tax upon timber going out of the country. It would appear, as M. Wrangel observes in his *Histoire de la Legislation Forestière de la Russie*, that at that time government itself considered the usufruct of the state forests as a species of commonty ; and it is of course only by degrees that new ideas, based upon a necessity which is not obvious to their senses, will take root amongst the rural population. It may, however, be observed, that, even in countries such as Germany, where a good forest economy has long prevailed, cases of waste are not unknown. M. Steffens, head forest master (*Oberforstmeister*) of Rhenish Prussia, has recently published a sketch of the sylviculture of that province, from which it appears that at the beginning of the present century the forest land, now occupying 3,000,000 morgens, was covered with foliaceous wood (*Laubholz*), appropriate to the nature of the soil and climate ; but that, in consequence of waste occasioned by the irregular exercise of servitudes, such as fire-wood, free pasture, and the like, a large portion has had to be replaced by plantations of

are better preserved than any where else ; and observes that they entertain a sort of veneration for old and fine trees, which they have inherited from their pagan ancestors.

coniferæ (*Nadelholz*), the impoverishment of the soil not admitting of the other description of timber.

One of the greatest scourges of our forest economy is the frequent and sometimes immense conflagrations. M. Kœppen, in one of his statistical works, mentions that, in 1839, no less than 200,000 dessiatines (= 540,000 acres) were consumed by fire in the single government of Kostroma — these accidents invariably arising from the carelessness of the inhabitants. The peasants employed in the woods kindle fires, either to warm themselves or to cook their victuals, and then, when their purpose is served, they forget to put them out: the smouldering remnant gains by degrees the dry leaves and brushwood, and next attacks the stems, till at last the entire forest falls a prey to the flames. Such accidents are particularly frequent in pine and fir forests, the dry acerose leaves of which, covering the ground, readily catch fire, and rapidly communicate it to all around. This cause of destruction is one of the main objects of surveillance; but surveillance over a forest some thousand square miles in area is no easy matter. We ought, however, to observe that, independently of the measures taken by government, private proprietors are now beginning to bestow increased attention on the subject.

Retimbering of the Steppes and other naked Districts.

As we have already had occasion to observe, it appears from experiments already made, that in some districts of the steppes retimbering is perfectly practicable, whilst in other very extensive districts it is opposed by the nature of the soil, as where the base is saline, or the humus is too thin. But again, where the soil is fertile, planting would be an unprofitable speculation, for the culture of corn and the rearing of cattle can be carried on with little trouble and at little cost, whilst, by a singular combination of circumstances, wood has by no means the value that might be imagined, its place as fuel being supplied by straw, dung, reeds, and dried thistles. Thus the burden of retimbering these countries, being an enterprise which, with a few isolated exceptions, offers little chance of profit to the private proprietor, falls entirely upon the state, which alone can undertake it upon a large scale, and, with a view to the prospective interests of the country, incur the required temporary sacrifice of outlay. This sacrifice is so much the greater, that in our climate more time is requisite for forest reproduction than in the other countries of Europe. At the forest-school of Lissino it is considered an axiom that coniferous trees (pines and firs) require 120 years, and foliaceous trees

60 years, to attain their full growth*; and, moreover, the excessive cold often kills the young plants. M. Haxthausen asserts that, on the northern belting of the steppes, even old trees sometimes perish from the cold in a very severe winter unaccompanied by snow; but he adds that such cases are of very recent observation, which would seem to indicate a recent fall of temperature in these regions. But, however this may be, government does not recoil before the difficulties of its task, and, with a full apprehension of its importance, the administration of Forests has taken it in hand, with the intention of carrying it out at once systematically, and with a due regard to local circumstances. In regard to the system to be pursued, opinions have been divided. M. von Brinken's proposal of planting the ravines and valleys is not generally applicable, *first*, because the soil of these lower regions has frequently a saline basis, and, *secondly*, because even were such plantations to succeed, they would not effect one of the main objects desired, namely, the protection of the higher grounds from the dry scourging influence of the east winds.† The scientific committee, therefore, approved of the plan of one of its own members, M. Petersen, which is just the converse of M. von Brinken's. This plan, which consists in covering the heights of the steppes with forest trees, has been partly carried into effect on a colony of Mennonites, and on a farm lately established at Veliko-Anatole: but it could exert a salutary influence upon the climate and culture of those districts only in case of its extension over a fifth or sixth part of the steppe territory. Under existing circumstances the plan cannot be carried through on such an extensive scale by government alone; the larger portion of the steppes having been long ago alienated to private parties, or colonised by the peasants of the domains, and the heights being now occupied in great measure with the culture of cereals, the state could not undertake to cover them with plantations, except at the expense of either violating vested rights, or buying back the lands. The extent of land suitable for sylviculture remaining at the state's free disposal is but

---

* It is asserted by some practical men, that the time requisite for forest reproduction is not by any means so great; or that such a period is at any rate inapplicable to the whole of Russia, especially as regards foliaceous trees, — the birch, for example, often beginning to decay after thirty years' growth, and, when cut down after that age, being, in many districts, almost always found hollow inside.

† Although the planting of the ravines and valleys would exert no sensible influence on the climate of the steppes generally, yet, wherever practicable, it would be productive of local advantage. Such partial plantations would be so many reservoirs of a moister atmosphere, which would soften the climate of the surrounding districts. They are beginning to be undertaken in the best peopled districts of the steppe countries.

very limited; whilst the scrubby plantations made by individuals and by the peasants of the domains can at present make but small progress for want of capital; nor are they of sufficient body to exert any sensible influence on the climate : they can scarcely stand out against the droughts, or the strong snowless frosts. For these reasons it has been thought necessary to have recourse to other measures with a view to mitigate the temperature of the steppes, and intercept the malignant influence of the easterly winds; and amongst others it was resolved to try the plan of planting hedge-rows at short distances from each other, employing for the purpose those sorts of trees and shrubs which seemed best calculated to support the climate and the ravages of cattle and insects. The Ministry of Domains is now occupied with these experiments, the result of which will in due time be communicated to the agriculturists of the districts. One of the main difficulties attending the whole question is the limited number of species of forest trees which can stand the soil and climate of these regions.

Before concluding this chapter, it may not be amiss to give a brief summary of the measures undertaken by government for the promotion and improvement of agriculture in general. In referring to the various branches of our rural economy we have already noticed the most important measures which have been adopted in regard to some of these branches, as the encouragements held out for the culture of potatoes, tobacco, and vines, for the rearing of bees and of silk-worms, of cattle and horses — the inquiries instituted concerning the culture of flax and hemp, and the means devised for its improvement. Our present purpose is to give a slight sketch of some general measures which embrace the complex of our agricultural interests, and the welfare of our cultivators.

I. *General Survey and Measures for a better ascertainment of Marches.*

The boundaries between landed properties, both of the state and individuals, were, down to last century, exceedingly vague and ill ascertained, so that great uncertainty in the state of possession was the consequence. Under the reign of the Empress Catherine II. the grand task was undertaken of a general survey, which was commenced in 1766 and finished in 1835, thus occupying 69 years. At the same time a special department was instituted at the senate as a court of last resort for all law-processes arising out of the new ascertainment of boundaries, whether betwixt individual proprietors or betwixt the latter and the administration of the state domains. This general measure laid the foundation of our present rural economy, and may be regarded as having formed, by consolidating the rights of territorial property, the starting point of agricultural improvement; in some governments, however, property was and still is affected by conditions exceedingly adverse to improvement, namely, the great number of enclaves within the various estates themselves: the measures taken by government to remedy this evil, together with their hitherto attained results, have been already adverted to (*antè*, p. 240, *et seq.*). In 1846 there was founded at Tiflis a school of land surveyors, which in 1851 turned out twenty-two pupils who had finished their studies,— the majority with distinction in their own department. During the five years 1846—50 the operation of surveying, including the preparation of plans and relative documents, was completed over an extent of 600,000 dessiatines (=1,600,000 acres),— an operation which will advance with accelerated rapidity in proportion as the Institution of Surveyors turns out more pupils ready for service.

II. *Measures concerning the Conversion of the Corvée.*

The corvée, being one of the most important questions affecting the future prospects of our rural economy, is also one of those which have most particularly attracted the attention of government. Every one who has had a fair opportunity of forming a correct idea of our agricultural position must agree that, in the present state of things, the conversion of the corvée into a money-rent by means of a general legislative measure, is an impossibility, and that such a measure must be gradual in its operation and greatly dependent upon local circumstances. Referring to what we have already said upon the subject (*antè*, p. 221, *et seq.*), we may observe that all that government could do was to encourage the gradual emancipation of the serfs by means of administrative measures — to consolidate arrangements having that object in view — and, as much as possible, to remove abuses from the prestation where it still exists. Such are the aim and spirit of the ukase of 2d September, 1842, and of the regulations known under the name of *Inventories*, which refer to the prestations in kind exigible, in the provinces of the west. The latter measure, regarding which opinions are divided in the provinces in question, is still too recent to admit of our appreciating its results. We have already seen (*antè*, p. 224.) that about two-thirds of the productive soil

are now no longer worked by the corvée system. This prestation, which existed from ancient times in some of the state
domains in the western governments, has been gradually abolished and replaced by a pecuniary rent (*obrok*): there are now
only about 150,000 peasants of the domains still subject to it ;
and these will probably soon be emancipated, as the arrangements for that purpose are being actively carried on.   In
the Appanage lands, the corvée has been entirely abolished,
and replaced by a money-rent.

Perequation of the Imposts borne by the Cultivators in the State
Domains.

Of all the countries of Europe, Russia is unquestionably
one of those whose burden is lightest in regard to direct contributions and other pecuniary charges, if we take into consideration merely the amount of these charges and the extent
and fertility of the productive soil : but they are often rendered
severe by the inequality of their distribution.   All the direct
imposts, as well as communal charges, are levied in the form
of a poll-tax, at so much per head, taking no account of the
capability of the contributor, or of the extent and quality of
the soil which he labours.   This is also the mode in which the
obrok is levied when the corvée has been converted into that
pecuniary payment to the over-lord.   In the distribution of
these various assessments, which is made by the *starchina* or
elders of the commune, the inequalities resulting from this
mode of imposition are diminished — the poorer contributors
being relieved by means of a sur-charge upon the more wealthy :
but though this may be a practical palliative, the system is
radically defective.   Government has long recognised its inconveniences ; and the question of the conversion of this personal impost into a land tax has frequently engaged its attention.   The task is attended with much difficulty for want of
the necessary elements for a cadastral valuation of the landed
property to serve as a rational basis for the whole direct imposts.   Such a reform of our financial system involves the
necessity of an immense deal of preparatory labour, effected at
the cost of much time and much money.   Meantime, government, impressed with the necessity of equalising as much as
possible the charges borne by the peasants of the domains (who
form about $\frac{3}{8}$ of the agricultural population) has placed this
task in the first class of those to which the new administration
of Domains was instructed to direct its attention.   The imperial
ukase of 1838 addressed to the head of this administration bears
the express injunction, "to place the imposts levied on the

peasants of the Domains in equitable harmony with the benefit
which the latter derive from the lands laboured by them, and
the industries connected therewith." The Report of the
Department of Rural Economy to the Ministry of Domains,
published in 1849, contains some interesting information on
the result of the labours undertaken for this purpose, the substance of which is as follows:—

The ministry turned its attention, in the first instance, to an
examination of all the old plans proposed for a reform of the
existing system, and at same time caused detailed information
to be collected regarding the surveys and valuations of foreign
countries, and the different systems of taxation of landed property practised in Russia. After collecting these materials,
they proceeded to local inquests on the resources of the villages
belonging to the state domains, and the mode of distributing
the imposts among the peasantry, endeavouring to trace, for
the conversion of these charges into a rent levied not upon the
individuals but upon the presumed product of the land and
relative branches of industry, the basis of a system of valuation
and conversion which should, through its simplicity of plan
and facility of execution, be appropriate to the immense extent
of the state domains, to our agricultural situation, and to the
pecuniary circumstances of our cultivators. These preparatory
labours were pursued during the years 1838, 39, and 40, and the
information collected in the different parts of the empire showed
that whilst it is impossible to apply to Russia the cadastral
systems of other countries, yet there are circumstances peculiar
to ourselves, such as the equal division of the lands amongst
the peasantry and the communal organisation of the villages,
which afford the means of simplifying the more difficult cadastral operations. We may therefore hope to be able in the
course of time to improve the system of imposts, without either
extraordinary effort or great innovation upon popular use and
wont, and to create, if we may use the expression, a national
survey and valuation which shall embrace the principal advantages of those adopted in foreign countries, but shall be
less expensive and more simple in its application. The information collected as above was submitted to the examination of several governors of provinces, of the heads of the
chambers of Domains, and of the corresponding members
of the scientific committee of the Ministry of Domains.
With a view to facilitate execution, the ministry has been
careful to form in its establishments a nursery of young
men to whom cadastral operations might be entrusted: of
these a certain number have been sent to the governments

of St. Petersburg and Nowgorod to acquire the necessary experience in the valuation of landed property.

It was only after all this preparation that the Ministry of Domains determined on submitting for the sanction of the supreme authority its plan for the conversion of personal into real assessment, and on soliciting authority—which was granted—to make trial of its application in two governments, namely, St. Petersburg and Woronèje; the former of these governments serves as a model in all the economical arrangements of the Administration of Domains; the latter is one of the most important in regard to the extent and population of the crown villages, and, from its exclusively agricultural character was very suitable for a first attempt at cadastral operations. These experimental operations, which were begun in May, 1842, were finished in the short space of five months, in the course of which time there were surveyed 1339 crown villages, containing a population of 446,000 souls and 2,626,000 dessiatines of productive soil, and all the returns were collected which were to serve as basis for the conversion of the personal assessment. The promptness with which the work was concluded shows the practical utility of the mode of survey adopted; but in order to test the correctness of the estimates before applying them, they were submitted to the peasants themselves — commissioners being dispatched to both governments with instructions to hear the parties interested and to give relief wherever there appeared well-founded complaint. In this way many errors, inseparable from a work of the sort, were discovered and corrected. These operations were seconded by the good will of the peasants themselves, who in many cases solicited the prompt introduction of the new system. In some villages of the government of Woronèje, where arable land is so abundant that part of it was allowed to lie waste and the remainder laboured without any regular division,—every one taking possession at his own option of what seemed good unto himself, the peasants were found quite willing to introduce regularity into the state of possession and distribute the land *per capita;* in others the superfluous lands were converted into small farms (*obrotchnyia statia*): a number sought permission to form excambions with their neighbours, or to remove a portion of their population into some other village where the arable land was more abundant. These demands were, as far as possible, complied with; and thus the cadastral operations— independently of the more equal distribution of the impost — had the effect of improving the economical arrangements of the peasantry, and have greatly tended to diffuse amongst them juster ideas with regard to the relative value of the lands, and of the advantages to be derived from their local positions.

These operations having been finished in 1843 in the two governments in question, the Ministry of Domains received the imperial authority to put in execution in 1845 the conversion of the personal imposts after coming to an understanding on this subject with the Ministry of Finance ; and was further authorised to proceed gradually with the cadastral operations in the other governments upon the same principles, but with such practical improvements as they had derived from the experience now acquired.

The cadastral surveys and valuations were accordingly continued in the governments of Penza and Tambow, and subsequently in those of Toula, Riazan, Orel, and Koursk, so that by the end of the year 1849 the new system had been introduced into the whole of these eight governments, in which the State Domains contain 8,263,476 dessiatines of productive land, with a rural population of 1,707,279 individuals, contributing in imposts of every sort the sum of 8,673,540 silver roubles. The expense of these operations amounted *in toto* to 597,000 silver roubles, or at the rate of $7\frac{1}{4}$ kopecks per dessiatine—a very small expense if we compare it with what similar operations have cost in other countries. In France the expenses of the cadaster come to $82\frac{1}{2}$ kopecks, in Rhenish Prussia to 81 kopecks, and in Austria to 53 kopecks per dessiatine. The survey and valuation is at present proceeding in the governments of Moscow, Pskow, and Ekathérinoslaw.

The experience acquired in the course of these operations has shown that, wherever agriculture constitutes the main source of the peasant's subsistence, the introduction of the new system is attended with little difficulty ; but that in localities where industry is more developed the task is one of harder solution. In industrial governments, where the quantity of arable land is small, the imposition of the present taxes upon the produce of the land alone would press with excessive weight on agriculture, and raise the land tax in many cases beyond the rent payable to land-owners ; whilst on the other hand the taxing of various branches of industry, with us still in their infancy and producing very variable returns, is a matter that requires great delicacy of management. Alive to these considerations, the Administration of Domains has proceeded in its important labours with every possible tenderness towards existing interests,—preceding its actions by careful inquiry, and turning to no less careful account the experience which it has gradually gained. After the new system had been introduced into the governments of Woronèje, Tambow, and Penza, which are essentially agricultural, it was introduced experimentally into those of Toula and Riazan, where industry has attained a certain degree of importance, and which form a sort of transition between the industrial and the purely agricultural districts. Commissioners were at same time dispatched to the industrial governments of Jaroslaw and Kostroma, to collect information with regard to the industries carried on upon the State Domains, and to ascertain the fairest methods of estimating the return therefrom derived by the peasants.

The taxation of industry has formed, at all times and in all countries, one of the most difficult problems of finance; the difficulty is enhanced in Russia in its application to the peasants of the Domains because their industry is confounded with their agriculture; their time and their talents are divided between the labours of the field and the labours of their trade; and this epicene character renders an estimate of their contributive forces a nicer and more complicated operation. Still, as the matter on hand was not the introduction of a proper industrial impost, such as exists in France under the denomination of *patentes* and in Austria under that of *Gewerbsteuer*, but the conversion of a moderate personal impost already in existence, and representing at same time the rent of the land, the estimate of the return derived by the contributors from their trades and employments was to be regarded as merely a subsidiary means of rendering the new distribution more equitable. The arrangement is still too recent to admit of our judging as yet of the influence it is likely to exert on the welfare of the contributors; but it has in general been well received, and even in cases where increased taxation has been the result, an intimate conviction on the part of the peasantry of the scrupulous fairness with which the redistribution was effected, has prevented any thing like grumbling. The conversion will, of course, be more difficult in those governments where industry is largely developed and constitutes the main dependence of a large number of the peasantry, as, for example, in the governments of Moscow, Wladimir, and Jaroslaw; but it is hoped that by dint of proceeding cautiously, and not seeking to go beyond the limits of a more or less approximative estimate of the contributory capabilities of each village, the new system may be introduced into these governments, as into the others, without damaging any existing interest. When this task shall have been accomplished for the State Domains throughout Russia, it will be a great step gained in the reform of our system of taxation, and the cadastral operations will afford most useful materials for the introduction everywhere of a land tax in lieu of the present capitation impost.

In the Appanage domains the *obrok* has long been regulated in conformity with the extent and quality of the land; this has had a favourable influence on the situation of the peasants, whose thriving condition is evidenced, *inter alia*, by the punctuality with which they pay up their mails and duties, and the rapid increase of their communal fund. The latter amounted in 1850, according to a Report of the Ministry of the Appanages (without taking into account the fund for the relief of discharged soldiers amounting to 62,000 roubles) to the sum of 1,791,000 silver roubles (= 283,500*l.* sterling), being at the rate of more than a rouble per head for the population of both sexes (1,725,000 souls).*

4. *Colonisation and Distribution of Land in the South of Russia.*

The first manifesto concerning colonisation in the thinly peopled districts of the empire appeared in 1762. By virtue of this manifesto, all strangers without distinction (Israelites excepted) who came to settle in Russia as cultivators, received concessions of land on very advantageous terms. Afterwards, under the reign of the Emperor Alexander, colonisation became more regularly organised; a certain guarantee was required from the colonists, and it became a principle to admit only good cultivators, vine-dressers, gardeners, shepherds, and certain classes of artisans, as tailors, shoemakers, carpenters, potters. The first important colonies were established between the Don and the Volga in the government of Saratow; afterwards colonies of Mennonites were established in the government of Ekathérinoslaw, and these are now the most important and flourishing of any. In most of them we perceive an improved mode of culture and a higher development of those branches of industry which are most directly connected with agriculture; but their influence upon the neighbourhood has hitherto been less perceptible than could be wished.

Besides colonisation, government has, in the south of Russia, made concessions of vacant lands (*poustoporojnyïe*) to indigenous agriculturists for the rearing of sheep and cattle. Partial donations have been made, sometimes in life-rent, sometimes in absolute ownership, by way of encouragement and reward to those who had distinguished themselves in this branch of rural economy. Special regulations published in 1804 and 1806 fixed the principles of these distributions. In 1815 there was

---

* The capital of the Appanages amounted at the end of 1850, according to the official Report above mentioned, to 8,321,000 silver roubles (= 1,317,000*l.* sterling).

founded, from the proceeds of the sale of unappropriated pasture lands, a capital destined to encourage and promote the progress of agriculture in the governments of Kherson, Ekathérinoslaw, and Tauride. These measures have produced satisfactory results, and the progress of those southern countries of the empire is exhibited in the rapid rise in the value of the land.

We must not omit to mention one important measure adopted with a view to the future welfare of the agricultural class, namely, that in establishing colonies and making concessions of separate lands to the peasants, the latter have been empowered to attach to their possessions the right of *majorat*, so as to prevent the dismemberment of their little properties.

5. *Measures for the Instruction of the Agricultural Classes.*

It was under the Emperor Paul that the idea of imparting special instruction in husbandry was formed; and the first practical school of agriculture was founded at 24 versts from St. Petersburg. This branch of instruction has been considerably extended since. A new school was founded in 1804 in the immediate vicinity of St. Petersburg; it was placed under the patronage of the Administration of the Appanages; and is organised in a manner exceedingly appropriate to the wants and social condition of our agricultural classes. Theory is there adapted to the degree of their intelligence and education, and is closely followed up with practical instruction, which is made to extend not only to the culture of the soil, the various rotations, and the like, but also to the trades most useful for the agricultural classes, as the weaving of linen, the preparation of leather, the making of wearing apparel and various household implements. In 1832 there was founded a special school of agriculture for the peasants of the Appanages with the view of diffusing, by means of their instruction, agricultural knowledge amongst the other classes of cultivators. In 1834 an agronomic institute was established at Dorpat, under the direction of Professor Schmalz, for superior instruction in the different branches of rural economy; and in 1840 a new agronomic school, richly endowed and organised on a grand scale, was founded in the government of Mohilew on the domain of Gorigoretzk belonging to the crown. A capital of 38,580 roubles ($=6,100l.$ sterling) and a considerable extent of land, with an agricultural population of 2,735 inhabitants, were appropriated to this establishment, which is divided into two departments, one, of inferior instruction, for simple cultivators, with the view of enabling them to carry out the praxis, and the other, of superior instruction, for the special purpose of training agriculturists capable of managing large estates, and introducing upon these improved systems of cultivation; attached is a farm for the practical instruction of simple peasants. In 1836, the Minister of Public Instruction was authorised to found chairs of agriculture in the universities in proportion as pupils might offer, and to introduce, at the expense of the state, public courses of lectures on agriculture in some large towns where there is no university. Of establishments of special instruction in various subsidiary branches of rural economy, such as forest institutes and schools of viticulture and gardening, we have already spoken in treating of these different cultures.

At the period of instituting the first agronomic schools, the idea was first formed of instituting model establishments of rural economy. A model farm was founded in 1801 in the government of Smolensk to facilitate the introduction of an improved cultivation in the Appanage domains, and a similar establishment, termed *the English farm*, was founded in 1802 near St. Petersburg; but both establishments were suppressed shortly afterwards, in consequence of their expense so greatly exceeding the value of any benefit that seemed likely to be derived from them; at that period our agricultural classes were too little familiar with the very elements of a rational system of culture to be able to appreciate their advantages. This first want of success did not prevent the government from again directing its attention to the subject. In 1825 the Minister of Finance was authorised to institute model farms in those districts where they might be most useful, appropriating to each a foundation capital of 50,000 roubles and an annual rent of 15,000. By virtue of this authority, a model farm was established at Lougansk in the government of Ekathérinoslaw, which was afterwards suppressed for local reasons, and replaced by another founded in 1848 in the same government on an estate belonging to the crown in the district of Alexandrowsk. Besides this farm, seven others have been established in the governments of Wologda, Saratow (two farms), Tambow, Mohilew, Kazan, and Kharkow. The lands appropriated to these eight farms occupy an extent of 10,490 dessiatines (= 28,220 acres). Both crown and private peasants are admitted as pupils into the whole of them. In 1849 the total number of pupils amounted to no more than 706 ; but it is yearly augmenting : a complete course of studies occupies four years. Different systems of agriculture are practically taught in these establishments, each being appropriate to the particular circumstances of the region in which the farm is situated.

The diffusion of useful knowledge by means of the press has

also been recognised as one of the most effectual means of promoting the improvement of agriculture. In 1802 the Emperor Alexander manifested a desire to see the Academy of Sciences systematically engage in publications, derived from periodical writings and foreign works, on all agronomic inventions and improvements of recognised utility. From this epoch date the numerous agricultural publications which have been made at the expense of the state. In 1830 the practice was introduced into most of the governments of issuing periodical publications under the title of Government News (*Goubernskïa vedomosti*), containing useful hints in matters of agriculture, industry, and commerce. In 1834 there was established, at the expense of the state, an Agricultural Gazette, of which a certain number of copies are distributed gratuitously to the village clergy. Of this paper about 5,000 copies are now thrown off. The Ministry of Domains has issued since 1841 a monthly journal, which conveys to the public a knowledge of its operations, and contains essays upon various subjects connected with rural economy, and information about agricultural improvements both at home and abroad. Besides these two periodicals, the Colonial Protection Committee has, since 1846, published at Odessa an agricultural gazette in the German language, specially intended for the colonists in the south of Russia. There are also published, under the superintendence of the scientific committee of the Ministry of Domains, and by some of its members, useful works on different branches of agriculture, of which several are specially intended for the moral and agricultural instruction of the peasant class. The impulse given by government roused the literary activity of the enlightened classes; and since then publications on agricultural affairs are yearly becoming more numerous. A list of all the works published on this subject during the years 1843-48 is given in the report of the Department of Rural Economy to the Ministry of Domains, published in 1849. We have still to mention one other measure, which we consider of great importance, and likely to be attended with the best results. With the view of diffusing agricultural knowledge amongst the peasantry by the instrumentality of the village curates, government has introduced a course of agriculture into the seminaries, which send to the institute of Gorigoretzk pupils intended to become professors of this branch of instruction; and the Ministry of Domains has just published a complete course of agriculture specially intended for seminarists. The village curates of the dominant church have considerable endowments in land well rounded off, and every way suitable for forming little model farms; and an improved system of culture, seen in operation upon the minister's glebe, cannot fail to exert a favourable influence upon the whole parish, not to speak of the good counsels which an intelligent parson, without going far out of the way of his duty, may be able to impart to his parishioners about their rural as well as their spiritual affairs.

6. *Farmer Clubs.*

The utility of these associations has been recognised in every country. They facilitate to enlightened agriculturists the means of concerting about improvements, of communicating to each other the result of their observations and experiments, and of affording each other generally the benefits of their respective knowledge. The first Russian farmer club was instituted at St. Petersburg in the reign of the Empress Catherine, in 1765, that is to say, at a period when there were not half-a-dozen societies of the sort in all Europe. Under the reign of Alexander the agricultural society of Livonia was founded in 1805, and that of Moscow in 1818. Since then, several others have been formed, in the Baltic provinces, in the south of Russia, and in some of the central governments : they amount now to the number of nineteen, whereof four, namely, the Imperial Society of Rural Economy at St. Petersburg, the Agronomic Society of Moscow, the Central Society of Sheep Farming (also at Moscow), and the Agronomic Society of South Russia at Odessa, enjoy an annual subsidy from the state, amounting, for the whole four, to 34,285 silver roubles (= 5,430*l.* sterling). Besides these clubs, there was instituted in 1833 a special commission, charged with the investigation of the best means for promoting agricultural improvement. The journal of this commission, which has been superseded by the Scientific Committee at the Ministry of Domains, contains some interesting information, and various proposals of which several have been carried into execution.

7. *Prize Essays.*

Since 1842 the scientific committee of the Ministry of Domains has offered gold and silver prize medals for the solution of important questions connected with our agriculture, by ascertaining the causes which impede the progress of any particular branch, and suggesting the best remedy. The successful essays are published in the Journal of the Ministry. These competitions operate as an encouragement by awakening the attention of thoughtful men to the given subject, and stimulating investigations which may often conduct to useful results. The Department of Rural Economy, in its report published in 1849, gives

a list of the themes given out for discussion : the following are
a few of the more important :—

On the means of improving meadow cultivation in Russia;

On the most simple and least expensive means of procuring
supplies of water in the southern and eastern steppes;

[On this subject forty-seven essays were given in, for several
of which the larger or smaller gold medal or the silver medal
was awarded ;]

On the causes of the degeneration of horses and cattle amongst
the peasantry ;

On the causes of the unsatisfactory state of agriculture in
the northern regions of the empire, and the appropriate remedies.

On the condition of those branches of industry which are
exercised by the peasants in some governments, and the means
of encouraging and improving them ;

On the best system for building peasants' cottages, as regards
economy, solidity, and their preservation from fire.

8.   *Agricultural Shows and Prizes.*

Shows of agricultural produce promote the improvement of
rural economy by stimulating competition ; they serve also to
exhibit the progress which agriculture actually makes in the
different provinces.   The first shows were held in 1844 at
Odessa and Jaroslaw : they now take place in several other
governments. In the report of the Department of Rural Economy already referred to, there is a complete notice of all the
res gestæ down to the end of 1848, and of the medals adjudged
to successful candidates.

9.   *Measures concerning Agricultural Implements.*

To facilitate the acquisition by agriculturists of these instruments, government allows them to be imported duty free : and
in 1836 it established at the Technological Institute of St.
Petersburg a cabinet of models, duplicates of which are trans-
mitted to the chambers of finance of every government for the
purpose of forming collections.   The agricultural machine-
makers of Moscow have also received pecuniary subsidies to
enable them to extend their establishments. These measures cannot fail to exert a favourable influence on agricultural progress;
but here more than in any other department the effects of the
best devised measures will be slow to show themselves, especially
over a vast empire, where immense distances render communication so difficult. In manufactures every new invention or
improvement produces an almost immediate return, whilst it

often happens in rural economy that the fruits of improvement can be gathered only at the end of a series of years, or that even a future generation may have to wait for their ripening.

CHAP. II.

INDUSTRY.

Position of Russia in regard to her industrial Interests in general. — Branches of Industry most directly connected with Agriculture. — Distillation. — Brewing. — Manufacture of Beet-root Sugar. — Linen Manufacture.

BEFORE entering on a special examination of the various more important branches of our industry, it may not be amiss to direct our attention for a moment to the peculiar position in which Russia stands in regard to her industrial interests in general, and to the degree of importance which she ought to attach to these.

In common language we often hear states distinguished as agricultural, manufacturing, or commercial countries: but this nomenclature possesses only a very relative value: it serves to indicate the degree of importance occupied in a given country by one or other of these three branches of the productive industry of man, or rather the degree of development at which its industry or commerce has arrived; for at all times and in all countries agriculture forms the basis of a country's productive forces. Every people is more or less agricultural, more or less manufacturing, more or less commercial; but in every country (of a certain territorial extent) the values created by the culture of the soil greatly exceed in amount those produced by commerce or manufactures. On this subject we have already cited the case of England, the industrial and commercial state *par excellence* (*antè*, p. 217.). It is possible that in a small country very densely peopled, where the soil does not produce a sufficiency for the subsistence of its own inhabitants, industry and commerce, favoured by geographical position, by local circumstances, by the relations of the state with its neighbours, by the special aptitude of its inhabitants for a particular manufacture, may assume the first rank in importance and become the main basis of national wealth: but this is scarcely possible in a large one. States occupying a considerable extent of territory and endowed with a fertile soil may, if they have ready outlets for their produce, attain a certain degree of wealth with very little manufactures; but they cannot attain prosperity by means of their manufactures if their agriculture remain in a depressed condition. In great empires it is requisite, as a general rule, for the progressive and natural development of their productive forces, that manufacturing industry should go hand in hand with the progress of agriculture, but not that it should be favoured at the expense of the latter; and what is true in this respect of all large states, is true especially of those which, from their soil and geographical position, have a peculiar vocation to agriculture. Those modern economists who have constituted themselves the zealous champions of industrial interests are fond of setting forth the advantages which agriculture more or less directly derives from the progress of industry. They cite the prosperity of agriculture around manufacturing towns and in manufacturing districts; and we do not dispute the fact: but we demur to some of the conclusions as regards the general economy of states, which they seek to draw from it. Granted that the progress of industry exerts a favourable influence on that of agriculture,—the influence is more or less local: what is true of a district is not always true of a whole country,— especially if that country be a great state occupying a vast territory, composed of various provinces differing from each other in regard to their material interests. Nor can we admit the invariable and unqualified correctness of the observation, even if we limit it to a single province, as will appear from an example supplied by ourselves. The governments of Moscow and Wladimir — none of the largest—are the chief centres of our manufacturing industry; and yet in these two provinces agriculture is in a comparatively backward condition. They belong, no doubt, to the category of those of which the soil is but moderately fertile, and where there is a deficiency of meadow land,—a circumstance which checks the progress of cattle-rearing, and therewith the means of a plentiful supply of manure: but this should just be a reason for augmenting the fertility of the soil by a better system of husbandry, and for increasing the amount of the hay crop by drainage, irrigation, and the formation of artificial meadows,— such improvements being encouraged by the high price of grain, of which these governments do not raise enough for their own consumption. It is by such means as these that the Baltic provinces have succeeded in placing their agriculture in a satisfactory condition, although their soil, in its natural state, is certainly not more fertile than that of Moscow and Wladimir. Now this absence of agricultural improvement in these two governments must be attributed, in part at least, to the scarcity of capital; and this scarcity of capital for agricultural purposes arises from the circumstance that the capital is absorbed in various branches of industry: and, indeed, it is natural enough that parties should not feel inclined to invest large sums in improvements which will require a length of time to become remunerative, when they can at once obtain 10 or 12 per cent. for their money by investing it in a spinning mill or a calico manufactory. But even if this *un*favourable influence of manufacturing industry upon the agriculture of these governments could be contested, the undeniable fact remains, that while it may benefit some districts in the immediate neighbourhood of the principal industrial *foci*, it does nothing whatever to promote the rural economy of the remainder.

In large states, industry is never equally distributed over the whole area: it is almost invariably concentrated in certain districts, often of no great extent. Quite close to the centres of industrial activity, agriculture may, no doubt, derive considerable advantages from the ready markets thus presented for its produce. As facilities of communication increase, these advantages may become wider extended; but their extension is nevertheless always limited, and often shackled by local circumstances; and the distant provinces, which must look to foreign countries for their market, have no interest in the matter. Or rather their interests will suffer if the manufacture be excessively protected at their expense; that is, if it oblige them to pay a high price for home-manufactured articles, and deprive them of their means of exchange in foreign commerce. The sacrifices imposed on them by such a state of things are of course more severe and uncompensated, if the dearness of the articles they consume extend to necessaries as well as to luxuries.

We do not intend by these observations to depreciate the advantages of manufactures, even for great states, in which the interests of agriculture ought to predominate. We will not dispute, that, precisely in countries of very large extent, there may be this or that district or province whose vocation it is to sacrifice its own special interests to the general prosperity of the rest: but such sacrifices must have a certain object, a certain term, and certain limits: if it be for the interest of the state to enrich certain districts or provinces by protecting their manufactures, it is no less for the interest of the state to abstain from impoverishing other districts or provinces by ruining their agriculture. We view this question by the lights of a generally recognised political economy: we do not pretend to lay down any new general principles of our own: the question has already been amply discussed by publicists of talent and learning, to which we make no pretension: committing our studies and opinions to the reader's criticism, we endeavour to grasp the various circumstances requiring to be taken into account, when we seek to balance the agricultural, industrial, and commercial interests of a great country, and to determine, (with more or less precision,) the degree of importance which fairly belongs to each.

Let us now proceed to the matter more immediately before us, namely, an examination of the condition in which Russia stands in regard to the development of her productive forces by means of the industrial activity of her inhabitants.

The empire of Russia is so vast—it embraces within its limits so many extensive provinces essentially differing from each other in geographical position, soil, and climate, in the condition of their rural economy, their various products, the density and character of their population, their grade of well-being, the very nature of their productive forces, the elements of their prosperity, the local circumstances favourable to this or that department of labour—that it must be considered, in regard to its social economy, as a congeries of different countries, each with its own set of material interests to be managed and devel-loped. This assemblage of various interests spread over an extensive surface offers a vast field for the operations of inland commerce, and the development of different branches of industry. Taken as a whole, European Russia is a very thinly peopled country, since it contains only 650 inhabitants to the (geographical) square mile: but there are certain regions in which the population is dense enough to be in disproportion to the extent of the productive soil. It is natural that in such districts a portion of the inhabitants should either migrate into localities where there is more land than hands to labour it, or seek the means of subsistence in some branch of industry: both expedients are commonly enough had recourse to. This necessity of seeking a subsidiary resource in industry may also arise in governments where there is no want of arable lands, but at same time no market for their products, so that the inhabitants — the lower classes especially — would be unable to supply themselves with necessaries and with the means of paying their imposts, unless they had recourse to some sort of industry apart from the cultivation of the soil. But there is another circumstance more general in its influence, which augments the necessity for industry in Russia, and may be said, up to a certain point, to favour its progress, and that is the severity of our climate, and the length of our winters. The season of agricultural labour being with us much shorter than in the countries of the west and south, the cultivator has much more free time at his disposal. In countries where the climate is temperate and the population dense, where there are a number of small towns, and the home trade is active, the peasant, whose labours in the field last from the beginning of March into the month of November, will find little difficulty in turning his time to account during the three or four months of winter: he can carry his produce to market; he can fell and carry home timber; he can look after the fattening of his cattle; he can hire out his labour as a carrier for the conveyance of merchandise, or engage in some other subsidiary branch of rural economy. With us such resources are very much more limited, whilst the labours of the field are interrupted for a much longer time. Now what a loss of productive forces must arise, and what a cause of impoverishment must be in action, if, for want of any sort of industry, of the 60 millions composing the population of Russia in Europe, more than 50 millions should remain unoccupied during the six or seven months that the labours of the field stand still? But to avoid this loss we are thrown upon our industrial resources; and it is this peculiar situation of ours, joined to the abundance and variety of our products, and to the natural and instinctive intelligence of our people, which gave the earliest impulse to our industry, and impressed it with the peculiar and national stamp which it bears. From these peculiar circumstances, and from our communal organisation, has sprung up that village industry which, unlike that of other countries, has preceded the industry of the towns, and attained a considerable development without the aid of custom-houses or other forced and artificial means. It is long since we possessed populous villages where all the peasants are either weavers, or tanners, or shoemakers, or smiths, or cutlers, or cabinet-makers, or manufacturers of some other single article of commerce. It is this industry which has assumed with us in some sort a national character—which is so appropriate to the manners and customs of our people—which is so well adapted to the patriarchal organisation of our rural communes, that fundamental basis of our social order—which withdraws no hands from tillage—which does not interfere with the peasant's family life—which does not carry in its train the present grave inconveniences, or the future fatal consequences, of the concentration of the working classes in overgrown cities—which produces no proletariate, that scourge of modern society,—it is this village industry, we say, which, above all others, ought to be most carefully preserved and most specially protected.

Here, then, the question naturally occurs, up to what point is manufacturing industry, in the large wholesale meaning of the term, indispensable or useful in Russia; and how is it to be reconciled with our agricultural interests, and brought into harmony with our social organisation and economic position? This question is undoubtedly one of the most important that can arise touching the future prosperity of our great empire; but it is also one of the most complicated and hardest of solution: we shall esteem ourselves happy if the few following observations contribute to throw any light upon it.

During the first phases of our social organisation and of the development of our productive forces, our village industry, such as it had existed from time immemorial, was sufficient for our wants and our economic position. The principal products of our soil,—our cereals, flax, hemp, tallow, and timber, our leather, sailcloth, and cordage,—found an easy outlet in our foreign commerce. We received in exchange colonial wares, wine and spirits, the finer manufactured goods, and other articles of luxury. In this state of things there was nothing prejudicial to our interests; but, after the introduction of the continental system, the industrial and commercial interests of Europe in general, and of Russia in particular, underwent a change. England, which was, and indeed still is, the principal market for our produce, sought and found other sources of supply; and, adopting a system of protection in favour of her own agriculture, industry, and colonies, imposed heavy taxes on several of our principal articles of export. France, again, ever since the revolution of 1793, had adopted a tariff carried to the extreme of prohibition, and exceedingly prejudicial to our export trade. On the return of peace, every branch of industry, and specially the cotton manufacture, became vastly developed on the European continent. The prodigiously increased consumption of cotton manufactures produced an immense revolution in the social economy and industrial interests of every country. In the midst of this general movement it was impossible for Russia to remain passive and unconcerned. Perceiving, on the one hand, diminished chances of outlet for her products, in consequence both of the changes that had taken place in the social economy of other countries, and of the increasing competition with herself from across the Atlantic, and perceiving, on the other hand, that there was an increasing demand for manufactures abroad arising from the progress of wealth and population, Russia considered that she, too, required to seek, in the extension of her industry, a new means of aiding the development of her productive forces. Influenced by these considerations, she adopted, in 1822, the prohibitive system, which succeeded, without the least transition, the momentary experiment of the moderate tariff of 1819.

A great country like Russia, containing so many resources within herself, could not condemn herself to remain stationary in the development of her industry, and to refuse to profit by the new inventions, discoveries, and improvements with which the human mind had enriched itself in every branch of manufacture: but it does not follow that we were bound to enter the lists without taking into consideration the *ensemble* of our social economy, and to run the risk of all the inconveniences which the over-excitement of industrial interests has produced in other countries. On the contrary our duty rather is to profit by the experience of others, keeping in view our own special situation and the nature of our resources. Making no pretensions, as we have already observed, to lay down principles *ex cathedrâ*, we shall merely announce our opinion in general terms, and leave it to the judgment of our readers: In according protection to our manufacturing industry, we must not push it to the extreme of endeavouring to fabricate every thing for ourselves, and to reject every thing manufactured by others:—this is an object which no people can aim at without injury to itself. By concentrating our energy and resources upon the branches of industry most appropriate to the wants of the country, and the means at its disposal, we obtain surer and more durable results than we could obtain by dispersing them from a desire to do too much at a time. Capital and credit are the two great levers of industry: where either is wanting, the situation of the other must be precarious; and, if even in countries where both are abundant it would clearly be ill advised to undertake and force every branch of industry simultaneously, the absurdity of such a course must be still more palpable in a country where capital is scarce, and the resources of private credit very limited: but this is just the position in which Russia, like all countries whose productive forces are still in the early phases of their development, stands at present. Many of our manufacturers not being possessed of sufficient capital for their business, work up a raw material for which they have paid 12 or 15 per cent. more than the ready money price, which is of itself enough to enhance greatly their cost price and to entail a heavy burden on the consumer.* With the exception of a few articles, such as certain qualities of linen, ordinary cloths, and some sorts of silks, we may aver, without the slightest exaggeration, that in all purchases made at St. Petersburg and

---

* We have, no doubt, at Moscow, Petersburg, and elsewhere, wealthy manufacturers, who own large establishments worked with their own capital : but these are merely happy exceptions to the general rule.

Moscow, the price stands to the price of the same articles purchased in Germany exactly as the silver rouble does to the
convention florin*, being a difference of 60 per cent.; and many
articles are even 80 or 100 per cent. dearer. To form a just
idea of the position and prospects of our manufacturing industry,
we require to take into account both the favourable and the
unfavourable circumstances by which it is affected. The rigour
of our climate and the length of our winters, which have greatly
contributed to the development of our village industry, are also
favourable to the establishment of various factories; for the
workman, who is at the same time agriculturist and has nothing
whatever to do with his time during a great portion of the year,
can afford to work at much lower wages than the artizan who
looks to the factory alone as his source of subsistence. Moreover, the cheapness of articles of prime necessity produced in
the country contributes to keep wages low. Our people, also,
is exceedingly intelligent: it possesses in a high degree the
spirit of imitation, and easily adapts itself to every sort of trade.
These are the natural circumstances which favour the development of industry in Russia. We are far from disputing their
importance: but we find their advantages counterbalanced —
especially as regards the more complicated and skill-requiring
branches — by other circumstances, some of which we have
already indicated. These are, scarcity of capital, and the high
rate of interest — the great distances and the difficulties of
communication, which impede the transport of the raw material
on the one hand, and of the manufactured article on the other —
the dearness of the agents of fabrication, as machinery, chemical
productions, and colouring matters imported from abroad — the
dearness of iron, which renders the construction of all sorts of
machinery and tools very expensive — the dearness of fuel in
some industrial districts, where it has to be fetched from a great
distance: this is felt the more inasmuch as we have few water-
falls which could be used as a motive power, so that it is generally
necessary to have recourse to steam, — a very expensive agent,
especially when it is necessary, as it is with us, to import the
engines† — lastly, the state of culture amongst our burgher
classes: the majority of our manufacturers do not possess that
amount of knowledge which would be required to enable them
to conduct their establishments in a systematic manner, and to
avail themselves of mechanical and chemical improvements as

---

* As 3s. 2d. to 2s.

† In Russia there are but very few establishments where steam-engines are
manufactured, and their extension is trammelled, as we have already observed,
by the dearness of iron.

they arise: from this there results a great loss of time and labour, and the cost of production is consequently enhanced. To all this we have still to add, 1st, that amongst our factory undertakers there are a number of proprietors, who, having embraced the business as amateurs, without having received the necessary industrial education, are obliged to have recourse to managers, who, being often themselves imperfectly instructed, and often negligent or unfaithful, commit all sorts of errors, which their master has dearly to pay for, and who at best will never carry into the concern the interest, zeal, and activity of the manufacturer by profession, who conducts his affairs himself and saves the manager's salary as well as his blunders*; 2ndly, that the majority of our great establishments are obliged to stop for want of hands during the season of field labour; this likewise augments the cost of production by causing a heavy loss on the interest of capital and on the general expense of management; 3rdly, that, for certain branches of industry, the workman who interrupts his labours at the manufactory for a period of several months to return to the labours of the field, can never acquire the same aptitude and dexterity as the one that is constantly employed in the same department of skilled labour†; 4thly, the necessity which our manufacturers find of bringing over from abroad overseers, designers, colourists, mechanics, &c., all of whom require the inducement of large salaries; and of having attached to their factories small foundries for the preparation of moulds, and workshops for the repair of tools and machinery; for even in our centres of industry there are very few establishments for the manufacture of mechanical instruments or for the repair of machinery, such as we see in foreign countries, and especially in every manufacturing town in England.

The workmen in the factories form two classes — the one paid by wages; the other working *corvée*, in factories belonging to the owner of the land. The latter sort of labour, unpaid, it is true, but sometimes not very well performed, often leaves the owner of the establishment under some delusion in regard to the cost of manufacture. It happens not unfrequently that

---

* Amongst these proprietors we could name some men of great capacity, who have embraced their career with all the knowledge of the accomplished tradesman, and would scarcely be surpassed by the most distinguished foreign manufacturers: but they form only individual and exceptional cases.

† This mixed character of cultivator and artizan preserves us from proletarianism, which has become the sore of so many other countries, and from the violent crises apt to occur in manufacturing countries, when, from a stagnation in trade, a number of hands are thrown out of employment; but, viewed in regard to industrial economy, it presents the inconveniences we have mentioned.

the owners of factories, where the labour is performed under the corvée régime solicit permission to cede to the state the excess of population attached to their establishments, which they find to be a burden. In such cases government colonises the affranchised workmen, or allows them the option of entering into the class of burgesses.

From all this we think it may fairly be inferred that Russia, not being in a position to equal or outstrip other countries in the career of manufacturing industry — not combining the requisite conditions for becoming a great manufacturing country —we should rather seek to stimulate those branches of industry which are best adapted to the situation of our eminently agricultural country, and best combine with the industry of our villages ; and that, as a general rule, we should endeavour to protect those manufactures of which our own soil supplies us with the raw materials. This, as a general rule, is applicable to all countries, but more especially to Russia. We may here refer to an objection which we have often heard propounded by persons who are fond of drawing inferences from facts alone, leaving out of sight the causes to which these facts owe their existence. " See," say they, " how absurd a thing is the theory of political economy : it lays it down as a rule that those departments of industry which employ some product of the country as their raw material are entitled to a preference of protection, as being best adapted to the nature of the country and likely to be most successful ; but experience has shown that the cotton manufacture (of which the raw material had to be fetched from abroad) has made immense progress in Russia, whilst the linen manufacture (which seemed so natural to the country), far from progressing, is declining." This somewhat specious observation will pass current with those superficial thinkers who are fonder of cutting with a sentence the gordian knot of a difficulty, than of disentangling it by patient inquiry ; but it loses its force upon a closer examination. In political economy there are no absolute principles applicable alike to all countries, times, and circumstances. Political economy is a science of observation, consecrated to an examination of the facts which manifest themselves in the creation of wealth, and of the causes by which they are produced. The principles which it admits are derived from experience, and subject, like others drawn from the same source, to occasional exceptions which do not detract from their value as general rules. The study of social economy, as of all moral and political sciences, must be guided and corroborated by practice and experience ; theory and practice are not antagonistic ; but each ought, on the contrary, to aid and supplement

the other.   He who would found his judgment solely upon the
facts which come under his observation, ignoring their antecedents
and their attending circumstances, will run as much risk of
error, and perhaps more, as he who would take theory for his
infallible guide, without ever condescending to consult experience or practice.   As regards the comparison between the
cotton and the linen industries of Russia, where the manufacture of the exotic raw material thrives, whilst that of the indigenous seems tending to decay, this is explained by causes which
nowise strike at the general principle which this example is
supposed to overturn.   Cotton, as a textile plant, combines the
great advantages of fineness and lightness of filament, facility of
being spun with machinery into the finest yarn—and great
aptitude for receiving upon its fabric every colour and impress.
By dint of these advantages, and of the thence resulting cheapness of cotton manufactures, the latter have invaded every
market, and to a great extent supplanted linens.   In proportion
as the use of cotton cloth has more and more penetrated into
the habits of every class of the population, the linen manufacture has more and more felt its effects, and for the last twenty
years it has been in a distressed condition, not only in Russia
but in every other country except England, where the invention of flax-spinning by machinery has been turned to such
admirable account.   We are indeed somewhat worse off than
our neighbours.   Germany, which formerly carried on a very
extensive linen trade, still contrives to find a foreign outlet;
and although this trade has now lost much of its former importance, the states of the Zollverein still export in linen cloth of
every description to the value of about 10 millions of silver
roubles, whilst the value of our exports does not exceed from
800,000 to 900,000.   Thus our linen industry, restricted to a
home market invaded by cottons, had no encouragement to
augment its production *, whilst the cotton manufacture, removed by a prohibitory tariff from the apprehension of foreign
competition, has seen the home market, of which it holds the
monopoly, enlarging before it to an enormous extent.   It has
attracted a large proportion of the capital of the country, and
there need be little room for surprise that, under these circumstances, the one manufacture should pine whilst the other
prospers.   But without allowing ourselves to be dazzled by
its success, it will be worthwhile to compare its intrinsic merits
with those of such industries as work up an indigenous raw
material.

* We shall have occasion to return to this subject, and to refer to the means
most suitable for improving the condition of our linen manufacture.

Notwithstanding the severe competition of cotton cloth our linen manufacture still holds up its head. It almost entirely supplies the home market, for the value of foreign linens imported does not exceed 500,000 roubles; whilst, notwithstanding our very prohibitory tariff, the importation of cotton stuffs amounts to the value of nearly 4 millions. Our common linen cloths enter the home market at prices so moderate that they need fear no foreign competition, even if the import duty were reduced to a minimum. This is proved by the fact that, independently of sail-cloth, we export linens known in commerce under the names of *Flems* and *Ravensduck* to the value of upwards of 500,000 roubles, notwithstanding the duties to which these are subject on entering foreign countries. In this exportation we find even diapers figuring to the amount of from 60,000 to 70,000 roubles. The case is nearly similar with our woollen fabrics; our common cloths up to the price of 1 rouble 50 kopecks per archine (= 6s. 2d. per yard), are, relatively to this price, so well woven and so durable, that foreign cloths could not compete with them in our markets. We even export in our commerce with Europe from 15,000 to 20,000 archines (= 11,600 to 15,500 yards), and the fabrication of medium qualities is also progressive. At the same time it is certain, and undeniable even by the stoutest champions of our cotton manufacture, that we have not the slightest chance of ever being able to succeed in forcing our cotton fabrics into the markets of Europe, and that even in our own markets they will never be able to sustain foreign competition except so long as they are bolstered up by high protective duties. China and some other Asiatic countries on our own border are our only foreign outlets, and this commerce, although favoured by the geographical position of those countries, which have no direct or continuous relations with others, is limited enough. For some time past it has been found necessary to stimulate it by bounties on exportation. We do not export at an average to all Asiatic countries cotton goods of all descriptions to the value of more than 2,150,000 roubles, whilst the average exportation of our woollen cloths amounts to about 2,750,000 roubles; in 1847, it reached 3,121,000 roubles. All this, we think, goes to prove, that an industry based upon an indigenous raw material rests on a more solid foundation than one where the raw material is imported from abroad.

We do not mean to imply or to assert that the cotton manufacture does not deserve to be protected. Since the use of cotton stuffs has become so common in every country and amongst every class as to be an article of almost prime necessity, Russia could not condemn herself to remain for that article tributary to the foreigner. Our only object has been to rectify some erroneous or exaggerated notions with regard to the real utility of this branch of our industry and the degree of importance that fairly belongs to it. We will have occasion to return to this subject in detail in treating specially of the different branches of manufactures; and we now begin that part of our inquiry with those which are more immediately connected with rural economy.

Brandy Distillation.

The severity of our climate renders the use of spirituous liquors a necessary of life. Except in the vinicultural countries of the south, brandy is an article of almost prime necessity for the common people, being nearly indispensable for health. Important in itself as a branch of industry from its extent, brandy distillation has a special importance from its bearing on our agricultural interests. In those provinces which abound in cereals and have little outlet for their produce, it is the main and sometimes almost the only money resource for landed proprietors, who either distil themselves or sell their grain to distillers in their neighbourhood. These provinces furnish brandy to those where grain is too dear to admit of much distillation.

We have no complete data with regard to the consumption of brandy throughout Russia, but we can form an approximative estimate. In all countries where the common people are accustomed to the use of ardent spirits, their consumption will depend greatly upon the retail price; and this price is determined, not merely by the cost of production, but likewise, and generally to a greater extent, by the amount of excise duty imposed upon it, and the mode in which this impost is levied. Hence the relative consumption of spirits in Russia varies considerably in the different possessions of the empire according to the régime of impost to which they are subject. The governments of Great Russia and Siberia have, from a remote period, been under the farming régime; and in all these provinces, embracing a population of about $38\frac{1}{2}$ millions, brandy being sold by the farmers at a much higher price than throughout the rest of the empire, its consumption is greatly restricted. In those provinces termed privileged, which embrace the western and southern governments, namely, the Polish provinces of the empire, Little Russia, White Russia, New Russia, and the Baltic provinces of Courland, Livonia, and Esthonia, containing a population of more than 20 millions, the proprietors had preserved, down to the end of 1850, the right of free sale, upon paying to the crown an impost calculated upon the number of their peasants. In these provinces brandy was much cheaper, and much more of it was sold. Since 1850 an excise has been laid upon its manufacture, and an impost (which is farmed) upon its sale in the towns. The Baltic provinces have not been included in this measure, and there the old order of things still subsists. In the kingdom of Poland the duty is levied on the manufacture. In the Grand Duchy of Finland, every landed proprietor has a right to distil brandy during eight months of the year, upon paying a certain tax calculated upon the extent of his estate and the size of his still: the towns have a similar right, upon paying an impost proportioned to the amount of their population.

The production of brandy in the kingdom of Poland, as officially ascertained, amounted in 1846 to 15,000,000 garnietz = 4,950,000 vedros (= 16,000,000 gallons), which gave for the population of that period (about 4,700,000 inhabitants) 1·05 vedros (= 3·4 gallons) per head; but adding 10 per cent. for the surplus which in all countries escapes control* we may carry the effective production of the year to 1·15 vedros (= 3·8 gal.) per head. During the following years the production of brandy in the kingdom of Poland fell off considerably: in 1848 it had fallen to 3,211,550 vedros, but in 1849 it had again risen to the officially ascertained amount of 4,283,236 vedros, or at the rate, allowing for increase of population, of $\frac{9}{10}$ vedro per inhabitant. Taking into account these fluctuations in the annual production, which depend chiefly on the prices of corn and potatoes, and taking also into account the quantities manufactured which escape the gauger's control, we think we may admit a minimum consumption of 1 vedro per head, which would afford for the present population a consumption of about 4,800,000 vedros. We will perhaps not be far wide of the mark in assuming the same proportion for the western governments, the Baltic provinces, and the Grand Duchy of Finland, which would give for the united population of all these provinces 21,500,000 vedros. In the provinces which are under the farming régime, embracing, with the governments of Siberia, a population of more than $38\frac{1}{2}$ millions, the total ascertained sale amounts to about 20,000,000 vedros, giving about $\frac{1}{2}$ vedro per inhabitant; but adding the quantities illicitly sold, we may probably carry the total to

* In well-organised distilleries it is usual to obtain a much higher product than the official estimate, which is formed from the quantity and quality of the fermented matters employed.

22 millions of vedros.   These three quantities together give for
the total consumption of Russia only 48,300,000 vedros; but we
do not think we will go beyond the mark if we estimate the total
production at 50 millions of vedros (= 162 millions of gallons),
representing, at the medium price of 60 kopecks per vedro*, a
value of 30 millions of roubles (= 4,750,000*l.* str.).   Deducting
three-fifths of this amount for the value of the grain and other
produce employed in the distillation, which have been already
taken into account in our estimate of the gross value of our
agricultural products, there remains a sum of twelve millions of
roubles, which the distillation of spirits adds to this gross value.
But the main advantage which our agriculture derives from
this industry consists in the facility which it presents for obtaining a return from grain in those provinces which have no
good outlet for that article.   In order to appreciate this advantage at its proper value, we must take into consideration the
part which the employment of grain in distillation occupies in
the *ensemble* of our corn trade.   Reckoning 6 vedros of brandy
of 20° Beaumé as the average yield of a tchetwert of rye, there
would be required for 50 millions of vedros 8,333,000 tchetwerts
of grain; but, as in large and well-organised distilleries 7
vedros, and even more, are now obtained from a tchetwert of
rye, and as for some time past the use of potatoes in distillation has been extending in some provinces, we do not consider that we can reckon more than 6 or 7 million tchetwerts
of grain to be employed in the whole distilleries of the empire,
Finland and the kingdom of Poland included.†   Now, according to an estimate already given (*antè*, p. 267.), we cannot
hold the quantity of grain coming into actual commerce to
exceed 50 or 60 millions of tchetwerts, of which three-fourths
or thereby are absorbed in the provisioning of the army, of the
towns, and of those districts where there is a deficiency: the
remainder must either be exported or distilled.   Distillation,
therefore, absorbs about the half of our surplus harvest, and it
is in this that its principal benefit consists: to this must be
added the encouragement which potato distillation holds out to
the culture of that tubercle, and the facilities which distilleries
afford for the rearing and fattening of cattle; to this latter
circumstance, so important for countries where much manure is

---

* This is pretty nearly the average price paid for the crown magazines during
the six years 1845—50.

† M. Protopopoff estimates the quantity of grain at 10,000,000; but this would
infer a much larger production of brandy than is actually distilled. M. Kœppen's
estimate is 5,000,000, without the kingdom of Poland, which comes much nearer
to that which we have adopted.

requisite, the progress of agriculture in the Baltic provinces must in no small degree be attributed.

This important branch of industry is susceptible with us of great improvements both in its apparatus and in its processes. In many distilleries they make use of old-fashioned apparatus which has been condemned by experience; often, indeed, for want of the capital required to purchase better. The processes employed are likewise often very defective. The results of distillation, as regards both quantity and quality, depend, first, on the due mixture of the fermented matters; secondly, on the means employed to set fermentation a-going; thirdly, on the care and skill with which the proper moment is seized for the disengagement of the alcohol. For this reason there may be obtained from the same substances, and with the same apparatus, very different results, according to the skill of the operator. Professor Balling* publishes the results obtained in various distilleries of Bohemia and Austrian Silesia; we shall cite but a single example: in a distillery of the circle of Bunzlau in Bohemia, there had been obtained during the season 1837—38, from a mixture of 100 lbs. Vien. (= 123½ lbs. avoird.) of potatoes with 6·18 lbs. (= 7·6 lbs. av.) of barley and rye malt, only 6·04 mass (= 2·2 gal.) of brandy, of 20° Beaumé; this same distillery, having been placed in 1838 under the charge of a better manager, yielded during the season 1838—39, from 100 lbs. Vien. of potatoes with 7·06 lbs. (= 8·7 lbs. av.) of malt, 8·36 mass (= 3·1 gal.) of brandy of 20°. Thus, by the addition of ⅘ per cent. of malt, there was obtained an increase of spirit of more than 38 per cent. A large number of our distillers and their managers are still greatly behind in the march of improvement; and yet it is to one of our distinguished chemists, the celebrated Kirchoff, that the distiller owes one of the most important discoveries in his art, namely, the conversion of amylaceous fecula into fermentable saccharine matter by the reaction of sulphuric acid. This branch of industry is one of those for which the Technological Institute of St. Petersburg, and the instructions in chemistry applied to the arts given at the University of Moscow and other establishments of public instruction, may become of the greatest consequence; but, apart from improvements, its progress will essentially depend on the facilities for sale, and the system of impost, which so materially affects the price and production. As we here confine ourselves to a treatment of the question as it bears

* See the volume entitled " Die Branntweinbrennerei," p. 354., forming part of the author's valuable work on industrial chemistry applied to the processes of fermentation (Die Gährungschemie), published at Prague, in 1845.

upon the interests of national industry, we refer, for the financial view, to what we have said upon this subject in our work
on the Finances of Austria, vol. ii. p. 44., *et seq.;* but we may
observe that the numerous difficulties which have been found in
every country in regard, both to imposition and the control of
perception, are much greater than elsewhere in Russia, where
the means of surveillance are greatly more limited, owing to
the immense area over which the distilleries are scattered, to
the difficulties of communication, and to other circumstances
peculiar to the country.

Besides the industrial and financial interests, there is still the
moral side of the question to be taken into account. It has
been considered, and not without reason, that cheap brandy has
a tendency to foster the vice of drunkenness. It is sure enough
that the low price of liquor may hold out a temptation to persons of the lower classes, but it is difficult to draw a line which
shall discourage abuse and yet leave moderate use untouched.
Nor is it the habitual drunkard that the high price of spirits
will chiefly restrain from their consumption; the man of pru-
dence and economy, when the price of brandy is high, will
stint himself in its use; but the drunkard, to satisfy his craving,
will go with his last penny to the public-house. Experience has
also shown that the consumption of spirits depends much less
upon the habitual drunkards than upon the decent sober consumers, who regularly drink their moderate allowance. Of this
fact the excise accounts of Prussia during the period 1833—38
furnish a striking example. In the Grand Duchy of Posen,
where drunkenness is much more common amongst the lower
classes than in the German provinces, the mean consumption
per inhabitant was only 7·46 *quarts* (= 2·2 gallons), whilst in
the province of Saxony, where the peasant is much more
orderly and economical, the consumption was 10·77 quarts
(= 3·2 gal.), and in the province of Brandenburg it was 15·3
quarts (= 4½ gal.) per head, that is to say, more than double
the relative consumption of the Grand Duchy of Posen.* The
cause is natural enough. The drunkard is generally a bad
workman; he often idles away his time, and often after a
debauch he remains for a long period without the means of
purchasing the moderate ration of spirits which the temperate
man drinks at his daily meal. Considering the general use of
spirits with us, and that the climate renders them almost a
necessary for the working man, we think that, even under a
pretty high, but not an excessive duty, the consumption for the

---

* See Hoffman, "Die Lehre von den Steuern," p. 286.

whole empire (the transcaucasian provinces excepted) might easily attain the figure which it has reached in the kingdom of Poland (1 vedro per inhabitant), which would bring the total production of spirits throughout the whole Russian possessions (Transcaucasia excepted), to 64 millions of vedros (= 208 millions of gallons), and it might even be much larger.

This estimate may be justified by the following approximative calculation. From the total 64 millions of inhabitants we deduct 10 millions, or $15\frac{2}{3}$ per cent. as representing the easy classes (who do not drink ordinary spirits), and the wine countries of the south; from the remaining 54 millions, we deduct for children under the age of 14 years complete, who form 35 per cent. of the total population*, 18,900,000, leaving again a remainder of 35,100,000 individuals. Taking one half of this, or 17,550,000, for the male population, with the addition of only $\frac{1}{10}$ of the female population, we obtain a total of 19,305,500 consumers of spirits. We cannot reckon for an ordinary drinker less than $\frac{1}{10}$ *schtoff* (= 1·07 imp. gill) per diem; this is the smallest measure by which spirits are retailed. Now $\frac{1}{10}$ schtoff (= $\frac{1}{100}$ vedro) per diem gives 3·65 vedros (= 12·2 gal.) per annum, or for 19,305,000 drinkers, 70,463,250 vedros, which exceeds our slump estimate by nearly $6\frac{1}{2}$ millions.

It may, perhaps, be objected to this calculation, that of the 19,305,000 individuals whom we have reckoned as habitual drinkers, there are probably some whose circumstances do not permit them to take their daily moderate allowance; but if we consider, first, that of the said number there are some who take a double or even a triple allowance; secondly, that we have thrown out 10,000,000 of the population as non-consumers; thirdly, that amongst the women of the lower classes certainly more than $\frac{1}{10}$ are spirit-drinkers; fourthly, that whilst we have thrown out all the children under fourteen years complete, the boys amongst the peasantry often begin drinking before that age; and fifthly, that no inconsiderable amount of alcohol is consumed in chemical preparations, in pharmacies, and for different industrial purposes, which we have not taken into account;—if we consider all this, we will be satisfied that the estimate made is not excessive.

As regards the economical view, this branch of industry is so favourably situated in respect to the abundance and cheapness

---

* We borrow this proportion from the statistics of Prussia, in this respect the most complete we are acquainted with. In Prussia, out of 100,000 inhabitants there are reckoned to be 20,064 children of seven years and under, and 14,891 of fourteen and above seven ; in all 34,955 not above the age of fourteen years complete, which gives about 35 per cent.

of grain in various parts of Russia, that our brandy might become an important article of export. We could, if it were requisite, deliver 50 or 60 millions of vedros (= 162 to 195 million gall.), were it not that the import duties upon spirits are so high in foreign countries. In this respect we may hope that things will take a more favourable turn, seeing the tendency now more or less manifested in every country towards customhouse reforms and lowering of tariffs, especially in reference to raw materials and alimentary substances. The export of our brandies was formerly very considerable. In 1824 it amounted to about 400,000 vedros (= 1,300,000 gall.); but, after that date, it gradually sunk to below 10,000. In 1847 it suddenly rose to 159,000; but this increase was merely temporary; for, during subsequent years, not more than from 10,000 to 15,000 vedros have been exported.

The largest and most numerous distilleries are found in the western provinces, in Little Russia, in the governments of Saratow, Woronèje, Twer, Koursk, Orel, Toula, and Orenburg, in the kingdom of Poland, and in the Baltic provinces, where they prefer distilling from potatoes, in consequence of the high price of grain.

Beer-brewing.

This branch of industry is by no means so extensive as the former—not attaining one-tenth part of its pecuniary value. In the kingdom of Poland, where, in proportion to the number of inhabitants, much more beer is drunk than in the empire, there was brewed in 1846, according to official data, 22,500,000 garnietz (= 24,800,000 gal.); which, at the rate of 5 kopecks per garnietz, gives a value of 1,125,000 silver roubles. The product of distillation the same year was, as we have already observed, 15 millions of garnietz = 4,878,000 vedros; which, at the rate of 60 kopecks per vedro, represents a value of 2,926,800 roubles; so that the value of the product of the breweries was to that of the distilleries as 10 to 26; but there are many governments of the empire in which the former value does not amount to a tenth of the latter. The following figures exhibit these comparative values in 1846 in those governments where the same were officially ascertained. The numbers, as in most official data of the sort, may be assumed to be somewhat below the reality.

Governments.	Value of Beer.	Value of Spirits.	Proportion of Value of Beer to Value of Spirits.
	Roubles.	*Roubles.*	As 100 to
Twer - - - -	20,000	370,000	1850
Smolensk - - -	10,000	75,000	750
Kiew - - - -	26,600	753,000	2813
Saratow - - - -	38,000	700,000	1842
Toula - - - -	30,000	577,000	1923
Kazan - - - -	25,000	280,000	1120
Total - - -	149,600	2,755,000	1842

At the rate of 5 kopecks per garnietz, the value of 149,600 roubles would represent a quantity of 2,992,000 garnietz = 987,360 vedros,—a quantity which, distributed over the population of these six governments in 1846 (8,392,600 inhabitants), gives only $\frac{12}{100}$ vedros per head; whilst, in the kingdom of Poland, the 22,500,000 garnietz = 7,425,000 vedros, brewed in 1846, distributed over a population of 4,700,000 inhabitants, give 1·58 vedros per head. In the western governments, which were not under the farming régime in regard to the sale of liquors, the consumption of beer is larger than in the others, but not nearly so large as in the kingdom of Poland; and it could not be estimated for the whole empire, the kingdom of Poland excepted, at more than $\frac{15}{100}$ vedro per head, which would give for a population of 57,200,000 inhabitants (Finland included) 8,580,000 vedros. Adding the 7,425,000 vedros brewed in Poland, we obtain, as the total consumption of beer made in this country, in round numbers, 16 millions of vedros, which gives for the total population of European Russia (60,000,000) $\frac{26}{100}$ vedro per head. The 16 millions of vedros, reckoned at the average price of 15 kopecks per vedro, give a gross value for the products of this manufacture of 2,400,000 roubles; but if we deduct the value of the malt (which has already been entered in our estimate of the gross produce of our agriculture), we cannot carry our approximative estimate of the value which this branch of industry adds to the gross products of our soil beyond 1,000,000 roubles.

In the states of the Zollverein the consumption of beer is estimated, from official statistics, (see Dieterici's *Statistische Uebersicht*, vol. ii. p. 310.) at 38 quarts = 3·42 vedros per head; in Bavaria alone it is 106 quarts = $9\frac{1}{2}$ vedros; in Austria, 19·74 mass = 2·17 vedros; in France (from the agricultural statistics of 1840), 0·12 hectolitre = 0·94 vedro; in England (from M'Culloch's and Dieterici's calculations, founded on the

quantity of malt consumed in the breweries) 46 (Russian)
quarts = 4·14 vedros per head.   These results may be exhibited
in the following tabular form : —

	Consumption of Beer per Inhabitant.	
	Vedros. =	*Gallons.*
In Russia, including the kingdom of Poland - -	0·26	0·87
Ditto, without the kingdom of Poland	0·15	0·50
In the kingdom of Poland alone - -	1·55	5·19
In France - - - - -	0·94	3·14
In Austria - - - - -	2·17	7·26
In the States of the Zollverein - -	3·42	11·45
In Bavaria alone - - - -	9·00	30·15
In England - - - - -	4·14	13·86

The consumption of beer is restrained in Russia by the
greater use of spirituous liquors, which in winter the severity
of the climate renders necessary.   During summer its place is
supplied in a great part of Russia by *kwass*, a fermented liquor
prepared from rye meal: the use of mead also is tolerably
general in the two capitals and in some provinces.   But the
consumption of beer would be much larger than it is if it were
but better prepared.   Except at some large breweries at St.
Petersburg, Moscow, and Warsaw, and at a few other establishments, the beer is generally very light, insipid, apt to spoil,
and to derange the digestive organs, whereas the moderate use
of good substantial beer is very conducive to health.   The
consumption of beer always depends to a great extent upon
the skilfulness of the manufacture, which mainly determines its
price and quality: nowhere is so much drunk as in Bavaria and
England, and nowhere is it so well manufactured.   The best
proof of the influence which a good process of manufacture
exerts on the consumption is, that wherever good breweries
have been established they have never wanted custom, and
their owners have become wealthy.   At Vienna, and throughout
Lower Austria, where the manufacture of beer was very much
behind thirty years ago, the consumption of that article has
tripled since the organisation of good breweries, like those of
Bavaria and Bohemia, and it is constantly augmenting notwithstanding the extensive use of the country wines.   But independently of the mediocre quality of the beer brewed in Russia,
its consumption will always be small as long as the price is
kept so high as it is at present.   An ordinary sized bottle of
the best beer, which would sell in Bavaria for 3 kopecks, costs
at St. Petersburg from 25 to 27, or about nine times as much,
so that this drink has become an article of luxury inaccessible
to the common people.   Were it not for this highness of price
and lowness of quality, the use of spirits, extensive as it is,

would never have reduced the consumption to such a low ebb as it has sunk to in Russia. The best proof that the consumption of the two articles might extend side by side is furnished by the kingdom of Poland, where the consumption of beer is at the rate of 1·58 vedro, whilst that of spirits exceeds the rate of 1 vedro for each inhabitant.

Manufacture of Beet-root Sugar.

In the preceding chapter we have pointed out the importance of the cultivation of the beet-root for our rural economy. It may be considered as the first step gained towards the system of alternating the culture of grain with that of other plants which less exhaust the soil and furnish at same time food for cattle : but its main advantage for Russia consists in this, that it stimulates the industry of the country people, helps to put money in circulation, and procures for proprietors, in districts where there is little outlet for the other products of the soil, the means of deriving a certain income from their land, by the production of an article which finds a ready sale and can be transported even great distances without difficulty.* We are now to consider the manufacture of beet-root sugar as a branch of industry.

Favoured more than in any other country by the protection of a very high tariff, which subjects raw colonial sugar to an import duty equivalent to cent. per cent. on its value, and entirely prohibits the importation of refined sugar, the beet-root sugar manufacture has, within the last ten or twelve years, assumed a very rapid development. We have seen (*antè*, p. 150. that in 1848 there were throughout the empire and in the kingdom of Poland 337 manufactories, which were officially ascertained to have produced that year 902,960 poods of raw sugar. Allowing for the quantities which escape control, and for the progress of this manufacture during the last three years, we think we will not go beyond the mark in estimating the present production at about 1,200,000 poods, representing, at the medium price of 6 roubles per pood, a value of 7,200,000 silver roubles. The quantity amounts to nearly a third of the production of France, which amounted in 1850 to 65 millions of kilogrammes = 3,973,000 poods, — to three-fifths of the production of the Zollverein, which is about 660,000 (zoll) centners = 2,018,000 poods, — and to more than double the production of Austria, which is about 150,000 (Vienna) centners = 513,000

* These are the considerations which have long induced the Ministry of Domains to encourage this culture, and protect its interest on all occasions.

poods. Assuming an average yield of 4 per cent. *, the manufacture of 1,200,000 poods of sugar supposes the consumption
of 30 millions of poods of beet-root, representing, at the price of
5 kopècks per pood, a value of 1,500,000 roubles, which we
have to deduct, as already included in our estimate of the gross
produce of the soil : there thus remains a value of 5,700,000
roubles added by this branch of industry to the products of our
agriculture.

The importation of colonial sugar, including the importation
into the kingdom of Poland, amounts now to about 2,300,000
poods, which quantity, added to 1,200,000 poods of indigenous
sugar, gives a total consumption of 3,500,000 poods, of which
the indigenous forms somewhat more than a third.   In France,
the indigenous sugar forms more than half the consumption,
being (in 1850) 65,000,000 out of 121,000,000.   In the Zollverein it forms about a third, and in Austria about a fifth of
the total consumption.

The 3,500,000 poods distributed over a population of
64,000,000†, gives a consumption of 2·2 lbs. Russian per head.
The relative consumption of other countries is as follows : —

					lbs. Russian per Head.
Great Britain	-	-	-	-	24
Belgium	-	-	-	-	18·3
Holland	-	-	-	-	17·1
France	-	-	-	-	8·3
Denmark	-	-	-	-	6·1
States of the Zollverein	-	-	-	5·5
Sweden and Norway	-	-	-	3·7
Austria	-	-	-	-	2·8

Thus the relative consumption of sugar in Russia is 21 per
cent. lower than that of Austria, and 40 per cent. lower than
that of Sweden, the two countries occupying the next lowest
places to itself in the scale.   In Austria there are several provinces, as Gallicia, Bukowina, Hungary, Transylvania, and the
Military Frontier, where the use of tea and coffee is confined to
a few of the larger towns and of the least numerous classes of
the inhabitants, and where, in consequence, the common people
have scarcely any share in the consumption of sugar ; and these
provinces embrace more than half the population of the whole
empire.   This explains the small relative consumption of sugar

---

* In well-organised manufactories six per cent. and upwards is extracted ; but
the great proportion of our manufactories are so backward that we cannot assume
a higher average than four per cent.

† The total population of the whole Russian possessions amounts, according to
the last census, to about 65,500,000 ; but we have deducted Finland, which is not
included in the above estimate.

in the Austrian empire as compared with other countries. Russia is in a somewhat analogous position: the consumption of coffee is greatly more limited there than even in Austria; but, on the other hand, the use of tea, confined in Austria to the upper classes, is very general in Russia even amongst the common people.* One circumstance peculiar to Russia may, no doubt, contribute a little to restrain the consumption of sugar: as bullock's blood is used in the process of refining, the strict observers of Lent use honey instead during three months of the year; but this custom is not general enough to keep down the consumption so much below that of other countries; and there can be no doubt that it would increase considerably if the article were procurable at a lower price. Its dearness proceeds from the high duty (3 roubles 80 kopecks per pood) on raw sugar, which is equivalent to more than cent. per cent.

It has been proved by the experience of every country that there are few articles upon the consumption of which the influence of a high duty is so sensibly manifested as it is upon that of sugar. In England, in the space of four years, from 1844 to 1848, after a reduction of the duty, the consumption increased nearly 50 per cent.

It is an indisputable fact, that it is precisely this high price of sugar which has given the main impulse to the home manufacture of that article; but the extravagant bounty which the tariff secures to the home manufacturer has been attended with the disadvantage of calling a number of establishments into existence, under local circumstances not favourable to their prosperity; and many proprietors, who have become manufacturers without sufficiently weighing these circumstances beforehand, have not found their speculations to answer, notwithstanding the high prices. Now, however advantageous well-organised manufactories may be, both to their owners themselves and to the locality in which they are situated, it is clear that such as can merely protract a sickly existence by dint of the extreme dearness of the article which they produce, are indefensible on the principles of a sound political economy. The trifling benefit which they produce to their owners is out of all proportion to the pecuniary sacrifices which they entail upon the state, by depriving it of the duty which would be levied on the corresponding quantity of colonial sugar, which they prevent from entering the market. It is a well-ascertained fact that

* In Austria, the consumption of coffee is $\frac{70}{100}$ lbs. per head; in Russia it is only $\frac{15}{100}$ lbs. On the other hand, the mean consumption of tea per head is, in Russia, $\frac{19}{100}$ lbs., and in Austria only $\frac{1}{1000}$ lbs. Russian.

beet-root sugar manufactories can never become paying concerns, except where they use the best apparatus — are under
the direction of parties possessing the requisite technical knowledge and experience — and are placed in suitable localities,
that is, in localities where soil and climate are favourable to
beet-root cultivation, where fuel is cheap, and where the hands
requisite for weeding* and harvesting are easily procurable at
the right time and at reasonable wages. Wherever any one
of these conditions is wanting, it is impossible for the sugar
manufacture to prosper. Thus, for example, a well-found
manufactory, provided with all the best apparatus, may be a
commercial failure, if the boiling-master be inexpert at his
business, or if the hands necessary for the culture and in-gather-
ing of the beet-root can be procured only at high wages. For
this reason, in foreign countries, sugar manufactories are generally found concentrated in densely peopled districts. With
us, those proprietors who establish manufactories on their
estates can have recourse to the corvée; but this is a species of
culture requiring a degree of care and attention with which
corvée labour is not always conducted. We should, therefore,
apprehend that this branch of industry will never attain with us
the degree of prosperity of which it is susceptible, until the
culture of the beet-root shall have been sufficiently propagated
amongst our peasants. It is easier for a cultivator to take care
of his own little plantation, weeding it and watering it, with
the assistance, when necessary, of his wife and children, than it
is to see that all this is done on a large plantation undertaken
by a manufacturer. In this respect, some slight progress has
already been made. In the principal sugar districts the peasants are beginning to acquire a taste for this culture, and to
appreciate its advantages; but, whatever these may be, there is
one grave evil which is insurmountable, namely, the frequent
droughts, which sometimes ruin the whole crop.

As regards the process of manufacture, this branch of industry, taken as a whole, is with us far behind what it is in other
countries. We possess, no doubt, model establishments, as, for
example, that of Count Bobrinsky, in the government of Kiew,
which will bear an advantageous comparison with the best manufactories of France or Germany; but these are rare. In a number of manufactories the apparatus is so badly constructed, and
the management is so defective, that they scarcely obtain a yield
of 3 per cent. of the raw material. We have already seen (*antè*,

---

* It is well known that parasite plants exercise a great influence on the saccharine substance of the beet-root, and that the produce of an ill-cleaned plantation
is always of very mediocre quality.

p. 150.), that the average yield with us is only $3\frac{1}{3}$ per cent., whilst in France and Germany it is generally above 5 and often above 6 per cent.

In speaking of the culture of the beet-root as a sacchariferous plant, we have impartially examined the benefits which it confers on the localities in which it is cultivated, and the degree of importance which falls to be assigned to the sugar manufacture, as promoting the interests of agriculture. We shall now endeavour to examine with the same impartiality the sacrifices which are made on its account. Hitherto these sacrifices have affected only the financial interests of the state, for originally the high duty laid upon colonial sugar in our tariff was established, not with a view to protect the indigenous article, but for the purpose of revenue. Although therefore the home manufacture has profited by the duty, it would be a mistake to saddle it with the exorbitant price of the article; it formed, on the contrary, a competing interest with the refiners, who had previously enjoyed a monopoly of the market, though, no doubt, it has not hitherto had the effect of sensibly bringing down their prices. The badly organised establishments, producing dearly, cannot afford to sell at a lower price than colonial sugar can be sold for, notwithstanding the heavy duty with which that article is burdened: they therefore cannot compete with the well-conducted establishments; so that these, in their turn, have no occasion to undersell the refiners. This may be merely a fortunate circumstance for them, so long as the present duties are maintained as a matter of fiscal policy; but when we consider that these duties have the effect of doubling the price of the article to the consumer, it is obvious that the interests of the latter must be very seriously prejudiced, if they are now to be continued for an indefinite period for the sake of the benefit which they afford to the home manufacturer. The direct sacrifices imposed upon the treasury are easily calculated. As the home manufacture has not lowered the price, it is obvious that it has not, in any degree, contributed to increase the consumption, and that the progress which consumption actually makes is referable merely to the progress of population and wealth in the community; every pood of sugar, therefore, produced in the country merely takes the place of another pood of colonial sugar which would pay a duty of 3 roubles 80 kopecks at the custom-house. The indigenous manufactures now produce about 1,200,000 poods, which quantity, replaced by colonial sugar, would bring into the treasury 4,560,000 roubles. Deducting from this amount the duty of 45 kopecks per pood payable on home manufactured sugar, which (assuming that the duty is regularly paid on the whole quantity actually manufactured) ought to produce 450,000 roubles, there remains the sum of 4,110,000 roubles annually sacrificed by the treasury.

The sugar manufacturers deny the reality of this sacrifice, because, say they, the importation of colonial sugar, instead of falling off, has increased, notwithstanding the increasing production of indigenous sugar. This argument is entirely void of substance. The consumption of sugar has in every country a natural tendency to augment; but its indigenous manufacture can have no conceivable influence in stimulating this augmentation if it do not bring down the price; now this our home manufactured sugar has not done; and, not having done so, it cannot attribute to itself any share in producing the increased consumption; it is therefore plain that the increased importation of colonial sugar would have been much greater than it has been, had it not been for the competition of the indigenous article, and therefore that the loss suffered by the state finances has been, and is, a very real one. But additional light will be thrown upon this question by a glance at the following figures, which exhibit the quinquennial averages of importation of sugars of every sort during the twenty-five years from 1826 to 1850:—

Years.			Mean Importation. Poods.			Increase. Poods.			Proportion per cent.
1826—1830	-	-	1,230,700						
1831—1835	-	-	1,497,300	-	-	266,600	-		21·7
1836—1840	-	-	1,709,300	-	-	212,000	-		14·2
1841—1845	-	-	1,936,700	-	-	227,400	-		13·3
1846—1850	-	-	1,942,100	-	-	5,400	-		0·3

Thus in the space of twenty years the increase of importation has entirely disappeared, and it is more than probable that, as the manufacture of beet-root sugar progresses, importation will follow a decreasing movement.

It is well known that the duties on colonial produce, and especially on sugar, form in all countries one of the main items of the customs revenue. The following is the proportion of these revenues in the principal states of Europe, (see p. 469.):—

The most zealous advocates of the home manufacture cannot claim from the treasury an indefinite sacrifice to their interest of such an important branch of revenue. Accordingly, they confine themselves to asking time to allow their industry to consolidate. With the view of granting them this, government, having seen proper to impose a duty upon beet-root sugar, with the view of partially repairing the loss of its duties on colonial sugar, proceeded to this measure with every possible precaution, and after carefully listening to the representations of the sugar manufacturers. The impost was fixed, in 1848, for that and

	Total Revenue from Customs.	Product of Sugar Duty.	Proportion of Sugar Duty to total Customs Revenue per cent.
	Silver Roubles. '	*Silver Roubles.*	
Great Britain (average of 1847 —48) as per official registers, 20,472,800*l*. = - - -	132,049,600	28,716,800	21·7
France (in 1847) as per "Moniteur," 136,484,000 francs -	34,121,000	12,198,500	35·7
States of the Zollverein (average of 1848 — 49) per official tables, 23,454,000 thalers -	21,812,200	5,816,000	26·7
Austria (average of 1845—47) 16,993,000 florins - -	10,909,500	2,952,000	27
Russia (average of 1848—50) -	31,370,000	7,485,200	23·9

the following year at 30 kopecks; for the two subsequent years, at 45 kopecks; and for the years 1852-54 at 60 kopecks per pood: for the small establishments, producing not more than 500 poods, these duties were lowered, during the periods in question, to 15, 30, and 45 kopecks respectively. From and after 1854 the whole question of the sugar duties, indigenous and colonial, is to be subjected to a fresh inquiry. The question is both important and complicated, involving as it does the reconciliation of the interests of the home manufacture — with which the agricultural interests of the localities of their industry are intimately connected — with the interests of the treasury and those of the consumer. It is not easy to find a solution that will satisfy all; the matter has occasioned much embarrassment to the government of every country in which this industry has taken root. We have the advantage of their experience, keeping in view those circumstances which are peculiar to ourselves; and this experience may help to guide, not only government in its financial measures, but also the manufacturers in their processes and management.

If we take a retrospective glance at the progress of this industry in foreign countries, we will find that it originated during last century. The chemist Marggraf, director of the section of physics at the Academy of Sciences of Berlin, was the first who attempted to employ various sacchariferous plants as a substitute for the sugar-cane, and he analysed for this purpose the parsnep, the carrot, and the juice of the birch. These experiments, not having been attended with a satisfactory result, fell into oblivion, and it was not till about half a century later, when the continental system had raised the price of colonial sugar in the proportion of 1 to 8 that the chemist Achard of Berlin renewed them upon the beet-root; and, after having obtained from a cwt. of beet-root 5 lbs. of white sugar and 3 lbs. of molasses, established a sugar-manufactory in Silesia upon an estate conceded to him by the king for that purpose. The most celebrated chemists of France, Cels, Chaptal, d'Arcet, Fourcroy, Tessier, and Vauquelin, were successively dispatched to Silesia by the National Institute to examine Achard's process. From this time the manufacture began to be carried on in France with more or less success, whilst in the country of its birth it was almost entirely abandoned. However, it is only since 1830 that even in France it has attained much consequence; in 1828 the total production did not amount to 3 millions of kilogrammes; in 1836 there were 466 manufactories producing 49 millions of kilogrammes; and this industry, protected at that time by a duty on colonial sugar of $42\frac{1}{2}$ to $49\frac{1}{2}$ francs per 100 kilogr., became a dangerous rival for the colonies; the importation fell from $82\frac{1}{2}$ to $67\frac{1}{2}$ millions of kilogrammes, which led to the imposition of a duty on beet-root sugar of $16\frac{1}{2}$ to 22 francs per 100 kilogr. according to quality. In consequence of this measure the home production was reduced by more than a half, whilst the importation of colonial sugar was but slightly increased. In 1841 it amounted to no more than $74\frac{1}{2}$ million kilogrammes. During the same period indigenous sugar, still favoured by a differential duty of 26 francs per metrical quintal, rapidly recovered from its depression. Out of 600 manufactories, a fourth — for most part badly organised establishments — had been abandoned; but the remaining 450 increased their business, and the total production, which in 1839 had fallen off to 22 millions of kilogrammes, amounted in 1842 to 41 millions. During these different phases, the product of the sugar-duty underwent the following variations. From 1831 to 1837 the mean revenue maintained itself at about 31 millions of francs; in 1838 it fell to 30,381,000, and, in 1839, to 28,407,000. In consequence of the changes in the tariff in 1839 and 1840, the revenue rose in 1840 to 34,896,000, and in 1842 to 40 millions of francs. It was then calculated that, if the home manufacture were suppressed, the revenue would rise to at least 60 millions, and this gave occasion to the *projet de loi* presented to the Chambers in the session of 1842-43 for the suppression of the entire manufactories, which were to be allowed from the treasury a compensation of 50 millions of francs. This project was rejected, and in its stead was passed the law of 1843, by which the duty upon indigenous sugar was, during the course of five years, to be gradually assimilated to the duty on sugar imported from the French colonies. This measure was attended with the downfal of some of the more rickety establishments; but the solid houses weathered the crisis, as they had done the former one, and indigenous production again assumed an ascending movement. During the season 1846-47, that is to say, immediately before the duty attained its maximum, it amounted to 43,394,000 kilogrammes, and during the following season of 1847-48, the home manufactories produced 53,350,000 kilogrammes, being 4,350,000 kilogrammes beyond the maximum it had reached before it was ever subject to a duty at all. In 1850 it attained the figure of 65 millions of kilogrammes, and it is now a dangerous rival to colonial sugar.

The question has been greatly agitated both in France and in Germany whether the manufacture of beet-root sugar upon the European continent could attain the degree of perfection necessary to enable it to compete with colonial sugar without the protection of a differential duty. Analyses have been made by the most distinguished chemists to ascertain the quantities of saccharine matter contained in the cane and in the beet-root respectively, and careful estimates have been formed of the costs of production both in the colonies and in the European manufactories. In the calculations of M. Stölzel, a technologist of the university of Heidelberg[*], the various local circumstances are taken into account which may affect the cost of production at home or in the colonies, and it may be worth while to state the chief results. Chemical analysis has proved that the contents of crystallisable sugar are just as variable in the cane as in the beet-root, depending on the quality of the plant, and on soil and climate. In the juice of the cane the saccharine matter varies between 10 and 30 per cent., and 18 per cent. is considered the most admissible average. In the beet-root, the quantity of saccharine matter varies, according to Einhoff, Hermann, Deyeux, Chaptal, Pelouze, and Péligot, between 5 and 13 per cent. Ludersdorf found in the different sorts of beet-root submitted to his analysis a range of 3 to 13 per cent. The proportion of 10 per cent. as an average is that adopted by the majority of chemists. Thus the difference in favour of the cane would be as 9 to 5; but this difference is considerably reduced in the effective results of the manufacture. Besides that the cane contains only 90 per cent. of substances more or less liquid and 10 per cent. of solid and filamentous substances, whilst in the beet-root the proportions are 95 and 5, there can be obtained from the latter plant, by mechanical means, especially since the application of the hydraulic press, a comparatively much larger extraction of juice. According to the most recent experience there can be

[*] See his pamphlet, "Die Entstehung und Fortentwicklung der Rübenzucker-fabrication," published at Brunswick in 1851.

extracted from the beet-root from 75 to 85 per cent. of the
juice.   In most of the colonies they are obliged, for want of
wood, to use the residue of the canes for heating the coppers,
for which reason they cannot be reduced into small enough
fragments to express all the juice which they contain, so that
the quantity of the latter obtained does not in general exceed
50 per cent.   In Bengal the quantity of juice is as small as 30
per cent.   On those plantations where the best apparatus is
made use of, 60 per cent. of juice is obtained.*   Now, of the 95
per cent. of juice contained in the beet-root, from 75 to 85
per cent. is extracted, and consequently, of the 10 per cent. of
saccharine matter which the plant contains, there is realised
from the juice from $7\frac{1}{2}$ to $8\frac{1}{2}$ per cent.; whilst of the 90 per
cent. of juice contained in the cane, there is extracted but 50 or
60 per cent., and consequently, of the average 18 per cent. of
saccharine matter, there is realised not more than 10 or 12 per
cent., and in Bengal, from 35 per cent. of juice, only 7 per cent.
of sugar.   This difference in material result is modified still
farther in favour of the beet-root by the form under which the
sugar is produced.   The sugar extracted both from the one
plant and from the other is produced under the form of crystallisable sugar and uncrystallisable sugar, or molasses.   In
his first experiments, Achard had obtained from the beet-root a
product of a very inferior quality, containing more molasses
than sugar; but by means of certain chemical processes he succeeded in obtaining from 8 lbs. of raw sugar 5 lbs. of crystal-
lised sugar and only 3 lbs. of molasses.   Since Achard's time,
immense improvements have taken place in the manufacture,
and it is now considered a fair average proportion when, of the
$7\frac{1}{2}$ to $8\frac{1}{2}$ per cent. of sugar contained in the extracted juice, 6 to
7 per cent. is in the state of crystallisable sugar and $1\frac{1}{2}$ to $2\frac{1}{2}$
per cent. in the state of molasses.   In the colonies, the results
obtained have been very variable.   The chemist Avequin found in
four analyses made in Louisiana, each time with 100 lbs. of cane
juice, that the quantities of crystallisable and uncrystallisable sugar
obtained were respectively as follows: 10 lbs. and 4 lbs.; 12 lbs.
and 5 lbs.; 10 lbs. and 3 lbs.; 11 lbs. and 5 lbs.   Dupuis obtained
at Guadaloupe from 100 lbs. of cane 8 lbs. of sugar and 3 lbs. molasses; and, on another analysis, 7 lbs. sugar and 3 lbs. molasses,
that is to say, the proportions of 2·3 and 2·6 crystallisable sugar
and 1 of uncrystallisable.   Dumas found in the plantations of
Louisiana, on an average of six years' production, out of 500

* According to recent information procured in England, as much as 70 per
cent. is now extracted in some colonies by means of improved presses ; but such
cases are exceptional.

kilogrammes of raw sugar, 286 of molasses, which gives the proportion of 7 crystallisable to 10 uncrystallisable. The French, English, and Spanish colonies in the West Indies, yield, according to the same chemist, out of 500 kilogrammes of raw sugar, 208 kilogrammes of molasses, or the proportion of crystallisable to uncrystallisable sugar is as 14 to 10. On combining these numerical data, the following result is obtained: of the 10 or 12 per cent. of saccharine matter expressed from the cane, the saccharine contents vary in the following proportions:—

Crystallisable sugar - - - - - -	4 to 8
Uncrystallisable sugar - - - - - -	6 to 4

From this we may judge what quantity of crystallisable sugar contained in the cane juice must be lost in the process of manufacture; and thus the natural superiority of that plant, as to its saccharine contents, is sensibly modified. But there is another circumstance still requiring to be taken into consideration: the growth of the cane till it comes into arrow lasts nearly a year. In some plantations, as in Brazil and Jamaica, it is not cut down until it becomes yellow and soft, which requires a period of fourteen or sixteen months: throughout the greater part of the West Indies, it is cut immediately after coming into arrow, which generally takes place during the twelfth month: in the East Indies, it is cut even before coming into blossom, after ten or twelve months' growth; but reckoning the time requisite for preparing the land and for planting, we may reckon, upon an average, an interval of fifteen months between one crop and another, so that for 4 crops of beet-root there can be reckoned only 3 crops of canes. Taking this proportion, and combining it with the preceding data, M. Stölzel makes the following calculation: 100 lbs. cane yield *per annum* $\frac{3}{4}$ of 8 = 6 per cent. crystallisable, and $\frac{3}{4}$ of 4 = 3 per cent. of uncrystallisable sugar: that is, nearly the same proportion that is yielded by 100 lbs. of beet-root.

We have now to ascertain the difference in the cost of manufacture. It has been ascertained by statistical researches that the price of labour in the colonies is in general higher than on the European continent — even slave labour, where it exists, coming high, especially since the measures which have been taken against the slave-trade.

	Kopecks.
At Cuba the maintenance of a slave, including interest of capital and sinking fund upon his cost price, comes to $\frac{1}{3}$ dollar per day -	27
At Porto-Rico the day's work of a slave, as that of a free man, comes to $\frac{1}{4}$ dollar - - - - - - - - -	34
At St. Domingo the free man's day's work comes to $\frac{1}{4}$ to $\frac{1}{3}$ dollar -	34 to 43
In Jamaica, it is $1\frac{3}{4}$ to 3 shillings - - - - -	46 to 82
In Guiana, it is 2 to $4\frac{1}{2}$ shillings - - - - -	55 to 124

The following, *per contra*, is the usual price per day for field labour in Europe:—

	Kopecks.
In Austria and Bohemia (according to Hagemeister) - - -	12
In Eastern Prussia (according to Hoffmann) - - - -	12
In the environs of Magdeburg, in Saxony, and in Silesia (according to Gaspari) - - - - - - - - -	18
In the Bavarian Rhenish provinces - - - - - -	21
In the district of Brandenburg (according to Hoffmann) - -	23
In the district of Düsseldorf (according to Vieban) - - -	28
In France - - - - - - - - - -	31 to 37
In England (according to Senior) - - - - - -	37 to 53

On comparing these figures we perceive that the day's work in the colonies is much the dearer of the two. It is, moreover, to be observed, that the lowest West India rates are based upon the cost of maintaining slaves, whose labour is not, as a general rule, very productive. There are but a few exceptions, as, for example, the Island of Barbadoes, where the day's work of a free man comes to only 10 or 12 pence = 23 or 28 kopecks, which arises from the redundancy of the population: but even this rate corresponds to the highest wages for field labour in Germany. The lowest rate of wages is found in the East Indies, where, according to Neumann, a day's work in some districts, as, for example, at Benares, costs only 9 kopecks: this proceeds from the ruin of the cotton manufacture, which, having been driven out of the market by the English manufacture, has left a great number of hands without employment: and to this circumstance it is owing that these countries, although extracting from the cane only 35 out of the 90 per cent. of its contained juice, can still compete with the West Indies.

Capital forms the second element in the cost of production: but in this respect also the colonies are at a disadvantage. In all countries which have not got beyond the first period in the development of their material forces—where industry is little advanced—where there are virgin lands to cultivate, and a multitude of things to be undertaken, the supply of capital is scarce in proportion to the demand, and this has, of course, a great effect on the rate of interest. In the United States the current rate of interest is 10 or 12 per cent.; and when in 1807 the legal rate was lowered to 6 per cent., the merchants could no longer obtain credit, so that in consequence of their solicitations it was raised again to 8 per cent. In Brazil, the common rate is 12 per cent.; in Mexico 30 per cent.; in the East Indies 24 per cent. The colonial planters have, no doubt, the advantage of working with simpler means and apparatus; but, on the other hand, even this simple apparatus is exceedingly expensive in those countries. If, as we have already seen, the wages of ordinary field labour is higher than on the European continent, the difference in cost of the labour of an artisan is more considerable still: at Buenos-Ayres the most simple artisan receives 1 piastre = 1 rouble 33 kopecks; at Rio-Janeiro, from 1 to 2 piastres; at Demerara a carpenter's assistant receives nearly 18 shillings. From this high price of labour it is found less expensive to import apparatus from England than to have it made in the country.

The difference of cost is also great in the article of fuel, which is scarce in most of the colonies, with the exception of Java and Porto-Rico, where there are fine forests. The refuse of the cane is one of the main substitutes; but it is an expensive sort of fuel, for, in order that it may be of avail, the juice must not be fully expressed: in Jamaica it is found more profitable to import coal from England. Notwithstanding the dearness of fuel, the construction of the furnaces is so imperfect that even in the best of them 1,700 lbs. of wood are consumed in the manufacture of 100 lbs. of raw sugar. If they seek to save fuel by diminishing the intensity of the fire, the result is that the juice, passing but slowly into a state of ebullition, is exposed to fermentation, and thus the quantity of crystallisable sugar is diminished.

Besides these circumstances, the value of the land occupied as plantation forms an important element in the cost of production. In this respect the advantage is entirely on the side of the colonies; in these countries, for most part thinly peopled, there are immense tracts in a state of nature; the price of the productive land is very moderate, and the natural fertility of the soil affords abundant crops.

The following, according to M. Hagmeister, is the mean price of land in Europe and in the colonies.

In Europe.	A Prussian Morgen costs: Prussian Thalers.	An Imperial Acre costs: £ Sterling.
In Prussia - - - -	94 to 106	£22 7s. to £25 5s.
In the Province of Magdeburg -	406 „ 437	£96 3s. „ £104
In Austria - - - -	66 „ 70	£15 15s. „ £16 16s.
In Bohemia - - - -	66	£15 15s.
In Würtemberg - - -	98	£23 6s.
In France and Belgium - -	135 to 168	£32 3s. to £40
In the Colonies.		
In St. Domingo - - -	9 to 36	£2 2s. to £8 8s.
In Jamaica - - - -	13 „ 26	£3 2s. £6 4s.
In Guiana - - - -	17 „ 22	£4 1s. £5 5s.
In Porto-Rico - - - -	45	£10 7s.
In Cuba - - - -	45 to 90	£10 7s. to £20 14s.
In Barbadoes - - - -	440 to 880	£104 15s. £209 10s.

From this comparative table it appears that, with the exception of Barbadoes, where there is a population of 10,000 inhabitants to the geographical square mile, the value of land is much higher in Belgium, Germany, and France, than in the colonies ; the average price of the land in Cuba, where it is highest, scarce exceeds the price in Bohemia, where it is lowest. Striking an average of the whole, with the exception of Barbadoes, we obtain, for the colonies $33\frac{2}{3}$ thalers per morgen = $8l.$ per acre, and for the European countries 171 thalers per morgen $=40l.$ $17s.$ per acre, so that the average value of colonial land is scarcely one fifth of the average value of land in Germany, France, and Belgium, taken together, which necessarily makes a great difference in the cost of production in favour of the cane.

As regards the difference in the produce of crops, the following information, collected from various economists, is reproduced by M. Stölzel.

In *Austria*, there is gathered from a joch of land, according to Krause, from 216 to 300 centners of beet-root; according to Bürger, there is gathered, with good culture, from land of average fertility, from 350 to 400 centners. The mean of these figures is 316 centners per joch (= 245 cwt. per acre). In *Bohemia*, according to M. Neumann, the mean crop is estimated at 240 centners per joch (= 186 cwt. per acre). In *Prussia*, according to Ludersdorf, a morgen yields 146 centners: Thaer considers the average to be 180 centners. In the district of Magdeburg the average (deducting $\frac{1}{4}$ for failures) is reckoned to be 176 centners. Combining these three figures we obtain as the general average of Prussia 167 centners per morgen (= 259 cwt. per acre). In the neighbourhood of *Heidelberg*, the average crop is estimated at 140 centners per morgen (= 225 cwt. per acre). In *France*, according to Dumas, and to the report presented to the Chambers in 1836 by a committee appointed for that purpose, the crop in the northern departments averages 40,000, and in the other departments 25,000, kilogrammes per hectare : Boussingault gives for the whole of France an average of 30,000 kilogrammes per hectare (=230 cwt. per acre). Deducting from all these quantities 15 per cent. for waste in preparing them for the press, and assuming a yield of raw sugar equivalent to 6 per cent. on the remainder, we obtain the following results.

	Average Crop of Beet-root per Acre.	Product of Crystallisable Sugar.
	Cwt.	*Lbs.*
In Austria - - - - - -	209	1405
In Bohemia - - - - -	158	1061
In Prussia - - - - - -	228	1532
In environs of Heidelberg ' - -	191	1283
In France (département du Nord) -	272	1827
In Do. (other departments) - - -	170	1142
In Do. (general average) - - -	204	1370

In *Bengal,* an acre of land yields, according to Busch, 1,094 to 3,053, or at an average 2,073 lbs. of raw sugar: according to Backford, it yields 2,300 lbs. ; the two latter figures give an average of 2,186 lbs. per acre. In *Vera-Cruz,* according to Ward, there is obtained from a hectare 2,800 kilogrammes of raw sugar (= 2,413 lbs. per acre). In *St. Domingo,* according to Page, a hectare yields 3,489 lbs. avoirdupois (= 1,418 lbs. per acre). In *Louisiana,* where the cane is beginning to degenerate, a hectare yields, according to Dumas, only 1000, sometimes 1,500, rarely from 2,000 to 3,000 kilogrammes. Taking as the average 1,500 kilogrammes, this will be = 1,343 lbs. per acre. In *Martinique,* according to Dumas, the yield is 2,500 kilogrammes per hectare (= 2,238 lbs. per acre). In *Guadaloupe,* it is 3,000 kilogrammes per hectare (= 2,686 lbs. per acre). In *Bourbon,* it is 5,000 kilogrammes per hectare (=4,476 lbs. per acre). At the *Havannah,* where every circumstance concurs to make the produce a rich one, it amounts, according to Dumas, to 6,000 kilogrammes per hectare (= 5,370 lbs. per acre). In the *Brazils,* according to the same authority, the produce is 7,500 kilogrammes per hectare (= 6,700 lbs. per acre). In order to place the product of the colonies in a line with that of the European continent, we must deduct a fourth of the preceding quantities, seeing that, as we have already explained, the beet-root gives 4 crops during the time that the cane yields 3. This deduction made, we obtain the following quantities of raw sugar as the gross produce of an acre in the respective colonies.

		Lbs.
In Louisiana	- - - - - -	1000
In St. Domingo	- - - - -	1066
In Bengal	- - - - - -	1626
In Martinique	- - - - -	1680
In Vera-Cruz	- - - - - -	1880
In Guadaloupe	- - - - - -	2000
In Isle of Bourbon	- - - - -	3333
In Havannah	- - - - -	4000
In Brazil	- - - - - -	5000

Thus the mean produce of raw sugar in the colonies varies between 1,000 and 5,000 lbs. per acre, whilst the mean return per acre in the manufacture of beet-root sugar is between 1,060 and 1,826 lbs. The plantations of Louisiana and St. Domingo are behind the best districts of Germany; but in all the other colonies the product exceeds in very various proportions,— sometimes near quadrupling,— that of all the sugar establishments of Europe, with the exception of the manufactories in the north of France, where the soil is particularly favourable to the culture of the beet-root, and the manufacture has attained a high degree of perfection.   The sugar manufactories of that district may be advantageously compared, not only with the two colonies just named, but also with Bengal, Martinique, Vera-Cruz, and Guadaloupe.

In striking an average of all the foregoing figures we find that the mean annual produce of beet-root sugar is at the rate of 1,360 lbs., and of colonial sugar at the rate of 2,400 lbs. per acre, being nearly in the proportion of 10 to 18.

As the cane and the beet-root differ from each other both in form and composition, and as these differences have an influence on the process of manufacture, they also require to be taken into consideration.   The cane, containing nearly twice as much solid matter as the beet-root, the processes for extracting the juice are different in the two cases.   For the cane, grooved iron cylinders are made use of, whilst, to express the juice of the beet-root, it has to be grated and then subjected to the action of the hydraulic press, which requires a more complicated apparatus; but though this of itself does not create much difference on the cost of production, there are other circumstances which render the manufacture from beet-root more difficult and expensive.   The beet-root juice contains a quantity of saline substances, and possesses a certain peculiarity of flavour, which it can be freed from only by means of highly-improved filtering apparatus and the use of animal charcoal.   The sugar is also in a lower state of concentration, so that a larger expenditure of time and fuel is required for the evaporation of the watery particles; these two circumstances combined exert a sensible influence both on cost and quantity, though the expense of additional fuel in Europe is no doubt counterbalanced by the dearth of that article and the defects of the heating apparatus in the colonies.   The profit which may be derived from the accessory products forms no unimportant item in the financial results; of these, molasses forms the chief.   In the colonies it is partly consumed on the spot as a substitute for sugar, and partly sent home in the form of syrup; but it is chiefly employed in the distillation of rum, which forms a main article of export, especially from Jamaica.   In the West Indies the proportion of molasses obtained from the cane is about 4 to 6 per cent.; in the East Indies it must be much larger.   In the beet-root manufactories the molasses amounts to only about 2 per cent. of the raw material; it is very inferior to the cane molasses and fetches only half the price; it retains the disagreeable flavour of the plant, and yields only a very ordinary spirit on distillation. The other accessory products are the cane refuse, used as fuel in the West Indies, and the beet-root leaves, waste, and solid residue after pressure: all these parts contain saccharine matter, and are suitable for the feeding of cattle.   Of these accessory products there are obtained in Germany about 50 centners of leaves per morgen (=80 cwt. per acre), about 15 per cent. waste from the root, and 5 per cent. residue after the extraction of the juice.   In this respect, therefore, the advantage is on the side of Europe.

On a general view of both sides of the account we perceive that the advantage is sometimes on the one side, sometimes on the other; but the chief natural advantages are on the side of the cane : these are, 1., the natural fertility of the soil of the tropics, the vigour of vegetation, and the abundance of the crop; 2., the low price of land; 3., the relatively larger quantity of saccharine matter in the cane, and its state of concentration in the expressed juice; 4., the quantity and quality of the molasses.   Though these natural advantages are modified by various circumstances already adverted to, it is only up to a certain point that the beet-root manufacture can counterbalance them, by the greater perfection of its processes, with all the artificial appliances of chemistry and mechanism, and by the aid of a more advanced rural economy, which affords the means of turning several of the accessory products to account. From the best information we have been able to collect regarding the cost price of indigenous sugar in France and Bohemia, and that of colonial sugar, including the expenses attending its transport to Europe, it would seem that the latter could be landed at Havre or Hamburg at an average cost price of about 13 per cent. less than beet-root sugar could be produced at.   From this it might appear likely that the latter would soon be able to support the competition of colonial sugar without any protection at the custom-house; but independently of the great variety of price in the different qualities of colonial sugars, the results which they yield in the refinery are so variable, that it is exceedingly difficult to specify a limit at which competition may turn in favour of the one sort or of the other.   In this, as in many similar questions, we must take experience for our guide.   France is the only country which has hitherto succeeded in solving the problem in a satisfactory manner; but it must not be forgotten, 1., that the French colonies belong to the number of those in which the processes of fabrication are still backward, and, 2., that in regard to sugar from other countries, French sugar, whether colonial or beet-root, is still protected by a differential duty of from 15 to 30 francs per 100 kilogrammes. In the states of the German Zollverein, beet-root sugar, subject to a duty of 2 thalers per centner, whilst colonial sugar pays 5, enjoys a protection of 3 thalers per centner = 90 kopecks per pood; but from the manner in which the duty is levied, the difference amounts in good manufactories to more than 1 rouble per pood, or on an average to about 40 per cent. on the value of colonial sugar. Still the experience of the last ten years has shown that there is a vitality about the beet-root sugar manufacture on the European continent which was far from being imagined twenty or thirty years ago. Considering that in France it so quickly recovered from the blow dealt it in 1843 by the introduction of a system of impost placing it gradually on a level with the sugar of the French colonies; —that the terror of free competition, which formerly alarmed the French manufacturers so much that many of them abandoned their establishments, and the whole were at one time inclined to do so upon receiving compensation from the state, has now passed from the home manufacturer to his rival in the colonies; — that in Germany, under the tax imposed in 1842, the manufacture, although for a moment arrested in its progress, immediately resumed its ascending movement, so that from 124,000 centners produced during the season of 1842—43, the production rose in 1848—49 to 660,000 centners, that is, more than quintupled in the short space of six years *; — that with the present differential duty, even moderately well-organised establishments do a good business, and that new ones are constantly starting up; — considering all this, it may be inferred that this manufacture, if unable to stand competition with the cane on a footing of perfect equality — which is still questionable — is at least robust enough to stand its competition with less protection than it enjoys at present, and that it is only badly organised or unfavourably situated establishments which could be compromised by an increase of the duty on indigenous, or a lowering of the duty on colonial sugar. As regards the future fate of this industry, independently of secondary considerations, there are two main circumstances which must exert a very important influence on the question: these are, the vigour of tropical vegetation, which gives rise to such abundant crops, and the superiority of the cane in regard to its saccharine contents. We have already seen that the quantity of saccharine matter in the cane varies between 10 and 30 per cent., and in the beet-root between 3 and 13 per cent., the average contents being,

---

* It still continues to increase rapidly : in 1850—51 it had risen to above a million centners, and in 1852—53 it amounted to 1,700,000 centners. The number of manufactories has also increased from 96 in 1845—46 to 238 in 1852—53. See Baron v. Redens, " Deutschland und das übrige Europa," p. 478. — Tr.

according to the best scientific authorities, 18 per cent. for the
one and 10 per cent. for the other : farther, that this difference
is modified in favour of the beet-root by the two following
circumstances, namely, 1st, the cane contains only 90 per cent.
of liquid to 10 per cent. of solid substance, whilst the beet-root
contains 95 per cent. to 5 ; and, 2ndly, of the above quantities
of liquid substances there can be extracted from the cane, by
the processes hitherto adopted, not more at an average than 50
per cent., whilst, since the application of the hydraulic press,
there has been extracted from the beet-root 75 to 85 per cent.
of its juice.   Thus the difference in saccharine contents between
those two plants, which in nature stands as 9 to 5, is considerably modified as to the results of extraction.   It is evident that
this conquest of European over colonial industry, due to the
progress of the physical and mechanical sciences, has powerfully
contributed to enable the home sugar to make head against its
colonial rival: but the question arises, Will circumstances in
this respect always remain the same?   The progress of the
sugar manufacture on the continent has been so rapid that, as
regards the process of fabrication, it seems to have almost
reached its culminating point already.   In the well-organised
establishments of France and Germany they succeed in extracting from the beet-root from 7 to 8 per cent. of raw
sugar, that is to say 80 per cent. of its average saccharine
contents, so that in this respect there remains but a narrow
margin for farther improvement.   To whatever perfection the
mechanical process may be brought, it will never be possible to
extract *the whole* saccharine contents which chemistry reveals,
and it seems exceedingly doubtful if more than 9 per cent. will
ever be drawn from the raw material.   On the other hand the
manufacture from the cane, so negligently and defectively
carried on hitherto, presents a vast margin for improvement.
If once the intelligence and the capital of Europe were turned
in that direction, which is far from improbable, and has even
already partially taken place, — if chemical, mechanical, and
economical reforms were introduced into the colonial establishments,—if a number of these establishments, now in the hands of
indolent and half bankrupt planters, were to pass into the hands
of skilful, intelligent, and enterprising capitalists, who instead
of being satisfied with extracting from the cane one-half of its
contained juice would contrive to extract $\frac{3}{4}$ or $\frac{4}{5}$, — in that case
the colonies would become much more dangerous rivals for the
home fabrication than they are at present.   Recent accounts
inform us that European speculation has already directed its
attention to the improved manufacture of colonial sugar: im-

proved presses are introduced, and the new process of boiling
in rarefied air.   The great London Exhibition has made known
M. Brunfault's invention, which consists in extracting from
molasses about 50 per cent. of crystallisable sugar.   This invention will no doubt be useful for beet-root sugar likewise;
but it will turn greatly more to the account of colonial sugar,
which yields much more molasses, containing a much larger
proportion of crystallisable sugar.   With these and other improvements, for which there is still abundance of room, the
colonies may be able to furnish sugar at a price so low that the
beet-root manufacture could not stand the competition without
a higher protecting duty; and though this may be a question
of the future rather than the present, it is one not to be overlooked on a general survey.   We have also to observe that at
present, besides the duty upon raw sugar, the indigenous
article is protected on the continent by the legislation with
regard to refined sugar.   The duty on this latter is so high
that only raw sugar can be imported, — a circumstance which
greatly augments the cost of freight, whilst the beet-root sugar
manufacturers either refine upon their own premises, or sell to
refiners in their own immediate neighbourhood.

In regard to the sugar manufacture of Russia in particular,
it seems to us that, apart from the protection of the tariff, it is
not in a much more disadvantageous position than in other
countries.   Its progress may, no doubt, be trammelled by the
want of capital—the apparatus for an improved manufacture
may cost more money than in France or Germany—it may be
more difficult to procure good managers for the large establishments, particularly good boiling masters, and it may be necessary
to pay them higher salaries; but, on the other hand, common
labour costs little, and the rent of land for the culture of the
beet-root is very low.   Moreover both the cost of apparatus
and the salaries of overseers may diminish in the course of time,
as the establishments for the construction of machinery become
more numerous, and as the technological institutes gradually turn
out more and more well-trained pupils.   But one circumstance
exceedingly difficult to be got over is, as we have already said,
our frequent droughts, which often destroy the greater part of
the crop, and throw a number of manufactories idle.   Early
frosts also sometimes injure the quality of the root.

According to official information collected in 1848, the product of the beet-root crop that year in twenty-two governments
was at the average rate of 600 poods per dessiatine (see *antè*,
p. 150.): in Germany the average crop is from 1300 to 1900,
and in the French departement du Nord it is 2,270 poods per

dessiatine; so that, even assuming our crop to exceed by 20 per cent. the officially ascertained quantity, it would amount to less than half the relative product of Germany, and less than a third of that of the département du Nord in France. This inferiority must be attributed, not solely to our climate, but likewise to a less careful culture — a fault which may mend with time. But, however this may be, the rapid progress of the manufacture in Russia proves the importance that it is capable of acquiring, and it has now become a difficult problem to reconcile its interests with those of the consumer and of the treasury. It is sure enough, as we have already observed, that it received its main stimulus from the high duty laid upon colonial sugar, without which, considering the difficulties that every new branch of industry has to struggle with in Russia, it never could have developed itself in the manner it has done in such a short period of time: but this encouragement, we must repeat it, has called a number of sickly establishments into being, and there can be no doubt but that, under existing circumstances, the state is yearly making large pecuniary sacrifices on their account, whilst the consumers pay a much higher price for their sugar than they do in any other country in the world. For the ill-organised establishments these sacrifices are made in vain: they do good to nobody. Such a manufacture gains less than a rouble, perhaps hardly 50 kopecks a pood, whilst the state loses 3 roubles 35 kopecks of import duty upon every pood of sugar manufactured in the country. This is not the place for surmising what measures government may adopt for the future, with the view of bringing the protection due to the home manufacture in harmony with the interests of the consumer and the fisc, but we may state our conviction that a more rational and natural state of matters cannot be attained without the sacrifice, as in other countries, of a certain number of ill-organised establishments, which can only protract their precarious existence by dint of an excessive bounty.

We will now subjoin some statistical data with regard to the Russian sugar manufactories. In 1849 there were reckoned 390 establishments, distributed as follows:

Government of Kiew	-	-	71		Brought forward	-	302
„ Tschernigow	-		40		Government of Tambow	-	13
„ Podolia	-	-	36		„ Orel	-	13
Kingdom of Poland	-	-	35		„ Wolhynia	-	12
Government of Kharkow	-		27		„ Kalouga	-	10
„ Koursk	-	-	26		„ Minsk	-	10
„ Toula	-	-	25		„ Penza	-	8
„ Woronèje	-		21		„ Riazan	-	5
„ Poltawa	-		21		„ Mohilew	-	4
Carried forward	-		302		Carried forward	-	377

Brought forward	-	377
Government of Smolensk	-	4
„ Kherson	-	3
„ Nijni-Nowgorod		2
„ Grodno-	-	1
Carried forward	-	387

Brought forward	-	387
Government of Witebsk	-	1
„ Twer -	-	1
„ Saratow	-	1
Total	-	390

Of 350 establishments in operation within the empire during said year, there were only 49 which employed steam apparatus*; of these, 25 are in the government of Kiew, 7 in that of Podolia, 6 in that of Wolhynia, 2 in that of Kharkow, 2 in that of Toula, and 1 in each of the seven governments of Tschernigow, Woronèje, Tambow, Orel, Kalouga, Smolensk, and Penza. We perceive, therefore, that the government of Kiew is the most advanced in this species of production; it has the largest number of establishments, and of these more than a third are worked by steam.   Hydraulic presses were employed in 266 manufactories, and screw presses in 38 ; in 80, the juice was extracted by maceration, and, in 69 of these, by means of cold water.   During the season 1848-49 the production of raw sugar officially ascertained amounted in the manufactories of the empire to 962,000 poods, and in those of the kingdom of Poland to 102,700, making in all 1,064,700 poods ; but as the official figures founded on the quantity of beet-root manufactured (which quantity again is only approximately estimated from the dimensions of the apparatus) are always considerably below the real amount, the product of this season may be estimated at 1,200,000 poods at least, and this figure we have accordingly adopted.   For the season 1849-50 the production was officially estimated at 1,000,000 poods, without including the manufactories in the kingdom of Poland : for the following season it was estimated at only 800,000 ; but during season 1851-52 it must have been much larger, owing to the good beet-root crop.

The principal establishments are those of the Counts Bobrinski (3 establishments), Potocki, Branitski (3 establishments), of MM. Poniatowski and Holovinski, and of Messrs. Jakhnenko and Simirenko, merchants,—all in the government of Kiew; of Count Bobrinski and M. Chischkoff in the government of Toula; of M. Chepeleff in the government of Kalouga; of Prince Wassiltschikoff and Count Chouwaloff in the government of Tambow; of M. Tchélischtscheff in the government of Smolensk; of Prince Galitzine and M. Rakhmanow in the government of Kharkow ; of Prince Dolgorouki and Count Kouscheleff-Bezborodko in the government of Tschernigow ; of MM.

* We have not ascertained what proportion of the establishments in the kingdom of Poland use steam.

Gaïsmar and Soulatitski in the government of Podolia; of Count Branitski in the government of Wolhynia; and of Count Kouscheleff-Bezborodko in the government of Woronèje.

The Report of a commission of inquiry, appointed in 1849 by the Ministers of Finance and Domains, to ascertain the present condition of beet-root culture and sugar manufacture in various governments, contains some very interesting information, from which we extract the following: — In the government of Kiew the cultivation of the beet-root is carried on principally upon the estates of the large landed proprietors — rarely by the peasants. A number of sugar manufacturers find it more economical to cultivate the beet-root upon rented land, by means of hired labour, than to purchase it for ready money. They state that in this manner the *berkovetz* (10 poods) comes only to 43 kopecks, whilst, if they were to purchase it, they would have to pay 57 kopecks. Those proprietors, who are also manufacturers, do not encourage this culture amongst their peasants, because the latter prefer sowing the beet-root upon low moist lands, which produce abundant crops, but of inferior quality, the roots containing more nitrous and less saccharine matter. In this same government, however, some manufacturers find it more profitable to purchase the beet-root than to raise it for themselves, so that much must depend on local circumstances. In the government of Poltawa, likewise, the beet-root is much more extensively cultivated amongst the proprietors than amongst the peasants. In the government of Tschernigow it is cultivated by proprietors, peasants, Cossacks, by the burgesses in their fields and gardens, and even by the village curates. In the government of Mohilew it is cultivated by those proprietors who are at the same time manufacturers, and by their peasants: the peasants of the Domains are also beginning to take part in it. In the government of Toula it is the peasants solely who supply the large establishment of the Counts Bobrinski, at a certain agreed on price. Each family consecrates to this culture from 240 to 500 square *sagenès* (= 1 to $2\frac{1}{4}$ roods). A peasant with his family cannot well cultivate more than $\frac{1}{6}$ dessiatine (= $1\frac{4}{5}$ roods); and from this he derives a return of from 8 to 10 silver roubles (= 56s. to 70s. per acre). For the other establishments, the beet-root is principally cultivated on the lands of the proprietors; still, both in this government and in that of Riazan, it is making way amongst the peasants, thanks to the encouragement of the landowners; and even the crown peasants of the neighbouring villages are beginning to try it. In the government of Kharkow it has made but little way amongst the peasants: on the lands of the proprietors it is carried on partly by means of the corvée and partly by hired labour: the corvée alone is not sufficient: hired labourers are generally employed for weeding and harvest work. There have been instances, especially in the government of Kiew, of sugar manufactories having gone to wreck for no other reason than that all the labour, both in the field and in the house, was carried on upon the corvée system; while there have been instances in the same government of proprietors who have found their advantage in employing nothing but hired labour, even at wages amounting to double the price of corvée labour. In the governments of Tschernigow and Poltawa, the beet-root is cultivated on the lands of the proprietors solely by corvée labour: hired labour is used only when there is a scarcity of hands for weeding or harvest work. In the governments of Toula and Riazan the culture is mostly carried on with labourers hired by the year; and horses and oxen are also kept for that purpose: women, besides, are hired for weeding and harvest work; and there is no difficulty found in procuring hands, as these operations take place at a time when there is little other field work going on.

In the government of Kiew the crop of beet-root returns, at an average, 650 poods per dessiatine (= 76 cwt. per acre); on the better cultivated lands the return is 850, and in some districts as high as 1,000 or 1,200 poods per dessiatine (= 99,110 and 140 cwt. per acre). Comparing these returns with those of France and Germany (antè, p. 476.), we perceive in what a state of inferiority this culture still is with us. In the government of Poltawa the crop varies between 600 and 3,000 poods, — a crop of the latter abundance being exceedingly rare; the average may be about 1,000. In the northern portion of the government of Tschernigow the crop, after hemp, returns as much as 1,500 poods per dessiatine; whilst, cultivated alternately with cereals, it seldom returns more than 700, and the average is 600. In the southern portions of the government, the peasants, who cultivate the beet-root several years in succession upon the same land, obtain, the first year 1,000, the second year 800, and the third year 600 poods. In the governments of Toula and Riazan the lands, which are highly manured, yield a return of as much as 2,000 poods per dessiatine; but the quality is so inferior in saccharine contents, that the excess in quantity does not make up for it. It has been observed that the large-sized beet-roots, the juice of which indicated only two degrees of Beaumé's areometer, did not yield a third of the produce obtained from small beet-roots of good quality: the manufacturers, accordingly, are shy of purchasing large beet-roots off highly manured land. In the government of Koursk, where this culture dates only from 1845, the average crop is 620 poods per dessiatine.

The expenses of cultivation vary greatly both from place to place and from year to year, so that it is very difficult to form a general estimate. Upon an estate in the government of Kiew, where M. Dupan, manager of Count Bobrinski's establishments, keeps an exact account of the expenses of cultivation, these are found to amount to 95 paper or 27 silver roubles per dessiatine, and this agriculturist considers that they ought in no case to exceed 30 silver roubles per dessiatine, (= 35s. 4d. per acre), even including the renewal of agricultural implements. M. Chischkoff, one of our most experienced proprietors in this branch of culture, gives the following estimate of expense per dessiatine.

	Roub.	Kop.
32 days' work of a man @ 15 kopecks - - - -	4	80
77 „ a woman @ 8 „ - - - -	6	16
18½ „ a horse @ 30 „ - - - -	5	50
Total per dessiatine -	16	46

The same proprietor furnished the commission with the following account of the expenses of culture of 250 dessiatines, taken on an average of seven years:

	Roub.	Kop.
10,412 days' work of a man @ 15 kopecks - - -	1561	80
6,411 ditto of a woman, for sowing and weeding @ 8 kop.	512	88
9,115 ditto of ditto, for harvest work @ 8 kop. - -	729	20
1,922 ditto of horse @ 30 kop. - - - -	576	60
1,036 ditto of pair of oxen @ 30 kop. - - - -	310	80
Rent of 250 dessiatines of land @ 6 roubles - - -	1500	0
Cost of seed - - - - - - - -	581	14
Total -	5772	42

This is at the rate of 23 roubles 9 kopecks per dessiatine, of which 14 roubles 76 kopecks are for field labour. Assuming an average crop of 800 poods, the cost price would be at the rate of 2¾ kopecks per pood. The nett return of course depends greatly on the distance of the land from the manufactory. Experience has shown that beyond 15 versts (= 10 miles) of carriage, the benefit either for grower or for manufacturer is very problematical; and those establishments which have drawn their raw material from a greater distance — of which, however, the examples are but rare — have almost always worked at a loss.   Yet there are establishments in the government of Koursk which receive their beet-root from plantations 40 or even 70 versts off.

In the government of Kiew the beet-root is paid for at a price agreed on before-hand, which is generally at the rate of 57, sometimes at that of from 50 to 55 kopecks per berkovetz, or from 5 to $5\frac{1}{2}$ kopecks per pood.   When delivered at the manufactory, 11, 12, or sometimes as much as 15 poods are reckoned to 1 berkovetz, according as the beet-root is better or worse cleaned, that is, freed of the small roots and the adhering earth.   The manufacturers consider this over-weight necessary likewise to make up for the loss from drying during the time it lies in the barn.   In the government of Tschernigow, to save the trouble of weighing, the beet-roots are taken off by measure, — $1\frac{1}{2}$ tchetwerts being held equivalent to 1 berkovetz, of which the ordinary price is 60 kopecks = 6 kopecks per pood.   In the government of Toula, very few proprietors raise beet-roots for sale: those who have manufactories pay their peasants for it at the rate of from 60 to 85 kopecks per berkovetz.

The inquiries made by the commission as to the revenue which may be derived from the culture of the beet-root as compared with other sorts of culture, led to the following results: In the government of Kiew, a dessiatine of land occupied in the culture of beet-root gives a nett return of about 30 roubles, whilst a good wheat crop affords a return of not more than 20, or a third less.   In the southern part of the government of Tschernigow, and in the northern part of that of Poltawa, the culture of tobacco holds the balance pretty even with that of beet-root: the latter is found profitable only where the plantation is quite in the neighbourhood of the manufactory.   From an account handed to the commission by M. Chischkoff, founded on the average expense of culture and proceeds of return obtained in the governments of Toula and Riazan, it would appear that a dessiatine of beet-roots gives a nett return of 43 roubles 54 kopecks, whilst a dessiatine of cereals cultivated on the three-shift system gives an average return of not more than 15 roubles 54 kopecks: the difference in favour of the beet-root is therefore 28 roubles 10 kopecks per dessiatine.   According to another account, presented by the same proprietor, the mean produce of seven years from his own plantations in the government of Toula amounted, notwithstanding partial failures of the crop, to 65 berkovetz per dessiatine, affording, at the rate of 60 kopecks per berkovetz, a nett return of 16 roubles 15 kopecks; but taking the rate of 85 kopecks, being the price paid by other establishments of the district, the nett return per dessiatine would be 32 roubles 50 kopecks,— a return never to be derived from the culture of any sort of grain.

In most of the sugar manufactories the fuel employed is wood; but in districts where wood is dear, turf or coal is employed, and, in the south of Russia, straw and rushes. The quantities of fuel used in the different manufactories seem to be very different, depending on the quality of the wood, the mode of manufacture, and the apparatus. Where fuel is very plentiful, no exact account of the quantity consumed is kept. In the government of Kiew, where forest land is abundant, some partial destructions of forests have resulted from the large consumption of fuel, and in some localities a scarcity of this article is felt: in some of the towns of this government the price of fire-wood has doubled since the introduction of the sugar manufacture. The price of hard-wood delivered at the manufactories, cost of transport included, comes to about 6 or 7 roubles per cubic sagène, (1 sagène = 7 feet). The consumption of wood in the sugar manufactories of the districts of Tscherkassk, Tschihirinsk, and Zwenigorod in the government of Kiew, amounts to 40,000 cubic sagènes, and the production of these manufactories is estimated at 272,000 poods of raw sugar, which gives $6\frac{4}{5}$ poods of sugar to a cubic sagène of wood; so that the cost of fuel comes to about a rouble upon the pood of raw sugar. In the northern part of the government of Tschernigow, which is also well wooded, the proprietors of the sugar establishments provide themselves with fuel from their own forests; but in the southern districts, the wood is beginning to get scarce, and its price is sensibly augmenting: the proprietors, after exhausting their own forests, are now obliged to purchase; and many of them, from the dearness of wood, have recourse to straw, which costs $\frac{1}{4}$ to $\frac{1}{2}$ kopeck per pood. In some establishments the consumption of wood is reckoned to be at the rate of 1 cubic sagène to 100 poods of beet-root; in others it is estimated at only $\frac{1}{2}$ or $\frac{3}{4}$ sagène, so that the average may be taken at $\frac{3}{4}$ sagène to 100 poods: at this rate, and reckoning the price at 6 roubles per cubic sagène, fuel would come, with a return of 3 per cent. of raw sugar, to 150 kopecks; with a return of 4 per cent., to $112\frac{1}{2}$ kopecks; and, with a return of 5 per cent., to 90 kopecks per pood. The government of Poltawa is situated, in regard to fuel, pretty similarly to the southern part of Tschernigow. In the government of Toula, the manufacturers have to fetch their wood from a distance of 10 to 30 versts, and a cubic sagène costs them from 7 to 10 roubles. This high price has induced some proprietors to have recourse to peat; and several large establishments use that sort of fuel exclusively. In the steppe districts straw is made use of.

The quantity of fuel required depends in no small degree on the mode of extraction of the juice; the thicker the juice is the less fuel is needed; according to M. Chischkoff's experiments, there is required for 10,000 poods of beet-root from which the juice is extracted by pressure, 30 cubic sagènes of wood; when extracted by maceration in cold water, 40 sagènes; and in hot water, 45 sagènes. Thus, assuming a return of 3 per cent., and a price of 6 roubles per sagène, the cost of fuel would amount, in the three cases respectively, to 60, 80, and 90 kopecks upon the pood of raw sugar; with a return of 4 per cent., it would be 45, 60, and 67½, and with a return of 5 per cent., 36, 48, and 54. M. Chischkoff is of opinion that fuel might be greatly economised by a better construction of the furnaces, which, in most of the establishments, is exceedingly defective.

The animal charcoal employed in the manufactories has often to be procured from distant localities. In the government of Kiew a pood of calcined bones costs 57 kopecks: some establishments get their bones raw from the ports of the Black Sea, where they cost from 7 to 10 kopecks per pood, which, adding the expense of transport, brings them to from 10 to 15 kopecks laid down at the manufactory. In the government of Tschernigow the Jews collect the bones from amongst the peasants, and sell them to the manufactories; sometimes they receive payment in money, but generally in kind, the price being a pound of sugar for a pood of bones. In the government of Toula the peasants themselves of the neighbouring villages carry their bones to the manufactories — in small quantities of course; and the manufacturers procure them also from Moscow and other towns; the average price of a pood comes to 30 to 35 kopecks. M. Chischkoff calculates that for 1,000 poods of beet-root there is required 250 poods of animal charcoal powder, or a pound of the one for a pood of the other, and that for the above quantity of the powder 850 poods of bones are required; other proprietors reckon only ½ to ⅔ lb. of the powder to a pood of beet-root.

The labour at the manufactories is performed partly by corvée, partly upon wages; it is seldom that the latter mode is not had recourse to — the only exceptions being where the domains of the proprietor are large compared with the extent of his establishment. Where the manufacturer is not a landed proprietor, the whole work is performed by hired labourers, and this is sometimes the case even in establishments belonging to landed proprietors. The number of workmen employed depends not only on the extent of the establishment, but also on the mode of manufacture and the distribution of labour. According to M. Chischkoff's opinion there are required, for the purpose of converting 1,000 poods of beet-root into sugar within the space of twenty-four hours, working day and night, at least 100 workmen who relieve each other; and as the season lasts from three to four months, an establishment consuming 1,000 poods of beet-root in the twenty-four hours would consume at least 100,000 during the season, which would give 1,000 poods of beet-root per workman. But the number of workmen employed is generally larger: for example, Count Kouscheleff-Bezborodko's manufactory in the government of Tschernigow, which consumes 1,000 poods of beet-root in the twenty-four hours, employs two hundred workmen during three months, which would give about 90,000 poods for the whole season, and 450 poods per workman. M. Essimontowski's manufactory in the same government, which works off from 30,000 to 40,000 poods of beet-root, employs from 120 to 140 workmen during the season, and 10 or 12 permanently, which gives an average of 1 workman for 248 poods. We apprehend that we may reckon at the lowest 1 workman for 500 poods of beet-root; and as the production of 1,200,000 poods of sugar, assuming a yield of 4 per cent., implies the consumption of 30 millions of poods of beet-root, we may estimate the total *minimum* number of workmen employed in this manufacture at 60,000 individuals, whereof nine-tenths are employed from three to four months, and one-tenth have employment during the whole year.

The workmen's wages are paid sometimes by the day, but oftener by the month, and do not vary greatly in amount in the different provinces. In the government of Kiew the ordinary rate is 15 kopecks a day with food, for twelve hours' work; and if the wages are paid by the month the rate is never under 3 roubles. In the government of Tschernigow the rate is 4 roubles per month with food, or 6 roubles per month without. In the government of Poltawa the rate in some establishments is 28 roubles for seven months, and in others 4 roubles per month with food. In the government of Toula the rate in almost all the establishments is 3 to $3\frac{1}{2}$ roubles per month.

The expenses of manufacture depend on the extent of the establishment, the apparatus employed, and the length of the season. According to M. Chischkow they amount at an average to $1\frac{1}{2}$ roubles per berkovetz, or 15 kopecks per pood; the following is an abstract of the expenses of his own establishment during the seven years from 1842 to 1849, in the course of which 179,770 poods of beet-root were converted into sugar: —

	Silv. Roub.
Fuel (wood) - - - - - - - - -	8339
Wages of superintendence - - - - - - -	1299
Workmen's wages - - - - - - - -	5332
Horse-hire - - - - - - - - - -	495
Light - - - - - - - - - - -	395
Oil, tar, and grease - - - - - - - -	61
Animal charcoal - - - - - - - - -	3493
Chalk, fullers' earth, &c. - - - - - - -	121
Casks and hoops - - - - - - - -	381
Costs of transport and sale - - - - - - -	1301

Total	-	21,217
Tear and wear	- -	3109
Total expense	-	24,326

This gives a result of 13½ kopecks per pood. We perceive also that the cost of fuel comes to 34¼ per cent.; salaries and wages to 27 per cent. and bone black to more than 14 per cent. of the total expenses of manufacture :—

	Silv. Roub.
Adding to the above sum of - - - - - -	24,326
the value of 179,770 poods of beet-root @ 6 kop. per pood -	10,786
We obtain a total expense of - -	35,112

The 179,770 poods would give a return, at the rate of 4 per cent., of 7,191, and, at the rate of 5 per cent., of 8,988 poods of raw sugar, of which, therefore, the cost price would be at the rate, in the first case, of 4 roubles 88 kopecks, and, in the second case, of 3 roubles 90 kopecks per pood.

Most of the manufactories send their raw sugars to the nearest refineries, which again send them, in a refined state, to the nearest fairs and towns; in some establishments the raw sugar is sold upon the spot; the cost of transport varies according to season and locality. In 1849, the carriage of refined sugar from Kiew to Nijni-Nowgorod cost 1 rouble per pood; in the government of Poltawa and Tschernigow, the common rate is 10 kopecks per pood for a distance of 100 versts; in the government of Toula, for a distance of 300 to 350 versts, the summer rate is 25 to 35, and the winter rate 15 to 18 or 20 kopecks per pood.

In concluding its Report, the commission observes, *inter alia*, that beet-root does not require a particularly fertile soil—it may be grown wherever rye is grown:—but it is exceedingly dependent upon climate, and the crop becomes very uncertain as we approach the regions of excessive cold; it is to this cause that the commission attributes the bad success of this culture in the government of Moscow, and of course its chances would be less in the countries situated to the north and east of that government; on the other hand, in most foggy climates, the beet-root yields abundant crops, but contains little saccharine matter. In the steppe countries of the south, the climate, although sufficiently warm, is subject to rapid changes, and the droughts generally commence at the season when the young plants are most in want of warmth accompanied by moisture, so that in these regions the culture becomes very uncertain. Its most favourable locality is considered by the commission to be the countries situated to the south-west of the government of Moscow, where the climate is temperate and great droughts are rare; the soil also has preserved sufficient virgin fertility to be able to dispense with much manure, which is a great advantage, as the experience of all countries has proved that the beet thrives best on a well ploughed and well cleaned but undunged soil. Manure always communicates to it saline substances, which it is difficult to separate from the saccharine matter; but the difficulties of raising a crop without manure are yearly increasing, and now amount almost to an impossibility in the northern districts of the region, which form the chief seat of the sugar manufacture. For this reason the commission considers the most favourable districts for this culture to be the governments of Kharkow, Poltawa, and Kiew. Amongst the chief benefits to our rural economy which have attended its introduction the commission specifies the following : — that it has occasioned the introduction by our proprietors of improved agricultural implements, which the peasants, after becoming familiar with their use, have also begun to employ in the culture of cereals; — that the beet-root, readily adapting itself to a system of rotation, has put the proprietors in the way of several improvements in this respect; — and that the sugar manufacture furnishes the rural population with the means of turning their time to profit during the season when there is but little to do in the fields.* It is only to be regretted that these advantages are restricted within the narrow limits which the culture occupies.†

* According to information collected by the commission, the wages of workmen employed in the sugar manufactories amounted to 1,800,000 roubles annually, without including the kingdom of Poland : to this we may add 300,000 roubles for animal charcoal, which pass for most part into the hands of the poorer classes in exchange for an object formerly entirely destitute of value.

† We are induced from information gathered since the earlier part of this work was written to reduce our estimate of the quantity of land employed in beet-root culture to something between 35,000 and 40,000 dessiatines ; our former estimate (ante, p. 150.) is too high. The estimate of the commission is 30,000 dessiatines, without the kingdom of Poland.

Linen Manufacture.

Notwithstanding the heavy blows continuously dealt out to it by the increasing use of cotton goods, the linen manufacture still maintains the foremost rank in Russia in point of extent and importance. It is not, like the cotton manufacture, concentrated in large establishments which strike the eye by their size, their machinery, and the numbers of workmen collected on the premises; but, confined within the modest walls of the peasant's cottage, it is diffused over the whole length and breadth of the land; there is scarcely a village to be found within the wide limits of the empire where the wheel, the distaff, and the loom are not likewise to be found. With regard to the product of this industry, however, it is but an approximative estimate that we are able to form, as our statistics on the subject are still very imperfect.

Linen cloth forms one of those articles of prime necessity which no individual, rich or poor, can entirely dispense with. Reckoning only two shirts per annum for each inhabitant, and 4 archines at an average for each shirt, this single article would infer for a population of 65½ millions, a consumption of 524 millions of archines.* In an article on the exposition of the products of Russian industry at Moscow in 1843, published in the *Gazette de Commerce* of the same year, M. Weretennikoff strikes an average of 20 archines as the quantity of common linen cloth consumed in Russia by each inhabitant; and he estimates the value, at the rate of 12½ kopecks (paper) per archine, at 150 millions of paper (= 42,857,000 silver) roubles. M. Scherer, adopting this estimate in his work on the exposition of the products of Russian industry at St. Petersburg in 1849, makes the following calculation as to the products of linen industry : common cloths 40 millions of silver roubles; other cloths and articles manufactured for home consumption 20 millions; flax and linen manufactures exported 20 millions; total 80 millions of silver roubles. This estimate gives room for some observations.

The average of 20 archines per inhabitant, or 100 archines per family, annually, seems too high, especially considering that linen fabrics are much more durable than cotton; it implies, amongst the common people, more ease of circumstances than is generally the case. On the other hand, the value of 12½ kopecks paper (= 3⁴⁄₇ kop. silv.) per archine is far too low: it is the price of the coarsest sackcloth. A pound of linen yarn,

* An archine is 28, or, more exactly, 27·992 English inches.

such as is used in the manufacture of the coarsest cloth, costs 10 kopecks silver, and will not turn out more than 3 archines at the utmost. This of itself makes $3\frac{1}{2}$ kopecks for the semi-raw material, leaving only $\frac{1}{14}$ kopeck for the weaving. Moreover, besides the common cloth of which the peasants' shirts are composed, the females in most governments use handkerchiefs and other articles of a somewhat finer sort of stuff. Now, the most ordinary household linens sell for 5 to 7 paper roubles per piece of 30 archines, being at the rate of $16\frac{2}{3}$ to $23\frac{1}{3}$ paper, or $4\frac{3}{4}$ to $7\frac{1}{3}$ silver kopecks per archine; and we do not think that we can estimate the average value of the ordinary linen cloth consumed by the lower classes of the population at less than 6 silver kopecks per archine.

Let us now endeavour to estimate the average consumption. We have already estimated the population of the empire of Russia in Europe for the year 1852 (see *antè*, p. 66.) at $55\frac{1}{2}$ millions; but as, according to the last census, the decrease during the cholera years was larger than we had supposed, we think it will be safer, in order to keep within the mark, to reduce that figure to 54 millions, being pretty nearly the number given by M. Kœppen for the year 1846.

Adding to this number of				54,000,000
1. Population of the Grand Duchy of Finland	-			1,500,000
2. Ditto of kingdom of Poland per latest returns	-			4,800,000
3. Ditto of Asiatic possessions	-	-	-	5,200,000
We obtain a total population of		-		65,500,000

Of this total, the urban population amounted, in the towns of European Russia, to 5,356,000, and in those of Asia to 340,000, together to 5,696,000 inhabitants; from which we may deduct about 10 or 12 per cent. for that portion which has preserved its rural habits and costume, and belongs more properly to the rural than to the urban or burgess class of the population. In round numbers, then, we may state the entire population of the whole Russian dominions, Asia included, at $60\frac{1}{2}$ millions of rural, and 5 millions of urban inhabitants. Now we can hardly reckon, for body linen, a lower average than two shirts per annum; this of itself comes to 7 to 8 archines per inhabitant. Adding to this other articles of apparel for man, woman, and child, bed-linen, towels, &c., we are safe in carrying the average quantity used by an individual as high as 10 archines*, which

* In the states of the Zollverein the home consumption of linen is estimated at 406 millions of ells for a population of 29 millions, which gives an average of 14 ells, or about $13\frac{1}{2}$ archines for each inhabitant.

gives, for the rural population of $60\frac{1}{2}$ millions, 605 millions of archines. This, at the price of 6 kopecks per archine, represents a value of 36,300,000 silver roubles. But if we consider that, of these $60\frac{1}{2}$ millions, at least a tenth of the males and a third of the females use body linen of a somewhat finer quality than the sort which we have estimated at 6 kopecks per archine*, this estimate will appear to be certainly under the mark, and we believe that we may, without exaggeration, estimate the value of linens consumed by this class of the population at the same slump sum that M. Scherer does, namely, 40 millions of roubles. †
As regards the urban population of 5 millions, in which are included the nobility, burghers, clergy, employés, and officers of every rank, and all the classes in easy circumstances, who use more and finer linen of every description, we allow them at an average 20 archines per inhabitant—in all 100 millions of archines, representing, at the rate of 20 kopecks per archine, a value of 20 millions of silver roubles: this, added to the preceding sum, gives 60 millions, to which we may still add 5 per cent., or 3 millions, for the manufacture of fine table napery, sail-cloth, stockings, bonnet-work, thread,— giving a total value of 63 millions of silver roubles, without reckoning exports.

The hempen manufacture is greatly inferior in importance to the linen. In the article already cited, M. Scherer estimates its value at 50 millions of silver roubles; but we consider this estimate excessive for the following reasons: The quantity of hemp produced is estimated at 6 millions of poods, without reckoning the production of the kingdom of Poland: this figure we admit to be below the mark; but it is notorious, first, that the culture of hemp is much less extensive than that of flax, and, secondly, that the linen manufacture augments the value of the raw material in a much higher proportion than the hempen manufacture does. Linen fabrics, even of the most ordinary description, represent thrice or four times the value of the raw material, and the finer fabrics can augment this value in the proportion of 1 to 20, and even more; whilst hemp being em-

---

* A number of the female peasantry, especially in Little Russia and the Polish provinces, wear linen that costs from 10 to 15 kopecks per archine, and even more.

† If it be objected that in Asiatic Russia, especially in the transcaucasian provinces, part of the population wear silk shirts, instead of linen, we answer that considering that this practice exists amongst $\frac{1}{50}$ at the utmost of the population of the empire — that in the Caucasian provinces not more than 6,000 or 7,000 poods of silk at most are employed in the preparation of fabrics suitable for the lower classes — and that we have reduced both average consumption and price to the most moderate possible figure, — it must be obvious that any difference that could possibly proceed from such a limited use of silk is amply counterbalanced by the moderation of our estimates.

ployed for most part only in the manufacture of coarse fabrics, such as sail-cloth, baggings, and packing-cloth, the manipulation can only double or triple the value of the article in its raw state; and, when it is employed in the fabrication of cables and cordage, this value is raised only by 50 or 100 per cent. During the years 1848, 1849, and 1850, there were exported in the commerce with Europe 8,424,000 poods of hemp and hemp-codilla, representing, at the official valuations, 20,700,000 silver roubles, which gives an average value of 2 roubles 46 kopecks per pood; and 1,236,000 poods of cables and cordage, representing a value of 3,511,000 roubles, which gives a mean value of 2 roubles 84 kopecks per pood, so that the value of the hemp was to that of the cables and cordage as 100 to 115, or, in other words, the manipulation had added only 15 per cent. to the value of the raw material. Assuming that the whole cables and cordage exported had been manufactured from hemp codilla, which figures at the mean price of only 1 rouble 28 kopecks per pood, the value of the raw material would be to that of the manufactured article as 100 to 222. The augmentation of value is more considerable in the manufacture of sail-cloth, being nearly as 10 to 32; but on the other hand it is less for packing-cloth and bagging. Putting all these circumstances together, we do not consider that we can adopt at an average for the value of the whole manufactures of which hemp forms the raw material more than $2\frac{1}{2}$ times the value of the latter. Now the average annual export of hemp and codilla during the three years 1848—50, was 2,808,000 poods, estimated at the average value of 2 roubles 46 kopecks per pood. At this rate, we cannot adopt for hemp used upon the place of production a higher value than 2 roubles at the utmost. But assuming that there is used in the country (without including what is employed in the manufacture of the sail-cloth and cordage exported) about double the quantity exported in a raw state, or 5,600,000 poods, and reckoning a value of 5 roubles per pood of worked hemp, we obtain 28 millions of roubles as the total value of the products of this branch of industry. The value of the products of the linen manufacture consumed in the country, having been already estimated at 63 millions, these two branches together give a value of 91 millions of roubles, to which we must add the flax, hemp, yarn, cloth, cables, and cordage exported. The mean annual value of the exportation of these articles during the three years 1848—50 was as follows :

					Roub.
Flax and flax-tow	-	-	-	-	11,022,000
Hemp and hemp-tow	-	-	-	-	6,900,000
Flax and hemp-yarn	-	-	-	-	238,000
Cables and cordage	-	-	-	-	1,174,000
Sail-cloth, raven-duck, and other fabrics		-	-	-	1,552,000
Total	-	-	-	-	20,886,000

Adding this sum to the 91 millions representing the value of the linen and hempen products consumed in the country, we obtain a total value from these two branches of industry, including the value of the raw material, of about 112 millions of roubles ($=17,730,000l.$ sterling), or nearly $2\frac{1}{4}$ times the value of the product of the same branches of industry in France, estimated by M. Schnitzler at about 200 millions of francs.* Deducting from this amount the value of the raw material, which we have already estimated (*antè*, p. 157.) at 36,523,000 silver roubles, there remains about $75\frac{1}{2}$ millions of roubles ($=12$ millions sterling) added by the linen and hempen manufacture to the gross value of two of our agricultural products—an addition which no other branch of industry has hitherto succeeded in effecting. It thus occupies the highest rank amongst all the departments of national labour, and is so much the more deserving of preference and encouragement inasmuch as the raw material which it employs is produced upon our own soil—as it is intimately connected with the prosperity of our agriculture—as it has its seats in the humblest cabins—as it withdraws not a single cultivator from the labours of the field—and as it is most perfectly adapted to the family life and the patriarchal organisation of our rural communes. To this we may add that it is the support of several little subsidiary trades, as wheel-, spindle-, and loom-making, which give employment to a number of hands amongst our country population. In some governments there are whole villages which find employment in these little branches of industry, and we may count by millions the number of hands to which the linen manufacture, in some form or other, affords occupation.

Of the total quantity of flax produced throughout the possessions of Russia, amounting at a very moderate computation to about 12 millions of poods, there remains, after deducting exportation, about $7\frac{1}{2}$ millions of poods for home consumption. Of this, deducting a fourth for waste and for the flax employed for other purposes, there would still remain 5,625,000 poods

---

* In Austria the products of the linen manufacture which find their way into commerce, home or foreign, are valued in the official statistics at 31,000,000 convention florins ($=3,100,000l.$): but in this estimate are not included the household stuffs manufactured and consumed by the peasantry without entering into commerce.

for spinning; with us this operation is always performed by hand, and as for an average spinner' we can scarcely reckon more than $\frac{1}{3}$ lb. per day *, or—reckoning 240 days' work—2 poods per annum, the spinning alone of this quantity of flax would occupy 2,812,500 individuals — a number which will not be considered excessive when it is considered that the work is done by women in the intervals of their domestic occupations and partly also by children.† The weaving occupies much fewer hands than the spinning. According to information collected in the government of Jaroslaw, a weaver can manufacture in a day from 3 to 6 archines, according to fineness, of a fabric of medium quality; of coarse fabrics a complete days' work may turn out as much as 10 archines; but considering that in Russia the women often weave during the intervals of their domestic occupations, we can scarcely reckon more than $7\frac{1}{2}$ archines as the average quantity fabricated per diem, or, for 240 days' work, 1,800 archines per annum; this, for 705 millions of archines consumed in the country, allows 392,700 weavers; adding a surplus of 6 per cent. for very fine fabrics and exports, we will not go beyond the mark in carrying the number of individuals employed in weaving to 425,000. Adding the number of hands occupied during a part of the season in subsidiary operations, as steeping, scutching, and heckling, and in the manufacture of wheels, spindles, looms, and other accessory implements, the total number of the rural population which finds a useful employment for its time by means of the linen manufacture, may be estimated at little less than 4 millions. The hemp manufacture must occupy, according to an approximative estimate, at least a fifth of the number of hands engaged in the linen manufacture, so that the total number of individuals more or less interested in these two branches of industry cannot be much under 5 millions.

This much premised with respect to the importance of these manufactures, we will now direct our attention to their progress and present position.

In Belgium and some other countries, the whole operations which flax undergoes from the time it has been pulled, belong, in a manner, to the domain of industry: in Russia, and other countries where industry is less advanced, the steeping, scutch-

---

* The commission already referred to found that, in the government of Jaroslaw, a good spinner could spin in a day 18 zolotnik, or less than $\frac{1}{3}$ lb., of yarn selling for about 75 kopecks per lb. Of coarser yarn as much as $\frac{1}{2}$ lb. or more could be spun; but for finer sorts twice as much time is required. We do not therefore think that the average quantity can be taken to exceed $\frac{1}{3}$ lb. per diem.

† In Gallicia, with a population of 5,000,000, there are reckoned, according to the official statistics published in 1843, to be 450,000 spinners, or 1 to every 11 inhabitants: the above figure gives only 1 spinner to every 23 inhabitants.

ing, and, to a certain extent, the sorting of the flax belong to the occupations of agriculture, and the linen industry, properly so called, commences with the operation of heckling. This is a very important process, as it is upon it that the fineness and equality of the yarn mainly depend: in England, Belgium, and other countries, it is performed in two manners, either by means of machinery, or with the hand by means of metal heckles: but hitherto even the best heckling-machines do not turn out work equal to good hand heckling, which is still preferred by the majority of manufacturers; and it is no uncommon thing to heckle over again by hand flax that has been already heckled by machinery, in order to bring it into the highest condition of fineness and smoothness. In Belgium two sorts of heckles are used; in England, three sorts are in use, and the tow remaining from the different sorts of heckles is separately collected to serve for different sorts of yarn. In Russia this process is generally conducted in a very negligent manner, by means of bristle brushes, often ill made and greatly the worse for wear: this is one of the main causes of the backward state of our linen manufacture. From brush-heckling there results in truth more line and less tow; but the line is less smooth, less supple, and less silky; and of the tow more is lost by waste. Flax heckled in the Flemish manner, with metallic heckles, is much more suitable for the manufacture of fine fabrics, and two sorts of tow are obtained, of which that proceeding from the second heckling is very superior to that remaining after the dressing with the hogs'-bristle brushes. The experiments of the two methods, performed under the eyes of the commission already mentioned, in the government of Jaroslaw, gave the following results: —

From 1 lb. flax dressed in the Russian manner with bristle brushes,

$54\frac{1}{4}$ zolotnik line;
$36\frac{3}{4}$,,   tow;
5   ,,   waste.

From 1 lb. flax dressed in the Flemish manner with metal heckles,

$23\frac{1}{4}$ zolotnik line;
$48\frac{1}{4}$,,   tow first heckling;
22   ,,   do. second heckling (with a finer heckle);
$2\frac{1}{2}$,,   waste.

Thus, by the second process, there results less than half the quantity of line, but the loss in this respect is compensated, 1st, by the superior quality of the line itself, and secondly, by the quantity of the tow and the superior quality of what is obtained from the second heckling; tow of a good quality, that is to say, well cleaned and freed from its short fibres, sometimes fetches nearly as high a price as good flax, and yields yarn suitable for the manufacture of good linen cloth of medium quality, whereas tow from bristle heckles yields a very inferior sort of yarn, suitable merely for very coarse fabrics.* In Russia it is only line that is used for the manufacture of flems; whilst in England and Belgium the tow is made to answer. Nor must it be forgotten that by using the iron heckle there is a saving of more than 2 per cent. in the waste.

The method followed with us may suit our cultivators in this respect, that the machinery required is inexpensive: the bristle brushes are made in the villages, and cost but little: it may likewise answer well enough for the manufacture of household linens for the use of the peasantry; but it is a real impediment to progress in the higher branches of the manufacture. It would therefore be very desirable that metal heckles should come into more extensive use, especially in those districts where manufacture with a view to sale has already made some progress, as in the governments of Jaroslaw, Wologda, and Kostroma. The high price of the instruments is one great difficulty, there being very few artisans that make them. M. Karnovitsch was the first to introduce them into the government of Jaroslaw, but the maker charges him 40, and for the finest sorts 70 paper (=20 silver) roubles per pair, which is four or five times over what would be their cost in Germany. A diligent workman is able, with the help of a single assistant, to make a pair of heckles in five or six days; the requisite material costs but 5 roubles; the remainder of the price represents the labour; thus an artisan with his assistant gains 35 paper, or 10 silver, roubles in five or six days, which is equivalent to 1 roub. 70 kop. or 2 roubles (=5s. 4d. to 6s. 4d.) per diem. This is just one example of the dearness of artisan labour in Russia, the moment a certain amount of capacity or skill is required, whilst for ordinary labour it is the cheapest country in the world; and this dearness of skilled labour is one of the causes which arrests the progress of industry with us in several of its branches, and renders manufactured articles so dear, especially such of them as are not produced in large quantities. It is evident enough that, at a price so exorbitant, the use of iron heckles can never become general amongst our rural population. The commission so repeatedly mentioned had occasion to convince itself that the Jaroslavian peasants perfectly recognise the superiority of these

* In Russia the tow is generally so indifferent that it fetches but 1 rouble per pood, whilst good flax costs 3 to 3½ roubles.

instruments, but find them too dear to purchase. A remedy, we think, might be provided, either by establishing manufactories of them in centrical situations, and granting to these certain encouragements, or by ordering them to be made at Moscow, where there are establishments for analogous purposes, in which they could be manufactured in large quantities at a moderate price, or by importing them from abroad duty free (as allowed by the tariff), and establishing entrepôts for their sale at prime cost. This could be done either through the intervention of agronomic or industrial societies, or under the auspices of the Department of Manufactures. The Ministry of Domains has already taken the initiative by sending models of the best heckles into those districts where the linen manufacture is most widely diffused; and the preparation of these instruments at a reasonable rate, and the propagation of their use, might be introduced into the list of measures for which government awards medals and premiums.

The second question, no less important for the future prospects of our linen manufacture, regards the spinning. Ever since the invention of spinning-machines, the effects of that invention upon the linen manufacture and upon the lot of the numerous population engaged in hand-spinning, has been a subject of intense interest, especially for Russia, where, as we have already seen, this branch of the manufacture gives employment to nearly 3 millions of individuals. Philanthropy, upon the continent, was long sceptical as to the real benefits of spinning by machinery; but the example of England gave a new turn to men's ideas, as well as to their interests. Experience showed that it was solely to machinery that England was indebted for the progress of her linen manufacture, and that without the aid of this powerful agent the continental linen manufacture could not long stand the English competition. We have already observed (*antè*, p. 349.) that the export of linen manufactures from Germany has fallen off by a third— a decline which has repeatedly occasioned much distress in various districts, especially in Silesia. This painful experience produced the conviction that the only chance for the linen manufacture was the introduction of spinning machines — that if it continued to depend solely upon hand-spinning, it ran the risk of entire decay, which would be equally fatal for spinners as for weavers—and that it would consequently be a blind philanthropy which should renounce the powerful aid of machinery for fear of interfering with the occupation of the numerous class of hand-spinners. On the other hand, the investigations made in Germany by order of the different states and industrial societies have shown that hand-spinning may maintain itself, up to a certain point, alongside of machine-spinning—the latter being suitable where fabrics are to be furnished for wholesale commerce, and the former for the household linen, spun, woven, and used by the agricultural classes themselves. Machine-spinning, moreover, is attended with difficulties for the higher numbers; and even in Belgium, where every branch of the linen manufacture is in such an advanced state, hand-spinning is preferred where fabrics of great fineness are wanted. Still, it is impossible to foresee what degree of perfection machine-spinning may attain in that respect; at the London Exhibition there were shown fine assortments of Leeds yarn up to No. 300: on the other hand, Courtrai yarn was shown which went as high as No. 1,200 for the warp and No. 1,600 for the weft, which may probably be considered as the *ne plus ultra* of hand-spinning. For the very finest fabrics, therefore, the latter mode still preserves its superiority; but we must not forget that of these superfine numbers neither the demand nor the supply will bear a large proportion to the total consumption, and that if machine-spinning has got the length of No. 300, a large portion of the hand-spinning territory is already invaded. On the other hand, careful inquiry has shown that hand-spinning is itself susceptible of many improvements in the way both of economising time and producing a better article, and that a good means of introducing these would be the establishment of spinning-schools,—a plan which has been successfully adopted in Germany, where it has been shown that a hand-spinner bred in one of these establishments can turn out yarn in much greater quantity, and of much better quality, than an ordinary spinner.

In Germany machine-spinning has of late years made very rapid progress. In Prussia, for example, there were in 1837 only four spinning mills, with 10,300 spindles, and in 1846 there were 14, with 45,000 spindles, showing an increase of the latter in the space of nine years in the proportion of 10 to 45 [*]: the present number of spindles cannot be under 50,000. In Austria there were in 1843, according to the official statistics, eight spinning mills with 20,800 spindles; the number of the latter must now be at least 30,000, and there must be quite as many in the remainder of Germany, so that we approximately estimate the number of spindles in all Germany, Austria included, at about 110,000. In 1850 there were reckoned in England 364 spinning mills with 1,025,031 spindles,—an extent of spinning power which furnished her with the means of an extensive trade both in linen cloth and in linen yarn. The exportation of the

* See Dieterici, *Mittheilungen*, II^{er}. Jahrgang, p. 97.

latter amounted in 1844 to 25,970,600 lbs., of which more than half went to France, and about a fifth to Germany. This was its culminating point : the increase of the import duty in France, and the rapid development of machine-spinning there which was the result of that measure, occasioned a sensible decrease in the exportation of English yarn, which gradually fell off, till in 1848 it had sunk to 11,722,200 lbs. In 1849 it resumed an ascending movement, and the figure of exportation for that year was 17,264,000 lbs.* In France there were reckoned in 1846 more than 150,000 spindles, and the Minister of Agriculture and Commerce then declared that the number would soon amount to 200,000. In Belgium there were reckoned at the same period 60,000 : the number must now be very much larger. We may thus safely estimate the extent of flax-spinning machinery in England and on the continent together, at 1,400,000 spindles at the very least; allowing 3 poods per annum for each spindle, this would infer the consumption of 4,200,000 poods of flax — which is about the extent of our average export of that article — and a production (allowing 30 per cent. for waste) of 2,940,000 poods of linen yarn.†

Whilst such rapid progress is making in spinning by machinery, both in England and on the continent, our linen manufacture would be ruined, past hope of redemption, if we refused to profit, like our neighbours, by the new invention which has enriched English industry. Besides the other advantages which would arise from the extension of spinning by machinery, it would greatly contribute to improve the dressing of our flax, and would give this branch of commerce in general a better direction. The great impediment in the way of its rapid development is the want of capital: a flax spinnery will scarcely be successful unless conducted on a large scale; and for this a large capital is requisite. The flax-spinning machines, being more complicated than the cotton-spinning, are proportionally dearer ; and the flax to be spun by machinery requiring to be of good quality and well dressed, the result of the dressing gives a much smaller proportion of line, and a larger proportion of

---

* In 1844 the declared value of linen yarn exported from the United Kingdom amounted to 1,050,676*l.*; in 1848 it had fallen to 493,449*l.*; the re-action which commenced in 1849 (when the declared value was 732,065*l.*), has proceeded so rapidly, that in 1852 and 1853 (since the original text was printed), the value of the exports exceeded that of 1844 by 89,889*l.* and 98,427*l.* respectively.— *Tr.*

† In Austria the estimate per spindle is 100 lbs. (= 137 lbs. Russ.) of flax, yielding 20 lbs. of waste to 80 lbs. of spinning material; of the latter, 30 lbs. are line and 50 tow ; in the spinning *there is a farther waste of 12½ per cent. on the line and 20 to 25 per cent. on the tow, so that the nett product in yarn would be only 63 to 66 lbs. But in the lower numbers the waste is smaller, so that we have thought we might adopt the proportion of 70 lbs. yarn to 100 lbs. flax.

tow: it therefore becomes indispensable that the tow also should be spun, and this augments the required capital by necessitating the use of a second set of machines. In Austria it is calculated that for the establishment of a flax spinning-mill there is required a capital of 80 to 100 florins = 50 to 63 silver roubles per spindle, whilst for a cotton spinning-mill the requisite capital per spindle is only 12 florins = 8 roubles 15 kopecks.*
According to this estimate, based on experience, we ought to reckon in Russia, where iron and mechanism are so dear, not less at any rate than 60 to 65 silver roubles per spindle†; but, assuming only 50 roubles, a spinning-mill of the moderate size of 10,000 spindles would cost 500,000 roubles; whilst to attain the number of 100,000 spindles, which would work up 300,000 poods of flax, or about a twentieth of the raw material consumed in the country, a fixed capital of 5 millions would be requisite, besides a floating capital of 1½ more. It is evident that, in a country where capital is scarce, a manufacture requiring such a large amount of it can be developed but slowly, by the aid of government encouragement and joint-stock companies.

The first spinning mill established in Russia—about twenty years ago—was that attached to the factory of Alexandrovsk, near St. Petersburg, belonging to government; but it works only for the establishment in question, which is chiefly for the manufacture of sail-cloth. The first one undertaken on private account was that of M. Élizaroff, at Wiazniki, in the government of Wladimir; but, having been established on a small scale, and working, it would appear, with defective machinery, it was not successful, and has lately been abandoned. ‡ Mr. Wright's mill at St. Petersburg, which began by spinning the finer numbers, now turns out only about 5000 poods of yarn, which is woven on the premises into ordinary fabrics destined for America. Besides the above, there are still a few of small importance, mostly gone into decay. The whole of them set out with spinning fine numbers, and ended—owing to the imperfection of their machinery,—with confining themselves to the coarse yarn suitable for sail-cloth, flems, and other ordinary fabrics. A joint-stock company undertook the establishment of a spinning mill at St. Petersburg, but from defects in the mechanism employed, and mistakes in the organisation of the

---

* See the official statistics of Austria published in 1845.

† The spinning-mill with 1,900 spindles lately built by M. Mertwago in the government of Moscow, cost 79,000 silver roubles, or 41¾ roubles per spindle, exclusive of the cost of buildings and steam-engine.

‡ This seems to have been the fate of most of the spinning-mills established on the continent before the machinery had been brought to the requisite degree of perfection.

company itself, the undertaking was unsuccessful. In 1841 a new company for a similar purpose was formed at Riga, but resulted in nothing in consequence of the death of its principal promoter, M. Wermann, the banker. These several failures have arrested at the outset the development of this branch of industry; but they prove nothing against its future prospects. Other countries have had to pass through similar trials; and most of the spinning mills founded on the continent at the period when flax-spinning was rapidly improving in England have had the same fate. Now that we are in a condition to profit by the improvements introduced within the last twenty years, a new enterprise would have every probability in its favour, if it were based upon a well-laid plan, and carried on with a sufficiency of means.

In Russia the high price of machinery may be largely compensated by the advantage of having at hand a cheap supply of the raw material. In this respect, we stand to England, as concerns flax, much as England does to us as concerns cotton; and we have the additional advantage of the low price of labour. We may, therefore, hope that the three new spinning-mills, lately established in the governments of Moscow and Wologda, will succeed better than the former ones; and that they will give a favourable impulse to a manufacture which government, by the protection it has accorded those establishments, has shown the utmost disposition to encourage. One main condition of success may be considered the choice of a locality where the flax can be had at first hand, and situated at the same time in the centre of a weaving district: in both these respects the government of Jaroslaw is well placed. In regard to government encouragement, the first idea that naturally presents itself is custom-house protection; but this, at present, would be quite illusory. The importation of foreign machine-spun yarn is almost *nil*: the employment of this article will become more general only with the gradual extension of its manufacture at home. Machine-spinning, no doubt, took a great start in France, in consequence of the additional duty imposed on yarn in 1842; but at that period the use of machine-spun yarn was already so extensive, that more than 13,000,000 lbs. of it were imported from England alone.

In regard to the influence which machine-spinning might exert upon the welfare of the numerous classes who occupy themselves in hand-spinning, any inconvenience resulting from the progress of the former will be the practical question of a remote futurity; and it can never attain with us the gravity which it may present in other countries. We have already seen that more than 5,000,000 poods of flax are spun in the country: if this were to be done by machinery, the number of spindles required would be about 1,500,000, or nearly 50 per cent. more than could be mustered in all England. But we have already seen that the extension of spinning-mills in Russia can be but very slow; and it may be safely predicated that they will never more than very partially displace the household wheel, which, be it observed, still maintains its ground, even in countries where spinning by machinery has already made notable progress. For a long time to come, machine-spun yarn will be employed with us only in the manufacture of flems, table-linen, and other fabrics of medium fineness intended for commerce; and hand-spinning will continue, as in time past, to supply the manufacture of household linens for the lower classes, and of very fine fabrics. The latter sort will also probably become greatly improved when the intentions of the Administration of State Domains, in regard to the establishment of good spinning-schools, have been put in execution.

In Russia both the wheel and the distaff are made use of. The results of the two modes depend a good deal upon the spinster's dexterity. With the wheel, more work is done in a given time; with the spindle, the thread is more equal; spindle yarn is better for very fine fabrics, and is generally preferred for the warp; but, taken as a whole, the wheel presents greater advantages, and is gradually encroaching on the spindle. This has been the case in the government of Jaroslaw for the last fifteen or twenty years; but in the government of Kostroma and many others the distaff maintains its sway. An apprenticeship in well-organised spinning-schools will probably produce considerable improvement in the handling of both implements. The negligence with which the spinning is very generally executed — the little care which is displayed in the assortment of the yarn — the little bits of trickery which the spinners sometimes perpetrate in making up their hanks, which sometimes contain less than the full quantity of yarn, and sometimes coarser yarn inside than outside — all these are impediments to the progress of the trade. The manufacturers are obliged to lay in a larger stock of yarn, in order to assort the different qualities and select what suits them: they find themselves also losers in regard to the quantity and quality of their purchases, and there is often a considerable quantity of yarn of which they can make no use whatever. In regard to all these matters, the introduction of machine-spinning could not fail to be attended with benefit, both directly, by supplying a better article itself, and indirectly, by stimulating the production of a better one by the hand-spinners.

The weaving of linen cloth by the power-loom is one of those recent inventions of which the utility has not yet been sufficiently tested by experience. It is possible that, in the course of time, these may take the place of the domestic loom; but this is a question of the future, which has for us no immediate interest. There are in Russia, at present, only two linen manufactories in actual operation where the power-loom is used — that of Alexandrovsk, belonging to government, and Mr. Wright's, at St. Petersburg — both producing only sail-cloths and other ordinary fabrics, and these in small quantity. Besides these, M. Mertwago has just been organising a new establishment for weaving linen by machinery at Wiblovo, near Moscow; but these do not require to occupy our attention, and we shall confine our notice to the ordinary domestic hand-loom. These looms are made by the peasants after very old patterns, and sell for from three to five silver roubles, according to the breadth of the fabrics for which they are intended: inferior looms may be had for even less. A good workman can make one in ten days or a fortnight, and gain 2 to $2\frac{1}{2}$ roubles per week. The metal parts, made also by the peasants themselves, are generally badly finished; and the whole construction is defective enough, which of course impedes the progress of the manufacture. They are commonly too slight, — not strong enough for properly stretching the warp. Sometimes also the yarn is not strong enough to admit of its being properly stretched, and this is a frequent cause of the thinness of our fabrics: moreover, in Russia, the looms are generally kept in very warm rooms, which puts them out of order by drying up the wood, whilst in other countries they are kept in unfloored and somewhat damp apartments. To remedy this inconvenience our weavers sometimes wet the floor during the time the weaving is going on, but that does not preserve the loom at other times. The weaver's stays are generally made of rushes, often simply of wood. Copper or steel stays are only beginning to be introduced into the best factories: the peasants do not yet well understand the use of these metal stays, and consider them very dear; however, they are beginning to use them for the broader sorts of linens: the dressing is also often performed in a very slovenly manner: nowhere do we see the improved apparatus for this operation, which in other countries are regarded as indispensable. Jacquard looms have been introduced into the principal manufactories of damask table linen, and even begin to be introduced amongst the peasants who manufacture fine table linen : for common damask fabrics the old-fashioned loom is still preferred: the price of Jacquard looms has considerably fallen off of late : at Moscow a wooden one can be purchased for from 11 to 17, and an improved iron one for from 29 to 46 roubles. Since the introduction of the Jacquard loom, the fabrication of damask tissues has undergone considerable improvement: so long as the common loom was used for this purpose the quality turned off was very inferior, and fine home-manufactured table napery was a rarity which sold at an exorbitant price. Now beautiful napery is made in several manufactories, and the price is considerably reduced.

The dimensions given to the size of the piece, both as regards length and breadth, are very variable from one locality to another: there is no established rule or custom in the matter, except for sail-cloth, raven-ducks, and flems, the size of which was regulated by government in the time of Peter the Great. For fine piece fabrics the breadth of $\frac{5}{4}$ archine was at one time quasi-adopted, but this rule has been deviated from of late, and it is now rare to find linen which ought to have $\frac{5}{4}$ archine, or 20 verchoks, having even so much as 19 verchoks when it comes to be measured: more frequently it has only 17 or 18. Fabrics which used to measure 1 archine, or 16 verchoks, now measure only 14 ; nor are the weavers very conscientious in regard to the length of the web. This abuse of confidence, and the absence of well-established rules, deprive the trade of all regularity, and do it infinite mischief both at home and abroad. It would be a great point gained if our weavers could be brought to understand that honesty is the best policy, and that by their faithful adherence to certain well-understood rules nobody would be so much the gainer as themselves. The fineness of the fabric is judged of entirely by the eye : the use of small microscopes for determining the precise number of threads in the warp is almost unknown. Fabrics of $\frac{5}{4}$ archine in breadth are manufactured of the fineness of 2,100 to 5,600 threads, and sell at from 17 kopecks to 2 roubles per archine : the bulk of the fabrication is 2,400 to 2,600 threads to the warp: fine fabrics of 4000 to 5,600 threads are seldom manufactured by the peasants on their own account: this manufacture is concentrated at Wéliko-Sélo in the government of Jaroslaw : even in the establishments belonging to landed proprietors it is rarely that linen of greater fineness than 3,600 threads to a $\frac{5}{4}$ archine warp is manufactured. The following, according to the information collected in 1844 by the commission, at Wéliko-Sélo, is an account of the expenses of manufacture of a piece of linen cloth 30 archines long, by $\frac{5}{4}$ wide, and 2,400 threads fine :

						Roub.	Kop.
18 hanks yarn for warp @ 45 kop. paper	-	-	-	-	-	8	10
18 do. do. for weft @ 50 kop.	-	-	-	-	-	9	0
Weaver's wages @ 20 kop. per arch.	-	-	-	-	-	6	0
Scouring of yarn @ 3 kop. per hank	-	-	-	-	-	1	8
Reeling of ditto @ 3½ kop. per hank	-	-	-	-	-	1	26
Bleaching web @ 10 kop. per archine	-	-	-	-	-	3	0
Other expenses	-	-	-	-	-	0	56
Total expense = 8 roub. 29 kop. silver					-	29	0

Assuming the very moderate selling price of 110 kopecks paper per archine, which comes to 33 roubles for the piece, there would remain for the manufacturer a nett profit of 4 paper roubles, or nearly 14 per cent.

According to the same authority, the following is an account of the expense of manufacturing a web of 30 archines $\frac{5}{4}$ wide and 4800 threads to the warp: —

					Roub.	Kops.
40 hanks yarn for warp @ 115 kop. paper	-	-	-		46	0
50 ditto ditto for weft @ 125 kop.	-	-	-		62	50
Weaver's wages	-	-	-	-	50	0
Scouring of yarn @ 3 kop. per hank	-	-	-		2	70
Reeling of do. @ 6 kop. do.	-	-	-		5	40
Bleaching web @ 14 kop. per archine	-	-	-		4	20
Other small expenses	-	-	-	-	4	10
Interest of capital @ 5 per cent.	-	-	-	-	8	60
Total expense = 52½ roub. silver				-	183	50

Assuming a selling price of 200 paper roubles (= 1 rouble 2 kopecks silver per archine), there would remain for the manufacturer a nett profit of 16 roubles 50 kopecks paper, or 9 per cent.*

A good weaver can weave daily 5 or 6 archines of 2400 threads to the warp, which, at the rate of 20 kopecks per archine, makes a wage of 1 rouble to 1 rouble 20 kopecks paper, or 28½ to 34¼ kopecks silver (= 10¾d. to 1s. 1d.) per day: sometimes as much as 30 kopecks per archine is allowed, which comes to 43 to 51½ kopecks silver (= 1s. 4d. to 1s. 7½d.) per day. For the household linens used by the peasantry, which are sold at from 5 to 7 paper roubles per piece of 30 archines, a weaver gains only 50 paper kopecks (= 5½d.) per day, receiving 1 rouble 50 kopecks paper for a web of 30 archines, which he can weave in three days. In some districts of the government of Jaroslaw, where there is not much arable land, the peasants are employed in weaving the whole year round; but in general they are thus occupied during only seven or eight months of

---

* Although we give the above calculation as we find it, we may observe that linen of this quality and price — the price of the best foreign linens — is very rarely manufactured in Russia, and more by way of experiment or for show than for sale : we have never seen any of it.

the year. In many districts it is usually the women who
weave : young lads and girls are also employed at the same
work ; the fabrics manufactured by the latter are often found
wanting in equality and consistence. In the government of
Jaroslaw, where this manufacture is most advanced, there are
villages in which weaving is carried on as a regular trade —
the father bringing up his son to the business, and making it
over to him entirely when he reaches a certain age.   The
linens manufactured in the districts where this custom prevails
are reputed the best : in those districts where a great deal of flax
is cultivated, the peasants spin and weave their own flax, and,
when they have not enough, they purchase from their neighbours ; others weave only to order, and receive the yarn from
the manufacturer or proprietor ; this sort of customer work
often gives occasion to disputes, from the inequality of the yarn
and inexactness of measure — defects to which we have already
alluded.

The household linens, which are sold without being glossed,
are usually woven by women in the rooms inhabited by the
family ; but the professional weavers generally work in a sort
of bothy with several windows, commonly built near a running
stream.   Sometimes a single peasant builds one of these bothies
or workshops, and lets workmen's places in it at the rate of
2 silver roubles per winter ; sometimes several weavers club to
build the bothy, and then draw lots for the window which each
of them is to occupy.   There are in Russia no schools for
weaving, properly so called ; spinning and weaving are learned
in the family ; at Wéliko-Sélo, for instance, the girls, by the
time they are seven years old, begin to spin ; they are then
taught to reel, and at twelve they learn to weave household
linen ; by the time they are sixteen they begin weaving the
finer sorts for sale.   In districts where weaving forms a
regular business, the weavers take pupils to board with them—
the parents paying from 7 to 11 roubles for their board and instruction during seven months ; but in most cases the apprentices are, up to the age of thirteen or fourteen, employed in
winding the yarn and preparing the bobbins, for which they
receive a wage of 2 to 6 silver roubles per winter.   Weavers
that have a number of orders hire journeymen upon wages,
allowing them as much as 23 silver roubles per winter, besides
board.   Some proprietors have manufactories on their estates,
into which they receive young pupils as apprentices, employing
them afterwards as workmen ; this is attended with a good
effect on the manufacture amongst the peasantry.

The faults commonly found with our linens are, first, a want
of compactness in the fabric, — a fault which proceeds not only

from the weakness of the yarn and the slightness of the looms, but also from the circumstance that the weavers, to get on more quickly with their work, do not strike very hard with the batten. Linens thus woven generally reckon in a square archine more yarn in the warp than in the weft; whilst good linens present more regular squares, and in very fine sorts there is more yarn in the weft than in the warp. Sometimes, also, too fine a thread is taken for the weft as compared with the thread of the warp. Secondly, the streaks or grooves in the cloth, proceeding sometimes from the weakness of the thread, and sometimes from the weaver's negligence in mending the warp yarn when it breaks. Thirdly, the double threads in the weft, proceeding in like manner from carelessness. Fourthly, the knots or spots arising from the inequality of the threads, or from several of them breaking all at once. Fifthly, the nap, which covers the web, — a fault which proceeds from the circumstance that the yarn, for want of proper twisting, and from the bad heckling of the flax, divides and becomes downy after being scoured. In other countries the light hairy filaments are destroyed, either by beating the yarn with flat hammers previous to weaving, or passing the web between strongly-heated rollers; but it is seldom that either of these operations is had recourse to in Russia. Lastly, inequality of the fabric, arising sometimes from the warp not being always in a perfectly horizontal position, and sometimes from the (not always undesigned) negligence of the workman, who makes better work at the two ends of his web than in the centre.

The bleaching is performed by the peasants in a very defective manner. In some districts lime is used with a view to accelerate the process; and, being often used without proper knowledge and precaution, it corrodes the fabric; so that, after being awhile in the shop, it tumbles into tatters. Really good bleach-fields are seldom found except in the neighbourhood of manufactories of flems, raven-ducks, and the like, which require superior apparatus. M. Karnovitsch, to whose enlightened exertions the linen manufacture of the government of Jaroslaw is under such weighty obligations, was the first to establish a well-organised bleachery on the plan of those of Bielefeld in Westphalia; from which place he got over for that purpose a bleacher and a finisher. Guided in all his undertakings, not by a single eye to his own interests, but by the interests of our linen industry in general, M. Karnovitsch receives for bleaching and finishing whatever cloth may be sent him; and his great object has been to familiarise our peasants with the advantages resulting from having these finishing operations conducted in a proper manner. Not being desirous of pecuniary benefit for himself, he fixed the price of bleaching at the very moderate rate of 4 kopecks per archine; but it is to be regretted that our weavers have shown little anxiety hitherto to avail themselves of the advantages thus placed within their reach. This arises, first, from the little inclination which they show in general to adopt any improvement which interferes with their ordinary habits; and, secondly, from the circumstance, that the common bleaching and finishing is executed by the females with such simple means and appliances as to cost next to nothing; so that bleached and unbleached linen sell at very nearly the same price. The expense of good bleaching, however moderate, forms a new expense which they do not like to incur; and they have not foresight enough to appreciate the benefit which they would derive in time from furnishing a better article; they are, moreover, often hard pressed for money; and this induces them to hurry into the market without waiting the few weeks that it would require to have their napery bleached. To these particular causes of the want of success of M. Karno-vitsch's undertaking may be added a cause of a more general nature. In other countries bleaching establishments commonly belong to manufacturers, who give out the yarn to the weavers, and receive back the green napery, which they then bleach and finish on their own account; but amongst us it is the peasants who are themselves the manufacturers; and they prefer per-forming all the operations themselves the best way they can, to having some of them performed in an improved manner by others at the expense of advancing money out of their pockets, which they would often find very inconvenient. We think M. Karnovitsch's enterprise would have a better chance of suc-ceeding if he were to purchase the unbleached webs from the peasants, and finish and sell them on his own account.

Chemical bleaching by chloride of lime is of very recent in-troduction into Russia. M. Karnovitsch was the first to orga-nise an establishment of this sort in his factory at Talitsa, and the experiment succeeded beyond expectation. At first the peasantry were a little doubtful on the subject; but, dazzled by the celerity of the process, which took only from four to nine days at the utmost, they took rather a liking to it, and it has been upon the whole more successful than any preceding attempt. Besides the celerity of the process, chemical bleach-ing has the advantage of being independent of the variations of the atmosphere; and experience has shown that, when employed with care and the requisite degree of skill, it can be used with-out injury to the stuff: but its application to linen cloth is a nicer affair than its application to cotton. In several countries, especially Belgium and some parts of Germany, common atmospheric bleaching is still preferred. In these countries, common bleaching having attained a high degree of perfection, the application of the chemical mode is an improvement that is less urgently called for; but in Russia, where this is any thing but the case, chemical bleaching in well-organised establishments might be attended with the very best consequences. To the various defects in the manufacture which we have mentioned, we may add a circumstance, which, though seemingly a very trifling one, does nevertheless exert a prejudicial influence on our linen trade, and that is, the mode of rolling up the cloth, which is such as to make it impossible for an intending purchaser to judge of the equality of the fabric without unrolling the entire piece.

The manufacture of fine linens, especially of those that have a breadth of $\frac{5}{4}$ archines ($=35$ inches) like foreign linens, is chiefly confined to the government of Jaroslaw: its principal seat is Wéliko-Sélo, which is also the centre of the linen trade in general. At the fairs of this place 60,000 pieces are sold annually, the fine sorts being sent to Moscow and St. Petersburg and the fair of Nijni-Nowgorod, and the household sorts chiefly to the Ukraine, but partly also to Nijni. It was at Wéliko-Sélo that the manufacture of fine linen began, not more than five or seven and twenty years ago: before that period nothing was manufactured but household linen, known in commerce under the name of *noviny:* fine linens are also manufactured in the government of Kostroma, but in small quantities, and only by a few proprietors: the peasants of this government prefer manufacturing household linens, whether for their own use or for sale: this sort is also manufactured in the governments of Jaroslaw, Kostroma, Wologda, and various others: for domestic use it is manufactured more or less throughout Russia.

The manufacture of damasks, requiring a somewhat more complex apparatus, forms a sort of transition from household industry to that of the factory: ordinary damasks are still within the domain of the industry of our peasants: taken in its largest sense, this branch belongs principally to the government of Kostroma—the government of Jaroslaw standing only in the second rank: its centre is formed by the village of Wytschouha (government of Kostroma), and extends from thence to the town of Kineschma. In this district are situated the principal manufactories of fine table linen, belonging to General Mengden, M. Mindowski, and M. Konowalow. The chief branch of manufacture is common damask for towelling, in pieces of 24

French ells long by 10 verschoks ($=17\frac{1}{2}$ inches) wide, manufactured at Wytschouha and its neighbourhood. There is
usually required for the weaving of a piece 10 hanks of yarn,
costing from 86 kopecks to 1 rouble silver: the piece sells at
from 1 rouble 14 to 1 rouble $28\frac{1}{2}$ kopecks, and sometimes as low
as 1 rouble, so that the gain by the weaving can be but small:
the weaving is executed principally by the female peasants, who,
when they work to order, are paid at the rate of 13 to 17 kopecks per piece: a diligent worker can weave three or four
pieces weekly, and thus gain $6\frac{1}{2}$ to $11\frac{1}{2}$ kopecks ($=2\frac{1}{2}d.$ to $4\frac{1}{2}d.$)
per diem. Formerly these fabrics sold for 2 roubles or 2 rou-
bles 30 kopecks per piece; but then the piece contained 30
archines by $\frac{3}{4}$ or even $\frac{4}{4}$ arch. in breadth: we still find Wytschouha damasks 27 by $\frac{3}{4}$ archines which sell for 2 roubles, 57
to 3 roubles 14 kopecks per piece. For a piece of this sort,
which he can weave in three days, the weaver receive 1 rouble
20 kopecks paper, which amounts to a wage of 40 kopecks
paper ($4\frac{1}{4}d.$) per diem. These fabrics are bought at the bazaars
of Wytschouha, Kineschma, and Pless, at first or second hand,
by Armenian or Russian merchants, who send them to the
Ukraine: they used to be sent in considerable quantities to
America; but this trade has greatly fallen off of late, owing to
bad bleaching, bad weaving, and bad measure — faults of ours
by which our friends the English have not failed to profit.

Next to the common damasks of Wytschouha falls to be
ranked the table napery of a more improved manufacture, which
is sold in sets of 1 table cloth, 8 archines by 3, and a dozen
table-napkins of an archine square. This napery is woven in
more complicated looms (*iz priborami*) than the common sort;
but the attempts to introduce into their construction the improvements adopted in other countries have not hitherto been
successful; the Jacquard loom, however, has been partially introduced. The weavers generally work in the glazed bothies
of which we have already spoken, sometimes on their own risk,
sometimes to order,—receiving in the latter case from 71 kopecks
to 1 rouble for a dozen table napkins, and $28\frac{1}{2}$ to $34\frac{1}{2}$ kopecks for
a table cloth 3 archines broad. A good workman can weave a
dozen napkins per week, which allows him 12 to 17 kopecks
($=4\frac{1}{2}d.$ to $6\frac{1}{2}d.$) per day. A weaver that owns his own loom
can gain, with the help of an assistant, 500 paper roubles ($=22l.$
12s.) per annum, out of which he pays 100 paper roubles to his
assistant, and 50 to the winder who attends to his bobbins; so
that there remains for himself only 350 paper roubles ($=15l.$
16s.), out of which he has still to pay for the scouring of his
yarn 5 paper kopecks ($=0\cdot542d.$) per hank. The yarn used in

this manufacture is of medium fineness, and costs from 13 to 17 kopecks (5d. to $6\frac{1}{2}d$.) per hank. A dozen napkins of this sort sell at first hand for 3 roubles 14 to 3 roubles 71 kopecks, and table cloths 3 archines broad at the rate of 70 kopecks to 1 rouble 14 kopecks per running archine; they are sent for sale to the fair of Nijni-Nowgorod or the Ukraine; a small part are also exported. For the last ten or a dozen years there has also been manufactured in the government of Kostroma a good deal of table napery in which there is a mixture of cotton—the weft being formed of the latter material; this sort of stuff is manufactured much quicker and sold at a much lower price.

Very fine table linen is made only in large factories; but this branch of manufacture is visibly decreasing in importance. The three principal factories in the government of Kostroma are those of General Mengden, M. Konowalow, and M. Mindowski; the latter gentleman is chiefly a cotton manufacturer; linen fabrics are but a secondary article in his factory ; in all the three Jacquard looms are used. The finest articles made in the two last named factories are towels, which sell at 14 roubles 86 kopecks per dozen, and table linen, of which the set of two dozen napkins with a table cloth of 8 archines by 3 sells at $31\frac{1}{2}$ roubles. The weaver receives for a table cloth of 3 archines in breadth 34 to 40 kopecks per running yard, and for a dozen napkins 1 rouble 28 kopecks to 1 rouble 41 kopecks. A good workman, with an assistant, can weave 1 archine of table cloth and gain 37 kopecks ($=1s.\ 2d.$) per day ; at weaving napkins a single weaver can gain 23 to 26 kopecks ($8\frac{3}{4}d.$ to $9\frac{5}{4}d.$) per day. In General Mengden's factory, very fine table napery is manufactured ; this is the first of all our linen factories in respect both to the perfection of its fabrics and to its internal organisation : it might serve as a model for all establishments of the sort. By means of a good distribution of labour, of improved processes of manufacture, and of an active and enlightened superintendence, this establishment is able to turn out at a profit fine fabrics which others could manufacture only at a loss ; its products have figured at several expositions of national industry, and have attracted the attention of all connoisseurs. For certain sorts of fabrics English yarn, Nos. 70. to 120. is employed, sometimes with a mixture of home-made yarn costing 39 kopecks per lb.; the very fine fabrics are for most part made to order of the Moscow and St. Petersburg shopkeepers; the medium fabrics are sent chiefly to Riga and Nijni. There are also manufactured in this establishment linen of the fineness of 4000 threads to the warp of $\frac{1}{4}$ archine broad ; these are generally woven by the peasant's wives; the greater number of the weavers are peasants belonging to the general's own estate, together with their wives and children, though there are a very few hired on wages. The whole work-people receive, besides their food, payment at a rate which is very little under that of free workmen, and the looms with their appurtenances belong to the proprietor.* The weavers who have finished their apprenticeship in the factory can gain from 26 to 36 roubles per annum, whilst their wives, between weaving and bleaching, can gain from 17 to 26 roubles, and each boy about 14 roubles by winding and preparing the bobbins, so that a peasant's family may earn amongst them about 71 roubles 40 kopecks (= 11l. sterling) per annum. This establishment unites the advantages of diffusing comfort over the district, and setting an example of good organisation and the introduction of improved methods of manufacture.

There is also at Jaroslaw a large manufactory of table-linen, belonging to M. Jakowlew, the fabrics of which have long enjoyed a certain degree of repute ; it is the oldest establishment of the sort in Russia, having been founded in 1722 : attached to it was a population of nearly 2,000 individuals, which, on the application of the present proprietor, was purchased by government and incorporated in the burgher class of the town of Jaroslaw. The establishment has lost much of its former importance ; it gives occupation to about 150 weavers, and only free men are employed. In its present condition the profits it brings in are but small ; the buildings are in a state of decay, continually wanting repairs ; and the processes of manufacture are antiquated ; altogether it would require a thorough re-organisation.

At Moscow there is now only a single table-linen manufactory of any importance ; it belongs to M. Kouzmine, a merchant ; it formerly used for three-fourths of its fabrics foreign mill-spun yarn, but of late it has mostly used home-spun yarn. The wages there paid to a weaver is 1 rouble 14 kopecks for a cloth 1 ell long by 3 archines broad ; and as a good workman can weave $1\frac{1}{2}$ archines per day, he may gain about 7 roubles per week ; for a dozen towels, which sell for 17 roubles, the weaver receives 7 ; the weaving of the dozen occupies about two weeks, which allows him a wage of 58 kopecks per day, Sundays deducted ; this is a tolerably large expense of production. The linen from this factory is about the best we produce

---

* It must be obvious that an establishment based upon economical arrangements of this sort, however good may be its organisation in regard to the processes of manufacture, cannot be worked at a cheap rate, for the labour comes high.

as regards compactness and equality of fabric, but leaves much
to be desired on the score of bleaching and finish.

We must also mention a new factory of table-napery and
fine linen, established within the last few years, by M. Janke,
in the neighbourhood of Riga, the products of which, especially
the fine linens, attracted the attention of connoisseurs at the
St. Petersburg exposition of 1849. The cloth of this manufactory, which employs mostly English yarn, fetches from 34
to 68 silver roubles the piece of 48 archines, and can compete
with the best foreign linen; the table linens of the same factory belong to the best fabrics of their kind, but their price is
comparatively higher. The establishment promises to become a
very important one; it already employs upwards of 20 Jacquard
looms.

The orders for very fine table linen fell off considerably in
the principal factories, especially in General Mengden's, in
consequence of the lowering of the tariff which took place in
1842, for foreign linens imported by dry frontier; and yet the
duty of 1 rouble 20 kopecks per lb. represented, for very fine
table-linen, a duty of 20 to 30 per cent., and, for ordinary
table-linen, 100 per cent. and upwards, which proves that our
best manufactories cannot yet stand foreign competition without a high protection. The same is the case with regard to
common linen, as we may perceive by the following facts mentioned in the report of the commission so repeatedly referred to.

A piece of Bielefeld linen, which cost on the spot 13 roubles,
and weighed 12 lbs. Russ., paid, under the tariff which was in
force to the end of 1850, an import duty (at the rate of 1 rouble 20 kopecks per lb.) of 14 roubles 40 kopecks, or 108 per
cent. upon its cost price; adding expense of transport, commission, &c., amounting to 2 roubles 50 kopecks, the piece cost the
merchant by the time it got to St. Petersburg, 29 roubles 90
kopecks, and was sold for 34 roubles 30 kopecks; so that there
was still a profit of 4 roubles 40 kopecks or $14\frac{2}{3}$ per cent.
Again, a piece of fine linen costing at Bielefeld 70 roubles,
and weighing 10 lbs., paid an import duty of 12 roubles, equivalent to 17 per cent. Adding 2 roubles 50 kopecks for carriage and commission, the piece came to 84 roubles 50 kopecks,
and was sold for 100 roubles, thus leaving the Petersburg
merchant a profit of 15 roubles 50 kopecks, or $18\frac{1}{2}$ per cent.
Down to 1842, linen of every sort, whether arriving by land
or sea, was subject to a duty of 1 rouble 85 kopecks per lb.,
which nearly amounted to a prohibition; for it was only the
very finest sorts which could partially support such a heavy
duty; but the above mentioned facts sufficiently indicate that

the prohibitory system adopted in 1822 did little to forward the progress of our linen manufacture, and that this object is to be attained only by introducing improvements into our manufacturing processes, under the shadow of such a moderate amount of protection as does not exclude the healthy stimulus of a little foreign competition. Accordingly, the commission reported unfavourably of the demand urged by some manufacturers for a return to the prohibitory duties of 1822; and the inexpediency of excessive protection was also recognised by government; the duty of 1 rouble 85 kopecks, and 1 rouble 20 kopecks, for linens imported by wet and dry frontier respectively, without distinction of qualities, has been reduced in the new tariff to 40 and 60 kopecks respectively for the ordinary, and 60 kopecks and 1 rouble respectively for the finer sorts.

The Commission gives in its Report the following comparison of the prices of Belgian and Russian linens. A piece of linen cloth of 2,600 threads warp to a breadth of $\frac{5}{4}$ archine, costing in Belgium 26 kopecks per archine, comes in the government of Jaroslaw to 34 to 37 kopecks per archine, being a difference of 30 to 42 per cent. A piece of similar breadth and 3,400 threads to the warp, costs in Belgium 53 kopecks per archine, and in the government of Jaroslaw 65 to 85 kopecks, or 22 to 60 per cent. more. A piece of 4,200 threads costs in Belgium 68 kopecks per archine, and at Jaroslaw 1 rouble 14 kopecks to 1 rouble 43 kopecks, or from 68 to 110 per cent. dearer. We perceive that the difference augments in proportion to the fineness of the fabric, being only from 30 to 40 per cent. for cloth of medium quality, whilst it amounts to 100 per cent. and upwards for the very fine qualities; so that in the higher regions of this industry we have a very long lee-way to make up. The difference in price may be accounted for by the difference in the price of labour. In Belgium, a weaver is paid for weaving cloth of 3,400 threads to the warp at the rate of 12 kopecks per archine; and at Wéliko-Sélo the rate of payment amounts to $23\frac{3}{4}$ kopecks per archine, or about double the remuneration of the Belgian weaver; the latter, moreover, weaves both better and quicker; he gets through with $1\frac{3}{5}$ archines per day, whilst at Wéliko-Sélo, where the weaving is generally performed by females, the worker seldom executes more than 1 archine per day, so that the Belgian workman, paid at the rate of only $17\frac{1}{5}$ kopecks per day, furnishes nearly 50 per cent. more work—and better done work into the bargain—than the Russian workwoman, who is paid at the rate of 26 to 28 kopecks per day. This is one proof more that, whilst unskilled labour is nowhere so cheap as in

Russia, no sooner is anything like skill required than wages become dearer there than anywhere else—a fact which meets us in every department of industry.   From this we may infer that our industry ought to apply itself by preference to the manufacture of common fabrics of medium quality, and engage but sparingly and with caution in the fabrication of articles of luxury.   When a branch of industry has once been thoroughly established for those articles which form in all countries the bulk of the consumption, the finer articles are manufactured by degrees, as the skill of the workman becomes more and more improved; but if an attempt is made to manufacture fine articles, whilst the processes of manufacture are still backward, whilst skilled labourers are scarce, and can be obtained only at a high rate of wages, it is obvious that the manufacture must be a very expensive one.   No doubt if prices were to be allowed to rise to an unbounded height, and if no sacrifices on the part of the consumer were to be recoiled from, it would be possible to manufacture in any one country whatever it is found possible to manufacture in any other; but an industry carried on at such a cost as that it could furnish its article only at twice the price for which it could be purchased elsewhere, would not be an industry in the true sense of the term, but a sham which would never compensate the sacrifices which it entailed.

Our linen manufacture is so natural to the country that it will be able, in the course of time, to arrive at perfection by dint of its own resources, without the help of prohibitory duties. If some manufactories were put to inconvenience by the diminution of orders for fine fabrics which supervened upon the modification of the tariff in 1842, the inconvenience was but temporary and partial: in the course of two years afterwards a new manufactory of fine and table linen, which we have already spoken of, was established at Riga; three years ago it had 20 Jacquard looms in operation; and, being organised on the plan of the best foreign factories, it will, it is hoped, be so much the better able to sustain foreign competition.

The duties fixed by the new tariff of 40 and 60 kopecks per lb. for ordinary linens, amounts at an average, upon the common household cloths which are sold at St. Petersburg for 10 kopecks per archine, to 130 and 200 per cent. of the value*, and upon cloths of medium quality of $\frac{5}{4}$ archine in breadth, containing 5

---

* A piece of 30 ells of common household linen, 15 verchoks broad, the retail price of which at St. Petersburg is 10 kopecks per archine, weighs about 10 lbs. A piece of foreign linen cloth of this quality would pay on arriving by land (at 40 kopecks per lb.) a duty of 4 roubles, or 133 per cent., and, on arriving by sea (at 60 kopecks per lb.) a duty of 6 roubles, or double the cost price of the home-made piece.

square archines to a Russian lb., to 37 and 55 per cent. of their value at the place of production, which is certainly more than sufficient protection for this sort of cloth. For the very fine linens sold at Bielefeld for 70 roubles per piece of 48 archines, weighing 10 lbs., the duty of 60 kopecks, or 1 rouble, according as they enter by dry or wet frontier, comes to $8\frac{1}{2}$ and $14\frac{1}{4}$ per cent. respectively; and if we add for carriage, commission, &c., $2\frac{1}{2}$ roubles per piece, the total premium in favour of the home manufacturer will run from 12 to 18 per cent. This is certainly a very moderate protection: but these fabrics of luxury, of which the consumption is always very limited, constitute but a very trifling proportion of our linen manufacture; and a long experience has shown that protective duties of thrice the amount had no other result than to encourage smuggling. Since the last reduction of duties the import of these articles has more than doubled, while the contraband trade has considerably fallen off; so that the smuggler has been the only loser.

The manufacture of the strong fabrics known in commerce under the name of flems and raven-ducks *, which require more extensive apparatus, is concentrated in the towns of the governments of Wladimir, Kostroma, and Jaroslaw, and principally at Mourome and Wiazniki. They are also known in commerce under the names of these two towns. The manufacturers purchase the yarn at first hand, or through the medium of petty merchants, who purchase it up in detail amongst the peasantry in the governments of Jaroslaw, Kostroma, and Wologda. The yarn intended for flems is paid for at the rate of 5 roubles 14 kopecks, and that for raven-ducks at 3 roubles 71 kopecks per pood: it is scoured and bleached at the manufactory, and loses in the process of scouring 14 or 15 lbs. per pood: there seldom remains more than 25 out of the 40 of raw yarn. The weaving is partly performed — especially for cloths of the best quality requiring more care and superintendence — in barracks belonging to the factories, but more generally in the peasants' own houses. For the weaving of a piece of flems, which a good workman can accomplish in from three to five days, the payment is from 71 to 81 kopecks; and for a piece of raven-duck, which requires only from two to four days' work, it is from 37 to 46 kopecks, so that the weaver gains at an average for the first sort of fabric 20 kopecks, and for the second nearly 12 kopecks per day. In order to facilitate the weaving of those stuffs which require a very strong thread, the warp, after being starched, receives a coat of tallow. Those strong fabrics have

---

* A piece of flems 50 archines by $1\frac{1}{2}$ weighs nearly 30 lbs., or at the rate of $\frac{3}{5}$ lbs. per archine, and a piece of raven-duck 50 archines by $\frac{3}{4}$ weighs 20 to 23 lbs.

at all times formed the bulk of our linen trade with foreign countries; but for the last thirty years this branch of our commerce has been in a depressed condition, for want of an effective demand, and in consequence of a great fall in the price of the article since 1823. The flems, which formerly sold for 52 paper roubles the piece, now fetch only 27; and the raven-ducks, which sold for 25 paper roubles, have fallen to 19 roubles 50 kopecks.

The following, according to the information collected by the commission, is the cost price of these fabrics : —

For a piece of Flems, medium quality.

	Paper. Roub.	Kop.
41 lbs. yarn - - - - - - - - -	18	45
Expense of scouring ditto at 3 roub. per pood - - -	3	8
Arranging bobbins and warp - - - - - -	0	30
Weaving - - - - - - - -	2	50
Petty expenses - - - - - - - -	0	65
Carriage to St. Petersburg, and commission - - -	1	30
Total = 7 roub. 51 kop. silver. -	26	28*

The price at St. Petersburg in 1850 was from 8 roubles to 9 roubles 75 kopecks; but in 1844 the prices were, for first quality, 7 roubles 71 kopecks, second quality, 7 roubles 42 kopecks, so that the manufacturer was working without profit, or even at a loss.

For a piece of Raven-duck.

	Paper Roub.	Kop.
35 lbs. yarn - - - - - -	11	81
Expense of scouring - - - - -	2	62
Arranging bobbins, and warp - - - -	0	25
Weaving - - - - - -	1	60
Petty expenses - - - - - -	0	45
Carriage to St. Petersburg, and commission - -	1	0
Total = 5 roubles 7 kopecks silver -	17	73

The price at St. Petersburg in 1850 was 6 or 7 roubles, giving a profit of from 93 kopecks to 1 rouble 93 kopecks per piece; but sometimes the price falls as low as 5 roubles 50 kopecks, so that the profit is reduced to 43 kopecks per piece.

* Since this calculation was made (in 1844) the cost of fabrication must have diminished ; for the flems of Mourome are sold at the place of production for 7 roubles 28½ kopecks, and those of Wiazniki for 7 roubles. M. Mertwaho now furnishes the mill-spun yarn for these fabrics for 5 silver roubles per pood, so that the price of 41 lbs. would be only 17 roubles 94 kopecks, instead of 18 roubles 45 kopecks, ut suprà, which of itself makes a difference of 51 kopecks paper or 14½ kopecks silver.

In consequence of the fall of prices, which has been felt principally in flems, raven-ducks, which give a surer profit, have become the favourite article of manufacture. There is also manufactured in the government of Kostroma, and in some other districts, a sort of raven-duck, called semi-sail cloth, which is thicker than common raven-duck, and is used for light sails and other maritime purposes; but it is seldom manufactured except to order, and does not constitute a current article of merchandise.

In consequence of the fall of prices, the manufacture of flems and raven-duck has greatly fallen off in importance. At Kostroma, where, twenty years ago, there used to be manufactured 70,000 pieces, there are now made not more than 20,000; at Wiazniki, likewise, the number has fallen from 73,000 to 20,000, and several factories have entirely stopped work. This stagnation proceeds mainly from the circumstance that England and the United States, formerly our chief customers, now manufacture considerable quantities of these articles for themselves. The exportation of flems which, during the three years 1824—26, averaged 72,960 pieces, averaged during the three years 1848 — 50 only 19,391; and that of raven-ducks, which during the former period amounted to 70,699, had fallen during the latter to 38,785. The establishments which were exclusively occupied with the manufacture of these fabrics naturally suffered most from the change; those which at the same time manufactured fabrics for which there was a greater home demand got through the crisis without entirely discontinuing their manufacture of the former article; other manufacturers betook themselves to the weaving of cotton. The chief establishments for the fabrication of flems and raven-ducks are those of M. Senkow at Wiazniki, and of M. Souzdaltsew at Mourome in the government of Wladimir —the former employing nearly 1000 looms with 1150 workmen, and producing 17,000 pieces, and the latter producing about 10,000 pieces per annum.

Besides the strong cloths which we have just been mentioning, there are also manufactured several sorts of ticks and other fabrics of the sort, certain qualities of which are specially intended for the China trade. Holland used to be a good customer for our ticks; but this branch of commerce has also fallen off, the article being now, in a great measure, replaced by cotton fabrics. Most of the ticks now manufactured in Russia contain a mixture of cotton; it is seldom that they are wholly of linen; but sometimes they are of cotton entirely.

We have mentioned the governments of Jaroslaw, Kostroma,

Wologda, Moscow, and Wladimir, as those in which the linen manufacture, in the widest acceptation of the term, is chiefly concentrated; but large quantities of linen cloth of different sorts, especially for the home market, are manufactured in the governments of Pskow and Witebsk, in Livonia, and in Lithuania. In these countries the manufacture is almost entirely in the hands of proprietors: many of the establishments employ 30 looms and upwards: both the spinning and the weaving are generally performed under the corvée system: the household cloths for domestic use, and the common table napery, are everywhere manufactured more or less amongst the peasants.

Manufactures from hemp, as compared with those from flax, occupy but a secondary place. Of all fabrics from the former substance, sail-cloth is the only article which in Russia constitutes a branch of industry, properly so called. Our sail-cloth has long enjoyed a justly merited reputation, which, notwithstanding the decline of this branch of industry amongst us from its extension in England and the United States, it still retains; and of this no better proof need be sought than the fact that, to procure their article a readier sale in America, English manufacturers have been known to imitate the stamp of M. Briouzguine, one of our principal manufacturers, whose sail-cloth is in great demand in that country. The imperial factory of Alexandrovsk, near St. Petersburg, manufactures very superior sail-cloth with mill-spun yarn. The principal sail-cloth factories belonging to private parties are those of M. Briouzguine and of M. Zotow at Kozelsk, in the government of Kalouga, of Messrs. Plotnikow at Serpouckhow, in the government of Moscow, and of M. Maslow at Toula. The trade, as we have already observed, has greatly fallen off, both from the extension of the manufacture amongst our best customers, and from the use of cotton fabrics. The exportation, which during the period 1824—26 had amounted to 60,400 pieces, did not, during the period 1848—50, exceed the average of 23,280. On the other hand our export of cables and ropes has followed during the same interval an ascending movement. During the period 1824—26 it averaged 259,383 poods, representing a value of 2,151,340 paper roubles, equivalent, at the exchange of the day (27 per cent.) to 580,861 silver roubles; and during the period 1848—50 it attained the figure of 449,100 poods, representing a value of 1,163,613 silver roubles. The principal establishments for the manufacture of ropes and cables are those of M. Cazalete and M. Sazonow at St. Petersburg, of M. Mieschkow in the government of Orel, and of M. Smyschlaiew in the government of Perm. There is also a large cordage manufactory at Nijni-Nowgorod. The two manufactories at St. Petersburg are furnished with perfect machinery, and their products enjoy a justly merited reputation.

Our trade in fabrics of flax and hemp with Europe and Asia during the period of 27 years, from 1824 to 1850 inclusive, exhibits the following movement:—

Triennial Averages of Value of Exportation and Importation.

	Exportation.	Importation.	Excess of Exportation.
	Silv. Roub.	Silv. Roub.	Silv. Roub.
Average of 1824 to 1826 - -	3,114,600	139,200	2,975,400
1827 „ 1829 - -	2,601,600	259,300	2,342,300
1830 „ 1832 - -	2,308,200	208,500	2,099,700
1833 „ 1835 - -	2,850,500	241,900	2,608,600
1836 „ 1838 - -	2,757,500	356,500	2,401,000
1839 „ 1841 - -	2,763,200	400,200	2,363,000
1842 „ 1844 - -	1,968,400	350,200	1,618,200
1845 „ 1847 - -	1,862,500	384,200	1,478,300
1848 „ 1850 - -	1,551,800	519,600	1,032,200

It results from this table that exportation has fallen off by one-half, whilst importation has augmented in the proportion of 10 to 37, and the excess of exportation has been reduced by nearly two-thirds. This result proceeds from the cause already adverted to, which has considerably reduced the demand for our sail-cloths, our flems, and our tickings in England, Holland, and America; whilst in Russia the greatly augmented consumption of fine linen and table napery has caused a considerably increased importation of these articles, notwithstanding the sensible improvement that has of late taken place in the home manufacture.

If to the exportation of linen and hempen fabrics we add that of ropes and cables, we will obtain the following total result of the exportation of linen and hempen products:—

	Value.
	Silv. Roub.
Total export during three years 1824—1826 - - -	3,374,000
Ditto during three years 1848—1850 - - - -	2,715,400
Decrease = 19½ per cent. -	658,600

The only means of restoring this important branch of our commerce would be to improve the manufacture, and this depends entirely upon the manufacturers and workmen themselves. The industry possesses all the elements of vital force necessary to insure its prosperity, notwithstanding the competition of cotton, which has paralysed it for a time, first, by taking the place of flax for various purposes, and secondly, by withdrawing capital and intellectual productive forces from the

one channel to the other.   With these disadvantages the linen
manufacture has had to struggle in other countries as well as
with us, and the linen manufacturers of England and Belgium,
setting their shoulders to the wheel, have been successful up
to a certain point at any rate.   Our own natural advantages
over most other countries are immense: our soil yields the
raw material in the richest abundance; and, from the low value
of land, we can raise it much cheaper than it can be raised
elsewhere: our spinners and weavers are at same time cultivators of the ground; each sees in the products of his field his
resource against want and pauperism; and, manufacturing
industry being his staff and not his crutch, he can afford to be
satisfied with much lower wages than the spinners and weavers
of other countries, who have nothing but their weekly wages
to depend on for their daily bread.   These circumstances ought
necessarily to exert a favourable influence on the cost of manufacture.*   All, then, that is requisite to enable us advantageously to support competition with other countries, not only
at home but in foreign markets, is to improve our manufacturing
processes: our superiority exists in the nature of things, if
we but knew how to turn it to account.   Now that cotton
industry has attained, as it were, its culminating point, and
absorbed all the capital and intellectual productive powers that
it was capable of absorbing, a good impulse given to our linen
manufacture by a few active and enterprising men could not
fail in soon bringing forth its fruits.

In pointing out the principal defects in the different branches
of our manufacture, including the preparation of the raw material, we have at the same time endeavoured to indicate the
remedies, founded on the opinions of various well-informed men
who have directed their attention to this important subject;
and we cannot too often repeat that one of the most desirable
improvements—inasmuch as all the others would naturally
spring from it—would be the introduction of spinning by machinery.   Besides improving the quality and diminishing the
cost of our fabrics, machine-spinning would also give a better
direction to the preparation and assortment of the flax, and to
hand-spinning.   Nor is it less essential to introduce better modes
of bleaching and finishing; for this is altogether our weakest
side.   The Wéliko-Sélo merchants say that linen might be

---

* The examples we have already cited of the expense of weaving might seem to lead
to a different conclusion ; but we have also explained the cause of these : the price
of weaving is generally high only for fine or damask fabrics, for which we have
a deficiency of skilled labourers, and the consequent want of competition raises the
price of labour.

manufactured in Russia for half what it costs abroad; but that it will always lose in comparison from the defective bleaching and finishing. It is only slowly, no doubt, that these improvements can be effected; for, besides activity and intelligence on the part of the industrial classes, they require considerable capital. But let us only begin; and, once begun, let us persevere. If we cannot reconquer in foreign markets the trade in certain fabrics, which we used exclusively to supply, we can replace them by other articles, which we are able to furnish at a very low price. Thus, for example, we are very advantageously situated for the manufacture of certain tickings, and other fabrics of linen and cotton mixed. Several manufacturers have availed themselves of this, and thereby found the means, as we have already observed, of supporting their establishments when their existence was threatened by the crisis which occurred in the linen trade; but the greater number of our tradespeople are too open to the reproach of not sufficiently studying the oscillations of industry and commerce in other countries, arising from changes of habit and demand, — changes, however, which we must study and conform to, if we are to hope for regaining the ground we have lost in our foreign commercial relations. Notwithstanding the numerous crises which the linen manufacture of the Zollverein has undergone within the last twenty years, these states export linens to the value of 11 or 12 millions of roubles; and there is nothing to hinder us, with our superiority in natural productive forces, from attaining still better results, not, of course, at a bound, but in the long run, by dint of application and perseverance. What, in truth, is wanting to attain this end? Nothing but to improve the preparation, assortment, and dressing of our flax, to introduce spinning by machinery, and good schools for hand-spinning, to employ better looms, and form good establishments for bleaching and finishing; and though all this cannot be done in a day, it is all perfectly within the bounds of possibility. The improvements of which this industry is susceptible might soon augment, by at least 50 per cent., the value of its products; and this would give an addition of more than 30 millions of silver roubles ($4\frac{3}{4}$ millions sterling) per annum to the national wealth.

Finally, we must repeat what we had occasion to observe when speaking of the culture of flax, — an observation which is referable to the whole economic organisation of this branch of industry, from the most elementary preparation of the raw material. In order that the whole processes which the flax undergoes, down to the time that it is delivered in the form of a web into the hands of the merchant, may be conducted in a rational manner, the cultivator would require to sell it in its raw state to the tradesman, whose business it would be to steep, scutch, and heckle it, and from whom the spinner would purchase the heckled flax to be spun by the hand or by machinery. The yarn should then pass into the hands of the manufacturer, who would distribute it to the weavers in the villages, and the latter would return him the raw webs to be bleached and finished in his own establishment. It is to an organisation of this sort that the immense progress made by Ireland in the linen manufacture is mainly owing; and similar results would attend its introduction elsewhere; for it is founded on a wise subdivision of labour, without which perfection is unattainable in any branch of industry.

END OF THE FIRST VOLUME.

London:
A. and G. A. Spottiswoode,
New-street-Square.